Counseling Today

Foundations of Professional Identity

Darcy Haag Granello
The Ohio State University

Mark E. Young
University of Central Florida

Boston Columbus Indianapolis New York San Francisco Upper Saddle River
Amsterdam Cape Town Dubai London Madrid Milan Munich Paris Montreal Toronto
Delhi Mexico City São Paulo Sydney Hong Kong Seoul Singapore Taipei Tokyo

Vice President and Editor in Chief: Jeffery W. Johnston
Senior Acquisitions Editor: Meredith D. Fossel
Editorial Assistant: Nancy Holstein
Vice President, Director of Marketing: Margaret Waples
Senior Marketing Manager: Christopher Barry
Senior Managing Editor: Pamela Bennett
Senior Project Manager: Mary M. Irvin
Senior Operations Supervisor: Matt Ottenweller
Senior Art Director: Diane Lorenzo
Cover Designer: Candace Rowley
Cover Art: fotolia
Full-Service Project Management: Thistle Hill Publishing Services, LLC
Composition: Integra Software Services, Inc.
Printer/Binder: Courier
Cover Printer: Courier
Text Font: Slimbach

Photo Credits: All photos provided by the subjects of the Snapshot features or by the authors.

Every effort has been made to provide accurate and current Internet information in this book. However, the Internet and information posted on it are constantly changing, so it is inevitable that some of the Internet addresses listed in this textbook will change.

COUNSELING TODAY: FOUNDATIONS OF PROFESSIONAL IDENTITY is an independent publication and has not been authorized, sponsored, endorsed, or otherwise approved by the American Counseling Association (ACA). The American Counseling Association (ACA) makes no representations or warranties with regard to the author or organizations mentioned in the text.

Library of Congress Cataloging-in-Publication Data

Granello, Darcy Haag.
  Counseling today : foundations of professional identity / Darcy Haag Granello, Mark E. Young.
    p. cm.
  Includes bibliographical references and index.
  ISBN-13: 978-0-13-098536-1 (pbk.)
  ISBN-10: 0-13-098536-8 (pbk.)
  1. Counseling—Vocational guidance—United States—Textbooks.   2. Educational counseling—United States—Textbooks.   3. Counselors—Professional relationships—United States—Textbooks.   I. Title.
  BF636.64.G73 2012
  158'.3023—dc22

                                                                                              2011000766

8   16

www.pearsonhighered.com

ISBN 10:   0-13-098536-8
ISBN 13: 978-0-13-098536-1

To my dad, Douglas M. Haag, who gave me my roots, and to my husband, Paul, who gives me my wings.

—DHG

To J. Melvin Witmer, Professor Emeritus, Ohio University, with deep respect.

—MEY

Darcy Haag Granello, PhD

Darcy Haag Granello is Professor of Counselor Education at The Ohio State University and a Licensed Professional Clinical Counselor in Ohio. She has published over 60 articles, co-authored two books, made more than 100 national and international presentations, and secured more than $750,000 in grants. Darcy's research and interests are in the areas of suicide prevention and assessment and in methods to promote the cognitive development of counselors and counseling supervisors. She is co-author of *Suicide: An Essential Guide for Helping Professionals and Educators* (Allyn & Bacon, 2007) and *Suicide, Self-Injury, and Violence in the Schools: Assessment, Prevention, and Intervention Strategies* (John Wiley & Sons, 2011). She has received state and national awards for her research in counselor development, and she seeks to find ways to enhance the training and education of counselors to promote professional identity and cognitive complexity.

Darcy is a certified suicide gatekeeper trainer and a Red Cross Mental Health First Responder. She is founder and listowner for COUNSGRADS, the national listserv for graduate students in counselor education.

Mark E. Young, PhD

Mark Young is Professor of Counselor Education at the University of Central Florida, which is located in Orlando. For more than 20 years, he worked as a counselor in community mental health, college counseling centers, private practice, and corrections. He has been a state and national leader in counseling. For the past 10 years, he has conducted research and provided services for couples at the UCF Marriage and Family Research Institute. His writing is focused on practical issues that counselors face, including maintaining their personal wellness, understanding clients' religious and spiritual perspectives, developing a theoretical orientation, and understanding the client/counselor alliance. His most recent books include *Learning the Art of Helping: Building Blocks and Techniques*, Fourth Edition, (Pearson, 2009) and *Counseling and Therapy for Couples* (Wadsworth, 2007).

■■■ Brief Contents ■■■

Contents

▪▪▪ To Our Students ▪▪▪

Welcome to the profession of counseling! As counselors, we are always thrilled and excited to see people follow their passion in life. We know that our profession offers wonderful opportunities for you to evolve into the professional you want to be and to have a career filled with meaning and purpose. It is our hope that you will find in the profession of counseling a lifelong career that challenges you to learn and grow.

We need only look to the world around us to see how badly we need counselors. There are so many examples of human suffering and pain as well as stories of remarkable courage and resilience. There are, in short, countless opportunities for counselors to make a difference.

We think it only fair to let you know that you are in for quite a journey. Becoming a counselor changes you and tests you. Counseling is not just something that *you do*; it is someone *you become*. In that way, counseling is different from many other professions. In your graduate program, you will be asked to read books, write papers, and take tests. But even if you master all of these academic skills, you will not have everything you need to be an outstanding counselor. You can be a straight A student, and of course we believe it is vitally important that you learn all the material in your courses. But A's are not enough. After all, no client will ever ask you what grade you made in your Foundations of Counseling course. Ultimately, you will need to integrate everything you are learning with the person you already are, to become the counselor you wish to be. You must constantly monitor your own reactions and be willing to grow and change. It's a tall order, and one that none of us should take lightly. The good news, however, is that it is the most exciting, challenging, and energizing experience that you can imagine!

We encourage you to strive to become more intentional—to be more clear about what you want from your graduate education, from your career, from your relationships with others, and from yourself. In order to do this, you will need to adopt a self-reflective approach in which you continually stop and think about what the material you are learning means to you. A self-reflective approach can help guide you to develop clarity about your goals. Rather than just allowing life (or classes, or counseling skills) to happen *to* you, it is important that you take control of your own experiences and learning.

We want to remind you that your journey toward becoming a counselor is a long developmental process. We hope you will give yourself permission to be in the moment, to learn new things, to take risks, and to not know. We encourage you to allow yourself time to explore ideas and options, and try not to rush to a decision or conclusion. It's okay to relax, take a deep breath, and think before you respond. Sometimes students get frustrated with themselves because they take longer than they would like to develop new skills, understand new material, conceptualize client problems, or know the appropriate thing to say. Keep in mind that counselors develop slowly, over time, and they continue to grow and change and learn long after graduate school is over. As much as you can, try not to hold yourself to unrealistic expectations about what you "should" know or how fast you "should" learn. The type of learning you will encounter is like nothing you have experienced before, and it will require patience.

We hope you will find this book helpful as you begin your journey toward becoming a professional counselor. Our intent is to provide you with a text that helps share our passion and enthusiasm for counseling, gives you an understanding of how your graduate training can help shape you as a counselor, and takes a strong stand that all counselors need to be trained to the highest possible standards. After all, the world doesn't need any more mediocre counselors. The world needs you to be the absolute best counselor with the strongest sense of professional identity and professional integrity that you can possibly have. You, and your future clients, deserve no less. So, welcome to the start of your professional journey.

Darcy Haag Granello

Mark E. Young

▪▪▪ Preface ▪▪▪

We first conceptualized this textbook at an American Counseling Association conference many years ago, as we were sharing experiences about helping our students develop a sense of professional identity in our Foundations of Counseling courses. We wanted a book that helped students get excited about the career choice they were making. We believe that the decision to become a professional counselor must be an active one. Students must *decide* to become counselors, not just slide into it. Therefore, we tried to write a book that takes a stand about being a member of this specific profession rather than trying to appeal to everyone. There are many other paths to becoming a professional helper, but this book is about the profession of counseling. Over countless conversations and pieces of high-quality chocolate, the idea for the book started to take shape. We believe that the result is a book that helps students understand the world of counseling and begin to envision themselves as professional counselors.

Helping students in counseling programs to develop a sense of professional identity is one of the most important tasks that educators face. As students learn about the profession of counseling, they must also begin to see themselves as professionals. To do this, they must learn, and then begin to internalize, the knowledge, standards, ethics, and skills that are at the foundation of the profession. We believe that this sense of internalized, professional identity can be strengthened with an intentional and self-reflective approach to learning that can begin from the very first course a student takes in the counseling program. Thus, this book is intended to help set a solid foundation for the student's journey toward becoming a professional counselor.

In this book, we use a developmental perspective that encourages students to take a self-reflective stance toward becoming counselors. Counseling students who are self-reflective continually stop and think about what the material they are learning means to them; they consider how their own personality, beliefs, values, thoughts, and experiences influence the way they look at the world, and reflect on their own development as professionals. We offer ideas and suggestions for students to adopt a self-reflective approach to the topics that we cover in this book. This approach to self-discovery, however, should not stop at the end of this text or even when they finish graduate school. Professional counselors who are self-reflective spend their entire careers seeking to better understand themselves and their work so that they can continually improve the care that they provide to others. Self-reflection, then, is an ongoing process of self-evaluation and self-awareness that enhances both our personal and professional lives. Helping counseling students learn the skills and habits of self-reflection is a core idea that is infused throughout this text.

Counseling is about understanding people's stories, and exposure to those stories can motivate counseling students to apply the information they are learning to real-life situations.

Students also have different learning orientations than they did in the past as a result of the infusion of technology. Because today's students have been raised reading content in Web-based formats, which typically appear in snippets that highlight important elements of the content, the narrative of this text is heavily punctuated with first-person stories from counseling students and professional counselors. It is also interspersed with current developments in the field that will certainly change the course of our profession, and ideas that are intended to challenge students to engage with the material presented.

One of the primary goals of this text is to get students excited and energized about the counseling profession and to help them begin to see it as a vibrant, ever-changing field that is populated with people who are trying to make a difference. Thus, the text does not merely repeat static information about the profession that will most certainly be covered in depth in other classes. We believe that the presentation of so much material in a dry, narrative format can leave students feeling overwhelmed with information and can drain them of the passion and energy that they once had for their new profession. Instead, the foundations text should help students envision themselves as part of the profession by providing the context for application of their learning to their own lives. For example, the chapter on theories of counseling (Chapter 6) is not simply a recitation of existing counseling theories. Instead, this chapter discusses the major underpinnings of counseling theories and then helps students understand *why* counselors need theories, *how* counselors choose a theory, and what steps they can take to begin to develop their own theoretical stance. In short, the book provides content and then focuses on the application of that information to the world of the counselor.

Organization of This Book

Our organizational framework for the text first introduces students to the profession of counseling by helping them understand how the profession fits within the greater context of the helping professions (Chapter 1). It then focuses on helping students build an understanding the many facets of the counseling profession. We were surprised to find that foundations textbooks do not typically include information on what counselors actually *do*. Because we find this to be a critical component of our book, we have spent several chapters discussing the many roles of the counselor and what a counseling session might look like in practice (Chapters 2, 8, and 9). Also included are chapters to help students place the different content areas in context, such as chapters on how counselors use theories (Chapter 6), engage in research (Chapter 7), work in a diverse and vibrant society (Chapter 10), and apply ethics (Chapter 12). The role of social justice and advocacy is increasingly becoming important for counselors, as we recognize the role that social context plays in an individual's mental health. Thus, we include perspectives on these important roles in several of the book's chapters (e.g., Chapters 2 and 10). We also have included a chapter specifically designed to help counseling students get the most from their graduate programs (Chapter 5). Finally, because the process of becoming a counselor can be emotionally as well as physically draining, we include a chapter on maintaining wellness and balance in life as students go through the journey toward becoming professional counselors (Chapter 13).

The following provides an overview of what you'll find in each chapter:

- *Chapter 1* provides a brief historical overview of the profession of counseling through a discussion of the key ideas and values that have emerged and moved the profession forward. Students are encouraged to understand how counseling differs from other helping professions as well as how their own values and beliefs might coincide with—or differ from—those at the foundation of the counseling profession.
- Chapter 2 highlights the many roles of the counselor. Students are often surprised to learn the diversity of roles within the profession, and this chapter highlights 20 different counseling roles, stories from practicing counselors about how they engage in these roles, and opportunities for students to reflect on how they might fit in these roles.
- Chapter 3 moves to a discussion of professional identity through an exploration of the education and professional qualifications of counselors and an introduction of the professional counseling associations. In this chapter, a counseling student shares her perspective on why joining a professional association is important.
- Chapter 4 introduces students to the developmental journey of professional counselors. The chapter helps students understand the complexity of mixing personal and professional identities, and provides a perspective on lifelong learning and growth.
- Chapter 5 helps students get the most from their graduate programs. The chapter provides strategies for learning and then focuses on helping students have healthy interactions with faculty, peers, and professionals as well as setting appropriate expectations for relationships with family and friends.
- Chapter 6 gives students a framework to understand how counseling theories can inform practice. Current controversies, including efforts to move to brief therapy models or evidence-based practice, help students see the ever-changing role of theory in practice.
- Chapter 7 introduces students to the connection between research and practice. With the introduction of a practitioner-scientist model, students see how keeping up with the current research, as well as conducting their own outcome studies, can enhance their counseling programs and the care they give to their clients.
- Chapter 8 gives students a peek into the counseling session. Students are exposed to the counseling process from different perspectives, including a first-person account by a counseling client about what she thought was beneficial about the counseling process.
- Chapter 9 introduces students to the many different settings where counseling takes place. Through stories of visits to various counseling offices as well as first-person accounts by those who work in these settings, students learn that counseling is truly a diverse and exciting profession.
- Chapter 10 challenges students to think about the diverse world in which they will practice. Although multicultural perspectives are infused into

every chapter, this chapter encourages students to stop and reflect on their own cultural identity, to learn about the counseling profession's efforts to encourage a multicultural perspective, and to consider the important role of social justice and advocacy.

- Chapter 11 helps students understand the important role that assessment has in counseling. Students learn that effective counseling is based on a full understanding of the client's problems and strengths.

- Chapter 12 encourages students to understand the important role of ethics and the law in the counseling profession and introduces the concept of aspirational ethics. Students are given opportunities to reflect on how their own beliefs and values might impact their counseling practice, and they are introduced to several ethical decision-making models to help them make appropriate ethical choices.

- Chapter 13 reminds students that to help our clients, we must also take care of ourselves. This chapter encourages students to develop their own individualized wellness plans and provides resources and ideas for staying mentally, emotionally, and physically healthy during graduate school and beyond.

- Chapter 14 is a glimpse into the future of counseling. Students reading this text represent our profession's future, and we provide some insights and ideas about where the profession might be headed, including a first-person account from a counselor (and his Web-based avatar) about the role of technology in counseling.

Special Features

There are many special features throughout the text that help provide differing perspectives and approaches to counseling. We believe it is important to share these diverse ideas and expose students to the complexity of the counseling world. After all, ours is not a profession filled with absolutes or fixed positions, but one that is changing and growing and filled with challenges. Our students need to understand these complexities so they are prepared to meet these challenges head on. To help convey these complexities, we include the following in each chapter:

- *Words of Wisdom* provide advice and guidance from experienced counselors, clients, and famous people whose words can inspire.

■■■ *Words of Wisdom* ■■■

"I've learned to stop trying to give clients answers and let them find their own through our work."

—Andrew Moss, Licensed
Professional Counselor

- *Spotlights* highlight current trends and important viewpoints that help readers develop a sense of professional identity.

Spotlight
The Social Atom

The concept of the "social atom" may help here. The social atom, modeled on the structure of the physical atom, helps describe, explain, and predict how people develop and maintain long-term interpersonal relationships. Based on the work of Joseph Moreno (1951), the concept is intended to help us see the influence of these relationships in our lives. In a social atom, the nucleus represents the individual and the electrons represent the many groups with which the individual identifies. The distance of each group from the nucleus could be said to represent the emotional or psychological distance of the person from the group. In the example in Figure 3.1, a somewhat "stripped down" social atom demonstrates the concept.

family occupies a spot on the innermost ring. There might be other groups that are equally important, and they would be on this ring as well. The next ring contains several groups of friends (sorority sisters, church youth group), while the third ring out has extended family, friends from high school, roommates, and peers in the counseling program. Each of these rings can have many more groups in it, and the rings can extend out indefinitely. The point of the social atom is to help clients (or in this case, students in counseling programs) see the extent of their relationships. Take a moment and draw a social atom of your own, and you will see the many groups of people in your life who help you feel connected and help you define

- *Snapshots* are first-person stories by real counselors who work in the field and have influenced the profession as well as counseling students who will help shape the future of the profession.

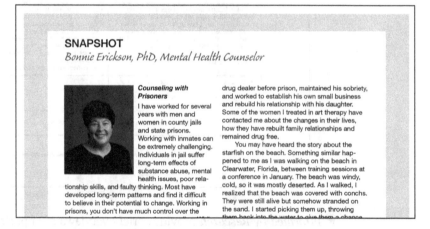

SNAPSHOT
Bonnie Erickson, PhD, Mental Health Counselor

Counseling with Prisoners

I have worked for several years with men and women in county jails and state prisons. Working with inmates can be extremely challenging. Individuals in jail suffer long-term effects of substance abuse, mental health issues, poor relationship skills, and faulty thinking. Most have developed long-term patterns and find it difficult to believe in their potential to change. Working in prisons, you don't have much control over the

drug dealer before prison, maintained his sobriety, and worked to establish his own small business and rebuild his relationship with his daughter. Some of the women I treated in art therapy have contacted me about the changes in their lives, how they have rebuilt family relationships and remained drug free.

You may have heard the story about the starfish on the beach. Something similar happened to me as I was walking on the beach in Clearwater, Florida, between training sessions at a conference in January. The beach was windy, cold, so it was mostly deserted. As I walked, I realized that the beach was covered with conchs. They were still alive but somehow stranded on the sand. I started picking them up, throwing them back into the water to give them a chance

- *Fast Facts* offer interesting snippets of data about counseling and counselors.

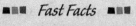

Fast Facts

Counselors are licensed in all 50 states and the District of Columbia. Requirements vary. Counseling students who want to work in a state different from where they are receiving their degree should consult the American Counseling Association website, www.counseling.org, where state professional counselor licensure boards are listed with their contact information.

- *Counseling Controversies* feature two sides of an issue that is currently being debated in the field, such as, "Should counselors engage in diagnosis of mental and emotional disorders?"

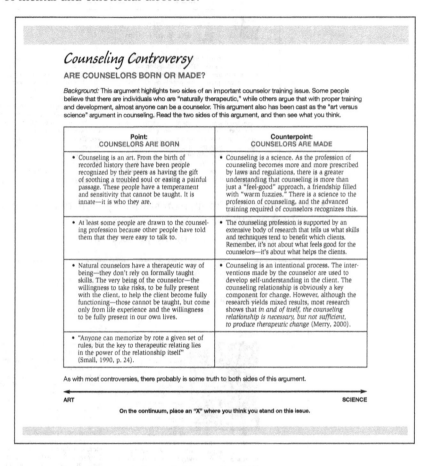

Counseling Controversy

ARE COUNSELORS BORN OR MADE?

Background: This argument highlights two sides of an important counselor training issue. Some people believe that there are individuals who are "naturally therapeutic," while others argue that with proper training and development, almost anyone can be a counselor. This argument also has been cast as the "art versus science" argument in counseling. Read the two sides of this argument, and then see what you think.

Point: COUNSELORS ARE BORN	Counterpoint: COUNSELORS ARE MADE
• Counseling is an art. From the birth of recorded history there have been people recognized by their peers as having the gift of soothing a troubled soul or easing a painful passage. These people have a temperament and sensitivity that cannot be taught. It is innate—it is who they are.	• Counseling is a science. As the profession of counseling becomes more and more prescribed by laws and regulations, there is a greater understanding that counseling is more than just a "feel-good" approach, a friendship filled with "warm fuzzies." There is a science to the profession of counseling, and the advanced training required of counselors recognizes this.
• At least some people are drawn to the counseling profession because other people have told them that they were easy to talk to.	• The counseling profession is supported by an extensive body of research that tells us what skills and techniques tend to benefit which clients. Remember, it's not about what feels good for the counselors—it's about what helps the clients.
• Natural counselors have a therapeutic way of being—they don't rely on formally taught skills. The very being of the counselor—the willingness to take risks, to be fully present with the client, to help the client become fully functioning—those cannot be taught, but come only from life experience and the willingness to be fully present in our own lives.	• Counseling is an intentional process. The interventions made by the counselor are used to develop self-understanding in the client. The counseling relationship is obviously a key component for change. However, although the research yields mixed results, most research shows that *in and of itself, the counseling relationship is necessary, but not sufficient, to produce therapeutic change* (Merry, 2000).
• "Anyone can memorize by rote a given set of rules, but the key to therapeutic relating lies in the power of the relationship itself" (Small, 1990, p. 24).	

As with most controversies, there probably is some truth to both sides of this argument.

ART ←————————————————————————————→ SCIENCE

On the continuum, place an "X" where you think you stand on this issue.

- *Informed by Research* provides brief overviews of important research studies to help students recognize the relationship of research to practice.

Informed by Research
School Counselors and Outcome Research

The Center for School Counseling Outcome Research conducted research to determine the most crucial needs for research in the area of school counseling (Dimmitt, Carey, McGannon, & Henningson, 2005). The researchers used the Delphi Method, a strategy that employs a panel of experts in the field to generate ideas, gain consensus, and identify areas of discord about a specific topic. In this study, 21 school counseling experts, all national leaders in the field, were questioned about their beliefs regarding the best

2. Documenting effectiveness (validating that what school counselors do makes a difference in the lives of children)

3. Understanding how research can affect change in the field (evaluating the impact of training and research on the field of counseling as well as education overall)

4. Identifying the most effective educational and supervisory approaches for training (understanding how counselor preparation

Teaching with This Text

Our goal is to have students actively interact with the material in this book, rather than passively read the chapters in preparation for a class exam. Toward that end, we have integrated many opportunities throughout the chapters for students to stop and reflect on the material, providing prompts, questions, checklists, and spaces for students to take notes. We encourage you to include time in class for discussion of these ideas and/or to encourage students to complete them on their own. For example, in Chapter 2 (*What Do Counselors Do?*), we provide a table of the many roles of counselors, with a column that asks students to consider their reactions to the fit that each of these roles might have for their own professional careers. In Chapter 3 (*How Are Counselors Trained and Regulated?*), we give descriptions of each of the divisions of the American Counseling Association, providing space for students to check boxes by the divisions they would like to explore more. Chapter 5 (*How Do Counseling Students Get the Most from Their Graduate Programs?*) provides prompts in the text for students to develop personalized strategies to maximize their success in school. Chapter 10 (*How Do Counselors Work in a Diverse Society?*) asks students to respond to questions about their own cultural identity. In other words, each of the chapters contains opportunities for students to engage in self-reflection through guided activities and exercises that are intentionally designed to challenge students to develop their own professional identity.

In addition to the activities embedded within each chapter, end-of-chapter activities include **Prompts for Personal Reflection** and **Journal Questions** that can be done independently or as class assignments. **Topics for Discussion** provide ideas for engaging students with some of the most complex and challenging material in each chapter. **Experiments** are suggestions for students to seek out more information or feedback about a particular topic or engage in active outreach with counseling professionals, associations, or the community. **Explore More** gives students (and instructors) important resources for more in-depth exploration of the ideas presented within each chapter. Finally, several chapters contain links to specific information in **MyHelpingLab**. This online content contains links to videos that correspond with the information provided in the chapter, and watching the videos can help students better understand what counselors do.

Instructor's Supplements

Online Instructor's Resource Manual with Test Bank

The Online Instructor's Resource Manual with Test Bank is a comprehensive resource available to adopting instructors. For each chapter, there is a chapter overview, discussion questions, and sample test items with an answer key.

Online PowerPoint Lecture Slides

These lecture slides highlight key concepts and summarize key content from each chapter of the text. Both the Online Instructor's Resource Manual with Test Bank and Online PowerPoint Lecture Slides are available on the Instructor Resource Center at www.pearsonhighered.com. To access these materials, go to www.pearsonhighered.com and click on the Instructor Resource Center button. Here professors can log in or complete a one-time registration for a user name and password.

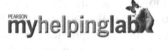 MyHelpingLab is the online destination designed to help students in counseling make the transition from academic coursework to professional practice. The online content consists of video clips of authentic counselor/client sessions, video interviews with professionals in the field, written case examples, and licensing information with valuable information for students who are beginning their careers. For a demonstration of the website and to find out how to package student access to this website with this textbook, go to www.myhelpinglab.com or contact your Pearson sales representative.

■■■ Acknowledgments ■■■

During the writing of this book, we were blessed by encouragement, support, and care from family, friends, and colleagues. Chief among these are our spouses, Paul Granello and Jora Young, both writers themselves, who offered their love and opinions. We must also acknowledge that there has never been a more patient and understanding editor than Meredith Fossel, who "inherited" us from Kevin Davis, our first editor, who saw and immediately understood the vision for this rather unconventional text. Thank you, Kevin, for helping us define with more intentionality what we were after. Meredith, your wonderful and sustained support and guidance have been truly amazing. You helped us create the book that we knew we wanted to write, and you struck a balance between support and challenge that, in the end, was exactly what we needed. Thanks to those who reviewed various drafts of the manuscript:

James F. Calhoun, University of Georgia; Yvonne Callaway, Eastern Michigan University; Audrey L. Canaff, University of Tennessee at Chattanooga; Stephen Feit, Idaho State University; Jeannine Feldman, San Diego State University; Norma Gaines-Hanks, University of Delaware; Sharon Jones, University of Georgia; Jeremy Linton, Indiana University, South Bend; Michael Mullen, SUNY Oswego; Kelli Saginak, University of Wisconsin, Oshkosh; Aaron B. Stills, Howard University; Sherri Turner, University of Minnesota, Twin Cities; and Robert Urofsky, University of Wisconsin, Oshkosh.

We would also like to thank the staff at Pearson who have been patient and kind during so many steps in the process. A special thank you to Max Effenson Chuck and Angela Urquhart (Thistle Hill Publishing Services), who worked diligently to prepare the final manuscript and attend to all the details. Your work is much appreciated. We also wish to recognize our colleagues in counselor education who share our passion for creating a strong sense of professional identity and upholding the highest professional standards among future generations of counselors. We hope that this text provides you with a starting place for these important conversations with your students. We are particularly indebted to several colleagues who have been instrumental in the development of the ideas in this book, including Colette Dollarhide, Kara Ieva, Jonathan Ohrt, Marisol Tobey, and especially Tracy S. Hutchinson, who worked tirelessly on so many of the special features in this text.

Finally, we wish to extend our heartfelt gratitude to the many students who have been part of our counselor education programs over the years. You have shared your excitement and passion with us, and you have taught us through your learning. It is through you that we have defined and refined our ideas, and it is because of you that we know that our profession is in good hands.

Who Are Counselors?

In this chapter, we will:

- Show you the layout of the book and describe our approach. It is based on the reflective practitioner model that asks you to pause and evaluate as you read.

- Describe the various mental health professions and compare them with the profession of counseling.

- Identify the key values that have emerged in counseling's short history.

- Introduce you to the American Counseling Association.

As you read the chapter, you might want to consider:

- How counseling compares with other mental health professions

- Whether and how the important values of counseling fit with your own ideas and goals

- What points in the chapter raise questions in your mind that you might want to ask in class, or places where you disagree or strongly agree with what is presented

Professional Counseling and Professional Identity

Because this is an introductory counseling book, it is very likely that you are exploring the field of counseling for the first time. While *professional* counseling may be new to you, being in a helping relationship will not be a novel experience. Our everyday relationships frequently involve taking on a therapeutic role. You may already have mentored someone at work, listened to a friend's romantic difficulties, consoled someone after a loss, or tried to help mediate the difficulties of family members. These experiences give you a background to reflect on as you read about the profession of counseling. You probably have also experienced some of the joys of helping others—and perhaps some of the pitfalls as well. A few readers will already possess considerable helping experience,

1

perhaps working with children, in schools, in corrections, helping with substance abuse problems, or working in a social service agency. Regardless of your background, you may not yet think of yourself as a counselor. In other words, you may not have established your professional identity as a counselor.

Establishing a professional identity means more than completing the degree requirements, passing the state or national examinations, and having a plaque on the wall. It means finding a professional home in a field. Selecting a professional identity as a counselor is a fork in the road. It means that you have decided to become a counselor rather than a social worker, psychologist, or some other mental health professional. It also means that you have made a decision *for* something. You have selected the values, organizations, and traditions of the counseling profession. This step, like marriage, should not be undertaken unadvisedly. You should take time in all of your introductory courses to thoroughly investigate the profession you are entering and determine if counseling is the proper fit for you. As you will soon learn, some of counseling's origins spring from career counseling; therefore, you may want to consider receiving professional career counseling. At any rate, you should visit practicing counselors, attend professional meetings, and see what the life of a counselor is really like. In this book, we will suggest experiences and provide you with information that will help you take the next step in your entry into the field.

Reflecting on What You Are Learning

Part of establishing a professional identity is to compare yourself with others in the field. Do you find common values and interests? Although you need basic knowledge of the counseling field, you also need to go through a process of personal examination to see if this profession fits you. We have tried to bring in those elements that will help you recognize the professional standards, look at your own beliefs, and see if there is a match. For this reason, we have adopted a "reflective practitioner" model in this book. This model assumes that you must synthesize what you are learning with the person you already are—comparing as you go along. At every new puzzling step, at every uncomfortable thought, take the opportunity to grow through reflection and consider what you are taking in. Thinking or reflecting can take place in your head, but it is almost always better written down or expressed aloud with another person or small group. Reflection means weighing what you have learned through your previous experiences and trying to put that together with new information. It means critically evaluating what the textbook and teacher say rather than swallowing it whole. It means being open to new ideas even if they challenge precious beliefs. Reflecting can lead to "Aha" experiences (when an insight comes suddenly) or alternately to a gradual recognition that you have changed over time. The only way you may recognize these changes is to document them as you grow. In many ways, the process of change you will experience is very much like what a client goes through. Frequently, clients do not recognize the ways they have evolved unless they can compare their states before and after counseling.

This Text Is a Field Guide to Counseling

Entering a new field can be a bit like visiting a foreign country where the customs and language are unfamiliar. We decided to write a book that gives you the information you need in an easily accessible format similar to what you would find in a travel guide to a foreign country. If we are successful, you will find this book to be up-to-date and practical. You may benefit most from hearing the stories of other travelers, including their warnings and best experiences. You will also find an introduction to the language and key definitions. Like a field guide, this book will also show you some pictures of people and things you will encounter. It will describe what is really out there.

To make this a useful guide, we included a number of special features that appear in most chapters. Each chapter begins with **Advance Organizers** that outline what you will be learning, as well as some **Reflective Questions** to consider as you read. These reflective questions frequently ask you to review what you already know about the chapter topics and to think about the personal importance of the topics.

Spotlights are sections in the chapter where we focus on current trends and important viewpoints that help you develop a sense of professional identity. For example, in this chapter, we look at the American Counseling Association's national convention where many counseling professionals find like minds, continuing education, and a forum for common concerns. **Counseling Controversies** highlight two sides of an issue that is currently being debated in the field. We present both sides and then ask you to examine your own thinking about this debate. In fact, this is the approach we have tried to take throughout the book. Rather than give you the "party line" about such issues as medication and insurance, we have tried to highlight the disagreements, not just report the middle ground. **Snapshots** are words and pictures about real people who are working in the field or who have influenced the profession. Snapshots bring leaders and everyday counselors from the field to the classroom. **Informed by Research** provides a brief overview of an important research study bearing on the chapter's topic. We hope that counselors in training will appreciate from the beginning that they can learn from the discoveries of others as well as from their own experiences. As you become a professional, you will want to look at the critical research in counseling and related fields as sources of ideas and evidence for good practice. In **Words of Wisdom**, we have compiled helpful advice, comments, or quotes from counselors, clients, or famous people whose words can inspire. Throughout the text you will also see **Key Definitions** highlighted and **Fast Facts**, which are interesting data about counseling and counselors.

What Is Counseling?

Counseling occurs when a professionally trained individual develops a contractual relationship with a client and communicates with that person in a way that is deemed helpful. By contrast, counseling cannot occur when a friend gives advice to a friend, when fellow church members share their difficulties, or when the school principal brings parents to a conference to change a child's behavior. These activities are better described by the generic term *helping*. **Helping** occurs in a wide variety of settings, but it is not counseling unless it involves the key provisions that the counselor is professionally trained and that client and counselor have agreed on the issues of remuneration, confidentiality, time limits, and responsibilities.

Why is it important to make this distinction between helping and counseling? Let us take the example of plumbing. We like the comparison to plumbing because, like counseling, plumbing is considered to be rather simple, and most people think they could probably do it themselves if they had the time. (Also, we believe that counselors should be paid at least as well as plumbers!) Let us say that you have a dripping faucet. Although you might be able to solve this problem yourself or have a next-door neighbor help you change the washer, you are not a plumber! In the same way, most problems that people face are handled alone or in collaboration with family and friends. It is usually only when the situation is desperate that people seek professional help. Your neighbor, trying to solve a major plumbing problem, may make things worse. That is why we have licensure, professional organizations, and state boards for plumbers *and* counselors. It is the best way of ensuring that the client receives the most up-to-date procedures, a contract, the best-trained person, and a means for redressing grievances. Nevertheless, there will always be people who believe that they are born plumbers or counselors and that they do not need any training or a contract.

Another term similar to counseling is *psychotherapy*. **Psychotherapy** is a way of describing counseling as a treatment, something akin to medicine. The term was coined in the late 19th century and originally referred to "suggestive psychotherapy" and hypnotism (Jackson, 1999). The word went through many permutations. By the beginning of the 20th century it meant treating physical illness by psychological means. Sigmund Freud used it synonymously with "catharsis," emotional venting. Today, the term describes the entire spectrum of change theories and techniques.

Many writers have struggled to differentiate counseling and psychotherapy over the years, and most have decided to use the terms interchangeably (cf. Capuzzi & Gross, 2001; Gilbert, 1952; Patterson, 1973; Wrenn, 1954). In many states counselors, psychologists, social workers, psychiatrists, and marriage and family therapists can all practice "psychotherapy." In most cases, the techniques and theories employed are the same whether they use one term or the other. The reason to call what we are doing *psychotherapy* is mainly an economic one. Insurance forms require this medical language. In truth, like the term *counseling*, *psychotherapy* has become a generic term for professional helping. Those who prefer the term *psychotherapy* may see themselves as operating within a medical model and aiming more at longer-term personality change. They may emphasize assessment and testing, arrive at a diagnosis, and develop a treatment plan. This process from assessment to treatment plan is called **the diagnostic treatment planning model**. Others like to reserve the term *psychotherapy* for their treatment of clients with severe problems. They are more

■■■ *Fast Facts* ■■■

Counselors held about 665,000 jobs in the United States in 2008. Of these practitioners, about 276,000 worked in schools, 130,000 were rehabilitation counselors, 113,000 were mental health counselors, 86,000 worked in substance abuse and behavior disorders, and 27,000 were in marriage and family.

Source: Data courtesy of the *Occupational Outlook Handbook*, published by the U.S. Department of Labor (2010), Bureau of Labor Statistics. The handbook can be explored on the Web at www.bls.gov.

likely to be licensed as psychologists or psychiatrists, although counselors can work with these clients too. The term *counseling* is more likely to be used by people trained in counseling programs and who may not rely on a diagnostic treatment planning model but focus more on client-defined problems, wellness, the therapeutic relationship, and client strengths. In the end, counselors practice what psychotherapists call therapy and psychotherapists practice what counselors call counseling.

Guidance or **guidance counseling** is a term still used in schools, but it is unpopular among counselors. School counselors used to be called "guidance counselors." Guidance has a historical connotation connecting it with the term *vocational guidance*, as we will see when we look at the history of the profession. Guidance suggests advice and a directive approach, steering students into professions, college, or technical schools. Certainly, many counselors are involved in helping students make major life decisions, but it is doubtful that school counselors do any more "guiding" than any other helping professionals. Because school counselors are working mainly with children, the quasi-parental term has stuck. The American School Counselor Association now prefers the terms *school counseling* and *professional school counselors*.

 ## The Helping Professions Today

Before we go any farther, we need to clarify the terms we will be using in this text. We will use the generic terms *therapist, clinician,* and *professional helper* to refer to a member of one of the five major mental health professions: counseling, social work, marriage and family therapy, psychology, and psychiatry. Although there are many subspecialties, licensure (granted by state legislatures) is normally granted in one of these five professions. Training imbues each with a certain perspective and a philosophy of helping. Space does not allow us to adequately describe the entire training philosophy of each profession. Instead, we will try to contrast the training of other professions with that of counseling where possible. It is difficult to be objective in this comparison because we tend to see other ideas through our own counseling "lens." As you explore your professional path in a helping profession, you will want to carefully examine the issues and gain more information about all of the helping professions by talking with other clinicians, reading the *Occupational Outlook Handbook*, and examining the websites of professional organizations.

Ideally, the five major helping professions should work together to help clients benefit from their combined philosophies, tools, and skills. Everyone benefits when professionals collaborate to help meet the varying needs of an individual client or to advocate for the collective mental health needs of an entire school or community. Schools and mental health agencies across the country are filled with counselors, psychologists, social workers, marriage and family therapists, and psychiatrists who work together on a daily basis and treat each other with professional respect and dignity. In practice, most members of the helping professions recognize the important and distinct contributions that each profession makes to a mentally healthy society.

Unfortunately, the history of interdisciplinary cooperation of the helping professions at the national or state organizational level has been quite sad at times. At the level of professional organizations, professional collaboration remains an important, yet sometimes elusive goal.

There are clearly strong commonalities that bind these professions together, and pioneers and famous clinicians have come from all of the helping disciplines. Nevertheless, there is still a fierce rivalry. For example, psychiatry fought a long and expensive battle to contain the profession of psychology. At this writing, psychiatrists and psychologists are locked in a struggle about prescribing medication. Psychologists and social workers spent millions in the 1980s trying to defeat counselor licensure, while counselors have consistently opposed the entrance of bachelor's-level practitioners into the licensure fold. These struggles continue today despite the fact that in many agencies, schools, and even private practices, professional helpers in all fields work in concert or even in teams for the welfare of clients.

What Is a Counselor?

As you enter the profession of counseling, you should know that there are some unifying concepts that help define who we are and what we do. In the following paragraphs, we highlight some of the foundational principles of the counseling profession for you to consider.

A counselor has specific training. Most counselors receive their degrees in colleges of education. Counselors hold a master's degree, Education Specialist (EdS), or doctorate (PhD) in counseling or counselor education. Many school counselors go on to achieve an EdS degree to receive more advanced training. Doctoral-level counselors work mostly in academia as counselor educators, supervisors, or private practitioners.

Counselors typically have a degree in one of the following specialties:

- School counseling
  Working with students in public and private schools
- Mental health counseling or community counseling
  Community agencies, hospitals, private practice

- Marriage and family therapy or marriage, couples and family counseling
  Community agencies or private practice
- Rehabilitation counseling
  Working for private or government agencies or residential facilities helping people cope with stresses associated with a disability, including vocational counseling, training, and placement
- College student counseling and personnel services
  Working in college counseling centers or in college departments of student life

Common core curricular experiences. The semester hour requirements for a master's degree in counseling programs are substantial compared to, say, a master's in mechanical engineering, which may be 36 hours. Counseling master's programs normally range from 48 to 60 graduate hours, depending on the specialization, and take between two and two and one-half years to complete on a full-time basis.

Eight areas of preparation are required for all counseling specialties under the Council for Accreditation of Counseling and Related Educational Programs (CACREP) (2009), the counseling accrediting body, and you can use them to compare counseling training with other mental health professions. The core areas have labels that describe large areas of training, yet they show what counseling training emphasizes as well as the history and values of the profession. The eight areas are the following:

1. Professional Orientation and Ethical Practice
2. Social and Cultural Diversity (multicultural counseling)
3. Human Growth and Development
4. Career Development (helping people choose and develop in their work and leisure)
5. Helping Relationships (how to form a therapeutic alliance)
6. Group Work (group dynamics and group therapy)
7. Assessment (testing and diagnosis)
8. Research and Program Evaluation (conducting research, gathering statistics, and evaluating counseling programs)

A counselor belongs to professional organizations. Counselors are members of the following national organizations: the American Counseling Association (ACA), the American Mental Health Counselors Association (AMHCA), and the American School Counselor Association (ASCA). AMHCA and ASCA were once part of ACA and now are listed as divisions, but one may belong to the school counselors or the mental health counselors (MHCs) but not the American Counseling Association. While they often work together to promote school counseling and mental health legislation, these three organizations have separate executive directors and are self-governing. The American Counseling Association has divisions for marriage and family counseling (International Association for Marriage and Family Counseling), college counseling (American College Counseling Association), and rehabilitation counseling (American Rehabilitation Counseling Association).

Psychiatry

Every state has licensure requirements for psychiatrists. Board-certified psychiatrists are medical doctors (MDs or DOs) who, following medical school, become residents in psychiatry, an internship program that may last as long as five years. Residency training is accredited by the American Medical Association. During this time, psychiatric residents learn about therapeutic relationships and psychological and biological theories of behavior. They are also trained in psychopathology and diagnosis and in human development, as well as receiving extensive training in psychopharmacology and other biological treatments. The psychiatric residency places less emphasis on skills and intervention methods and vastly more emphasis on biological bases of behavior, organic brain syndromes and prescribing medication.

Psychiatrists are members of the American Psychiatric Association, which also publishes the *Diagnostic and Statistical Manual of Mental Disorders* (DSM), the listing of accepted mental disorders. In the past, psychiatry produced some of the greatest thinkers in the mental health field, including many of its founders and pioneers. This began with Sigmund Freud (who may have been the first psychiatrist) and his contemporaries, such as Alfred Adler, Otto Rank, and Karen Horney. Later, major contributions were made by J. L. Moreno (psychodrama and group therapy), Fritz Perls (gestalt therapy), William Glasser (reality therapy), Aaron Beck (cognitive therapy), Jerome Frank, Milton Erickson, Eric Berne (transactional analysis), and Irving Yalom (group therapy, existential therapy), to name only a few.

Things have changed since the early days of psychiatry. Although some psychiatrists practice as therapists today, the vast majority help determine diagnoses and prescribe and evaluate the effects of medication, especially on people with severe mental disorders such as schizophrenia or bipolar disorder. Frequently, psychiatrists lead interdisciplinary teams in hospitals. They often receive referrals from physicians and other mental health professionals including counselors. Counselors rely on psychiatrists when a client has confusing physical symptoms or needs an evaluation for medication.

Social Work

A social worker may have a bachelor of social work (BSW) or a master of social work (MSW). Social workers are licensed in all 50 states. Those who work as licensed therapists possess the MSW. A doctoral degree (DSW) is possible, but it is relatively rare and seems to be mainly confined to academics. The typical length of master's programs is about 60 semester hours, but a proportion may be undergraduate hours. Thus, with 30 bachelor's hours, in some programs, it is possible to finish an MSW degree in one year. A comparison of social work training and master's degree training in counseling reveals that social workers are generally better trained than counselors in utilizing and understanding the environmental, social, and economic forces on clients. They advocate on behalf of clients. They are knowledgeable about social agencies and the workings of community referral sources. While counseling training has become more multicultural and sensitive to special populations, social work training emphasizes this area even more. Normally, psychological testing is not within the scope of practice of a social worker.

Compared to social work, counseling prepares students more in the skills and knowledge of the helping relationship. Counselors have more emphasis on individual and group therapy techniques and interventions. Still, the MSW degree is a versatile, highly regarded degree, because social work has a long history and jobs have been available in hospitals and community services agencies. Some state licensure boards and most training programs differentiate between administrative MSWs and those trained as clinical social workers. Social workers have been major players in family therapy and several are quite well known, including solution-focused pioneers Steve de Shazer, Insoo Kim Berg, and Michele Weiner Davis.

Marriage and Family Therapists

Marriage and family therapists are currently licensed in all 50 states and the District of Columbia. The major professional organization representing marriage and family therapists is the American Association for Marriage and Family Therapy (AAMFT) with about 25,000 members. The AAMFT holds an annual convention highlighted by "master sessions" where expert therapists perform live sessions with actual clients. The founders of AAMFT were mainly psychiatrists, social workers, and psychologists who became interested in couple and family work. AAMFT, through its accrediting body, the Commission on Accreditation for Marriage and Family Therapy Education (COAMFTE), certifies about 110 programs in North America. The accreditation extends to both universities and private training institutes that offer master's, doctoral, or training certificates.

Counselors and psychologists have their own organizations for members interested in couples and families. The American Psychological Association (Division 43) and

■■■ *Fast Facts* ■■■

Counselors are licensed in all 50 states and the District of Columbia. Requirements vary. Counseling students who want to work in a state different from where they are receiving their degree should consult the American Counseling Association website, www.counseling.org, where state professional counselor licensure boards are listed with their contact information.

 ## Spotlight
In Their Own Words—The Major Mental Health Organizations Describe Their Professions

In this section, we gleaned from the professional association websites how each of the professional organizations describes what their members do. Notice the language used by each of the associations as they describe their practice. Do you notice any overlaps? Any differences? You might take a moment to visit the websites of the different organizations for a more in-depth look at what they do.

The American Counseling Association (ACA)

What is professional counseling? Professional counselors work with individuals, families, groups, and organizations. Counseling is a collaborative effort between the counselor and client. Professional counselors help clients identify goals and potential solutions to problems which cause emotional turmoil; seek to improve communication and coping skills; strengthen self-esteem; and promote behavior change and optimal mental health. Through counseling you examine the behaviors, thoughts, and feelings that are causing difficulties in your life. You learn effective ways to deal with your problems by building upon personal strengths. A professional counselor will encourage your personal growth and development in ways that foster your interest and welfare.

_____

Source: www.counseling.org/consumers/FAQs.htm
Organization website: www.counseling.org

The American Psychological Association (APA)

What is psychology? Psychology is the study of mind and behavior. The discipline embraces all aspects of the human experience—from the functions of the brain to the actions of nations, from child development to care for the aged. In every conceivable setting from scientific research centers to mental health care services, "the understanding of behavior" is the enterprise of psychologists.

_____

Source: www.apa.org/about/
Organization website: www.apa.org

The American Psychiatric Association (APA)

What is a psychiatrist? A psychiatrist is a physician who specializes in the diagnosis, treatment,

the American Counseling Association's International Association for Marriage and Family Counselors (IAMFC) are large and active. Other associations such as the American Family Therapy Association (http://afta.org) also represent family therapists from a variety of professional backgrounds. Very few noted therapists were originally trained in marriage and family therapy. Family therapist pioneers such as Jay Haley (anthropology), James Framo (psychology), and Murray Bowen (psychiatry) have come from other disciplines.

Psychologists

Psychologists in the United States have a doctorate in psychology and are members of the American Psychological Association (APA) or the American Psychological Society (APS). The APA is the larger organization and represents most clinical psychologists. APA does not offer full membership to master's-level

and prevention of mental illnesses and substance use disorders. It takes many years of education and training to become a psychiatrist: He or she must graduate from college and then medical school, and go on to complete four years of residency training in the field of psychiatry. (Many psychiatrists undergo additional training so that they can further specialize in such areas as child and adolescent psychiatry, geriatric psychiatry, forensic psychiatry, psychopharmacology, and/or psychoanalysis.) This extensive medical training enables the psychiatrist to understand the body's functions and the complex relationship between emotional illness and other medical illnesses. The psychiatrist is thus the mental health professional and physician best qualified to distinguish between physical and psychological causes of both mental and physical distress.

Source: www.psych.org/public_info/what_psych.cfm
Organization website: www.psych.org

National Association of Social Workers (NASW)

What is the practice of social work? Social work practice consists of the professional application of social work values, principles, and techniques to one or more of the following ends: helping people obtain tangible services; counseling and psychotherapy with individuals, families, and groups; helping communities or groups provide or improve social and health services; and participating in legislative processes. The practice of social work requires knowledge of human development and behavior; of social, economic, and cultural institutions; and of the interaction of all these factors.

Source: www.socialworkers.org/pdev/default.asp
Organization website: www.socialworkers.org

American Association of Marriage and Family Therapists (AAMFT)

What is a marriage and family therapist? Marriage and family therapists (MFTs) are mental health professionals trained in psychotherapy and family systems, and licensed to diagnose and treat mental and emotional disorders within the context of marriage, couples, and family systems. Marriage and family therapists broaden the traditional emphasis on the individual to attend to the nature and role of individuals in primary relationship networks such as marriage and the family. MFTs take a holistic perspective to health care; they are concerned with the overall, long-term well-being of individuals and their families.

Source: www.aamft.org/faqs/index_nm.asp#what
Organization website: www.aamft.org

practitioners, although it trains them. They are not eligible for licensure as psychologists and frequently obtain licensure as counselors. The doctoral training of psychologists is about the same number of credit hours as doctoral training in counseling. The difference is that counselors must have a master's degree before entering the doctoral program. Psychologists receive a master's degree along the way to the doctoral degree. In addition, counseling doctoral students normally have several years of experience before entering doctoral training. Therefore, psychology doctoral students are younger, usually going into doctoral training directly out of a bachelor's program. They normally do not possess the 48 or 60 semester hours master's degree training of a counselor in addition to their doctoral training.

There are three major options for a doctorate in psychology that emphasizes therapy. The most traditional is the **clinical psychologist** (PhD), whose training is a heavy helping of research and testing along with a clinical internship. This model of scientist/practitioner was challenged in the late 1970s by the development of a pure therapist doctorate, the PsyD or **doctor of psychology**. The training necessary for a PsyD is similar to medical school training for a three- or four-year period in the APA-accredited programs. Nonaccredited programs vary in the length and type of training. Psychologists with a PsyD work mostly in private practice and rarely teach in universities. Like MDs, they are not academics but practitioners.

Counseling psychologists have a PhD in counseling psychology. Their primary province has been the college counseling center. Counseling psychologists may be members of Division 17 of the American Psychological Association, and some belong to the American Counseling Association too. Division 17 was founded in 1945 and was originally called the Division of Guidance and Counseling—now the Division of Counseling Psychology. For most of the last century, counseling programs and counseling psychology programs intermingled in universities with a large percentage located in colleges of education. Counseling psychologists frequently have more background in research than counselors, and their internships may focus more in the college counseling arena rather than community agencies. There are now only about 68 APA-accredited programs in counseling psychology in the United States and Canada.

The training of a psychologist. Making a gross generalization, psychology training emphasizes psychological testing, research, and biological bases of behavior much more than counseling programs. There is more emphasis on behavioral learning theory and cognitive therapy. Counseling programs, by contrast, focus more on skill development, the therapeutic relationship, career counseling, cultural issues, group work, and the needs of children. Counseling programs philosophically are closer to the humanistic versus the behavioral approach to helping clients.

Counseling and psychology have many overlaps and a shared history. Counselors read psychology journals, especially the *Journal of Counseling Psychology*, and often work side by side with psychologists in agencies, educational institutions, and corporations. Psychologists who have contributed to and influenced counseling include B. F. Skinner, Carl Rogers, Albert Ellis, Arnold Lazarus, Donald Meichenbaum, Albert Bandura, and many, many others.

Counseling Yesterday: The History of the Counseling Profession

When we read history, we tend to think that the story is a collection of facts. Actually, all historians have biases and see the events from the fortress of their own loyalties. Just as the history of the American Civil War can be told from at least two opposing angles, the history of counseling has many different threads. Frequently when we read about the history of counseling, we learn what happened chronologically—as if each decade were a building block leading to the present age of enlightenment. As you study the history of counseling, we think you will see that things are not so cut and dried. There have been violent upheavals, gradual shifts, and along with the forward steps there have frequently been backward ones and full-scale retreats. While it might have been neater to arrange our story by decades, we have decided to tell the history of counseling as a history of ideas. In other words, what are the grand passions and philosophies that shaped the profession, in some cases creating national movements? Along the way, we will identify some of the influential people and historical figures who served the profession. Finally, we will tell the story of the professional counseling associations and look at how their actions and composition affect the life of counselors today. We have portrayed the major ideas and their related movements to convey how the ideas about counseling affected and interacted with each other, creating a complex web of lived history, rather than a simple chronology. Just as in counseling where client stories seldom follow a simple linear path, the story of the counseling profession requires us to listen to the many related strands that weave together to form a history.

In telling this story, we have tried to be practical. What should a counselor know about his or her professional origins? Why should we know about the history of counseling ideas and philosophies? One reason is, as the song says, "Everything old is new again." In other words, ideas, enthusiasms, and models appear and disappear over time. Popular books and professional papers frequently fail to acknowledge that many of the same debates are still going on and many of the so-called revolutions in therapy have been tried before. Furthermore, we can solidify our sense of professional identity by looking at the ideas that form the basis of the profession. As you read through this history, you may want to take a moment to think: Are these ideas important to me? Are these values consistent with my own?

The ideas and philosophies that formed counseling are alive and well and can be discovered in the professional writings, worldviews, and philosophies of counselors. For example, the American Counseling Association (the main professional organization for counselors) publishes books and advertises them on its website, www.counseling.org. The major headings in the newest catalog are Multiculturalism, Advocacy and Empowerment, Holistic Counseling, Child and Adolescent Development, and Career Counseling and Development. Perusing the list of new releases, one finds a number of new books on multiculturalism, testing, career issues, and integrating family and school counseling, as well as clinical issues regarding trauma. As you read this chapter, we think you will find that these ideas are not new but stem from counseling's roots at the turn of the 20th century. The values formed by ideas, individuals, and organizations continue to influence what you will be reading in books and journals and hearing from your professors. By being aware of these ideas early in your career, you may be better able to critically evaluate them and see if these professional clothes fit you.

SNAPSHOT
Frank Parsons: Counselor (1854–1908)

Frank Parsons, First
Counselor

Parsons has been called the "Father of Vocational Guidance," but some claim that he was merely an easily identifiable symbol of the vocational guidance movement, a shooting star rather than a founder (Blocher, 2000). Parsons was trained both as an engineer and a lawyer. After being admitted to the bar, he suffered from exhaustion and camped for three years in New Mexico. Later, he taught art in public school and worked in publishing. During the Depression, he was a laborer for an iron mill. He was a college professor in social sciences in Kansas and later taught at Boston University Law School. One of his students described him as having a great intellect with the heart of a woman and the methods of a scientist (Davis, 1969). Throughout his life, he was a social activist railing against the excesses of big corporations and the "wild capitalism" of the time. He traveled widely, giving speeches that influenced Theodore Roosevelt and his friend Oliver Wendell Holmes. It must also be said that Parsons was prejudiced against some ethnic minorities and used phrenology (the study of bumps on the skull) to assess personality (Gummerre, 1988).

Parsons always considered his own career path to have been a series of mistakes so, in 1908 in Boston, he called a meeting of neighborhood boys who were graduating to find out what they were planning to do and what they knew about the world of work. When he discovered that they were woefully uninformed, Parsons began advising them and established the Vocation Bureau, the first vocational guidance center. His title was Director and Vocational Counselor. The center grew and stimulated interest in vocational guidance across the country. Parsons wrote 14 books including *Choosing a Vocation* (1909), published posthumously. It is fitting that one who struggled with so many abilities and careers became interested in helping others make good choices. His tombstone reads "Frank Parsons, HERO–TEACHER–PROPHET" (Davis, 1969).

What we owe to Parsons:

- Developed the first self-inventory or questionnaire for interests and aptitudes, and personality to match work environments. Designed the first counseling agency.
- Sparked the development of vocational guidance in schools.
- Conceived of counseling as a mutual process involving cooperation, an expert, and a client—and the client makes the final choice.
- Left a legacy of activism and advocacy for clients.

The Big Ideas of Counseling

In the next sections of this chapter, we will highlight some of the most important ideas that have influenced the development of the counseling profession. They are:

1. The values of equality, client advocacy, the importance of career
2. The potential for personal growth

3. The belief in science

4. The influence of health, human development, and biology

Some of these key values were a reaction to the world wars, the Depression, new laws, and other external changes. Others grew from the minds of a few thinkers and practitioners. All of these ideas have had strong adherents—people who fervently believed in them and made them a part of counseling today through their work and their personal examples. As you read, we hope you will be aware of your own personal reactions to these ideas. Note where you become interested, excited, and where you disagree.

Two graphical representations of the contents of this chapter might help you get an overview as well. Figure 1.1 shows the four major ideas and some of the associated trends and movements associated with them. Figure 1.2 includes a traditional time line so that you can trace the events we have talked about in a more linear fashion.

The values of equality, client advocacy, and the importance of career. The values of equality, client advocacy, and the importance of career may seem to be separate entities, but it is hard to unfasten them because they all began as part of a larger philosophy called **progressivism**. The years 1900 to 1920 have been called the Progressive Era because a large segment of the American population became awakened to negative changes wrought by rapid industrialization, corruption, and the overwhelming influx of immigrants. Although Mark Twain referred to this time as the Gilded Age, this was true mainly for the Carnegies and Rockefellers, not for the masses of newly arrived Americans who swarmed into the northern cities. Out of this confluence of events came the progressive movement. Progressivism was a

FIGURE 1.1 The Big Ideas of Counseling

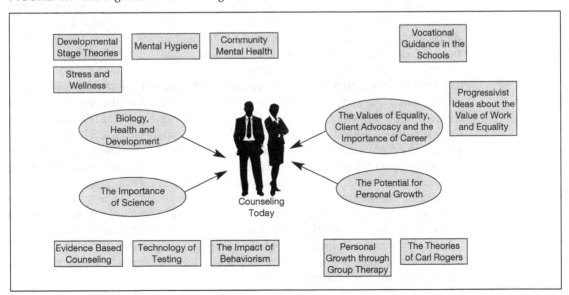

FIGURE 1.2 Events, High Points, and Key Moments in Counseling

World Events, Legislation, and Movements		Progressivist movement takes shape			World War II gives impetus to psychologists and testing GI Bill offers education to vets
High Points for the Profession	Frank Parson starts Vocational Bureau	First National Vocational Guidance Convention, 1910			
Key Discoveries and Publications	Freud publishes *Studies in Hysteria*, 1895 Parsons publishes *Choosing a Vocation*, 1909	Adler and Jung separate themselves from Freud	Strong publishes interest test, 1927	Axelrod, Roe, and Super propound theories of career development	Carl Rogers publishes *Counseling & Psychotherapy*, 1942 Frankl publishes first version of *Man's Search for Meaning* Existentialism flourishes
	1900–1910	1910s	1920s	1930s	1940s

social philosophy affecting many fields of study. It included election reform, antitrust legislation, women's rights, immigration reform, the needs of youth, and prohibition. Leadership came from the educational philosopher John Dewey and from the Christian Socialist Jane Addams. Both worked in Chicago, and that city became a stronghold of the movement.

Progressivism affected school reformers who shared the common ideal that education could be democratized without being reduced to the lowest common denominator. Alternative schools flourished. Maria Montessori's ideas about early childhood education were compatible with progressivism. The Montessori philosophy maintains that students should be allowed to follow their own interests and respect others. Progressivist educational ideas included character education and movement, and emphasized the importance of work. Progressivist ideas such as physical education, interest stations in classrooms, industrial arts, technical schools, and extracurricular activities are the remnants of this movement in today's schools. The election of the reformer Woodrow Wilson to the American presidency was the culmination of the progressivist movement's political aims. The administration was successful in passing legislation that ended child labor and established vocational education.

1950s	1960s	1970s	1980s	1990s	2000–2010
Sputnik is launched, 1957 NDEA passes, sets up institutes to train counselors	NDEA funding continues for elementary, then middle, and alternative school counselors End of the Vietnam war increases awareness of veterans' needs The special education movement means that all handicapped students must receive help			Congress rejects national health care War focuses counselors on PTSD	Congress passes a health care bill
Number of school counselors triples School counselors become 5th division of APGA		Virginia passes first counselor licensure law, 1976	Private practice of counseling flourishes	AACD changes its name to American Counseling Association	All states achieve licensure for MHCs or PCs
C. Gilbert Wrenn writes about counseling as a profession and a cultural perspective	Theoretical schools abound Group counseling becomes popular Mental health for school students becomes an important function of school counselors Developmental approach to school counseling gains momentum		CACREP created, 1983 The schools of counseling diminish Accountability becomes a watchword for school counselors	Computers and telephones become a part of counseling	ASCA model focuses on role of counselor as educator
1950s	1960s	1970s	1980s	1990s	2000–2010

Jesse B. Davis of Grand Rapids, Michigan, is considered to be the first individual to utilize vocational guidance practices in the classroom, but it was the charismatic reformer, Frank Parsons, who opened the Vocation Bureau in Boston's Civic House and who is most identified with the profession (McDaniel & Watts, 1994) (see Snapshot: Frank Parsons: Counselor). Blocher (2000) points out that Parsons was not the founder of the field of vocational guidance, nor was he an early pioneer, and his professional experience as a counselor only lasted six months or so. However, Parsons's book *Choosing a Vocation* (1909) has been immensely influential, probably because there was virtually nothing else available at the time it was published.

As time went on, the emphasis on agencies to help unemployed youth gave way to a focus on schools as the medium for guidance. This was partially due to the new wave of mandatory education laws. In the 1920s and 1930s, the progressive philosophy dominated school guidance, although teachers, not counselors, mainly delivered these lessons. Group guidance and career or vocational exploration was first used in this time period. The development of specialists in guidance grew slowly but steadily because the progressive ideas were compatible with promoting the overall growth of the students.

Progressivism today. Progressive ideas are still alive in counseling today. For example, the emphasis on multiculturalism in counseling is a direct offshoot of progressivist ideas of equality and mutuality. Multiculturalism is the idea that culture is a prime ingredient in a person's makeup and that counseling must consider a person's culture before appropriate treatment can be rendered. More than that, counselors believe that all cultures should be celebrated, not merely tolerated, and that counselors should possess skills, attitudes, and knowledge about cultures and cultural differences to practice ethically and effectively. The idea that individuals have differences but possess the same rights—the value of equality— still affects counseling today. Counselors still have a reformist attitude. They frequently discuss, write about, and teach client advocacy and ways of reforming organizations to make them more humane. Counselors are a diverse group, and so they are sensitive to the needs of minorities and those deprived of power.

Counseling still maintains a strong focus on career counseling too. Eight universities have graduate degree programs in career counseling accredited by CACREP. It began with the vocational guidance movement and drew from the progressivist philosophies. Career counseling is taught in virtually every counseling program at the master's and doctoral levels. In your career counseling class, you will learn about career development theories, career testing, and helping children and adults cope with vocational choice and career planning. Counselors find that one's career and work are frequently tied to one's self-esteem and overall wellness. Job stress and job dissatisfaction can lead to significant mental health problems, and it is sometimes difficult to differentiate problems caused by career difficulties from a person's overall mental health concerns.

The potential for personal growth. One of the enduring values in counseling is that human beings are viewed as being in the process of becoming. We are not finished. We can change, adapt, create, and do more than we expect. One of the founding divisions of the American Counseling Association is the Counseling Association for Humanistic Education and Development (C-AHEAD), now called the Association for Humanistic Counseling. C-AHEAD is the institutional keeper of the flame, but the value of humanism exists in the accreditation standards, in the curriculum, and in the philosophies of professors and practitioners.

The Legacy of Rogers. Carl Ransom Rogers is probably the most important name in counseling, not because of his professional leadership but because of his ideas and to a large extent because of his personal warmth and genuineness. *Counseling and Psychotherapy* (1942) was the compilation of his revolutionary concepts and research on the helping relationship. In 1951, he published his major work, *Client-Centered Therapy,* which formed the basis not just of a theory, but also of a set of values. His work sparked a humanistic movement among clinicians. *On Becoming a Person* (1961) has been cited as one of the most influential books among counselors and counseling professors as well (Young & Feiler, 1994). His idea that the counselor must create the "core conditions" of genuineness, empathy, and unconditional positive regard have become institutionalized in counseling. Rogers's legacy is that counseling is a profession that values the client and believes that clients have the inner potential to solve their own difficulties. Helping means implementing the core conditions and implies the need for a counselor to become a mentally healthy person. It is the therapeutic relationship mutually created by counselor and client that has the potential to heal.

The Group Therapy Movement and the Proliferation of Counseling Theories. During the late 1960s and the early 1970s, group therapy swept this country both in the form of therapeutic groups run by clinicians as well as groups led by nonprofessionals. On college campuses, in community mental health centers, hotels and corporate boardrooms, the country became fascinated with the power of the group to bring about personal growth. Groups bloomed at a time in American history when people yearned for a connection to community, having abandoned small towns and farms for the suburbs. Many people found their new lives to be sterile and disconnected. A sense of alienation between individuals and between generations had widened into a "generation gap" and a felt lack of intimacy in personal relationships. There were many innovations in group work during this time and many abuses too. Marathon group therapy was born, where participants worked for an extended period of time (usually 24–48 hours) without respite. There were harmful extremes including nude group therapy and highly confrontive group therapy (Yalom, 2005). The enthusiasm for groups waned in the 1980s, but the American Counseling Association's Association for Specialists in Group Work remains a strong division whose members are interested in therapeutic groups, task groups, and educational uses. Group work is a skill that every counselor learns and needs because of its tremendous ability to produce therapeutic change as well as its cost effectiveness.

The prominence of group work in the 1960s and 1970s cannot really be separated from the creative climate that was also affecting all of the helping professions. New counseling theories and techniques proliferated during this period. There was a good deal of rivalry between camps, and there were frequent debates among the founders and their followers. During this time, Rogers's client-centered therapy was pitted against strict behaviorists. Transactional analysis, rational emotive therapy, gestalt therapy, reality therapy, and many, many smaller schools of therapy arose. It has been estimated that by 1980, there were between 100 and 460 forms of therapy (Corsini, 2001; Herink, 1980; Parloff, 1979). While this created controversy and confusion, one result of this proliferation was a strengthening of one of counseling's key values: People can change and counseling helps them grow.

The belief in science. At the time that progressivist ideas were taking hold in the industrial cities, another powerful idea was sweeping the universities in America and abroad. The emergence of mass-production consumer goods, inoculation against disease, and technologists like Thomas Edison were creating a belief that science held the answers to every human misery and unhappiness. Perhaps to call it a religion is too strong a word, but the vehemence with which science and scientific progress were promoted was not less than that of the most fervent evangelist. Those who grew up in the 1950s and 1960s were bombarded by the dreams and horrors that science would someday make possible, from atomic energy to flying cars and the three-day workweek. The reliance on scientific findings and the value

Counseling Controversy

HOW DO EVIDENCE-BASED ARGUMENTS STACK UP AGAINST THEORETICAL AND CLINICAL WISDOM ARGUMENTS?

Background. A major trend in medicine and in mental health is a call for **evidence-based** treatment. This is the idea that clinicians should use only use scientifically validated treatments. Practitioners have long relied on "clinical wisdom," measuring success through experiences with clients. Practicing counselors and other clinicians are not always able to stay abreast of new research findings (Sexton, Whiston, Bleuer, & Walz, 1997). **Outcome research** is a term for research studies that try to compare the efficacy of different treatments based on client improvement. The results of outcome research often provide startling results. For example, for several years we treated clients with panic disorder (panic attacks and other anxiety symptoms) with relaxation training. Relaxation training had become a standard technique that had been refined since the 1930s. Unfortunately, it is not very effective with this type of highly anxious client (Beamish, Granello, & Belcastro, 2002). As the saying goes, "When the only tool you have is a hammer, everything looks like a nail." In other words, we tend to use our favorite counseling tools on all sorts of different problems rather than consulting outcome research. On the other hand, most therapists are not working scientists. Many practitioners rarely read journals, and they have accumulated data and beliefs about what works from their experiences with clients. Read the following arguments and see what you think.

POINT: EVIDENCE-BASED ARGUMENTS	COUNTERPOINT: THEORETICAL AND CLINICAL WISDOM ARGUMENTS
• A "seat-of-the pants" approach to counseling means that counselors use whatever is familiar rather than what works.	• Counseling is an art. The great therapists are artists, not scientists.
• Scientific study is the only rational method for determining what works. We can then develop manuals to guide treatment.	• The therapeutic relationship is crucial to good outcomes in counseling. Maximizing this relationship is more important than the technique that is used.
• Counselors sometimes use fad treatments rather than those that have been tested.	• Counselors who do not use theories to guide their work do not have a systematic way of working nor do they have the ability to plan treatment.
• Scientific study frequently reveals that approaches one thinks might help actually do not lead to improvement. Intuition and "wisdom" are subject to error.	• Research is mainly based on averages. Individual clients do not always respond to the standard treatment because of their differences.
• No theory of counseling has been shown to be more effective than any other.	• Through the accumulation of experience, a counselor gains important knowledge about what works in the real world.
	• Outcome research limits clinical innovation by encouraging clinicians to do only what has been proven effective, rather than to try new ideas and techniques.

Perhaps you have never thought about the issue of how a counselor should choose treatment methods. As you look at counseling theories, you will have the opportunity to think more about this because many counselors use these theories as the basis for their approach—not the research literature. As we address the importance of science in counseling, it seems important to think about this current controversy in counseling.

After reading the Counseling Controversy, think about the following questions.

1. One underlying assumption of the evidence-based approach is that using what works is more important than the experience level of the clinician who delivers it. What are your thoughts on this?
2. How important is it for a counselor to have proper training in research?
3. What are the practical reasons a counselor might not be keeping abreast of the new developments and effective treatments?

←———→

As with most controversies, there probably is truth on both sides of this argument.

Evidence-based   **Clinical wisdom**

On the continuum, place an "X" where you think you stand on this issue.

of data to validate counseling ideas has been a constant theme and influences counseling today. The role of science in the "art of counseling" has also been controversial. For example, Carl Rogers posed the question "Persons or Science?" in a landmark article (1955), pointing out the difficulties of reconciling scientific rigor and the need to recognize the uniqueness as we try to understand individuals.

The Technology of Testing. Wilhelm Wundt's laboratory in Germany in 1879 showed that it was possible to identify individual differences such as reaction time. Wundt is given credit for putting psychology on a scientific basis, separating it from philosophy and religion. James McKeen Catell first used the term *mental tests* in 1890 (see Blocher, 2000). His notion that personality traits could be measured was one of the most revolutionary psychological ideas of the time. In 1904, Alfred Binet and his doctoral student, Théodore Simon, began describing and measuring intelligence. Eventually they developed the first test of intelligence, which was described in Binet's paper, "New Methods for the Diagnosis of the Intellectual Level of Subnormals" (1905). The first IQ tests were developed around this time (Simon & Binet, 1916). As the title of Binet and Simon's article suggests, the purpose of such tests was to identify children who would not have been appropriate for public school. From its origins testing has aimed at classifying individuals using quantitative methods so that different educational and therapeutic treatments can be applied.

In 1927, E. K. Strong published the Strong Interest Inventory, the first vocational interest test. Strong's test was a bold step to move career assessment to a new scientific plane. Following Strong's lead, career testing inventories proliferated. Soon, personality testing became popular, especially with psychologists. Testing became an industry and a trusted tool of decision makers beginning in World War I, when American psychologists developed the Army Alpha and Army Beta tests to classify millions of people in the service. By the 1920s "applied psychology programs" using testing were developed in universities around the country. World War II added more impetus when the need arose to place individuals in service jobs. After the war, the GI Bill funded both education and counseling for returning service people. Career counseling and testing helped veterans enter new jobs.

Today in schools and clinics, testing is used to identify clients who are depressed and suicidal, who have specific learning disabilities, and who may be suffering from undiagnosed substance abuse problems. On the career side, every high school, college, and university uses interests, values, and aptitude testing to help students make decisions about higher education or careers. As a counselor, you will definitely learn to use the standard career instruments and probably utilize online and computer-assisted career instruments as well.

While psychologists and school psychologists usually have the most training in testing, many counselors also possess this background. In many states, counselors have the right to use psychological tests, providing they have the requisite training. Counselors and psychologists will continue to battle over this right and the right to use such terms as *psychological test* and *psychological report*.

The era of testing that accompanied the enthusiastic embrace of everything scientific was in decline by 1955. Its decline has been due to expense, disappointing results, and ethical concerns. Testing has been accused of being inaccurate, culturally biased, and clinically irrelevant. For example, much has been written about the cultural loading of intelligence tests (Flanagan, Genshaft, & Harrison, 1997) but less has been said about the irrelevance of some forms of testing. For example, testing cannot yet reliably predict violence, suicide, or even success in graduate school! Many argue, however, that even though tests are not yet accurate or cannot predict the future with specificity, they remain some of the best tools we have to help understand our clients.

The emphasis on testing by some members of the profession frequently clashes with some of counseling's main values, namely, the importance of personal growth, individuality, and autonomy. Personality and intelligence tests categorize people and portray them as having a certain measurable potential. In addition, tests do not necessarily benefit our clients by providing them knowledge about themselves. Many people are given tests (especially children) but never profit from the results, while institutions, schools, and employers use this information to make decisions about the individual. In some ways, it is like having a credit report that you cannot challenge or amend. The debate about the uses and misuses of testing will continue as we try to solve the dilemma posed by two contrasting values, the wish to be scientific and the need to respect individuality.

Achievement Testing. One of the most controversial uses of testing is the new trend in education to use achievement testing to measure the effectiveness of the educational curriculum (Kohn, 2000). The new testing fervor is due to the perception that student achievement has diminished and that to really improve achievement, we need a baseline and quantifiable goals. There is no national achievement test yet, so every state makes its own selection. Testing is an expensive, time-consuming operation. The results of testing can determine whether principals and administrative staff are retained and in some states, schools receive grades (A, B, C, D, or F) based partially on the results of the testing. In many school districts, teacher raises are based on how well students do on tests.

Frequently school counselors administer and safeguard the security of state achievement tests. In many cases, counselors are asked to explain the results to parents and to the students themselves. Recently, one of our internship students was asked to hold a "pep rally" to increase student motivation for the test. This trend places the responsibility for learning squarely on the school and the teachers. Some in the counseling profession have raised concerns about the emphasis on testing and the No Child Left Behind Act. They argue that the idea of standardized testing clashes with the values of counseling. If we look at the developmental guidance movement, counselors generally believe in maximizing the growth of all students. Testing means that teachers now "teach to the test," molding their curriculum around the standards, and they must therefore be oblivious, to some extent, to children's individual learning needs. Children cannot really follow their interests but must study what legislators feel are the "basics."

Behaviorism. In 1953, B. F. Skinner, the American behaviorist, published *Science and Human Behavior,* his appeal to apply science to human affairs. Skinner had also published *Walden II,* a fictional account of what life would be like in a utopian world governed by psychological science. Skinner had been an English major and his vision of a scientific society was persuasively written. It suggested that in the future, humans would be rational, and that we would need to work only a few hours per day. But his most important predictions involved how we would manage each other. In essence, we would learn to predict and control human behavior and engineer society to reward good behavior and eliminate problems through withholding rewards.

Behaviorism revolutionized psychology because it boldly asked to be evaluated by the same tools as physical sciences. This idea flew in the face of traditional methods of psychological inquiry and placed behaviorism in direct opposition to the clinical science of the Freudian analysts. Behaviorists began carefully collecting data and publishing their results. Since the 1970s behaviorism or *cognitive behaviorism* has been the major theoretical basis of most psychologists and most psychology programs. The appeal of behaviorism is that it is quantitative, that is, behavior is reduced to numbers and evaluated. Those who feel that therapy research, in an attempt to be precise, also became too narrowly focused have criticized this reductionism. More studies were done on eliminating or acquiring specific behaviors than in evaluating treatment programs. Much psychological research was found to be irrelevant to the practitioner and worse, it was rarely read. It must be said that behaviorism and modern cognitive behavioral therapy have contributed scores of important techniques and have challenged counselors to be more systematic in their practice. The behavioral approach to setting quantifiable goals has helped counselors evaluate client improvement.

Sputnik and the National Defense Education Act. On October 4, 1957, the Soviets launched Sputnik, the first man-made satellite of the earth (see Figure 1.3). Sputnik was only 22 inches in diameter, but its incessant beeping, picked up by

FIGURE 1.3 Sputnik

One of the authors (Mark) under a replica of Sputnik, the small round silver object hanging from the ceiling of the Smithsonian Air & Space Museum in Washington, DC. In this photo, it is easy to see how small Sputnik was (less than two feet in diameter). In spite of its small size, the first artificial satellite to orbit the earth had a large influence, including a significant boost to the profession of counseling.

radio, and its visibility in the night sky frightened the American public and embarrassed the government. America recognized that it was behind in the space race and number two to the Russians in science. In order to combat the newly perceived communist threat, a number of initiatives were created. One of these was the National Defense Education Act (NDEA) of 1958, which appropriated money for loans for teachers to go to graduate school for science, math, and modern language instruction. The section that has had a lasting impact on counseling was Title V. Part I gave money for training secondary school counselors to encourage students to attend college. Part II funded guidance and counseling institutes to train counselors. Schoolteachers and counselors were given stipends to attend university institutes that trained them in the technology of helping. Some of the training lasted as long as a year or went on for several summers, leading to a master's degree. Over time, the universities developed a complete curriculum and by the 1960s counseling had gained an institutional foothold.

Health and development: Is biology destiny? The idea that biology and psychology are intimately linked has a long history in the helping professions. Many of the clinicians who made important contributions to counseling today began as physicians. The "big three" of the psychoanalytic approach, Sigmund Freud, Alfred Adler, and Carl Jung, were all trained as physicians and saw their work as the first scientific approach to mental healing. All three showed sustained interest in the interaction between the body and the mind. Freud once said that biology is destiny, suggesting that we are inevitably affected by our physical makeup and the changes our bodies go through over time. Freud began his serious work in psychiatry treating what we now call *conversion disorder.* Conversion disorder is the psychologically caused loss or change of a physical function suggestive of a physical disorder. For example, Freud treated "hysterical blindness," as it was called in those days. The affected client reports being unable to see, but there is no physical cause for the disability. Many of Freud's original clients showed these kinds of symptoms, but today such cases are rare. Freud's theories about how the mind functions are in part based on his training as a neurologist. The observation that physical illness can be caused or exacerbated by psychological problems is still with us.

Biological Treatments. A number of biological treatments have been tried for mental disorders, including hydrotherapy (baths), insulin shock, and the most infamous, electroshock therapy (ECT). Today only electroshock therapy remains, and its use is confined to treating severe depression when the client fails to respond to medication. All mental health fields have been deeply affected by advances in medication for severe mental disorders. For example, few clients with schizophrenia were significantly helped by "talk therapies" alone. With the introduction of antipsychotic medications in the 1950s, clients with schizophrenia have been able to lead more normal lives with more freedom from confinement. This led to a conclusion that most (if not all) mental disorders can be cured with medications, and today, psychotropic medication is a major industry. However, these drugs did not come without a price tag. Until the 1990s many antipsychotic drugs led to irreversible neurological damage and had more of an effect on **hallucinations** (a sensory experience that a person perceives as real) and **delusions** (false beliefs about reality), but frequently did nothing to help other symptoms of schizophrenia. Modern medications have fewer side effects and eliminate more symptoms.

Since the 1980s new antidepressant medications have also been available. While these drugs may be considered important agents in the treatment of severe and chronic depression, many clinicians worry that the medications are overprescribed and overused by people with the normal "blues" due to advertising by drug companies. Prescription of antidepressant medication has increased rapidly, and rates of adult use of antidepressants tripled between 1994 and 2000. In 2002, 11% of women and 5% of men in the United States were prescribed antidepressants (Stagnitti, 2005).

One of the most frequently prescribed drugs is Ritalin. Although some alternatives are now available, Ritalin continues to be used to treat attention deficit disorder and hyperactivity in children on a grand scale (Greenhill & Osman, 2000). The United States now utilizes 90% of the Ritalin produced. While it can significantly help many children with attention problems, there are medical risks and many mental health professionals feel that it is prescribed more often than necessary for misbehavior rather than attention deficit disorder. Counselors in schools are alarmed at the growing rate of prescription drugs given to children—even preschoolers (Kalb, 2000).

In short, counselors work with clients who receive medication and so they must be informed about the effects of these drugs. Counselors find themselves in dilemmas at times because they want their clients to receive proper dosages, be prudent consumers, and receive the best treatments available. Yet they cannot advise their clients to discontinue a medication, take a higher or lower dose, or disparage a physician's treatment. Instead, counselors often find that they can be helpful teaching clients skills to work with their psychiatrists to make sure their medication is managed properly.

The Mental Health Movement. At the same time Frank Parsons was establishing the Vocation Bureau, Clifford W. Beers (1876–1943) was founding a movement to help mental patients. Beers suffered a bout of manic depression illness, what we would now call bipolar disorder. He was hospitalized for three years. Following his recovery, he wrote his famous (and horrifying) book, *A Mind That Found Itself* (1908). For example, he describes how he planned to commit suicide and his delusion that his brother was a spy. This book was so influential that it created a national outcry for more humane treatment of mental patients. Beers went on to organize the National Association for Mental Health to advocate for clients. He traveled widely and spread his message abroad. Originally, the idea was called the "mental hygiene movement," a name suggested by the psychiatrist Adolf Meyer, presumably to add a medical connotation. Using a biological/medical approach

Spotlight
Mental Health Advocacy Organizations

Persons with mental illnesses often have little political, economic, or social power. There are many organizations (including the organizations of the mental health professions) that advocate for persons with mental health problems. Two major advocacy groups are the National Mental Health Association (NMHA) and the National Alliance on Mental Illness (NAMI). You might want to check your local web and/or telephone listings to see if either of these groups have local affiliates, as they are great resources for information and may provide opportunities for volunteer work in the profession.

NMHA is the country's oldest and largest nonprofit organization addressing all aspects of mental health and mental illness. With more than 340 affiliates nationwide, NMHA works to improve the mental health of all Americans, especially the 54 million individuals with mental disorders, through advocacy, education, research, and service. For more information, see the NMHA website: www.nmha.org.

NAMI is a nonprofit, grassroots, self-help, support, and advocacy organization dedicated to improving the lives of persons living with mental illness. With more than 220,000 members, NAMI is the largest organization of its type. Founded in 1979, NAMI now has more than 1,200 state and local affiliates. For more information, see the NAMI website: www.nami.org.

evoked sympathy for the sufferers and decriminalized those with mental disorders. The term *mentally ill* became widespread, although today the term *person with mental illness* is preferred.

Beers and Meyer originated many of the modern ideas of agency work including outreach and prevention. The establishment of the National Institute of Mental Health and the community mental health center were built on Beers's initial work. The National Mental Health Association is the present-day organization that continues Beers's advocacy work. It has been instrumental in lobbying and doing educational work for clients of mental health services.

Before 1960, most mental health treatment was provided to patients in hospitals or private or state asylums. It is estimated that one of every two hospital beds in the country was for mental patients. The development of antipsychotic and antidepressant medication emptied hospitals of clients diagnosed with schizophrenia and depression, the two largest diagnostic categories. But it soon became evident that medication alone would not be enough. **Deinstitutionalization** (moving patients out of large institutional facilities such as state hospitals) required community support to make it permanent. Under the Kennedy administration, the Community Mental Health Center Act was conceived and finally passed in 1963. Communities received funding through grants, and mentally disabled patients became eligible for benefits from Medicare, Medicaid, and Social Security. Every community or "catchment area" was eligible to have a community mental health center (CMHC) providing inpatient, outpatient, education and consultation, partial hospitalization, and emergency services. At this same time, counseling programs were creating graduate degree programs in mental health counseling to meet the needs of the CMHCs. This new group of counselors with mental health training and experience began to develop a professional organization and vie for licensure.

Throughout the 1970s and 1980s, deinstitutionalization continued at a rapid pace along with legal precedents allowing mental patients to refuse treatment if they were not dangerous to themselves or others. In 1981, the Omnibus Budget Reconciliation Act under the Reagan Administration reduced funding for mental health services by 25%. In addition, money was shifted away from prevention and outpatient services for the community as a whole and was focused almost entirely on the treatment of the severely mentally disabled. The economic downturn of the 1980s, deinstitutionalization, and decreased funding to community mental health centers resulted in a large population of homeless mental patients. It is estimated that 20–25% of the homeless population suffer from a severe mental disorder, a startling number that does not even include those with substance abuse disorders (Koegel, Burnam, & Morton, 1996). The federal funding decline and shift in priorities means that community mental health centers in most states have changed from a comprehensive education, counseling, and prevention resource to an emergency hospitalization facility and partial hospitalization program. Consumers of counseling services, or their insurance companies if they have comprehensive mental health insurance, must pay a high price for counseling offered by private practitioners or community agencies.

The Importance of Development. Human beings go through physical, sexual, emotional, moral, spiritual, social, and psychological changes through life. **Stage theories** have been developed in each of these areas of human functioning to organize our knowledge about what is happening. As you study human development more deeply, you will find stage theories proposed by Freud (psychosexual), Erikson (1950) (psychosocial), Piaget (1964) (cognitive), Kohlberg (1975) (moral), Fowler (1995) (religious faith), Perry (intellect and ethics), Loevinger (the ego), and many others. Most stage models propose that like steps on a ladder, conquering each stage is a prerequisite for taking the next leap. In other words, the stages are sequential and cannot be skipped.

One of the first psychological stage theories was Sigmund Freud's controversial claim that children move through stages of psychosexual development called the oral, anal, latency, phallic, and genital stages as they physically mature. These stages were thought to be associated with psychological changes and became the basis for predicting psychopathology. For example, if a child was fixated at the oral stage, his or her difficulties might manifest as oral issues, such as drinking or eating disorders, later in life.

Jean Piaget was a biologist who proposed a cognitive developmental model based on physical maturation. Prior to his observations of children (including his own offspring), Piaget worked primarily with mollusks. He held a doctorate in natural history. He studied briefly with Carl Jung and began working on intelligence testing at the Sorbonne. His human studies led to one of the most persuasive models of how the human mind develops, the **stage model of cognitive development**, which he began writing about in the 1920s. His model was most influential during the 1950s and 1960s. The theory suggests that individuals move through four major stages of *cognitive* development as they physically mature. These stages are sensorimotor, preoperations, concrete operations, and formal operations. Piaget's work has been carefully studied, and it is safe to say that his ideas of human cognitive development are good descriptions in "broad strokes," but the exact sequences and stages are not as tidy as we first guessed. For example, it has been found that young infants have much more ability than Piaget suspected (Baillargeon, 1993). Many notions about the steplike nature of these stages have failed to hold water and have been criticized as sexist, culturally inappropriate, and unsupported by data (Gilligan, 1982). Despite these significant limitations, it must be recognized that Piaget's ideas and extensions of his ideas had tremendous influence on education, psychology, and counseling.

The concept of development and the influence of stage theories have been powerful in the counseling profession, much more so than in other mental health professions. In the core areas for accrediting counseling programs, Human Growth and Development is the first content area. There are two main reasons for its prominence. First, counselors generally have a psychological growth philosophy that is compatible (though not identical) with the notion of physical growth. They see human beings as moving in a positive direction and like the idea that a counselor is someone who removes blockages to the normal hurdles that each life stage produces. Second, counselors continue to struggle with how to treat people of differing ages and want a comprehensive structure that will make sense of the vast differences in clients at different ages. Many counselors work primarily with children and college counselors work mostly with a very restricted age range. Counselors frequently find that methods that work with adults fail miserably with first graders or college sophomores because of differences in all areas of development and because the environmental issues that they are dealing with are quite different. For example, eighth graders are dealing with complex social situations, college students are trying to separate from parents and form romantic relationships, and older adults are dealing with declining health and isolation. Advocates of stage theories suggest that if we understand the normal stages of physical and psychological development, we can utilize stage-appropriate methods for helping the client move to the next step.

The concept of *developmental guidance* is an offshoot of the developmental models. Developmental guidance aims at teaching schoolchildren life skills to improve academics and bolster self-esteem (Myrick, 1997). A developmental guidance approach in schools is generally more preventive and educational than problem oriented, meaning that school counselors spend less time on crises and more on teaching skills through group guidance and improvement of the school climate. In a developmental guidance program, the counselor is trying to influence the development of all the children by a knowledge of developmental, educational, and preventive mental health principles (Gysbers & Henderson, 1994).

Developmental guidance has been proposed as an alternative philosophy for school counselors who are frequently called upon to put out fires rather than thinking about growth (American School Counselor Association, 1984).

Stress and Wellness. In the 1960s, the word *stress* entered the American vocabulary. The work of Hans Selye (1974) awakened many in the medical and psychological field to the dire consequences of psychological stress on many human illnesses including heart disease, headaches, gastrointestinal disorders, and a wide variety of other illnesses. It was found that coping techniques significantly influenced the impact of negative life events on physiology (Folkman & Lazarus, 1980). This finding led to the conclusion that people might lead healthier lives if they could learn better coping techniques for living in a stressful world.

One of the results of the renewed interest in the mind-body connection was a flood of "stress workshops" given by professional and lay people during the 1970s and 1980s (cf. Tubesing, 1981). In the field of psychology, a new term, *health psychology,* was being utilized and an American Psychological Association division by the same name was formed along with a related journal. Psychology began to study coping and the benefits of psychotherapy for health problems.

Counseling began to focus on the word *wellness* in the late 1970s. Wellness is defined as "the whole person approach for improving the quality of life in proactive and positive ways" (Witmer, 1985, p. 45). The term recognizes that an individual's outlook and self-care skills are an important part of health and that physicians need to recognize and activate these healing forces (Travis, 1981). In the counseling field, the special issue of the *Journal of Counseling and Development* edited by Myers, Emmerling, and Leafgren (1992) was apparently the high-water mark for the wellness movement in counseling. It was suggested that this should become the training paradigm for counseling that the stage models or developmental model failed to provide (Myers, 1992; Witmer & Sweeney, 1992; Witmer & Young, 1996). The bold notion that counselors are wellness professionals aimed at enhancing physical, mental, and emotional wellness across the life span never became an organizing force for the profession. Some counseling programs have courses in wellness that promote a holistic approach by exploring physical, mental, and spiritual methods and techniques. The term *wellness* is used in community health prevention facilities and in university campus "wellness centers" that help students learn coping skills and preventive strategies in a nonclinical environment.

Looking at the historical interaction among biology, medicine, and physical health, counseling has led a rather separate life, unlike psychology, which struggled for recognition from psychiatry (Blocher, 2000). Psychology has a history of interest in diagnosis and treatment of neurological problems. Recently psychologists received the

■■■ *Fast Facts* ■■■

According to the American Academy of Family Physicians, two-thirds of office visits to family doctors are prompted by stress-related symptoms.

Source: Cotton, D. H. G. (1990). *Stress management: An integrated approach to therapy.* New York: Brunner/Mazel.

ability to prescribe psychotropic medication in one U.S. state. In general, however, the illness model has not been attractive to counselors. Most do not fully embrace the diagnostic treatment-planning model, and they prefer to talk about clients rather than patients. Frank Parsons's (1909) idea that counseling is a based on "mutuality," a confiding relationship (similar to a lawyer/client relationship), has been more influential than the medical metaphor of expert/patient.

Recent Issues in Health Care. In the early 1990s the U.S. Congress refused to institute a national health care plan to deal with the health care crisis, which involves skyrocketing medical costs and large numbers of uninsured people. Recently, a health care bill was passed, but at this writing many of its provisions are not yet in effect. Millions of Americans do not have health insurance, meaning that in addition to lack of services for physical health problems, they are not covered for counseling or inpatient treatment for a mental disorder. **Managed care** companies have flourished as employers try to cut costs. Managed care companies include health maintenance organizations (HMOs) or preferred provider organizations (PPOs). While managed care companies show record profits, many Americans are dissatisfied with this system that lowers health care costs and quality of care at the same time. In general, an HMO or PPO contracts with employers to pay a certain rate for insurance and then bargains with providers (such as doctors, dentists, and mental health care professionals) to provide services at a bargain rate. For the private practitioner in counseling, it has meant a lowered per hour rate but a higher client volume. Clients (also called consumers) and providers have been frustrated by these payment systems and by the fact that they cannot deliver the treatments they think best. Managed care companies dictate the length and types of treatment based on their cost effectiveness. Maintaining quality services while operating within managed care is one of the key challenges that counselors will face in the upcoming decades.

 # History of the American Counseling Association

Later in this text, we describe the structure of the American Counseling Association and its divisions as well as its efforts in licensure and credentialing. For now, let us look only at how the structure of the organization changed as a result of world events, legislation, and social movements. This brief history may echo the values and philosophies that you have been reading about.

In 1910, the meeting of the National Society for the Promotion of Industrial Education (NSPIE) was attended by Jane Addams, G. Stanley Hall, and Jesse B. Davis and was hosted by Meyer Bloomfield, Parsons's successor at the Vocation Bureau. The meeting invigorated this group of progressivists, but some were more interested in political change. It was Jessie B. Davis, high school teacher and counseling pioneer, who helped to found a breakaway organization at the NSPIE's Grand Rapids Conference in 1913. It was called the National Vocational Guidance Association (NVGA), the forerunner of the American Counseling

 ## Spotlight
The American Counseling Association (ACA) Annual Convention

Every year, the American Counseling Association hosts an annual convention in a major American city. Counselors from around the country and from many foreign nations come together to learn and mingle. Visit the ACA website, www.counseling.org, to get a schedule of this year's program, but you can expect the following main events:

- **Keynote Speeches.** Keynote speeches are spread throughout the conference. Frequently they are inspiring talks by important thinkers.

- **Learning Institutes.** Full-day and half-day workshops by noted experts in the field that take place before the convention actually begins. Some institutes are for those who are just beginning to explore a topic; others are more advanced.

- **Division Meetings.** ACA's 19 divisions represent counseling specialties such as group work, counselor education and supervision, assessment, and so on. Most groups hold board meetings and luncheons and give national awards at the convention.

- **Exposition.** Book publishers from all the major houses (including ACA) display and sell titles, videos, and CDs at the convention. Testing companies demonstrate the latest technology for administration. You also find school counseling curriculum materials and play therapy equipment.

- **30-Minute Project/Research Poster Sessions.** These sessions present research findings or innovative counseling methods. The format is interactive with many people stopping by a session for only a few minutes to get a handout while others can linger and go into more depth.

- **90-Minute and 3-Hour Sessions.** These sessions go into greater depth. The following list is a sample of the workshop titles from a recent ACA annual convention, and you can see the great diversity of interests represented:

  "The Schoolyard Bully: Mean Kid or Victim Too?"

  "Creating Employment Opportunities for First-Time Offenders"

  "Gestalt Dreamwork in Group Counseling"

  "Self-Injurious Behavior: Diagnosis, Assessment, and Intervention"

Association. Rather than political change, the NVGA was a group of practitioners who wanted to develop a profession (Blocher, 2000).

Over the years, the organization and its major journal changed names and focus several times. Until 1952, the organization's focus was clearly on vocational guidance. In 1952, the American College Personnel Association (ACPA) merged with the NVGA. ACPA was an organization that represented student life workers and administrators at colleges and universities. The merger created the name change to the American Personnel and Guidance Association (APGA). This compromise set of letters was later discarded when ACPA disaffiliated in the early 1980s. At about the same time, the American Mental Health Counselors joined APGA, creating a new clinical division. One of the key events that triggered the change was the first licensure law in Virginia in 1976. For the first time, counselors

"Doctoral Written Exam Replaced with Portfolio Assessment"

"Dual Relationships in Academia"

"Attitudes toward Wheelchair Users"

"Hepatitis C and Substance Abuse"

"Family Counseling in School Settings: Measuring Outcomes"

"Facilitating Spiritual Wellness with Gay, Lesbian, and Bisexual Clients"

"The Experiences of First-Year School Counselors: A Qualitative Study"

"Utilizing Play Therapy with Culturally Diverse Families"

- **Parties.** ACA conventions always include one grand get-together either at the beginning or the end of the conference.
- **Ancillary Receptions.** Universities hold hotel-room receptions for their alumni, and ACA divisions provide networking opportunities at hotel salon gatherings.
- **Counseling Career Network.** An opportunity to meet employers and possibly be interviewed for a position.

What to Do at the Convention:

- **Volunteer.** Students can volunteer to work for 12 hours and receive a discounted registration fee. Sometimes this means clerical work, or you might monitor education sessions, meet the presenter, and have a chance to listen to his or her workshop.
- **Browse the Exposition Exhibits.** Take at least four hours to discover the newest publications and technology.
- **Schmooze.** Talk with presenters, attend division receptions and parties. Some of the most interesting networking occurs when you are on a shuttle bus, loitering in a lobby, or munching at a buffet table. The value of the convention is making contact with other counselors. ACA usually hosts a lounge for graduate students where you can learn about special events and meet other students.
- **Attend a First-Timers Orientation.** Because the convention is so vast, this orientation can get you started in the right direction.
- **Go to Education Sessions.** Go through the convention program and circle the "must see" education sessions, keynote talks, and ancillary meetings. Make a schedule for yourself. It is easy to get swept away when so much is happening.
- **Go to Preconference Institutes.** Here you can explore a topic in depth and learn practical skills for a few hours or a day.

received state licensure, allowing their members to conduct private practice and vie for insurance dollars. The complexion of the organization changed with two groups dominating, mental health counselors and school counselors.

In the early 1980s it was clear that counseling, not guidance, was the chosen identity of the profession, but the organization was not ready to give up its developmental roots. Another compromise name was accepted and in 1983, we temporarily became the American Association for Counseling and Development. In 1992, the name was simplified to the American Counseling Association. The name changes are important not simply because they portray changes in thinking but because they also show the diversity of the profession and the need to negotiate at every step. They also reveal some of the major values of the organization: the importance of career guidance and a view of the individual as a developing entity.

Summary

In this chapter, you learned about the historical roots of the counseling profession. Rather than present these concepts in a linear fashion, we presented four major ideas and discussed how these interrelated concepts have shaped the counseling profession today. You learned that counselors share some common values, including the belief in equality, a passion for client advocacy, and an understanding that all human beings have great potential for personal growth and development. You read about the importance of science and the influence of health and biology to the counseling profession, and how these values sometimes clash with the humanistic beliefs that are at the core of the counseling profession. The overarching message in the story of counseling, however, is one of change, growth, and dynamism. The counseling narrative continues to evolve and change as the profession evolves and steps up to meet the ever-changing needs of society. Changes in technology, the economy, health care, politics, education, cultural diversity, and the social climate all influence the story of the counseling profession.

This chapter also highlighted the five major helping professions: counseling, social work, marriage and family therapy, psychology, and psychiatry. The story of counseling has been shaped by the interplay of these five major professions, and counselors today understand that they must find ways to be collaborative with these other professionals in order to best serve the needs of their clients and of the people in the communities in which they work.

Additionally, this chapter introduced you to the layout of this text and the premise that becoming a *self-reflective practitioner* will help you develop a mindset that will be useful not just in reading this text, but in your journey toward becoming a professional counselor.

End-of-Chapter Activities

The following activities might be part of your assignments for a class. Whether they are required or not, we suggest that you complete them as a way of reflecting on your new learning, arguing with new ideas in writing, and thinking about questions you may want to pose in class.

Student Activities

1. **Reflect.** Now it's time to reflect on the major topics that we have covered in Chapter 1. Look back at the sections or the ideas you have underlined. What were your reactions as you read that portion of the chapter? What do you want to remember?

   _____

   _____

_____

_____

_____

2. Take a look at the time line in Figure 1.2 that gives a brief review of the
   world events, highlights of the professional organizations, and new discoveries and theories. What particularly interested or surprised you? What, if
   anything, did you find disturbing?

_____

_____

_____

_____

_____

3. The four key values issues in this chapter were (1) equality, advocacy, and
   career; (2) the importance of science; (3) biology, health, and development;
   and (4) the potential for personal growth. Are there other important values
   in counseling that you noticed? Any other reflections or ideas that you want
   to get on paper so you don't forget them?

_____

_____

_____

_____

_____

■■■ Journal Question ■■■

Frank Parsons (1909, p. 5) was earlier quoted
as saying that a good choice of career involves:
"(1) a clear understanding of yourself, your
aptitudes, abilities, interests, ambitions,
resources, limitations, and their causes; (2) a
knowledge of the requirements and conditions
of success, advantages and disadvantages,
compensation, opportunities, and prospects in
different lines of work; (3) true reasoning on
the relations of these two groups of facts."

As you consider entering the counseling
profession, do you think you have a clear
understanding of yourself and knowledge
of the profession? If not, what information
about your self or about the profession do
you need?

■■■ Topics for Discussion ■■■

1. In this chapter, the authors try to justify the study of history by saying that professional identity involves understanding the basic values of the profession and that those values are revealed in its history. Do you agree? Are there any other reasons to study history?

2. The reformist attitude is still alive in counseling today. Counselors are trying to cure society's ills by changing institutions and through client advocacy. American Counseling Association's division Counselors for Social Justice is an example of the fact that such sentiments are still alive. Some writers feel that counselors must be activists to really make changes in the forces that are creating mental health problems and obstacles to optimal functioning. Do you think it is the counselor's job to take social action or is it sufficient to help individuals, couples, and families lead happier, more productive lives?

3. Reflect on the standardized tests that you have taken in high school or college, perhaps to get into college or graduate school or for career planning and placement. Has a significant goal in your life hinged on your test performance? For most students, a licensure test is in your future. How will the results of that assessment affect your ability to become a professional counselor?

■■■ Experiments ■■■

1. Look at some university websites or catalogs and compare social work, counseling, and psychology master's programs. Do you notice a difference in emphasis on testing, administration, and practicum experiences? Is a thesis required? What do you think is unique about the training of each program?

2. Attend a state or national counseling conference. Students get very low rates on conferences and on membership dues of professional organizations. During the conference consider whether the ideas and the topics presented pique your interest. Does this organization fit you?

■■■ Explore More ■■■

If you are interested in exploring more about the ideas presented in this chapter, we recommend the following books and articles.

Books

Kaplan, B. (1964). *The inner world of mental illness.* New York: Harper & Row.

> This is a collection of first-hand experiences by people with mental disorders including Clifford Beers, Tolstoy, Saint Augustine, Sartre, and many others.

Locke, D. C., Myers, J. E., & Herr, E. (Eds.), *The handbook of counseling* (pp. 3–26). Thousand Oaks, CA: Sage.

> Sweeney's history helps link philosophy, history, and the idea of professional identity.

Rogers, C. R. (1961). *On becoming a person.* Boston: Houghton Mifflin.

> Rogers's manifesto for the client-centered (now person-centered) movement in counseling explains the humanistic theory in layperson's terms.

Sweeney, T. J. (2001). Counseling: Historical origins and philosophical roots. In D. Locke, J. West, D. L., Bubenzer, D., &

Osborn, C. J. (Eds.). (2003). *Leaders and legacies: Contributions to the counseling profession.* New York: Brunner Routledge.

> This is a series of biographies of key historical figures and current leaders written by their peers. The editors use these biographies as a springboard to discuss the notion of professional identity.

◼◻◼ MyHelpingLab ◼◻◼

To help you explore the profession of counseling via video interviews with counselors and clients, some of the chapters in this text include links to MyHelpingLab at the Pearson.com website. There are some videos that correspond with this chapter, and watching them might challenge you to think about these concepts at a deeper level.

- Under the heading Ethical, Legal, and Professional Issues, go to "Professional Identity of Counselors" to watch this video clip:
  - What is a counselor? (and then video clip response)

- As you watch this beginning counselor struggle with describing to a client who she is and what she can offer, think about ways that you might describe to future clients, parents of students, colleagues, or others what it is that counselors do.

2

What Do Counselors Do?

In this chapter, we will:

- Discuss the many different roles that counselors play and describe the most common roles a counselor might assume.

- Ask you to consider what your ideal counseling job looks like, and which of the counseling roles would be most appealing to you.

- Hear from four practicing counselors in different settings. They will tell us, in their own words, what their life as a counselor is like, what their "typical day" looks like, and what parts of their job they particularly like or dislike.

As you read the chapter, you might want to consider:

- What image comes to your mind when you think about counselors? How has this image been affected by the media? Your exploration of the profession? Your own personal experiences of counseling? Do you think your image is an accurate one?

- What do you think counselors do on a day-to-day basis? How do they spend their time? What components of the job do you think you would like? Find stressful?

- How will you decide what counselor roles are a good fit for you?

If you stop for a moment and think about it, you probably already have some ideas about what counselors do. You undoubtedly were drawn to the profession because you had an image of what counseling looks like, how people are helped by counseling, and how you might fit into this process. You may even want to close your eyes for a moment and engage in a bit of imagery. What do you imagine the job is like? Can you picture yourself in the role of a counselor? Take a moment and imagine yourself at the end of your graduate training, the day after you graduate or receive your license. What are you doing? What does it look like?

A picture may come immediately to your mind. Where did that picture come from? Do you have images from television or the movies about what a "typical" counseling session looks like? Are your pictures influenced by your own experience in counseling? Or that of your friends or family members? Did you imagine a client lying on a couch telling you about his past? Or a teary-eyed child in your office, confiding in you? Did you see yourself out in the community? Did you picture yourself actively solving problems, or is your vision more in line with a counselor who is more reflective?

Perhaps you are having difficulty envisioning what a "typical" counselor does or how or where you will fit into the role of the counselor. That's not unusual. Our images of counseling can be distorted by many factors. For example, a quick search of YouTube finds thousands of "hits" for the words "counseling" or "counselor." Yet very few of these videos portray an accurate representation of the world of the counselor.

The point is that there are many different images of counseling, and we all come to the profession of counseling with our own preconceived ideas of what counselors do. Some images are accurate, but others will require some alteration and refinement over the course of your training. Whatever your images of counseling, they have helped provide you with the motivation to embark upon this career path.

Part of the difficulty many people have in developing a mental picture of counseling may be related to the extremely large diversity of jobs, settings, clients, and responsibilities within the counseling profession. To be sure, some of the confusion comes from the word itself. *Counseling* is a generic term that is used when two people work together to solve a problem. It is for this reason that we see job titles like "financial counselor," "camp counselor," "real estate counselor," or even, as one of us recently experienced, "vinyl siding counselor." Even in the context of mental health, however, there is still great diversity in where counselors work and what they do.

In this chapter, we will discuss what counselors do by talking about the many different roles that counselors take on. We will highlight some of the most common roles, with the understanding that there are many more roles and functions than we can possibly include here.

In Chapter 1, we discussed some of the ways that the role of the counselor compares with that of other helping professionals. The emphasis was on the differences in roles and functions *between* the helping professions. In this chapter, you will learn about the great diversity of roles *within* the profession of counseling. What counselors do depends in great part upon what roles they assume, and within the field of counseling, there are many, many options.

Table 2.1 on pages 40–41 lists 20 different roles that counselors can engage in, and it is a good place to begin the discussion of counselor roles. Clearly, not all counselors engage in all of these roles, and not all counselors are trained or qualified for every role. Additionally, there are other roles and functions that counselors in highly specialized settings may perform. But the chart will give you a general idea to get you started. As you read through the list, you may wish to indicate which roles are particularly appealing to you and which ones you are less enthusiastic about. You also may encounter some roles that surprise or intrigue you, or which you know very little about. Indicate this as well. This process of clarification may help you in your own search for a personal sense of professional identity.

TABLE 2.1   The Many Roles of the Counselor

Counselor Role	Major Responsibilities	My Level of Interest in This Role (Indicate response, and jot down notes to help clarify your interests.)
Counselor as Therapist	Conducting individual or family counseling; career counseling	A B C ‼ ? *Comments:*
Counselor as Group Leader	Coordinating and running psychoeducational or therapeutic groups	A B C ‼ ? *Comments:*
Counselor as K–12 Guidance Curriculum Expert	Program planning; conducting guidance lessons in K–12 classrooms or through small group guidance activities; educating parents, conducting teacher inservices	A B C ‼ ? *Comments:*
Counselor as Diagnostician	Making appropriate mental health diagnoses for clients	A B C ‼ ? *Comments:*
Counselor as Assessor	Assessing client strengths and weaknesses, personality traits, interests, etc., sometimes through the use of formalized instruments	A B C ‼ ? *Comments:*
Counselor as Consultant	Working with other mental health or educational professionals on specific clients, cases, or groups	A B C ‼ ? *Comments:*
Counselor as Administrator	Scheduling clients, students, or projects; organizing office responsibilities; managing and/or supervising (nonclinical) staff	A B C ‼ ? *Comments:*
Counselor as Record Keeper or Case Manager	Completing paperwork, scheduling, and billing; assisting clients with functions of daily living, including navigating social services (e.g., housing, food stamps) as well as ongoing management of chronic mental illnesses	A B C ‼ ? *Comments:*
Counselor as Researcher or Scientist	Conducting research on counseling or program effectiveness; surveying clients, families, parents about counseling programs	A B C ‼ ? *Comments:*
Counselor as Learner	Keeping up-to-date with the field, attending workshops, classes, reading journals, etc.	A B C ‼ ? *Comments:*

Counselor as Educator or Trainer	Teaching others within the context of a formalized educational institution, through workshops or writing, or other venues	A B C ‼ ? *Comments:*
Counselor as Supervisor or Supervisee	Supervising counselors in training, or being supervised by more advanced practitioners	A B C ‼ ? *Comments:*
Counselor as Crisis Interventionist	Stepping in to assist individuals to cope during periods of individual or widespread crises and disasters	A B C ‼ ? *Comments:*
Counselor as Advisor	Assisting students and clients with academic and/or career decisions	A B C ‼ ? *Comments:*
Counselor as Expert Witness	Interacting with the legal system to provide testimony on behalf of clients, agencies, etc.	A B C ‼ ? *Comments:*
Counselor as Prevention Specialist	Working with individuals to promote wellness and prevention; working with systems (e.g., schools, employers, public agencies) to promote wellness and prevention	A B C ‼ ? *Comments:*
Counselor as Businessperson or Entrepreneur	Setting up and maintaining a private practice, developing products or services for commercial sale, obtaining funding for projects or social services agencies, writing grants to provide services	A B C ‼ ? *Comments:*
Counselor as Mediator	Assisting parties in a dispute to find an amenable solution	A B C ‼ ? *Comments:*
Counselor as Advocate or Agent of Social Change	Advocating for clients, for the profession, or for broader concerns (e.g., mental health, anti-stigma); working for systems change, widespread political and/or social activism	A B C ‼ ? *Comments:*
Counselor as Member of Professional Associations	Participating in associations and organizations that promote professionalism and a sense of professional identity within the profession	A B C ‼ ? *Comments:*

A = I am very interested in this role.
B = I am not sure if this would be a good fit for me.
C = I don't believe that this would be a good fit for me.
‼ = This role surprises or intrigues me. I want to learn more.
? = I don't know enough about this role to have an opinion.

As you pay attention to the many roles of the counselor, notice that there are some roles that you did not see in this chart. For example, you did not see "Counselor as Disciplinarian," a role that school counselors may sometimes be asked to play. We argue that this is never an appropriate role for a school counselor. School counselors are not disciplinarians and do not possess the proper credentials for disciplining students. More importantly, stepping into the punitive role undermines the school counselor's credibility as a person a student can go to for help. The American School Counselor Association (ASCA, 2007) has developed a position paper on the issue. ASCA states that school counselors can best make use of their education and experience not by punishing students, but by helping them understand the consequences of their behaviors and participating in schoolwide efforts to make schools safe and healthy places for learning. Being a disciplinarian sets the counselor in an adversarial role—*against* the student. Counseling, on the other hand, literally means "to come alongside." Clearly these two roles—counselor and disciplinarian—are generally at cross-purposes.

You also did not see the role of "guidance counselor." Although this term has been in use for many years, in 2003, the American School Counselor Association

 ## Spotlight
Appropriate and Inappropriate Activities for School Counselors

The American School Counselor Association (ASCA) National Model for school counseling programs helps school counselors focus on the appropriate use of their time. The overarching goal of school counselors is to engage in activities that contribute to a comprehensive school counseling program. Therefore, school counselors contribute to the school environment in ways that best make use of their training and experience. Although school counselors understand the need to be team players and "pitch in" when necessary, they cannot be fully effective in schools if they are not performing the roles that they are best trained to do. When school counselors coordinate tests or schedule classes or engage in other administrative duties, they are not available to implement the comprehensive school counseling programs, and ultimately, the students suffer.

Consider this comment from one state's survey of school counselors: "I am filling out this survey based on my responsibilities last year. I was the testing coordinator. Testing is a *full-time* job. I would work most weekends, Sunday mornings included, to keep my head above water. It was *awful.* This year, my high school hired a test coordinator. I *love* counseling! I'm working like a dog, and it is *great!"* (North Carolina School Counselor Survey, 2000). It's clear from this comment that counselors are not afraid of hard work or taking on their share of responsibilities—it's that they want to (and should do) the job they are trained and hired to do. On the same survey, another counselor wrote, "So many children's individual needs are going unmet because school counselors are being forced to spend most of their time in classrooms, cumulative records, testing, committee meetings, etc., rather than focusing on the children's needs" (North Carolina School Counselor Survey, 2000).

developed national standards and replaced the term *guidance counselor* with *professional school counselor*. Professional School Counselors engage in a wide variety of the roles listed in the chart, but for many reasons that will be discussed throughout the book, the term *guidance counselor* has fallen into disuse.

Finally, a role that you did not see on the chart is "Counselor as Multicultural Expert." We did not include this as a separate role because we do not see this as a distinct role or an optional choice. We believe that *all counselors in all settings and all roles* must be multicultural experts, and multicultural counseling competence must be at the foundation of *all* counseling roles, whether working directly with clients or students, running a private practice or agency, conducting research, or supervising or teaching others.

In the following Spotlight, you will read more about some appropriate and inappropriate roles for school counselors. Then, in the following sections, you will read more in depth about each of the appropriate counselor roles listed in Table 2.1. As you read more about each of these roles, consider whether the description of the role has changed your initial reaction to it and make a correction to your original ranking, if appropriate.

Inappropriate (Noncounseling) Activities	Appropriate (Counseling) Responsibilities
Registering and scheduling all new students	Designing individual student academic programs
Administering cognitive, aptitude, and achievement tests	Interpreting cognitive, aptitude, and achievement tests
Signing excuses for students who are tardy or absent	Counseling students with excessive tardiness or absenteeism
Performing disciplinary actions	Counseling students with disciplinary problems
Sending home students who are not appropriately dressed	Counseling students about appropriate school dress
Teaching classes when teachers are absent	Collaborating with teachers to present guidance curriculum lessons
Computing grade-point averages	Analyzing grade-point averages in relationship to achievement
Maintaining student records	Interpreting student records
Supervising study halls	Providing teachers with suggestions for better study hall management
Clerical record keeping	Ensuring student records are maintained in accordance with state and federal regulations
Assisting with duties in the principal's office	Assisting the school principal with identifying and resolving student issues, needs, and problems
Working with one student at a time in a therapeutic, clinical mode	Collaborating with teachers to present proactive, prevention-based guidance curriculum lessons.

Source: ASCA National Model: A Framework for School Counseling Programs (2005, p. 56).

Counseling: A Multi-Faceted Profession

Regardless of the setting, professional counselors are trained to help people with personal, family, social, environmental, educational, and career decisions. The American Counseling Association defines professional counseling as "the application of mental health, psychological, or human developmental principles, through cognitive, affective, behavioral, or systematic intervention strategies, that address wellness, personal growth, or career development, as well as pathology" (ACA, 1997). The American School Counselor Association defines counseling as addressing "all students' academic, personal/social, and career development needs" (ASCA, 2008). Counseling is typically viewed as a collaborative effort between the counselor and the client (and others, as appropriate), rather than something that is done by the counselor "to" or even "for" the client. In general, professional counselors help clients identify goals and potential solutions to problems that cause emotional turmoil, seek to improve communication and coping skills, strengthen self-esteem, and promote behavior change and optimal mental health.

Within the broader field of counseling, the different specialties have specific emphases. Professional counseling specialties include mental health, school, career, gerontological, rehabilitation, substance abuse and behavioral disorders, marriage and family therapists, and many more. Each of these specialties is more "narrowly focused, requiring advanced knowledge in the field founded on the premise that all Professional Counselors must first meet the requirements for the general practice of professional counseling" (ACA, 1997). That is, all counselors, regardless of setting and specialty, are first and foremost counselors.

Counselor as Therapist (Direct Service Provider)

Counselors in many different settings work with individuals, couples, and families to treat mental and emotional disorders and conditions and to promote optimal mental health. In this context, counselors apply a variety of therapeutic techniques and theories to address a wide range of concerns, from mental health diagnoses (e.g., depression, anxiety disorders, psychotic disorders), to problem behaviors (e.g., suicidal impulses, bullying, addictions, parenting, relationship issues), lifestyle concerns (e.g., stress management, job and career concerns, issues associated with aging, educational decisions), and other presenting problems (e.g., self-esteem, self-awareness; identity development, interpersonal skill development; coping strategies). The role of "counselor as therapist" is central to all professional counselors. In other words, although not all counselors in all settings will work in intensive one-on-one psychotherapy with clients, all counselors will work with individuals in therapeutic ways to help clients make appropriate choices and changes in their lives. Whether through

---

■■■ *Words of Wisdom* ■■■

"I've learned to stop trying to give clients answers and let them find their own through our work."

—Andrew Moss, Licensed
Professional Counselor

brief interventions that focus on making behavioral changes, through assistance with a decision-making process that may occur in career counseling, or through long-term relationships that have the goal of restructuring the personality, counselors serve in a therapeutic role.

Counselor as Group Leader

Some counseling interventions are done through group work. Counseling groups can be particularly beneficial for individuals who share common problems or who have interpersonal/relationship concerns. Group members provide feedback, support, alternatives, and encouragement for behavior changes. Often people in groups begin to feel less alone when they hear that others face similar problems. Group counseling has been demonstrated to be effective for many problems, including anxiety and panic, chronic pain and illness, depression, eating disorders, social anxiety and other interpersonal problems, substance abuse, and traumatic experiences, just to name a few. In schools, groups are often used to help address problems such as difficulties in relating to others, adjustment to parental divorce, behavior problems, learning disabilities, teenage parenting, and alcohol/drug addiction or abstinence (Corey & Corey, 2006).

Groups are used in many different settings, including schools, mental health agencies, rehabilitation centers, and substance abuse settings. There are many different types of groups, ranging from preventive and psychoeducational, to remedial and therapeutic. The role of the group leader varies with the type of group, clients, and setting. In general, however, the group leader establishes the group, selects members, and facilitates group meetings.

Counselor as K–12 Guidance Curriculum Expert

In this role, professional schools counselors develop and provide structured lessons to students, parents, school staff, and the community that are designed to help students "achieve desired competencies and to provide all students with the knowledge and skills appropriate for their developmental level" (ASCA, 2008). As guidance curriculum experts, school counselors emphasize preventive and developmental counseling to provide students with life skills needed to address problems before they occur and to enhance the students' mental health and wellness in three broad

---

■■■ *Fast Facts* ■■■

ASCA National Standards (ASCA, 2005) recommend that professional school counselors spend a certain percentage of their time in the role of implementing the guidance curriculum. For elementary counselors, 30–40% of their time should be spent on curriculum; for middle school counselors, the percentage is 20–30%; and for high school counselors, it is 15–25%.

A study of practicing school counselors in North Carolina found that only 18% of the elementary school counselors spent the recommended time on curriculum activities, and just 10% of the middle school counselors spent the recommended time on guidance curriculum. Comparatively, 36% of high school guidance counselors met the recommended time for guidance curriculum activities.

Source: How North Carolina School Counselors Spend Their Time (2000).

SNAPSHOT
Susie Boggs, Licensed Professional School Counselor

I was 40 years old when I finally figured out what I wanted to be when I grew up! I had been many things during my work life—I taught music, worked as a legal assistant, a customer service representative, and a trainer and middle manager at a large insurance enterprise. Throughout this time, I truly enjoyed each opportunity to learn and grow, and have really appreciated the many transferrable skills I have accumulated. However, I never loved my job. I missed young people and wanted to believe that I was making a difference, so I enrolled in graduate school to become a professional school counselor and I have never regretted it!

Since then I have spent the past eight years working as a school counselor at a career-technical high school. Here junior and senior high school students from seven different regional school districts enroll in technical laboratory programs ranging from automotive technology and welding, to firefighting/EMS, computer science and nursing. Students work in their technical programs for half of the day and take their core academic studies the other half. My students are from very diverse economic, academic, and racial/ethnic backgrounds who want to learn in a different way and get a head start on a career of their choosing; it is very rewarding. Finally, I love my job.

If you choose this career, know these three things: (1) No two days will ever be alike, (2) you will never accomplish everything you want to, or even everything you think you should, and (3) you may never know the impact you might have had on a young person's life. But I promise you, you *will* have an impact, you may even save a life. Believe me, regardless of the frustrations, it's worth it!

The role of a school counselor is challenging to define. Due to our history, and despite the profession's many efforts, our "job description" is often debated. What you may learn in your graduate program may not always be what your administrator, and even seasoned colleagues, will say you should be doing. Generally, you will be dividing your time between individual counseling and planning, developing, and leading small groups and large group/classroom lessons on academic, career, and personal/social needs. Additionally there will be work on student academic records, counseling notes, data collection and analysis, scheduling and enrolling students, parent conferences, teacher consultations, as well as duties within your school building. Not only that, do not be surprised to find a building colleague in your office seeking your advice and needing a shoulder to lean on. Public education can often be stressful and even isolating. Your fellow educators will see you as a helper and sounding board. I will tell you what my graduate advisor told me—at the end of the day, you will be tired!

As in any profession, you will find things you love and you will find things you hate. Paperwork, however necessary, is the bane of my existence. My best times are in direct contact with students, formally and planned, or as I chat with them in the hallway or during lunch breaks. Remember that any contact, however short or seemingly inconsequential, has the potential to make the day for that student. Would I prefer not to have lunch duty? Of course! Can I use it as an opportunity to talk with students? Absolutely!

If there was one piece of advice that I could give someone considering this career, it would be to remember self-care. It is so easy to take your work home with you, to internalize the issues your students face, and feel you must "save" everyone—you can't. You must take care of yourself physically and mentally to avoid burnout and maintain your life outside of school. Focus on stress reduction/relief—exercise, yoga, meditation, etc. and stay engaged in your professional development and networking. Join the American School Counselor Association and become active within your state association. I remember my first year on the job when a fellow counselor invited me to call anytime because "no one else really ever knows what you are going through besides another school counselor." How right he was.

This profession is not for the faint-hearted; each day is a challenge. But know that each day is also a fresh opportunity to advocate for a child and have a lasting impact on a young person's life. Oh, did I mention that I love my job?

Susie's Breakdown of Time Spent on Daily Activities	
Individual student academic planning	15%
Individual counseling and crisis management	35%
Small group development and counseling	10%
Large group/classroom lessons	10%
Program planning	5%
Paperwork, clerical activities, building duties	25%

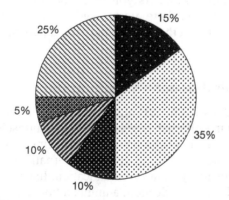

■ Individual student academic planning
▨ Large group/classroom lessons
▨ Individual counseling and crisis management
▨ Program planning
■ Small group development and counseling
▨ Paperwork, clerical activities, building duties

areas: academic development, career development, and personal/social development. The accompanying Snapshot by Susie Boggs, Licensed Professional School Counselor, will give you even more insight into the roles of a school counselor.

Counselor as Diagnostician

Most mental health counselors consider diagnosis of mental and emotional disorders to be one of their major responsibilities as counselors (Altekruse & Sexton, 1995). Mental health professionals in America use a common language to diagnose mental and emotional disorders. Criteria for all recognized mental disorders are listed in the *Diagnostic and Statistical Manual of Mental Disorders, Fourth Edition, Text Revision*, published by the American Psychiatric Association (2000; DSM-IV-TR, for short). This manual contains over 300 different diagnoses grouped into 16 major categories. The DSM-IV-TR is used by clinicians and researchers in all fields related to mental health, and it provides information that is usable and relevant across a variety of settings. The DSM is a work in progress, and each iteration of the manual contains the latest research and clinical expertise available at the time of going to press.

Not all states have counseling licensure laws that allow counselors to diagnose mental and emotional disorders. Of the 50 states with counseling licensure, 31 states specifically allow professional counselors to diagnose their clients. See Table 2.2 for a breakdown of counselors and diagnosis by state. Even in states that allow counselors to diagnose their clients, not all counselors believe that such a practice is appropriate. As you will read about in this chapter's Counseling Controversy feature, there are markedly different opinions among those in the profession about whether counselors should participate in the diagnosis of mental disorders.

Counselor as Assessor

Psychological assessment is any method used to measure characteristics of people or programs. Proper assessment helps counselors and those they serve to more fully understand the nature of problems, strengths, or interests; to select appropriate interventions; to generate alternatives; and to evaluate the effectiveness of treatments, programs, or education. In general, good assessment practice includes skills in test selection, administration, and interpretation (Tymofievich & Leroux, 2000).

When counselors are in the role of assessor, they are in the role of investigator. They are seeking to learn more about a person or situation so that they can formulate or evaluate treatments, interventions, or programs. If counselors are not skillful at assessment, or if they conduct an incomplete or inaccurate assessment, everything else in the counseling process can be negatively affected (Whiston, 2005). Assessment is used in counseling by counselors in all settings.

TABLE 2.2 Counselors and Diagnosis: A Breakdown by State

States in Which a Licensed Counselor Can Diagnose Mental and Emotional Disorders	States in Which Diagnosis Is *Not* Within the Scope of Practice for Licensed Counselors
1. Alaska	1. Alabama
2. Arizona	2. Arkansas
3. California	3. Connecticut
4. Colorado	4. District of Columbia
5. Delaware	5. Georgia
6. Florida	6. Idaho
7. Hawaii	7. Illinois
8. Kansas	8. Indiana
9. Kentucky	9. Iowa
10. Louisiana	10. Maine
11. Maryland	11. Mississippi
12. Massachusetts	12. Missouri
13. Michigan	13. New Jersey
14. Minnesota	14. New York
15. Montana	15. Oregon
16. Nebraska	16. Pennsylvania
17. Nevada	17. Puerto Rico
18. New Hampshire	18. Rhode Island
19. North Carolina	19. Wisconsin
20. North Dakota	
21. Ohio	
22. Oklahoma	
23. South Carolina	
24. South Dakota	
25. Tennessee	
26. Texas	
27. Utah	
28. Virginia	
29. Washington	
30. West Virginia	
31. Wyoming	

Source: American Counseling Association and California Counseling Association. Information accurate as of September 2010.

Assessment in counseling can be formal or informal. In other words, assessment can consist of standardized instruments that have fixed instructions for administration and scoring and yield specific information for individual clients. Assessment also can be very informal and make use of intake interviews, reviews of records or charts, observations of clients or students, completion of ratings scales or checklists, or discussions with members of a client's support system or other mental health professionals.

All counselors use informal assessments. In addition, most counselors, regardless of setting or population, engage in some type of formal assessment with their clients, and most counselors consider assessment fundamental to the

Counseling Controversy

SHOULD MENTAL HEALTH COUNSELORS ENGAGE IN DIAGNOSIS OF MENTAL AND EMOTIONAL DISORDERS?

Background. The *Diagnostic and Statistical Manual of Mental Disorders* uses a multiaxial assessment system that is the primary language of communication within the mental health system. Those who argue against its use believe that the use of diagnostic labels is contrary to the positive and developmental approach of counseling. Read the following arguments and see what you think.

POINT: PROPER DIAGNOSIS LEADS TO PROPER TREATMENT	COUNTERPOINT: LABELING CLIENTS IS HARMFUL TO THEM
• Counselors who operate outside of that system cannot hope to engage in effective practice, to receive third-party payments, or to use the current research and knowledge to implement effective treatments (Eriksen & Kress, 2006).	• Diagnosis is at best unnecessary and at worst is psychologically damaging to clients who are labeled by their counselors. Counseling has its roots in a humanistic philosophical stance that values the worth of individuals, rather than reducing them to mere medical labels (Hansen, 2003).
• The process of diagnosis in and of itself is not dehumanizing, and, in fact, can help ensure quality treatment by counselors who are informed of the best practices in the field. Many (79) of the 400 DSM-IV-TR classifications include specific cultural information, and there is nothing inherent in the diagnostic system that limits the understanding of how culture affects behavior.	• The use of diagnostic labels encourages counselors (and others) to abandon their traditional focus on wellness and holism and instead look for pathology and illness in all of their clients.
• Diagnosis benefits clients by giving them concrete explanations for their behaviors and experiences and gives them hope for a better future, with less psychological pain and suffering, once proper treatment has begun.	• The concept of the medicalization of mental illness has been challenged for decades. Szasz (1961), one of the fiercest critics of psychiatry and the field of mental health, argued that mental illness is defined based on the prevailing norms of the day. Individuals who deviate from society are labeled "abnormal," and societies use the threat of that label to constrain free will. One need look no further than the label of homosexuality, which was once considered a mental illness, but now that society is generally more accepting of homosexuality, it is no longer contained in the DSM.

• The practice of diagnosis allows communication of complex ideas between treating professionals; allows researchers to compare treatment approaches, which may allow for prevention and improved outcomes; relieves clients of the guilt and self-blame for their behaviors and experiences; encourages family members and others to be less blameful of the client and more focused on the "external enemy" of the illness; and helps clients feel understood and validated.	• The practice of diagnosis has been criticized for leading to a self-fulfilling prophecy, where clients begin to believe that their situation is hopeless and they are indeed "sick"; narrowing a counselor's focus, so all the counselor sees is the illness; ignoring the social context in which clients live that can perpetuate unproductive behavior problems; imposing societal values on individuals; and ignoring the effects of culture and diversity.

As with most controversies, there probably is some truth to both sides of this argument.

Diagnosis is necessary and important and SHOULD be done

Diagnosis undermines the dignity of the client and SHOULD NOT be done

On the continuum, place an "X" where you think you stand on this issue.

general practice of counseling (Sampson, Vacc, & Loesch, 1998). A 1998 study of counselors in a variety of settings found that only 9% indicated that they are never involved in formal assessment activities (Elmore, Ekstrom, Shafer, & Webster, 1998). A 2004 survey of practicing school counseling found that all respondents stated that they were involved in testing in some way, with 98% stating that they had responsibility for referring students, when appropriate, for additional assessment and appraisal. In addition, most respondents had more direct involvement in testing, with 29% stating they were responsible for selecting tests, 63% for administering tests, and 71% for interpreting tests (Ekstrom, Elmore, Shafer, Trotter, & Webster, 2004).

Counselor as Consultant

Consultation generally refers to a problem-solving process, and in counseling, *consultation* is typically the term that is used for indirect services. In other words, when counselors work directly with their clients, that is considered direct services. When counselors work with others in order to help improve *their* direct services, that is consultation (Doughtery, 1990). Gelso and Fretz (1992) defined consultation as "a professional service that uses knowledge of human behavior, interpersonal relationships, and group and organizational processes to help others become more effective in their

> ■▤▤ *Words of Wisdom* ■▤▤
>
> "The answers you get depend on the questions you ask."
>
> —Thomas Kuhn

roles" (p. 515). Formal consultation involves contracts, goals, and outcomes. But consultation also can be a very informal process that is done over the phone, at lunch, or in brief discussions. A few examples may help. Counselors are consultants when . . .

- A mental health counselor helps another mental health professional with problems he or she may be having with a client.
- A career counselor helps a worksite create job descriptions for the variety of staff employed there.
- A rehabilitation counselor receives a phone call asking what types of assistive or adaptive technology are available for a colleague's spouse who is recovering from a stroke.
- A school counselor works with a schoolteacher to discuss classroom management techniques.
- A counselor provides information on recognizing suicide warning signs to the staff at a mental health agency.

In short, consultation is a way for counselors to affect the direct services provided by others. Consultation is always voluntary, nonjudgmental, and based on the premise that the consultee is free to accept or reject any or all recommendations or ideas provided by the consultant (Hershenson, Power, & Waldo, 1996). Regardless of the setting or the informality of the consultation process, it is important to remember that the rights of the client must be protected at all times. Client names and/or identifying information should not be part of the consultation process, and the consultant must protect the privacy and rights of the consultee. There is an entire section of the ACA Code of Ethics (2005) that covers the ethical responsibilities of counselors when they act in the role of consultant.

Informal consultation is a very common experience in the field of counseling. In fact, it is so common for counselors to engage in informal consultation that they often do not even realize when they are serving as consultants. Perhaps it is not surprising that counselors, with specialized knowledge, training, and experience, are sought after for input and recommendations regarding a wide variety of problems. In discussions we have had with practicing counselors, it is not uncommon for them to initially say they "never" engage in consultation. However, when we talk about the many types of informal consulting that they may do, they typically find that this type of interaction is an integral part of their jobs. School counselors in particular find themselves serving as consultants to teachers and administrators who may need assistance or recommendations to work with a troubled student. School counselors also may function as consultants to parents who are concerned about their child's behavioral or academic problems. Mental health counselors may serve as consultants to their peers if they have expertise in a working with a particular type of client or diagnosis that others may need assistance with.

Counselor as Administrator

Administrators are individuals who oversee or manage organizations or agencies and thus are responsible for making and implementing major decisions. The role of administrator is one that is seldom discussed in the counseling community. Nevertheless, each year countless professional counselors are asked to assume administrative roles in schools, colleges and universities, state and federal government offices, community agencies, and foundations (Herr, Heitzmann, & Rayman, 2005). Some counselors seek the role of administrator, while others become administrators as they rise to higher and higher levels of responsibility within an organization or agency. In the role of administrator, counselors use many of the human relations skills that are the hallmark of their counseling training, such as setting goals, working with diverse staff, managing conflict, and working with difficult or angry clients. They also are called upon to develop skills that may not have been included in their counseling training, such as strategic planning, budgeting, recruitment and development of staff, organizational risk management, meeting with constituent groups or lawmakers, and facilities management. For counselors to be successful administrators, they must posses a range of diverse skills in both the counseling and business worlds (Sullivan, 2006). In some small agencies, administrators have job responsibilities that are incredibly diverse. Consider this "job description" by N. J. Groetzinger, an executive director of a mental health agency in Chicago.

> I was the executive director, I was also the chief financial officer; I did all the financial work. I didn't have a bookkeeper, let alone a controller. I was the human resource manager, and I was the development officer. Because of the size, I was even the backup receptionist. (Gumz, 2004, p. 364)

The job of a counselor who becomes an administrator is shaped by a range of forces, often beyond his or her control (e.g., accreditation policies, local/state/federal contracts, state and federal laws and requirements, and accountability demands). Effective administrators are able to manage these external demands while simultaneously creating an environment that puts the principles, purpose, and guiding beliefs of the organization first (Sullivan, 2006). Obviously, this is a significant challenge, and the role of counselor as administrator is not for everyone. But, for those who have the temperament and skill set to become administrators, there is tremendous opportunity to have a positive impact on the field of mental health, thereby helping to improve the lives of clients in significant and meaningful ways. The accompanying Snapshot of Grant Schroeder in this chapter provides additional highlights and insights into the role of a counseling administrator.

Counselor as Record Keeper or Case Manager

Paperwork, paperwork, paperwork! It is probably no one's favorite role, but at least some of a counselor's time must be spent on logistics—filling out paperwork, keeping records, scheduling (of tests, groups, or clients), and billing. Counselors in

SNAPSHOT

Grant Schroeder, Licensed Professional Clinical Counselor and Administrator

I currently serve as the vice president and chief operating officer at Maryhaven, a large behavioral health care organization in Columbus, Ohio, that specializes in the treatment of substance dependence and co-existing mental, emotional, and behavioral problems. Maryhaven offers 20 various programs and services ranging from care of the homeless, to outpatient and residential treatment, driver intervention programs, residential care for youth under the temporary custody of children services, contractual services for federal offenders, and halfway house services for women who have completed primary treatment.

I initially served in a supervisory role and subsequently in administrative roles with increased management responsibility at this agency from 1985 to the present time. Prior to this I had worked in a variety of substance abuse counseling roles in the public and private sector since 1975. I love the field of addiction treatment and the challenges and successes of our clients! I was driven to the management side of the work because of business and management courses in my undergraduate degree and because I wanted to lead and influence events that affect patient care.

My workdays are often a "wide-angle" view of all of what is happening in our agency. As chief operating officer, I am the manager who makes sure that we are providing effective services in a timely manner. This means being concerned with staffing, incidents that arise, coverage issues, and clinical decision making. I oversee our medical staff, supervisory staff, counseling staff, nursing director and her staff, as well as the case aides, students, and volunteers who all contribute to helping patients recover from addictive illness and mental health problems. Although I frequently feel like a fireman, running from one problem to the next, I very much enjoy the change of pace and challenges my work offers me every day. In addition to my work at Maryhaven, I have continued some private practice work and teaching throughout my career to keep my skills fresh and to experience the pleasure of providing direct counseling services. However, I am better suited for the change of pace and challenges of the administrative functions. Earlier in my career I found counseling all day—whether in group therapy or individual counseling—caused me to get restless and somewhat burned out.

Today my struggles at work involve dealing with many things that require essentially an immediate response, such as staff evaluations, budget and utilization reviews, hiring and firing issues, staff meetings, and the many meetings with funders and government agencies that are stakeholders in our business. At times I see myself as balancing on a seesaw, the balancing point being my day-to-day responsibilities. At one end of the seesaw are meetings with clients and staff and "managing by walking around" (MBWA). On the other side of the seesaw is having the time to think, read, and plan on how we might improve the effectiveness and efficiencies of our services. Increasingly, I find great rewards when I take time to talk with clients about our services and ask if they feel cared for, if they are receiving what they need to recover, what our customer service is like, or what has upset them about what we do or how we do it. Speaking with staff about the challenges they face with paperwork, clients, and our agency policies is equally rewarding. When I take time to do this and follow up with time to discuss my thoughts and feelings with other trusted managers, I am almost always rejuvenated and my thinking and planning for the future becomes more focused.

Grant's Breakdown of Time Spent on Daily Activities	
Administrator	70%
Learner/investigator	10%
Educator/trainer	10%
Supervisor	5%
Entrepreneur	5%

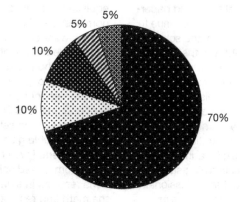

all settings are accountable for paperwork. They set up appointments for clients or schedule groups or meetings. Mental health counselors often complete accountability logs or billing paperwork. They make referrals for clients to receive social services, they follow up with other providers to coordinate intervention efforts, or they fill out paperwork to certify that court-ordered clients have attended their mandated sessions. Counselors serve as case managers when they monitor ongoing services for persons with chronic mental illness. School counselors often schedule and coordinate testing. In this chapter's Informed by Research feature, we discuss results of a study of school counselors, highlighting the importance of time spent in counseling practice, rather than paperwork or clerical duties.

Informed by Research
Does Implementing a Research-Based School Counseling Curriculum Enhance Student Achievement?

The ASCA National Model (2005) delineates appropriate roles and functions for professional school counselors that focus on implementing a comprehensive school guidance curriculum, engaging in individual student planning, using responsive services to needs that arise in the school, and supporting students, teachers, and administrators as they work to enhance student academic achievement. Nevertheless, school counselors have long complained that they have been asked to perform clerical tasks and paperwork in their schools, and principals continue to hold assumptions about the role of the school counselor that are incongruent with the national standards. For example, a 2004 study (Pérusse, Goodenough, Donegan, & Jones) found that more than 80% of school principals identified the following activities as appropriate for school counselors, even though they are not endorsed by the ASCA standards: (a) registration and scheduling of all new students; (b) administering achievement tests; and (c) maintaining student records. Kaplan (1995) found that professional school counselors often view themselves as misused because they are assigned to tasks such as scheduling, handling disciplinary matters, and performing clerical functions.

One of the efforts of the Transforming School Counseling Initiative has been to find ways to validate the effectiveness of time spent in appropriate school counseling activities. The argument is that unless school counselors can justify the effectiveness of the ASCA National Model, they will continue to be asked to perform clerical duties. In 2003, one of the first rigorously designed research studies on the effectiveness of a comprehensive school

counseling program investigated whether a combination of curriculum-based and group-based interventions that focused on cognitive skills, social skills, and self-management skills had a measurable impact on students' test scores on state standardized achievement tests.

Brigman and Campbell (2003) compared a treatment and a control group that were randomly selected from middle schools with equivalent racial composition and socioeconomic levels. Pretests demonstrated that both groups were comparable on their achievement levels. The treatment group included 185 students who engaged in classroom-based and small group format interventions. The researchers found that school counseling interventions that focus on the development of cognitive, social, and self-management skills can result in sizable gains in students' academic achievement. Involvement in small group and classroom-based school counseling interventions resulted in significant improvements on the math and reading scores of the Florida Comprehensive Assessment Test.

This study represents an important milestone for school counselors who wish to use research to support their claims that implementation of a comprehensive school counseling curriculum can have positive effects on student academic achievement. Clearly, more research will need to be conducted, but these results are promising. High-quality research, such as this study conducted by Brigman and Campbell (2003), allows school counselors to say with confidence that their time is best spent in accordance with the ASCA National Standards.

Counselor as Researcher or Scientist

In order to make use of the accumulated knowledge in the field, to contribute new knowledge to the field, and to understand the effectiveness of their own practice and programs, counselors in all practice settings must be willing to take on the roles of researcher and scientist. Today's counseling students will graduate to face an environment in which the ability to assess treatment outcome and program effectiveness will be essential to success (Plante, Couchman, & Diaz, 1995). As a result, counseling students can graduate with outstanding clinical skills and a sound theoretical foundation, but without the ability to choose treatments or interventions that have research to support them, these same students will be at a disadvantage in a competitive marketplace (Granello & Granello, 1998). Bridging the gap between research and practice is essential (Whiston & Coker, 2000), and it serves as the foundation for a scientist-practitioner model that is often used in counselor education.

The scientist-practitioner model is based on the premise that all counselors should use sound decision making when determining treatment strategies and programs and should select interventions that are supported by empirical evidence, when available. A more controversial component of the scientist-practitioner model is belief that all practitioners should conduct and publish rigorous research that contributes to the field, although most within the field of counseling and psychology recognize that few practitioners engage in this type of research (Gelso, 2006). Because of this, Houser (2008) (and others) argue that counselors are really *practitioner-scientists*, with the emphasis on counselors as *consumers* of existing research, rather than *producers* of new knowledge. Regardless of terminology, it is clear that the ability to read, understand, and implement the *existing* research in the field has become the foundation of good counseling practice (Sexton, 1999). Sexton and Whiston (1996), in their call for the integration of research and practice, wrote:

> First, practitioners must be aware of what research is available; second, they must have the ability to identify the implications of those research findings; and, finally, they must have the knowledge and skill to integrate those findings directly into practice. (p. 588)

Counselor as Learner

The field of counseling continues to grow and change, and competent counselors recognize that to be effective in their careers, they must commit to being lifelong learners. The role of counselors as learners encompasses both an innate desire and a professional requirement. Ongoing learning is so important to professional counseling that licensing and certification boards in all states require continuing education to maintain the counseling credential. All licensing and certification boards have specific requirements regarding continuing education units (CEUs). The importance of engaging in ongoing

■■■ *Fast Facts* ■■■

A survey of 129 school counselors revealed that 97% routinely read at least one school counseling publication to stay abreast of the latest research. Topics that were of the most importance to the counselors in the study were (1) divorce and family issues; (2) aggression/violence/gangs; (3) bullying; (4) death, loss, and grief; and (5) attention deficit disorder and other mental health disorders.

Source: Bauman, Siegel, Davis, Falco, Seabolt, & Syzmanski (2002).

learning is encapsulated in the ACA Code of Ethics, where continuing education is mandated.

Most writers who discuss professional development in the helping professions recognize that there are generally two options that professionals can choose: continue to grow and change professionally and personally or stagnate and burn out (Echterling et al., 2002; Gladding, 2002). The recognition that lifelong learning has a personal benefit, as well as a professional advantage, is the reason that many practicing counselors find that they more than fulfill the minimum number of hours of continuing education for licensure or certification requirements. Clearly, graduate training in counseling is not the end of the learning process, and a degree in counseling is just one step in a lifelong process. In fact, both qualitative (e.g., Skovholt & Ronnestad, 1992) and quantitative (e.g., Granello, 2010) research support a model of professional development that begins a trajectory of growth and development during graduate school and continues throughout a counselor's entire professional career. Adopting a stance as a lifelong learner means seeking opportunities for new learning in a multitude of contexts and situations. In fact, in their research to uncover common characteristics of master therapists, Skovholt, Jennings, and Mullenbach (2004) found that they are "insatiably curious" and have an "intense will to grow" (pp. 134–136). Master therapists see themselves as lifelong learners, active learners, and eager to learn.

Counselor as Teacher or Educator

At times, counselors take on the role of teachers or educators. Sometimes this is within the context of a counseling relationship, where, when done sparingly and appropriately, supplying information or facts can help a client reach his or her goals. At other times, counselors teach graduate courses or conduct workshops or trainings. In both of these circumstances, counselors impart information and help their clients, students, or peers engage in new learning.

According to the REPLAN model, which provides a listing of factors that improve therapeutic outcomes, providing new learning is an essential component of the counseling relationship (Young, 2005). New learning can be in the form of providing information or referrals to clients, or simply arming clients with the facts they need to make wise decisions or goals. In many therapeutic settings, giving clients important information about their psychiatric diagnoses or medications can help them become partners in their own behavioral health care. Once clients understand, for example, how panic attacks affect the body's physiology, they are more able to understand how to get control over their bodies when a panic attack strikes. In other contexts, new learning can be in the form of giving clients information that they can then integrate into their own behaviors. For example, counselors might teach their clients basic human relations skills or how to get along with others (Ivey, 1976). This is the premise behind a particular type of group work called psychoeducational groups. In psychoeducational groups, clients or students learn about a concept (assertiveness, for example), and then learn how to apply that concept to their own lives. In this example, without the "education" of learning about assertiveness, the "psychological" portion of the group, where the material is applied to one's own life, would be meaningless.

Counselors are also in the role of teacher or educator when they are conducting trainings or workshops or teaching courses. At a professional conference for counselors, the workshops are typically presented by counselors or counseling students. Counselors provide trainings in organizations and businesses, where they may provide workshops on specific interpersonal skills or on methods to improve organizational functions. The professor or instructor of the course for which you are reading this text is undoubtedly a counselor in the role of educator, and the term *counselor educator* refers to a counselor who has taken on the role of college professor or instructor. In this context, counselors use the skills, training, and experience they have in the field, as well as specialized knowledge and training in teaching, research, and supervision, to teach others to become professional counselors. The accompanying Snapshot of Dr. Daniel Cruikshanks provides additional highlights and insights into the role of a counselor educator.

Counselor as Supervisor or Supervisee

In all states, professional counselors in training must spend at least some of their time in supervision, and supervised experience has long been considered one of the most significant aspects in the training of professional counselors (Bernard & Goodyear, 2004). Supervision requirements vary by state and type of licensure, but minimum requirements set forth by the learned association of the profession are 100 hours of practicum and 600 hours of internship for the master's degree (CACREP, 2001). In addition, many states require supervised experience (1500 to 4500 hours, depending on the state) after the completion of the degree for those wishing to become independently licensed mental health counselors. Supervision is based on the belief that some type of learning occurs in supervision that is *qualitatively different* from what occurs in the classroom. That is, although classroom-based learning is essential to becoming a counselor, it is not sufficient. Supervised experience in an actual setting, with real clients or students, also is required. Supervised experience provides meaningful learning, a diversity of experience, and an opportunity to put the classroom learning into practice.

In this context, counselors take on the role of supervisors and supervisees. Supervisors are more experienced counselors who guide supervisees as they acquire the skills, experience, and professionalism needed to become professional counselors. Bernard and Goodyear (2004) defined supervision as "an intervention provided by a more senior member of a profession to a more junior member or members of that same profession [based on a] relationship that is evaluative, extends over time, and has the simultaneous purposes of enhancing the professional functioning of the more junior person(s), monitoring the quality of professional services offered to the clients . . . and serving as a gatekeeper for those who are to enter the profession" (p. 8). Hawkins and Shohet (1989)

SNAPSHOT
Daniel Cruikshanks, PhD, Licensed Professional Clinical Counselor and Counselor Educator

I am a professor of counseling at a small college, a clinical counselor in private practice, and a counselor supervisor. As a professor of counseling, I have a wide range of responsibilities including teaching courses, coordinating internship, serving on university committees, advising and mentoring students and working on various research projects whenever I can. There are a great number of misconceptions about what university professors do. I often hear people suggest that we just work a few hours a week teaching a couple of classes and then have a lot of time on our hands. Even though I am at a teaching institution (rather than a research institution) where I teach three to four courses per semester, teaching actually comprises the smallest amount of my time as a professor. A surprising amount of my time is spent working on ongoing accreditation and curriculum development issues.

When I am not professing, I am typically working with clients in my clinic. I see about eight to ten clients weekly doing individual, couples, and family counseling. As a doctoral-level Professional Clinical Counselor, I can and do perform psychological evaluations as part of my practice and have carved an interesting niche doing forensic evaluations for the Department of Job and Family Services. It's very interesting work. In the meantime, I also serve as a counselor supervisor for a small clinic in my town. This means that every week I spend two hours at the clinic alternately meeting with four counselors.

The great thing about being a counselor and a counselor educator is that I have the opportunity to do so many different kinds of work. For example, as a clinical counselor, I work with clients in an effort to help them work through their mental and emotional problems. I work with physicians, inpatient units, case workers, and other health care workers in various ways in the service of my clients. I love this work, but it has a kind of intensity that, for me, can be too much without some kind of interruption of routine. As a professor, I get to work with students, which is a lot of fun. I discovered that teaching is a kind of performance art that allows me to tap into the stand-up comic that I would never manage to be in real life. But I also discovered that there is a complex and interesting dance that unfolds between students and faculty as we negotiate their learning. The professor/student relationship is always loaded and, in a way, antagonistic, like a tug-of-war. In the end, my experience is that the best students appreciate the challenge and pain, but sometimes only later on, after they discover the benefits of the quality education they got.

By all rights, I shouldn't be here. I nearly failed high school, was actively steered away from college by my guidance counselor, and only was able to get "back on track" because I was fortunate enough to live in California, which has an education system that allowed me a second chance once I had developed enough to become educated. Thus it's a little ironic to me that I find myself in a profession that is based on the idea of growth and human development—that people grow and change over time, and readiness varies depending on circumstances. I started on a path that didn't work for me, and then I discovered that I could change that path and create the life that I wanted. I became a counselor and a counselor educator and, in many ways, I believe that my personal development and my professional development have evolved together such that they cannot really be separated.

I have been a mental health counselor for the past 14 years and a counselor educator for the past 10. I have had the opportunity to work with hundreds of clients, many hundreds of students, and numerous counselor supervisees. Over the years, I have often been frustrated, irritated, overwhelmed, and yet more often, I have found my experiences to be exciting, interesting, and generally an amazing adventure, and I can think of nothing I would rather be doing. I have heard it said that the greatest satisfaction in life comes from the meaning we get in the service of others rather than the money we make or the materials we acquire. As a professor and a counselor, I work hard and I work a lot. I have become well regarded and respected, but I will never make the kind of money that many others can make with much less education. On the other hand, I enjoy incredible variety in my work. Perhaps most surprising to me, among the most satisfying parts of the work that I do is mentoring students toward doctoral training. I will never be famous, nor will I ever be financially wealthy, but if I am remembered for anything, it likely will be by those professors who pursued doctoral training because I suggested it to them and believed that they could.

Dr. Cruikshank's Breakdown of Time Spent on Daily Activities	
Therapist	10%
Diagnostician	5%
Assessor	5%
Advisor	5%
Record keeper	10%
Researcher/scientist	10%
Teacher/educator	25%
Supervisor	10%
Advocate	8%
Expert witness	2%
Member of professional assoc.	10%

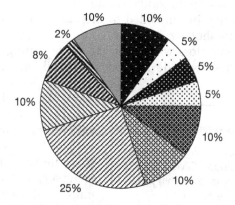

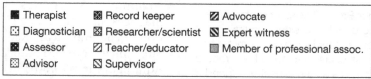

said that the goal of supervision is to help the counselor-in-training develop a healthy internal supervisor, so that after the required hours in supervision were completed, the professional counselor was able to self-regulate his or her own counseling practice.

The requirements regarding who can become a counseling supervisor, who needs to be supervised, and the rights and responsibilities of supervisors and supervisees are all regulated by state licensing and credentialing boards and by the ACA Code of Ethics (2005). In spite of these very straightforward requirements, other aspects of supervision are less clear cut. There is much controversy and discussion in the professional literature about the many roles and functions of counseling supervision, to what degree supervision is a developmental process, the place of theory in supervision, how to implement multiculturally appropriate supervision, and how the effectiveness of supervision can be measured. Counseling supervision is a vibrant area of research and study and a topic of lively debate within the field. When you have the opportunity to be supervised, or when you eventually become a supervisor, you will gain even more understanding of the complexity of these counselor roles.

Counselor as Crisis Interventionist

Counselors in this role step in after a crisis to help individuals, families, groups, or communities cope with tragedies. Crisis counseling is typically short-term (less than 3 months) and focuses on single or recurrent problems that are devastating or traumatic. Crisis counseling often is a combination of counseling, education, guidance, and support. It is not a substitute for long-term counseling, but intended to help individuals get through the immediate trauma and its short-term effects.

Crisis counselors work in a variety of settings, and counselors in many types of settings who do not focus primarily on crisis intervention may find themselves put in the role of crisis interventionist. Crisis counselors may conduct initial assessments, find referrals, and provide information to clients who present in such places as emergency rooms, rape crisis centers, or domestic violence shelters, or who call suicide hotlines. In other settings, crisis counselors reach out into the community. Still others maintain regular practices and are "on call" for crisis situations. The American Red Cross and the Substance Abuse Mental Health Services Administration (SAMHSA) train Disaster Mental Health Responders who come to the assistance of everyone from individuals who lose their home to a fire, to families

■■■ *Words of Wisdom* ■■■

"I was left, like most Americans, wishing I could do something to help. Give blood? Give money? Well, I had an opportunity to give something that I am eternally grateful for, I gave myself."

—Christopher Brown, assistant professor and Clinical Director of Professional Counseling at Southwest Texas State University, commenting on his decision to go to New York to participate as a mental health responder after the 9/11/2001 attacks, quoted in *Counseling Today* (September 2002, p. 19).

devastated by school shootings, to thousands affected by natural disasters, such as Hurricane Katrina. These individuals are often licensed mental health professionals who go through additional training to serve as mental health first responders. After the attacks of September 11, 2001, many licensed counselors across America left their homes and practices to go to New York, Washington, DC, and Pennsylvania, where they worked not only with the victims and their families, but with the emergency personnel who were experiencing "secondary trauma" from hearing the stories and seeing the effects of the devastation.

A study by Norris (1992) found that 69% of the general population had experienced at least one extremely traumatic event during their lives, underscoring the importance of crisis counseling skills for all counselors in all settings. Many of the counseling interventions needed for crisis counseling are the same as for other types of counseling, such as developing rapport, expressing empathy, and listening. Other skills are more specialized, such as debriefing or creating survival stories (Echterling, Presbury, & McKee, 2005).

Counselor as Advisor

In counseling skills courses, beginning counselors are taught to resist the role of advice-giving. In most situations, it is not particularly helpful for counselors to give clients advice. Clients are unlikely to act upon the advice that is given to them, and most individuals who engage in helping others change behaviors recognize that there is far more involved in behavior change than just being told what to do (Young, 2005). (If it were that easy, we would all follow the advice of our doctors, be thin and fit, and always eat nutritious meals!)

There is a type of advice-giving, however, that counselors do regularly engage in, particularly in schools and colleges. When counselors are in the role of advisor, they provide recommendations and suggestions (as well as advice) to their students and clients. Career counselors offer career or educational advice. In her book *Career Advising*, Virginia Gordon (2006) reminds counselors that they must help clients see the connections between their academic and career choices and the impact that their decisions have on their future professional and personal lives. Academic advising is "a developmental process which assists students in the clarification of their life/career goals and in the development of educational plans for the realization of these goals. . . . The advisor serves as a facilitator of communication, a coordinator of learning experiences through course and career planning and academic progress review, and an agent of referral" (Habley & Crockett, 1988, p. 9). Academic advisors in colleges and universities may help students with course selection or meeting institutional requirements (Alexitch, 2006), and undergraduate academic advising has been identified as a high priority by students (Axelson, 2007).

School and college counselors who engage in the role of academic advisor take on a significant responsibility in the lives of their students and clients. A 2001 court case (*Sain v. Cedar Rapids Community School District*) determined that school counselors must use reasonable care when providing specific academic information to students. The court found that school counselors can be held accountable for providing accurate information to students about credits and courses needed to pursue post–high school goals. Although this legal requirement may seem daunting, academic advising is an important role for school counselors as it is a tangible way to help level the playing field for students (Stone, 2002). School counselors who provide academic advising to students help close the information gap between those students who already know what they need to do to be eligible for postsecondary education and those who do not have this information. In this way, academic advising serves to help fulfill a social justice agenda.

Counselor as Expert Witness

Although this role is not particularly common in the counseling profession, some counselors find that they enjoy the challenges of participating in the legal system as expert witnesses. Expert witnesses are individuals who have specialized knowledge, training, and experience in a particular field. Expert witnesses are hired by either prosecutors or defendants, and they can be used to evaluate documents, to provide insights, and to provide expert testimony in court cases. Counselors can assist juries with understanding the complexities of cases involving mental health; they can assist attorneys by reviewing documents that may be difficult to comprehend without training in mental health; and they can help judges and juries make informed decisions (Kwartner & Boccaccini, 2008).

Counselors who serve in the role of an expert witness are obliged to follow all ethical and legal guidelines of the counseling profession. Important court cases, such as *Murphy v. A. A. Mathews* (1992), hold that even when mental health professionals are hired to promote the stance of prosecutors or defendants, this does not exonerate them from following the ethical mandates of the profession. In other words, counselors must carefully balance both perspectives, remain neutral in their presentation of facts and information, and not allow the inherent pressures of the situation to affect their judgment and decision making (Shuman & Greenberg, 2003).

Counselor as Prevention Specialist

Philosophically, the concept of prevention is congruent with the profession of counseling. In 1993, Kiselica and Look called prevention "a defining characteristic of the [counseling] profession" (p. 3). A survey of experts in the field of counseling revealed that most described prevention as one of the criteria that distinguished counselors from other mental health professionals (Ginter, 1991). Indeed the focus on a proactive, rather than a reactive, approach to mental health is intrinsically appealing to most counselors.

Prevention specialists in the field of mental health have more traditionally been employed in the area of drug and alcohol prevention. Many K–12 school systems offer prevention programming to help students learn to make smart choices, to resist harmful peer pressure, and to become more assertive in standing up for their rights.

In more recent years, prevention services have been moving out of the schools and into other areas of mental health care. There is emerging evidence that with appropriate preventive care, certain mental health problems can be prevented altogether, while others can have delayed onset or less severe symptoms (Matthews & Skowron, 2004). Prevention focuses on building resilience and encouraging healthy development throughout the lifespan. Examples of effective prevention programs include parenting education programs, school-based social competency programs, and programs for persons experiencing stressful circumstances, such as divorce or recent unemployment (Surgeon General, 1999).

In spite of the growing emphasis on prevention in mental health, however, financial reimbursement remains a significant barrier to its widespread use outside the school system. Just as the medical profession was slow to promote prevention activities in health care, and insurance companies have been slow to reimburse for health-related prevention activities, the same has held true for mental health. It is only recently that businesses, agencies, communities, and insurance companies have begun to advocate—and pay—for prevention in mental health.

Counselor as Businessperson or Entrepreneur

Most people who enter the field of counseling are more oriented to the world of people than to the world of business or finance. It is perhaps not surprising, then, that there is little discussion in the field about the role of the counselor as businessperson or entrepreneur. The lack of available information can send the message to new counselors that somehow discussing money is bad or inappropriate for persons who should be interested in caring for people rather than making money.

The reality, however, is that the role of counselor as businessperson or entrepreneur can be critical for counselors who need to finance their work, whether through grants and contracts to fund programs or through reimbursement agreements with insurance companies to pay their salaries. Professional counselors must get paid for their work, and they must have sufficient resources to implement needed programs. Some counselors work in schools or agencies where funding is provided through an established budget, but others must find ways to finance themselves.

Counselors can receive funding through grants and contracts, but in order to receive this funding, they (or others, on their behalf) must write proposals to organizations and foundations. Typically, grant proposals identify specific programmatic objectives and how these objectives will be met. Foundations are targeted whose missions align with those of the grant proposal. Grants are available for many different types of counseling interventions, such as specialized curricula in the schools, domestic violence prevention, suicide prevention, and gerontological programming. Counselors can support their work through contracts with schools, agencies, businesses, governmental departments, or communities. For example, a counselor might contract with a community to provide court-mandated counseling for individuals charged with driving under the influence. Another counselor may contract with a school to provide mental health services, or with a business to provide employee assistance counseling. In these instances, counselors reach out to those whose constituents may need their services and offer to provide counseling or other programs for a set fee.

Counselors also receive funding for their work from clients who pay for counseling out-of-pocket or from insurance companies. Counselors in private practice who wish to receive insurance reimbursement typically must get onto provider panels with insurance companies or managed care organizations. Counselors may have to advertise to attract clients, and learning how and where to advertise in an effective, appropriate, and ethical manner requires business acumen. Regardless of their funding source, counselors need to feel comfortable in the role of entrepreneur—reaching out to potential funders or clients to let them know the benefits of the programming and services that they provide.

Counselor as Mediator

Mediators are individuals who help two or more parties involved in a dispute reach a resolution that they can agree upon, rather than having a resolution imposed on them by a third party. Mediators use many counseling techniques, such as mechanisms to improve communication and listening, increase problem-solving, and de-escalate emotions. Mediators are impartial in the dispute, and they can offer opportunities for the involved parties to hear different perspectives in a safe environment.

Not all mediators are counselors by training, and there is a separate credentialing process for professional mediators (although a mediation credential is not required to engage in mediation). Many counselors engage in informal mediation. For example, a school counselor may mediate between students who have been caught fighting, or between a parent and a teacher, when conflict escalates. Mental health counselors may mediate between partners in a divorce to find a solution to parenting that is amenable to both parties or between co-workers at a worksite.

■■■ *Words of Wisdom* ■■■

"You must be the change you wish to see in the world."

—Mahatma Gandhi

Counselor as Advocate or Agent of Social Change

Advocacy is "the process or act of arguing or pleading for a cause" (Lee, 1998, p. 8). For counselors, advocacy means becoming agents of social change, intervening not just to help individual clients, but to work

■■■ *Fast Facts* ■■■

In one national survey, more than half of all national, state, and local counseling associations (52%) had a statement that required involvement in advocacy activities for professional counselors.

Source: Myers & Sweeney (2004).

to change the world in which our clients live. When counselors are advocates, they fight injustices through both individual and collective actions. Advocacy has been termed "a professional imperative" for counselors (Myers, Sweeney, & White, 2002, p. 394).

The American Counseling Association (ACA) recognizes the importance of advocacy for professional counselors, and in 2003, the Governing Council endorsed a set of Advocacy Competencies (Lewis, Arnold, House, & Toporek, 2001) that encourage counselors to empower their clients, make systems change interventions, and negotiate relevant services and educational systems on behalf of their clients. In 2004, ACA formed a new division to emphasize this role, called Counselors for Social Justice (CSJ).

School counselors are ideally positioned within schools to become agents of social change. There is a well-documented academic achievement gap between poor and middle class students (House & Hayes, 2002). When school counselors serve as educational leaders who advocate for all students, they can help make systemic changes to ensure all students have equal access to quality education that helps unlock their full potential (House & Hayes, 2002; Trusty & Brown, 2005). Professional school counselors have a set of advocacy competencies that include (a) having the disposition to advocate on behalf of students; (b) possessing the knowledge of resources, parameters, advocacy models, and systems change to advocate for students; and (c) using communication, collaboration, problem solving, organizational, and self-care skills to become advocates in their schools (Trusty & Brown, 2005). Although speaking up against the system can sometimes be uncomfortable, school counselors should remind themselves that the goal of social and educational equality is well worth the discomfort!

Mental health, community, and rehabilitation counselors also have an important role to play in advocacy and social justice. Counselors often work with clients in the aftermath of oppression and related social injustices (Vera & Speight, 2007). Kiselica (2004) reminded all counselors that they have a duty to advocate for clients who are too overwhelmed or ill to advocate for themselves. This advocacy can occur on an individual level, such as working with an insurance company to gain approval for more counseling sessions, or on a systemic level, such as lobbying for laws and regulations that will help improve clients' lives. Because of the importance of advocacy at the legislative level, ACA sponsors a Legislative Training Institute each year where all types of counselors can learn how to lobby their legislators on behalf of mental health promotion. Many state-level counseling associations also offer "Legislative Days" when counselors can advocate for mental health. In the accompanying Spotlight, we highlight counselors who are advocates for their clients and for the profession.

Spotlight
The Many Faces of Advocacy

Sometimes, counselors can read or hear about tremendous social injustices, the need that exists for social change, and the advocacy efforts of others in the field and feel overwhelmed by the challenge. It is easy to believe that counselors who are advocates must dedicate countless hours to big causes. And for some advocates within the profession, that is certainly accurate. Other counselors advocate on a much smaller scale, but their contributions are still very important to their clients, to the profession, and to society as a whole. This Spotlight briefly highlights 13 different counselors who have taken up the role of advocate. The point is for beginning counselors to recognize that advocacy can take many forms, and there is a place within this role for everyone. Just as with all counseling roles, there are many different paths to take within the overarching role of professional advocacy.

Susan Sears was one of several counselors who developed what was to become one of the first and strongest clinical licensure laws in the country. Dr. Sears and her colleagues set guidelines for board rules and policies as well as required qualifications of applicants. Dr. Sears believed strongly in the counseling profession, and she lobbied hard to include the provision of diagnosis and treatment of mental and emotional disorders into the wording of the law, in spite of pressure from legislatures, lobbyist, and some of her colleagues to drop this provision in order to ensure easier passage of the law. In recognition of her hard work on behalf of Ohio counselors, Dr. Sears holds license #1 in Ohio.

Michael D'Andrea is a tireless advocate for multiculturalism and anti-oppression. A professor at the University of Hawaii, Dr. D'Andrea is consistent in his efforts to bring discussions of social inequality to the counseling profession. He is a self-described outspoken advocate for peace and social justice issues. His tactics have been challenged by some, but Dr. D'Andrea contends that he is trying to bring attention to the status quo of racism and sexism.

Jenny Renfro is a counselor in New York City. She works in a mental health setting in Spanish Harlem. Although Jenny didn't know any Spanish when she started her work, she is learning to speak the language and is actively engaged in outreach and programming to the Latino/a culture.

Anita Young is a school counselor and consultant for the Education Trust Transforming School Counseling Initiative. She is active in her state school counseling association, and she co-authored a book on how school counselors can use data to help improve students' achievement. As a doctoral student, she implemented a program in an urban high school that resulted in a 50% increase in the number of high school seniors who applied and were accepted to college.

Jerry Juhnke is a counselor and professor in Texas. After Hurricane Katrina, more than 13,000 displaced people were transported to San Antonio, Texas. Rather than sit helplessly by and watch this human drama unfold, Dr. Juhnke organized his students, who provided more than 300 direct service hours of counseling in the weeks following the disaster.

Erin Bruno is a college counselor who does outreach to urban high schools, preparing low-income/first-generation college students for postsecondary education.

Mark Kiselica is a counselor who began advocacy work by organizing consciousness-raising events about the needs of Teenage Fathers, a group that has been largely ignored by society. As his efforts grew, he brought attention to the issue to a national level, including becoming the founder and coordinator of the American School Counseling Association's Taskforce on Teenage Parents. In 1996, Dr. Kiselica served as a consulting scholar to the Federal Fatherhood Initiative, advising officials from the U.S. Department of Health and Human Services about how to better serve fathers in federally sponsored social service programs.

Natalie Turner was a student in a master's internship class working at the homeless shelter in a large city. She was surprised to learn that the shelter did not have a standard policy for mental health programming or standardized access to mental health care. Rather than wait for someone else to develop such a protocol, Natalie researched the project and developed one on her own. When it was presented to her supervisor, word of Natalie's initiative quickly spread throughout the agency and was soon adopted by the board as the official policy for the shelter. The protocol was widely shared with other homeless shelters throughout the state and quickly became the standardized policy in the state.

Paul Granello was impacted personally by suicide when his brother took his own life in September 1999. As a result, Dr. Granello became a tireless advocate for suicide prevention and founded the Ohio Suicide Prevention Foundation in September 2005. The foundation provides information and resources to local suicide prevention coalitions and works to raise public awareness of suicide, reduce stigma, and increase help-seeking behaviors among the general public.

Suzanne Lynah is a counselor in Vermont. Suzanne is a deaf person born into a hearing family. At age 16, she decided she wanted to be a counselor. Now, she is the only licensed deaf therapist in Vermont. She travels all over the state to meet the needs of deaf clients in schools and other agency settings. Through her work and outreach, she advocates for deaf persons to receive culturally and linguistically appropriate therapeutic care.

Barbara Mahaffey is a Licensed Professional Clinical Counselor in a small Appalachian town. Late one Friday afternoon, she received a call from a crisis worker at a local jail who said there was a man in custody who said he planned to complete suicide that night. The man had asked the crisis worker to contact Barbara, whom he had never met, because he heard from some friends that she was a compassionate and caring person, and he wanted Barbara to take care of his cats after his death. Barbara spent the rest of the day and into the evening helping get the man the mental health care he so desperately needed. After multiple calls to the psychiatric hospital, the emergency room, the lieutenant at the jail, the insurance company, and a judge, Barbara was able to get the man admitted to the hospital, many long hours after she received the first phone call about a stranger in need. After a long day, Barbara headed home, but not before stopping at the man's house to feed his cats.

Keith Liles is an LCDC (Licensed Chemical Dependency Counselor) in Texas. He spent 12 years in the banking industry before beginning his training as a counselor. He first became involved in the Texas Association of Addiction Professionals as a student volunteer, then as a part-time counselor, and now as director of clinical services for a behavioral health care organization. Keith had a strong vision of what addiction professionals could and should do in Texas and how they should be trained. He is a tireless legislative advocate on behalf of persons with addiction. In 2005, Keith received the National Association for Alcoholism and Drug Abuse Counselors' "Outstanding Professional of the Year" Award.

Anne Lombardi is a college counselor at a small liberal arts college. She is passionate about student safety and ways that colleges can help students find appropriate mental health care. She knew that if college counselors in her state had a way to communicate with each other, they could share important and life-saving ideas. As a result, she organized a statewide meeting for college counselors, with an emphasis on mental health problems on small college campuses where resources are often scarce. Thanks to Anne, college counselors who used to work in isolation on small campuses now have an entire statewide network to assist them in their important work.

You

_____Take a moment to think about what your contribution to advocacy might be. What "story" would you like to read about your efforts? Remember, there is plenty of work to be done to help advocate for clients and for the profession. Find your niche, tap into your potential, and look for ways to express your advocacy *in ways that make sense for you.*

SNAPSHOT

Jean Underfer-Babalis, Licensed Professional Clinical Counselor, Counselor in Private Practice, Supervisor, Advocate, Leader in Professional Associations

Note: We put the snapshot of Jean here, under "Member of Professional Organizations," because she has been a leader in professional organizations at the state and national level for many years. However, like many counselors, her story could go under many of the different headings because, just like many counselors, Jean's professional life involves commitments to many different roles. In fact, as you read Jean's story and look at her chart of percentages of time spent in each of these roles, you will discover that she has clearly mastered one of the keys to being a successful counselor: *flexibility!*

Jean:

I have been a professional clinical counselor (PCC) for over 20 years, and it is a passion for me. I have had a private practice for 15 years. I love the independence, freedom, and autonomy of private practice, and with my leadership responsibilities and speaking engagements, I need the flexibility in my schedule.

Most days, my day starts at 9 a.m. and ends between 7–9 p.m. I work three to four days a week. In the morning, before seeing clients, I review charts, answer phone messages, and if time permits, I check my e-mails. I schedule clients straight through without any breaks. I hold to a 45-minute clinical billable hour and do my paperwork, return phone calls, call insurance companies if needed, attend to office duties, and take care of personal needs as time permits.

Anything can happen during the day. I can have large gaps with no clients, or every client attends and has some kind of emergency. Fielding calls from clients, family members, referrals, and anyone associated with a client is part and parcel of what I do on a daily basis. Routine and structure are nonexistent in my world.

I have learned to expect the unexpected, because it will happen. Some days I go 12 hours right through, and I feel like I am on roller skates. At the end of the day, I realize I have not eaten or even gone to the bathroom. Sometimes, I have to deal with crises with clients, another health professional, an emergency service, or something as boring as cleaning the office.

The days I do not see clients, I am usually involved in some sort of activity related to professional counseling. I am an officer in several of the professional counseling organizations, so I travel frequently and have volunteer work to do in that capacity. Being a leader costs me money in lost revenue, but it is my belief that it is important to be involved in the counseling profession and represent what is happening in the clinical world.

When I am supervising interns or professional counselors working toward independent licensure, I usually have them come to my office. I do site visits about once a month. At times, I take a contract to provide supervision for an entire group of beginning counselors at an agency. At those occasions, I go to that agency on a specific day of the week for a half a day.

Watching clients gain strength and insight into their lives and situations is such a joy to not only watch but to be a part of the process. To be there with a client with empathy and compassion and share in the pain and the joy is a privilege that cannot adequately be explained in words. One of the most rewarding parts of my professional life is learning about the impact my counseling has had on a human life.

The distasteful part of my career is dealing with insurance companies and bureaucracy. It is terribly annoying and sometimes maddening to have a reviewer tell me (the professional who has worked with the client directly) that the client only needs a few more sessions to draw counseling to closure. Of course, if I share my harsh thoughts with the reviewer, I might only hurt the client, because the reviewer has the power to discontinue treatment.

The wisdom I would like to impart to an aspiring professional counselor going into private practice is to surround yourself with excellent people. Being in private practice requires flexibility, patience, and being able to handle some level of anxiety (your income fluctuates). Learn to go with the flow and hire people to do the things that are not directly related to seeing clients. Your time is better spent generating income and paying someone to file charts.

Most importantly, love what you do. Having a passion and love for being a PCC will get you through those times when you wonder if what you are doing is helpful. Beware, doubts will occur. Being in private practice requires patience, self-motivation, tolerance, being able to weather the storm, and being able to see the big picture.

Jean's Breakdown of Time Spent on Daily Activities	
Therapist	29%
Diagnostician	5%
Assessor	10%
Administrator	3%
Researcher/scientist	3%
Learner/investigator	10%
Teacher/educator	5%
Supervisor/supervisee	3%
Crisis interventionist	2%
Advocate	4%
Social activist	1%
Expert witness	2%
Entrepreneur	3%
Member of professional organization	20%

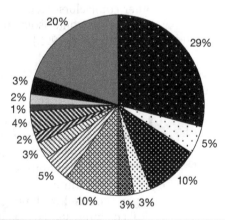

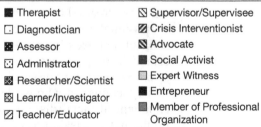

■■■ *Fast Facts* ■■■

Most professional counselors recognize the importance of membership in their state and national counseling associations. One study of school counselors found that more than three-quarters (76%) were current members in at least one state or national professional association (Wheaton, Bruno, Granello, & Moore, in press). A similar study of clinical counselors found 81% were members of these associations (Whitney, 2007). In the preceding Snapshot, a professional counselor discusses the importance of participation in professional associations and how her own career has been enhanced by her active membership and involvement in these organizations.

Counselor as Member of Professional Associations

Professional associations are critical to the future of the profession and to the ongoing development of the individual counselor. Professional associations at the national, state, and local levels act as advocates for the profession and provide organized and unified lobbying and public awareness campaigns. Counseling associations help set standards for the profession of counseling and develop ethical guidelines for members to follow. Professional associations provide members with new knowledge and information through books, journals, newsletters, and conferences. Professional associations also provide leadership opportunities for counselors. Those who wish to become involved can help create a vision for the future of the profession and can use their knowledge, skills, and motivation to encourage and support other counselors. Counselors who do not belong to their professional associations can become isolated and deprived of the newest information in the field (Lee & Remley, 1992).

Summary

In this chapter, you learned about the many roles that professional counselors play. Some of them were probably what you expected, while others may have been new or surprising to you. Of course, the list of roles in this chapter is not all-encompassing, and there are many, many other roles that, although less common, are no less important. Since the profession of counseling began, counselors have been carving out niche roles that use their special skills or interests. For example, we have had students come into our programs who are already lawyers, doctors, nurses, government executives, morticians, professional athletes and coaches, or engineers, and they have combined the skills of their existing professions with their newly learned counseling skills to establish unique roles and employment niches. We have worked with counselors who have very specialized clientele, and therefore, highly specialized roles. A counselor who works primarily with burn victims and those who have experienced facial disfigurement finds that although she engages in several traditional counseling roles, such as direct service, case management, advocacy, and assessment, she also has some unique responsibilities. Among these are helping client maneuver the complex medical world of plastic surgery and facial reconstruction. In this role, she accompanies clients on their visits to doctor's offices. Another counselor who works with athletes retiring from professional sports found that he has added "media consultant" to his list of counseling roles. A school counselor who is employed by an online high school found that (limited) technical support is among her roles when one of her students is frustrated by technical problems that keep him or her from learning.

The point is that with a strong background in counseling, you can create the job of your dreams. If your ideal position doesn't exist, then it is possible for you to create it. Counselors are, by training and temperament, resourceful and flexible individuals who look to find ways to help others and to apply their skills and training where they are needed most.

 ## End-of-Chapter Activities

Student Activities

1. **Reflect.** Now it's time to reflect on the major topics that we have covered in Chapter 2. Look back at the sections or the ideas you have underlined. What were your reactions as you read that portion of the chapter? What do you want to remember?

   _____

   _____

   _____

   _____

   _____

2. Take a look at the Spotlight on the many faces of advocacy. Whose stories did you connect with? What part of advocacy appeals to you? What role do you see yourself playing in both the personal and professional advocacy of the profession?

   _____

   _____

   _____

   _____

   _____

   _____

   _____

■■■ Journal Question ■■■

A Counselor's Professional Setting. Imagine for a moment that you've completed your formal training in counseling and you're in your ideal counseling job. In what type of work setting do you see yourself? What kinds of counseling interventions are you doing (e.g., individual, group, family, rehabilitation, adventure therapy? Long-term or brief counseling?) What does your client population look like? At this point, when considering your future work setting, are there any clients or populations that you would *not* consider working with or any setting that you would rule out? Why? What is it about these clients/populations/settings that you believe would make it difficult for you to be an effective counselor? Is there anything you could do in the coming weeks and months to expose yourself to this population in order to make sure you haven't ruled them out prematurely?

■■■ Topics for Discussion ■■■

1. Do you think counselors should focus on social justice and advocacy at the systemic level, or should they focus on the needs of their individual clients? Do counselors have the right to ask their clients to engage in social justice issues? How can counselors find a balance between the needs of individual clients and greater social needs?

2. Counselors clearly can engage in many different roles and functions. This may contribute to an overall problem with professional identity. In a field with such diversity, how can counselors develop an overall definition of counseling that fits with all the specialties and roles?

■■■ Experiments ■■■

1. Look again at the chart on pages 40–41 that you completed before you read this chapter. Now, complete the chart again, based on your new understanding of these many roles that counselors can play. What has changed? What has been confirmed? Do you have different thoughts now about your future involvement in the profession?

2. Interview three different counselors, one in each of the following categories:

   a. A counselor who holds a role that you are attracted to

   b. A counselor who holds a role that you are not attracted to

   c. A counselor who holds a role that you don't know much about

After your interviews, consider what you learned about the many roles of the profession based on your experiences. Did any of your interactions change your beliefs about the kind of counselor you would like to be?

3. Develop a brief (1–2 sentence) description of what it means to be a counselor that could be shared with others outside the profession. Use your own words, rather than descriptions taken from this text or websites of the profession. Is it challenging to develop a brief but inclusive definition for counseling? What are the difficulties you encountered when you attempted this experiment?

■■■ Explore More ■■■

If you are interested in exploring more about the ideas presented in this chapter, we recommend the following books and articles.

Herr, E. L., Heitzmann, D. E., & Rayman, J. R. (2005). *The professional counselor as administrator: Perspectives on leadership and management in counseling services.* New York: Routledge.

> This book explores a role that many counselors find themselves in with little preparation. Counselors who seek administrative roles, or who find themselves in these positions, will benefit from the practical advice and information.

Kiselica, M. S. (2004). When duty calls: The implications of social justice work for policy, education, and practice in the mental health professions. *Counseling Psychologist, 32*(6), 838–854.

> This article helps those in the helping professions better understand how to incorporate social justice and advocacy into their professional role.

Sullivan, W. P. (2006). Mental health leadership in a turbulent world. In J. Rosenberg & S. Rosenberg (Eds.), *Community mental health: Challenges for the 21st century* (pp. 247–258). New York: Routledge.

> Counselors in community mental health must find ways to use their leadership skills for the good of their clients and of the profession. This chapter (and the entire book) helps counselors find a way to use these skills in their roles as professional counselors.

Trusty, J., & Brown, D. (2005). Advocacy competencies for professional school counselors. *Professional School Counseling, 8*, 259–265.

> School counselors have been called upon to become advocates for all of their students, and this article provides not only a listing of the necessary competencies, but practical strategies for implementation of them.

◼◼◼ MyHelpingLab ◼◼◼

To help you explore the profession of counseling via video interviews with counselors and clients, some of the chapters in this text include links to MyHelpingLab at the Pearson.com website. There are some videos that correspond with this chapter, and watching them might help you get a better idea of the kind of work that counselors do.

- Under the heading Counseling Children and Adolescents, go to "Career Interventions" then "Career Explorations" and

finally click on "counseling" to launch a website with a series of videos where counselors discuss what they do. We recommend:

- Ed Guzowski, Elementary School Counselor

- Mario Moraga, Addictions Counselor

- Rachel Henderson, Family Therapist

- Allen Kirkpatrick, Vocational Counselor, JA Director

3

How Are Counselors Trained and Regulated?

In this chapter, we will:

- Discuss what it means to have a strong sense of professional identity as a counselor.
- Survey the education and qualifications required to become a licensed counselor.
- Review the professional associations and organizations to which counselors belong.
- Learn how professional counselors are regulated throughout their careers.

As you read the chapter, you might want to consider:

- What do you think differentiates professional counselors from friends who reach out to help others or other nonprofessional helpers?
- How can a sense of professional identity help individual counselors and the profession as a whole?
- Do you believe that all counselors, regardless of setting, have the same core professional identity?

Becoming a counselor certainly means different things for different people, and the road you took to get to this moment in time is as unique as you are. Yet from now on your path, at least in terms of professional experience and training, will have some commonalities with all other graduate students in counseling. These commonalities bind our profession and give us all a sense of professional identity. Having an identity as a professional counselor is not just a job title or the listing on your license. Being a professional counselor means that you have achieved a high level of education and training, have met agreed-upon standards of the profession, and have committed to a vocation that upholds certain principles and values. Being a counselor means that you believe that all human beings have value and are worth helping, that people can and do change their lives, and that you have something to offer them in their journey. Being a professional counselor is both an awesome responsibility and a wonderful privilege. It is because of this responsibility that professional counseling remains a tightly regulated profession. As you learned in Chapter 2, almost anyone can use the term *counselor*, but having identity as a *professional counselor* is much, much more.

In this chapter, you will learn about the education and training of professional counselors. You will learn about the professional associations that foster the growth of counseling and about state licensing and certification boards that regulate counselors. There is no national certification or licensure of counselors. Regulation of the profession is done on a state-by-state basis. Nevertheless, there are some generally agreed upon principles for the education of professional counselors, and there are several national organizations and associations that help regulate and promote the profession. Becoming a counselor and maintaining your status as a professional counselor is a very involved process, and this chapter will help you negotiate the many diverse and complicated regulations and guidelines for becoming a counselor.

 ## How Many Counselors Are There?

The American Counseling Association (ACA) states that there are over 80,000 professional counselors who are licensed in 50 states and the District of Columbia. However, this number represents only mental health counselors who are licensed by their state licensing boards. When all the counseling specializations are included, the number of practicing counselors in the United States is much higher. According to the U.S. Department of Labor's Bureau of Labor Statistics (2008), there were approximately 665,000 counselors in the United States in 2008. According to the same source (U.S. Bureau of Labor Statistics, 2008), the health care and social assistance industry employ about 47% of counselors, and state and local governments employ about 11%. According to projections, job opportunities for counselors in the next several decades should be *very good*, with job openings expected to exceed the number of graduates from counseling programs, although this varies by location and occupational specialty. The overall employment of counselors is expected to increase by 18% from 2008 to 2018, much faster than the average for all occupations (which is approximately 10%). Specifically, projections are that demand for some specialties will increase dramatically:

- Mental health counselors—24% growth

- Substance abuse and behavioral disorder counselors—21% growth

■■■ *Fast Facts* ■■■

Counselors represent three of the top five *fastest growing occupations* for all occupations requiring a master's degree:

1. Mental health counselors
2. Mental health and substance abuse social workers
3. Marriage and family counselors
4. Physical therapists
5. Physician assistants

Counselors also represent three of the top five occupations projected to have the *largest numerical increases in employment* for all occupations requiring a master's degree:

1. Clergy
2. Physical therapists
3. Mental health and substance abuse social workers
4. Educational, vocational, and school counselors
5. Rehabilitation counselors

Source: U.S. Bureau of Labor Statistics (2008).

- Rehabilitation counselors—19% growth
- Educational, vocational, and school counselors—14% growth
- Marriage and family therapists—14% growth

Because the federal government does not regulate counselors and there is no national standard for what is included in these federal reports, there are varying levels of education, experience, licensure, and certification represented in this listing. Nevertheless, it is clear that counselors represent a significant (and increasing!) proportion of the U.S. workforce.

 ## The Education of Counselors

To become a professional counselor, most states generally require, at a minimum, a master's degree in counseling (in some, but not all, states a master's degree in a related field is acceptable). Graduate degrees in counseling typically are offered through counselor education programs in colleges of education, although at some universities, the programs are located in other colleges or departments. There are many subspecialties in counseling, and new counseling students may be surprised that they can specialize in "college student affairs, elementary or secondary school counseling, gerontological counseling, marriage and family therapy, substance abuse counseling, rehabilitation counseling, agency or community counseling, clinical mental health counseling, and career counseling" (U.S. Bureau of Labor Statistics, 2008, p. 2). Of course, not all universities or counselor education programs offer all of these specializations. The most common ones offered are school counseling, clinical/community counseling, and college student affairs.

The specific course and education requirements for counselor licensure are dictated by state laws and regulations. However, most states follow the guidelines that have been established by CACREP—the Council for Accreditation of Counseling and Related Educational Programs. CACREP is an independent agency that was founded in 1981, after the American Counseling Association (then the American Personnel and Guidance Association) formed a task force in the late 1970s to look into the development of national standards for counseling accreditation. As we discussed in Chapter 1, during the 1970s and 1980s, counseling was not licensed in most states, and there were no agreed-upon standards for the training of counselors. Without licensure or certification to guide this process, each counselor education program was free to develop its own unique program. In fact, it was common for school counselors trained in the late 1960s and early 1970s to have only one summer's worth of counseling classes before they began their school counseling careers. Even into the 1990s, colleges and universities (in states without counseling licensure) could offer "counseling" programs with far fewer courses and credit hours than were required in other states.

CACREP (and CORE—Commission on Rehabilitation Education in rehabilitation counseling) represents a professional accreditation standard. Professional accreditation is a process whereby an educational program at a college or university voluntarily undergoes review by an accrediting body. Professional accrediting bodies evaluate and qualify educational programs that have met the standards for accreditation. CACREP was developed so training programs throughout the country would train their students in the same basic curriculum and with the same minimum standards. The eight core areas of counselor training that were developed by CACREP serve as the basis for most counselor education programs today. These are:

1. Professional Orientation and Ethical Practice
2. Social and Cultural Diversity
3. Human Growth and Development
4. Career Development
5. Helping Relationships
6. Group Work
7. Assessment
8. Research and Program Evaluation

In addition, CACREP's eight core areas are used as the basis for the educational requirements for most state's licensure requirements, and the core areas serve as the foundation for the test questions in the National Counselor Exam for Licensure and Certification (NCE). As a result, the curriculum guidelines developed by CACREP have had a major influence on the education of all counselors in all states. In this chapter's Informed by Research feature, you will read about a study conducted to help validate the importance of each of the eight core areas of CACREP to the practice of professional counseling.

Colleges or universities can have their programs accredited by CACREP if they meet certain criteria and voluntarily submit to the accreditation process. CACREP accredits both master's and doctoral programs in counselor education. The doctoral standards build upon the successful completion of a master's-level program in counseling. At the doctoral level, students focus their educational experiences primarily on research, teaching, supervision, and leadership within the counseling profession. As of 2008, CACREP had accredited 228 institutions in at least one of the CACREP specializations. Of those, 53 institutions were CACREP accredited at the doctoral level (CACREP, 2008). The number of program accredited through CACREP continues to increase.

Not all programs are CACREP accredited, and CACREP accreditation is not necessarily a prerequisite for counselor education programs to train high-quality counselors. In fact, there is no research to support a finding that graduates from CACREP programs are any better prepared or more proficient than graduates

Informed by Research
The Eight Core Areas of the Counseling Curriculum

The eight core areas that make up the counseling curriculum in most states and in all CACREP programs are firmly established and generally well accepted within the counseling profession (Schmidt, 1999). Studies of counseling students, faculty, and graduates consistently find support for the relevance of the eight core areas to the counseling profession (McGlothlin & Davis, 2004).

McGlothlin and Davis (2004) set out to explore whether graduates in different specialties (school counseling and mental health counseling) and faculty in counselor education programs had different perceptions of the relative benefits of the eight core areas. They conducted a national survey of practicing school counselors ($N = 256$), mental health counselors ($N = 242$), and faculty members in counselor education ($N = 143$).

Results indicated that overall, all three groups had favorable perceptions of all eight core areas (3.09 on a 4.0 scale). Helping Relationships and Human Growth and Development were perceived as the most beneficial by all three groups, with Social and Cultural Diversity ranking a close third and Group Work fourth. Practicing school counselors saw the least benefit in Research and Program Evaluation. Both practicing mental health counselors and counselor education faculty ranked Career Development last, although faculty, even though they ranked

this core area last of the eight, still perceived Career Development as significantly more beneficial ($p < .05$) than did practicing mental health counselors.

It is perhaps not surprising, given the importance of counseling skills and the developmental nature of counseling, that Helping Relationships and Human Growth and Development were perceived to be the most beneficial core areas for all three groups. The lower ranking of Research and Program Evaluation and Career Development are consistent with how individuals score on the National Counselor Examination (NCE), where counselors typically score lowest on career, research, and assessment (Loesch & Vacc, 1994).

The results of the study support the inclusion of the eight core areas in the counselor education curriculum. Even areas with the lowest level of support are still perceived to be beneficial to the counseling curriculum. It is because of the findings from these studies that the CACREP standards revision committee elected to keep the eight core areas the same in the 2009 CACREP revisions. Meaningful research conducted by McGlothlin and Davis (2004), Schmidt (1999), and Loesch and Vacc (1994) all help counselors, counselor educators, and accrediting bodies to make sound decisions that are truly informed by research.

from non-CACREP-accredited programs (Schmidt, 1999). What is important is that training programs meet the state licensure requirements for the state within which the program is located. In other words, since state licensure programs set out specific training and education requirements before individuals are eligible to sit for licensure, it is these requirements that a counselor education program must follow. As long as your program meets your state's licensure requirements for education and training of counselors, regardless of whether the program is accredited by CACREP, your degree will allow you to sit for the licensure exam within your state.

Educational Requirements

The education and training that you receive during your graduate program is the result of many years of research and practice into the most effective methods for training new counselors and professionally agreed-upon standards regarding the core educational content and experiential components of your training. Because of the awesome responsibility that professional counselors face as they work with their students and clients, training programs must be both far-reaching in content and rigorous in process. It is not uncommon for students to feel overwhelmed by all that is required of them in their counselor preparation programs. New students might look ahead to the required curriculum and think that it seems almost insurmountable. You may have experienced this, too. Each term, when you are handed a syllabus for a course, you might be excited by the possibilities and energized by the opportunities it presents, but you may feel a bit overwhelmed as well. You may start to think that you are in over your head and that the requirements are more than you will be able to complete. The good news is that this feeling is very common among graduate students in counseling. The *even better news* is that faculty in your program have worked hard to develop a program that not only prepares you to become an outstanding counselor, but is done in a way that best facilitates your success. Faculty frequently discuss how to structure courses (or the entire counseling curriculum) in ways that both support and challenge the student learners. Courses may challenge you in ways that you have never been challenged before, but there are typically supports in place to help you. Chapter 5 of this text will give you some practical strategies to help you get the most from your graduate program.

Core Curriculum

The eight core areas that are required by CACREP and most state licensure boards have remained the same since CACREP was founded in 1981, although the specific information and educational experiences that are contained within these core areas change with the needs of the profession. In your graduate program, you will have at least one course or educational experience in each of the eight core areas. What follows is a brief description of each of these areas, which is intended to give you a broad overview of your graduate program and to whet your appetite. More important than just listing the content included in each of these areas, we will focus this discussion on *why* the core areas serve as the foundation for your training. You will have entire courses to help you understand what is included in each of the core areas, and any overview we can give you of the actual content would be cursory, at best. We believe that in a textbook that introduces you to the profession, the most important thing for you to understand about these core areas is their importance to your training and to the counseling profession, and the rationale for basing a curriculum around these topics.

Professional orientation and ethical practice. Often called "Foundations of Counseling" or "Introduction to Counseling," the goal of this educational experience

■■■ *Words of Wisdom* ■■■

"Contemporary definitions of professional identity highlight three themes: self-labeling as a professional, integration of skills and attitudes as a professional, and membership in a professional community. During training, new professionals are immersed in a professional culture in which they learn professional skills, attitudes, values, modes of thinking, and strategies for problem solving. This equips new counselors with the tools they need to be ethical, effective, and self-reflective professionals."

—Colette Dollarhide, counselor educator and researcher on issues of professional identity in counseling

is to provide an overview of the history and philosophy of the counseling profession as well as an understanding of the current context within which counselors work. Counselors-in-training learn about the professional roles and functions of counselors, the professional organizations and agencies that license, regulate, and promote the counseling profession, the importance of advocacy, and the ethical standards of the profession. The goal of this core area is to help counselors-in-training understand the profession and to begin to envision themselves as future counselors. It is in the Professional Orientation course(s) that the emerging sense of professional identity is forged. Clearly, we believe that the Foundations of Counseling course is an important one to start you on your journey, and the textbook you are holding is part of this important first step.

A sense of identity as a professional counselor will frame all of your future professional decisions and goals. The experiences you have in your Professional Orientation course(s) are specifically designed to help you understand this identity. Whether you are asked to interview practicing counselors, attend local or state counseling meetings or conferences, or read the journals of the counseling profession, the goal is to help you start to see yourself as a member of the counseling profession.

Social and cultural diversity. In a world of ever-increasing diversity, the counseling profession has taken a strong stance in its efforts to be at the forefront of culturally appropriate services. The need for culturally responsive counseling is evident, as the U.S. population is becoming more multicultural, multiethnic, and multilingual. According to the U.S. Census Bureau, by 2050, non-Hispanic whites will represent less than half of the U.S. population (2009), and there will be significant increases in the percentages of the population who are Hispanic American, African American, and Asian American. Counselors must demonstrate an ability to work with clients who represent a broad diversity in race, ethnicity, national origin or ancestry, socioeconomic status, religion, sexual orientation, gender identity, and ability or health status. In 1992, Sue, Arrendondo, and McDavis developed the Multicultural Counseling Competencies (MCCs), which are comprised of three domains: skills (behavioral component), attitudes and beliefs (affective component), and knowledge of relevant research and theory (cognitive component). These competencies were met with wide acclaim within the counseling profession. The American Counseling Association, as well as many of its divisions, has formally adopted a position that supports the MCCs and recognizes multicultural counseling competence as a priority for all counselors in all settings.

The core area of social and cultural diversity emphasizes the need to train counselors to be multiculturally competent in their counseling and to take a strong stance to work to "eliminate biases, prejudices, and processes of intentional and unintentional oppression and discrimination" (CACREP, 2008), wherever it occurs. Most professional counselors would agree that the goal of multiculturally competent counseling is using our professional skills to *promote and celebrate* diversity (Hill, 2003). Traditional theories and techniques in counseling and psychology have been criticized for perpetuating culture-bound value systems (e.g., individualism) that may contradict the beliefs and values of diverse clients. Multicultural counseling represents a paradigm shift beyond this monocultural perspective. Because of its importance to the entire profession, multicultural counseling has been called counseling's "fourth force," building on the existing forces of psychodynamic, behavioral, and humanistic perspectives in counseling (Pedersen, 1991).

Although almost all graduate programs offer separate courses in multicultural counseling, there is a strong emphasis in most training programs to infuse issues of diversity in every course, regardless of course topic or sequence in the curriculum. Training in multicultural counseling typically includes an exploration of one's own beliefs, attitudes, and understandings of diversity, as well as information about theories of multicultural counseling and identity development, and specific counseling skills for diverse populations.

Human growth and development. One of the key identifying characteristics of counseling is its emphasis on human development. Whereas other helping professions focus on pathology and illness, counselors focuses on wellness and growth. Therefore, it is probably not surprising to see that human growth and development is one of the core content areas of the counseling curriculum. When counselors understand clients and their problems from a developmental context, they are able to intervene more appropriately. For example, two clients facing a similar problem (let's say, alcohol dependence) may need different interventions based on their chronological age. The treatment protocol for an adolescent with an alcohol problem would be very different from the protocol used with a retiree. In schools, counselors spend much of their time addressing the developmental needs of their students. Elementary school counselors, for example, provide a type of counseling that is different from that of their high school counterparts, and these differences include not just the *content* of what they do, but the *process* of how they do it. When we work with clients, we strive to understand them in the context of their developmental level so we can provide the most appropriate interventions.

Many of the early theorists in counseling and psychology recognized the importance of understanding people and their problems in the context of their developmental life cycle. Freud theorized that children and adolescents go through a series of psychosexual stages (oral, anal, phallic, and genital) that include developmental tasks that had to be mastered to allow for healthy transition to the next developmental stage. Later, Carl Jung recognized that healthy development does not stop at adolescence, and in his work, *The Stages of Life* (1931/1962), he wrote about important developmental milestones in midlife and beyond. Erik Erikson famously proposed eight stages of human development throughout life (1950). Because Erikson's work provided a framework that was based on a growth and wellness perspective that meshed with the wellness perspective in counseling, it became an important foundation that is frequently applied to the field of counseling. More recently, these theories were challenged by feminists who argued that the existing developmental models were "male-normative," meaning that they assumed that models based on healthy male development were applicable to females, which may not be the case.

The body of knowledge represented by the core area of human growth and development, like all of the core areas, constantly changes to incorporate the latest research and thinking in the field. The one constant is the widespread belief that we must work to understand clients in their developmental context, whether that means understanding the life tasks they are facing because of their age or working through stages of healthy identity development in a sexual minority client. The point is that each of us is always in a process of change and growth, and counselors use developmental approaches to help clients navigate those changes in appropriate and healthy ways.

Career development. The profession of counseling has its roots in career development. In Chapter 1, we discussed Frank Parsons, often called the Father of Vocational Guidance. Nowadays, we recognize that career development is a life-long process that goes beyond just our initial selection of a field of work. Whereas traditional vocational guidance focused on dispensing information about career options, career counseling is now seen as complex, multifaceted, and lifelong. Crites (1981) was among the first to recognize this shift. He conceptualized career counseling as an *interpersonal* process. He wrote: "Ideally, it [career counseling] involves active participation in the decisional process, not simply passive-receptive input of information" (p. 11).

Career development is not just a counseling specialty for career counselors, it is an area of interest for all types of counselors. Career development is one of the three major content areas (along with academic development and personal/social development) in the American School Counselor Association National Standards (ASCA, 2005). Within the field of rehabilitation counseling, career interventions are so important that the specialization of Vocational Rehabilitation specifically addresses the specific career needs of individuals with disabilities. It is now clear that the distinction between career counseling and mental health counseling is somewhat artificial as well. For example, individuals unhappy in their careers find that it is difficult to be happy in other areas of their lives. Alternatively, persons with mental health problems typically find that these problems affect their careers. People with depression, anxiety, substance abuse problems, post-traumatic stress—all of these individuals may present at a counselor's office with vocational problems that affect or are affected by their mental health status (Hinkelman & Luzzo, 2007).

Career development, like all of the core content areas in the counseling curriculum, is a subject area that is constantly changing and growing. Importantly, career counseling benefits greatly from the use of the Internet and electronic resources. More and more career resources are available online, and electronic delivery of career information is quickly becoming the preferred method for high school and college students (Venable, 2008). Counseling professionals have identified career counseling as the specialty area that most readily adapts to electronic format (Boer, 2001; Lewis & Coursol, 2007). Whatever the mechanism for delivery, however, career development uses appropriate interventions, assessments, resources, and techniques to help individuals make appropriate and meaningful choices in their lives.

Helping relationships. It is fair to say that most students enter graduate training in counseling because they want to help others, and the topics included in this core area give counselors-in-training the specific skills that they need to *actually do* counseling. This is where "the rubber hits the road" so to speak, and counseling students try out the skills they are learning, practicing on their peers *before* they work with actual clients. Students learn counseling theories, skills, and techniques as well as appropriate counselor characteristics and behaviors. In Helping Relationships course(s), counselors-in-training practice case conceptualization and interviewing skills. Most students are asked to record their work, so they can get feedback on their developing skills. And, although most of us cringe at the sight of ourselves on camera or the sound of our voices on the audio recordings, it is important not to miss the bigger picture here. We practice on peers and in laboratory settings, where the stakes are lower and we can get feedback and support, so that when we face our first clients, we are ready. Learning the basic helping skills can be challenging, confusing, exhilarating, and overwhelming. The more open you can be to the process of receiving feedback, the better your skills will become.

Group work. Group interventions are essential to counseling, and counselors in all types of settings, with all types of clients, use groups in their work. Groups are an important and meaningful type of intervention because human beings are primarily social animals. We learn about ourselves from our interactions with others. Each of us belongs to many different groups. For example, you may identify as part of your family, your counseling cohort, your church or religious congregation, your college graduating class, and your yoga class. These connections that you feel are important, and they help define you. In the accompanying Spotlight, you will learn how counselors use the concept of

 ## Spotlight
The Social Atom

The concept of the "social atom" may help here. The social atom, modeled on the structure of the physical atom, helps describe, explain, and predict how people develop and maintain long-term interpersonal relationships. Based on the work of Joseph Moreno (1951), the concept is intended to help us see the influence of these relationships in our lives. In a social atom, the nucleus represents the individual and the electrons represent the many groups with which the individual identifies. The distance of each group from the nucleus could be said to represent the emotional or psychological distance of the person from the group. In the example in Figure 3.1, a somewhat "stripped down" social atom demonstrates the concept. You can see that for this person, immediate family occupies a spot on the innermost ring. There might be other groups that are equally important, and they would be on this ring as well. The next ring contains several groups of friends (sorority sisters, church youth group), while the third ring out has extended family, friends from high school, roommates, and peers in the counseling program. Each of these rings can have many more groups in it, and the rings can extend out indefinitely. The point of the social atom is to help clients (or in this case, students in counseling programs) see the extent of their relationships. Take a moment and draw a social atom of your own, and you will see the many groups of people in your life who help you feel connected and help you define who you are.

FIGURE 3.1 Example of a Social Atom for a Graduate Student in Counselor Education

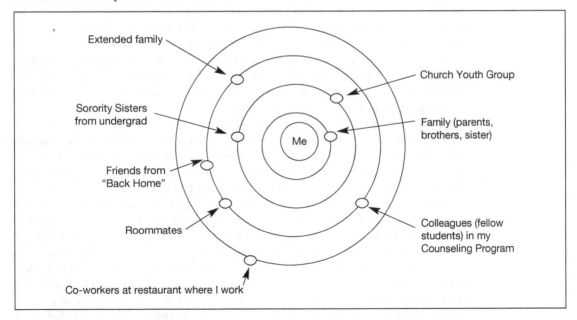

a social atom to help clients recognize the importance of connections with others in their lives.

Within the field of counseling, group work "involves the application of group theory and process by a capable professional practitioner to assist an interdependent collection of people to reach their mutual goals, which may be personal, interpersonal, or task-related in nature" (Association for Specialists in Group Work, 1991, p. 14). The purpose and goals of groups in counseling can be conceptualized along a continuum, with one end representing groups focused on prevention and growth and the other including groups that provide remediation and therapy. Prevention- and growth-oriented groups are intended for individuals who are relatively well functioning, but could benefit from some specific life-skills training. Psychoeducational groups are a particular type of group intervention that, as the name implies, employ both psychological and educational constructs. These types of groups are often used in schools and counseling settings to teach specific life skills (e.g., assertiveness training, stress management, parenting). Psychoeducational groups help to educate and prepare individuals who are facing a potential threat, a developmental life event, or an immediate life crisis (Brown, 2004). For example, a child with a parent in the military who is being deployed may benefit from a psychoeducational group within a school setting that includes other children in similar situations. Or, an adult recently diagnosed with a chronic illness, such as diabetes, may benefit from a psychoeducational group that includes both information about the condition and therapeutic interactions with other adults who have diabetes. Therapy groups, which are at the other end of the continuum, provide participants with mental health problems opportunities to do more in-depth therapeutic work. Counseling or therapy groups help individuals develop interpersonal relationship, receive feedback, and practice new behaviors within the context of the group.

Group counseling has been found to be effective for a wide variety of client populations and presenting problems. Even a cursory review of the research reveals hundreds upon hundreds of research articles demonstrating the overall effectiveness of groups for many mental health diagnoses, including substance abuse, eating disorders, anxiety disorders, depression, and personality disorders. Groups have been demonstrated to be effective in helping people without a psychiatric diagnosis as well. Survivors of sexual abuse, persons living with HIV/AIDS, children of divorcing parents, persons quitting smoking—all of these and countless others have been shown to be helped by group interventions.

One of the most powerful components of counseling groups is the benefit that members receive when they recognize that although everyone is different, we all share universal struggles. This concept, called *universality*, is one of the core curative factors identified by Irving Yalom. Yalom (1970) found that in all counseling groups, regardless of population or setting, certain core elements occur that are, in and of themselves, curative. He called these the **curative factors**, and concepts such as universality, altruism (helping others in the group), instillation of hope (allowing the experiences in the group to make one feel hopeful about the future), and group cohesiveness (feeling connected to the group), among others, are some of these curative factors.

Because working with clients in groups requires specialized training beyond the individual counseling skills that are learned in the Helping Relationships class(es), separate training experiences in group counseling are a required part of the counseling curriculum. In addition to the classroom learning, this core area includes a requirement for a minimum of 10 clock hours in a small group setting. That is, students must not just *learn about* groups in a class, they must experience a group *as a member*. Most students find this a very powerful experience, and it is a good reminder of the power (and the potential) of group counseling.

Assessment. Assessment in counseling is broadly defined as "any method used to measure characteristics of people, programs, or objects" (American Educational Research Association, American Psychological Association, & National Council on Measurement in Education, 1985, p. 89). The terms *assessment* and *testing* are sometimes used interchangeably, although assessment is a broader, more inclusive term that includes testing, interviews, observations, and other formal and informal measurement procedures. Accurate assessment is the key to any intervention. To use a medical analogy, why work on the right leg, when the left leg is broken? In other words, the more we understand about a person, program, or situation, the better and more effective our work with clients can be. All counselors in all settings use both formal and informal methods of assessment to better understand their clients, the needs of their constituents, and the effectiveness of their interventions and programs.

Assessment is the cornerstone of any intervention or decision. Counselors who fully understand the domain of assessment and the appropriate use of tests find that they have more complete and complex understandings of their clients and programs and are better prepared to assist. Assessment can include intake interviews, client or student observations, self-reports, standardized tests, needs assessments, and program evaluations, just to name a few. The American Counseling Association developed a core set of assessment competencies required of all counselors in order to be considered properly trained in the area of assessment (American Counseling Association, 2003). These seven competencies include:

1. Understanding of the role of assessment in counseling, including the practitioner's counseling specialty

2. A thorough understanding of testing theory, including test construction, reliability, and validity

3. A working knowledge of statistical concepts in testing

4. Ability to review, select, and administer tests appropriate for clients or students

5. Skill in administration of tests and interpretation of test scores

6. Knowledge of the impact of diversity on testing accuracy

7. Knowledge and skill in the professional responsible use of assessment and evaluation practice

Sadly, assessment is one of the core areas in which counselors are sometimes not adequately trained. Students attracted to careers in the helping professions are often less comfortable with concepts that involve math and statistics. As a result, they may be reluctant to fully engage in assessment courses and may perceive these classes as just "something to get through." Prediger (1994) wrote, "Unfortunately, the response to student preferences by some counselor educators has been to water down [assessment] courses" (p. 228). Childs and Eyde (2002) found that many assessment concepts receive only limited coverage in counseling programs. In fact, standardized assessment training has decreased in quality, intensity, and scope over the last two decades (Dana, 2003). Counselor education faculty, themselves people who joined the profession because of their interest in people rather than numbers, may be intimidated by teaching assessment courses. That attitude may be perceived by students as evidence that the testing course(s) are less important than other counseling courses. Consider the reaction from one of the author's experiences.

Darcy: When I was a practicing counselor in a day treatment program, I conducted a lot of comprehensive psychological evaluations with clients, and I eagerly read existing psychological evaluations of my clients in order to more fully understand them in all of their complexities. When I became a professor, I jumped at the chance to teach the testing classes and was surprised when no one else on our faculty objected or expressed any interest in teaching the classes. I had (mistakenly) thought I would have to fight for the opportunity to teach these core classes. After all, I knew so well how important assessment is to really understanding our clients.

My experience working with students in these courses has taught me that our students come to graduate school feeling rather "beat up" in the area of testing and statistics. So many of our students have horror stories. They have been taught to believe that they "can't do math" or that because they prefer working with people, it means they can't work with numbers. These are bright students. They are top achievers in their undergraduate programs and people with confidence and self-assuredness in other areas of their lives. Yet they have been told over the years that they shouldn't worry about math. That it's too complicated for them. That they will never "get it." And, sadly, they've learned to believe it.

I talk to my students about how their willingness to accept this (inaccurate) assessment of themselves is not unlike what many of our clients face. Our clients often have been told they are stupid, not worthy, not likeable—whatever—and they have come to believe it about themselves. Counselors help clients write new life stories, develop new self-awareness, and make positive determinations about who they want to be. I believe we have this opportunity in assessment as well. I think it's important that counselors refuse to see themselves as "stupid when it comes to math" or believe assessment is something foreign or irrelevant. Assessment isn't difficult—or at least no more difficult than any other area of counselor training. Like anything else, it takes effort and a willingness to see the connection between the work in class and the need in the profession. More importantly, it's important that counselors-in-training recognize the negative self-messages that they are perpetuating and work to challenge them. After all, it's exactly what we ask our clients to be willing to do.

The need for understanding and appropriate use of assessment has never been greater. More counselors are using more types of tests in their work than ever before. Since the 1980s, there has been a dramatic upsurge in the number and types of tests used in counseling (Nugent, 2008). The wide availability of assessments, including electronic testing and instruments available on the Internet, the pressure on counselors to make quick decisions regarding diagnosis or treatment interventions, and the use of computerized scoring and interpretation of tests mean that counselors have access to more assessment information and resources than ever before. In addition, the increasing diversity of society adds to the complexity of assessment. In recognition of this diversity, the American Counseling Association has adopted Standards for Multicultural Association (Association for Assessment in Counseling, 2003). These standards adhere to an ethical mandate to move counselors to cultural competence in all areas of their counseling, including assessment (Dana, 2005).

Research and program evaluation. The last core area, research, provides counselors with the knowledge, skills, and confidence they need to read, understand, and use the latest research to make decisions in their counseling. Research and evaluation courses also give counselors skills to conduct their own research to determine the effectiveness of their programs and interventions and to evaluate the impact of decisions to implement a single treatment protocol or an entire counseling program. Just as with the assessment area, counseling students may be reluctant to fully engage with the research course(s). But just as with assessment, the skills learned in this core area are fundamental to all other components of the counseling program.

Let's say, for example, that a client comes to you with an anxiety disorder. What do you do? What interventions have been demonstrated to be effective? How do you know? Perhaps you learned (or will learn) the fundamentals of treating someone with an anxiety disorder in your program, but what if the presenting problem is more complicated or more obscure? How will you work with someone who has a hoarding compulsion? What if the client is a 9-year-old girl? Or an 80-year-old man? Does age make a difference in treatment decisions? What if the client is a Somali refugee who has fled to the United States from his

■■■ *Words of Wisdom* ■■■

"The integration of research into practice should be a primary objective of counseling practitioners, educators, and researchers."

Source: Sexton, Whitson, Bleur, & Walz (1997, p. 16)

own war-torn country? Is hoarding still a sign of pathology? Is it a normal and expected response to stress? The point is, no matter how comprehensive your graduate program, no matter how much you learn, no matter how great and experienced your professors might be, you can never learn in graduate school all you need to know to work with the great diversity of clients and presenting problems. You will need to learn to make extensive and effective use of the vast amount of research that is available to help you make appropriate decisions in your counseling. Classes in your research core will help you. You will learn to analyze and evaluate existing research. Through this process, you will learn how much confidence to place in research results that have been published in professional journals and other outlets. You also will learn how to conduct (and evaluate the quality of) your own research.

Clinical experiences (practicum and internship). In addition to the eight core areas outlined above, graduate programs in counseling require both a practicum and an internship, also called *field experiences.* These supervised field experiences provide counseling students with the opportunity to *apply, evaluate, and refine* their counseling skills, and to integrate these skills with the theoretical knowledge gained through coursework. The purpose of field experiences is to provide students with real-world experiences while they are learning how to become effective counselors. Field applications provide students with opportunities to practice individual and small group counseling skills, consultation, collaboration and teaming, advocacy, and leadership skills. Both practicum and internship are "on-site" field experiences, which means that the counseling students work with actual clients in an agency or school, or in a university-based counseling clinic.

Practicum differs from internship in both length and purpose. The practicum (typically 100 hours) is intended to provide the student with a limited supervised experience in a specialized area of counseling. Counseling students in practicum are expected to see clients or students, develop relevant paperwork, and discuss cases both with the on-site and university supervisors. In addition to the hours that they spend at their sites each week, practicum students are required to attend a university-based practicum class for regular group supervision and to discuss other issues that arise at their practicum sites. Reviewing recordings of counseling sessions, role playing, presenting cases, learning about community resources, discussing how to work effectively with diverse cultures, and evaluating relevant legal and ethical issues are examples of seminar activities.

The internship (typically 600 hours, although certain specialty areas and/or states may require more hours) is an arranged supervised experience with a broad range of counseling functions. Internship is intended not only to provide the student with counseling experience but with greater exposure to all aspects of professional role and function.

The supervised field experience has long been considered one of the most significant aspects in the training of professional counselors (Granello, 2000). Learning and experiences that occur within the field experience simply cannot be replicated in the classroom, and field experiences allow students to capture, understand, and integrate the essence of the counseling process (Holloway, 1992). As a result, counselor educators and supervisors generally believe that the counseling practicum and internship experiences are an integral and indispensable part of the total program of counselor education. Ideally, practicum and internship should provide an opportunity for the student to develop his or her own unique style of counseling while working within the theoretical and therapeutic framework of the site.

In addition to the eight core content areas and the supervised field experiences, the graduate curriculum in counseling has many other courses, workshops, and experiences that vary by specialty, state, or college/university program. Examples include:

- Consultation
- Diagnosis and treatment planning
- Counseling children
- Crisis intervention and trauma counseling
- Wellness and prevention
- Theories of counseling supervision
- Grief/bereavement counseling
- Gender issues in counseling
- Personality testing
- Intelligence testing
- Substance abuse counseling
- Couples and family counseling
- Suicide prevention, assessment, and intervention
- Counseling students in special education
- Community and agency counseling
- School counseling
- Rehabilitation counseling

In addition to regularly structured courses, many counselor education programs offer a variety of workshops, weekend classes, and other learning opportunities to explore special topics. Taking advantage of these opportunities is a wonderful way to learn about current and important issues in counseling.

Beyond Graduate School

Learning does not stop at graduation. Professional counselors see themselves as lifelong learners. The field of counseling is ever changing, ever growing. There are new ideas, new research, new client problems, and new sources of inspiration for treatment and programming. Counselors recognize that no matter how good their graduate training is, it represents only the foundation of their professional knowledge. Counselors keep up-to-date throughout their professional careers by taking university-based courses, attending workshops and trainings, and keeping up with the latest research in the professional journals. Counselors who wish to specialize with a particular population or presenting problem know that they will need additional training beyond what is offered in graduate school and perhaps even specialized supervision. Continuing education and lifelong learning is a philosophical stance that encourages counselors to provide the best possible service to their clients.

 ## Counseling Licensure and Certification

State Licensure

A counseling license, issued by the state, is what allows individuals counselors to practice in a particular state or jurisdiction. There is no national counseling licensure. Licensure is a government-sanctioned credential that is based on the legal concept of the regulatory power of the state. States wishing to regulate the profession of counseling have their state legislatures pass a licensure law. Once the licensure law has passed, it becomes illegal for any individual who is not licensed by the state or specifically exempted from licensure to engage in the activities of the licensed occupation (American Counseling Association, 2009). In the accompanying Spotlight, you will read about the many different acronyms that are used to describe professional counselors in states throughout the country. The different initials can contribute to the public's confusion about the profession, but the differences exist because the titles are decided by the laws and rules governing counseling in each state, rather than at the national level.

Each counseling law contains a "scope of practice," which lists all of the activities a counselor with a specific type of licensure can legally engage in within the state. However, the state's counseling scope of practice is typically much more broad than that of the individual counselor. For example, just because a state law allows a counselor to diagnose a mental disorder or perform a comprehensive psychological evaluation, individual counselors cannot claim these tasks within their scope of practice unless they have appropriate education and training. A good analogy is a medical license. Although a medical license technically allows a doctor to perform any type of medicine, all doctors understand that they cannot do everything. Instead, they choose to specialize

 ## Spotlight
Counseling Licensure—What's in a Name?

Many states have several different types and levels of counseling licensure. Some states have a single license for their mental health and community counselors, while others have a two-tiered system. The names vary from state to state, and at least part of the confusion that the general public may have about the counseling professions stems from the lack of consistency in licensure titles and scope of practice across states. It is important to check with the licensure board in your state to see what type of licensure counselors in your state might hold.

Some of the most commonly used counseling licensure titles are the following:

- Licensed Professional Counselor (LPC)

- Licensed Clinical Professional Counselor (LCPC)

- Licensed Professional Clinical Counselor (LPCC)

- Licensed Mental Health Counselor (LMHC)

- Licensed Professional Mental Health Counselor (LPCMH)

- Licensed Clinical Mental Health Counselor (LCMHC)

- Licensed Professional Counselor—Mental Health (LPC-MH)

and only claim their scope of practice to be those areas of medicine that they are fully trained to perform.

The primary purpose of professional licensure is to protect the citizens of the state by ensuring that all licensed individuals meet the agreed-upon professional standards in education and experience. There are other benefits to professional licensure. For example, benefits of professional counseling licensure for the *consumer of counseling* include:

- Provides proof of competency to consumers and employers and assures accountability

- Provides consumers with a wide range of mental health professionals who are competent to work with diverse populations, issues, and programs

- Protects consumers' rights, as licensed mental health providers must follow standardized protocols and ethics with regard to issues such as record keeping confidentiality, and so on

- Ensures consistency for minimum standards for training and competency

Benefits for the *licensed professional counselor* include:

- Enhances the standing and advancement of the profession

- Helps maintain the integrity of the profession

- Provides clear mandates for education, experience, and continuing education
- Assists with recognition outside of the profession, for insurance panels, third-party payors, consumers, and so on

Counselors who wish to become licensed in a particular state must meet all the standards and criteria written in that state's licensure laws and in the rules that regulate the profession in that state. In addition, all states require applicants to pass a licensure examination, although the specific test(s) required varies by state. The American Counseling Association publishes a book listing the major criteria for each state's licensure laws (*Licensure Requirements for Professional Counselors*), and information also is available on the ACA website, accessible by individuals who are members of ACA.

School Counselor Licensure

Professional school counselors are required by law and/or regulation to be credentialed in every state and the District of Columbia. In some states, this credential is called *licensure*, while other states use the terms *certification* or *endorsement*. Graduate education in school counseling is an entry-level prerequisite for state credentialing as a professional school counselor. A master's degree in school counseling or a related field is required by 43 states and the District of Columbia. Fifteen states and the District of Columbia require applicants to have previous counseling or teaching experience. In 37 states, a licensure test is required. Each state's requirements are available through the state's Department of Education.

Certification

Certification is typically a voluntary action by a professional group to "institute a system by which it can grant recognition to those practitioners who have met some stated level of training and experience" (ACA, 2009). Individuals who meet the standards set by the credentialing organization are entitled to hold themselves out to the public as having the certification. Licensed or credentialed counselors may hold a variety of certifications indicating that they have specialized education or experience. For example, counselors can be certified in Dialectical Behavior Therapy (DBT), Eye Movement Desensitization and Reprocessing (EMDR), Gestalt Therapy, or many other techniques or interventions in counseling. Other types of certifications, such as Addictions Counseling, Marriage and Family Counseling, or Art Therapy, are broader in scope than an individual technique or intervention, and they may have their own specializations within a college or university. None of these certifications are what allow a counselor to practice, however; only the state-issued license or credential allows counselors to practice in the state. Given the very broad scope of practice within the counseling profession in general, certifications allow counselors—and their clients—to feel confident that the counselor has highly specialized skills or training.

 **Spotlight**
The NBCC

The National Board of Certified Counselors (NBCC) offers a national certification as a National Certified Counselor (NCC). Counselors certified through NBCC have met certain standards that may be higher than those required by some state counseling licensure boards. Thus, the NBCC assures the public and employers that counselors with this certification have met these agreed-upon standards. Founded in 1982, the NBCC is the largest national counselor certification program in the world. Although certification from NBCC is not a license to practice, in some states, holding a national certification can assist the counselor in obtaining a state license.

In addition to the overall certification as an NCC, the NBCC also certifies counselors in three specialty areas. The certification types are the following, with the number of counselors holding each certification type (as of 2010):

• National Certified Counselor (NCC)—45,090
• Certified Clinical Mental Health Counselor (CCMHC)—999
• National Certified School Counselor (NCSC)—2321
• Master Addictions Counselor (MAC)—622

For more information on NBCC, visit their website: www.nbcc.org.

 ## Counseling Associations and Organizations

So far in this chapter, we've considered how counselors are educated and licensed and the standards that regulate the profession. In this section, we turn our attention to the associations and organizations that advance the profession and advocate for professional counselors.

The American Counseling Association

The **American Counseling Association** (ACA) is the world's large association representing professional counselors in all practice settings. With more than 50,000 members in all 50 states and the District of Columbia as well as many international locations, ACA is the major voice of the counseling profession. The mission of ACA is "to enhance the quality of life in society by promoting the development of professional counselors, advancing the counseling profession, and using the profession and practice of counseling to promote respect for human dignity and diversity" (ACA, 2008).

ACA provides its members with services that benefit both the individual counselor as well as the profession at large. Some examples include the following:

• Advocacy—ACA provides a single, powerful voice to the influence national legislation and provides members of the association a voice in policy development at the federal, state, and local levels. ACA advocates on behalf of counselors (e.g., working to get counselors reimbursed through Medicaid or assisting states to obtain counseling licensure) as well as on behalf of consumers (advocating for mental health parity in insurance or working to get appropriate mental health services for veterans).

- Professional development—ACA provides members with up-to-date information and guidelines on a variety of topics, such as ethical guidelines, multicultural counseling competencies, or spiritually counseling competencies.
- Resources—ACA and its divisions participate in the publication of 20 different national counseling journals. In addition, ACA and each division publish national newsletters and maintains websites with information for counselors and consumers. ACA also publishes a variety of books and video materials for counselors.
- Networking and mentoring opportunities—ACA is well known for its annual international conference, which attracts more than 3,000 counselors and counseling students each year.
- Liability insurance—All counselors, regardless of setting, should carry malpractice insurance, and ACA provides its members with insurance at greatly reduced fees.
- Ethical guidelines and support—In addition to developing the *Code of Ethics and Standards of Practice* for the counseling profession, ACA staff answer thousands of individual ethics inquiries each year, assisting counselors as they navigate the challenging ethical boundaries of the counseling profession.

ACA was founded in 1952 and originally was called the American Personnel and Guidance Association (APGA). Today, there are 19 specialized divisions of ACA that are organized around specific interest and practice areas. In addition, there are 56 branches that organize counselors based on locality (one branch in each state, Washington, DC, and several specific territories in Latin America and Europe). Individuals who join ACA may join one or more divisions that relate to their practice area or special interest. They may also choose to join their state's branch of ACA, which mirrors the larger national association, but on a much smaller scale. For more information about ACA, visit www.counseling.org.

In 1995, the executive councils of the American School Counselor Association (ASCA) and the American Mental Health Counselors Association (AMHCA) voted to disaffiliate from ACA in order to pursue their own separate goals. Currently, ASCA maintains its status as a division of ACA, but it does not require ASCA members to also be members of ACA, so its status represents more of an affiliation with ACA, rather than a true division. The decision by ASCA and AMHCA raises difficult questions about whether an association originally formed to unify counselors from many disparate practice settings can continue to do so when two of its major divisions have disaffiliated from the association. The executive committees from ACA, ASCA, and AMHCA continue to be in close communication, but only time will tell how these decisions will ultimately affect the professional identity of the counseling profession. In this chapter's Counseling Controversy feature, we present some of the ideas that have been used to emphasize what unites all of us as one profession as well as the arguments that have been made to argue for the specializations of counseling as distinct professions.

In 2005, representatives from the 19 divisions and 4 geographic regions of ACA, as well as other related organizations and associations, established a task force to continue to strengthen the profession of counseling. Called *20/20: A Vision for the Future of Counseling*, delegates continue to meet several times a year to address what the counseling profession wants to be in the year 2020 and what it will take to get there. The seven principles identified by the 20/20 task force to help create a unified vision for the profession of counseling are:

1. Sharing a common professional identity is critical for counselors.
2. Presenting ourselves as a unified profession has multiple benefits.
3. Working together to improve the public perception of counseling and to advocate for professional issues will strengthen the profession.
4. Creating a portability system for licensure will benefit counselors and strengthen the counseling profession.
5. Expanding and promoting our research base is essential to the efficacy of professional counselors and to the public perception of the profession.
6. Focusing on students and prospective students is necessary to ensure the ongoing health of the counseling profession.
7. Promoting client welfare and advocating for the populations we serve is a primary focus of the counseling profession.

By 2010, 29 of the 31 member organizations and associations of the 20/20 Taskforce had agreed to a consensus definition of counseling, which has now been adopted by ACA. Two divisions, the American School Counselor Association and Counselors for Social Justice, declined to endorse this definition: *Counseling is a professional relationship that empowers diverse individuals, families, and groups to accomplish mental health, wellness, education, and career goals* (www.counseling.org).

The Divisions of ACA

ACA has 19 different divisions. As you read through the descriptions of each of them, take time to consider which of these divisions might hold the most interest for you (you may wish to make a mark in the box ☑ next to their names to remind you to investigate these divisions further). If you can, visit their websites or look through their journals or newsletters. Remember, most divisions (and ACA itself) have student rates that are greatly reduced, making graduate school the perfect time to try out membership.

☐ *American College Counseling Association (ACCA)* Chartered in 1991, the focus of ACCA is to help counselors in colleges, universities, and community colleges foster student development. The mission of ACA is to "support and enhance the practice of college counseling, to promote ethical and

Counseling Controversy
IS COUNSELING ONE PROFESSION OR MANY?

Background: Since the introduction of the first professional counseling associations, counselors have struggled to develop a professional identity that represented them both within the profession and to the external world. As counselors become more and more specialized, some wonder whether the original foundational roots that connected us all no longer apply. Read the arguments below, and see what you think.

POINT: COUNSELORS ARE COUNSELORS, REGARDLESS OF SETTING	COUNTERPOINT: THERE ARE SIGNIFICANT DIFFERENCES BETWEEN COUNSELORS, AND THEY REPRESENT TRULY DISTINCT PROFESSIONS
• Professional counselors work in a variety of settings and specialize in many different interventions, populations, and disorders. Nevertheless, we are all still counselors— part of a larger profession that serves as an umbrella and binds us all together.	• There are multiple professions of counseling, not a single profession with multiple specializations. School counselors, mental health counselors, rehabilitation counselors, college counselors— each of these professions is distinct and unique. While there may be some overlapping issues, it is sufficient to have affiliations between these professions to keep lines of communication open so they can work together on policy or advocacy, as needed.
• The American Counseling Association defines professional counseling as "The application of mental health, psychological, or human development principles, through cognitive, affective, behavioral or systematic intervention strategies, that address wellness, personal growth, or career development, as well as pathology" (ACA, 1997). This broad-based definition allows counselors in all specialty areas to fit comfortably within the professional identity of "professional counselor."	• There is no need to artificially force members of different professions to adhere to one model of professional counseling. Forming one organization with lots of different divisions does not help. Divisions within organizations are just that—they are divisive. No matter what is done, people within different divisions may feel slighted, as though their viewpoint is lost among the association at large. This is particularly true among a large association, such as ACA, where the voices of a few thousand individuals representing one area of practice can be drowned out.
• The push for a solid, unified professional identity does not mean that counselors cannot specialize. Indeed, counseling specialties have different needs and agendas, and the ACA divisions are intended to help address these specific interests.	• AMCHA and ASCA voted to disaffiliate from ACA because they recognized that mental health counseling and school counseling are distinct professional identities. Their missions are different, their clientele are different, their licensing bodies are different, and their interventions are different—what is the point of pretending that all counseling is the same?

• A specialty is a role that a counselor might assume *on top of* the already existing role of professional counselor. This is similar to the medical profession, where doctors hold different specialties, but still identify themselves as medical doctors first and foremost.	• Counselors must have their distinct voices heard within the areas of advocacy and legislation. If counselors are part of a larger organization that does not view the needs of one specialization as a priority, then it is difficult for individuals within those specializations to get their needs met.
• Counselors are unified by a core set of experiences in training. These experiences define counseling and help establish a strong sense of professional identity.	• When the different counseling professions are forced to combine, it is inevitable that there will be "turf wars," distrust, and disenfranchisement of the membership (Eriksen, 1996).
• The counseling profession is stronger and able to do more and better advocacy as a unified profession. This argument is best summed up by a discussion that took place in 1991 when ACA was challenged to decide its professional identity by a representative from the National Institutes for Mental Health (NIMH). He asked: "You have to decide one fundamental question: Are you a group? Or a group of groups? If you come to me as 3000 rehabilitation counselors, or 10,000 school counselors, or 12,000 mental health counselors, or 4000 career counselors, I really don't need to listen to you. But if you come to me as 50,000 professional counselors, then you will get my attention" (as quoted in Myers & Sweeney, 2001, p. 50).	• Members who more closely identify with their specific profession are far more likely to become actively involved in it. When counselors are members of a more generic organization, such as ACA, they may not feel closely connected. However, when counselors can identify professionally with others who are just like them, they become more active and engaged.
• The public, already confused by the multitude of helping professionals in the marketplace (e.g., counselors, social workers, psychologists, psychiatrists), is only further confused by the artificial divisions within the profession.	• Separate organizations and separate professional identities means that counselors within each of these professions can choose where to spend their professional association dollars, putting money and effort into the causes that are most important to them.
• When energy goes into divisiveness instead of unity, it keeps us from accomplishing the real mission of the counseling profession: helping those in need (Eriksen, 1996).	

As with most controversies, there probably is some truth to both sides of this argument.

⟵————————————————————————————————⟶

There is just one profession,
and all professional counselors
are part of it

The specialties in counseling
are so distinct, they represent
truly unique professions

On the continuum, place an "X" where you think you stand on this issue.

responsible professional practice, to promote communication and exchange among college counselors . . . [and to] provide leadership and advocacy for the profession of counseling in higher education." *The Journal of College Counseling* is published twice a year, and ACCA holds biennial conferences. To further explore ACCA, visit their website: www.collegecounseling.org.

☐ *American Mental Health Counselors Association (AMHCA)*   Chartered in 1978, AMHCA represents mental health counselors, advocating for client access to quality services within the health care industry. AMHCA strives to be the national association representing licensed mental health counselors with consistent standards for education, training, practice, advocacy, and ethics. Although not technically a division of ACA (it disaffiliated in 1995), AMHCA remains closely connected to ACA through its executive committee. AMHCA publishes the *Journal of Mental Health Counseling* and holds an annual conference for its members. For more information, visit www.amhca.org.

☐ *American Rehabilitation Counseling Association (ARCA)*   ARCA is an organization of rehabilitation counseling practitioners, educators, and students who are concerned with enhancing the development of people with disabilities throughout their life span and in promoting excellence in the rehabilitation counseling profession's practice, research, consultation, and professional development. ARCA collaborates with other professional associations in rehabilitation counseling to publish *Rehabilitation Counseling Bulletin*. Further information can be found at the ARCA website: www.arcaweb.org.

☐ *American School Counselor Association (ASCA)*   Chartered in 1953, ASCA supports school counselors' efforts to help students focus on academic, personal/social, and career development so they can achieve success in school and are prepared to lead fulfilling lives as responsible members of society. ASCA members also work with parents, educators, and community members to provide a positive learning environment for students. ASCA provides professional development, research, and advocacy to more than 24,000 professional school counselors worldwide. Although not technically a division of ACA (it disaffiliated in 1995), ASCA remains closely connected to ACA through its executive committee. ASCA publishes the journal *Professional School Counseling* and holds an annual conference. Learn more about ASCA at www.schoolcounselor.org.

☐ *Association for Adult Development and Aging (AADA)*   Chartered in 1986, AADA serves as a focal point for information sharing, professional development, and advocacy related to adult development and aging issues. AADA's mission is to improve the standards of the professional service to adults of all ages by (1) improving the skills and competence of members, (2) expanding professional work opportunities in adult development and aging, (3) promoting the lifelong development and well-being of adults, and (4) promoting standards for professional preparation for counselors of adults across the lifespan. The journal, *Adultspan*, is published twice per year. For more information, visit www.aadaweb.org.

☐ *Association for Assessment in Counseling and Education (AACE)*   Originally the Association for Measurement and Evaluation in Guidance, AACE was chartered in 1965. The purpose of AACE is to promote the effective use of assessment in the counseling profession. AACE holds biennial national conferences and publishes two journals: *Measurement and Evaluation in Counseling and Development (MECD)* and *Counseling Outcome Research and Evaluation (CORE)*. AACE has developed or contributed to many guidelines and practice models for assessment in counseling, including *Rights and Responsibilities of Users of Standardized Tests* (RUST Statement) and *Standards for Multicultural Assessment*. AACE's website has much more information. Explore it at www.theaaceonline.com.

☐ *Association for Counselor Education and Supervision (ACES)*   ACES was one of the founding divisions of ACA in 1952 under the name of the National Association of Guidance and Counselor Trainers. ACES emphasizes the need for quality education and supervision of counselors in all work settings and strives to continue to improve the education, credentialing, and supervision of counselors. The journal of ACES, *Counselor Education and Supervision*, publishes information on the preparation and supervision of counselors in all settings, and the ACES national conference is a biennial occurrence. For more information, visit www.acesonline.net.

☐ *Association for Counselors and Educators in Government (ACEG)*   ACEG was originally chartered in 1984 under the name of Military Educators and Counselor Association. The name was changed to reflect the desire to serve the needs of all government employees, including military personnel and their families. ACEG is dedicated to counseling clients and their families in local, state, and federal government or in military-related agencies. ACEG publishes a newsletter for members, but does not have a professional journal. The ACEG website can be found at www.dantes.doded.mil/dantes_web/organizations/aceg/index.htm.

☐ *Association for Creativity in Counseling (ACC)*   The Association for Creativity in Counseling (ACC) is a forum for counselors, counselor educators, creative arts therapists, and counselors in training to explore unique and diverse approaches to counseling. Established in 2004, ACC's goal is to promote greater awareness, advocacy, and understanding of diverse and creative approaches to counseling. The *Journal for Creativity in Mental Health* focuses on interdisciplinary discussion and research on practical applications of using creativity to help deepen self-awareness and build healthy relationships. For more information, visit www.creativecounselor.org.

☐ *Association for Humanistic Counseling (AHC)*   The Association for Humanistic Counseling (formerly the Counseling Association for Humanistic Education and Development or C-AHEAD) was a founding division of ACA in 1952. The association changed its name in 2011 to reflect a more clear focus on their mission. AHC provides a forum for the exchange of information about humanistically oriented counseling practices and promotes changes that reflect the growing body of knowledge about humanistic principles applied to human development and potential. Humanistic counselors (1) base their practice upon a philosophical foundation that affirms the dignity of every human being; (2) acknowledge the responsibility of human beings for their own destiny; (3) recognize and respect the ability of human beings to employ reason, science, intuition, and creativity; and (4) believe that wellness and health are best achieved by combining personal growth with avid service for the greater good of humanity. The *Journal for the Association of Humanistic Education and Development* is a publication of AHC, although the name of the journal will need to change to reflect the division's most recent name change. As AHC reorganizes under its new name, it has a new website address (http://afhc.camp9.org). This address may change, and the American Counseling Association website will always have the most up-to-date web address for all of the divisions.

☐ *Association for Lesbian, Gay, Bisexual and Transgender Issues in Counseling (ALGBTIC)*   The mission of ALGBTIC is to educate counselors on the unique needs of GLBT clients and communities and to promote greater awareness and understanding of GLBT issues among members of the counseling profession. In addition, ALGBTIC strives to identify conditions that create barriers to the human growth and development of GLBT clients and to develop counseling skills, programs, and efforts to help clients overcome these barriers and promote development. The division publishes the *Journal of LGBT Issues in Counseling*. To learn more about ALGBTIC, visit www.algbtic.org.

☐ *Association for Multicultural Counseling and Development (AMCD)* Originally the Association of Non-White Concerns in Personnel and Guidance, AMCD was chartered in 1972. AMCD strives to improve cultural, ethnic, and racial empathy and understanding by programs to advance and sustain personal growth. Additionally, AMCD seeks to develop programs specifically to improve ethnic and racial empathy and understanding and to advance and sustain personal growth for members from diverse cultural backgrounds. The Multicultural Counseling Competencies are an important contribution for all counselors, regardless of practice setting. AMCD publishes the *Journal of Multicultural Counseling and Development*. For more information, visit www.amcdaca.org.

☐ *Association for Specialists in Group Work (ASGW)*   Chartered in 1973, ASGW was founded to promote quality in group work training, practice, and research. ASGW provides professional leadership in the field of group work, establishes standards for professional training, and supports research and the dissemination of knowledge. In addition, ASGW seeks to extend counseling through the use of group process; to provide a forum for examining innovative and developing concepts in group work; to foster diversity and dignity in groups; and to be models of effective group practice. ASGW holds national conferences and publishes the *Journal for Specialists in Group Work.* There is much more information on their website: www.asgw.org.

☐ *Association for Spiritual, Ethical, and Religious Values in Counseling (ASERVIC)*   Originally the National Catholic Guidance Conference, ASERVIC was chartered in 1974. ASERVIC is devoted to professionals who believe that spiritual, ethical, religious, and other human values are essential to the full development of the person and to the discipline of counseling. ASERVIC defines itself as an organization of counselors and human development professionals who believe spiritual, ethical, and religious values are essential to the overall development of the person and are committed to integrating these values into the counseling process. ASERVIC holds national conferences and publishes the journal *Counseling and Values.* For more information about ASERVIC, visit their website: www.aservic.org.

☐ *Counselors for Social Justice (CSJ)*   CSJ is a community of counselors and counseling students who seek equity and an end to oppression and injustice affecting clients, students, counselors, families, communities, schools, workplaces, governments, and other social and institutional systems. The mission of Counselors for Social Justice is to work to promote social justice through confronting oppressive systems of power and privilege that affect professional counselors and clients and to assist in positive change through the professional development of counselors. Together with the association of psychologists for social responsibility, CSJ publishes the *Journal for Social Action in Counseling and Psychology.* For more information, visit the CSJ website: http://counselorsforsocialjustice.com.

☐ *International Association of Addictions and Offender Counselors (IAAOC)*   Originally the Public Offender Counselor Association, IAAOC was chartered in 1972. Members of IAAOC advocate the development of effective counseling and rehabilitation programs for people with substance abuse problems, other addictions, and adult and/or juvenile public offenders. IAAOC members are concerned with improving the lives of individuals exhibiting addictive and/or criminal behaviors. The *Journal of Addictions and Offender Counseling* publishes reports of research that focus on addictions and offender counseling. For more information about IAAOC, visit www.iaaoc.org.

☐ *International Association of Marriage and Family Counselors (IAMFC)*   Chartered in 1989, IAMFC members help develop healthy family systems through prevention, education, and therapy, regardless of employment setting. The organization provides leadership, skill building through workshops and training, and information and research through publications in couples and family issues. IAMFC holds national conferences and publishes *The Family Journal.* For more information on IAMFC, the largest division within ACA, visit www.iamfc.org.

☐ *National Career Development Association (NCDA)*   Originally the National Vocational Guidance Association, NCDA was one of the founding associations of ACA in 1952. The mission of NCDA is to promote career development for all people across the lifespan through public information, member services, conferences, and publications. NCDA developed the *National Career Development Guidelines* to assist career counselors in their work. They hold national conferences and publish a journal, *Career Development Quarterly.* For more information about NCDA, visit www.ncda.org.

☐ *National Employment Counseling Association (NECA)*   NECA was originally the National Employment Counselors Association and was chartered in 1966. The commitment of NECA is to offer professional leadership to people who counsel in employment and/or career development settings. Additionally, NECA promotes the use of job information tools and techniques to better serve the client, advocates for legislation that positively influences employment counseling and job opportunities, and promotes research into employment counseling. The association publishes the *Journal of Employment Counseling.* For more information on NECA, visit www.employmentcounseling.org.

There are other counseling associations besides ACA and its divisions and affiliated organizations. For example, you might have an active mental health board in your community that provides workshops, trainings, and advocacy. There are national associations for counselors that are not affiliated with ACA, such as the American Association of Pastoral Counselors (AAPC), the National Association for College Admissions Counselors (NACAC), the National Association of Alcohol and Drug Abuse Counselors (NAADAC), and the American Association for Marriage and Family Therapists (AAMFT). In many cases, there are multiple professional associations with very similar goals and memberships. For example, there are seven different national rehabilitation counseling professional organizations, and all have adopted the same definition of a rehabilitation counselor as "a counselor who possesses the specialized knowledge, skills, and attitudes needed to collaborate in a professional relationship with persons with disabilities to achieve their personal, social, psychological, and vocational goals" (CORE, 2005, p. 49). Nevertheless, although the seven associations can agree on the same definition of rehabilitation counseling, many in the field believe that the multitude of professional associations is divisive and confusing. A 2006 study of practicing rehabilitation counselors found the most significant problem in professional identity among rehabilitation counselors was "the extreme segmentation of the rehabilitation counseling profession" (Shaw, Leahy, Chan, & Catalano, p. 176). They found that rehabilitation counselors wanted better integration of rehabilitation counseling into the counseling profession as a whole, recognizing that this move is a "survival strategy" for rehabilitation counseling. Additionally,

■■■ *Fast Facts* ■■■

A survey of 450 practicing school counselors in one state found that 83% belonged to at least one professional association. Of those who were members:

- 89% believe professional organizations increase the visibility of the field.
- 85% believe that their professional organizations help them keep current in the field.
- 85% regularly read the newsletter of their professional organization.
- 69% believe membership in professional organizations is one of the hallmarks of a professional person.
- 65% regularly read the scholarly journals published by the professional organization.
- 63% regularly visit the organization's website.
- 28% are actively involved in their local, state, or national professional organization (e.g., hold office, serve on committees).

Source: Bauman (2008).

participants in the study argued that the competing agendas of the multiple organizations and the splinter groups within the profession were serving to undermine the rehabilitation counseling profession.

Unlike some other professions, such as law, for which the professional association controls entry into the profession via the bar exam, thereby virtually guaranteeing 100% membership, joining a counseling association is a voluntary decision. Nevertheless, state and national counseling associations are essential if the profession is to remain viable and strong. Counselors with a strong sense of professional identity join their counseling associations. In one study, 96% of ASCA members endorsed a statement saying professional organizations are important for school counselors. That same study found that those who join professional associations believe that (a) being a professional includes belonging to professional organizations, and (b) professional organizations advance the field (Bauman, 2008). Additionally, counselors cite membership in professional counseling organizations as one of the key factors that contribute to their sense of professional identity (Lafleur, 2007).

State counseling associations serve important connections between counselors and the counseling profession. Most state associations hold annual conferences, and there is added emphasis on networking and support as members tend to live in closer proximity than the national association. State associations provide an excellent mechanism for students to get more involved in the counseling profession, and we encourage you to consider involvement in your state branch of ACA and/or ASCA. In the accompanying Snapshot, a graduate student talks about her involvement with professional counseling associations at the state and national level.

Chi Sigma Iota

One professional association was developed specifically with graduate students in counselor education in mind. Chi Sigma Iota (CSI) is the international honor society for professional counselors, counselor educators, and students in counselor education programs. CSI is intended to "promote scholarship, research, professionalism, leadership and excellence in counseling and to recognize high attainment in the pursuit of academic and clinical excellence in the profession of counseling" (CSI, 2009). CSI was established in 1985 at The Ohio University to provide recognition for outstanding achievement and outstanding service within the profession.

SNAPSHOT

MAUREEN JOHNSON, MA Student in Clinical Mental Health Counseling

When I first started my counseling program, my professors discussed the importance of joining a professional organization. I talked to other graduate students, explored websites, and decided to see what the organizations could offer me. I found that not only was it easy to join, but I received a lot of great benefits as a student member. I joined the American Counseling Association (ACA) and my state counseling organization during the first year of my program. I also joined a division of ACA, the Counseling Association of Humanistic Education and Development (C-AHEAD). One of my professors was the president of C-AHEAD at the time, and I volunteered to help her with the Web page and listserv. I have continued serving in these roles and found them to be rewarding and fun. Although not everyone gets involved at this level, I have enjoyed helping with this division and plan on continuing in this role in the future, even after graduation.

One very big reason for joining professional counseling organizations as a student is that student memberships are extremely cost efficient, and students still get all the benefits that professional level members receive. As a student, you also can join the divisions at a greatly discounted rate, and state organizations (and their divisions) also typically offer discounts for student members.

Another reason to join as a student is that you will be able to add these memberships to your resume. These associations speak volumes about your commitment to the profession. Additionally, the networking experiences may help you find a job once you are finished with school. When you meet other students and other professional counselors at events, you start building connections with your colleagues that can help you with your professional practice.

When you join a professional association, you will receive journals and newsletters. ACA and my state organization both have publications. The *Journal of Counseling and Development* (JCD), the journal of ACA, is a quarterly journal that publishes the highest quality research in the field. The monthly news magazine, *Counseling Today*, updates members about the activities of the divisions within ACA and provides articles about the latest news and research findings. ACA also sends an online newsletter out to all members twice a month. In addition, the divisions each have their own journals. When I joined C-AHEAD, I began to receive the *Journal of Humanistic Counseling Education and Development* twice a year. The ACA website also provides a bookstore, with reduced costs for members.

An important benefit of joining professional organizations is attending conferences and workshops at the reduced cost of a student member. These events can also help you with your professional training, give you an opportunity to promote and support your profession, and offer great networking opportunities. Students can volunteer at conferences, which usually leads to reduced cost or free attendance at these events. During my first year as a student, I attended the ACA conference. The conference was a great experience, and the presentations by practicing counselors gave me practical information to help me with my current (and future) work. During my second year as a student, I participated in the student poster

presentation at the state conference. It was exciting to be one of the presenters, and it gave me a
great experience to put on my resume.

Once you join organizations, you will get more
information about upcoming events and workshops
from national and local providers. You may request
to be added to e-mail listservs, which can provide
additional information about trainings. In the few
years I've been a member of ACA and my state
organization, I've received early notification about
trainings and have received even more discounts on
these trainings through being an association member. In addition, the liability insurance through ACA
has been great for practicum and internship.

By joining organizations as a student, you will
have a voice in the profession. I was asked to
provide my input on future presentations for the
upcoming ACA conference because I chose to be
involved in leadership in a division of ACA. When
you attend conferences, your input is solicited to

help presenters improve their presentations. You
also have an opportunity to help shape the profession. You may choose to participate in conferences
as a student member, and you can provide the
knowledge you have gained to other members
of ACA and your division and state organizations.
I also became a member of my state's government
relations committee, which helps update me on
political issues important to counselors.

Joining professional organizations can be very
valuable for graduate students. I've enjoyed being a
member of ACA, my state organization, and their
divisions, and it's been interesting and fun to
become active within the divisions. There are so
many benefits to joining a professional organization
while in graduate school. I encourage you to see
what organizations have to offer you as a student
member. Like me, I hope you will find that the numerous benefits and reduced cost make joining these
organizations a very wise professional decision.

There are over 250 active chapters of CSI, with over 12,000 active members
worldwide (more than 60,000 members have been initiated in the organization).
CSI chapters are often active at the local level. University chapters might, for example, host workshops, guest speakers, and service projects for the students in
their counselor education programs. At the national level, CSI has a fellowship
program to promote leadership in the profession, provides grants and funding for
research on professional identity and leadership, develops resources in the field
of counseling, and publishes a newsletter.

Chi Sigma Iota promotes leadership in the counseling profession, and it has
worked to address leadership in counseling perhaps more than any other counseling-
related organization. Local chapters are places for counseling students to begin to
take on leadership positions within the profession as they organize professional development, advocacy, outreach, and social activities for their members. At a national
level, CSI is deeply committed to leadership development. CSI provides leadership
training through "CSI Day" at the American Counseling Association annual conference and fellowship and internship programs for students.

Your program faculty will know if your university has an active chapter of Chi
Sigma Iota. If you do, see what kinds of opportunities and projects are sponsored by
the chapter. Chances are, there is a lot going on. If you have an active chapter, you
will be invited to join after you complete one term of graduate study in a counseling
program, provided you have earned a grade point average of 3.5 or better on a 4.0

scale. Membership in the local chapter includes membership in the national organization. If your counseling program does not have an active CSI chapter, it is not difficult to start one. Full instructions are available on the CSI website: www.csi-net.org.

Summary

In this chapter, you learned about the educational requirements for licensure as a professional counselor. You learned how the eight core areas of CACREP are incorporated into counselor training programs, and you were challenged to think about *why* these core areas are important to the development of a counselor. In this chapter, we also discussed the role of credentialing and licensure and the many different ways that counselors can become specialists within the profession. We also covered the major counseling associations and organizations that are important to the profession and gave you some insights into how you might best use these associations for your own professional development. Finally, we gave you lots of information and websites for further exploration.

It is, of course, extremely important to remember that education and training to be a professional counselor do not end at graduation, or even when you are granted a license to practice. Learning to become a counselor is a lifelong endeavor. Licensure and certification require counselors to continue their education, but most counselors recognize that even without such a mandate, ongoing learning is essential to stay current. Counselors who continually challenge themselves to be lifelong learners are more fully engaged in the profession and, as a result, are better counselors for their clients.

There are many facets to becoming a counselor. This chapter focused on the required education, training, and licensure, but that is just part of the picture. *Becoming a counselor* is much more than logistics—it is a pathway of personal growth, development, and learning. It is developing the counselor as a person, not just as a professional. This combination of the personal and professional is both exciting and challenging, and it is to this that we turn our attention in the next chapter.

End-of-Chapter Activities

Student Activities

1. **Reflect.** Now it's time to reflect on the major topics that we have covered in Chapter 3. Look back at the sections or the ideas you have underlined. What were your reactions as you read that portion of the chapter? What do you want to remember?

_____

_____

_____

_____

2. Do you think the amount of regulation over the counseling profession and the programs that regulate counselor training is appropriate? In what way do you think the counseling profession can best determine who is eligible to be a counselor? In your ideal world, what qualifications should counselors have, and how should we determine who has them?

_____

_____

_____

_____

3. As you read the Snapshot of Maureen and her experiences in professional associations during her years as a graduate student, what are your reactions? What type of involvement in professional associations is most interesting to you?

_____

_____

_____

_____

■■■ Journal Question ■■■

Reactions to the Graduate Program. Think for a moment about the remainder of your graduate program and your upcoming classes. Which classes are you looking forward to? Which ones do you find intimidating? Boring? If there is some flexibility in your program of study, how will you make decisions about what classes to take and when to take them? How can you keep yourself flexible enough to make changes in your program to accommodate your changing and evolving interests as a counselor?

■■■ Topics for Discussion ■■■

1. Consider the eight core areas of the counseling curriculum. Are there other major areas that you think should be included? If so, what topics, and why? Why do you think these eight areas have remained the core of the educational experience for more than 30 years? Is it time for a change? If yes, what do you recommend?

2. Do you think the counseling profession is made up of one profession or many? Should there be an overarching counseling association that includes of all the specialties, or does that make it too difficult for the voices within every specialty to be heard?

3. As you look forward to practicum and internship, what are your reactions? Are you excited? Nervous? Ready to jump in? Wary of the experience? All of these? It's common to have a mix of emotions as you think ahead to seeing your first clients.

■■■ Experiments ■■■

1. Find out the specific qualifications licensure/certification for your specialization within your state. You may need to contact your state counselor board, the state's Department of Education, or other licensing bodies. In addition to the coursework and experiences required by your graduate program, what else is required to become licensed?

2. Go to the ACA, ASCA, and/or AMHCA websites to explore what these associations have to offer. As you explore these associations (and other divisions of ACA or your state branch), what are your reactions? What excites or engages you?

3. Attend a state workshop or conference to learn more about the counseling profession in your state. If you have the opportunity, volunteer to work at the conference for a reduced conference admission fee and the opportunity to network with professionals in the field.

■■■ Explore More ■■■

We encourage you to learn more about the topics in this chapter. For this chapter, the best resources for exploration are the websites of the state and national associations.

- Check the website for your state-level licensure or certification to learn more about the requirements for counselors in your state. Be sure to read the rules that govern counselors, and check out the latest newsletters on the site for the most up-to-date information.

- Go to your state-level counseling association website for information about upcoming conferences and workshops, as well as information about current topics important to the counseling profession in your state.

- Other websites to explore:

  American Counseling Association: www.counseling.org

  American School Counselors Association: www.schoolcounselor.org

  American Mental Health Counselors Association: www.amhca.org

  Chi Sigma Iota: www.csi-net.org

4

How Do Counselors Develop?

In this chapter, we will:

- Consider the personal aspects of counseling and of being a counselor. What are the personality types of counselors, and who is drawn into the counseling profession?

- Discuss how counselors develop, both personally and professionally, over time.

- Encourage you to adopt a self-reflective approach to becoming a counselor that involves synthesizing the new learning with the person you already are—comparing as you go along and remaining open to new ways of looking at the world.

As you read the chapter, you might want to consider:

- What drew you to the counseling profession? What are your strengths that will enhance your ability to be a counselor, and what are your personality traits that might get in the way?

- What personality traits do you think counselors should possess? Do you think that there is a "best fit" personality profile of counselors? Can people with lots of different temperaments and personalities be effective counselors?

- How will you monitor your own growth and development as a counselor? What sorts of activities can you engage in to help you become more self-reflective?

Who Are Counseling Students?

Some students enter graduate training in counselor education directly from their undergraduate programs. If you are in this category, you may have majored in psychology or a related field and may even have known from an early age that you wanted to pursue a career in mental health. Going to graduate school in counselor education is just the next step on that path. Maybe you majored in education, knowing that you wanted to work with children in

113

schools. Or perhaps you had a completely different major and came to the realization during your undergraduate years that you wanted to pursue a graduate degree in counseling. Maybe you're coming to graduate training in counseling because you want to stay in school, where you feel comfortable and safe, and the choice of major is less important than just continuing to be in college. You may even be among the group who came to graduate training in counseling as your second choice after not being accepted into a graduate program in another field.

Counselor education programs also attract adult learners—those of you who have been out in the world for several or many years, either in a different profession, or busy raising a family. You may be embarking on a second or maybe even third or fourth career. You may be returning to graduate school because you found your career to be personally or professionally unfulfilling and you want a career that offers meaning. It is not uncommon for students who come to counseling from the world of business to talk about how their job left them feeling empty, or as one student put it, "I just couldn't sell one more insurance policy—I need to really make a difference in people's lives." Perhaps you decided to come into the counseling profession because somewhere along the line, a counselor helped you and now you want to give back. This is particularly common in the counseling specialty of substance abuse, where clients often believe that their counselors and the mental health system "gave them their lives back" and now they believe that they owe it to the profession, and to themselves, to dedicate their lives to helping others get their lives back as well. Maybe you are among the group that has postponed your professional dreams until your children were in school or grown, and now you can finally focus on yourself. It could be that you want the prestige or money that graduate education can offer. More than likely, it is a combination of your personal goals, beliefs, and opportunities that brought you to a graduate program in counselor education.

Some counseling students are scholars; others barely made it through their undergraduate training. Some are the first in their family to go to college, much less graduate school. Others are following a long tradition of education in their families. Some have experienced firsthand the devastation that mental illness can cause in families; others have more removed experiences with mental illness. Still others are managing their own mental health problems. In this chapter's Counseling Controversy feature, you will read about two different perspectives on whether anyone can be trained to become a counselor or whether becoming a counselor is more innate to a person.

The point is that there are as many motivations to enter graduate training as there are students. Counselor education programs are often a mix of students with diverse experiences and goals. The demographic data about counseling students (primarily female, primarily Caucasian) belies the reality of the diversity of personal experiences in our profession.

■■■ *Fast Facts* ■■■

According to one study, 82% of counselor education students are female, with an average age of 33 . . . but students in that study ranged in age from 21 to 59.

Source: Granello (2002).

Counseling Controversy

ARE COUNSELORS BORN OR MADE?

Background: This argument highlights two sides of an important counselor training issue. Some people believe that there are individuals who are "naturally therapeutic," while others argue that with proper training and development, almost anyone can be a counselor. This argument also has been cast as the "art versus science" argument in counseling. Read the two sides of this argument, and then see what you think.

Point: COUNSELORS ARE BORN	Counterpoint: COUNSELORS ARE MADE
• Counseling is an art. From the birth of recorded history there have been people recognized by their peers as having the gift of soothing a troubled soul or easing a painful passage. These people have a temperament and sensitivity that cannot be taught. It is innate—it is who they are.	• Counseling is a science. As the profession of counseling becomes more and more prescribed by laws and regulations, there is a greater understanding that counseling is more than just a "feel-good" approach, a friendship filled with "warm fuzzies." There is a science to the profession of counseling, and the advanced training required of counselors recognizes this.
• At least some people are drawn to the counseling profession because other people have told them that they were easy to talk to.	• The counseling profession is supported by an extensive body of research that tells us what skills and techniques tend to benefit which clients. Remember, it's not about what feels good for the counselors—it's about what helps the clients.
• Natural counselors have a therapeutic way of being—they don't rely on formally taught skills. The very being of the counselor—the willingness to take risks, to be fully present with the client, to help the client become fully functioning—those cannot be taught, but come only from life experience and the willingness to be fully present in our own lives.	• Counseling is an intentional process. The interventions made by the counselor are used to develop self-understanding in the client. The counseling relationship is obviously a key component for change. However, although the research yields mixed results, most research shows that *in and of itself, the counseling relationship is necessary, but not sufficient, to produce therapeutic change* (Merry, 2000).
• "Anyone can memorize by rote a given set of rules, but the key to therapeutic relating lies in the power of the relationship itself" (Small, 1990, p. 24).	

As with most controversies, there probably is some truth to both sides of this argument.

←——→

ART   **SCIENCE**

On the continuum, place an "X" where you think you stand on this issue.

Why Do People Become Counselors?

Most people who enter the field of counseling know they want to work with people, to make a difference, to help where they can. They find counseling to be an outgrowth of their personality, and they want to receive graduate training to develop the necessary skills and education required by licensure or certification bodies. Most counselors would agree that it is a privilege (as well as a responsibility) to help people survive and thrive during difficult life situations. Some counselors talk about their intrinsic desire to understand people, to engage fully with others, to have a career that helps them live a life of meaning and purpose. Others say they are fascinated to see the theories and concepts of human nature come alive in their work with others. Day (1994) conceptualized three main reasons why people entered the profession of counseling: (1) to do for others what someone has done for me; (2) to do for others what *I wish* someone had done for me; and (3) to share with others certain insights I have acquired or to help inspire others to make changes in their lives. Take a moment to think of the reasons that you decided to enter the counseling field, and make some notes here.

_____

_____

_____

_____

What Types of People Become Counselors?

Counseling is not something that is external to self. The major tool you have as a counselor is yourself. It is not just learning to do a set of skills (solve a math problem or play tennis). Counselors are who we are. Becoming a counselor changes you—it becomes a part of everything you do. For example, your helping interactions with friends and family may radically alter as you learn more about how people change and grow.

As a graduate student, you may be prepared for the academic rigor of the counseling program in which you are studying. However, you may be less prepared for the expectations that you will face regarding your personal development. Counseling is unlike other professions, where academic preparation alone may be sufficient. Counselors are expected to attend to their personal development, to their ever-changing *personhood*. Personhood is the evolving sense and understanding of self, of being truly human and aware of who you are. Understanding your own subjective experiences, feelings, and private concepts and your own views of the world and self—these are the key components of attending to your own personhood.

■■■ *Words of Wisdom* ■■■

"What lies behind us and what lies before us are small matters compared to what lies within us."

—Emerson

Carl Rogers, one of the most important figures in the history of counseling, wrote about this blending between becoming a practitioner and growing as a person in one of his most significant books, *On Becoming a Person* (Rogers, 1961). In it, Rogers argued that the personhood of the counselor—and the counselor's awareness of his or her own personhood—is more critical to the success of the counseling session than scholarly knowledge, professional training, theoretical orientation, or techniques. The premise is that as counselors, we must be willing to work to understand ourselves before we can be truly present for our clients.

Rogers believed that people who make the best counselors are those who are naturally warm, spontaneous, real, understanding, and nonjudgmental (Rogers & Stevens, 1967). He believed that the personality traits necessary for counselors could be summed up by the core conditions of therapy: congruence, unconditional positive regard, and empathy.

Congruence refers to congruence between thoughts and behaviors. Counselors who are congruent are genuine in their behaviors. They act how they feel. They do not put up a professional front or distance themselves from their clients. Rogers described congruence as follows: "The feelings the counselor is experiencing are available to him, available to his awareness, that he is able to live these feelings, be them in the relationship, and able to communicate them if appropriate" (Rogers & Stevens, 1967, p. 90).

Unconditional positive regard is the constant and unwavering respect that the counselor has for the client. Clients can present themselves in a multitude of ways, with a variety of problems, varying levels of insight or intelligence, and the counselor always respects and values the client. Counselors distinguish between people and actions—that is, even when the person in front of you has committed terrible actions, the value of the person is not diminished. Unconditional positive regard is what allows counselors to work with people whose values are very different from their own, or who have committed crimes. Valuing the basic worth of the person and differentiating the person from the behavior allow us to have empathy (Hazler, 1988).

Empathy is the desire to fully understand the world view of the client, to have a profound interest in sharing the "client's world of meanings and feelings" (Raskin & Rogers, 1989, p. 157). Empathy involves both understanding and the ability to communicate that understanding to the client. True empathy involves the moment-to-moment experiencing of the inner world of the client. It is not merely the counselor acting "as if" he or she understands or using a standard phrase or expression that labels the client's feelings without true understanding. Clients recognize when counselors are using empathetic words but have no real empathy behind the words (Young, 2009). Rogers acknowledged that complete empathy was probably unattainable, but saw the ability to empathize as a lifelong goal that should always be under development for counselors.

What Are the Personality Traits of Counselors?

Rogers's core conditions of congruence, unconditional positive regard, and empathy clearly are important for counselors. They have been validated as important components of the counseling relationship through research studies (Truax & Carkhuff, 1967). Many other writers and researchers have added to the list of desirable traits for counselors (e.g., Bayne, 1995; Carkhuff, 1987; Hackney & Cormier, 1996; Kush, 1997; Langman, 2001; Pope & Kline, 1999; Softas-Nall, Baldo, & Williams, 2001; Weaver, 2000; Williams, 1999; Witmer, 1985). Several of these personality traits are listed in the following paragraphs. Although the list is not exhaustive, you may notice as Witmer (1985) did that many of these traits are similar to personality traits of psychologically healthy individuals. As you read the personality traits, you may want to consider whether you believe these traits are important for counselors. Additionally, you might want to consider the degree to which you believe you possess each of these personality characteristics.

Counselors are self-aware (introspective). Counselors understand themselves and are willing to examine their beliefs and behaviors. Self-awareness helps counselors focus on who they are. Self-reflection encourages counselors to evaluate what they have learned about themselves, and self-discovery allows counselors to take risks and try out new ways of becoming.

Counselors are trustworthy (have personal integrity). In order for the counseling relationship to grow, clients must feel safe. Counselors must be trustworthy *and* have the ability to translate that trustworthiness into behaviors that the client can see.

Counselors take risks. Regardless of theoretical orientation, most counselors believe that you can only take a client as far as you are willing to go yourself (Wilkins, 1997). Therefore, counselors must be willing to take risks in their own lives if they want to encourage clients to take risks and make changes in their lives. Risk-taking can mean moving out of your comfort zone to try new behaviors or interacting with people who are different from you. Risk-taking also is important because there is no way any counselor can plan for every eventuality in a counseling session. You always take a risk when you engage with a client— you risk going to a place that forces you to change or grow.

Counselors have a sense of humor. Counselors who can see the humor in life and can remember to laugh are less likely to suffer from emotional burnout (Skovholt, 2001). In one study, 82% of therapists ranked maintaining a sense of humor as the number one career-sustaining behavior (Kramen-Kahn & Hansen, 1998). Humor that is ironic or playful, rather than sarcastic or cynical, tends to be more useful in avoiding burnout (Witmer, 1985).

Counselors have an innate curiosity about the world and the people in it.
Part of counseling is an investigation into the life of the client. Counselors must
have a desire to learn "what makes people tick" or how the world looks from the
eyes of their clients. This is not the same as voyeurism (simply learning the
details of a client's life or story for your own enjoyment or even morbid curiosity), but trying to understand the client so you can truly empathize with his or
her situation. Counselors look for clues that further their understanding of the
world of their clients and become co-discoverers, along with their clients, in the
client's journey to self-understanding.

Counselors are emotionally stable. People who are emotionally volatile—
whose temperament changes on a daily or even hourly basis—do not provide the
kind of consistency that is needed by most clients. Clients in counseling must
be allowed to work through their own issues without regard to the changing
emotional state of the counselor. This is another reason a counselor must be constantly aware of his or her personal reactions, so that they do not interfere with
the client's work.

Counselors believe that people can change (optimistic). Fatalistic people—
those who believe we are powerless to make changes in our lives—rarely become
counselors. After all, the goal of most counseling is to help clients make positive
changes in their lives—even if that simply means helping them to reframe their
reactions to those negative aspects of their lives that they truly are powerless
to change (e.g., being diagnosed with a terminal illness, having parents who are
alcoholics).

**Counselors are not afraid of psychological pain and do not shrink back
from people in pain.** Counselors are not uncomfortable with tears and sadness
and do not try to "make things all better" for their clients. They allow clients to
fully experience their emotions, and in turn, counselors are willing to be present
and involved with their clients' emotional reality. However, counselors cannot become so invested in the emotional lives of their clients that they no longer can be
objective or offer useful assistance. Counselors walk the line between being fully
present to allow clients to experience their emotions, and emotional contagion,
which is the belief that other people's strong emotions will overcome the counselor as well. Research shows that people in the helping professions who are susceptible to emotional contagion are more vulnerable to stress and burnout
(Bakker, Schaufeli, Sixma, & Bosveld, 2001; LeBlanc, Bakker, Peters, van Heesch, &
Schaufeli, 2001). Thus, counselors must be open to experiencing the psychological pain of their clients without finding themselves overcome and paralyzed by it.

Counselors respect their clients. Robert Carkhuff (1987) took Rogers's unconditional positive regard and operationalized it as respect. To respect a client
means that you believe that the client has the capacity to determine his or her
own future. Counselors who respect their clients do not offer simple answers to

the complex problems in clients' lives; they believe that clients are the experts when it comes to understanding and changing their own lives.

Counselors have the capacity for self-denial. People come to counselors when they are in emotional crises. The counselor must be able to put aside whatever is going on in his or her own personal life and focus totally on the client. If you are having a bad day or just had a fight with your significant other, your mind cannot wander to your own life and interfere with the attention you are giving to your clients. Clients cannot be used for monetary gain when they do not need counseling, as a support mechanism to validate or reassure the counselor, nor as a source of sexual satisfaction. The clients' needs must come first.

Counselors are nonjudgmental (open-minded, tolerant, accepting). Counselors are open to new ideas and experiences. They are not critical or judgmental of others who are different from themselves. They are careful to avoid preconceived ideas or stereotypes about their clients. This open-minded approach is an essential component of counseling in a multicultural and diverse society. As a result, a nonjudgmental approach to others is often considered one of the most critical personality characteristics of effective counselors. In one research study, counseling experts ranked acceptance at the top of their list of necessary personality traits of counselors (Pope & Kline, 1999).

Counselors are comfortable with their power. Whether we like it or not, the role of counselor carries some inherent power. Clients may see us as able to help them in ways other people can't. A counseling license or certification may "open doors" for us, both personally and professionally. And even your family might now consider you "able to read people's minds" in ways they hadn't before. The role of professional counselor carries weight, and counselors are comfortable using their role to advantage their clients (e.g., to advocate for a student in a school system or negotiate with a managed care company for continued sessions for a client), but counselors do not use the power and status that is ascribed to them for their own benefit or to dominate their clients.

Counselors are verbally fluent; they are effective communicators. Talk therapy relies on counselors who have the ability to communicate with others. That means that counselors typically have an innate ease in talking with others and with listening. They tend to be social, to put other people at ease, and to find it easy to talk with others. They communicate well, are precise in their choice of words, and easily read the nonverbals of those around them.

Counselors are flexible. Beginning counselors often want their professors or supervisors to tell them what to do. They might ask, "When a client says *X*, what should I say?" But counselors-in-training soon realize that there are no scripts in counseling. Counselors use a variety of techniques and interventions based on differing theoretical approaches, and clients respond to lots of different kinds of approaches. Therefore, a counselor must have a repertoire of skills and techniques, but even more importantly, must be able to think on his or her feet. The ability to be creative and to approach each session with freshness is important to moving the session in a direction that is helpful to the client, rather than in some predetermined or counselor-imposed direction.

Counselors tolerate ambiguity. Most people like closure or definitive answers. But in counseling, clients and their counselors have to live with not knowing, with being "in flux," and with not having clear right and wrong answers. Clients present with problems that are complex and do not have solutions that respond to a "quick fix."

Counselors are patient. Sometimes clients make big changes in their lives and counseling sessions move a client quickly toward resolution of a problem. Sometimes the changes are small—almost imperceptible. Clients move and change at different rates, and they need counselors who will stay with them and not become frustrated. Sometimes beginning counselors make large and unrealistic goals for their clients (e.g., by the end of the quarter or semester, my client will no longer be using inappropriate methods to gain attention from his parents). Patient counselors recognize that counseling must move at a pace that is beneficial to the client, not at a pace determined by the counselor.

Counselors possess good mental health and have a sense of their own well-being. Witmer and Sweeney (1992) used the work of Alfred Adler to develop a model of well-being. They included in their model of a well person five life tasks: (1) spirituality (a sense of purpose and connectedness), (2) self-direction (including sense of worth, sense of control, realistic beliefs, emotional awareness and coping, problem-solving and creativity, sense of humor, nutrition, exercise, self-care, stress management, gender identity, and cultural identity), (3) work and leisure (to provide a sense of enjoyment and a sense of accomplishment), (4) friendship (connections with others), and (5) love (sustained, long-term, mutual commitment). Counselors are aware that to be fully present with their clients, they need to be as psychologically well as possible. Counselors can use this model to consider their own wellness and to strive to achieve balance in their lives. (We will discuss the concept of counselor wellness and how to work to achieve and maintain balance in your life as a counselor in Chapter 13).

Counselors are aware of their own limitations. Not all counselors can work with all clients. Counselors do not engage in practices for which they have not been fully trained, and they do not work with clients for whom they cannot find empathy. In other words, counselors recognize that just because *legally* they have the credential to engage in a certain practice or counsel a particular client does not mean that *ethically* they should. We recognize the limitations of our professional training and our personal limitations as well. We refer clients who need a counselor with a specialized type of training. We also take care to make sure that our own personal issues— our "unfinished business"—does not interfere with the work we are doing with our clients.

Counselors are human. Remember, no one possesses all of these personality traits. No one is the perfect listener, always empathetic, never judgmental, and always able to give the client his or her full attention. Counselors are human, and we bring that humanity into the counseling session. Each of us has our strengths and our areas to work on. The goal is not perfection, but a continued striving to be the best counselor that you can be. Although it may be difficult and painful at times to engage in self-awareness, self-reflection, and self-discovery, it will become a cornerstone of who you are in the counseling relationship. Some writers have referred to this concept as "self-as-instrument"—when it is just you and the client in a counseling session, your ability to be fully present, to engage with the other person from the essence of your personhood, is all you have. In the accompanying Spotlight, you will read about a concept at the core of the helping professions, which is that counselors use their own experiences of hardship and pain to help understand and empathize with their clients. Although our own suffering can help us connect, it can also cause us to lose perspective and put our own needs ahead of those of our clients.

When practicing therapists reflect on their careers, they typically believe that practicing their profession *enhanced* their positive personality traits. It wasn't so much that they believed that they had them all right from the start, but that they grew into the personality traits that they now value. Riessman (1965) called this the "helper therapy principle" (p. 27). By this he meant that the helper, as well as the client, benefits from the process of helping. A study by Radeke and Mahoney (2000) confirmed the benefits of helping. They found that high percentages of practicing therapists believe that their practice positively influenced their personalities. They found that when reflecting on their practice:

- 94% believed it "made me a better person."
- 92% believed it "made me a wiser person."

Spotlight
The Wounded Healer

The *wounded healer* is a concept that dates back to Greek mythology, and it has become important to the helping professions. The belief is that many people who are called to help others have themselves been through difficult experiences, and those experiences sensitize them to the sufferings of others. Wounded healers are assumed to have an unconscious connection with their clients or a deep sense of empathy, which assists the clients in their healing process. The counseling profession appears to have a disproportionate number of people who are psychologically wounded, and studies have found that counselors and counselor trainees have higher levels of psychopathology than is found in the general population (see Hanshew, 1998).

Rollo May observed that many geniuses had physical illnesses or disabilities (for example, Mozart, Beethoven), and that these challenges seemed to bring out their genius. He noted that Harry Stack Sullivan, a noted psychiatrist, had severe interpersonal problems—but he made his greatest contributions to psychiatry in the field of interpersonal relations. Thus, May proposed "that we heal others by virtue of our own wounds" (May, 1995, p. 98).

Being a wounded healer might provide you with some empathy into your clients' suffering, but it can also negatively affect your ability to be objective and fully present with your clients. If your own suffering or personal experiences are affecting your counseling sessions, then you might find yourself responding more from your own "unfinished business" than to the needs of your clients. All counselors, and particularly those who have had difficult emotional experiences in their past or present, are reminded that receiving your own counseling as a client can be an essential part of becoming—and of being—a counselor.

- 92% believed it "increased my self-awareness."
- 90% believed it increased my "appreciation for human relationships."
- 89% believed it "accelerated [my own] psychological development."
- 81% believed it "increased my tolerance for ambiguity."
- 75% believed it "increased my capacity to enjoy life."
- 74% believed it "felt like a form of spiritual service."
- 61% believed it "resulted in changes in my value system."

In the accompanying Spotlight, we examine the role that personality plays in the development of counseling professionals. The Myers-Briggs Type Indicator (MBTI) is a popular assessment for identifying preferred ways of interacting with the world, and it can be a useful tool to help beginning counselors reflect on the strengths and limitations that they might bring to their new profession.

Spotlight
Counselors and the Myers-Briggs Type Indicator (MBTI)

One of the ways that counselors help clients understand their strengths and how their personality types can influence their interactions with others is through an assessment called the Myers-Briggs Type Indicator (MBTI). This same test can be used to help beginning counselors understand the potential strengths and limitations they bring to their new profession.

The MBTI is based on the work of Carl Jung, a psychoanalyst and theorist who was interested in understanding psychological types (Jungian archetypes) that he believed were present across all cultures. During the 1930s, Katherine Cook Briggs and her mother, Isabel Briggs Myers, set out to develop an instrument to measure these psychological types, believing that such an instrument could help match soldiers to their ideal military jobs during WWII. The MBTI is now the most popular measure of personality typology in the world and has been translated into more than 30 languages (Geyer, 2002). The MBTI measures personality traits on four continua: extraversion versus introversion (E/I), intuitive versus sensing (N/S), thinking versus feeling (T/F), and judging versus perceiving (J/P).

The extraversion/introversion (E/I) scale measures the degree to which a person is oriented to the external world of people versus the internal world of thoughts and ideas. Extraverts draw energy from action and recharge and get their energy from spending time with people. Introverts seek depth (rather than breadth) in interactions with others and recharge and get their energy from spending time in reflection and quiet time alone. The sensing/intuitive scale (S/N) measures the primary method for intake of information, either through the concrete method of sensing or the more abstract method of intuition. Sensing individuals like hands-on methods and are more realistic and practical. Intuitive people prefer the big picture and are more conceptual, seeking inspiration, rather than facts and details. The thinking/feeling scale (T/F) measures how a person prefers to use information to make decisions. Thinkers are more logical and rational, and they make decisions based on the facts and information. Feelers are more emotion-based, subjective, and relationship-oriented in their decision making. The T/F scale is the only one affected by gender. More males (about 75%) score on the thinking side of the continuum, and more females (about 75%) on the feeling side. Finally, the judging/perceiving (J/P) scale defines how an individual interacts with the environment. Persons who fit in the judging category face the world with a plan. They are organized and structure their time. Conversely, those who fit into the perceiving category take the world as it comes. They are more spontaneous, easily distracted, and value creativity over neatness and order. The results of each scale are brought together to form a four-letter personality type. For example, a person who is primarily extraverted, intuitive, thinking, and judging would be an ENTJ. Thus, there are 16 possible personality types.

Although the MBTI has been criticized for forcing the entire population of the world into 16 code types (Dahlstrom, 1995) and for questionable validity (Healy, 1989), the inherent usability of the results make it very appealing for use in research and practice. Counselors use the MBTI to help clients understand their basic temperaments. In career counseling, the MBTI helps match people with jobs and work environments that suit their personalities. In couples counseling, the MBTI helps partners realize the inherent strengths that each partner brings to the relationship and to recognize differences in temperament and the communication styles that result from those differences. The MBTI is also used in education to help learners and teachers recognize their different approaches to understanding the world.

There is no specific personality type necessary to be a counselor. Counselors are represented in all 16 categories. However, counselors with different personality types tend to have different strengths and enjoy different aspects of the profession. The most common personality type for counselors is ENFP (extraverted, intuitive, feeling, and perceiving), and a higher percentage of counselors are in this category than the percentage of ENFPs in the general population (Vanpelt-Tess, 2001).

Bayne (2004) argued that counselors with certain MBTI personality types will have particular strengths and areas for growth. These are listed in the following table, and they may provide a good starting place as you consider your own strengths and limitations as a counselor.

	Likely Strengths	Likely Aspects to Work On
E	• Helping the client explore a wide range of issues • Easy initial contact • Thinking "on feet"	• Using silence • Helping clients explore issues in sufficient depth • Reaching the action stage too early
I	• Helping the client explore a few issues in depth • Reflecting on strategies, etc. • Using silence	• Helping clients move to action • Helping clients explore all relevant issues • Ease of initial contact
S	• Observing details • Being realistic • Helping clients decide on practical action plans	• Taking the overall picture into account • Brainstorming (strategies, challenges, and actions) • Using hunches
N	• Seeing the overall picture • Brainstorming • Using hunches	• Being specific • Testing hunches • Helping clients decide on practical action plans
T	• Being objective • Challenging (i.e., from counselor's frame of reference)	• "Picking up" feelings • Being empathetic (i.e., in client's frame of reference) • Being warmer • Challenging in a timely way (not prematurely)
F	• Being warm • Being empathetic	• Taking thoughts into account as well as feelings • Coping with conflict and "negative" feelings • Being more objective • Challenging
J	• Being organized • Being decisive	• Helping clients to make decisions in a timely way (not prematurely) • Being flexible
P	• Being spontaneous • Being flexible	• Being organized (keeping to time and structure of session) • Helping clients make decisions

Source: Bayne (2004), p. 137. Strengths and aspects to work on for counsellors or coaches.

If you have an opportunity, you may wish to take the MBTI. Many people, however, find that they are able to correctly identify their personality type when they are presented with the descriptions of the four scales. Remember, there is no "right or wrong" type—but having an understanding of how you primarily view the world will help you in your journey to better understand yourself and the way you interact with your clients.

How Do Counselors Develop?

With all this diversity, you might think it would be impossible to say anything about the general development of counselors and counseling students. Indeed, it would be foolish to suggest that all counselors come from the same mold and follow the exact same steps toward their personal and professional development. Nevertheless, there are several models that can be used as a foundation for understanding the developmental path of graduate training and beyond. These models can help you as you embark upon your journey toward becoming a counselor.

Theorists have generated some ideas about how therapists develop over time. Most of these models suggest that in the beginning of training, counseling students are more dependent on others (particularly faculty or supervisors) to tell them what to do. As students learn and grow over time, they become more independent and more confident and able to make decisions on their own (Bruss & Kopala, 1993; Kreiser, Ham, Wiggers, & Feldstein, 1991). This sounds natural for any new learner, but it frequently becomes a roadblock in counseling when you are practicing your skills without an expert present. Beginning students often want their faculty or supervisors to provide more answers, more didactic instruction, and more structure. Students who are nearing the end of their programs often desire faculty and supervisors to act more like a consultant. Students at this stage do not want answers and structure as much as they want the opportunity to try out new ideas with a more advanced practitioner who will provide guidance and support (Stoltenberg & Delworth, 1987).

Other models, taken from the adult development literature, research on college student development, and novice-to-expert literature, also help us understand the path that many counselors take in their development over time. Several of these models are outlined in the following paragraphs. Perhaps you will recognize yourself in these models as you consider your own development as a counselor. The models might even provide a sense of relief. Your peers are going through a similar journey, and you are not in this alone. There is even a name given to the feelings that you may have right now. The **imposter phenomenon** is a term that describes the feelings of incompetence that many new professionals might feel. Beginning counselors sometimes feel guilty, as though they have deceived or tricked others into believing that they are more competent and more skilled than they actually are. Students in the beginning of their graduate programs may look around at their peers and begin to feel less competent, less able, and perhaps even as though they "slipped by" the admissions committee. Counselors-in-training and beginning counselors often comment that they believe they are "putting one over" on their clients, that if the clients knew that the counselor trainee was so inexperienced and unsure, they would certainly "run for the hills" rather than stay in the counseling session. The imposter phenomenon has been linked with students who are high achieving—have always been successful in the past—and now fear that they might be "found out" (Harvey, 1981; King & Cooley, 1995). It also has been associated more with women (Clance & Imes, 1978; Harvey, 1981; Hirschfeld, 1982), with students with perfectionist tendencies

(Henning, Ey, & Shaw, 1998); with introverts (Langford & Clance, 1993); and with first-generation minority students with low academic self-concept (Ewing, Richardson, James-Myers, & Russell, 1996).

Perhaps you find yourself feeling like an "imposter." The good news is that the feeling doesn't last long, and that by the time you see your first client, you actually will be more ready to see clients than you probably believe. Trust the process. The counselor education program is designed to make you ready to see clients. And there is hope—you won't always stay at the very concrete and structured place where you may find yourself right now!

Adult Developmental Models

Graduate students in counseling are adult learners. Adult learners typically move quickly past the traditional model of learning—the model where an instructor stands up and lectures on important material. Although lecture and didactic instruction can be an important component of any graduate class in counselor education, the "passive recipient model" of education no longer applies. Adult learners tend to want to direct their own learning and to take responsibility for their learning more than in traditional learning models. Adult learners see their professors and supervisors as facilitators and their student peers as collaborators, able to present alternative ways of thinking and acting. Adult learners also typically have more life experience to incorporate into their education and move quickly to incorporate what they are learning into their lives (Brookfield, 1989).

College Student Developmental Models

Although graduate students in counseling are no longer college undergraduates, the college student models can provide some useful insights as well. The most often cited model of undergraduate development is that of Perry (1970). Perry conducted a 20-year study of undergraduate students at Harvard University. He found that undergraduate students moved through a three-stage model of cognitive development. In the first stage, students were dualistic thinkers. Dualistic thinking is characterized by a black and white approach where there are right answers to all questions. Students then move into a multiplistic way of thinking—the belief that there are lots of possible answers, so every position seems equally correct. Finally, students move into a relativistic way of thinking—the recognition that although there may not be absolute right and wrong answers, decisions still can be made based on the best-available information. Although Perry's work was conducted with undergraduate students, his model has been applied to graduate students in counselor education by one of the authors (see the accompanying Informed by Research box).

Novice-to-Expert Models

A final model that is gaining acceptance in a variety of fields is the novice-to-expert approach. This model is based on the understanding that experts are better able than novices to encode (receive and make sense of) information, organize memory, retrieve relevant knowledge, observe inconsistencies, connect seemingly unrelated information, track multiple tasks, and develop novel responses to situations (Etringer, Hillerbrand, & Claiborn, 1995). Novices store information based on more superficial and irrelevant cues that often have little or no relationship to problem solving (Chi, Feltovich, & Glaser, 1981). Within the field of counseling, novice counselors ask more questions about details, attempt to learn by rote memorization, and have difficulty transferring classroom learning to hands-on situations. More advanced students are more likely to asked questions that connect classroom learning with practice, to relate information to their experiences, to more quickly recognize the important pieces of a problem, and to use their information more productively in counseling (Etringer et al., 1995).

What is interesting about all these approaches is that it appears that even though students may be more developed in other areas of their lives, the models are content-specific. In other words, you may be cognitively advanced in another profession—perhaps you came to counseling after years as a mortgage broker. Chances are you were developmentally advanced in that field, but when you enter counseling, you will probably need to progress again through the developmental stages (Granello, 2002; Simpson, Dalgaard, & O'Brien, 1986). Consider the following "Aha" moment taken from one of the authors' experiences:

> Darcy: I was surprised at my own developmental journey as I became a professor. Although I was cognitively advanced in other areas of my life, had completed a PhD, and had spent time as a counseling practitioner, when I became a professor, I immediately returned to a "dualistic" way of being. I had a million questions, and I just wanted someone to give me answers. I asked things like, "How do I write a syllabus?" "How should I determine student participation grades?" "What do I do if. . . ." It is a great example for me of how cognitive complexity does not necessarily transfer from one experience to another. When I study the development of counseling students, I am constantly reminded of the frustration we all feel when we enter a new field. We might be critical thinkers with advanced skills in other areas of our lives, but we typically return to the lowest level of thinking when we enter a new field. My own experiences in this cause me to have hope . . . I know that when I enter a new endeavor, I might regress to more concrete and dualistic thinking, but I won't stay there forever!

Although the developmental models that help us conceptualize professional growth can be useful, they have been met with some criticism. For example, it is clear that the models are overly simplistic insofar as the stages of development

 ## Spotlight
Feminist Responses to the Developmental Models

The developmental models are intended as a guide to help you understand your own development as a counselor. Nevertheless, it is probable that the models are not truly representative of *all the students* in counselor education, and they do not recognize that a person could get to the same end point of functioning through a variety of different developmental paths (Skovholt & Rønnestad, 1992).

Jean Baker Miller, in her foundational writing on feminism, developed *self-in-relation theory* (Miller, 1976). This theory posits that women tend to develop through affiliations and connections with others and that women tend to define and understand themselves through their relationships. Feminists who apply self-in-relation theory to stage models of development argue that the ultimate goals of independence and autonomy ignore the female goals of connectedness and relatedness. Miller argued that for many women, independence is perceived as the severing of relationships, which results not only in a loss of connectedness, but ultimately in a loss of sense of self.

In a similar vein, Carol Gilligan, in her book *In a Different Voice* (1982), argued that many developmental models are based on men (male-normative). Therefore, when females develop along a different trajectory, these differences are seen as deficits. For example, Perry's (1970) college student developmental model was originally based on a sample of white male students at Harvard. The model has since been applied to both males and females, and no differences in adherence to the model have been noted based on gender. Nevertheless, many feminists argue that this practice continues to use male development as the norm.

In a series of studies of counselor education students in their master's internships, Granello (Granello, Beamish, & Davis, 1997; Granello, 2003) found that female students interacted differently with their internship supervisors. Female students were more likely to defer to the suggestions of their supervisors (both male and female) and to ask their supervisors what they should do next. Male students were asked their opinions and ideas more than three times as often as female students. Additionally, female students were much more likely to use relationship-building comments, such as telling the supervisor that they agreed with the supervisor's ideas, making pleasing statements, smiling, or praising the supervisor. These studies lend support to the idea that female students in counselor education interact in ways that are different from—but neither better nor worse than— those of their male counterparts.

appear more orderly on paper than they are in real life (Granello & Hazler, 1998). In addition, all of the developmental models are based on research with men. In the accompanying Spotlight, you will read how some feminist researchers have responded to this male normative approach and advocated for research into developmental models for women.

In this chapter's Informed by Research feature, several research studies highlight the developmental models as they have been applied to graduate students and professionals in the field of counseling. As you read about these research studies, consider how an understanding of counselor development can help you in your own journey toward becoming a professional.

Informed by Research
Counselor Development

Research can help us understand clients and treatment interventions, but it also can help us better understand ourselves. Two series of studies, one qualitative and one quantitative, have been conducted on the general development of counselors and counseling students. The first, a series of qualitative studies by Skovholt and Ronnestad (Ronnestad & Skovholt, 1991, 1993, 1997, 1999; Skovholt & Ronnestad, 1995; Skovholt, Ronnestad, & Jennings, 1997) used an interview format to track the personal development of counselors and psychotherapists. They used both cross-sectional (comparing different practitioners at the same point in time) and longitudinal (comparing the same practitioners are different points in time) methodologies. These studies are summarized in a 2001 book by Skovholt called *The Resilient Practitioner.*

In general, Skovholt and Ronnestad found that as students enter graduate programs in counseling, they try to take in as much information as they can, leaving them feeling overwhelmed and exhausted. During the middle of their training, most students continue to imitate their professors and supervisors and feel uncertain of their own skills. By the time students graduate, they are feeling more confident in their skills, but it is not until they are in practice for a few years that they begin to develop a style that is more their own. As professionals move into the middle stage of their careers, they start to feel more authentic and genuine, leading ultimately to the self-understanding and self-acceptance that come with a lifetime in the field. Overall, the Skovholt and Ronnestad studies remind us that counselor development is a lifelong process. Many beginning counselors feel pressured to have all the answers. Take comfort in knowing that you don't have to be the expert by the time

graduation rolls around—it takes a lifetime to hone the craft of counseling.

The second set of studies used a quantitative methodology to study the cognitive development of counseling students and professionals (Granello, 2002, 2010). These studies also use both a cross-sectional and longitudinal design. In the first of these studies, 205 graduate students at different stages in their counselor education programs at 13 different universities completed a measure of cognitive complexity (designed to measure how people make sense of available knowledge in the field of counseling).

Overall, counseling students at the beginning of their programs tended to be in the dualistic stage of development. That is, students believed that there are right and ways to do counseling, and they expressed frustration because experts in the field do not have all the answers. Students at the end of their counseling programs were more fully entrenched in a multiplistic way of thinking—the belief that there is not so much a "right or wrong" answer when it comes to counseling, but that one should seek the "best available" answers that can be supported with data. The second part of the study used a longitudinal design of 41 counseling students at two universities and found similar results.

Granello (2010) also studied the developmental trajectory of practicing counselors. The results found a long, slow development over the course of counselors' professional careers. In fact, the first major shift in cognitive complexity occurred after counselors had been in practice between 5 and 10 years, with a second major developmental shift occurring after 10 years of practice.

The studies by Granello found that there is an ongoing developmental trajectory for counselors. For students, most growth in cognitive development occurred during internship. That is, students changed very little from the beginning of their program to the end of practicum, but made the biggest changes in their thinking between the beginning of their internships and the end of their graduate programs. For practicing counselors, growth continued decades into their professional practice. Clearly, practical experience in counseling has a large impact on counselor development.

How Do I Make Sure I Continue to Develop?

It is clear that the biggest changes in counselor development come after counselors-in-training start seeing clients, and the most changes occur after graduation. Development as a counselor is a lifelong process. Skovholt and Rønnestad's (1992) study and Granello's (2010) study with practicing therapists both found support for the belief that counselor development evolves long after formal schooling is completed.

Lifelong learning and continued development are important aspects of counselor development. Ongoing continuing education is required by most counselor licensure and certification laws. However, informal learning and continued attention to self-awareness is essential to maintain a positive personal and professional identity and to limit the possibility of burnout. **Burnout** is an emotional and physical exhaustion that leads to cynicism and ineffectiveness and "represents an erosion in values, dignity, spirit and will—an erosion of the human soul" (Maslach & Leiter, 1997, p. 14). Perhaps you have spoken with professionals who seem cynical and tired and not ready to do their best for their clients. Researchers on the causes of professional burnout are quick to note that even bright, energetic, and enthusiastic workers can become burned out if they work in an environment that draws energy from them, rather than reinvigorates them. Because of the high emotional demands of being a counselor, counselors can be at risk for burnout. In fact, burnout has been identified as the number one personal risk for counselors (Emerson & Markos, 1996). Although some of the inherent challenges of the profession that encourage burnout may be out of the individual's control, many of the methods for helping prevent burnout are individual in nature. Counselors are encouraged to take an active approach to preventing burnout by developing interests outside of counseling, maintaining clear and solid professional boundaries, and avoiding taking their work home with them. Additional methods to help prevent burnout have been identified (Coster & Schwebel, 1997; Hamberger & Stone, 1983; Romano, 1984; Smith & Steindler, 1983; Watkins, 1983), and these can be categorized into four major coping skills:

1. **Using problem-solving skills**, including anticipating problems and problem situations, using conflict resolution skills to mediate relationship stressors in personal and professional life, engaging in ongoing values clarification, and emphasizing flexibility and adaptability

SNAPSHOT

Patreece Hutcherson, School Counseling Student

At the time of this writing, Patreece was a graduating student in a school counseling graduate program. She was 24 years old and had known most of her life that she wanted to be a counselor so that she could help kids. Patreece was asked to reflect on her development during her graduate program in school counseling and her transition from student to counselor. Here's what she had to say.

Being a Student/Becoming a Counselor

Patreece started her program firmly entrenched in the student role. She thought she could be a passive recipient of the knowledge that her books and her professors had to share. She stated,

> When I started the Counselor Education program, I knew my purpose was to learn. I had no questions or challenges other than to read and listen and retain information. As I continued to develop in this program, I realized that being a student was not enough. Development in the Counselor Education program meant that I would not only have to read and understand but that I would also have to apply the theories and techniques. I then realized that applying theories and techniques meant that I had to be critical of others—I had to become a critical thinker. It meant I had to become a professional.
>
> At the beginning of my program I would always have specific questions for my professors. I would ask, "How do I act if this situation occurs? If that situation comes up, what will I do?" My professors would always answer the same way—that is to say, they wouldn't give me the answer I wanted. They would often say things like, "I don't know. How would you act if that situation occurred? Or what would you do if this situation comes up?" Although those were not the answers that I was looking for, it was what I needed to hear in order to develop as a professional. Learning my own counseling style would never be in a book, or an article, or even in my professors. The answers were locked away inside that mini-developing professional otherwise known as myself, the counselor-in-training.

As Patreece became more confident in her own developing skills, she began to recognize that simply transferring knowledge from the classroom to the client was not sufficient. She had to learn to *integrate* her new knowledge with her own personality.

> I use professional theories and techniques outside of the classroom. I evaluate which of the theories and techniques work best for me. As I apply the materials that I have learned, my main focus is on whether or not this concept truly works for me. Counseling is not only a profession but also a lifestyle. In this profession it is imperative to use concepts that fit your personality style. Using techniques that fit your personality type help counselors to remain genuine in the counseling session. Everyone cannot apply one technique or theory in the same way. Although the concepts hold consistent, the delivery varies. The theories and techniques help to guide us through the counseling process similar to an anatomy book guiding a brain surgeon. However, we must remember that the books are only a guide; no two surgeries are ever the same, just as no two counseling sessions or clients are ever the same. They may have similar traits but never the exact same treatments.

Finally, Patreece reflected on where she currently is in her journey toward becoming a counselor. As she graduated and stepped into her first school counseling job, she noted:

> *Do I still have questions . . . yes. Am I still sometimes confused as to what my next step will be . . . absolutely. But the difference between these questions at beginning of this program and now is that I am no longer looking for someone else to answer my questions. Instead, I use the expertise of others as a guide, not as a mandate. And given all that I have learned so far—about the profession and about myself—I look forward to my continued development as a counselor-in-training.*

2. **Finding a balance in life**, including developing outside interests, going on vacations, maintaining physical health (attending to proper nutrition, exercise, and sleep), and attending to spiritual dimensions

3. **Developing a social support network,** including communicating and collaborating with peers, finding support from mentors and supervisors and obtaining ongoing peer supervision, even after formal licensure requirements for supervision have ended, and making use of personal support systems (friends, family, significant others, etc.)

4. **Using stress management techniques**, including using time management skills, engaging in private reflection times for self-generation, making use of relaxation skills, and minimizing the use of substances, such as alcohol, caffeine, nicotine, or drugs

All of these strategies are important ones to engage in from the beginning of your counseling career—not just to avoid burnout, but to make sure that you are taking care of yourself as you balance self-care with "other-care" in an emotionally demanding profession.

Self-Reflection

Throughout this book, we focus on the importance of self-reflection as you go through your journey toward becoming a professional counselor. One practice that can help us focus our thoughts and be open to learning about ourselves is the practice of **mindfulness**. Originally based on a Buddhist concept, mindfulness is an empirically supported component of treatment for certain types of client problems (e.g., addictions, low sexual desire, anxiety disorders) and in certain theoretical

---

■▪▪ *Words of Wisdom* ▪▪■

"Remember, you don't have to be sick to get better!"

Source: Echterling et al. (2002, p. 161).

SNAPSHOT
FRANK PALMER, Clinical Counseling Student

At the time of this writing, Frank was a graduating student in a clinical counseling graduate program. He was 39 years old and came to the counseling profession after holding a wide variety of jobs, most recently as a truck driver. During his graduate program, Frank reflected on several key aspects of his development. The first occurred during practicum and reflected the imposter phenomenon that is so common in beginning counselors.

My overarching concern going into this is that I will not be good at it. That I'll find that I don't have the skills and gifts required to be an effective counselor, and I'll find myself a little lost and unfocused as I start to reach 40 years of age. I don't want to give too much power to that fear, but I would be an idiot to believe that it doesn't affect me. Another part of that is not only do I want to find that I can do this, but I want to be good at it. I don't want to be adequate, I want to be effective. I don't have any real fears yet that I will do any damage to clients, but it is on my mind. I hope I have enough perspective and concern to make sure I "do no harm." Ultimately the previous two concerns are very much tied together. For the most part if I am effective and empathetic I don't believe I will do any harm. The question for me is: Do I have what it takes to be effective and be as empathetic as I will need to be?

During a second writing at the end of practicum, Frank reflected on his experience.

Hopes and fears: I don't think these have changed much, except that my fears seem to have a clearer face. This is difficult to explain, but I can see where I could make mistakes and where I don't want to go. (Things are coming SLOWLY into focus and I think some of my anxiety is pressing on my patience. I mean, I realize I cannot be in a rush, but I guess I am a bit impatient.) The good news is that if I can see where the mistakes might lie, I can eliminate them and move on to other potential avenues. My hopes are getting clearer as well. They are becoming more focused on specific hopes with this particular client.

Finally, as Frank finished internship and graduated from the master's program, he reflected on his journey during graduate training.

Overwhelmed. That is the word that most accurately reflects my thoughts and feelings the first year of the counseling program. My brain was being loaded with ideas and information, and my emotions were being taxed with self-analysis of both my past and my present. This was a far cry from rolling around in a semitractor-trailer, which I was doing the year before. Being in a counseling program and the life change it symbolized for me made it something of an adventure as well: exhausting, challenging, and exciting. Both directly and indirectly I was challenged to reflect on who I am and to realize how my personality and worldview might impact (positively and negatively) my professional persona and my work with clients in counseling. I often questioned my ability to be an effective counselor. These doubts continued through the second year when the shock of being in graduate school and the work it requires had subsided. With practicum and internship, academia gives way to the practical application of what you are learning in the "real world." The learning obviously does not end, but it now has eminently more meaning and practicality.

Slowly, very slowly, the question of whether I can be a competent, effective counselor is being answered affirmatively. I am also realizing that counseling, for me at least, is a true vocation. It is a calling where the learning will never stop as long as I am open to being a student.

approaches (e.g., Dialectical Behavior Therapy; Acceptance and Commitment Therapy). Mindfulness also has application for counselors themselves. In general, mindfulness is a mental state of relaxed and reflective awareness that focuses the person on the present moment, without internal dialogue or judgment (Hick, 2009). Research indicates that mindfulness can help counseling students prevent burnout, compassion fatigue, and vicarious traumatization (Christopher & Maris, 2010). If you have an opportunity to learn more about mindfulness and how you can incorporate it into your counseling practice and/or your own life, we encourage you to explore this specialized technique for self-reflection.

Journaling can be another important method of self-discovery and self-reflection. Some of what you write might surprise you. We often hear from students that when they fully explore their own beliefs and experiences, they come to a deeper and richer understanding of themselves that is energizing and powerful. Other times, journaling can uncover material that is difficult for you. In fact, many of the activities we engage in as counselors-in-training (role plays, reading, discussions, working with clients) can remind us of our own emotional vulnerabilities. Our own "**unfinished business**" often emerges during the course of counselor training. When this occurs, it is important that you find ways to address these difficulties. We would like to suggest that you remain open to the idea of entering counseling as a client to help you work through any difficulties that emerge, either as a result of journaling or of other experiences you might have in your program. Many counselors have benefited—and continue to do so—from their own personal counseling.

■■■ *Fast Facts* ■■■

According to several studies, at least three-quarters of all practicing counselors have gone through a least one episode of personal counseling.

Source: Hanshew (1998); Norcross, Strausser, & Faltus (1988).

Finally, we remind you of the importance of social support to help you in your counseling training program and in your life as a counselor. Mentoring, supervision, peer support, and the support of family and friends is essential to maintaining the well-being of people in the helping professions. In the following snapshots, graduate students in counselor education reflect on their own developmental journey.

 ## Tips from Students

Because the concept of the developmental journey is so integral to becoming a counselor, we thought it was important for you to read the experiences of a wide variety of counseling students who are part of a national listserv for students in counseling graduate programs (COUNSGRADS). In this section, students from counselor education programs across the United States reflect on the process of their development as counselors. Your colleagues gave these responses to the question, "What changes have you noticed in yourself during the first year of your graduate training?"

Despite knowledge and education that told me differently, I wanted to solve people's problems when I first started "doing therapy." Part of it was a desire to truly help people that really needed help. Sometimes it was being able to see something that was so clear I wondered why they didn't see it, too. I was a mother, and I took on the job of "kissing it and making it better" for my children. As a counselor, why couldn't I do the same?

Of course, the answer is clear. Even with my children, I wish I had empowered them to take more control. With clients, it's not about my ability to solve their problems. It is letting them grow and use their own strength to deal with their conflicts, as they decide. Sometimes, their choice is not to solve them. Am I less of a counselor if the client leaves with the same conflict? I don't think so, if that is their choice. (I keep my magic wand handy, just in case). Therapy is about growth and perspective, and sometimes acceptance. In my first year, I am amazed at how much I have learned about myself and how I have grown through interactions with my clients.

—Laura M.

I believe that I am much more aware of the ecology of every person's story, including my own. By that I mean the interactions of their history with their personality and their environment. It has helped to dispel judgments made too quickly.

—Jeri G.

I have learned not only about the counseling profession but I have learned a lot about myself as well. We have been told since the beginning that this is an intense profession. I think that the hours I have spent at my site showed me how draining it can become. I now understand that seeing clients day-in and day-out can be very difficult. I have learned the importance of having an outlet to get your mind away from work for a while. I now understand the high burnout rate involved in this profession. Realizing the importance of having activities outside the counseling profession and actually utilizing these activities are two different things. It has been difficult to find time for myself. I really try to give 100% of myself to everything I do, however, I am learning that in this profession it is a fine line between giving it your all and giving too much.

—*Shawna G.*

I think the biggest change is increased self-confidence. As a 46-year-old (now 47), starting back to school after 25-plus years was very scary. I wasn't sure if I was capable of doing the work and keeping up with younger students. Imagine my surprise when I found myself in classes with others close to my age and also experiencing self-doubt. After one year, I am feeling better about myself and more confident in my abilities. I will say that taking a class on group counseling and participating in a personal growth group lab was probably the most challenging and painful experience of my graduate studies, and yet it has proven to be the most rewarding. It wasn't until I was forced to see myself as others see me and deal with the baggage from my past that I was able to really move forward. How liberating to no longer feel the need to be perfect! Group helped me realize that being real and genuine is more important than being right or perfect, which is an impossible goal.

—*Kym P.*

"Be the pebble in your pond."

I say this all the time because I believe in Internal Family systems—that each of us can act as a pebble with in our own pond—a change from within will ripple its effects outward and effect some sort of change in everyone we touch—for the good or for the bad. Change causes change.

—*Theresa K.*

An area of growth that has greatly impacted me from this experience is learning that people are human and that they will make mistakes. The idea that people can be perfect is wrong and it is wrong of me to hope for that. I experienced this with my clients when they would take a step back in our sessions. I had to learn that clients will not always continue to grow in a positive direction and when they do make mistakes, it does not have anything particularly to do with me. I also learned and used this knowledge in my personal life. Life is definitely more complex than I ever realized.

—*Jackie H.*

The power, manifested through influence and professional title, that comes with being a counselor and working within the profession is a bit scary. It is intimidating to know that you can help someone to get better or worse. While I know that it is okay to make mistakes, the fact that those mistakes may or may not directly influence another person's life is a big responsibility. Part of that fear I think is healthy, for it reinforces the need to stay abreast of new methods, techniques, and theories as well as consistent supervision and consultation. The one thing that I really began to understand was the need to have a solid counseling support network through which you can learn, grow, and maintain some sanity. Another thing that scared me was not knowing. This is something that I have struggled with for some time, and will probably continue to struggle with, but hopefully I will become more confident in my abilities as I go along.

—Liz Y.

Summary

In this chapter, you learned about the developmental trajectory that is part of the process of becoming a counselor. Although each counselor takes his or her own journey, understanding the typical path can help counseling students feel comfortable to explore and take risks, being in the process, rather than in a hurry to get to the end. We encouraged you to slow down and engage with what you are learning about the profession and about yourself.

Certain personality traits, such as flexibility, patience, self-reflection, and curiosity, can be of great benefit to beginning counselors as they approach their new profession. Although healthy counselors (and healthy people!) share many positive traits, it is not necessary to have mastered all of these before you start your new career. Becoming a counselor is a long journey that extends throughout one's professional life. Graduate school is just the first step.

End-of-Chapter Activities

Student Activities

1. In this chapter, we considered the personal aspects of counseling and of being a counselor. We talked about personality types of counselors and the different strengths that different types of people would bring to the counseling relationship. Perhaps you would like to look back at that section or the ideas you have underlined. What were your reactions as you read this portion of the chapter, and what do you think, feel, and believe about the personality types of counselors—especially as it applies to you? What are

your strengths that will enhance your ability to be a counselor, and what
are your personality traits that might get in the way?

_____

_____

_____

_____

_____

2. We also wrote about the development of counselors, both personally and
   professionally, during their counseling programs and beyond. We recognized that although there are some similarities in major developmental
   stages, everyone takes his or her own path toward becoming a counselor.
   What were your reactions as you read this portion of the chapter? How will
   you monitor your own growth and development as a counselor? What sorts
   of activities can you engage in to help you become more self-reflective? Will
   you be able to recognize normal stages of counselor development in your
   own training? How will you respond?

_____

_____

_____

_____

3. As you read the Snapshots of Patreece and Frank, or the comments from
   the students across the country on their development during their graduate
   training, what aspects of the stories are familiar to you? How can reading
   about the experiences of these students help you better understand—and
   prepare for—your journey as a counseling student?

_____

_____

_____

4. Is there anything else from Chapter 3 that you want to jot down? Any other
   reflections or ideas that you want to get on paper so you don't forget them?
   Now's your chance. Write them here, or if you would prefer (or need more
   room), write them in a journal.

_____

_____

_____

_____

_____

_____

■■■ Journal Question ■■■

Counselor Development. Beginning counselors often state that they feel overwhelmed with the importance of the role they are about to undertake, with the responsibility they will have in helping others, and with the fact that there is so much they do not yet know. This can lead to frustration with faculty who don't supply you with all the "right" answers, to anger at yourself for not learning as fast as you want, and to fear that you will somehow harm clients by your inexperience. All these feelings may exist even though you understand intellectually that learning to be a counselor is a long process. How are you handling these feelings? What strategies can you use to help yourself accept the fact that you are a beginner?

■■■ Topics for Discussion ■■■

1. One of the reasons we included the discussion of counselor development in this chapter was to "normalize" the experiences that beginners encounter. Do you think it is helpful to recognize that you are normal and on track? How can a practicing counselor normalize client experiences?

2. This chapter included some discussion of special issues that women face as they go through the developmental process. Think for a moment about men's development and upbringing. What unique issues do men face? For example, many men were raised to be competitive, but how useful is competitiveness and covering up one's mistakes as one learns counseling or practices as a counselor? Do you see differences in self-disclosure between men and women? If so, is this an asset or a challenge?

■■■ Experiments ■■■

1. Talk with someone who is an expert at something (other than counseling) and ask how he or she came to be an expert. What was the path they took? Can they reflect on the developmental process they went through? Have the person try to articulate how he or she knows what they know about their area of expertise. Can you

compare the person's developmental path with the path you will take in counseling?

2. Take the Myers-Briggs Type Inventory (MBTI) and consider your results in the context of being a counselor. (You can also take a test similar to the MBTI called the Keirsey Temperament Sorter on the Web at www.keirsey.com.) If you have clients who are of a different personality type than you, what difficulties might you have, and how might your differences enhance the counseling session? What if you have clients who are similar to you? Are there any traps or pitfalls that you will need to avoid with those clients? Any strengths that the similarities will enhance?

3. Consider the personal qualities of an ideal counselor. Make three columns on a sheet of paper. Pretend that you are going to select a counselor for yourself. In the first column, list the background (experience, education, life experiences), personal characteristics (such as gender or ethnic origin), and personality traits that you might want that counselor to possess. As an experiment, select a family member or friend and think how he or she might answer that question. List those traits in the second column. Now check your assumptions by actually posing this same question to that family member or friend and write his or her answers in the third column. Reflect in writing about what you learned from developing and comparing these three lists.

4. Join the national listserv for graduate students in counseling programs (COUNSGRADS). Instructions to join are available through the American Counseling Association website (www.counseling.org) under "students." This very active listserv averages over 1000 graduate students in counseling who are all seeking to get the most from their developmental journey toward becoming a counselor.

■■■ Explore More! ■■■

If you are interested in exploring more about the ideas presented in this chapter, we recommend the following books and articles:

Echterling, L. G., et al. (2002). *Thriving: A manual for students in the helping professions.* Boston: Lahaska Press.

> This book is a easy-to-read guidebook for students in counseling that includes tips and first-person accounts from students in the helping profession.

Schon, D. A. (1983). *The reflective practitioner: How professionals think in action.* New York: Basic Books.

> This book is a bit difficult to read, but provides an excellent and thought-provoking analysis of the importance of becoming self-reflective in our work as well as providing key strategies for how to infuse self-reflection into our lives.

Skovholt, T. M. (2001). *The resilient practitioner: Burnout prevention and self-care strategies for counselors, therapists, teachers, and health professionals.* Boston: Allyn & Bacon.

> Based on the research of Skovholt and Ronnestad (discussed in this chapter), this book uses the developmental perspective to help practitioners make plans to stay psychologically well.

■■■ MyHelpingLab ■■■

To help you explore the profession of counseling via video interviews with counselors and clients, some of the chapters in this text include links to MyHelpingLab at the Pearson.com website. There are some videos that correspond with this chapter, and watching them might challenge you to think about these concepts at a deeper level.

- To explore some of the challenges that counseling students might face as they develop into counselors, go to Ethical, Legal, and Professional Issues, then "Issues in Counselor Education" to watch this video clip:

- A difficult conversation (and the video response to that clip)

  As you watch this video, think about why it is so important for counseling students to develop strong counseling techniques and skills in addition to mastering the academic content of their counseling courses.

5

How Do Counseling Students Get the Most from Their Graduate Programs?

In this chapter, we will:

- Share strategies for preparing for graduate school, including preparing your friends and family for what to expect.
- Give specific study strategies for better understanding course material.
- Discuss methods for getting the most from interactions with peers, professors, and the professional community.
- Give specific ideas for helping diverse students (students from underrepresented groups, international students, and learners with disabilities) be successful in graduate school.

As you read the chapter, you might want to consider:

- What do I need to do to get the most from my graduate education?
- What study skills (including writing and reading skills) do I need to enhance to perform my best in graduate school?
- How can I be intentional and purposeful in my role as a graduate student?

As you have already learned in the first four chapters of this book, becoming a professional counselor is a lifelong journey that began long before you entered your graduate program and will continue long after you graduate with your degree. The life experiences, education, and passion you bring to your graduate training are critical components of your development as a counselor. Additionally, the lifetime of experiences you have after you become a counselor will shape your professional journey. However, the education and experiences you receive *during your graduate program* can have a significant impact on the type of counselor you will become. As such, it is important that you work to make the most of your graduate education in counseling.

■■■ *Words of Wisdom* ■■■

"I came to graduate school right after finishing my undergraduate degree in psychology. I kept thinking, 'I wonder what they [my professors] think happened to me over the summer?' I couldn't believe how much more intense it was, how much harder it was, and how much more I was expected to learn on my own."

—Sharon S., clinical mental health counseling student

This chapter is designed to help you approach your graduate program in counseling in an intentional manner that enhances your learning and gives you the foundational skills, knowledge, and awareness you need to become a counselor. As you will soon discover (if you have not already), graduate school is *very different* from undergraduate education. Students are sometimes surprised to learn that graduate school is not just an extension of their undergraduate years.

Students find that graduate school in counseling differs from undergraduate education in several significant ways. The following list can help you get started thinking about these differences, and to add any observations of your own.

1. **Difference in intensity.**   Coursework in graduate school isn't just more difficult than undergraduate work; it is more rigorous and intense. Beginning students often talk about the amount of material that is covered in classes and the amount of work that is required outside of class. Students who went through entire undergraduate programs with only a few required term papers now find that they have multiple research papers due each academic term. Of course, you would not have been admitted into your graduate program if your faculty did not believe that you could handle this extra work, but most students nevertheless find it a bit daunting when they first get started. In this chapter, we'll talk about some strategies to help you manage this intensity of work.

2. **Difference in focus.**   During undergraduate training, most students find that many of their classes do not relate to one another. Students taking required courses in biology, history, algebra, and psychology see these as separate, stand-alone curricular requirements. During your graduate program in counseling, you will find that all of your courses are interrelated. Learning experiences in each class have applications and significance for other classes. Although this can be exciting and energizing, it can also be a bit confusing and overwhelming at first. Students who have had a lifetime of learning in educational "silos" (the content from each class is discrete and separate from the others) will need to learn how to synthesize material across classes each term and across the entire counseling curricula over time. There are some strategies in this chapter that may help you learn to integrate the material from your different classes in ways that make the most sense for you.

3. **Difference in responsibility.**   One of the hallmarks of graduate education is increased self-directed learning (Brookfield, 1989). Graduate students are expected to take more leadership in planning, managing, and evaluating

their own learning experiences (Granello & Hazler, 1998). During your undergraduate education, your instructors were probably much more likely to give you strict guidelines to follow, to "hold your hand" through every step of the process, and to provide concrete answers to your questions. The faculty in your graduate program, however, are far more likely to give you some space to try to figure things out for yourself. That doesn't mean that you will be left to solitary learning without guidance and mentoring. Quite the contrary. You will often work in groups and will spend time talking or writing about your learning experiences. Additionally, your faculty will provide you lots of feedback and support. The difference is that *you* will be more and more responsible for taking charge of your own learning. If you don't understand something, *you* will need to find answers or seek advice or mentoring. If you are not being challenged, *you* will need to find ways to make your education meaningful. Successful graduate students take initiative. They are tenacious. They have good ideas, and they carry them out. Most graduate students are relieved to find that they are treated as adult learners, but many find that they have to work to learn this new way of being in the classroom. We hope that this chapter offers you some methods to help you begin this process of self-direction.

4. **Difference in meaning.**   As an undergraduate, you probably had to take classes whose subject matter was not particularly interesting to you. Maybe you told yourself, "I just have to get through this," and probably that worked for you. However, now that you are in your counseling program, *all* of the counseling courses have particular meaning for you. Even if you are less enthused about a particular course, you can probably still see the connection of the content to your future career. Most students find that it is energizing to be so passionate about *all* of their courses. However, it can also be a bit draining to have all of your courses compete for your passion and attention, and you will need to find ways to engage in other activities, besides your school work, to help you stay healthy. Chapter 13 of this text will provide you some strategies for keeping your life in balance during graduate school.

5. **Differences in peers.**   In graduate school, you are surrounded by bright, energetic, passionate people who are interested in the same topics that interest you. It's exciting and fun—but it can also feel intimidating. Students may find themselves feeling competitive with their classmates instead of cooperative. Students who are used to being "the smartest one" or "the best student in the program" in their undergraduate careers are suddenly surrounded by others who were also the "smartest" and "best" in *their* undergraduate programs. Although these feelings of inferiority or competitiveness are natural, they are not particularly useful. We hope that you will learn to recognize when these feelings are getting in the way of your education so you can work to manage them or seek assistance from others to help keep these feelings in check.

6. **Other differences.**   Perhaps you have already uncovered some differences between your undergraduate and graduate education. Take a moment to jot down any differences you have noticed as well as your reactions to these differences. If there is time in class, you may want to discuss your ideas with your classmates to see if they have noticed these differences, too.

Preparing for Success in Your Graduate Program

One of the concepts that we come back to again and again in this book is that of **intentionality.** That is, rather than just letting things happen, we ask our students (and our clients) to think about what they *want* to happen, how they *wish* to behave, or where they *desire* to end up so that they can be more intentional about the process of getting there. In this chapter, we use the concept of intentionality to help remind you how important it is that you assume responsibility for making the most of your graduate program. Being intentional means thinking about how you want to approach your education and planning to optimize the potential for your success. Being intentional is *not the same thing* as being inflexible. In other words, we are not asking you to micromanage every class or experience or to develop one strict way of approaching your education. In fact, rigid and inflexible ways of being are not compatible with success as a counselor, much less with happiness as a human being! Rather, we are asking you to step back and think about the *process* of your education while you are going through it. At each step of the way, ask yourself: What am I doing that is enhancing my learning? What is getting in the way of my learning, and what can I do about it? Starting on the process of self-reflection and intentionality now can help you develop good mental habits that will last throughout your professional career.

When we interview potential students in our counseling programs, we often ask them, "What kind of student do you plan to be?" Are you quiet and withdrawn? Do you participate in every conversation? Do you talk first and then think? Or do you think about what you plan to say so much that you miss the conversation? Are you a planner who includes every deadline in an academic planner? Do you get assignments done early or do you work well under pressure? Most students answer by describing the type of student they were during their undergraduate programs. When pressed, however, they say they never really thought about it, they just "did what came naturally" for them. We are asking you to think about it—to *plan* for your success, not just hope it will happen. In most cases that doesn't mean ignoring what has worked for you in the past, but it does mean making a conscious decision to build upon your strengths in intentional ways and to make plans for success.

Now it's your turn to think about becoming the successful graduate student you wish to be. Take a moment to complete the following mental imagery task.

It's graduation day. You are wearing your academic gown and sitting in the crowded auditorium with all the other graduates. You can see your family sitting in the audience, looking so proud and happy. You open your program and find your name among the list of graduates. As you listen to the speaker on the stage, your mind starts to wander. You can't believe graduation day is finally here. Finally, you are ready to leave school behind and begin your professional practice as a counselor. As you look back over your years of graduate preparation, you smile at the student you were when you entered the program—you hardly recognize that person any more! Now, you see yourself in such a different place. You recognize that you are more confident in your skills, more empathetic with your clients, more patient with yourself, and more willing to take risks and face new challenges. As you think about your path from the person you were when you entered graduate school, consider what aspects of your personality allowed you to grow into this new, confident counselor. Where did you have the most difficulties? Where did you have to work to let go of the parts of your previous self in order to become who you are today? Relax, and think about the journey that was necessary for you to become who you are today. What do you wish you could go back and tell yourself as you started your graduate program? What do you think you needed to do in order to be successful? Close your eyes for a moment and imagine this journey. Then take a few moments to write down some notes. What would your "future self"—the one looking back from graduation day—want you to know about how best to prepare for your journey through graduate school?

Notes to myself:

1. *In order to be the most successful I can be in my graduate program in counseling, I need to remember:*

   _____

   _____

   _____

2. *In order to be the most successful I can be in my graduate program in counseling, I will:*

   _____

   _____

   _____

3. *At times (particularly when I am under stress or overwhelmed), I may be tempted to:*

   _____

   _____

   _____

4. *I have many strengths that I bring to my graduate counseling program. These will help me through my journey, and they are important parts of who I am. Specifically, I want to remember to draw upon my strengths in:*

_____

_____

_____

Getting Ready to Start

Everyone who comes to graduate school has a life outside of school that needs to accommodate the changes that graduate school will bring. The better you prepare yourself, your family and friends, and your physical space, the greater the likelihood for success—and the greater the probability that you will encounter your program in the most productive way. In the following paragraphs, we share some of the preparation you might wish to do *early in your program* to maximize your potential for success.

Prepare Your Attitude

Becoming a counselor is a life-changing experience. It is not just *learning about* something, it is *becoming someone* different from who you are now. Students who have the best experiences in counseling programs share some common traits. They enter their programs:

- Open to new possibilities
- Energetic and passionate
- Willing to suspend "knowing" or their need to have immediate answers

Unfortunately, sometimes when people are under stress (say, for example, the stress of starting graduate school), they revert back to rigid and inflexible ways of thinking and behaving. It's a natural response. When we feel stressed, our bodies (and our minds) try to protect themselves by blocking out any new stimuli. In order to be open to the new learning presented to you in your counseling program, you will need to actively fight against this tendency.

One of the best ways to help prepare your attitude for graduate school is to actively work to overcome any self-defeating thoughts and emotions. Sometimes, we are our own worst critics. We convince ourselves that others are smarter, better students, or have more appropriate life experiences that we can never match. Some students worry that faculty will "find out that they made a mistake" in admitting them once the students are in class, or they obsess over

GRE scores or other admission requirements, comparing themselves to other students and worrying that they cannot measure up. Negative self-messages ("I can't do this," "I'll never be a good counselor," "Everyone will laugh at me when they see my practice counseling tape") can really get in the way of learning to become a counselor. There is no magic solution to this. However, the good news is that if you were admitted to a graduate program, your faculty saw in you the potential to become a professional counselor, and they are there to help you make your dream a reality. Trust the process—and seek help when you need it.

Prepare Your Support Network

To paraphrase John Donne, "No graduate student is an island." You have friends, family, and loved ones who are important parts of your life. Undoubtedly most, if not all, of these people really want you to succeed in your graduate program. But, when the thought of graduate school clashes with the reality of your new schedule, there is bound to be conflict.

Graduate students often talk about stressors they feel trying to stay connected with their friends and family as they transition into their counseling programs. Students may feel pressure from parents ("What do you mean you're going to miss your grandmother's birthday? Our family always gets together to celebrate") or friends ("We never see you any more!") or partners ("You are never around to help with the cooking and expect me to just have dinner waiting when you come home from class." Or "I need you to pick up the kids from school today, and I don't want to hear that you're too busy with your study group to help!") These conflicts are the result of natural and expected changes, but addressing them ahead of time, as well as when they occur, may help.

Hazler and Kottler (2005) recommend preparing your friends and family ahead of time for the new life you are embarking upon. Sit down with them and talk about your classes and the work you are doing. Show them your schedule and let them see how your time is allotted. Finally, and perhaps most importantly, remind them that they are important to you, and you still care about them, even if you are not able to spend as much time with them as you had previously.

In our experience, finding ways to include your friends and loved ones in your new life is important, too. They may worry that you are "growing out of them" and be fearful that you won't need them any more or will prefer your new graduate school friends instead. It's natural for you to be excited about what you are learning and the people you are meeting in graduate school. But talking about these experiences with your family and friends can make them feel excluded. Finding ways to help your loved ones understand your new world better can make them feel less threatened by your graduate experience. In the accompanying Snapshot, you will learn from a counseling student in the second

SNAPSHOT
Nimarta (Nimo) Singh

The biggest challenge I had with my friends and family during the first year of my graduate program in counseling was educating them about what I was doing. It was important to help them understand exactly what my program was like and how time consuming it could get. Many of my friends and all of my family members did not have a clear picture of how the program was structured. Further, they did not really understand what school counseling is and did not seem to appreciate my professional goal. I remember my parents were frustrated when I did not drive home on some weekends because they did not realize how busy I was at school. Looking back, I think the main reason they did not realize this was because I had never told them about the structure of the program, the profession of school counseling, and how busy I would get, especially during practicum and internship.

Now that I am in my second year in the program, my parents and friends are much more understanding because I talked to them all about my schedule and the classes I am taking. I informed them about my 20 hours/week internship at a middle school and my Graduate Teaching Associate position. I let them know about my passion for counseling and the importance of counselors. I even wrote out my schedule and showed it to my family so that they can be aware of where I am and what I'm doing each day. They now understand how busy I am and do not complain if I cannot take a whole weekend off to go see the Steelers game or come home for a weekend visit. If I had discussed all of these issues with my friends and family early on in the program, I think that I could have avoided many of the stressful arguments that arose throughout my first year. Once they understood exactly how passionate I was about becoming a counselor and how important it was for me to commit as much time and effort as I could during the program in order to maximize my experience and knowledge, they became much more understanding.

I would like to encourage all graduate students in counseling programs to stop and think for a moment. What can you do to help prepare your friends and family for your role as a graduate student in counseling?

year of her master's degree program about the importance of preparing friends and family for what to expect.

Prepare Your Physical Space

Preparing your physical space means creating the ideal learning environment in your home or apartment as well as finding a place to study on or near to campus. A campus study spot is the ideal place to do some work between classes or when there are too many distractions at home.

■■■ *Words of Wisdom* ■■■

"During the first week of classes in my program, I spent a significant amount of time exploring different places in the library and around campus that would be conducive to studying. This is something I could have probably done ahead of time, if I had thought about it."

—Lauren Schell, first-year school counseling student

Some suggestions for finding an ideal study spot:

- **Get comfortable   (but not *too* comfortable).** You may enjoy lying on your bed to read, but if it is lulling you to sleep, sit up and find a better place to study.

- **Set the right tone.**   Some students study at home while others use the library or a nearby coffee shop. Find a place that is right for you, preferably with few distractions and adequate space and lighting.

- **Make sure the space is ergonomically correct.**   Ergonomics is the science of designing the job, the equipment, and the workplace to fit the worker. Having a workspace that is engineered to fit your specific needs reduces stress on the body, fatigue, and the possibility of repetitive strain injuries.

- **Have plenty of room to spread out.**   You may need to have many books and articles open and available simultaneously. Don't crowd yourself with stacks of papers—have plenty of storage space for files and books that you are not using at the moment.

- **Organize your space.**   Use boxes, file drawers, organizers—whatever works best for you. In graduate school, you will create, and collect, a lot of information. Early in your program, you will want to consider how you will manage all of the different types of material and data that you will receive as well as the papers and research that you will generate. Most students find that they need to use a combination of paper files and electronic storage.

  - **Paper storage.**   You will receive handouts in class or at conferences, and you'll have hard copies of journal articles that you want to retain. Make sure you have a filing cabinet for storage, and buy plenty of file folders to organize everything. Resist the temptation to skimp on file folders by putting too many different kinds of materials in one folder. While it may save you a few pennies in folders now, in the long run, it will not be worth the extra time and effort needed to find the information you need (Kuther, 2008).

  - **Electronic storage.**   Graduate students use computers not only to write class papers, but to organize much of the material that they encounter in their programs. Kuther (2008) offers the following suggestions for organizing electronic information in graduate school:

    - Neaten your hard drive. Set up an organizational system that creates folders and subfolders with simple, clear names. For example, you may have a folder named Coursework, with subfolders for each of your classes. Another folder might be named Research or Presentations. Develop a system early so that you organize your material as you go through the program, rather than trying to fix it later on.

- Streamline your e-mail. Keep your inbox clean (or at least well organized). Check your university-issued e-mail account, or have the messages sent to that account automatically forwarded to the e-mail account you use. In many graduate programs, messages to students' university e-mail addresses are used for important updates and information.

- Purchase (and use!) antivirus and firewall software to help protect your computer from viruses. Many graduate students have horror stories about viruses that destroyed their computer files or papers that were lost.

- Back up your computer early and often. All electronic information is vulnerable. Protect your important files with backups. Some students e-mail their papers to themselves to serve as a backup system.

- **Keep visual reminders of your projects and deadlines.**   A bulletin board or white board can be divided into sections for current or future projects and can help you keep from feeling bogged down or overwhelmed.

- **Limit distractions.**   Turn off the television, the Instant Messaging, e-mail, your cell phone, and whatever other distractions might be available. Prepare a space to study that helps you focus on your work.

Prepare Your Schedule

Chances are good that when you entered your graduate program, you already had a busy life and quite a full schedule. Most students find it hard to make room for the many demands of graduate school without making appropriate accommodations to their schedules. Doing this in a mindful and intentional way means that you are more likely to keep the things that are most meaningful and important and drop the activities that are least useful to your life. Not everyone is a planner, and not everyone likes to schedule his or her time, but most graduate students find that they have to rely on these skills to make it through graduate school.

Many graduate students wonder about their ability to maintain a job while they are in their counseling programs. This is a topic you should discuss with your program faculty, as scheduling of classes and field experiences are specific to each university program. Your university may offer the possibility of Graduate Associateships (GAs), which can be a cost-effective method to pay

---

■■■ *Words of Wisdom* ■■■

"[The recent research clearly demonstrates that] even if you can learn while distracted, it changes how you learn to make it less efficient and useful."

—Russell A. Poldrack, professor of psychology, University of California, Los Angeles (http://www.amelox.com/study.pdf)

for your education. There are clearly trade-offs. If you are working full time you may need to take fewer courses each academic term, and you will undoubtedly have to miss some of the activities associated with the counseling program. Nevertheless, counseling faculty recognize that not all graduate students have the luxury of quitting their jobs and taking a moratorium on life to go to school.

Scheduling your life in graduate school can be a challenge. The following tips, offered by Caroline Baker, a graduate student in counseling at the time of this writing, might help:

1. Treat social events or personal time as a schedule item—block out time each week and treat these commitments as importantly as you would a class or meeting.

2. Even if you are single or have no family nearby, remember that your time is as valuable as that of your classmates who have partners and kids and other family commitments. It sometimes looks easier for the single person to take on more tasks in a group project or accommodate everyone else's schedule, but that's not fair. Everyone's time is valuable.

3. Learn to say "no" and choose your commitments wisely. Think: How will this help me in my development as a professional? Balance that with your social needs to help you maintain your stamina.

4. Find something that you really like to do that has nothing to do with counseling or your graduate program, and make sure you do it at least once every few weeks.

5. Pay attention to sleep and exercise and diet.

6. Give yourself lots of praise for the work you are doing. Notice the days when you accomplish everything on your list and keep to your schedule, and give yourself permission to have an "off" day when things don't get done. No one has to be perfect.

7. Schedule time for quiet reflection to consider your progress and future direction.

8. Seek help when you need it. Don't wait until you are so overwhelmed you are immobilized. Reach out to family, friends, faculty members, or a counselor.

No one is suggesting that being in graduate school means giving up all other commitments in your life. Rather, it's about making intentional choices about how you spend your time. Many students find that it is energizing for them to maintain at least some of the activities from their lives before graduate school, such as singing in the choir or coaching a Little League team. Ultimately, preparing your schedule is about finding a balance, maintaining your priorities, and seeking assistance when you need it.

Prepare Your Mind

The fact that you have been accepted into a graduate program means that you undoubtedly have a strong academic foundation upon which to build. Nevertheless, many graduate students find that to make the most of their counseling programs, they would benefit from enhanced study skills. Graduate students who were high achievers in college often admit that they did not have to do too much to earn their successes. In fact, if grades and school always came easily to you, it may be particularly challenging to motivate yourself when you are faced with the academic challenges of graduate school. If you haven't learned specific study skills to help you, you may be unprepared for the new challenges of your academic work and uncertain of how to proceed. In addition, you may find that many of the strategies that were particularly successful for the kinds of learning necessary in undergraduate courses are not appropriate for graduate school. For example, although undergraduate learning often has an emphasis on rote memorization, this skill is rarely utilized in graduate school, where the emphasis is more on understanding and application. Thus, if you always used flash cards or mnemonics to memorize lists, you will need to make sure you have additional study skills to complement your academic repertoire.

Although no two people study the same way, you may find the following tips to be helpful as you face your graduate work.

- Complete the reading before class. Try to keep up with the reading. Do not assume that the material covered in class will mirror the information in the book. In fact, in many graduate courses, professors assume that the students have already mastered the background information found in the textbook. If you haven't done the reading, you will quickly become lost.

- Learn how to read for the class. In some classes, students are meant to read each portion of the textbook carefully, learning the specific information included. In other classes, textbooks are meant to be used as reference guides, and the assigned reading is intended as a general overview. In many graduate classes, there is a lot of reading. We once had a student enter the program after a successful career as a mechanical engineer. Early in his fist term, he announced that he had to quit the program because he couldn't keep up with the reading. Turns out he was "reading like an engineer"—taking detailed notes on every chapter, memorizing facts and data, and trying to remember everything. He did not understand that when there are a hundred pages of reading or more for a class each week, the goal is general understanding rather than memorizing the details. Know what is expected of you in

■■■ *Fast Facts* ■■■

The Diagnostic and Statistical Manual of Mental Disorders (DSM) is an example of a textbook used in the counseling program that is intended to be a reference guide. Although you will be asked to read the information for the disorders before class, it is typically not expected that you would memorize all of the information within the book. When you diagnose clients with mental disorders, you will have the DSM with you to help guide your decision making.

your classes. Ask questions of your professors. Learn to read like a graduate student.

- Use specific strategies to read for understanding. Many undergraduates never learn how to read complex material. In fact, as many as 69% of college graduates are not proficient readers, where proficient is defined as the ability to read "lengthy, complex, abstract prose texts" (National Endowment for the Arts, 2007, p. 63). Of course, this is exactly the type of reading that is required in graduate education. If you haven't been exposed to specific reading strategies before, now is the time to learn. For example:

  - Look over the entire chapter or article first to get a feel for the structure of the reading, the main arguments, and the flow.

  - Pay particular attention to introductions and conclusions, as these often contain summaries or highlight important points.

  - Look for certain words or phrases, such as "in summary" or "the most important thing to remember is," as these can help you track the major points of the reading.

  - Consider reading the conclusion first. That way, you will know where you are headed, and that may make it easier to follow the reading.

  - Look up words you do not know. Don't just skip over them. Write the definitions in the margins.

  - Look back over the reading the next day, reading only the material you highlighted. Do this again in about a week. This will help you retain the information better.

- Take notes on the reading. Write in the margins, highlight text, or whatever you need to do to engage with the reading. Some students use different colors of highlighters (e.g., one color for something that they think is very important to know, another for something about which they have questions). Other students use multicolored tabs to mark important information and make it easy to find. Take care when using a highlighter, however, as some students end up highlighting nearly everything in the text, which defeats the purpose. Try not to highlight more than about 20% of the reading. It may also be useful to make a notation in the margin about *why* you highlighted particular information—what made it important to remember? This will help with retention. The important thing to remember (and if you were highlighting or making notes on this textbook, this would be a cue to tune in to the rest of this sentence) is that there is no one specific strategy that will work for everyone. Find a system that works for you. This takes patience and practice.

- Keep your textbooks. We know it is tempting to sell your textbooks back at the end of the term, but in graduate school this is seldom a good idea. You will refer to your textbooks throughout your graduate program

Spotlight
Top 10 List
Strategies for Getting the Most from Your Counseling Graduate Program

The officers of the counseling honor society, Chi Sigma Iota, in the Counselor Education program at The Ohio State University developed this "Top 10 List" for incoming master's degree students.

10. **Get to know other students in the program.** Counseling is all about collaboration, and you will need support. As students, you are all on the same team, so work as a team, including forming study groups for tests and proofreading each other's papers. In addition, ask the more advanced students for support, as they've been in your shoes. Be proactive. Seek advice and assistance.

9. **Learn about the program faculty.** Each professor is unique, and they specialize in different areas of counseling. They are great assets who want to help us become great counselors. Get to know your professors and consult them when making important decisions.

8. **Pay attention when the APA writing style is discussed in class and know that each professor has different APA expectations.** Purchase the APA handbook (latest edition) as soon as possible. There are several helpful websites with information about the APA writing style, but trust the printed text as your final guide.

7. **Textbooks are usually cheaper online than at the bookstore.** Do your best to find out what books you will need before classes start and shop for them on the Internet. Keep your textbooks. Many of them are important resources for the profession.

6. **Start a filing system for all of the great handouts and resources you will collect.** You will want to have access to these items during your academic and professional

and into your professional life, and you will need them to study for your counseling licensure exam. The few dollars that you will make in the short-term won't be worth it if you lose access to the information and notes that you will need.

- Take good notes in class. Some professors provide students with detailed handouts or links to websites with copies of PowerPoint slides. Although this can be helpful, it should not be used to replace active learning strategies. Note taking that focuses on summarizing material (rather than just verbatim copying of the lecture) has been demonstrated to improve retention and test scores (Hadwin, Kirby, & Woodhouse, 1999). Consider taking notes by laptop computer, if that is easier for you and approved by your professor (Note: Not

■■■ *Fast Facts* ■■■

The *Publication Manual of the American Psychological Association* contains a set of rules for scientific writing that are referred to as *APA style.* APA style is used in the counseling profession, and many professors expect graduate students to write in this style. There can be significant penalties for papers not submitted in this format, and the purchase of the most up-to-date edition of the APA manual is typically one of the first requirements of graduate counseling programs. For more information about APA style, visit http://www.apastyle.org.

careers, so save everything! The earlier you start a system for organizing your counseling courses, the easier it will be to maintain.

5. **Join a professional counseling association.**   These organizations will provide you with access to important information, resources, and current research in the field. Also, you will need the malpractice insurance they provide.

4. **Don't procrastinate.**   There is a lot to fit into each academic term, and time really flies! Do not save any coursework until the last minute. Graduate school requires a greater time commitment to assignments, readings, and other work than undergraduate programs. Start your research early in the term to prepare for projects that are due later on. Map out syllabi due dates in a planner to see when weeks may be the busiest for projects and assignments.

3. **Prepare your family and friends for the time commitment your program requires.** Balancing work, family, friends, and school with other activities can be stressful not only to you but to others who are used to seeing you on a regular basis. Family and friends may not understand your preoccupation with classes. Explain your schedule to them early so they can be prepared for how busy you may be in the upcoming year.

2. **Expect to be challenged academically and personally from day one.**   The more open you are to learning about yourself and taking risks, the more opportunity you will have to grow as a person and as a counselor.

1. **Enjoy your program. Take advantage of unique opportunities to learn and be involved.**   Because your program requires hard work and dedication to the field, it is crucial that you keep a healthy balance by taking care of your whole self (physically, emotionally, spiritually, etc.). Use your university's resources, including the recreation centers, counseling services, health services, student wellness centers, and spiritual or retreat centers. Enjoy the experience of your graduate program, learn a lot, take care of yourself, and have fun!

all professors allow laptops in their classroom, and it is important to ask permission first.)

- Review your notes between classes. In graduate school, most classes meet only once a week. That is a long time to try to retain information, and most students find that they need to pull out their notes and books between classes to keep the material fresh in their minds.

- Organize your class notes and materials. Keep notes for each class in a separate binder or computer file.

- Seek assistance with your writing skills. If your university has a writing center, consider a visit. Any writer can benefit from additional training and feedback.

- **For international/non-native speakers:**   Many English language learners (ELL) students find themselves a bit overwhelmed with the high expectations for written and oral English proficiency in counseling programs. Of course, counseling is all about communication, so the emphasis on these skills is not surprising. Try to find places to practice your spoken English, such as your university's English conversation groups or through volunteer opportunities. Resist the temptation to spend your free time with other students from your home country speaking your native language. Although this can be comforting when you are far from home, it doesn't help with your language skills.

- **For students with disabilities.** If you will require assistance with your classes, classroom materials, and tests (e.g., large print, electronic versions of materials, extra time for tests), it is important that you work with your university's Office for Disability Services. Register with them early in your program (even if you are not certain that you will need these accommodations). Registering ahead of time means that you will complete all the necessary paperwork and certifications before they are needed. If you wait until you are having problems in a class before you register, it may be too late in the term to get the accommodations you need. Your professors will not know that you are registered with this office unless you determine that you need to implement these strategies for a particular class.

You have just read a lot of ideas to help prepare your mind for graduate school. The overarching message, however, is that you may need to step back and think more intentionally (there's that word again!) about the kind of student you want to be and develop or adopt strategies to get there. Completion of an undergraduate program, even as a star student, does not guarantee academic success in graduate school. We have found, for example, that some graduate students enter our programs without ever having to write a research paper or without significant feedback on their written work. Faced with their first real critiques, these students are surprised to learn that their writing needs improvement. A student in one of our classes was surprised to see her feedback on a class assignment and the suggestion to attend the university's writing center for assistance. She said that she had always received a "check-plus" on her writing assignments in undergraduate classes, so she assumed that her writing was strong. In graduate school, the standards are higher. Take charge of your own learning. You can find even more strategies and ideas for success in your counseling graduate program in the Top Ten List that is part of the accompanying Spotlight.

 ## The Successful Graduate Student

Sadly, many of the commercially available books for students in graduate programs are focused on "surviving graduate school," as though it is something to be endured. We take a different approach. We think your graduate education in counseling is a time to thrive, to grow, to be energized and challenged. Of course there will be times when you will feel overwhelmed or eager for the academic term to end, but we argue that these feelings should be the *exception*, rather than the rule. In the following section, we offer some tips and ideas to get the most from your graduate program. The accompanying Spotlight offers some specific strategies and ideas to help minority students navigate their graduate school programs.

 ## Spotlight
Minority Students, Diversity, and Graduate School

Although graduate programs in counseling are becoming more and more ethnically and culturally diverse, the number of minority students in most programs is still disproportionately small. Nearly 70% of all graduate students in the United States self-identify as Caucasian (National Center for Education Statistics, 2008). Several hypotheses have been put forward to explain the lack of diversity in graduate school, including a lack of faculty from diverse groups, few diverse role models in the professional community, and a graduate educational system that does not sufficiently value diversity. Regardless of the reasons, if you are a member of a racial, ethnic, or cultural minority entering a counseling graduate program, you may find yourself feeling quite isolated. Many students of color note the lack of a "critical mass" of minority students within their academic programs (Ulloa & Herrera, 2008, p. 362). Other minority graduate students say that they feel pressured to represent the larger racial or ethnic group in class discussion, being asked, for example, to offer "the Asian" or "the Black" perspective on an issue. Others say that they struggle with defeating stereotypes or facing a lack of cultural understanding from faculty and other students. Some minority graduate students say they are challenged trying to figure out when to stand out from others in the department and when to blend in, in effect juggling their two identities.

The following tips may help facilitate the success of minority graduate students in counseling programs (adapted from the University of Georgia Graduate School, 2006):

1. Be aware of the pressures. Research shows that there is often undue pressure on minority students to succeed in graduate school.

2. Reach out to other minority students and faculty, even if you have to go outside your department to do so.

3. Don't take on so much that you set yourself up for failure. Be careful that your desire to present a positive representation of your cultural group does not cause you to take on too many responsibilities and commitments.

4. Cultivate a dual identity. Recognize that you will have to think of yourself both as a member of your profession and as a member of your racial, ethnic, or cultural group.

5. Find a mentor. A faculty member or advanced graduate student who is a member of your same minority group can offer advice about the challenges of navigating graduate school as a minority student.

6. Build cross-cultural alliances. Join campus organizations that represent your own culture and work with organizations representing other minority groups to help promote cross-cultural understanding.

7. Graduate, and get a job. Today's graduate students of color are tomorrow's professionals of color. Figure out what you need to do to be successful, and do it. You will be the role model to a future generation of minority graduate students, and you will change and diversify the profession from the inside.

Successful Peer Relationships

In your undergraduate program, you probably had a core group of friends you interacted with outside of class, and perhaps you gave little thought to the role of your peers and classmates in your courses. Graduate school is different. You will probably encounter many of the same classmates in many of your graduate

■■■ *Words of Wisdom* ■■■

"I got an A on my group proposal from Professor X, one of the most difficult and challenging professors in our program. When I told my parents, they said, 'Of course you got an A. You always do. You're very smart.' It was only when I told one of my peers in the class, and she said, 'An A? From Professor X? Wow. I'm impressed!' that I felt like anyone really understood this accomplishment. I learned that if I really want to feel supported in this program, I'm going to have to rely on my colleagues."

—Priscilla M., counseling graduate student

courses. You will quickly learn that your academic peers are invaluable to your learning experience.

Your peers in the graduate program will provide support and encouragement. Students in our programs often comment that the peers in their classes are the only people in their lives who truly understand what they are experiencing. In many programs where the same students are together in several classes, peers can challenge you to grow, push you to higher levels of learning, and confront you when you are not living up to your potential. Many graduate students form study groups with peers, read each other's papers before they are turned in, and offer important interpersonal feedback. After graduation, your academic peers become your professional colleagues. In our programs, we have seen former students set up counseling practices together, engage in peer supervision together, recruit each other for counseling positions, and hire our program graduates when counseling positions become available.

Finally, your peers will play an important role in the development of your counseling skills. In techniques classes, peers often portray clients for role plays. In group counseling experiences, academic peers provide interpersonal feedback. In practicum and internship, your classmates will help you conceptualize client cases and provide suggestions and ideas for next steps. In short, your academic peers are critical to your success. The accompanying Spotlight offers some concrete suggestions to help you make the most of peer-to-peer feedback during your graduate counseling program.

Successful Relationships with Faculty

Your program faculty are there to help you develop as a professional counselor. They act as professional role models, provide support and encouragement, challenge you to grow and change, and provide guidance in your professional journey. Hazler and Kottler (2005) and Kuther (2008) offer several ideas for getting the most from your program faculty.

■■■ *Words of Wisdom* ■■■

"The paradox of self-awareness is that you can't accomplish it alone. You need feedback from others to really understand who you are."

—Bob Towner-Larsen, PhD

- Ask for feedback, when appropriate. Seek input into your developing counseling skills, your academic work, and your interpersonal communication style. Remember, your program faculty are themselves professional counselors, and they notice your interactions inside and outside the classroom.

- Seek help from faculty if you need it. Don't wait until you are completely lost in a class or too far behind on a project to recover. To succeed as a graduate student, you must set aside your fears about asking for help or being intimidated and reach out to get the assistance you need.

- Read your program faculty's published research and writing. Not only does this provide you with insights about your faculty's passions, but it gives you the opportunity to engage in conversations with them about their research agenda and ideas.

- Volunteer to collaborate with faculty in their research or projects. Most faculty are engaged in a wide variety of research projects and service commitments, and students who volunteer to assist can gain invaluable experience.

- Make use of professors' office hours. This is a time when professors are in their offices and available to meet with students. Faculty are often surprised at how few graduate students take advantage of this opportunity. Use this time to get to know your program faculty. You may wish to discuss an upcoming paper or project or talk about your future career plans. Most professors are busy, and we are not suggesting that you just go by the office to "hang out" (unless that professor has indicated this is appropriate). Rather, come to the office hours with specific ideas or questions. Do some preparation ahead of time. For example, narrow the topic of your paper down to several ideas, or bring specific questions about a group you are conducting.

- Seek out a faculty mentor who can help you on your journey. Sometimes this will be your advisor, but it may be another professor or supervisor. Be proactive in getting what you need.

- Attend social gatherings in which program faculty will be available for informal conversations. Although not all programs or faculty offer these opportunities, it is always nice to see faculty members outside of their professorial role.

- Learn how faculty members prefer to be addressed. Some use first names, others use their full titles, and some use a combination, such as "Dr. G" or "Dr. Darcy." Until you are told otherwise, it is probably best to use the professor's academic title (for example, "Dr. Smith"). If you don't know what is preferred, ask. Use similar formality in e-mail formats. One of us (Darcy) once received an e-mail from an applicant to the graduate program that began "Hey Girl . . . " and although it wasn't a big problem, it did communicate a certain lack of understanding of professionalism on the part of the potential student!

- Don't be afraid to set boundaries. Unfortunately, there have been times when graduate students have been sexually or emotionally exploited by faculty. Professors are in a position of power, and they have an ethical responsibility not to abuse their authority by acting inappropriately with students. Be aware of your rights and protect yourself from harm.

Spotlight
Obtaining Feedback on Your Emerging Counseling Skills

Beginning counselors need feedback from their professors, more advanced counseling students, and their peers as they practice their counseling skills. Even though we know feedback is good for us and we should take it in the positive spirit in which it is offered, it isn't always easy to hear without becoming defensive. At its best, feedback both supports our current efforts and challenges us to grow. In undergraduate training, most feedback comes from professors or graduate assistants, but in graduate school, much of the feedback is peer-to-peer. All counseling students have a responsibility to their colleagues and to themselves to learn how to both give and receive feedback. The following ideas may help you develop and use feedback in ways that have the most potential to help.

Criteria for Giving Feedback

1. It is descriptive rather than evaluative.

   UNHELPFUL: "You did a terrible job figuring out the client's presenting problem."

   MORE HELPFUL: "In class we discussed three ways to try to help understand and clarify a client's presenting problem: paraphrasing, probing, and reflecting feelings. I heard you use probing, which is clearly an important skill. But when you use probes without reflecting the client's thoughts or feelings, the result can feel more like interrogation, instead of counseling."

2. It is specific rather than general.

   UNHELPFUL: "I don't think you're using the skills we are learning in class."

   MORE HELPFUL: "In class we learned how to paraphrase, and there are some times in your work with this client when paraphrasing could have helped clarify the situation. Let's review your tape and look for those opportunities and then practice ways to use paraphrasing."

3. It takes into account both your needs and the needs of the other person.

   UNHELPFUL: "You aren't taking this seriously, and I don't have time to work with someone who thinks this practice session is a joke."

   MORE HELPFUL: "I know it is difficult to hear feedback, and it seems to me that you are probably using the jokes to try to lighten the mood. When you do that, however, it makes me feel frustrated, as if you are not taking this seriously. I wonder what you think we can do so you feel comfortable enough to accept the feedback without making jokes?"

4. It is directed toward behavior that the receiver can do something about.

   UNHELPFUL: "Your accent is so thick—it makes it really hard for me to understand what you are saying to your client!"

   MORE HELPFUL: "Because of your accent, you will need to slow down the rate of your speech so clients are sure to understand you. It might also be helpful for you to remind your clients that if they are uncertain of what you are saying, they should ask you to repeat yourself or ask you for clarification."

5. It is solicited rather than imposed.

   UNHELPFUL: "I know you're tired and frustrated by how hard this is, but you should know that I think you still have a long way to go before you're ready to see clients."

   MORE HELPFUL: "I know you're tired and frustrated by this process. There is still work to be done, and I want to help you improve your skills. But right now, it seems as if you need a break. Should we take a few minutes before we continue?"

6. It is well timed, typically immediately after the given behavior has occurred (depending, of course, on the person's readiness to listen, on the support available from others, etc.).

UNHELPFUL: "I noticed that last semester you never confronted any of your clients, even when it would have been useful for you to do so."

MORE HELPFUL "I know confrontation is difficult for you. You agreed last week that you would confront this client on the inconsistencies between his statements and his actions, but I don't hear that confrontation in this tape. Let's talk about what stood in the way of your ability to confront the client and practice ways that you can use this skill in your upcoming session with him."

7. It is checked for clarity.

UNHELPFUL: " . . . So, that's what I think you should do."

MORE HELPFUL: "Okay, I've given you feedback in three essential counseling skills: facial expressions, paraphrasing, and eye contact. I wonder if you could repeat back to me your understanding of my assessment of your skills in each of these three areas."

Methods for Receiving Feedback

When we are on the receiving end of feedback, it's easy to let our emotions get in the way of our ability to truly hear and use the information. When the feedback comes from a professor or a more advanced counseling student, feelings of embarrassment or defensiveness can be amplified. After all, these are the very people that you might be trying to impress (or at least to reassure that allowing you into the counseling program was a good decision on their part!). Our students often tell us that when they are practicing with a partner in class, the moment that we stand beside them to listen or turn on the taping device, they suddenly freeze and have trouble remembering what to do. One student said that the "Murphy's Law" of counselor training is that a student's very best counseling intervention will

never be caught on tape! It's natural to feel threatened by feedback, particularly as you learn a new skill. But there are some things that you can do when others provide you with feedback. Some criteria for receiving feedback:

1. Seek feedback. It is the best way to learn. Students who openly seek feedback will typically find instructors and supervisors who are eager to assist.

2. Be open. Listen without interruptions or objections. Agree to hear the whole message until you respond. Once you take the focus off how you will defend yourself or why the statements that are made aren't true, you will listen more attentively.

3. Write down as much of the feedback as possible, using as many of the original words that the speaker uses as possible. That way, you can review the feedback later, when you are alone and feeling less defensive.

4. Be respectful. Giving feedback is difficult. Recognize the courage it takes for others to be honest and forthright. Try to be thankful for the risks they are taking and for their desire to help you improve. Don't sulk, withdraw, or lash out, as that seldom improves the process!

5. Be engaged and interested. Ask for clarification when needed. Summarize the feedback to be sure you understand the main points.

6. Consider which part(s) of the feedback you will use and accept. If you can't agree to all of the feedback, consider using the "Three P's for Receiving Feedback:"

a. Agree in Part—find one part that you can agree with, and acknowledge that part:

"I know you said I'm not taking this seriously and didn't give it my best effort in tonight's class. I agree that tonight I was tired and distracted, but I want you to know that I am interested in becoming a great counselor. In next week's class,

(continued)

(Continued)

I hope you will see that I am 100% engaged."

b. Agree to Probability—decide to what degree you agree, and acknowledge that:

"You said that I don't look interested in what my client is saying, and it's possible that I am not aware of how my facial expressions are interpreted as I listen to my client. Could you tell me more?"

c. Agree in Principle—agree to the underlying principle you share, without agreeing to all of the other person's statements:

"I agree that it is important to be engaged with our clients and demonstrate that engagement through our nonverbals as well as our verbal interactions. It sounds as if you have some ideas about how I could do a better job with this. Could you tell me more?"

Remember, becoming a counselor is a *process*, and feedback is an important method to help you on your journey.

In general, the relationships between students and faculty in graduate school are more collegial and less formal than those in undergraduate education. Multiple relationships (e.g., instructor, supervisor, mentor, advisor, role model) are common between faculty and graduate students. Learning to manage the differing expectations of these roles is an important part of graduate education. The relationships you develop with your program faculty will last far beyond your graduate education. One of the best parts of any faculty members' job is watching the success of their graduate students as they move through their careers and make significant contributions to the counseling profession.

A Note About Department Politics

Counseling programs are made up of people. Students can form cliques. Faculty can have interpersonal conflicts and petty jealousies. Rumors and gossip can be rampant. Try not to engage or "choose sides" in departmental politics. Stay focused on your work and your own development as a counselor. Remember that all of these students and faculty will be your professional colleagues someday. It is best not to burn any bridges.

Successful Interactions with Counselors and the Professional Community

The relationships that you develop with your faculty, supervisors, peers, and other professionals in the field will have a significant impact on your professional life. Use opportunities to interact with other professionals to your advantage. Most programs have relationships with professional counselors in the community, and you may have opportunities to meet these individuals at department-sponsored events.

Conferences and workshops are another place to network, not only in the educational workshops, but at conference social events and meals. We often find our graduate students sitting together or talking with each other at these events, and we have to remind them that this is their opportunity to branch out and meet others in the profession. It makes little sense to attend a conference, sit with your program colleagues, and attend workshops by your professors. Use the opportunity to branch out and spread your wings. Professionals are often thrilled to speak with graduate students. Remember, these are *counselors,* who are very much interested in the personal and professional growth of others and who will often go out of their way to be kind and welcoming to you. There are many, many examples in our programs of students who meet professional at conferences or interview them for a class assignment and then later use that contact to help secure internship or job placements.

Counseling students in other graduate programs are also an important part of your professional network. As you attend conferences or workshops, reach out to other students to form relationships. Interactions with students who are in other programs will broaden your understanding of the counseling profession and can be important resources for the rest of your professional career. There is a listserv for graduate students in counselor education programs throughout the United States to communicate with each other, share ideas and support, and provide learning opportunities that transcend the limitations of an individual program or university. Students can talk about classes, internships, papers, and ideas about the profession. The listserv, called COUNSGRADS, was founded in 1998 by one of the authors of this text. With more than 1000 members at any given time and many messages posted each day, it is an extremely active list that underscores the importance of communication among emerging counseling professionals.

Some other tips for networking:

- If you read an interesting article in a journal or section in a textbook and have questions or ideas about it, it is perfectly acceptable to e-mail the author (contact information is always included in journals or books). Authors typically love feedback on their work, and they are often happy to offer assistance in your professional development. Remember, however, that these are busy professionals, and we are not suggesting that you ask them to do your work for you. For example, we have both received e-mails from students around the country that are clearly requests for us to do their classroom work, which is inappropriate. Not long ago, Darcy received an e-mail from a student in another state that read, "I read your article on suicide assessment. I wonder if you could compare and contrast the use of two different counseling theories of your choice when working with a high school student with a drug problem. I need your answer today, please." It wasn't hard to figure out that this was a class assignment that had clearly been intended for the student to complete.
- Create a short speech about who you are, your research or practice interests, and your future goals. This is sometimes called an elevator speech—what would you tell the president of your state association if you were alone on an elevator with him or her?

- When talking with a counseling professional, make sure you ask the other person about his or her work. If you have read the person's work or attended a workshop she or he presented, ask specific questions.
- After the encounter, follow up with a brief e-mail or note to help maintain the connections that you made.

It is more and more common for interactions with others to take place via social networking sites on the Internet. As you read the accompanying Spotlight on counselors' use of Facebook or other social media outlets, think about what you believe is the appropriate role for on-line communication and networking in the field of counseling.

Success in the Classroom

One of the major components of graduate education is the coursework that is part of the counseling program. Graduate classes tend to be less didactic than undergraduate classes, and there is more room for dialogue and discussion. Graduate students are expected to be active learners who engage in class discussions, listen to other students, and bring outside information and learning into the classroom. Research supports the use of classroom discussion as an important method to enhance participants' critical thinking, self-awareness, appreciation for diverse perspectives, and self-confidence to take action (Brookfield & Preskill, 1999). In fact, one of the core premises underlying the counseling process is that talking through one's ideas and experiences is a meaningful process that allows the speaker to come to a deeper level of self-understanding.

Passive learners who do only the minimum of what is expected or who sit quietly taking notes during class discussions can be labeled by faculty as disengaged or unprepared. Some students argue that they are actively engaged with the discussion, even though they are silent. Many counseling faculty, however, argue that such silence not only deprives the students themselves of the opportunity to test their ideas in a public forum, it also deprives their classmates of the knowledge, ideas, and perspectives that would contribute to the discussion. It also deprives students of the opportunity to develop oral communication skills that are essential for the workplace. Thus, even students who are introverted or shy are expected to participate in class discussions, and this may take some practice. Active participation in professional discussions is an important skill in all counseling settings, however, and it is worthwhile to develop this skill while in graduate school.

In addition to active participation in classroom discussions, there are some specific

---

■■■ *Words of Wisdom* ■■■

"When I speak, I understand what it is I intended to say."

—Maurice Merleau-Ponty, French philosopher

 ## Spotlight
Facebook and Your Public Image
as a Counselor-in-Training

As you enter your graduate program in counseling, chances are you already have personal pages and accounts on social networking sites. In fact, more than 85% of college students have a Facebook page, and more than 60% log into their accounts daily. Although you probably created an account for social interactions, things are more complicated now that you are becoming a professional. There are no hard and fast rules about whether to keep your account or what to include on your personal page, but you will want to think about how you want to represent yourself in this medium. Counselors (and those in training) can be faced with difficult dilemmas. What types of pictures and personal information will you include on your page? What will you do, for example, if a client wants to "friend" you? Who will be granted access to your pages? An informal survey of professionals (Levy, 2007) resulted in three major paths professionals can take:

1. **Share Everything.**   Professionals who opted for this strategy gave all access to everyone. They argued that this shows your co-workers and professional network that you have nothing to hide. However, new counselors might want to think seriously about this option before they employ it. Do you really want your clients and professors to know *everything* about you?

2. **Share Nothing.**   The opposite stance is to share nothing. Either eliminate your Facebook page altogether (and many counselors-in-training come to this decision), or limit access only to very close friends. This requires, however, refusing the friend requests of clients, colleagues, and peers. Think this through.

3. **Go Half and Half.**   Some professionals say that they keep their professional lives

separate by using the "limited profile" feature on Facebook or setting privacy settings so that only certain friends or groups can see certain applications, photos, or the wall. Think through how you will divide your personal and professional lives.

The most important thing is to adopt a strategy early and revisit your decision often. Be cautious and thoughtful. Talk with other professionals and colleagues to respond to the ever-changing electronic environment. In general:

- Do not post inappropriate pictures (e.g., nudity, drunkenness).

- Talk with your friends about the pictures of you that *they* post. This is one of the most difficult things for many counselors-in-training. They complain that their friends don't understand "what the big deal is" about posting pictures of them partying with friends. Remember, once an image is on the Internet, it is impossible to ever truly eradicate it.

- Don't use foul or inappropriate (racist, sexist) language. In the words of one graduate student, "If you wouldn't show it to your professor, don't include it on Facebook."

- When you "become a fan" or join a group, remember that other people may think you are endorsing certain ideas/services/products. Be careful.

- Review your privacy settings frequently.

No one is asking you to forego who you are when you become a graduate student. But your role as a counselor-in-training does complicate your life a bit, and you want to be thoughtful and intentional about all of your choices, including the ones you make in the electronic world.

classroom strategies that can both enhance your learning and communicate to your professor that you are a serious and motivated learner. For example:

- Show up on time for class.
- Turn off your cell phone or set it to vibrate.
- Don't start putting your materials away before the end of class.
- Pay attention. Stay focused and *appear* focused. That is, don't look out the window or close your eyes. Don't do work for other classes, read the paper, surf the Internet, or read or send text messages.
- Be respectful. Don't roll your eyes when someone else is talking or use other body language to convey boredom or disagreement. If you would like to challenge something that another person has said, do so in a respectful manner.
- Submit assignments on time. If you have a problem meeting the deadline, consult with the professor.
- Use appropriate body language. Make it easy and fun to teach to you (professors are people, too!). All instructors find themselves giving more attention to students who make eye contact, nod, and in general, look interested in the class material.
- Dress appropriately. Most graduate classes do not require professional attire for each class meeting, but there are standards for appropriate dress and grooming that demonstrate that you take the experience seriously and respect the professor, your classmates, the process, and yourself. Wearing your pajamas to class or dressing in clothing that is inappropriately revealing does not convey the professionalism and maturity that is appropriate for graduate school.

Success in Navigating the Program Culture

Perhaps one of the most difficult things for graduate students to understand is that there are expectations in graduate school that are not clearly defined, not expressed out loud, and not attached to any specific course. These expectations encompass the intellectual life of the department that exists beyond the classroom, sometimes called the informal or hidden curriculum (Sullivan, 1991). Examples include lectures by visiting scholars or professionals, workshops, training sessions, service and leadership opportunities in local associations or the department's chapter of Chi Sigma Iota, study groups, and brown bag lunches. The ability to successfully navigate this curriculum is often hindered

■■■ *Words of Wisdom* ■■■

"Retain a copy of all syllabi for classes you take in a separate file because you will need to document your training, experiences, and skills when you apply for internship, licensure, and other opportunities."

Source: Kuther (2008, p. 61).

by the fact that many graduate students do not understand the importance of these opportunities or in some cases, do not even know that they exist. Faculty, supervisors, or doctoral students may announce upcoming events but typically note that they are optional. As a result, students who are unaware of the culture of graduate school miss out on these chances to enhance their professional development.

In the coming month in one of our programs, for example, the following opportunities exist for our master's degree students:

- Legislative Institute Day, sponsored by our state counseling association, to teach graduate students and professional counselors how to advocate for the profession
- A Dialectical Behavioral Therapy workshop, offered by a doctoral student completing a dissertation on the topic
- A Counseling Theories Workshop, comparing different theoretical approaches in counseling sponsored by the department's Chi Sigma Iota chapter
- A study session for graduating students to prepare for the state licensure test
- An opportunity to submit conference proposals to the state and regional counseling conferences
- An opportunity to volunteer at a state conference for counselor educators and supervisors, offering an opportunity to network with faculty in programs from around the state (particularly important for those students interested in doctoral programs)
- An opportunity to participate in a doctoral student's dissertation research involving assisting clients to learn to self-monitor the severity of their symptoms
- Opportunities to be involved with the campus suicide prevention program's education campaign and mental health awareness day
- An opportunity to be a counselor at a summer grief camp for children
- An invitation by the university's Psychiatry Department to a Grand Rounds seminar on interprofessional collaboration in mental health
- A request by the local mental health advocacy association to train students to complete depression screenings for an upcoming public health fair

There's more, but the message is clear. There is always a lot going on outside of the classroom. Participating in these activities and/or volunteering in schools and mental health agencies is an important way to hone skills, network with professionals, and learn more about the profession. Find out what opportunities exist in your program, and speak with faculty or more advanced students to better understand their expectations for your involvement.

Success in Maintaining Your Own Mental Health

As much as it is important to attend to the externally imposed demands of graduate school, counseling students cannot neglect the demands and challenges that will arise from within. It is essential not to neglect your own mental health as your go through your graduate program. Graduate students who are training to be counselors can feel enormous pressure to perform and may feel overwhelmed and anxious (Ronnestad & Skovholt, 2003). They may have jobs, families, and other responsibilities. Many of the activities counselors-in-training engage in (role plays, reading, discussions, working with clients) can tap into the student's own emotional vulnerabilities. When this occurs, it is important to find ways to address these difficulties. We would like to suggest that you remain open to the idea of entering counseling as a client. Most colleges and universities offer counseling for their students, and there are resources in the community as well. Many counselors have benefited—and continue to do so—from their own personal counseling. In fact, a meta-analysis of research studies (Neukrug & Williams, 1993) found that therapists who participated in their own counseling experienced:

- An increase in their own emotional health
- A deeper understanding of their own intra- and interpersonal functioning
- A decrease in therapeutic "blind spots"
- An increase in their belief in their own ability to do therapeutic work
- An increased respect for the role (such as not showing anger and frustration toward clients, not being seductive or sexual with clients) and the client
- A decrease in counselor acting-out behavior (such as showing up late or missing appointments)

 # Next Steps: Life After Graduate School

Ultimately, of course, the purpose of your graduate training is to secure a position as a professional counselor. Although for most students in an introductory graduate course in counseling the job search is off in the distance, it's never too early to start thinking about ways to prepare yourself. Keeping an open mind to the possibilities presented for career paths during your graduate education, networking with professional counselors, attending counseling conferences and workshops, and joining professional associations are all strategies that will assist with your job search.

Preparing Your Resume

It is extremely important to prepare your resume (in academia, a resume is called a *curriculum vitae* or *CV*) early in your program and keep it up to date. CVs do not need to adhere to the standard one-page format of a resume and

SNAPSHOT
Marjorie Adams: A Direct Path from MA to PhD

At the age of five, I informed my parents that I was going to get a PhD. Of course, I had no idea of what that actually meant, but I knew that I loved school and enjoyed learning new things. During college, I jumped from a major in psychology, to business, to pharmacy, to pre-medicine, and then back to psychology. By graduation, I had researched graduate programs and decided that I wanted to be a counselor. There was something about helping people change their lives and improve their quality of life that got me excited and motivated, so I enrolled in a master's program in counseling.

At the beginning of my master's program, I was unsure whether it made more sense for me to pursue a PhD right away or to wait until later in my life. Because I was unsure of how I would feel at the end of my program, I decided to leave my options open. I soon realized that a PhD in counselor education would help me to become a leader in the field. It would not focus as much on my clinical work as it would on helping me to learn to teach, supervise, conduct research, and find unique ways to contribute to the body of knowledge in the field. The more I learned about doctoral programs in counselor education, the more I believed that the PhD program would be a great fit for me. However, I also realized that in order to be a great counselor educator I would need to be a great clinician. I worried that I would not be ready by the end of the master's program.

Two things happened in my master's program that made me believe that I could continue straight through to pursue a PhD. First, I was accepted to a wonderful internship site, and I knew I would spend an intense but rewarding year dedicated to my development as a clinician. Second, I spoke with my advisor, and she reminded me that every doctoral student has strengths and limitations, and it would be my responsibility to develop in the areas where I was less experienced.

Because I had learned early in my graduate program that becoming a counselor was an all-consuming experience, I knew that if I were to continue into a doctoral program I had to be ready to dedicate a huge portion of my life to the endeavor. I worried about the amount of work as well as the commitment it would take. However, I could not ignore the fact that I was finally passionate about what I was doing. Even though parts of doctoral work, like the dissertation, seemed overwhelming, I was excited about the possibilities. I knew that the doctoral program would provide a chance for me to dive into interests that were piqued in the master's program. So, ultimately my passion and excitement for counseling influenced my decision to go straight through.

I was very hopeful upon entering the PhD program, but I must admit that I also worried that I was too young and taking on too many new identities at one time. I also worried that other professionals would not take me seriously as a leader in the field because of my age and inexperience. Looking back, however, I am very satisfied with my decision. Some of the potential drawbacks I feared, such as not having much experience as a counselor and being new to the field, are things that I had to consider when determining my plan of study, but they are not things that will automatically discount me or lessen my ability to contribute to the field. I am learning that I must be aware of potential drawbacks and find ways to overcome them. For instance, since I chose to go straight through to the PhD program. I have also committed to doing a substantial amount of clinical work while in the program to help overcome my lack of experience.

Although I believe I have some obstacles, I also believe that there are some benefits to my decision. Because I never took time away from school, I am still in "apprentice mode," and I am very comfortable seeing myself as a student and feel comfortable learning. I am aware of my strengths as a student and can use those strengths to help me develop as a counselor educator.

The one thing I've learned throughout this entire process is that there is no direct map to my dreams. This can be freeing, but it can also be uncomfortable. Without a clear path, there is always uncertainty. With this reality, I encourage you to relax and think about what gets you excited. I believe that if you find a passion and follow it, you will be motivated enough to make whatever academic or career goals you choose a brilliant step in achieving your dream.

typically include information about education, licensure or certification, honors and awards, counseling experience, publications, presentations, research involvement, teaching, professional service, and professional affiliations. Some master's students also list trainings attended, which is appropriate. In general, CVs do *not* contain personal information, such as age, marital status, ethnicity, or hobbies. As you enter practicum, submit a proposal for a conference, or apply for a graduate associateship or counseling job, others will ask for a current copy of your CV. It's best to keep yours active and consistently updated. Remember that the first impression that many professionals will have of you is your CV. Make sure it is comprehensive, accurately portrays your experiences and competencies, and does not have typos or grammatical errors. Have other people read through your CV to give you feedback. If your university has a career office, it is a good idea to work with their staff, who are trained in developing high-quality CVs and resumes.

Seeking References

All counseling positions will require professional references. Ask your faculty and supervisors if they are willing to serve as a "strong professional reference" for you—be sure to ask; don't just assume they will! If they are not prepared to speak highly of your work, then you will want to find others who can. Make sure the people who are your references know you well and can provide specific details about your counseling or academic skills, your motivation, and your interpersonal skills. Finally, offer to send a copy of your CV to the person who will serve as a reference to remind him or her what you have done. If you are asking for a reference letter, it is appropriate to ask if the person could highlight a specific experience or personality trait that you have. ("Professor X, would you be willing to write a strong professional reference for me for this position? It would be very helpful if you would highlight the work that I did on your research team so that the person in charge of hiring could see that I am a responsible and motivated member of a work team.")

SNAPSHOT

Felice Kassoy: A Returning Student's Journey to a PhD

It was a winter day in February 1981. I was a young 24-year-old newlywed living in Yucca Valley. I was a third-year teacher, coach, and cheerleading advisor when one of my freshman cheerleaders, Missy, a quiet, petite young lady, confided in me that she was pregnant. That moment was the beginning of a long professional journey. After 11 years in the classroom, the births of my own three children, and a steady part-time pursuit of my master's degree and professional counseling licensure, I became a counselor. For the past 20 years, I have been an elementary and middle school counselor, and most recently, a doctoral student in counseling.

Pursuing a doctoral degree in counselor education will enable me to reach my career goals for the next phase of my professional development. As a doctoral student, I will have the opportunity to engage in departmental research and begin my own original work. I will acquire the training and credentials necessary to teach and provide leadership at the college level and become an advocate for counselors both locally and nationally.

Having spent the last 20 years "in the trenches," I am eager to become more involved in academia. As schools have evolved over the last few decades, there are many critical matters we must address. I would like to have the opportunity to make a scholarly contribution that will provide useful information to enhance the work of current and future counselors.

In addition, I have always had a passion for teaching, guiding, and mentoring others. Taking my experience and enthusiasm into a graduate school classroom as a professor is a fulfilling prospect. Extensive experience as a school counselor coupled with my education in the doctoral program will make me well equipped to provide a "reality-based and research-guided experience" for the next generation of school counselors. After 20 years as a school counselor, I feel strongly about the integrity and value of our profession. One way that I can "give back" is to provide leadership both on the local and national levels.

From a personal perspective, this journey began for me at a very early age. I was raised by my mother and my stepfather, both of whom were children of Russian Jewish immigrants, who taught my parents the value of an education. I remember being reminded on many occasions that "they can take any *thing* they want from you, but they can never take your mind. So make the most of your mind." I was never quite sure who "they" were, but nonetheless, my parents heeded their advice (my mother and father both earned their master's degrees and my stepfather received his PhD in chemistry), and all of my siblings completed college, as well.

My stepfather has been the most influential in my decision to return to school. As he celebrates his 85th birthday this month, he continues to be my role model as a lifelong learner. His involvement in the interfaith community, his commitment to the English as a Second Language students he teaches every week, his volunteer work at a correctional facility with the prisoners, the hours he devotes to creative work, and the courses that he enrolls in at local universities are just a few of the ways he leads by example.

The biggest obstacle to this endeavor was me. I was intimidated by the thought of taking the GREs at age 51. I tried endlessly to uncover a "loophole" that might excuse me from this dreaded exam, but after running into multiple dead ends, I decided not to let me fear win. I hired a tutor, spent an entire summer studying, and then reluctantly sat for the exam. My hope was that my acceptance into the program would weigh more heavily on my 30 years of experience and not one standardized test. It wasn't easy, but I survived!

Once I was admitted into the program, I created another obstacle for myself. I began almost every sentence with an apology for my age. Thank goodness, I had a very caring professor during my first quarter who gently pointed out to me that this was unnecessary. As my confidence began to build, it was easy to let go of that "qualifying statement" and flip the lens. I began to view myself as a lifelong learner and a positive role model for others.

So last Christmas, my family and I went to Zionsville, Indiana. There we had the privilege of making 15 dozen authentic tamales with Missy, that little brown-eyed cheerleader from Yucca Valley, California. We were joined in this amazing family tradition by Monica, her 26-year-old daughter, and Mike, Monica's father and Missy's husband. With an enormous amount of hard work, unwavering commitment, and the support of many caring people, these two loving adults have overcome incredible odds to stay together and raise both of their children. I am proud to be one of those "caring people." I hope to utilize my doctoral degree to help train others in this vital profession, so they, too, can make a difference in the lives of the Missys of the world.

Getting a PhD

Some master's-level students ultimately decide that a PhD is right for them. If you are interested in pursuing doctoral work, it is important to discuss this possibility with your advisor early in your academic program so that she or he can help you get the experiences you need to prepare you for doctoral work.

In the preceding Snapshots, two doctoral students discuss their decision to obtain a PhD. In the first, Marjorie Adams talks about her decision to go into a doctoral program directly from her master's program. In the second Snapshot, Felice Kassoy discusses her decision to return to school for her PhD after years of practice as a school counselor. As you will see, neither of these decisions would be "right" for everyone, but you will learn the factors that went into their decisions to help inform your choices about doctoral study.

 ## Summary

In this chapter, we discussed some important strategies to help you get the most from your graduate program in counseling. Even extremely bright and talented students will find that they will benefit from introducing intentionality into their graduate experiences. Finding ways to prepare yourself as well as your loved ones about what to expect can help avoid difficulties in the future. Brushing up your study skills and preparing your work space also can be useful. Finally, making intentional choices in how you navigate the courses, the hidden curriculum, and relationships with faculty and peers can help you in your journey toward becoming a counselor.

End-of-Chapter Activities

Student Activities

1. Now it's time to reflect on the major topics that we have covered in this chapter. Look back at the sections or the ideas you have underlined. What were your reactions as you read that portion of the chapter? What do you want to remember?

   _____

   _____

   _____

   _____

2. As you read Caroline's tips on managing your schedule in graduate school, what specific strategies (from the list or other ideas) would you like to use to help maintain balance during your graduate program?

   _____

   _____

   _____

   _____

3. What type of student are you (or will you be) in your graduate program? Think about this with *intentionality*. What will it take for you to make the most of your classes and education, and what strategies can you use to ensure you get the best experience possible?

   _____

   _____

   _____

   _____

 Journal Question ■■■

Obtaining Counseling as a Client. Many counseling programs encourage counseling students to go into counseling as a client. What do you think might be the benefits of this practice? What might be some risks? What concerns might you have about entering counseling? Might you think, "I should be able to work things out for myself," or "I must be weak," or "I'm supposed to be the healer," or "I wouldn't want other people to know about this," or even, "I'm busy with my graduate program—I don't want to stir things up in my personal life"? If you are already a client in counseling, what fears and negative self-talk did you face when you decided to enter counseling? Reflecting on these reactions, what does this experience tell you about what it might be like to be a client in counseling?

■■■ Topics for Discussion ■■■

1. What are the differences that you have seen between your undergraduate and graduate education? Have your classmates noticed these same differences? What are the positive aspects of these differences, and where are you struggling to adjust?

2. What can you do to help your family and friends understand your life as a graduate student? Do your peers have suggestions that might be helpful?

3. The Spotlight on giving and receiving feedback points out some of the benefits—and challenges—of using your peers for feedback. How can you develop and maintain a culture among your peers that supports and promotes this type of professional feedback?

4. What is the role of Facebook, LinkedIn, MySpace, and other social media outlets for professional counselors?

■■■ Experiments ■■■

1. **Improve your study, reading, and writing skills.** Find out if your university has a study center or a writing center. If so, make arrangements to visit so you can learn more about ways to enhance your academic success in graduate school.

2. **Take a Learning Style Quiz.** Learn more about how you learn and the best ways to facilitate your learning at the following website: http://all.successcenter.ohio-state.edu.

3. **Review your own Facebook (or other social media) page** and consider what changes, additions, or deletions you would like to make as you enter your new role as a counselor.

4. **Review the CVs of professional counselors or other counseling students and get started writing your own.** If available, use your university's career services to get feedback on developing an appropriate format for your CV or resume.

Join COUNSGRADS, the national listserv for students in graduate programs in Counselor Education. Ask questions, engage in dialogue, or just read about what is on the minds of other students in the profession. Directions to subscribe or unsubscribe are always available on the ACA website (www.counseling.org), under "students."

◼▨◼ Explore More! ◼▨◼

Ellis, D. (2010). *Becoming a master student* (13th ed.). Belmont, CA: Wadsworth.

> Although this text was written for undergraduates, many graduate students find that the information and strategies are extremely helpful for navigating graduate courses, too.

Johnson, W. B., & Huwe, J. M. (2003). *Getting mentored in graduate school*. Washington, DC: American Psychological Association.

> Finding a mentor can be an important component of graduate education. This book offers practical advice and strate-

gies for getting the most out of this important relationship.

Walfish, S., & Hess, A. K. (2001). *Succeeding in graduate school: The career guide for psychology students*. Mahwah, NJ: Lawrence Erlbaum.

> This book offers strategies, advice, and guidance for navigating graduate education in the helping professions, including maintaining an ethical focus, making the most of internships, and building a career beyond the degree.

◼▨◼ MyHelpingLab ◼▨◼

To help you explore the profession of counseling via video interviews with counselors and clients, some of the chapters in this text include links to MyHelpingLab at the Pearson.com website. There are some videos that correspond with this chapter, and watching them might challenge you to think about these concepts at a deeper level.

- To explore some of the concerns that counseling students might face as they go

through their training, go to Ethical, Legal, and Professional Issues, then "Issues in Counselor Education" to watch this video clip.

- A student faces an ethical challenge (and the video response to that clip)
  - As you watch this video, think about how you might respond if you received a request like this from a classmate.

How Do Counselors Use Theories?

In this chapter, we will:

- Discuss common views of how people change. These dimensions of personality might influence your choice of theories.

- Help you become familiar with the most popular theories of counseling. The study of theories of counseling, however, is a mammoth undertaking, and you will not learn everything about counseling theories in one chapter, one course, or one book.

- Help you understand how to learn more about the theories that interest you.

- Share stories from counselors who practice a variety of different theories.

- Consider the research supporting the most common theories.

As you read the chapter, you might want to consider:

- Do I need to find a theory I can identify with and practice or can I be "agnostic"?

- Should I settle on one theory?

- Is any theory proven to be better than any other?

- What do I believe about human nature and the nature of change?

In this quote, Lewin is suggesting that theories are like flashlights; they help us find our way. The course of therapy is like a labyrinth, and counselors need theories as guides to look at the big picture and to choose methods and techniques that make sense. Theories provide you with a map and a rationale for your approach. They provide counselors with an orderly way to explain and conduct our practice.

Studying counseling theories is one way to get in touch with the wisdom of the ages. The struggles that you face with clients are not so different from those that the great therapists and theorists had to deal with. They started out like you, feeling that they were in the dark and that someone must be able to show them the way. Their writings provide us with courage and good practical ideas. With a theory, you have a rough idea about what assessments you need to conduct and what lies ahead in the therapeutic process. Along with a theory, you learn some techniques that are consistent with the theory. When you successfully implement these techniques, you will gain confidence.

Maybe clients need theories too. Recently we found an online guide to selecting a counselor that suggested that if a counselor cannot describe his or her approach—keep looking. A theoretical orientation can reassure a client by describing the process of therapy. Instilling hope and realistic expectations is part of many therapeutic systems, and they can help a demoralized client (Frank & Frank, 1991).

In this chapter, we will *not* attempt to help you make a final selection of a personal theoretical orientation to counseling. Instead, we introduce terms and concepts so you can talk about theories with your instructors and fellow learners. We take you through the basic ideas about how some theories work in practice, and we review some of the evidence supporting these theories so you can think about, "What works for whom?" Later on in your theories of counseling course, you will have a chance to learn, in depth, the major counseling theories, and we think it would spoil the surprise and make us unpopular if we made you read it twice. So what we have done is continue our field guide metaphor. First you need to be able to tell the beetles from the butterflies. So what may be helpful, at this point, is to recognize some basic ideas of each of the most common theories. More important, you will be able to feel where you are personally drawn and what general orientations you can focus on for further exploration.

 ## Theories of Change: Counseling Theories

What Are the Major Theoretical Positions?

The history of mental healing goes back to the beginning of human history from the magical incantations of the Babylonians to the practice of Yogic self-control in India and the analysis of dreams by the ancient Greeks (Ehrenwald, 1991; Jackson, 1999). But "talking cures" where people sit down and have a helping conversation have only become a distinct professional calling since the latter part of the 19th century (Bankart, 1997). Now, there are between 100 and 460 theoretical positions (Corsini, 2001; Herink, 1980; Parloff, 1979). In this forest of ideas, how can the beginning counselor find his or her way? One idea is to become familiar with a few of the most admired theories so that you know what people are talking about.

TABLE 6.1   Theoretical Orientations of Psychotherapists in the United States

Orientation	Clinical Psychologists	Counseling Psychologists	Social Workers	Counselors
Behavioral	10%	5%	11%	8%
Cognitive	28%	19%	19%	29%
Constructivist	2%	1%	2%	2%
Eclectic/Integrative	29%	34%	26%	23%
Existential/Humanistic	1%	5%	4%	5%
Gestalt/Experiential	1%	2%	1%	2%
Interpersonal	4%	4%	3%	3%
Multicultural	1%	—	1%	1%
Psychoanalytic	3%	1%	5%	2%
Psychodynamic	12%	10%	9%	5%
Rogerian/Person-Centered	1%	3%	1%	10%
Systems	3%	5%	14%	7%
Other	5%	9%	4%	3%

Source: From PROCHASKA/NORCROSS. *Systems of psychotherapy,* 7E. © 2010 Wadsworth, a part of Cengage Learning, Inc. Reproduced by permission. www.cengage.com/permissions

Twelve theoretical orientations are identified in Table 6.1. These are the major theories that are being practiced today. Traditionally, three big rivers of therapeutic thought (behavioral, psychodynamic, and humanistic/existential) have dominated the landscape. Thus, many older, more established theories fall into these categories. Because of its emergence as a very popular orientation, we must consider Eclectic/Integrative as a fourth category. Of the twelve orientations listed in the table, all but three (constructivist, family systems, and multicultural) fall under one of these four categories. The three that do not fit are all newer and represent the thinking of a new generation of counselors and therapists. In the following paragraphs we show you how they break out into these big categories.

Psychodynamic Theories

Psychodynamic theories (also called Freudian psychoanalysis, psychodynamic psychotherapy, or interpersonal psychotherapy) share a common belief that therapy takes place through psychological archaeology. Through understanding the conflicting forces within him- or herself, bringing them into consciousness, and recognizing the influences of the past, especially his or her childhood, the client is able to live more consciously, rather than be propelled through life by unconscious motivations. The notion of a Freudian analyst sitting behind the couch has been replaced by modern psychodynamic therapists who utilize the therapeutic relationship as a way of helping the person understand his or her past relationships and resolve conflicts.

Behavioral/Cognitive Theories

Behavioral and cognitive behavioral therapists help clients achieve behavioral change through self-control procedures, exposure treatments, and changing self-defeating thoughts and perceptions. Cognitive and behavioral therapies are often done in combination with each other, based on the belief that the solutions to many problems require intervention at both levels. In general, cognitive therapies are based on the belief that our thoughts precede our actions and emotions. That's important, because we have the ability to change our thinking (whereas changing our feelings can be very hard to do!).

Humanistic/Existential Theories

This category includes Rogerian person-centered therapy, gestalt counseling, and existential therapy. As a group, these theories believe that clients are helped when they are allowed to discover their own path. The therapist is a facilitator who may encourage clients to accept their own truths by bringing these out in the counseling session. The change in clients does not come about primarily through learning but by accepting disowned parts of the self.

Eclectic/Integrative Theories

Counselors adopting this orientation blend theories or acquire techniques from other theories in support of a central orientation. Thus a behavior therapist might use role playing (a technique that originated in psychodrama) to teach assertiveness to a shy client. For example, some have developed theoretical orientations that creatively blend psychodynamic and behavioral principles (Beier, 1962). Counselors who use eclectic or integrative approaches focus on using techniques or interventions that fit the client and the situation, rather than adhere to the counselor's theoretical approach.

Other Approaches

Of course, not all theories fit neatly into the four categories listed above. Some of the newer theories that are emerging in the profession may become core theories that require their own category at some time in the future. But for now, we simply list them under "other approaches," and encourage you to explore them as you think about your own developing theoretical approach.

Systems theory or family systems. People are part of complex systems, and those systems influence our thoughts, feelings, and behaviors. Family systems theorists believe that the family is an interacting whole that is both the basis for pathology and the nexus for change. One's family of origin is a crucial avenue of self-exploration for

Spotlight
Solution Focused Brief Therapy

Solution Focused Brief Therapy (SFBT) uses a positive approach focusing on what clients want to achieve in counseling, rather than on the problem(s) that made them seek help or keep them stuck. SFBT is not really a theory of counseling, but a set of techniques and interventions based on a social constructivist philosophy and a systems approach to counseling. The specific techniques and steps involved in the practice of SFBT are attributed to husband and wife team Steve de Shazer and Insoo Kim Berg (deJohn & Berg, 2002). Because components of SFBT are used by counselors in a variety of settings, we will highlight it here.

SFBT is highly focused on the present and future, with very limited attention to the past. Counselors adopt a stance of "respectful curiosity" and invite clients to envision what they wish their lives could be. Counselors who use SFBT are highly attuned to any movement toward positive goals, no matter how small. Clients are encouraged to notice when things go well or times when their current life is closer to the *preferred future* that they envision for themselves. By bringing small successes to clients' awareness and helping them repeat actions they are taking at moments when the problem is not there or is less severe, counselors help clients move toward their goals.

SFBT uses some very specific techniques to help move clients in the direction of their preferred futures. Some of the more commonly used techniques are in the form of questions.

- **The Miracle Question.** Counselors ask their clients a version of this question: "If you went to sleep tonight and a miracle occurred and your problems disappeared, when you woke up in the morning, *how would you know the miracle had occurred? What would you notice? What would be different, and how would you know it was different?"* Focusing clients on the changes that they can make helps them uncover the solutions that are already within them.

- **Scaling Questions.** These questions help clients determine where they are in their achievement of their goals. Questions are

the counselor as it affects how he or she sees the client. The client's family history is also relevant because it shapes how the client negotiates his or her interpersonal life. Systems theorists are concerned with interactions among family members and with families (or couples), rather than the individual client.

Constructivist theories. Constructivist theories such as narrative and solution-focused therapy believe that the client is the expert, not the counselor. The counselor aids the client in rewriting the story of his or her life and developing more constructive and effective frames of reference. Counselors who use these theories work with their clients in a collaborative approach to create meaning and new potential futures for the client.

Multicultural theories. The profession of counseling has been at the forefront in recognizing the important role of multicultural counseling. There is

similar to the following: *"On a scale of 1–10, with 1 being the worst [the problem] has ever been and 10 being the best it could be, where are you right now?"* Clients are then asked what it would take to make a small incremental step in the right direction: *"You are a 3 right now. What would it take for you to get to a 4?"*

- **Exception Questions.** Often when people are in distress, they use terms like "always" or "never." (Recognizing these catastrophizing approaches is important in cognitive therapy, too.) Recognizing when the problem *doesn't* occur can help counselors and clients understand what behaviors and skills are *already within the client's repertoire* for solving (or at least managing) the problem.

- **Coping Questions.** Recognizing the work that clients are already doing to cope with the situation (even when the problem *does* exist) is important. A stance that combines genuine curiosity and admiration can be useful: *"I know that you said coming to school is really hard for you because the other kids tease you, and yet you were able to get through the day today. I know it must have been really difficult for you. How did you do that?"* Such a question is another

way to help clients recognize what they are doing well.

SFBT is used in a variety of settings and with many different client problems. It is an approach that has been widely embraced by school counselors. Research has supported its use for a variety of academic and behavioral outcomes (Franklin, Moore, & Hopson, 2008). The social constructivist approach encourages involvement by parents and teachers, which fits with the mission of the school environment. The focus on interventions that lead to quick results to overcome current problems (rather than extensive understanding of past troubles or underlying personality problems), is consistent with the type of counseling that occurs in school settings. Critics of SFBT have argued that the approach is too simplistic to meet the complexity of human problems and does not pay enough attention to the therapeutic relationship or working alliance. Others argue that the focus on behavioral changes needed to address current problems fails to help clients understand or alter underlying personality traits or embedded ways of thinking. These individuals argue that SFBT does not give clients lasting skills for change (Wettersten, Lichtenberg, & Mallinckrodt, 2004).

clear awareness within the profession that to some extent, all counseling is multicultural, and there are numerous models for multicultural counseling, multicultural identity development, and multicultural training. Multicultural counseling as a *theoretical* stance, however, is less clear. Multicultural counseling theories are in their early stages of development, and more must be done to develop these theories in ways that contribute to the counseling profession (Kiselica, 2005). In general, counselors who adopt a multicultural orientation believe one's culture is the primary determinant of personality and must be considered when applying therapeutic techniques. Regardless of whether this approach has developed into a free-standing theoretical orientation, dealing with those who are culturally different is one of the most important jobs of the counselor. Every counselor must understand his or her own culturally instilled values and background and how they affect interactions with clients.

Focusing Your Search for a Theory

To give you your first taste of counseling theory, we used the twelve theories in Table 6.1 and selected the four most often utilized by counselors: behavioral, cognitive, eclectic/integrative, and Rogerian/person-centered. We have left out significant (but currently unpopular) theories, notably psychoanalytic therapy, originated by Freud. It may be wrong to focus only on the *therapies of the moment* rather than these historical giants. After all, this selection is based on a number of recent trends, including a change in cultural ideas that has made us lose touch with ideas spawned in Victorian times. For example, Freud's ideas about women and the centrality of childhood sexuality as the source of our problems are, for most of us, difficult to embrace. In addition, economics and the way health care is administered supports brief therapies where counseling only lasts 6–20 sessions rather than years. Nevertheless, many of Freud's concepts and ideas (e.g., defense mechanisms) have found their way into other theories and approaches. Throughout the history of the helping professions, older theoretical approaches have been modified and others have sprung up. These are not the "cutting edge." They are what counselors are practicing now.

Sadly, we also have to leave many interesting theories in the drawer that fall under the category of "Other." Among these is William Glasser's (1965) reality therapy. Although in an earlier study many counselors endorsed reality therapy as their primary orientation (Young & Feiler, 1994), in recent years, reality therapy has received little mention in the professional literature and little research support. Therefore, we have left it for your own discovery (or to be discussed further in your theories class). We also have not included a discussion of systems theory here. Previously, nearly all marriage, couples, and family counselors adopted this stance; now, despite the increase in the number of couples, marriage, and family counselors, their allegiance to systems theory has slipped considerably (Bike, Norcross, & Schatz, 2009; Freeman, Hayes, Kuch, & Taub, 2007; Young & Feiler, 1994). So, with apologies, we now focus on four theoretical groups—behavioral, cognitive, Rogerian/person-centered, and eclectic/integrative with the reminder that we see our job as acquainting you with the big picture while hoping we can help you appreciate the richness of the road ahead.

Dimensions of Personality Applied to Counseling Theories

Personality theory and counseling theories are two different animals. In this chapter we focus on counseling theories or theories about how people change. Previously, we talked about personality testing when we discussed the Myers-Briggs Type Indicator. Later, when we take up assessment and testing, we discuss more about personality theory and how this information can influence your view of your client. After all, personality theories are hypotheses about human nature: what makes us tick, what motivates us, our basic needs; and counseling theories (understanding what makes people change) are clearly rooted in these core beliefs about people.

Hjelle and Ziegler (1982) identified nine dimensions or controversies about human personality that are common to all personality theories. Their system helps us understand the similarities and differences among various theories of personality based on their philosophies about life. But here, we are trying to relate some of these same dimensions to counseling theories as a way of getting you to think about whether your view of human nature might affect the counseling theory you choose. Rather than look at all nine dimensions, we will only consider five that seem to be the most relevant to the therapeutic endeavor. In other words, we will examine those that seem to affect what we believe about *how people change*. As you read about these dimensions, try to indicate where on the continuum you might fall. Think about personal experiences that may have shaped your ideas.

1. **Freedom versus Determinism**   Are human beings the "captains of their fates" or are we mostly playing out the hand that we were dealt? Sigmund Freud, parent of psychoanalysis, believed that we were at the mercy of unconscious forces such as impulses originating in the id. He also felt that our early lives were the determinants of pathology (e.g., oral personality, anal personality). At the opposite end of the continuum Carl Rogers, the humanistic psychologist, believed that human beings are free to choose the course of their lives. This assumption about human nature affects how a counselor proceeds (see Wilks, 2003). Can everyone grow and change? Must we address the forces of the past in order to understand our present and future?

Determinism   Freedom

Freud			Adler	Rogers

External forces and   Human beings are free to choose
unconscious drives   and are responsible for actions

Where do you stand? Think of an experience that influenced your idea and note it here.

_____

_____

2. **Rationality versus Irrationality**   Do people make their decisions rationally and logically, or are they mostly driven by their emotions and other irrational influences? Probably no theorist contends that we are at either end of this continuum, yet some are more extreme. Albert Ellis (1989), founder of Rational Emotive Behavior Therapy, believed that human beings live best

when they are rational. Their neurotic behavior is based on infantile and unrealistic goals, such as "I must be loved!" "I must be perfect!" Psychodynamic therapists (influenced by Freud) might agree that humans function best when they are rational, but these theorists believe we are basically driven by irrational forces, such as sex and aggression.

Rational   Irrational

Albert Ellis (cognitive)	Rogers		Psychodynamic therapists	

Humans are basically rational and   Human beings are mostly irrational and
scientifically try to understand the world   more affected by biology and emotion

Where do you stand? Think of an experience that influenced your idea and note it here.

_____

_____

3. **Proactivity versus Reactivity**   Does change occur from within or from without? Does a person decide to change or do outer circumstances control human behavior? Alfred Adler (1927), a contemporary of Freud, was one of the first theorists to assert that it is the *subjective meaning* of an event that is important and not the event itself. For example, being the youngest child only affects you if you see yourself as the "baby." The causes of human behavior are, therefore, internal. On the flip side, Skinner's radical behaviorism asserts that behavior is the result of its consequences. Thus, people change because the world rewards or punishes certain behaviors. Other people and the world are largely responsible for changes in our behavior.

Humans are reactive   Humans are proactive

B. F. Skinner Behaviorism				Alfred Adler

External forces such as   Change occurs from within
rewards and punishments
change behavior

Where do you stand? Think of an experience that influenced your idea and note it here.

_____

_____

4. **Homeostasis versus Heterostasis**   Are people motivated to maintain the status quo (homeostasis), reduce stress, and maintain equilibrium, or are they motivated to grow and change (heterostasis)? Are they, like the turtle, more likely to pull their heads into a shell, or do they stick their necks out in order to move forward? Are we basically comfort seeking, or do we have a need to challenge ourselves to be fulfilled? Are both ends of the continuum true at different times? Family systems theories generally believe that families are seeking a state of balance and homeostasis, whereas existential/ humanistic therapists see people as naturally seeking growth, expansion, and change. Theorists like Maslow thought that self-actualization (to be all that you can be) was an inborn potential.

Homeostasis   Heterostasis

Systems theory	Freud and psychodynamic therapy			Existential/ humanistic

People seek to fulfill   People are questing to be
their needs, leading to a   all that they can be
state of quietude and balance

Where do you stand? Think of an experience that influenced your idea and note it here.

_____

_____

5. **Changeability versus Unchangeability**   There are two competing popular viewpoints about change. One is that people just do not change or that they change very little. This point of view is summed up in the expression, "A leopard never changes its spots." Another viewpoint is that people are constantly changing because we grow, develop, and react to the changes that the environment forces upon us—becoming different people as a result (Watzlawick, Weakland, & Fisch, 1974). Alfred Adler, one of the most important counseling theorists, said that all human qualities can be used either on the *useful* side of life or on the *useless* side

of life (cf. Adler et al., 1999). The con man can adapt his enterprising personality to legal pursuits, such as being a car salesman. Shyness may be difficult to eliminate but through counseling it is possible to learn to make small talk, become more assertive, and recognize the positive aspects of being socially sensitive (Carducci, 2000) (see also, www.shyness.com). Overall, counseling theories mainly agree that people can change. They differ on the degree to which it is possible. If you believe that people do not change much, then therapy is more a matter of adapting to life rather than changing one's basic approach to life.

Unchangeability (Better to Adapt)   Changeability

		Sigmund Freud	Alfred Adler	Carl Rogers

People do not have the   People must   People are constantly
capacity to change   adapt to life   changing and growing

Where do you stand? Think of an experience that influenced your idea and note it here.

_____

_____

Some professionals have argued that focusing on these core underlying constructs, such as the ones suggested by Hjelle and Ziegler (1982), is more important than the theories themselves. In this chapter's Informed by Research feature, you will read about a common factors approach to counseling, which relies on discovering core conditions that facilitate change and growth instead of selecting one theoretical approach over another.

Informed by Research
Common Factors in Counseling

Effectiveness research into counseling and psychotherapy allows counselors to state with confidence that, in general, counseling is effective in helping clients with a wide variety of presenting problems and psychiatric diagnoses.

More than seven decades of research supports several basic assumptions about counseling: (1) Counseling helps clients solve problems, reduce symptoms, and improve interpersonal functioning; (2) the positive effects of counseling can be achieved in a relatively short amount of time (5–10 sessions) for about half of all clients in all settings; (3) counseling outcome does not appear to be a function of any particular theoretical orientation of the counselor; and (4) the best predictor of success in counseling can be attributed to counselor-client relationship factors (Lambert & Cattani-Thompson, 1996).

Research to date has not found that any particular counseling theory is superior to others (#3 above), although there are certainly some theories that have more research studies to support their use with particular clients or problems than others. One possible explanation for the curative nature of a wide variety of counseling methods is that all of the counseling theories have similar features at their core, and therapeutic change is attributed to these **common factors**. In fact, common factors that transcend all of the counseling theories appear to account for the most therapeutic change within counseling (Lambert & Ogles, 2004).

Michael Lambert, together with his colleagues, has dedicated his professional life to researching client outcomes in therapy. His work on determining the amount of improvement in therapy that is due to common factors is considered foundational in the field of counseling and psychotherapy. Specifically, Lambert and his colleagues reviewed decades of outcome research and meta-analytic studies to draw conclusions about the contribution of these common factors to therapy outcomes (Lambert & Barley, 2001). They concluded that the percentages of improvement in client outcomes that can be attributed to therapeutic factors are the following:

- 40% extratherapeutic change (external or environmental changes, for example, client gets a job, or relationship that was causing stress ends)
- 30% common factors
- 15% specific techniques employed by the counselor
- 15% expectancy effect (placebo)

The 40% of improvement that comes from extratherapeutic change is, by its nature, out of the counselor's control. That means that the largest percentage of client change that the counselor can affect comes from the common (or curative) factors, the most important of which is the therapeutic relationship. In fact, in studies of the effects of counselor attributes on client outcome, counselor empathy is, by far, the best predictor of outcome. Even studies of behavior therapies, traditionally less invested in the counselor/client relationship than other theories, support this finding. Lambert and his colleagues theorize that empathy and a positive working relationship result in a "cooperative working endeavor in which the client's increased sense of trust, security, and safety, along with decreases in tension, threat, and anxiety, lead to changes in conceptualizing his or her problems and ultimately in acting differently by reframing fears, taking risks, and working through problems in interpersonal relationships" (Lambert & Cattani-Thompson, 1996, p. 603).

In this introductory chapter on counseling theories, there are two very important "take home" messages from the lifelong work of Lambert that are important for beginning counselors to learn as they develop their theoretical foundation.

1. There is no "magic" counseling theory— or at least no empirically derived answer to what counseling theory is best. Thus, there is no pressure for new counselors to choose the "right" theory—only the theory that is right for you.

2. Among variables that are at least partially within the counselor's control, the counseling relationship is the best predictor of client outcome. The development of skills and knowledge to enhance the counseling relationship, which has counselor empathy as its cornerstone, is the best investment of a new counselor's time and energy.

Behavioral, Cognitive, Eclectic/Integrative, and Rogerian/Person-Centered Theories

We now address our four theories, chosen from Table 6.1, by talking about the basic ideas or tenets, the historical contributors, and the settings and problems that have been helped by the approach. In addition, we utilize Hjelle and Ziegler's (1982) personality dimensions to analyze the theories so that you can understand their underlying beliefs and compare them with yours. We also have included a snapshot of a counselor who works from a specific theoretical stance to help you see how a counselor might adopt a personal theory and apply it in his work with clients.

Behavior Therapy

There is not one unified approach to behavioral counseling. The big difference among behaviorists is between those who focus on the role of thinking (cognition) and those who focus on classical behavioral techniques. More cognitively oriented counselors look at the role of thoughts and beliefs, whereas more behaviorally oriented counselors examine triggers for behaviors and the patterns that reward or reinforce behavior. Here, we will try to focus mostly on classical behavior therapy approaches (focusing on triggers and environmental rewards) while recognizing that, in reality, there are relatively few purely behavioral counselors. Most also use cognitive (thinking) techniques.

Basic tenets of behavior therapy. *Behavior therapy begins with assessment.* Assessment is the process of collecting information necessary for treatment. Assessment in behavior therapy often uses functional analysis. **Functional analysis** is a way of understanding a problem by looking at what precedes it (antecedents) and what happens after it (consequences). For example, a person who smokes cigarettes could work with a counselor who uses functional analysis to understand and change the behavior. The counselor assesses what happens before smoking (antecedents), such as meeting friends who smoke. Next the counselor analyzes the client's responses. How much does the client smoke? When does the client smoke? Where does the client smoke? Finally, the counselor analyzes the things that are rewarding the client's smoking behavior. Does the client experience reduced anxiety, acceptance by peers at the local bar, and so on? Armed with this information, the behavioral counselor then helps the client identify the current level of smoking (baseline) and set goals for reduction (target). By the way, most behavioral counselors would incorporate the client's thinking

---

■■■ *Words of Wisdom* ■■■

"The time has come when psychology must discard all reference to consciousness. . . . Its sole task is the prediction and control of behavior; and introspection can form no part of that method."

—J. B. Watson (1913, p. 158).

patterns and emotions as an important part of the assessment process. These counselors might be better labeled *cognitive behavioral* in their approach.

Learning is important in causing behavior and changing behavior. We learn to be afraid for a variety of reasons. We saw our parent jump when lightning struck (vicarious learning); we learned that certain foods made us sick, and after that, the mere smell could make us queasy (classical conditioning); and we are rewarded for pretending to be ill by getting extra attention (respondent conditioning). Similarly, we can unlearn these negative behaviors and replace them with positive ones. For example, we can learn to respond assertively to stressful situations rather than adopt the passive attitude that we learned from our parents. This makes the behavior therapist a teacher who helps us practice new behaviors and weaken unhealthy ones.

Behavior change is the gold standard. From its inception, behavior therapy has focused on behavior change rather than emotional change because behaviors can be measured more easily and reliably. Counselors practicing this theory normally set targets that can be defined in behavioral terms. For example, when a client says he or she wants to socialize more, the counselor might get the client to agree to three social events per week and spending at least 15 minutes at each event, chatting with two or more persons. This is a hypothetical example, but it points out how specific and simple behavioral contracts can be. When you begin working as a counselor or in your internship, you might be required to determine behavioral goals for your clients even if you are not practicing this theory. Agencies and insurance companies like these kinds of measureable goals. There are a variety of books that help you think about this and write these kinds of goals.

Problems and settings where behavior theory is used. Behavior therapy is often used with children, people with mental disabilities, individuals who are developmentally delayed, people with phobias, and those who suffer from disturbing habits. It is frequently used in mental hospital systems where patients earn points to achieve more freedoms. A behavioral counselor might help someone overcome fearful stimuli by exposing the person little by little to the things he or she is avoiding, such as crowds, cockroaches, or public speaking. A counselor practicing behavior therapy might treat a child's misbehavior by getting the parents to deliver and withhold rewards to strengthen good behavior and eliminate negative actions, or help an adult end his smoking obsession.

Some counselors shy away from behavior therapy because they see it as mechanical and manipulative. But behavior therapy is not just something that the counselor inflicts on the client. Behavior therapy is a theory of how people learn. Many psychoeducational procedures, such as assertiveness training and anger management, are best taught using behavioral principles. In fact, behavior therapy is often aimed at giving clients more self control. The counselor might teach clients methods and techniques of **contingency management** or **self-control** procedures such as rewarding or withholding reinforcement to achieve a desired end (e.g., Bellack & Hersen, 1985). For example, right now, I (Mark) have made a contract with myself to write for two hours on this chapter, after which I will give myself a bowl of ice cream—a big bowl. Can you see that clients can also use ordinary rewards such as watching TV to gain control over behaviors that they want to change?

Let's talk about another common treatment, **exposure**. Exposure means repeatedly facing a situation that creates an undesirable emotion or behavior. Usually, exposure is used when people have debilitating fears such as thunderstorms or public speaking. Eventually, through exposure the situation loses its power, because the feared consequence does not take place and the person no longer thinks of it as frightening. For example, you might fear heights because you are afraid you will fall. Repeated exposure to heights teaches you that you can be safe, lessening the fear that you traditionally associated with heights. Exposure can be done using imagery or **in vivo** by taking the client to the distressing place or slowly showing the client the feared object. For example, an exposure treatment for those afraid of flying involves gradually and repeatedly going on airplanes until the individual eventually actually flies in the plane. Exposure is a common treatment used by counselors of all theoretical persuasions. Even Freud advocated facing fears.

Is behavior therapy effective? Behavior therapy involves counting and charting success. As a result, research comes naturally to behavior therapists, and they are more prolific number crunchers than their counterparts in other theories. Also the number of cigarettes smoked is a lot easier to count than Oedipal complexes.

Compared to other theories, behavioral techniques have been well researched and have been shown to be effective. Behavior therapy and cognitive therapy are hard to separate in practice and in research. Still, it can be said that behavior theory has been shown to be effective in dealing with anger and aggression, anxiety disorders, cigarette smoking, children's behavior problems, and marital and family problems, to name just a few (Gottman & Notarius, 2000; Zinbarg & Griffin, 2008).

Common dimensions of human nature applied to behavior therapy. Previously, we discussed Hjelle and Ziegler's dimensions applied to personality theory. If we consider them in light of each of the counseling theories we discuss here, we will get an idea about their differences on these dimensions. In the case of behavior therapy, the underlying assumptions about change are that:

1. Freedom versus determinism: Human behavior is largely determined. Freedom is a myth (Skinner, 1972).

2. Rationality versus irrationality: This concept is not applicable to the theory. Human beings are shaped by the world and whether they are rational or irrational is not relevant.

3. Proactive versus reactive: Human behavior is the result of what the environment rewards and punishes. Therefore, humans are reactive.

4. Homeostasis versus heterostasis: This concept is not applicable because behaviorists make no assumptions about human personality, growth, or balance as human goals or drives.

5. Changeability versus unchangeability: Behavior therapy falls strongly on the changeability side of the continuum, but human behavior change over the lifespan is due to changes in the world and in the manipulation of rewards and punishments rather than human development.

Important contributors to behavior counseling.

John Watson showed that anxiety could be classically conditioned in the famous Little Albert experiments. Watson paired unpleasant noise with furry stuffed animals to cause Albert to fear furry animals. Unfortunately, 8-month-old Albert left the hospital before he could be treated for his fear of furry things that was caused by the experiment.

B. F. Skinner used animal models to understand human behavior. The Skinner box was created to conduct these experiments. Skinner kept his daughter in a similar environment. He showed that learning could be increased by the use of positive and negative reinforcers and decreased by punishment. Thus, mentally healthy behavior could be learned and unhealthy behavior could be unlearned.

Joseph Wolpe developed systematic desensitization, which theorized that relaxation was incompatible with fear. Thus, through graded exposure and simultaneous relaxation, phobias could be treated. Wolpe once treated a woman for fear of bugs without success until he found out that her husband was nicknamed after an insect. Marital therapy was eventually effective in helping her overcome her fears.

Albert Bandura demonstrated the power of models in his Bobo doll experiments, in which children exposed to violent models acted violently. His discovery of the role of models to teach positive behaviors has been a major contribution to therapy and education. Bandura has always been interested in how people disengage from immoral acts and has written about responses to homelessness, substance abuse, and terrorism. He is among the most influential psychologists in history.

Cognitive Therapy

Cognitive therapy proposes that changing people's cognitions is the way to help them lead happier lives. For example, people who are depressed dwell on discouraging thoughts. They possess negative beliefs about themselves, others and the future. Cognitions are not just thoughts. They include our "perceptions, memories, expectations, standards, images, attributions, goals and tacit beliefs" (Reinecke & Freeman, 2005, p. 230). We can easily see that someone's misery is often caused by a belief the person holds. For example, if someone believes he has been passed over unfairly at work, the belief can lead to anger, revenge, and depression. But it is not just thinking about specific past or present difficulties that causes emotional problems. Some common negative thought patterns also can be the source of emotional upset: **irrational beliefs** and **cognitive distortions.** Irrational beliefs include such things as believing that one should be perfect in all areas of human functioning. This thought can makes us anxious and then depressed when we inevitably fail. Cognitive distortions, on the other hand, are less specific errors in thinking. An example is *magnification,* which is the tendency of some people to make mountains out of molehills, to see things as more important than they are. The basis of the approach is to get clients to recognize their irrational beliefs or cognitive errors, challenge them, and replace them with more constructive beliefs and thoughts.

Although it seems obvious that negative and erroneous thinking is the cause of much human suffering, exclusively attempting to change people's thoughts and beliefs as the major emphasis of counseling did not take hold until the 1960s when Aaron Beck (1964) developed **Cognitive Therapy** and Albert Ellis (1962) developed **Rational Emotive Therapy.** Ellis later started calling his approach **Rational Emotive Behavior Therapy** as he recognized the important role that behaviors play in making changes (Ellis, 1989, 1999). Many people refer to both as examples of **cognitive behavioral therapy** or merely **cognitive therapy.** Most practitioners combine behavioral and cognitive theories. In other words, it is an integrative approach. The aim is not just to change behavior but to reduce distress-causing emotions that are preceded by disturbing thoughts.

Basic tenets of cognitive therapy. *Individuals interpret events in a unique way that affects their behavior and how they feel.* They interpret the world based on *schemas,* which are psychological structures that help process information and guide behaviors. Schemas are like maps that are referred to again and again as life progresses. For example, we may have a schema that guides our interaction with other people. We may automatically be cautious and untrusting because of experiences in our early life or the exhortations of our parents. These schemas are evoked automatically in corresponding environments.

Mental health is another name for having effective behavior patterns and realistic and rational beliefs. Pathology, on the other hand, is having unrealistic ideas that cause emotional distress and being unable to achieve one's goals because of self-limiting ideas (Kellogg & Young, 2008).

■■■ *Words of Wisdom* ■■■

"The best years of your life are the ones in which you decide your problems are your own. You do not blame them on your mother, the ecology, or the president. You realize that you control your own destiny."

—Albert Ellis

The major method of treatment is to uncover the client's dysfunctional belief system and to change it. Cognitive counselors help their clients understand cognitions that are sources of problems, as well as themes of cognition, emotions, and behaviors (Sharf, 2000). This involves assessment, individual or group treatment, and homework.

Problems and settings where cognitive therapy is used. Cognitive therapy has been widely used in inpatient and outpatient therapy, substance abuse treatment, couple relationship enhancement, and marriage therapy. Ellis's Rational Emotive Behavior Therapy (REBT) is often used to treat adults, adolescents, and children in individual counseling and group therapy. Beck's cognitive therapy has been the treatment of choice for many clinicians for the individual treatment of depression, but it has also been used for panic and social anxiety and in group and in couples counseling.

Is cognitive therapy effective? Cognitive therapy gained support initially because of its effectiveness in treating depression (Beck, Rush, Shaw, & Emery, 1979; Dobson, 1989) and anxiety (Butler, Chapman, Forman, & Beck, 2006). Today more research is being conducted on cognitive therapies than on any other approach. Prochaska and Norcross (2010) call it the "blue chip growth selection" of the next five years because it is "relatively brief, extensively evaluated, medication compatible, problem focused, and demonstrably effective" (p. 332).

Anxiety disorders such as social anxiety, panic disorder, specific phobia, and post-traumatic stress disorder have all been found to respond to cognitive therapy. In addition, cognitive therapy has been used extensively for the treatment of alcohol and drug addiction (Marlatt & Donovan, 2005) and as a treatment for marriage relationships (Baucom, Epstein, & La Taillade, 2002). In some instances, cognitive therapy has been effective with children and adolescents (see Butler et al., 2006), but it has been mainly used with adults.

Common dimensions of human nature applied to cognitive therapy.

1. Freedom versus determinism: Human beings are not only free but are responsible for their lives.
2. Rationality versus irrationality: Both Beck and Ellis believe that human beings would be better off if they were more rational, but it would be wrong to conclude that they suggest that human nature is basically rational. Rationality and irrationality are at war in human beings.
3. Proactive versus reactive: Human beings are more on the reactive end of the continuum. Ellis frequently quoted Epictetus, the Stoic philosopher who said that it is not what happens to you, but how you react to it that matters. On the other hand, some branches of cognitive therapy (constructivists) believe that humans are active and proactive and actively construct their worlds (Mahoney, 1991).

4. Homeostasis versus heterostasis: It appears that most cognitive therapies see human behavior as homeostatic. In other words, human beings are not motivated to grow as much as they are motivated to reduce negative emotions. As Ellis (2003) said, the goal is to stop "upsetting" oneself (p. 71).

5. Changeability versus unchangeability: Cognitive therapy falls towards the changeable end of the continuum, like all psychotherapies; however, changing thoughts and beliefs is still considered very difficult. Albert Ellis said that it can be as hard as convincing a Catholic priest that there is no God.

Important contributors to cognitive counseling. Both Aaron Beck and Albert Ellis, the two key founders of cognitive therapy, were former psychoanalysts who independently recognized the role of cognition in emotional distress. Both have been named among the most influential therapists in history.

Aaron Beck developed cognitive therapy based on his work with depressed patients. He identified the **cognitive triad**, a schema that involved negative views of self, others, and the world. His Socratic method and guided discovery techniques involve uncovering the client's schemas and helping the client develop experiments which can prove that his or her view of the world needs to change. The client weighs the options of keeping or revising his or her core beliefs. Beck published 17 books and about 500 articles.

Albert Ellis developed Rational Emotive Behavior Therapy in its original form in the 1950s. Until his death in 2007 at the age of 93, he continued to write and lecture in his charismatic, colorful, evangelical fashion. His confrontational approach as a therapist and in responding to critics as well as his espoused atheism and antagonism to religion made him unpopular to many. Ellis once claimed that he overcame his shyness at age 19 by introducing himself to 100 eligible women at the Bronx Botanical Gardens (with no luck). This incident taught him that one must test one's beliefs (such as "I will die if a woman rejects me!"). Ellis authored or co-authored about 80 books and more than 1100 articles.

Eclectic/Integrative Counseling

Eclecticism and *integration* are two words that essentially mean the same thing. However, *integration* sounds more as if you know what you are doing, so most of us prefer this term. Either way, it means that you do not have one particular theory that guides you; you may either combine two or more theories *or* have one central theory and utilize techniques from a variety of therapies. This hybrid seems attractive, but it has been roundly criticized, too. Eysenck (1970) declared that eclecticism is a "mishmash of theories, a hugger-mugger of procedures, a gallimaufry of therapies and a charavaria of activities having no proper rationale and incapable of being tested or evaluated" (p. 19). Big words! But eclecticism has come a long way in the 40 years since Eysenck's statement, and eclecticism/integration has gone beyond the mishmash stage and, in fact, has much to recommend it. For example, Prochaska and Norcross (2010) identify the following findings that have come to light since Eysenck's comments that support the progress of eclectic/integrative counseling:

1. There has been a growing awareness that no single theory works for all clients or for all problems.
2. In head-to-head comparisons, no one theory has emerged as superior.
3. Common factors such as the therapeutic relationship are far better predictors of outcome than any particular theory of the counselor.
4. Brief, problem-focused treatments are wanted by clients and by third-party payers.
5. Clinicians are now more exposed to other theoretical orientations and techniques, allowing us to see value in other points of view.
6. There are now organizations and journals that publish on eclectic and integrative practice (e.g., Society for the Exploration of Psychotherapy Integration and their *International Journal of Psychotherapy Integration*).

Some eclectic/integrative models are a blending of two or more theories (syncretism). The practitioner needs to (1) be fully trained in both, and (2) consider the inconsistencies that might result in the practice of this hybrid. Among the most common syntheses are cognitive and behavioral, Rogerian/humanistic and cognitive, and psychoanalytic and cognitive.

A systematic eclecticism is best. There is certainly a recognition that sloppy, wishy-washy eclecticism in which theories were unsystematically combined is theoretically unsound and rationally indefensible. On the other hand, a **systematic integration** is more than a combination; it is a new model that allows for the blending of what is best and what works. Using one theory and including interventions from other theories is called **technical eclecticism.**

Eclecticism/integration is practical. Because eclecticism/integration cannot rely on its theory, it must defend itself on pragmatic grounds. Eclectic/integrative counselors use what works rather than what is theoretically consistent. Thus an eclectic/integrative practitioner is able and willing to adopt newly developed and evidence-based practices more readily than one who is entrenched in a particular theory.

Eclecticism/integration means tailoring counseling to the client. Much more than other theoretical positions, eclectic and integrative models start with the client and develop an array of interventions to fit the client's needs and problems. Thus, eclecticism/integration easily includes client preferences, religious and spiritual beliefs, and multicultural considerations. As you can imagine, some counseling techniques might actually be culturally or religiously unacceptable to the client. Thus, the flexible, integrative counselor can utilize a wider variety of methods while one who chooses a single theoretical position normally stays with techniques associated with the theory.

Problems and settings where integrative/eclectic counseling is used. All counselors learn common curative factors (an integrative notion) when they learn the basic skills of counseling (Young, 2009). For example, they learn the importance of establishing a confiding alliance with the client that connects all the therapeutic approaches (Gelso & Carter, 1985). Although theories vary widely, the necessity of developing a relationship built on trust and mutual respect is vital. Thus, most counselors use an integrative element or a curative factor every day in their work, an approach that is not owned by any particular theory.

There are few settings or populations that have not been exposed to integrative therapies (Kellogg & Young, 2009). Integrative approaches have been used in settings that range from work with children (Gold, 1996) to couples therapy (Long & Young, 2007). Because integrative therapies often attempt to modify the treatment to fit the client characteristics (see Beutler's Systematic Treatment Selection and Prescriptive Psychotherapy; Beutler, Consoli, & Lane, 2005), the populations and conditions treated are diverse.

Is eclective/integrative counseling effective? The difficulty in assessing the effectiveness of integrative approaches to counseling is that there are no major types to measure. The approaches are suited to the situation. As a result, they differ so widely that a definitive answer to this question cannot be given. Still, a number of integrative approaches have been studied. In addition, the approach is young. In general, it can be stated that integrative therapies are as effective or of greater effectiveness than control groups over a wide range of problems (Schottenbauer, Glass, & Arnkoff, 2005).

Common dimensions of human nature applied to eclective/integrative therapy. Eclecticism, by its very nature, does not have one theoretical base, and thus it takes no stand on the basic assumptions about human nature applied to counseling theory. Each individual who practices eclectic/integrative counseling probably has individual answers to these questions based on her or his experience, beliefs, and study of other counseling theories.

Important contributors to eclectic/integrative counseling.

Arnold Lazarus (1981) developed multimodal therapy and introduced the concept of technical eclecticism. This approach advocated adding and modifying techniques to fit the therapist's own theory rather than merging or melding theories. Lazarus advocated "broad spectrum" assessment and client-specific interventions, key concepts of integrative therapy.

Paul Wachtel's (1977) work on integrating behavior therapy and psychoanalysis has become well known, especially in the area of the therapeutic relationship.

Marvin Goldfried (1980, 1995) and **Jerome Frank** (1961, 1974) both identify common factors and basic therapeutic principles.

James Prochaska and Carlo DiClemente's Transtheoretical model (1994) and stages of change have been significant contributions to research and treatment of addictions of all kinds. They identify client movement from pre-contemplation to relapse and recommend different treatments based on different levels of client readiness (Prochaska, Norcross, & DiClemente, 1994).

John Norcross, coeditor of the *Handbook of Integrative Psychotherapy* with Marvin Goldfried (2005), is the most prolific writer, supporter, and critic of integrative psychotherapy.

Rogerian/Person-Centered Theory

Carl Ransom Rogers developed an approach to counseling that he first called *client-centered* and later *person-centered.* As we have said, it has been the most influential theory for counselors, and Carl Rogers has been the most influential therapist of all time. His 1957 article, "The Necessary and Sufficient Conditions of Therapeutic Personality Change," has been cited more than 1000 times since 1980 alone (Elliott & Freire, 2007). In this paper, Rogers advanced his idea that the counselor must be genuine, have unconditional positive regard, and have accurate empathy (really understand the world of the client). Only when these conditions exist can the client make real change. What was so earth-shattering about this little nine-page paper? For one thing, Rogers focused on empathy rather than diagnosis as the first step. In postwar America, testing and diagnosis were in fashion. For another, Rogers focused the therapeutic endeavor squarely on the relationship. These relationship conditions were not only *necessary* but also *sufficient*—meaning no other methods were necessary. It was not what the counselor did, but who the counselor was. Rogers rejected any particular techniques as being crucial. Acceptance and understanding by the counselor were the vital elements. The therapy was nondirective, not emphasizing the counselor's expertise or cleverness but rather his or her humanity.

At least part of the decline of popularity that we see today in person-centered therapy may be due to its lack of "branding." Currently, every new technique has a certification program. Counselors who adopt a new technique often get a certificate and some letters after their name indicating that they are part of the *cognoscenti.* But, in the United States, Rogers never formed such an accrediting body and rejected attempts to regulate the practice of person-centered therapy.

■■■ *Fast Facts* ■■■

Carl Rogers was once named the most influential psychotherapist (Smith, 1982). Haggbloom et al. (2002) asked psychologists to rate the most influential psychologists including those in other non-clinical fields. Carl Rogers claimed sixth place. More than 25 years after Smith's study, Cook, Biyanova, and Coyne (2009) polled nearly 2600 therapists and again found Carl Rogers to be the most influential therapist by a landslide.

In the 1950s Rogers had conducted and emphasized research to support his ideas. But by 1964, he had all but given up university teaching, research, and individual therapy. He became involved in group therapy and world peace efforts. His absence from research in his later career certainly affected the direction and standing of the therapy he had created. Those interested in the fascinating life of Rogers should read Howard Kirschenbaum's biography and articles, which are informed by Rogers's personal diaries and extensive interviews (Kirschenbaum, 2004, 2007).

Despite Rogers's absence from research, person-centered therapy became immensely successful through the end of the 20th century. In fact, it is probably the success of the Rogerian approach that hastened its decline. It was up to others such as Truax and Carkhuff (1967) and Ivey (1971) to make Rogers's approach available by extracting the key techniques and describing them in detail so that they could be taught. Thus, Rogerian techniques became the basic skills that all helping professionals learn, and they are usually presented apart from the theory (Hill, 2004; Young, 2009). Empathy has been operationalized as skills such as paraphrasing, reflecting feelings, and reflecting meaning. In addition, these skills have been incorporated into other therapies (see Patterson, 1985) and now are seen as necessary *but not sufficient* for therapeutic change. Although person-centered therapy is changing in the United States, person-centered therapy is not dead. Today, European counselors are rediscovering the teachings of Rogers. Conferences, research, and institutes are proliferating.

Basic tenets of Rogerian person-centered theory. *Counseling should be **nondirective** in terms of allowing clients to talk about issues that are important to them.* Nevertheless, the counselor keeps the client focused on his or her cognitive and emotional experience of the problem, not just a recitation of the facts. Only the client understands the "true subtleties and complexities" of his or her life (Bohart, 2005). Clients need to arrive at their own decisions. In this regard, Rogers tells a story (Kirschenbaum & Henderson, 1989) that deeply affected him. In his early years, a prominent psychologist tried to talk him out of pursuing psychotherapy as a career. It was described as a mistake that "could never lead anywhere" (p. 24). Rogers's decision to continue in his career path and his ultimate success in the profession reinforced his belief that individuals know what is best for them. Goal setting is usually not a part of person-centered counseling. The person-centered counselor accepts people as they are and takes them where they want to go.

*The counselor tries to express **unconditional positive regard** for the client, not judging or evaluating the client's story.* The counselor strives to provide support, which is the optimal condition for growth. The counselor does not impose conditions of worth on the client, which helps increase the client's own sense of positive self-regard.

*The counselor shows **warmth**, which allows an emotional connection to the client.* Warmth allows clients to feel connected to their counselors in a manner that is accepting and nonthreatening. Warmth may be a difficult concept to quantify, but for person-centered counselors, it is important to expressing positive regard.

The counselor strives to be **genuine**. Counselors who are genuine act as their authentic selves and are not phony or fake. This includes self-disclosure by the counselor, when it is appropriate. It also means being congruent—where thoughts, feelings, and words match.

The work of the counselor is to reflect what the client is experiencing through **empathy**. Empathy is not merely reflecting the client's feelings but truly tuning in to the world of the client. The problem of low self-esteem is caused by the breach between "what I should be" and "how I experience myself." Empathy communicates **acceptance**, which allows the client to accept him- or herself.

Problems and settings where person-centered therapy is used. Because it is based on acceptance of the client, the person-centered approach has been influential in counseling clients who are culturally different (see Glauser & Bozarth, 2001). Much of the early studies were done with students (Champney & Schulz, 1983), including college counseling centers. Rogers's work with institutionalized individuals with schizophrenia had limited success (Rogers, Gendlin, Kiesler, & Truax, 1967). Rice (1988) found that person-centered therapy improved self-esteem more than other orientations.

In 1947, Virginia Axline published the book *Play Therapy*, extending nondirective counseling to children (Axline, 1989). Axline was among the founders of play therapy, and her work still forms the basis for much of what is practiced today. Person-centered counseling has become a mainstay of the approach to working with children and adolescents (Presbury, McKee, & Echterling, 2007). Unfortunately, person-centered work with young people has not been shown to be superior to other treatments (Weisz, Weiss, Han, et al., 1995).

Is person-centered therapy effective? In the 1980s person-centered therapy became less popular in the United States due to the factors mentioned above. Also, there were concerns about its effectiveness (Lambert, Dejulio, & Stein, 1978). In head-to-head comparisons, person-centered therapy has not been as effective as cognitive behavioral approaches (cf. Cottraux, Note, Yao, de Mey Guillard, Bonasse et al., 2008; Reicherts, 1998) but it is certainly better than no treatment (Greenberg, Elliot, & Litaer, 1994). What these conclusions miss is that person-centered therapy's emphasis on the *therapeutic relationship* has been incorporated into other therapies such as cognitive therapy.

Instead of leaving you with these ideas about the shortcomings of person-centered therapy research, we want to highlight two current trends: (1) the rise of motivational interviewing, and (2) a new emphasis on the centrality of the relationship as a common curative factor in all therapies. Motivational Interviewing (Miller & Rollnick, 2002) is a person-centered approach that includes a more directive therapist and an emphasis on focusing on the client's ambivalence about change. Motivational interviewing has been acclaimed by addictions professionals and other health care providers and its effectiveness is well documented. The second point is that when we look at **curative factors**, those curative elements that we find in most therapies, the therapeutic relationship is associated with change more than any specific technique, and the therapist is a crucial element in treatment outcome (Lambert & Okiishi, 1997). Norcross's (2002) book, *Psychotherapy Relationships That Work*, is an attempt to look at empirically supported relationships rather than specific techniques. In short, research is supporting the importance of the counseling relationship, something that Rogers espoused from the beginning. Many counselors now see the tenets of person-centered therapy as *necessary, but not sufficient* for therapeutic change.

Common dimensions of human nature applied to person-centered therapy.

1. Freedom versus determinism: Rogers's long experience as a counselor and working in groups convinced him that people make choices in their lives. On the continuum, he would be on the extreme end. Freedom is part of the basic makeup of human beings. People naturally grow throughout life toward more inner direction.

2. Rationality versus irrationality: Although Rogers may have believed that rationality was part of the basic personality of people and was enhanced as they grew, he did not necessarily believe that it was the best way to make decisions or deal with life. He sometimes talked about how he made some of his best decisions based on inner promptings and intuition (Kirschenbaum & Henderson, 1989).

3. Proactive versus reactive: Again, we find Rogers on the extreme proactive end of the scale. In Rogers's view, the fully functioning person was growing and was aimed at the future. People are naturally growing; what they need are the right conditions to flourish.

4. Homeostasis versus Heterostasis: According to Rogers, people are motivated to self-actualize, to be all that they can be. This places him firmly in the heterostasis camp. Thus the goal of human life is not to achieve balance, but challenge and growth.

5. Changeability versus unchangeability: While counseling theories all fall toward the changeability end of this scale, Rogers tips the scale with an emphasis on changeability built into the very fabric of his theory. People are constantly growing and changing due to the master motivating principle of self-actualization. Change is inevitable and one becomes more free and more rational through personal growth.

Important contributors to person-centered counseling.

C. R. Rogers formulated the basic tenets and did the initial research into person-centered counseling. His books and films had such an impact that he has frequently been named the most influential psychotherapist.

W. R. Miller (Miller & Rollnick, 2002) was not a disciple of Carl Rogers but developed his treatment of addictions based on person-centered treatment and rigorous research. His approach, called Motivational Interviewing (MI), involves expressing empathy, developing discrepancies, rolling with the resistance, and supporting self-efficacy (seeing the self as capable of changing).

 ## How Do Counselors Choose a Counseling Theory?

Sometimes the selection of a theoretical approach is predicated on the foundational beliefs a person holds and the type of counseling they wish to practice. For example, in this chapter's Spotlight on Pastoral and Christian Counseling, it is clear that the setting and goals of the counseling dictates the approach that the counselors will use.

For most counselors, however, the choice of a theoretical orientation is strongly influenced by their initial training program. Teachers and supervisors that they respect may have a personal perspective that seems sensible and available for learning. Some counseling programs ask students to adhere to a specific theory or philosophy, but most ask students to select one and use it as the initial foundation for their work with the understanding that they may later change their minds. As a personal research project, we suggest you talk to your professors and fellow students. Does your program subscribe to a particular viewpoint? Do the majority of the professors hold similar views? What are the orientations of your teachers? Ultimately, it is not a question of finding "the answers" but rather finding "your answer" (Halibur & Vess Halibur, 2006).

Your answer to the question about which theory to adopt might be to find one that is consistent with your personal life philosophy and past experiences. In the accompanying Snapshot, Dr. Richard Watts, a counseling professor and an Adlerian therapist, discusses how he decided to focus his theoretical approach.

Counselors also choose or change their theories as they gain experience. They see what works and what fits. In many ways this makes sense, because a theory should be able to work in the field. In fact, your theory might be shaped by the kinds of clients with whom you work. If you counsel adolescents, you might easily be persuaded to adopt choice theory (Glasser, 1998) (the new reality therapy). This theory places a great deal of emphasis, as the name suggests, on helping people recognize that the only person we can control is ourselves and that our choices are internal, not forced on us by the environment. You can imagine that this approach fits many of the problems affecting adolescents, who may have difficulty accepting responsibility for their actions. Similarly, if you work in a clinic where clients are limited

---

■■■ *Words of Wisdom* ■■■

"For most therapists, the choice of theory is a slowly evolving process, the result of study and, most important, supervised psychotherapy or counseling experience."

Source: Sharf (2000, p. 22).

Spotlight
Pastoral and Christian Counseling

Pastoral Counseling

Pastoral counseling is counseling provided by ministers, priests, rabbis, and other religious leaders primarily, but not exclusively, to their congregations. The American Association of Pastoral Counselors (AAPC) is an organization of ministers who work or practice counseling. The AAPC website (http://aapc.org) provides a registry of pastoral counselors with advanced degrees. Another related organization is the Association for Clinical Pastoral Education (www.acpe.edu). ACPE is primarily an educational organization that promotes better pastoral helping in all religious traditions. Their well-known training program leads to certification in clinical pastoral education.

Christian Counseling

There is not a single definition for Christian counseling because it is connected with a multifaceted religion (from Roman Catholics to evangelical fundamentalists) and not a therapeutic school of thought. Although some Christian counselors are trained and licensed as counselors, most are ministers or lay people practicing with little or no therapeutic training. This is possible because licensure laws for mental health counselors exempt pastoral counselors from the requirements for practice.

The American Association of Christian Counselors (AACC) is a Protestant evangelical organization. On its website, it offers referrals to licensed mental health providers with a similar viewpoint. Thousands of individuals belong to this and other organizations and thousands attend their conventions. The ethical foundations of the AACC, paraphrased from its website, are the following:

- Jesus Christ and the Bible are the models for counseling practice and ethics.
- Christian counselors are committed to a relationship with the church.
- Christian counseling is a "Spirit-led" growth process, helping people through spiritual, biological, and psychological interventions to "mature in Christ."
- Christian counselors owe their first allegiance to Jesus and also to client service, ethical integrity, and respect.
- Christian counselors respect the Bible's defense of human life, essential dignity of people, and sacred nature of marriage and family life.
- Christian counselors remember that they are representatives of Christ and the church and, therefore, they fulfill their social and professional commitments. See www.aacc.net/about-us/code-of-ethics.

Licensed professional counselors, whether they are working within a pastoral setting or not, often include the client's religious and spiritual

to six sessions, you might find that extensive history taking is not possible and that Solution Focused Brief Therapy or some other brief approach makes sense.

Finally, you might work in a place where everyone subscribes to the same theory, such as a substance abuse treatment center where everyone uses the disease concept or motivational interviewing. You might work in a family support center where everyone practices functional family therapy and receives training and supervision in that approach. So, your practicing theory might be guided by your place of employment rather than personal choice.

beliefs in their counseling. When counselors practice as Christian counselors, these beliefs tend to take a more forefronted stance. Those who engage in Christian counseling believe it enhances the therapy by building on the strengths of the client's beliefs. This is an argument for including these issues in counseling. Still, there are many controversies and criticisms that Christian counselors face, including the following:

- Is Christian counseling antigay? Or do individual Christian counselors differ on this?

- Can Christian counselors help those from different faiths or Christians of other denominations without trying to convert them to the counselor's beliefs?

- Does the Christian counseling stance of defense of life include those about to be executed or tortured or only preventing abortion?

- Is Christian counseling an actual theoretical position with a defined set of principles and techniques or are practitioners "making it up as they go along"? The Bible is not a counseling manual; it is a religious scripture.

- Should Christian counselors have to adhere to any counseling educational or experiential requirements? Currently, untrained Christians who advise people are not responsible to licensure boards and legal safeguards.

- Should untrained, unlicensed people be allowed to practice counseling when they do not have any required training in pathology,

suicide, marriage problems, or other serious issues that might arise?

- What happens to clients if theologically trained people emphasize guilt, sin, and shame, particularly when these concepts are unhelpful and unproductive, and possibly dangerous for some clients?

- If counselors operating within pastoral settings have little or no training in ethics or legal requirements, what happens to clients if the Christian counselor makes bad decisions about client relationships or client welfare or if he or she does not recognize legal or ethical situations when they arise?

- If some Christian counselors uphold certain values (e.g., the man as the head of the household, children should be physically punished for disobedience), what are the potential effects on marriage and family relationships?

- How can clients' rights (for example, those who wish to remain homosexual or want to end a pregnancy) be respected if they do not align with the counselor's beliefs, and how can unbiased counseling be ensured?

Although there is great interest in spirituality and religion in counseling (Miller, 2003; Richards & Bergin, 2005; Sperry & Shafranske, 2005), very little has been written on Christian counseling in the literature of the psychology and counseling organizations. This field is in its infancy, and there is little or no research data supporting, or refuting, the practices of Christian counseling.

On What Basis Should I Choose a Counseling Theory?

In true Rogerian fashion, we recognize that we cannot make this choice for you. It would be like buying you a suit without knowing the size. But we do have some suggestions to help you think about it. First, we suggest that you read extensively and, at the same time, withhold judgment if you can. Many people reject Freud out of hand until they actually read his work (try *On Dreams*, 1952). In short, you need more exposure to the varieties of theories before you can make a reasonable choice.

SNAPSHOT

Interview with Richard Watts, Adlerian Counselor

Richard Watts, PhD, Adlerian Counselor

What is your current job and experience as a counselor?

I am Professor and Director for the Center for Research and Doctoral Studies in Counselor Education at Sam Houston State University in Huntsville, Texas. I have been a counselor educator since 1994 and worked as a counselor in various private practice and pastoral counseling settings since 1989.

What kinds of clients seem to benefit most from an Adlerian approach?

A flexible and integrative approach, Adlerian therapy is used successfully with a diverse range of clients in a variety of settings because the focus is on tailoring the counseling process to the unique needs of each client rather than mere adherence to a theoretical model or therapeutic framework. Adlerian therapy allows counselors to be theoretically consistent and technically eclectic, and Adlerians use a wide variety of cognitive, behavioral, and experiential procedures. Adlerian practitioners include clinical psychologists, couple and family therapists, mental health counselors, psychiatrists, and school counselors.

What attracted you to this theory?

As I studied and tried on several counseling approaches in my counselor training, I saw many Adlerian ideas in the various other theories. As I studied the Adlerian model more closely, I was attracted to its flexibility. Using the Adlerian approach, I can be technically eclectic and theoretically consistent. I can go where the client needs to go and be who the client needs me to be as a counselor: a "therapeutic chameleon." Furthermore, Adlerian therapy was a positive psychology and strengths-based, encouragement-focused approach long before these ideas became popular in the field. Similarly, Adlerian therapy has historically attended to social equality/social justice and cultural diversity issues, and affirmed the positive role of religion and spirituality. These are a few of the reasons why I found (and continue to find) Adlerian therapy a useful approach.*

What is your favorite book about your theory?

It would be a tie between The Individual Psychology of Alfred Adler *(edited by Heinz and Rowena Ansbacher), published in 1956, and* Individual Psychology: Theory and Practice *(by Guy Manaster and Ray Corsini), published in 1982. The first book contains primary source material with annotations and explanations by the Ansbachers. The second was the book that first helped me grasp the complexity of Adlerian therapy.*

Can you describe a technique that you frequently use that comes from this theory?

One technique I frequently use that comes from Adlerian counseling is Acting "As If" and the extension I developed, Reflecting "As If" (RAI). The traditional Acting "As If" technique asks clients to begin acting as if they were already the person they want to be (e.g., a confident person). Using this technique, counselors ask clients to pretend and emphasize that they are only acting. The purpose of the procedure is to bypass potential resistance to change by neutralizing some of the perceived risk. The counselor suggests a limited task, such as acting "as if" one had the courage to speak up for oneself. The expectation is that the client will successfully complete the task. If the task is unsuccessful, then the counselor explores with the client what kept him or her from having a successful experience (Carlson, Watts, & Maniacci, 2006; Watts, 2003; Watts, Peluso, & Lewis, 2005).

What organizations and websites can serve as resources for someone interested in Adlerian Therapy?

North American Society of Adlerian Psychology (NASAP)
614 Old West Chocolate Avenue
Hershey, PA 17033
Website: www.alfredadler.org
Telephone: 717/579-9795
Fax: 717/533-8616
E-mail: info@alfredadler.org

Adler School of Professional Psychology
65 East Wacker Place, Suite 400
Chicago, IL 60601-7298
Website: www.adler.edu

After all, in this chapter, we only touched on four theories of the many hundreds that exist. Watch videos of famous and nonfamous people practice particular theories. Leave your options open as you collect the data on a wide range of theories.

Second, do not be afraid to consider the research evidence behind a theory or a technique. Just because a lot of people have faith in a particular point of view does not mean that it really works. Of course, one of the problems here is that behaviorists and cognitive behaviorists do most of the research. That does not mean that one should abandon everything else. At the same time, if a point of view has no evidence beyond the fame of the theorist, you might be skeptical.

Third, engage in self-examination. Go back over this chapter to see how your ideas match with the common dimensions of human nature that undergird the various theories. Reconsider those incidents and experiences that we asked you to note when you were thinking about those common dimensions. Does any pattern start to form? Another way to reflect is to engage with your fellow students whose ideas can help you become more aware of your own thinking. Ultimately, before you can pick a theory of counseling, you have to know yourself and your values, which will guide your selection of a particular theory. The opportunities for reflection at the end of this chapter and other chapters are ways of thinking about what you have learned, may help you consider whether you agree or disagree, and allow you to explore those theories that interest you. In this

■■■ *Fast Facts* ■■■

There are some common factors in all or most counseling theories. These include such things as developing a confiding relationship with the client and instilling hope. In general, common factors, when taken together, are more powerful predictors of success than specific techniques.

Source: Young (2009).

Counseling Controversy

ONE THEORY OR MANY?

Background: Some believe that counselors should, early in training, adopt a single theoretical position, while others believe that students should be exposed to a variety of theories. Consider the arguments on both sides of this controversy, and see what you think.

POINT: LEARN ONE THEORY	COUNTERPOINT: LEARN MANY THEORIES AND POSSIBLY COMBINE THEM
• Counseling is complex. Utilizing one theory simplifies the process. It is too early to branch out. Eclecticism or integration requires complete knowledge of many theories.	• One theory is severely limiting. What happens when a client does not respond to your theoretical position? For example, what if the client feels that discussing dreams and early childhood issues are irrelevant?
• If you know one theory completely, you, as a beginning counselor, will feel more confident. It is better to be fully versed in one theory than to have a little knowledge of many.	• In general, no theory has been shown to be more effective than any other, but some have specific techniques that have been shown to be effective. Therefore, it is better to learn the most effective techniques from a variety of therapies.
• Deciding on a technique to use with a client is simplified when you learn one theory. You learn the techniques associated with your theory and you apply them pretty much the same way with everyone.	• Probably no one except the founder agrees with all of the tenets of a theory. Not every aspect of a theory will be palatable to you. For example, if I were a psychodynamic practitioner, must I agree with the Oedipal complex since it is central to the theory?
• When using more than one theory, might a counselor include elements from one theory that are incompatible with another? In other words, is a person really making up his or her own theory?	• How can a counselor change and adapt to new findings while holding fast to one theory? If some new technique that does not fit with your theory is found to be effective with a particular problem, would you not use it?
• On what basis will you choose what is best from the theories you select? Will it be your own own feelings or thoughts?	• Many counselors choose a single theory based on what feels right to them. Is that a good way of selecting a set of guiding principles?

Questions to Consider

- Is there a middle ground between these positions? For example, could someone learn about two or three theories in depth?
- We have sidestepped the issue of eclecticism/integration here. Should the *beginning* counselor try to develop a hybrid of theories suited to his or her own personality?

As with most controversies, there probably is truth on both sides of this argument.

←———→

Evidence-based   **Clinical wisdom**

On the continuum, place an "X" where you think you stand on this issue.

chapter's Counseling Controversy feature, we offer two opposing opinions about the selection of a theory to guide your work. Now that you have read a bit about what theories can offer a counselor, consider what you believe about the two ideas presented. What strategy do you think you will follow?

Summary

I n this chapter, we discussed the role of theories in the practice of counseling. Counselors use theories of personality to help them conceptualize how people grow and develop, get their needs met, and interact with others and the environment. Counselors use theories of counseling to help them understand how people change. There are hundreds of theories that help counselors organize their thinking, but most counselors use one (or more) of about a dozen common theories of counseling. None of these theories has been shown to be better than any other, although some have more research than others to support their use with particular clients or problems. Theories are constantly evolving and changing, and counselors who adopt a theory (or theories) to guide their practice will want to continue to stay abreast of the research and writing in the field.

End-of-Chapter Activities

Student Activities

1. Now it's time to reflect on the major topics that we have covered in this chapter. Look back at the sections or the ideas you have underlined. What

were your reactions as you read that portion of the chapter? What do you want to remember?

_____

_____

_____

_____

_____

2. As you learned in the chapter, one of the reasons counselors adopt a particular theory is because of their own personal experiences. Select a theory from this chapter that most appeals to you. Consider messages from your family or experiences that you had as a child that align with this theory. How do your early experiences and messages influence your choice of theory?

_____

_____

_____

_____

_____

3. Now consider one of the theories that is _not_ appealing to you. What is it about that theory that makes it challenging for you to accept? Instead of just tossing the theory aside without further exploration, what can you do to more fully explore the theory so you have a clearer understanding of it?

_____

_____

_____

_____

_____

■ ■ ■ Journal Question ■ ■ ■

Review the common dimensions of human nature as the starting point for your journal. Recall your answers to the question "Where do you stand?" with regard to freedom versus determinism, rationality versus irrationality, homeostasis versus heterostasis, proactivity versus reactivity, and changeability versus unchangeability. As you think about these dimensions, what experiences shaped your beliefs? Did these beliefs mainly come from family, church, teachers, or were they the result of personal experiences? What personal factors other than these might influence you to adopt a counseling theory?

■■■ Topics for Discussion ■■■

1. As you can see, counselors are more likely to embrace cognitive and Rogerian/person-centered positions than most of their fellow professionals. As we said in Chapter 1, the person-centered theory of Carl Rogers is a foundational and historical element of the counseling profession. The adoption of Rogers by counseling may also be one reason that counselors are not usually psychodynamic, because these two theoretical groups differ sharply on their views of human nature. But why have counselors adopted cognitive therapy to such an extent?

2. Of the theories described in this chapter, which seem most attractive to you at the moment? Why?

3. We have not discussed psychodynamic/psychoanalytic theory very much in this chapter. We have mentioned Freud, but not those psychodynamic thinkers who came after him. Just because this theory is not popular, should it be neglected? Should every counselor understand the 12 theories identified in our list or merely adopt the one that seems best to him or her?

■■■ Experiments ■■■

1. Next time you have the opportunity to listen to a friend's problem, try using Carl Rogers's approach of listening, just being genuine, providing unconditional positive regard, letting the other person know that you understand. How hard was it to give up being judgmental and giving advice?

2. Consider the following list of words and phrases:

   a. I did great on the test, I was awful
   b. Large and small
   c. Easy and hard
   d. You are for me or against me

Now try to find a word or description that falls in the middle of each of these two positions. Human beings create these false dichotomies as if they must choose between two extreme positions. For example: I am good in math, I am terrible in math. In cognitive therapy, they call this black-and-white thinking. When a crisis occurs, do you imagine the worst that could happen or the best that could happen? Or do you recognize that the most likely outcome is somewhere in the middle? What are the consequences of thinking in extremes? What feelings might be activated by these opposing thoughts?

■■■ **Explore More!** ■■■

If you are interested in exploring more about the ideas presented in this chapter, we recommend the following books and articles.

Books

Halibur, D. A., & Vess Halibur, K. (2006). *Developing your theoretical orientation in counseling and psychotherapy*. Boston, MA: Allyn & Bacon.

Mearns, D., & Thorne, B. (2007). *Person centered counseling in action* (3rd ed.). Thousand Oaks, CA: Sage.

Norcross J. C., & Goldfried, M. R. (Eds.). (2005). *Handbook of integrative psychotherapy*. New York: Oxford University Press.

Schulyer, D. (2003). *Cognitive therapy: A practical guide*. New York: Norton.

Spiegler, M. D., & Gueveremont, D. C. (2003). *Contemporary behavior therapy* (4th ed.). Belmont, CA: Wadsworth.

Articles

Skovholt, T. M., & Ronnestad, M. H. (1992). Themes in therapist and counselor development. *Journal of Counseling & Development, 70*(4), 505–515.

Spruill, D. A., & Benshoff, J. M. (2000). Developing a personal theory of counseling: A theory building model for counselor trainees. *Counselor Education and Supervision, 40*, 70–80.

Watts, R. E. (1993). Developing a personal theory of counseling: A brief guide for students. *TCA Journal, 21*(1), 103–104.

Films

Kirschenbaum, H. (2003). *Carl Rogers and the person-centered approach* [60-minute DVD].

> Distributed by American Counseling Association, Alexandria, VA.

Shostrom, E. L. (Producer). (1965). *Three approaches to psychotherapy* [Motion picture]. (Available from Psychological Films, Inc., 110 N. Wheeler, Orange, CA 92669).

> These are the classic *Gloria* films. While the clothing and the words may seem dated, it is a chance to see three master counselors work with the same client. You may also find these at online video sites.

■■■ **MyHelpingLab** ■■■

To help you explore the profession of counseling via video interviews with counselors and clients, some of the chapters in this text include links to MyHelpingLab at the Pearson.com website. There are some videos that correspond with this chapter, and watching them might challenge you to think about these concepts at a deeper level.

• Under the heading "Theories," there are videos for more than 15 different theories and techniques. Take some time to explore the video clips that represent counseling theories and interventions that are particularly interesting to you.

How Do Counselors
Use Research?

In this chapter, we will:

- Discuss a model of counseling practice where counselors use research to help make decisions about their practice.
- Survey the major types of research that counselors can use and discuss ideas for how to translate the existing research into practice.
- Stress the importance of conducting your own research on your own clients or programs and give you general guidelines for how to accomplish this.

As you read the chapter, you might want to consider:

- How do counselors know that what they do works? What sort of steps might you take as a counselor to know if the interventions you are using or the programs you are designing have the best chance of success?
- What is your belief about the proper role of research in counseling? How will your belief about research affect your willingness to read and use, or conduct your own, research?

There is evidence that in general, counseling works. When clients go to counseling, most of them improve more than they would have if they were in a placebo or control group. More than 50 years' worth of research supports this statement. In fact, a seminal study by Smith, Glass, and Miller (1980) concluded that at the end of treatment, the average psychotherapy client is better off than 80% of the untreated sample. Clearly it is important for new counselors to know that there is strong evidence that counseling is effective for a multitude of client problems and concerns. But knowing that the general practice of counseling is effective does not mean that any *individual* counselor can have confidence that any *specific* client is improving, that any *isolated* technique or intervention is working, or that any *particular* program is effective. This is the goal of research. Counselors use research in a multitude of ways.

1. Counselors read existing research and scholarly writing in books and journals to know the most up-to-date interventions and programming that have been supported in the research.
2. Counselors measure the effectiveness of their own interventions and programs, typically with **outcome studies** that use pre- and postassessments.
3. Counselors engage in **action research** to better understand the process of their counseling and to reflect on the data they collect in order to develop an action plan for their counseling.
4. Counselors share the results of their research with others in the profession through conference presentations, publications, or reports, so that others might use the results to enhance their own counseling.

This chapter is about learning to *think* like a researcher, to be an investigator of understanding your clients, their world, and how best to help them. In some ways, adopting an investigative stance is like becoming a detective, and your client (or counseling program) is the mystery to be explored.

A note to the "statistic phobic": Most people enter the field of counseling because they prefer people over numbers. In fact, we have found that many of our students not only prefer *not to engage* in "number crunching," but, in fact, are extremely afraid of the whole idea of statistics and research. Many have had bad experiences in math or statistics classes and face their graduate-level statistics or research classes with dread. Rest assured. This chapter is not about statistics or math. It is about developing an inquisitive mindset—becoming an investigator—adopting a stance where you are constantly reflecting on your own work and looking for ways to make it better. Sigmund Freud viewed every case as its own research study. He believed the analyst (counselor) should become an investigator, learning the subjective world of the client and understanding the effects of the therapy for that person. That investigative nature has become a core belief in many more contemporary theories. Using scholarly research and writing and conducting research on your own counseling means carrying that inquisitive stance one step further—moving that investigative nature from a system of beliefs to a method of action.

Many counselors are afraid of research because they think it means complex methodologies and statistics. You might think that because those are most often the types of research studies that you see published in professional journals. But the reality is that collecting your own research can be as simple as asking a few questions before and after an intervention, and then making a simple graph of the results. It can mean collecting some written responses to open-ended questions after the completion of a program. Yes, research can be complex and statistically sophisticated, but it doesn't have to be. As long as your research answers the questions that you pose ("Do my students learn how to make assertive statements?" "Did my client become less depressed?" "Do the parents value the newsletters that I send home?"), then your research meets your needs.

Why Counselors Use Research

In an age of ever-increasing accountability, counselors are being called upon to show evidence that what they do works. Schools, agencies, hospitals, businesses, higher education—all of these settings have moved toward accountability-based operations. Traditionally, however, counselors have been more concerned about their relationships with their clients than with proving that what they do is effective. Many counselors, when asked what evidence they have that their work with clients is successful, might say, "I think they improve—or at least I hope they do. I know that I have very good relationships with my clients, and I put a lot of effort into working with them." Or, in the schools, "I know my work is successful because I am helping students develop essential life skills." However, few counselors are prepared to back up their claims with data.

But how do counselors really know that what they do works? How do they know what interventions have the best likelihood of success, and which ones may actually harm the client? How do they know that the programs they implement have the intended results? In this chapter, we will see why counselors need to use the existing research and literature to make decisions and how those decisions are made. We also will discuss how counselors can conduct their own research to determine their own effectiveness of their counseling or counseling programs. This chapter is not intended to take the place of a statistics or research class. Rather, we will encourage you to consider how research can inform your counseling practice and give you some general guidelines for how to use research effectively.

There are at least two major reasons why counselors use research. The first is a reactive approach that considers research as a response to external pressures. From this view, existing research is understood and research on our own counseling is conducted because other people, primarily those who pay for our services, want us to prove that what we do works. The second is a proactive approach that uses research to enhance the quality of client care. In this approach, research is a response to internal pressures—we want to know that we are providing the best possible care that we can for our clients. Both the reactive and proactive approaches are valid reasons for using research, and taken together, they underscore the importance of the role of research in counseling.

The Reactive Approach: Responding to External Pressures

More and more Americans are using mental health services. Estimates are that one in five adults will have a diagnosable mental disorder sometime during their life that will require treatment. In addition, many children require mental health intervention, and even more would benefit from interventions by a school counselor. Given this tremendous need, it is clear that there are insufficient resources. Therefore, priorities for funding must be determined.

In community and other agencies with limited funding, there is constant pressure to make sure funds are used in the most cost-effective way. There are a limited number of treatment hours available, or a limited number of groups or outreach programs that can be supported. Counselors who can prove the effectiveness of their interventions will have a greater chance of success in getting support for their programs, groups, and clients. In many hospitals and agencies, quality assurance models require ongoing investigation into the effectiveness of interventions in order to receive accreditation. Even counselors who do not conduct research on their own interventions must be sure that they are using the most up-to-date and relevant treatments for their clients.

Clinical and community mental health counselors as well as marriage and family therapists and rehabilitation counselors are faced with managed care and other third-party payors, such as insurance companies, that limit treatment. They also face funding for community treatment centers that is always inadequate to meet the needs. In this environment, counselors are increasingly being called upon to demonstrate the effectives of their counseling interventions. The ability to demonstrate treatment success is rapidly becoming the standard by which reimbursement is determined (Sexton, 1996). In other words, counselors who cannot demonstrate the effectiveness of their interventions may have difficulty getting on managed care provider panels or convincing insurance companies to pay for treatment.

The argument presented by these external funding sources is that counselors, just like all professionals, must be able to prove that what they do works. They must demonstrate that, in general, they use the most up-to-date and empirically supported treatment interventions. Further, they must support their claim that these interventions lead to treatment success. In this vein, insurers might argue, "We wouldn't allow treatment by medical doctors who couldn't prove that they were using the latest treatment with the greatest chances of success. Even if the doctor was using the most up-to-date treatment, we would also require that he or she demonstrate that the patients under his or her care actually gets better. The same standard should hold true for the counseling profession."

Within school systems in general, there is a large-scale movement toward accountability. Most people agree that what school counselors contribute to a school is important. However, in times of tight budgets, school counseling programs may be at risk. Whereas everyone in the school understands what the math teacher does—and math class is specifically linked to proficiency tests and other measures of accountability—fewer people understand and can demonstrate the direct impact that school counselors have on the success of the school and the students in it. School counselors must be able to show the effectiveness of their interventions, demonstrate to the principal and parents how their time is spent, and whenever possible, link their interventions to academic success. School counselors who can speak the language of accountability in relation to their own programs have a greater chance of receiving the support they need. The

---

■■■ *Words of Wisdom* ■■■

"A distinct professional identity [as a counselor] should integrate consumption and production of research as essential aspects of good practice."

Source: Wheeler & Elliott (2008, p. 133).

National Standards of the American School
Counselor Association (ASCA) recognize
the importance of evaluation of effectiveness. In their implementation guidelines,
they note, "You [the school counselor] will
need to continuously collect and evaluate
data and adjust your action plan accordingly"
(Dahir, Sheldon, & Valiga, 1998, p. 66). ASCA
includes in its rationale for this evaluation "to
be able to convey your successes to faculty,
parents, community members, and advisory
groups—and generate enthusiasm and sup-
port for your program" and "to have the data to demonstrate the success of your
program and its impact on students" (p. 66).

External pressures to work from a research base also can come from the legal
system. Counseling professionals must operate within the **standards of care** of
the profession. Standards of care can be defined as professional conduct as practiced by "reasonable and prudent practitioners who have special knowledge and
ability for the diagnosis and treatment of the relevant clinical conditions"
(Granello & Witmer, 1998, p. 372). These standards are determined by what others in the same discipline would do under similar circumstances. In order for
counselors to prove that they are operating within the standards of care of the
profession, they must be able to prove that the interventions that they used for a
particular client are "either considered standard practice or at least accepted by a
significant minority of other professionals" (Meyer, Landis, & Hays, 1988, p. 15).
One very effective way to support that what you are doing is considered the standard practice in the field is to point to existing research that supports your intervention. For example, if a counselor were using cognitive therapy with a client
suffering from depression, the counselor could point to a large body of research
that supports this intervention. If, on the other hand, the counselor were using
primal scream therapy with the depressed client, the counselor would have a
more difficult time proving that this intervention was supported by the most
up-to-date knowledge in the profession. Not meeting the professional standards of
care is considered negligence, which can ultimately lead to a determination of
malpractice (Granello & Witmer, 1998).

The reactive approaches, or pressures from external sources, are indicative of
the environment in which most counselors practice. Proving effectiveness to these
external sources may well influence—or perhaps even determine—whether funding is available (Granello & Granello, 2001). Using treatments and designing programs that are well situated in the research and scholarly literature can help justify
to courts, third-party payers, and school administrators why the chosen interventions have the greatest chance of success. All of these are valid and appropriate
reasons to keep abreast of the current research in the field and to initiate your own
research into the effectiveness of your own counseling. However, there are reasons
to monitor effectiveness that are internally derived that also must be considered.

The Proactive Approach—Responding to Internal Pressures

On the proactive side, counselors use research and data to make sure that their programs and interventions with their students and clients are the most up-to-date, have the greatest chances of success, and give every client the greatest opportunity for improvement. Keeping up with the research and literature as well as monitoring your own counseling and interventions is a form of quality assurance.

Imagine that you are a counselor working with a client who has come to counseling because she has panic disorder, a mental health disorder that is characterized by frequent and uncontrollable panic attacks. The panic attacks seemingly come out of nowhere and immobilize the client with fear. During these attacks, her heart races, her breathing becomes shallow, and her arms and legs begin to tingle. She thinks she is having a heart attack or running out of air. Her own cognitive reactions to the attack—thinking that she is dying—simply serve to escalate the physical sensations of panic. As her counselor, you use a variety of interventions, including teaching the client a relaxation technique called "progressive muscle relaxation." You reason that if the client is anxious and panicked, you should use several different techniques to try to teach her to relax, and you know that progressive muscle relaxation (PMR) is a standard relaxation exercise. Although this reasoning appears to make sense, the research shows that PMR actually has mixed results for clients with panic disorder, with some studies demonstrating that this technique can lead to higher rates of dropout among clients and may reduce the effectiveness of other interventions that may be used in conjunction with PMR (Beamish et al., 1996). In other words, even though you may know the general methods for interventions, and even though you may have the best of intentions for improving your client's functioning, not knowing the research in this instance could have unintended consequences. Although there are certainly external pressures to know the literature, this case represents an internal pressure. As a practitioner, you want to know that what you are doing with your clients has the greatest chance of success—or at the very least, the minimal chance of harm. As this case represents, keeping up with the research literature is essential.

Proactive approaches also mean using data—either existing data or data that are collected by the counselor—to make decisions. In agencies, hospitals, schools, and private practice, data-based decision making can be simply keeping track of the number of clients or students who need a particular service and then using that data to justify offering a particular service. It can be tracking client outcome so that counselors can monitor their success rates with different types of clients, making adjustments or seeking additional training as necessary. If, for example, a counselor collects data and finds that his or her clients show improvement overall, then that is validation for the types of interventions the counselor is offering. If, on the other hand, the counselor notices that clients who present with a particular problem or diagnosis do not seem to benefit from their treatment at the same level as other clients, then the counselor can focus his or her time and attention on learning more about the treatment of that disorder, including receiving more training or

Counseling Controversy

MANUALIZED TREATMENTS

Background: Within the mental health professions in general, there has been pressure by some to move toward manualized treatment. This movement recognizes that there has been a lot of research conducted on many different mental health problems (e.g., depression, PTSD, anxiety), and for many mental health diagnoses, there is an emerging consensus in the literature about the treatment that has the best chance of success. Those who support manualized treatment argue that the next step is to take the research results and develop them into a systemized method of intervention—a treatment protocol for the disorder. Counselors would simply follow a step-by-step manual that tells them what to do when working with a particular client. Those who oppose manualized treatment argue that counseling can never be brought down to these basics; it is more complex, multidimensional, and individually determined than can be outlined in a manual. Read the following arguments and see what you think.

POINT: MANUALIZED TREATMENT IMPROVES QUALITY OF CARE	COUNTERPOINT: MANUALIZED TREATMENT DIMINISHES QUALITY OF CARE
• Manualized treatments are empirically grounded. They make the most of what research has to offer. Rather than just a series of research studies tucked away in journals that no one reads, manualized treatments synthesize the existing knowledge to date on a topic and allow the clinician to know exactly what to do with a particular client. The clinician knows the specific interventions that have the greatest likelihood of treatment success. Manualized treatments are comprehensive, based in theory and research, and can be taught to clinicians to ensure optimal treatment.	• Treatment manuals limit the ability of counselors to deal with their clients as individuals. They are rigid, technique-driven, and typically come from only one theoretical stance.
• Manualized treatments may not work for every disorder, but there is a growing consensus in the literature about the best treatments for many mental health disorders. Manualized treatments provide the necessary guidelines for counselors to follow.	• Manualized treatment attempts to turn counseling and psychotherapy into a hard science, when it is not. Manualized treatments might make sense in medicine (e.g., take this much of this particular drug for the length of a treatment regime), but counseling is not medicine. Treatment manuals ignore the human side of the endeavor.

(continued)

(*Continued*)

• Manualized treatments are the most ethical—they make sure that everyone receives the treatment that has the highest chance of success. By doing so, they limit counselor exposure to charges of malpractice. They allow for further research to be conducted. If we know *exactly* what counselors are doing in any given session with a client, then we can make comparisons about treatment. Finally, they are time and resource efficient. Each counselor need not fully investigate the existing research on each disorder. Counselors can simply refer to the treatment manuals for a specific disorder to get a step-by-step guideline for treatment.	• The research upon which manualized treatments are developed is often done in laboratory-type settings, with clients who have just one specific disorder and therapists who rigidly adhere to a specific guideline. Because of the rigid adherence to a specific treatment strategy, other factors are, by necessity, neglected. Namely, the contribution of the individual qualities of the counselor, the nature of the therapeutic relationship, and the intricacies of clinical judgment are all ignored. In the real world of practice, clients often have several co-occurring mental health disorders and many differing demographic and individual characteristics. These real-world client differences make the rigid imposition of a set of guidelines culturally and therapeutically insensitive.
• The National Institutes of Health (NIH) is working to develop treatment manuals for adolescent substance abuse disorders and other mental health issues. The Clinical Psychology Division of the American Psychological Association began a Task Force as early as 1993 to begin to develop treatment manuals and has already released treatment manuals for several major diagnoses. The Center for School Mental Health Assistance is working to develop treatment manuals for children with mental health disorders in the schools. Clearly, all of these reputable national organizations recognize that treatment manuals provide a clinically useful and therapeutically valid tool for practitioners.	• Treatment manuals don't allow for clinical innovation. Rigid adherence to empirically supported guidelines means that counselors must follow only what has been supported in the past, rather than break ground with new treatment ideas that emerge from practice. In addition, treatment manuals are the imposition of research onto the field of practice, rather than a balance of research and practice. They force counselors to use methods that are most easily supported by research (e.g., cognitive and behavioral therapies) while reducing the emphasis on interventions that, although effective, do not lend themselves as easily to measurement (e.g., existential and humanistic interventions). Finally, and most importantly, they reduce counseling to something mechanistic and ignore the healing effects of the counseling relationship.

As with most controversies, there probably is some truth to both side of this argument.

◄───►

Manualized Treatment
Improves quality of care

Manualized Treament
Diminishes quality of care

On the continuum, place an "X" where you think you stand on this issue.

supervision. Because of the growing availability of research into treatment effectiveness, some researchers in the field of counseling have called for a greater reliance on manualized treatments. This approach standardizes interventions based on the latest available research. In this chapter's Counseling Controversy feature, we present the arguments for and against this type of regimented intervention strategy.

Within school systems, data-based decision making means using data (either new data or existing) to inform decisions. "School leaders who use data extensively have at their fingertips the information that supports a request or decision made" (Burgess & Dedmond, 1994, p. 52). Typically schools collect a lot of data, and much of it is stored away and never used. School counselors who use those data, or data they collect, can support both the need and the effectiveness of their programs. Existing data on attendance, for example, could be used to support programming decisions. Perhaps the counselor notices that attendance rates are significantly lower for children who live in single-parents households. In this case, the counselor might want to do some prevention programming for the children or assist parents with contingency planning. In other cases, school counselors might collect data on teacher or parental satisfaction with a particular counseling group or program. Those data could be used to support the extension of that program into other grades or with other children. In all of these examples, the use of data helps the counselor make the best use of the limited time and resources available. The Informed by Research feature in this chapter highlights the importance of research for school counselors.

Informed by Research
School Counselors and Outcome Research

The Center for School Counseling Outcome Research conducted research to determine the most crucial needs for research in the area of school counseling (Dimmitt, Carey, McGannon, & Henningson, 2005). The researchers used the Delphi Method, a strategy that employs a panel of experts in the field to generate ideas, gain consensus, and identify areas of discord about a specific topic. In this study, 21 school counseling experts, all national leaders in the field, were questioned about their beliefs regarding the best possible function of research in the field.

According to the study, the most important topics for future research, as identified by these experts, are the following:

1. Identifying best practices (providing school counselors with information on which interventions help students)

2. Documenting effectiveness (validating that what school counselors do makes a difference in the lives of children)

3. Understanding how research can affect change in the field (evaluating the impact of training and research on the field of counseling as well as education overall)

4. Identifying the most effective educational and supervisory approaches for training (understanding how counselor preparation programs can best prepare future school counselors).

Research studies such as this help develop a national research agenda for counselors. In this way, researchers in different settings across the United States can use their research to contribute to the profession in meaningful ways.

■■■ *Fast Facts* ■■■

A 2005 study asked practicing counselors to rate the degree to which research impacts their practice on a scale of 1 (low) to 10 (high). The average rating was 5.8, indicating the counselors, in general, recognize the relevance of research to the work that they do.

Source: Smith, Sexton, & Bradley (2005).

A 2004 study of practicing school counselors found 60% agreed or strongly agreed that research is relevant to their daily work as a school counselor.

Source: Bauman (2004).

Resistance to Research: Why Counselors Don't Engage in Research

Given all the reactive and proactive reasons to use research, it seems a bit difficult to understand why all counselors don't use research to guide their counseling practices. Nevertheless, several studies have revealed that there continues to be a segment of the profession who say they do not read research, do not engage in research, and believe that research has little or no impact on their counseling practices (Bauman, 2004; Cohen, Sargent, & Sechrest, 1986; Falvey, 1989; Smith et al., 2005).

Counselors who have resisted using research in their own work have articulated several major reasons for this stance. First, some clinicians have argued against research from a philosophical point of view. These persons argue that the invasion of accountability into practice negatively affects therapeutic decision making (e.g., Sherman, 1992). They argue that clinical decision making has always been the purview of the counselor, and to relinquish the selection of treatments or counseling interventions to other persons is to relinquish control of the counseling. Once counselors relinquish control to persons who have agendas other than client well-being (e.g., money) as their primary motivators, then treatment is affected. We agree that there are some important philosophical reasons not to base every therapeutic decision only on research or accountability. However, we argue that research and accountability can be useful ways to inform practice, not completely dictate every move a counselor makes.

A second reason that some counselors have resisted using research is based on the belief that the therapeutic process itself is not quantifiable (Mirin & Namerow, 1991). These individuals argue that describing what happens within a counseling session is impossible—even if a researcher were able to articulate the major therapeutic techniques or theories used, the interaction between the counselor and client is so highly individualized, it could never be repeated. Therefore, it does not make sense to try to describe it, replicate it, or measure it. We argue that the process of counseling may be difficult to capture (although not impossible, as you will see later in the chapter), but that the *outcome or impact* of counseling is more easily measured.

A third reason why practitioners resist research involves practical concerns. Many practitioners argue that they do not have access to journals and other venues for research, and if they do have access, they do not have the skills to interpret what they are reading. Others argue that engaging in their own research would be overwhelming, time-consuming, and complex. However, access to research is quickly becoming less and less of a problem as more and more information is available through the Internet and online journals. In addition, counselors who are members of the American Counseling Association and other professional organizations receive journals with the most recent and up-to-date research as a part of their membership benefits. As for skills, we argue that counselors must develop the skills to read, understand, and use research, and it is not sufficient to plead ignorance on this issue. Finally, we argue that conducting your own research need not be difficult. Research conducted by practitioners to measure their own effectiveness is not necessarily like the large-scale and statistically complex studies that are found in the research journals. This chapter, and other training that you will receive in your counseling courses, will help you understand how small studies with simple designs often are sufficient to answer the questions that you have.

How Counselors Use Research

We hope that we have convinced you that research is a fundamental component of the counseling process, regardless of setting. When counselors adopt an inquisitive stance about their counseling and clients, when they seek to find better ways to do their work, when they look for alternative solutions—we argue that all of these represent a "research approach" to counseling. In this section, we turn to a discussion of how specific types of research can inform practice.

In his book on using research to inform counseling practice, Rick Houser advocates for a **"practitioner-scientist"** model for counseling. This stands in contrast to the "scientist-practitioner" model, a common term in the field of psychology. The scientist-practitioner model emphasizes science and research as the major responsibility of clinicians. Houser (2008) turns the model around and argues that counselors are practitioners first, hence practitioner-scientist. However, counselors are *not only* practitioners, they also must be actively involved with the research in the field. Practitioner-scientists do not focus primarily on conducting their own research. They are primarily *consumers* of research. They use the research and literature for the benefit of enhancing practice. Practitioner-scientists use the existing research and literature to make practice-based decisions; they evaluate the quality of the information presented in the research and professional journals; and they determine the appropriateness of the research and literature for the populations with whom they work. Practitioner-scientists also typically engage in small-scale research studies on the job. That is, they evaluate the effectiveness of their own interventions and programs and make adjustments, as necessary, based on their results. This practitioner-scientist model is precisely the model that we advocate for in this chapter.

Counselors, then, use research to inform their practice. Research, as well as education and practice, all contribute to the knowledge base in the field. Practitioners draw from that knowledge base when they make their decisions in counseling, and they add to that knowledge base with the accumulated wisdom from their practice.

Using Existing Research and Scholarship to Inform Practice

By far the most common way that counselors use research is to read existing research and literature in order to help guide their counseling interventions and practice. You will undoubtedly be asked to use the existing research as you go through your graduate training. For example, you might be asked to develop a program or intervention that is based in the research literature, discuss appropriate interventions for certain types of clients or client problems, or analyze the appropriateness of specific assessment instruments for a particular multicultural population. You may be asked to write a research paper on working with clients with a particular diagnosis or problem. All of these assignments require you to use the research and scholarly literature in ways that are designed not only to answer a specific question, but also to prepare you for continuing to use the research literature after you graduate from your program.

When you complete your search of the literature and have copies of your articles, chapters, and books, you will see that the type of information you have collected comes in many different formats. Academic sources are scholarly articles and books that are written with the primary goal of advancing knowledge in a particular field. Academic (or scholarly) sources differ from information in the general knowledge base (see Table 7.1). Academic journal articles or books are rigorous, scholarly works that go through an extensive review process and are intended to help other scholars or practitioners in the field in their work.

Access to the Internet and online research databases has become the foundation for research in counseling. Counselors and counseling students use the Internet as the starting place for all of their inquiries, but using online resources for scholarly research requires specialized knowledge and skills. The accompanying Spotlight is intended to help you make the most of the Internet for your research, both as a graduate student and in your future work as a professional counselor.

There are many types of academic literature, and each contributes something important and useful to the overall knowledge base. The major classifications of scholarship and research are discussed below. As each type of scholarship is described, we offer a sampling of relevant

■■■ *Fast Facts* ■■■

Best practices come from an evidence-based perspective and empirical validation of what works. In the field of counseling, a special section is devoted to best practices in the *Journal of Counseling and Development* and other journals.

TABLE 7.1 Comparison Between Academic Sources and the Popular Media

	Academic Sources	General (Popular) Media
Purpose	Original research or scholarship, to advance knowledge in the field or to report on developments in the field. Discipline specific.	Current events, information, popular culture
Author	Written by scholars in the academic community or researchers in the field	Written by journalists
Audience	Intended for academic or scholarly audiences	Intended for general, nonspecific, nonspecialized audience
Reviewers	For journals, an editorial board of academic peers (with names listed in the front of the journal) engage in rigorous **peer review** process; for academic books, an editorial review process occurs at an academic publisher (or commercial publisher that specializes in scholarly books)	Typically not reviewed for accuracy of scholarship, although may be edited for content
Features	Lengthy, in-depth articles; graphs and charts, few or no ads, little color	Typically short articles with little or no in-depth coverage (although some literary and cultural magazines will include lengthy in-depth features); pictures, ads, often slick and colorful
Language	Academic or specialized language	Conventional or conversational language
References	Lengthy lists of references and citations so readers can refer to original sources	Typically do not contain references
Types	Academic journals, scholarly books	Newspapers, tabloids, newsletters, popular magazines, literary magazines, commercial books

articles from recent American Counseling Association journals. We hope you will start to get a feel for the breadth of topics that are covered within the journals and the ways that different types of scholarship can be used to help inform your counseling decisions.

Literature Reviews or Position Papers

Much of the information in counseling books and journals is in the format of a **literature review** or **position paper**. These narrative manuscripts do not include any new or original research, but instead organize, integrate, and evaluate previously published material into a meaningful and useful summary (Bem, 1995). As such, they clearly define and clarify a problem; summarize previous work in the area; identify relationships, contradictions, gaps, and inconsistencies in the literature; and typically suggest the next step or steps in solving the problem (American Psychological Association [APA], 2010). The authors of literature

Spotlight
Using the Internet for Academic Research

The availability of information on the Internet and its near-universal accessibility make it a tremendously useful tool for research. More and more, students are conducting their research exclusively on the Internet. Although the Internet can be a valuable source of information, it is important for counseling students, *emerging scholars* in the field, to recognize that the material on the Internet is of uneven quality. Academic journals and books have already been evaluated by scholars and publishers, but information on the Internet has no filters or review process. Thus, conducting academic research on the Internet is a specialized skill that requires thought, patience, perseverance, and a critical approach to the information.

Electronic Databases and Online Journals. Academic libraries at colleges and universities participate in a scholarly community of resources that includes electronic databases. These databases catalog academic journals and books that are available either online or through print resources. Electronic databases that catalog only scholarly works serve, in essence, as a clearinghouse for scholars. Material included in these databases, most commonly journal articles and scholarly books, has met the rigorous standards of the academic discipline. At present, most (but not all) academic journals are available in both electronic and print format. The electronic copy is a duplicate of what appears in print and has met the same rigorous standards of peer review. Your university pays a fee to allow students and faculty to access this material, just as they would

pay a subscription fee to have print copies available in the library. Other journal articles are not available electronically or do not have copies of the journal from previous years available in electronic format, and you will need to physically go to the library to obtain this information. There are hundreds of different electronic databases, and many are specifically tailored to particular disciplines. For example, your university might have access to PsychLit, PsychInfo, ERIC, or MedLine. All of these databases include scholarly information related to the field of counseling (PsychLit and PsychInfo are primarily for psychology and the social sciences, whereas ERIC is an educational clearinghouse, and MedLine contains information about medicine and health). Other databases are available and may be relevant to scholars in the field. You will need to search your library's electronic database collection to know what material can be accessed from your university. EBSCOHost is a popular, very inclusive database that many universities have available for their students and faculty. However, EBSCOHost contains both academic and nonacademic (general) resources, and users must differentiate between scholarly and general information. It may be useful for you to ask the faculty in your program which electronic databases they use and recommend for your college or university.

Search Engines. Popular search engines (e.g., Google, Yahoo!, MSN) allow users to access billions of websites that are available on the Internet. However, access to information is

reviews and position papers contribute to knowledge in the field not by creating *new* knowledge, but by aggregating *existing* knowledge in a way that others will find practical and useful. Position papers help set new agendas for the field, identify current trends, or pull together information from different sources in meaningful ways to help guide counselors in their work. Practitioners often rely on literature reviews or position papers to sum up existing research and provide insights for making practical use of the information.

not the same as access to *high-quality, accurate, useful* information. Google Scholar is a freely accessible search engine that indexes the full text of scholarly literature across a wide variety of disciplines. Students who have access to university libraries, however, will find that they often must pay a subscription fee to access the full text of articles in Google Scholar, whereas this same information may be available for free through the university's electronic databases. Thus, Google Scholar and other academic search engines (e.g., Elsevier, Web of Science) may be useful places to start an academic search, but to access the full text of articles, it may be most cost-effective to use the university's databases.

Websites. The Internet is a level playing field. Anyone can develop a Web page, and all information, from the highest quality to the most questionable, is equally available to anyone who browses the Internet. Kirk (1996) cautions that the Internet epitomizes the concept of *Caveat lector: Let the reader beware.* Students should exercise extreme caution in including information from commercial websites in their scholarly work, as most professors do not consider this information to meet criteria for academic work. If websites are to be used for scholarly purposes, there are five major criteria to help evaluate the quality of a website (Germain & Horne, 1997; Kapoun, 1998):

- Accuracy
  - Who is the author?
  - What are his or her credentials and affiliation(s)?
  - Do the affiliations indicate possibility of bias?
  - Does the website include contact information?
  - Is the information presented factual?
  - Does the author support information with evidence?
- Authority/Credibility
  - Who published the website (check the URL)?
  - If information is included from other sources, is it properly cited?
  - What is the domain designation:
    - .com: commercial, hosted by a company
    - .org: nonprofit organization
    - .mil: military branch of the government
    - .net: usually an Internet service provider
    - .gov: governmental website
    - .edu: educational institution
- Objectivity
  - What are the goals/objectives of the website?
  - What opinions (if any) are expressed?
  - Is the website a "mask" for advertising?
  - Use a critical eye and ask, Why was this written and for whom?
- Timeliness
  - When was the website produced? Has it been updated?
  - Are the links updated frequently?
- Coverage
  - Is the information accessible?
  - Do you have to pay an additional fee to access any of the material?

Consider some literature reviews or position papers published by ACA journals.

- Review of counseling children and adolescents through grief and loss.
  (2009) by A. Wilson. *Journal of Counseling and Development, 87,* 127–128.
- Motherhood in the 21st century: Implications for counselors.
  (2009) by S. Medina & S. Magnuson. *Journal of Counseling and Development, 87,* 90–97.

- School counselor accountability: The path to social justice and systemic change.

  (2009) by C. A. Dahir & C. B. Stone. *Journal of Counseling and Development, 87,* 12–20.

- Transgenerational trauma and child sexual abuse: Reconceptualizing cases involving young survivors of CSA.

  (2009) by K. N. Frazier, C. A. West-Olatunji, S. S. Juste, & R. Goodman. *Journal of Mental Health Counseling, 31,* 22–33.

- A strengths-based approach to promoting prosocial behavior among African American and Latino students.

  (2009) by N. L. Day-Vines & V. Terriquez. *Professional School Counseling, 12,* 170–175.

- When talking won't work: Implementing experiential group activities with addicted clients.

  (2009) by W. B. Hagedorn & M. A. Hirshhorn. *Journal for Specialists in Group Work, 34,* 43–67.

- Depression, sociocultural factors, and African American women.

  (2009) by V. L. Hunn & C. D. Craig. *Journal of Multicultural Counseling and Development, 37,* 83–93.

- Promoting overall health and wellness among clients: The relevance and role of professional counselors.

  (2009) by H. Fetter & D. W. Koch. *Adultspan, 8,* 4–16.

Counseling students who write research papers in their graduate courses are essentially writing literature reviews. Students are expected to make use of the existing scholarly research and literature to develop a synthesis that would be useful to practitioners or other scholars. That is, unless otherwise specified by the course instructor, a research paper in graduate school mimics the format and outline of a publishable literature review. A well-written paper in graduate school follows the same criteria for a well-written journal article and, in fact, can be submitted for publication in a professional counseling journal, as so aptly demonstrated by the graduate student authors in the accompanying Snapshot.

Quantitative Research

Much of the actual research that is conducted within the field of counseling is done through quantitative research. **Quantitative research** is a systematic, scientific investigation that uses quantifiable measures and employs statistical approaches to help understand certain phenomena under study. Quantitative research begins with the development of a research hypothesis, moves into collection of data, and then uses statistical methods to measure relationships or associations among the data collected.

SNAPSHOT
Graduate Student Authors

Graduate students may not think of themselves as potential authors or contributors to the professional counseling literature. Students typically see themselves as the *consumers* of journal articles, not the *producers* of them. Nevertheless, a well-written paper for a counseling class can be submitted for publication. Consider the experiences of these four student authors, all of whom had their class papers published in counseling journals while they were in their master's degree programs.

Maria Elliott was a first-year MA student when she wrote a paper for an assessment class. The assignment for the class was to use the existing research and literature to help counseling practitioners understand what they need to know when using a psychological assessment with a specific population. Maria submitted her paper to a state counseling journal, where it was published.

> **Elliott, M**. (2008). The Minnesota Multiphasic Personality Inventory (MMPI-2 and MMPI-A) and victims of childhood sexual abuse: A review of the literature. *Journal of Professional Counseling: Practice, Theory, & Research, 36*, 25–37.

Dallas Jensen was in his second year of an MA program in counseling and completing his internship at a college counseling center. He noticed that a lot of the students on his caseload were sleep-deprived, and he become interested in the topic of sleep disorders. When it was time to write a paper for his psychopathology class, he chose to explore the topic further. With some guidance and assistance from his faculty, the paper was submitted to a national counseling journal and was published.

> **Jensen, D**. (2003). Understanding sleep disorders in a college student population. *Journal of College Counseling, 6*(1), 25–34.

Sometimes students work more extensively with faculty members or other mentors to significantly expand upon work completed by the student. In these instances, students and faculty members might publish together, as in the following examples:

Matthew Fleming was in the second year of his MA program in counseling when he was struggling in his personal life to care for aging parents with Alzheimer's disease. Matt channeled his personal interest in the topic of caregivers into a class paper that eventually turned into an article in a national counseling journal. The article won the journal's Article of the Year Award in 2008.

> Granello, P. F., & **Fleming, M. S**. (2008). Providing counseling for individuals with Alzheimer's Disease and their caregivers. *Adultspan: Theory, Research, and Practice, 7*, 13–25.

Danielle Hayes was a first-year MA student who wrote a paper on using the psychological test, the Minnesota Multiphasic Personality Inventory, for persons diagnosed with multiple sclerosis. She worked with her professor and eventually submitted the paper to a national counseling journal, where it was published.

> **Hayes, D.,** & Granello, D. H. (2009). Use of the Minnesota Multiphasic Personality Inventory-2 with persons diagnosed with Multiple Sclerosis. *Journal of Counseling and Development, 87*(2): 227–233.

(continued)

(Continued)

The point is that all four of these students (and countless others who have published their work) were in their master's degree programs at the time they wrote these papers. All of them recognized (or were helped to recognize!) the potential use these papers had for other counseling professionals. We believe that this represents an important shift in how counseling students see themselves—moving from identity as a student to identity as a professional.

As you continue your work in your graduate program, why not consider moving one of your classroom assignments toward professional publication? We encourage you to talk with your instructor(s) if you are interested, to learn more about the process.

Quantitative studies use statistical procedures to determine relationships between variables. For example, if researchers want to know if a particular intervention is more successful for males or females, they would measure the differences between the genders on some measure of treatment outcome through statistical tests such as *t-tests, ANOVAs,* and *MANOVAs.* If researchers wanted to determine whether treatment outcome was related to other variables, they might use correlations or regression equations. All of these statistical tests (and others) are types of quantitative methods.

All quantitative methods make use of the concept of **statistical significance**, which is a mathematical tool used to determine whether the outcome of a study is the result of a relationship between specific factors or due to chance. If a finding is deemed statistically significant, it means that the phenomenon observed in the research is a significant departure from what might be expected by chance alone.

The significance level is usually represented as $p < .05$ (or sometimes, $p < .01$). In the social sciences, significance levels are typically set at .05 (less commonly, .01). Thus, if a finding is considered statistically significant, there is less than a 5% (or 1%) chance that the findings occurred simply by chance. Put another way, there is a 95% (99%) chance (the researcher has a 95% [99%] confidence level) that whatever phenomenon did not happen by chance. A "statistically significant difference" simply means there is statistical evidence that there is a difference; it does not mean the difference is necessarily large, important, or practically useful.

Efficacy studies. Much of the research on specific intervention or clinical treatments in mental health uses this approach. **Efficacy studies** use clinical trials to compare different approaches, most commonly different treatments for a particular disorder or problem. Clients are randomly assigned to either different treatment groups or, more commonly, to a treatment group or a placebo or control group. Participants must meet stringent criteria for a mental health disorder or specific problem, and the intervention protocols used are rigidly adhered to. Everything is held constant *except* the actual intervention. Efficacy studies have always been considered the gold standard of quantitative research and are the most common types of studies in the field of medicine.

Meta-analysis is a specific quantitative methodology where the results of many efficacy studies are combined into one large study to measure the overall effect of an intervention. Researchers who use meta-analyses do not conduct their own research. Instead, they use existing published research, pull out the data from these studies, and combine these existing data together. Meta-analyses use highly specialized statistical techniques to combine the data from all the published efficacy studies into one large data set so that the study has greater **statistical power**, or ability to uncover differences between groups in research. Small studies tend to have low statistical power. Studies with low statistical power often cannot distinguish differences between treatment and control groups, even if such differences do exist. Larger studies (either through large numbers in a single efficacy study or through combining several individual efficacy studies in a meta-analysis) are more powerful and can more easily detect these differences. Statistical power is an important concept in all quantitative research, not just meta-analysis.

The magnitude of the differences between treatment and control groups is expressed in **effect size**. Effect sizes help counselors who read research to know the amount of change that the treatment produced. Remember, just because a research study finds a statistically significant difference between two groups does not mean that the difference is very large or very useful to know. As a general rule, the stronger (or higher) the effect size, the more compelling the evidence that the statistically significant results are useful for counseling practice. Small effect sizes mean that the intervention being investigated produced negligible differences. Savvy consumers of research know that there is a difference between statistically significant findings and finding that are *practically significant*. Consider this example. Let's say an agency moves into your town and advertises that they have research that proves their clients have *statistically significant improvement* on their scores on the Graduate Record Exam (GRE). In fact, they advertise that if you are willing to participate in their program, they guarantee your score will improve. Here's the catch. The program costs $3,000 and takes 7 weeks of study. Would you do it? What if you needed to improve your GRE scores to get into graduate school, and this was *very, very important* to you? Would this be worth it? The point is, it's hard to make a decision without knowing the *effect size* of their research. What if their research shows that the average improvement is 5 points on the GRE? If there were enough individuals in the study, the 5-point difference on the GRE between the treatment and control group might be statistically significant (e.g., there is sufficient *statistical power* to detect this difference). However, the *practical significance* of the intervention is less impressive. Few students would be willing to engage in an expensive and exhaustive GRE preparation program for a 5-point improvement in their scores. Thus, the *effect size* is small, limiting the practical utility of the intervention. Counselors will want to know the effect size, or expected magnitude of the change that results from the treatment, before they implement interventions or programs based on the research.

Efficacy studies have high **internal validity**. That is, researchers have confidence that any differences between the groups at the end of the study are due to the differences in treatment interventions, as all other factors are controlled for by the random assignment (in other words, both the treatment and control group have the same demographic makeup, the same level of symptom severity, the same amount of time elapsed, etc.). For example, a study that compared Cognitive-Behavioral Therapy (CBT) versus antianxiety medications for clients with panic disorder could allow clinicians to have great confidence in knowing whether clients with panic disorder would benefit more from CBT or medication.

However, there are some significant problems that efficacy studies cannot overcome (Granello & Granello, 2001). For example, although in laboratory studies it is possible to find clients who have just the highly specific disorder under study, in the real world, clients come to counseling with a multitude of coexisting problems and disorders, a situation called **comorbidity**. It is impossible to know whether the treatment that was supported in the efficacy study would work well for these clients, too. Further, efficacy studies support only a very specific treatment intervention. Again, this might work well in laboratory settings, but in clinical practice, clients might have several problems and might receive several different types of interventions (for example, CBT for their panic disorder, medications for high blood pressure, vocational counseling, and case management for problems with housing due to unemployment). Thus, it is impossible to say which of these interventions (or all of them combined) truly had an effect on the client's outcomes. Additionally, most counseling is not for a specified period of time (as is the case in efficacy studies). Counseling continues until there is significant improvement. Counselors who use a particular type of intervention change course if clients don't improve. In other words, just because an efficacy study might support CBT for clients with panic disorder, a counselor might switch to another type of intervention if CBT does not help a client improve in a reasonable amount of time. Finally, in many real-world situations, there is no opportunity for "random assignment." School counselors do interventions with classrooms, and all students must be included. Half of the students can't be put into the hall as part of a control group. Clients who are suicidal must be given the best available treatment; they can't be put into a placebo group. The point is that efficacy studies, while important, cannot answer all questions. They have high internal validity but low **external validity**, meaning that the results of these highly controlled laboratory studies cannot be easily generalized to clients and programs in the real world. Counselors use efficacy studies to inform their counseling, but they must be open to using other types of research as well.

Consider some of the efficacy studies published by ACA journals. Each uses random assignment to compare the effects of an intervention versus an alternative treatment, a placebo, or a control group.

• Comparison of explicit forgiveness interventions with an alternative treatment: A randomized clinical trial.

(2009) by N. G. Wade, E. L. Worthington, Jr., & S. Haake. *Journal of Counseling and Development, 87,* 143–151.

- Exercise and functioning level of individuals with several mental illness: A comparison of two groups.

  (2009) by A. S. Perham & M. P. Accordino. *Journal of Mental Health Counseling, 29,* 350–362.

- The effects of Cuento Therapy on reading achievement and psychological outcomes of Mexican-American students.

  (2009) by S. Z. Ramirez, S. Jain, L. L. Flores-Torres, R. Perez, & R. Carlson. *Professional School Counseling, 12,* 253–262.

- The effectiveness of individual wellness counseling on the wellness of law enforcement officers.

  (2008) by H. Tanigoshi, A. P. Kontos, & T. P. Remley, Jr. *Journal of Counseling and Development, 86,* 64–74.

Effectiveness studies. Effectiveness studies attempt to assess outcomes in the less than ideal situations that often exist in the real world, focusing on how well clients fare under treatment as it is actually practiced in the field (Granello, Granello, & Lee, 2000). Effectiveness studies recognize that random assignment of clients may not be possible; that clients come with comorbid disorders, multiple treating professionals, and different interventions; and that everyone must receive the best clinical care possible, making placebo and control groups unethical in practice. As a result, effectiveness studies have high external validity (if clients in the study get better, in spite of all of the problems inherent in the design, then chances are the clients on the caseload of the counselor reading the study will improve, too), but low internal validity (it is impossible to say, since the variables in the study are not isolated, *what exactly* helped the client improve). Clearly, effectiveness studies have a place in counseling research, but they do not answer all the questions raised about effective treatment.

Consider some of the effectiveness studies published by ACA journals. Each explores the effectiveness of an intervention, but none uses true random assignment and several do not use a control or comparison group.

- Using personal growth groups in multicultural counseling courses to foster students' ethnic identity development.

  (2008) by P. C. Rowell & J. M. Benshoff. *Counselor Education & Supervision, 48,* 2–15.

- From childhood to adulthood: A 15-year longitudinal career development study.

  (2008) by A. A. Helwig. *Career Development Quarterly, 57,* 38–50.

- Increases in academic connectedness and self-esteem among high school students who serve as cross-age peer mentors.

  (2009) by M. Karcher. *Professional School Counseling, 12,* 292–299.

Nonexperimental quantitative research. Not all research involves implementing a treatment or intervention. Some research is based on the administration of surveys to counselors, counseling students, clients, or parents. Other research involves comparing characteristics, behaviors, or personality traits of different segments of the population or observing people in specific situations. Still other research attempts to development assessments or determine their appropriateness for certain groups.

Even without the introduction of an intervention to measure, this research is still quantitative because it involves careful quantification of the variables involved. Researchers use a variety of statistical methods, many of which may be familiar to you (e.g., ANOVAs, regression analysis, factor analysis, correlations, chi-square) to conduct these studies.

Consider some of the nonexperimental studies published by ACA journals.

- Factors affecting African American counselors' job satisfaction: A national survey.

  (2009) by C. Jones, T. H. Hohenshil, & P. Burge. *Journal of Counseling and Development, 87,* 152–158.

- Examining variation in attitudes toward aggressive retaliation and perceptions of safety among bullies, victims, and bully/victims.

  (2009) by C. P. Bradshaw, L. M. O'Brennan, & A. L. Sawyer. *Professional School Counseling, 12,* 10–21.

- A brief version of the Family Background Questionnaire.

  (2009) by T. P. Melchert & A. Kalemeera. *Measurement & Evaluation in Counseling and Development, 41,* 210–222.

- Perceptions of clients and counseling professionals regarding spirituality in counseling.

  (2009) by J. Q. Morrison, S. M. Clutter, E M. Pritchette, & A. Demmitt. *Counseling and Values, 53,* 183–194.

■■■ *Words of Wisdom* ■■■

"I see now that before I started to really read the therapy research on my own, my work was really narrow—basically reflective of my own theoretical views or that of my professors or program. This is understandable, all systems have constraints. Through delving into the research my eyes were opened to many, many new ways of working with clients."

—Kate V., Marriage and family trainee,
California State University, Sacramento

Qualitative Research

Qualitative research is used to gather a more in-depth understanding of behavior and the reasons that motivate that behavior. Qualitative methodologies are many (e.g., ethnographic studies, grounded theory, phenomenological research), but the primary purpose is for the researcher to gain an in-depth understanding of the "why" of a phenomenon, whereas quantitative research often focuses on the "what" or the "how." According to Kline, "the promise [of qualitative research in counselor education] is discovering concepts that further the conversation and deepen an understanding [about counseling], initiating research to address the gaps in knowledge . . . and challenging what we believe we know about our profession" (2008, p. 214). Unlike quantitative research, qualitative research is not concerned with concepts like generalizability, random sampling, or statistical significance. Rather, qualitative research seeks to describe in more detail the lived experiences of a few individuals to provide depth, rather than breadth, to the research.

Qualitative history does not share the same history as quantitative research in the counseling profession, and it has only been relatively recently that counseling journals have become open to publishing research with qualitative designs. Most in the profession see this shift toward acceptance of qualitative research as particularly appropriate for counseling, which by philosophy and approach shares many core principles with qualitative research. For example, qualitative research is open to describing the experiences of diverse people, to exploring emotions, and to abandoning search for "the truth" in favor of a search for understanding. Whereas quantitative research seeks to categorize the experiences of participants, qualitative research seeks to *explore* these experiences. Neither quantitative nor qualitative research offers a panacea for the counseling profession, as both have significant limitations. Taken together, however, they can provide a complementary approach to assisting counselors satisfy their innate curiosity about the counseling profession, clients, and the "research approach" to counseling. In general, the combination of quantitative research, in tandem with and often informed by qualitative research, helps counselor educators, supervisors, counseling students, and practicing counselors make informed choices about what interventions they choose to employ, or avoid, in their work. In fact, some studies make use of both quantitative and qualitative components, called **mixed methods** that allow for the strengths of each type of research to support the investigation.

Consider some of the qualitative studies published by ACA journals.

- Succeeding in school: A qualitative study of primarily American Indian students' use of an online intervention.

  (2008) by B. Zyromski, A. Bryant, Jr., B. D. Deese, & E. R. Gerler, Jr. *Professional School Counseling, 12,* 119–122.

- Partner-related rehabilitation experiences of lesbians with physical disabilities: A qualitative study.

  (2009) by B. Hunt, A. Milsom, & C. R. Matthews. *Rehabilitation Counseling Bulletin, 52,* 167–178.

- Triadic supervision and its impact on the role of the supervisor: A qualitative examination of supervisors' perspectives.

  (2008) by S. Hein & G. Lawson. *Counselor Education & Supervision, 48,* 16–31.

Program Evaluation

Program evaluation is used to measure the effectiveness of either a specific activity (e.g., a group counseling intervention for college students who self-injure) or an entire counseling program (e.g., a comprehensive school counseling program). There are four major types of program evaluation: context evaluation (needs assessment), input evaluation, process evaluation, and product evaluation (Gredlar, 1996). Within each of these types of evaluation, researchers use quantitative and qualitative data to inform decision making, and thus, this methodology does not fit neatly under the heading of either quantitative or qualitative design.

The central decision for all organizations is, what is the best way to spend the available resources, including time, money, and organizational efforts, to meet all the demands (needs) that compete for them? Such decisions may be based on intuition, political pressures, past practices, or personal preferences, but one of the most effective ways to decide such issues is through a **context evaluation** or **needs assessment** (Witkin & Altschuld, 1995). A needs assessment is a systemic set of procedures to determine the most pressing needs of any organization in order to set priorities. A needs assessment is, essentially, examining the gap between "what is" and "what should be." To conduct needs assessments, counselors gather information from a variety of sources (e.g., key informants, existing data, surveys of affected constituents) and develop action plans to implement the findings.

Input evaluation is assessing the available resources (Loesch & Ritchie, 2005). For example, school counseling students might engage in **community mapping**, a strategy designed to better understand the resources available in the neighborhood surrounding a school building. Developing an understanding of the existing resources is essential. It is easy to say "we don't have enough"—but in an age of tight budgets, it is important to make the best use of all available assets.

Process evaluation involves evaluating a program *as it is occurring*, rather than waiting until after its completion to measure outcomes (Hadley & Mitchell, 1995). The goal of process evaluation is to determine whether the program should continue as is, be altered, or be discarded (Loesch & Ritchie, 2005). It is appropriate for all direct service activities as well as model and demonstration projects. Sample questions for a process evaluation are used to prompt the counselor to critically analyze the progress to date and make intentional choices about next steps. In the following questions, "services" or "program" can mean any counseling program or intervention under scrutiny, and "clients" or "staff" can mean actual counseling clients, students, parents, school personnel, members of the community, or anyone affected by the program. Sample questions for process evaluation:

- What are the goals and specific objectives of [the project]?
- For each objective, what steps have been taken?
- How are the steps accomplished?
- What resources and inputs were/are needed for each step?
- What are the characteristics of the client(s) served?
- Do the clients served so far match the targeted group?
- What targeted groups continue to be underrepresented? Why?
- Does the number of clients receiving services match the projected goal? If not, why not?
- How satisfied are the clients with the services provided?
- How satisfied is the staff? Are there any aspects of the program's operation that the clients or the staff believe should be changed? Why?

Product evaluation is synonymous with outcome research. It involves assessing outcomes of a program after the program is complete. With product evaluation, the focus is *on the program* being evaluated, not the clients. Therefore, research not only answers whether clients improved, but what components of the program were most effective in producing change.

Consider some of the program evaluation studies published by ACA journals.

- The substance abuse counseling needs of women in the criminal justice system: A needs assessment approach.

  (2008) by J. M. Laux, P. J. Dupuy, J. L. Moe, J. A. Cox, E. Lambert, L. A. Ventura, & C. Williamson. *Journal of Addictions and Offender Counseling, 29,* 36–48.

- Combat stress reactions during military deployments: Evaluation of the effectiveness of Combat Stress Control Treatment.

  (2009) by A. R. Potter, M. T. Baker, C. S. Sanders, & A. L. Peterson. *Journal of Mental Health Counseling, 31,* 137–148.

Spotlight
How to Read a Research Article

Reading and understanding research articles are important skills for professional counselors. Students in counseling programs sometimes argue that they cannot read research articles because they do not understand all of the statistical methods employed. However, even novice researchers find that with the proper skills, they are well on their way to deconstructing the knowledge encoded in research.

Empirical (research) articles vary in format, but they generally follow a particular sequence (Granello, 2007). Understanding this sequence helps students decode the information in the article and provides a road map for making sense of the information.

Typical Components of a Research Article

Title, authors, and affiliations. After the title of the manuscript are the authors' names, generally in order of contribution to the research, with the project leader as first author. Institutions, affiliations, and contact information is always included. It has been our experience that students often fail to realize that this contact information is provided so readers can engage with study authors if they have follow-up questions or wish to learn more. Although authors are typically busy professionals who do not have time to do students' research for them, most authors are thrilled to receive an e-mail from a student who is using the author's work in counseling or academic work. We always encourage students to follow up with authors of articles that they find particularly compelling—it may even lead to a mentoring or networking relationship.

Abstract. The abstract is an "accurate, succinct, quickly comprehensible, and informative" summary of the manuscript (APA, 2010, p. 15). Abstracts are self-contained, and readers who

have access only to an abstract should have a basic understanding of all components of a manuscript. Typically, abstracts are written after the rest of the manuscript has been completed, thus allowing the author to identify and highlight the major findings of the research.

Introduction and Literature Review. The beginning of a research article introduces the specific problem and provides the reader with a background literature review. This review is focused and includes only research and writing that is relevant to the problem. The literature review is intended to "demonstrate the logical continuity between previous and present work" and to "develop the problem with enough breadth and clarity to make it generally understood by a wide professional audience" (APA, 2010, p. 16).

Methods. This section provides details on how the research was conducted. It typically includes the research design (what steps or procedures were undertaken, including an explanation of the treatment or intervention for experimental designs); sample (who was studied, the response rate if survey methodology was used, and sample demographics); and instrumentation (surveys, assessments, or other methods to measure quantitative data or record qualitative findings).

Results. The results section "summarizes the data collected and the statistical or data analytic treatment used" (APA, 2010, p. 20). In the results section, results from all statistical tests are included, whether or not they support the original hypotheses or are statistically significant. In many cases, data can be present with the aid of tables or figures. When reporting statistical information, authors should provide "sufficient information to help the reader fully understand the analyses conducted" (APA, 2010, p. 23). The results section is not a place for commentary or discussion. For quantitative studies, the results section should include the power of the statistical tests (the ability of the statistics to detect relationships between variables) and the effect size (or magnitude of the relationship between the variables).

Discussion. The discussion section of a manuscript focuses on "credibility, generalizability, and robustness" of the research (Wilkinson et al., 1999, p. 602). In this section, authors "examine, interpret, and qualify the results [of the study, and] . . . draw inferences from them" (APA, 2010, p. 26). This is where authors compare their results with those from previous studies and theory. Also included in this section is a discussion of the *limitations* of the current research Careful and thoughtful recommendations or implications for future research are essential components of the discussion section.

References. Scholars know that the reference section of any journal article is a good place to look for additional resources and references.

Appendices. Following the references are any appendices needed to fully understand the research, such as tables of findings, transcripts from qualitative research, and questionnaires, surveys, or examples of forms used in the research.

Tips for Reading a Research Article

In Chapter 5, we discussed some strategies for getting the most from your reading in graduate school. In addition to those general strategies, there is a specific standard, recognized strategy for reading a research article. Typically, research articles not read from beginning to end. Most beginning researchers find the following strategy particularly useful as they learn to read research (adapted from Wadsworth Cengage Learning, n.d.)

1. Read the abstract first. It is a brief summary of the research questions, methods, and findings. Abstracts often contain dense psychological language, and it may be helpful to read it over a couple of times and try to restate it in your own (nontechnical) language.

2. Read the introduction and literature review. This helps contextualize the research in the current state of research and professional literature about the topic. The literature review ends by stating the research hypotheses or purpose of the current study.

3. Read the discussion section. Skip over the methods and results for the moment. The discussion section will explain the major findings of the research in detail. This is particularly useful for students who are uncertain about their ability to comprehend the statistics and methodology employed in the study, as it will provide an important overview of the research.

4. Read the methods section. Now that you know the results and what the researchers claim the results mean, you are prepared to read about the methods. This section explains the type of research and the techniques and assessment instruments used.

5. Read the results section. This is the most technically challenging part of a research report, but since you already know the findings (you read about them in the discussion section), this section will be far more manageable. Don't get bogged down in the details of the statistics, but read for a general understanding of what was done.

6. Read the discussion section again. This time, it should make even more sense. Remember, this section often contains suggestions for future research, including issues that the researchers became aware of in the course of the study.

- Reducing alcohol use in first-year university students: Evaluation of a Web-based personalized feedback program.

  (2009) by D. M. Doumas & L. L. Andersen. *Journal of College Counseling, 12,* 18–32.

- Child sexual abuse prevention: Psychoeducational groups for preschoolers and their parents.

  (2009) by M. C. Kenny. *Journal for Specialists in Group Work, 34,* 24–42.

Other Types of Articles and Research

There are, of course, other formats for professional literature as well as other types of research that counselors might use. For example, counselors might read **single case studies** that discuss one counselor's experience with one particular client. Clearly there are problems with the generalizability of this research. Nevertheless, it can provide important insights and information. An example of a single case study from an ACA journal is:

- Relationship betrayal and the influence of religious beliefs: A case illustration of couples counseling.

  (2008) by D. M. Gibson. *Family Journal, 16,* 344–350.

Counselors might also read **anecdotal reports**, where the author has not conducted any research nor engaged in any analysis of the existing research or literature, but simply writes about his or her own experiences to help other counselors benefit. This can also include stories about or tributes to outstanding leaders or historical figures in the field of counseling. Although this is the type of writing that is most commonly seen in professional newsletters, anecdotal reports can also be included in counseling journals, as in the following example from an ACA journal:

- One veteran counselor's take on the future of rehabilitation counseling.

  (2009) by B. T. McMahon, *Rehabilitation Counseling Bulletin, 52,* 120–123.

Finally, counselors might use information they learn from attending professional presentations at counseling workshops and conference to inform their practice. However, in general, information contained in presentations does not undergo the same systematic and rigorous review of published resources, and counselors must take care to use a critical eye in assessing the quality and relevance of information included in presentations.

In the preceding Spotlight, we discuss an essential skill that counselors must develop in order to make the most of the available research. In your undergraduate program you may have been able to read summaries of research, but in your graduate program you will be expected to read and understand research articles as well as apply the information you learn to your own counseling practice. We hope that this Spotlight provides a review (for those already familiar with this task), or a good starting place if this is new to you.

Engaging in Your Own Research as a Counselor

The move from *consumers* of research to *producers* of research represents an important developmental milestone for counselors. Whereas many counselors are willing to read and use existing research, there appears to be more general reluctance about engaging in their own research. In fact, only 42% of practicing school counselors believe they have the skills to conduct research independently (Bauman, 2004). We believe that this disconnect between understanding the importance of research and *conducting one's own* research is due, at least in part, to a misunderstanding about the skills needed to conduct research. Assessing your work as a counselor need not be complex or overwhelming, and your research need not mirror the scientific rigor and scope of published articles.

Here are some examples of research you could do with your clients:

- Give one of your clients in an individual counseling session a pre/post measure of depression or anxiety (such as the Beck Depression Inventory or the Beck Anxiety Disorder) or a more global measure of distress (such as the Brief Symptom Inventory). Compare the results on the pre- and post-tests, either through simple statistics or by simply *looking at the results* to see if there are changes. Graph the pre and post scores to share with your client and supervisor. Or give the inventory each time you see the client to track changes over the course of treatment. You might find, for example, results that look like this (higher scores represent more distress):

Week One:	Beck Depression Inventory Score:	19
Week Two:	Beck Depression Inventory Score:	16
Week Three:	Beck Depression Inventory Score:	18
Week Four:	Beck Depression Inventory Score:	14
Week Five:	Beck Depression Inventory Score:	14
Week Six:	Beck Depression Inventory Score:	09
Week Seven:	Beck Depression Inventory Score:	11
Week Eight (Discharge):	Beck Depression Inventory Score	08

- Count the number of times a student in a school setting has a confrontation on the playground every day for a week. Average these findings to establish a baseline number of confrontations per day. After your anger management intervention, count the number of confrontations on the playground every day for a week. Did your intervention help?

  Perhaps your intervention might look something like Figure 7.1.

  You would not need much more information than this to know that after 5 weeks of the intervention, the number of playground confrontations has clearly been reduced.

FIGURE 7.1 Sample Graph of Average Fights at Baseline and Intervention

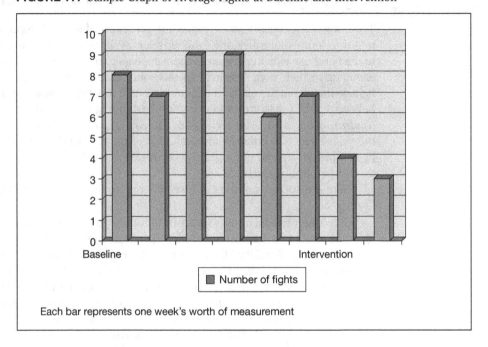

How about these examples?

- Give parents or teachers an open-ended questionnaire to assess any changes in behavior that they have noticed following a classroom guidance intervention in a school.

- Ask clients to rate their symptoms of depression on a scale of 1–10 every day and use that information when you meet with them in counseling. Assess the progress over time. Have the ratings improved, overall, with counseling? If so, why? Talk with the client about what he or she believes is contributing to improvement. If there is no improvement, why not? Again, talk with the client about the roadblocks that remain.

Give all of the clients on your caseload a measure of symptom distress as pre/post and 6-month follow-up. Imagine you found a result something like Figure 7.2.

- You would learn that your clients improve between admission and discharge. At 6-month follow-up, they are still improved when compared to admission, but they are not as well as when they were first discharged. (Incidentally, this

FIGURE 7.2 Sample Graph of Client Distress on a Measure of Symptomatology at Pre-Test, Post-Test, and 6-Month Follow-up

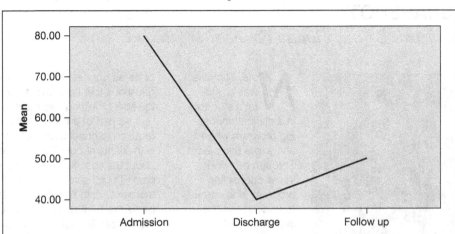

graph is actually taken from a research study that we conducted. Thus, this is *exactly* the type of information that you can get from your own research).

We could go on, but the point is, conducting your own research should be part of your ongoing approach to counseling. *Any* effort to assess the process or product of your own counseling will improve the work that you do. Ultimately, when you conduct your own research, you, your clients, and your entire counseling practice benefits.

For students who are willing to do more, we strongly suggest finding a faculty member who can mentor you in research. Becoming a part of a research team is a tremendous way to learn, and faculty members are often grateful for the additional assistance that student team members provide. Research mentorship benefits everyone. Students learn research expertise and contribute to the project's success while mentors gain valuable assistance and benefit from sharing their knowledge (Briggs & Pehrsson, 2008).

The counseling profession must take a strong a positive stance toward developing a research agenda to lead counseling into the 21st century and beyond. Expanding and promoting the research base in counseling has been identified by the American Counseling Association's 20/20 vision

■■■ *Words of Wisdom* ■■■

"The future of professional school counseling is at risk unless there is a shared commitment to conducting research that clearly documents how professional school counselors make a positive difference in students' lives."

Source: Whiston (2003, p. 447).

SNAPSHOT
Michelle Bruno, Clinical Counseling Student

Note: Michelle was a master's student in a clinical counseling program when she wrote this piece. Through her work in her counseling program, she came to understand the importance of collecting data on her clients to evaluate her own counseling. Like many agencies, the agency where Michelle did her internship had stacks and stacks of data on clients, but no one had ever moved that data out of the individual client files and into a format that could help inform the agency. As Michelle worked with the data at her agency, she reflected on the process that led her to engage in this research.

Michelle:

As I enter my last quarter of my master's internship, I have experienced a paradigm shift in terms of the meaning of research. I have always been someone who valued research and believed that it was an important part of learning, but it was not until recently that the impact of research in counseling became clear to me. I guess I always envisioned research as something that my professors and other experts in the field were responsible for conducting. I thought of it as something I would probably become involved in "later" in my career and did not really see how it fit in with my day-to-day work as a student. What I have learned this quarter is that research does not have to be a scary ambiguous notion conducted by someone else; it is a process that has importance and relevance for all

of us as counselors and students. It can answer questions that have direct relevance to clients and the staff providing treatment to those clients.

As part of our internship course, we are required to conduct an outcomes research project with clients at our sites. As I began to learn more about the specificity of how such a project is carried out, I discovered just how crucial such a project could be. My internship is in an adult partial hospitalization program, so I approached the clinical director with my assignment so that I could get permission and consent to gather some data. Because this program is part of a large hospital, they are required to collect certain data on clients anyway. The results from a report last year showed that some clients were leaving the program more anxious than others, which left the staff wondering what they could do differently. I decided to pursue steps to see how I could combine my assignment with the goals of the staff at the hospital. Along with my advisor, we set up a few meetings with the clinical director and another hospital staff person invested in outcome research. We are now in the process of learning more about how we can better serve our clients, especially those with high levels of anxiety, through an outcome study. We started this process by asking questions that can help provide descriptive information on the people who come to our program. Then we brainstormed questions that are not directly observable, but require some investigation. Such questions include how long patients remain in our program, whether this length is impacted by diagnosis, and differences in depression and anxiety scores upon entering and leaving the program.

These questions are important and can help us gain a clearer perspective on how we can better serve our clients. The results of this study will have an impact on how we do counseling, what group sessions we continue, and which ones we adapt or eliminate. This research process will provide us with answers to very important questions regarding the care we provide. As I have engaged in this process, it makes so much sense to gather information like this so we have some objective measures of how are clients are doing in our program. Conducting this research will help me have a better understanding of the clients I work with and has shown me how to find answers to questions that we as a staff were asking. This study will also have impact in other areas, too, such as future funding in the program. Using the information we gather in our study, we can observe, measure, and adapt so that we can provide the kind of care that people in our program seem to need. In this time of managed care, this kind of research also provides proof of effectiveness to those providers who decide on a person's care. What we learn from this phase of the research can help decide if we need to add more to our program in order to focus more on clients with high anxiety. I am not saying that conducting this large-scale study will be easy, but it's definitely something I can participate in and apply to the counseling world. Conducting research is not just something to read about in journals, but should be looked at as another way to impact our clients. This course assignment and subsequent large-scale study reduced the looming ambiguous "research monster" I had created in my mind, and provided guidance and clarification on how to use research as a student to help strengthen the program and impact clients.

statement as essential to the efficacy of professional counselors and to enhancing the public perception of the profession. We believe it is important for you to begin your research while you are still in your graduate program. For inspiration, you can read about the experiences of a counseling student who engaged in research during her graduate program in the accompanying Snapshot.

 ## Summary

I n this chapter, we discussed how counselors who adopt an inquisitive mindset can inform their counseling practice both by using existing research and by conducting their own studies of effectiveness. Ultimately, counselors with a research perspective engage in ongoing critical reflection about their work, seeking to make adjustments and improvements as they continue to learn and grow. Counselors who are practitioner-scientists see the benefit of incorporating a research perspective into all of their work.

Counselors who read scholarly books and journals, and who have the skills and knowledge to critically analyze what they read, become better counselors. Counselors who write articles, engage in their own research, participate in research teams, or present information at conferences and workshops not only benefit themselves and their own clients, but the entire field of professional counseling. We hope you are inspired to become a counselor who is always learning, always investigating, always improving.

End-of-Chapter Activities

Student Activities

1. Now it's time to reflect on the major topics that we have covered in this chapter. Look back at the sections or the ideas you have underlined. What were your reactions as you read that portion of the chapter? What do you want to remember?

_____

_____

_____

_____

2. What are your reactions to using existing research and conducting your own? What messages have you received in the past about research (either your ability or desire to conduct research, or simply other people's reactions to the idea of research), and how do you think these messages have affected your attitudes about research?

_____

_____

_____

_____

3. As you read about the graduate student authors, what are your reactions? Have you thought about publishing or presenting your work as a graduate student? What excites you about the possibility? What about this would be challenging for you?

_____

_____

_____

_____

■ ■ ■ Journal Question ■ ■ ■

As you think about your future as a professional counselor, what are some of the topics, problems, or populations that you would like to study? You don't have to commit to a research agenda, but just take a few moments to think about what questions you have that could lend themselves to research projects. Can you envision yourself as a researcher tackling these questions, either through the use of existing (published) research, or through your own exploration? What would it mean for you, as a person and as a professional, to be able to investigate these questions? In what ways would thinking of yourself as a researcher fit with your beliefs about yourself, and in what ways would your identity need to shift to accommodate this new role?

■■■ Topics for Discussion ■■■

1. Why do you think so many counselors are resistant to conducting their own research? What can you do to make sure that you have the necessary skills to read existing research and conduct research on your own?

2. Think about the type of setting where you might work as a counselor. What research question(s) might you have about your clients or setting? What types of research (general categories, not specific research designs) might help you answer your research questions?

■■■ Experiments ■■■

1. Individually or as a class, select a recent issue of a counseling journal, such as *Journal of Counseling and Development*, and classify all the articles as research (quantitative or qualitative), literature review/position paper, program evaluation, case study, or anecdotal report.

2. As you talk with counselors at professional conferences or meetings or interview them for class projects, be sure to ask them what the role of research is in *their* counseling practice.

3. Imagine you were a client who was considering going to counseling. Go on the Internet and select six websites that clients might explore to learn more about counseling. Don't look for the "best" websites or the "professional" websites—just six that might catch the eye of a person who is considering counseling. Use the criteria listed in the Spotlight in this chapter to review the quality of the information on the website. Consider what you discovered as you think about the messages the general public gets about counseling from the Internet.

■■■ Explore More! ■■■

Dimmitt, C., Carey, J. C., & Hatch, T. (2007). *Evidence-based school counseling: Making a difference with data-driven practices.* Thousand Oaks, CA: Corwin Press.

This book provides practical strategies for school counselors who wish to incorporate outcome research and data into their practice.

Granello, D. H. (2001). Promoting cognitive complexity in graduate written work: Using Bloom's Taxonomy as a pedagogical tool to improve literature reviews. *Counselor Education and Supervision, 40*(4), 292–307.

> This article describes a model for writing cognitively complex literature reviews that counseling students can use during their graduate programs.

Granello, D. H. (2007). Publishing quantitative manuscripts in *Counselor Education and Supervision*: General guidelines and expectations. *Counselor Education and Supervision, 47*, 66–75.

> This article gives general information on how to conduct methodologically sound quantitative research and present the results in a way that is suitable for publication.

Kline, W. B. (2008). Developing and submitting credible qualitative manuscripts. *Counselor Education and Supervision, 47*, 210–217.

> This articles gives general information on how to conduct methodologically sound qualitative research and present the results in a way that is suitable for publication.

Sexton, T. L., Whiston, S. C., Bleuer, J. C., & Walz, G. R. (1997). *Integrating outcome research into counseling practice and training*. Alexandria, VA: American Counseling Association.

> This foundational text on the use of outcome research in counseling practice offers ideas and strategies that remain relevant and useful for today's counselors.

8

What Happens in a Counseling Session?

What Is Counseling Like for the Client?

People have been consulting each other about their problems ever since we developed language. In many cultures, priests or elders have been consulted instead of professional helpers. Although counseling has become a helping specialty, the role of counselor is also an inherent part of parenting your children, teaching someone a skill, mentoring a fellow employee, coaching a soccer team, supervising someone in a work situation, and being a friend. Yet in these roles, we are sometimes stymied by the relationship itself. A friend can find it hard to be objective, and a parent can push too hard. That is why there is a role for a professional counselor to encourage, challenge, and bring us new perspectives when indigenous helpers like family, co-workers and friends are not available, are unreceptive, or do not possess the requisite skills or information. Clients come to make decisions about whether they should stay in their marriage, send a child to the drug treatment facility, choose a new career, or find ways to get over the disabling fear that keeps them cooped up in the house.

Although it may seem artificial and impersonal, the anonymous relationship also has many benefits. For one thing, clients can be seen as who they are in the present with no history or baggage. Counselors will not see us only as our parents do, and the counselor has no stake in how things turn out. The counselor can be more objective and help the client identify what he or she wants to do.

Imagine what it is like to publically ask for help by going to a counselor. First, you have to admit to yourself that you cannot handle your problems alone. Our society values independence, personal accomplishment, and picking yourself up by your own bootstraps. Going to counseling can feel like an act of weakness. You put off making the appointment, like going to the dentist. Things have to be pretty bad to make that call. None of your family or friends seems to be an option. Finally, you break down and schedule a time. Then, you have to face a receptionist or school secretary and probably some other clients or students and sit in a waiting room, wondering what it will be like and where you will start. It is a momentous occasion when someone gets to this point: needing counseling. It is not like a massage at a spa, something you do because it feels good. Some real pain has to motivate us. I try to remember that while this is just another *appointment* for me, the counselor, it can be a big *disappointment* for the client if he or she does not see some glimmer of hope when the session is over. If the client leaves discouraged, it may mean that he or she will not try counseling in the future.

People seek counseling during periods of upheaval and during developmental crises such as career change, just before marriage, and during the storm and stress of adolescence. For the person with a major mental disorder such as bipolar disorder, counseling may be required at various points along the lifespan. If counseling is a process during which an individual pauses in the full-court press of life and reflects on the direction life is taking, probably everyone could benefit from counseling at some point. Unfortunately, most people get the idea that counseling is for those with mental disorders or those whose lives are desperately out of control. As a student of counseling, you will have to consider the benefits of receiving counseling. Your program may even require it. As you do, you will have to struggle with the same prejudices that clients face: "Does this mean I am crazy?" "What will happen if someone finds out?" or "How deeply will I have to disclose?"

Typically, clients try a variety of strategies on their own before they seek counseling. Most commonly, they talk with other people in their lives (e.g., family, friends, peers), try to work things out for themselves, deny or ignore the problem,

■■■ *Fast Facts* ■■■

Brannon (1985) identified four themes that run through the lives of traditional males that may make it more difficult for them to seek counseling when needed.

1. *No Sissy Stuff.* Males may have been raised to believe that they must be masculine. Any signs of emotional vulnerability or help-seeking are labeled as feminine, and therefore, devalued and avoided.

2. *The Big Wheel.* Men who follow this axiom have been raised to believe that being male is equated with power, ambition, and success. This theme has also been called the "breadwinner bind" whereby men are socialized to feel they must work as hard as possible to provide the best life for their families, and then are criticized for neglecting family responsibilities because of their work commitments.

3. *The Sturdy Oak.* This theme is evidenced by rational and logical thought, rather than the emotionality of feminine thought. Men who have been raised to value this theme were not taught to recognize and acknowledge emotions, but rather to deny and fear them.

4. *Give 'Em Hell!* This theme of masculinity emphasizes the need to seek adventure, excitement, and risk, even through the use of violence. This theme includes the importance of physical strength and toughness, as well as aggression. The result of this theme is that men can feel valued only when they are declared the winner.

Taken together, these themes provide insight into some of the difficulties that traditional males might face when considering making an appointment with a counselor. Brannon's themes have been used by counselors to help find ways to make counseling sessions more appropriate for traditional male clients.

hope it goes away on its own, pray, or use alcohol or other substances to try to mask the pain (Manthei, 2007). In schools, sexually active adolescents are more than twice as likely to seek input or advice from their peers than from adults and more than five times more likely to tell a peer than an adult about being teased, hit, or threatened by another student at school (Vernberg & Ewell, 1995). Thus, by the time the school counselor knows about a young person's problems, it is likely that many of that student's peers already know all the details.

Some of the barriers that affect a person's willingness to receive counseling arise from family, religious, or ethnic mores. In other words, their culture may predispose clients to avoid "airing their dirty laundry" or admitting they need help. For example, some religions may consider seeking counseling to be a lack of faith. Families may feel disgraced and clients from some ethnic backgrounds might feel ashamed to admit to relatives that they are getting help. One of the cultural issues that has an impact on counseling is gender. Gender is the sex role that you learned as you were growing up. Men generally learn to ignore feelings, to hold them in and to solve problems independently. Being a man can be a handicap when you have an emotional crisis because, if you are a very traditional male, your "emotional intelligence" (Goleman, 2006) might be quite low. **Emotional intelligence** is recognizing what you feel and being able to accept and cope with distressing feelings. Being a traditional male makes it harder for you to accept help because you feel weak and ashamed (McCarthy & Holiday, 2004).

On the other hand, being an extremely traditional female may have conditioned you to be overly concerned about the feelings and needs of others to the extent that you are resentful and have lost your internal guidance system. Women are much more willing to come to counseling and accept help, but the counselor must be sure to empower them rather than direct them. Laura Choate (2008) makes the startling observation that because most counseling clients are women, all counselors need to be aware of women's issues and recognize the role of gender training in their clients' problems. We will talk more about these issues when we discuss multicultural issues in counseling; however, gender is mentioned here because, like religion and ethnicity, it can influence one's decision to get help in the first place.

Opening Up: Why Am I Afraid to Tell You Who I Am?

In his book, *Why Am I Afraid to Tell You Who I Am?,* John Powell (1995) says that we do not open up to others because we fear that disclosure will result in rejection. In addition, we are afraid to reveal ourselves because we fear that they will discover what a bad person we really are and we will have to face that fact, too (Goldberg, 2002). Conversely, James Pennebaker's book, *Opening Up* (1990), documents the health benefits of disclosing one's most troubling experiences through journaling or what is called *emotional writing.* It is now clear that even writing about disturbing issues can be very helpful. Being self-disclosing has long been known to be associated with mental health (Jourard, 1971; Pennebaker, 1989). But there are other reasons that should convince us of the need to disclose.

One of the powerful effects of counseling (or probably any intimate relationship) is finding out that the other person accepts you, despite your past and your problems. This can happen in a friendship or in a counseling relationship. When 10 people accept you, we call that group counseling. In fact, there is an exercise for groups called "Top Secret" in which clients write down an important secret and these are anonymously read to the other members (Yalom, 2002). The result is that people learn that their deepest, darkest disclosures are usually not met with the rejection they fear. What happens is that we become closer to people when we let them know who we are.

In the counseling relationship, we usually start with the most superficial topics and later disclose the deeper ones. It is sometimes said that clients begin by talking about "the thing next to the thing." Clients are testing the waters. When counseling is failing to get at important, deeper issues, the counselor can actually discuss this progression with the client to try to understand why counseling is staying superficial.

Does this mean that keeping secrets is a bad thing? After all, counselors consistently press their clients to be disclosing and honest. Yet it is probably not the keeping of secrets that is in itself the problem. Rather, it is a general tendency toward self-concealment that makes a person more likely to have psychological symptoms (Kelly & Yip, 2006). Therefore, it seems that the best route to take, as a counselor, is not to pressure clients to tell all their secrets but to gently show them that their fears may be unfounded and to provide an accepting environment conducive to self-discovery. After all, they may have good reasons in their personal histories to justify their reticence.

Secrets and Lies

Most counselors have never met their clients before the first session. They know only what the client tells them and they are cut off from the context of the person's life with no way to verify what they hear. One of the facts of the counseling relationship is that about 40–50% of clients keep secrets from their counselor about major life experiences and key facts and emotions (Farber, Berano, & Capobianco, 2004; Kelly, 1998). Kelly's study of client secrets reveals that they keep secrets from their therapist about relationships such as "desiring the wrong person" (p. 51), sexual secrets, health problems, drugs and alcohol, and lying. More than any other reasons, clients did not reveal secrets because they did not want to express their feelings; second, they were ashamed or embarrassed to tell the counselor. Interestingly, one study found that more than half of clients wished that their counselor would pursue their secrets a bit more actively (Farber et al., 2004).

In schools, counselors might know their student clients from interactions in the hallways or classrooms or from referrals by teachers or parents. Nevertheless, it is quite clear that even in school settings, students keep many secrets from their counselors. For example, national surveys consistently find that only 25% of adolescents say they would tell an adult if they knew a peer was suicidal (Granello & Granello, 2007). Other secrets that students often keep from their school counselors include self-injury, sexual activity, drug or alcohol use, or bullying/victimization.

Keeping secrets is an issue in individual, group, family, and couples counseling. Couples may conceal infidelities even when they are impinging on their primary relationship (Bass & Quimby, 2006; Cottone & Mannis, 1996), and families struggle with disclosing family histories and problems (McCurdy & Murray, 2003). Certainly, people who are having affairs, abusing drugs, or engaging in other addictive behaviors need to come clean. Keeping most things secret from others is associated with a number of physical and psychological complaints including depression (Kelly, 1998). Even more significant is the fact that when keeping secrets, clients may be misleading the counselor and delaying their own progress. For example, people who are in group therapy seem to benefit less if they keep important secrets (Wright, Ingraham, Chemtob, & Perez-Arce, 1985), and clients who withheld "relevant secrets" had poorer relationships with their therapists than those who did not (Kelly & Yuan, 2009). Clients who do not disclose that they have drug and alcohol problems undermine their current counseling work and do not get the help that they need.

Yet, it is probably not just embarrassment and fear of revealing addictions or acknowledging their moral missteps that motivates people from not sharing everything. It may have something to do with "preferred view of self." *Preferred view* refers to how we would like to act, how we would like to see ourselves and have others see us (Eron & Lund, 1998). We try to maintain this ideal to ourselves and we try to present it to the world. In short, people are trying to manage the impression they are giving to the counselor because this self-portrayal affects how they see themselves too.

When we lie or conceal we are, in a way, describing our possible selves (Markus & Nurius, 1986). Clients construct an identity in counseling that they

SNAPSHOT
My Counseling Experience by Ashley R.

Authors' note: Ashley was having problems finishing her master's degree in accounting. To most of the people she knew, she appeared depressed and unmotivated. She came to the college counseling center feeling that she needed to recover quickly from the fact that she and her fiancée had called it quits. This is her account.

I sought counseling in hopes of trying to move past the breakup of my engagement. As it had been almost a year since the relationship had ended, I was concerned that I was still struggling to let go of the pain and move forward. Although I quickly established rapport with my counselor and found it easy to open up and share my story with her, I soon realized that it would take time for me to be able to address one of my core issues . . . the shame and embarrassment I felt for still missing someone who had treated me so poorly and in the end had rejected me. Initially my friends and family tried to be there for me but after some time had passed, I started to feel as though they were all saying, "You've cried and held onto this past relationship long enough. It's not okay to still be this upset." I started to feel embarrassed that I could not let go of my pain because everyone around me seemed to be sending me the message that there is a time limit to grieving and yours is up. The one person who made me feel like where I was at was okay was my counselor. She validated my experience and created an environment in which I felt comfortable to begin the process of healing. She helped me to feel empowered, which allowed me to verbalize to my family and friends that yes, I was still grieving, and that I had to work this out in my own time and not on their time line. It is hard to put into words what strength that gave me. My counselor's constant support and validation set in motion my ability to eventually start to let go of my shame and embarrassment attached to still longing for my ex. My counseling experience also allowed me to gain insight into why I held onto the pain for so long.

wish they had, and that may not be such a bad thing. Let us say that you meet someone at the airport who presents herself to a fellow traveler as happily married and successful in business when in reality, she is single and struggling financially. One view of this is simply that the person is a liar. But it is also possible that the person is articulating a goal rather than reflecting reality. It is possible from this vantage point to see that that your client does not lie to you merely to mislead you but is afraid to face him- or herself by telling you the truth. The counselor tries to see what the client is intending, what is beneath the surface, what the client says *sotto voce*, in a whisper. When we are lied to as counselors, we do not react angrily to the client as if he or she were a friend or a partner. When we discover a deception our response is: "I wonder what you were trying to say to me by not telling me the truth?" This chapter's Snapshot describes the process of counseling, as written by a client. As you read the client's narrative, think about how the counselor allowed her to express her true self, rather than the self that others wanted her to be. It's a powerful story, and one that reminds us how important it is for others to validate our experiences.

What Do Clients Find Helpful in Counseling?

In American society, we are losing touch with our closest relations due to divorce and the need to move and travel for our jobs. We connect electronically because our friends and family are scattered. Even in the educational realm, with the advent of online education, the one-on-one, face-to-face relationship is becoming more rare.

Do these electronic relationships really substitute for being there? Is it a need for real human contact and understanding that makes people seek a counseling relationship? In general, clients are able to describe many things that their counselor did or said, as well as many relational or attitudinal factors that the counselor displayed, that they found particularly helpful (Manthei, 2007). Clients tend to appreciate counselors for their skill and experience as well as for treating them with respect, understanding, and as an intelligent person. Clients also appreciate explanations or interpretations that provide them with new ways of looking at their problems or situations. Finally, like all of us in all relationships, clients report that they like being made to feel that they are competent, capable, and insightful people, rather than being regarded as fragile, a failure, or unable to cope (Manthei, 2007). Following are some adjectives that clients have reported as traits and behaviors they appreciated in their counselors:

1. Sensitive, gentle, honest (Lazarus, 1971)
2. Warm, attentive, interested, understanding, respectful (Strupp, Fox, & Lessler, 1969)
3. Credibility, skill, empathic understanding, affirmation, attention to emotions, focusing on client problems (Orlinsky, Graves, & Parks, 1994)
4. Warm and supportive (Elliott & Williams, 2003)
5. Empathy, positive regard, and congruence (Greenberg, Elliott, & Lietaer, 1994; Rogers, 1980)
6. Encouraging and reassuring, someone who understands, gives hope (Murphy, Cramer, & Lillie, 1984)
7. Acceptance and understanding (Lorr, 1965)
8. Dedicated to serving their welfare and developing a meaningful relationship [clients of rehabilitation counselors] (McCarthy & Leierer, 2001)

■■■ *Fast Facts* ■■■

The average user on Facebook has 130 friends.

Source: Facebook (2010).

■■■ *Fast Facts* ■■■

Research indicates that client perceptions of the relationship with the counselor are the most consistent predictor of improvement, more so even than the therapists' perceptions of the relationship.

Source: Manthei (2007, p. 261).

Clients also appreciate counselors who:

1. Offer specific techniques to deal with problems.
2. Give advice but do not push (Murphy et al., 1984).
3. Act professionally.
4. Make useful referrals.
5. Are knowledgeable about the client and the client's problems.

 ## What Is the Counseling Relationship Like for the Counselor?

By now you have heard that counselors must always put the needs of their clients ahead of their own, and the counseling relationship is no exception. Counselors must work to provide a relationship that meets the needs of their clients. However, it is clear that counselors also benefit from the therapeutic relationship, and we now turn to a discussion of how helping relationships help us, too.

Joys and Satisfactions of Being a Counselor

One of the only studies that examined what counselors like about their profession was conducted by Barry Farber and Louis Heifetz (1981). They asked therapists to rate dimensions of their work on a 7-point scale. The therapists saw about 21 client hours per week and had on the average 10 years' experience. In Table 8.1, we graphically summarize their responses. As you can see, the *least* satisfying parts of the job are having access to juicy details and being a mysterious figure. Even the status aspect of the profession was not deemed very satisfying. Among the most satisfying elements were enhancing growth in self and in clients, learning more about clients, and using therapeutic expertise. Perhaps this last and most highly rated satisfaction requires some explanation. This response reflects a need by a highly trained person to utilize the skills he or she has acquired. It is like the quarterback on the bench who is watching the game but wants to play. It is like the craftsman who can make something beautiful and wants to exercise his or her skill. The counselors in this study had many years of experience, and it is doubtful that you will have this kind of counselor "high" in the near future. But take a look at some of the other areas. Counselors like the fact that their job involves self-awareness and personal growth, and they like the interpersonal aspects of the jobs. They like getting to know people at a deeper level and being of use, being helpful to and valued by their clients. As you look at this list, you will see that financial compensation does not even appear. As you think about becoming a counselor, this might be a good time to ask yourself: Is this what I am looking for in a career—becoming deeply involved with people?

TABLE 8.1   What Counselors Say They Like (and Don't Like) About Their Jobs

1	2	3	4	5	6	7
Not at All a Source of Satisfaction			*Moderate Source of Satisfaction*		*Major Source of Satisfaction*	
(Least)					*(Most)*	

Rankings from *most important* to *least important*	Score
1. Using therapeutic expertise	5.65
2. Enhancing growth in clients	5.47
3. Learning about many types of people	5.42
4. Self-growth	5.35
5. Self-knowledge	5.31
6. Being socially useful	5.09
7. Being valued by clients	4.60
8. Achieving intimacy	4.56
9. Status	4.53
10. Learning the intimate details	3.10
11. The mystique of the therapist	2.43

Dissatisfactions

Table 8.2 is also summarized from Farber and Heifetz (1981). This table shows how therapists in the study, on average, rate the most stressful aspects of their jobs. Note that several of the biggest stressors such as Excessive Workload (#1), Organizational Politics (#3), and Excessive Paperwork (#6) are not actually counseling problems but workplace problems. When we discuss self-care, we will look at the stressors on this list more carefully and think about ways of surviving and thriving with these challenges.

Countertransference

Countertransference is a word used to describe the counselor's conscious or unconscious emotional reaction to the client (Curtis, Matise, & Glass, 2003). Many people think this is Freudian mumbo jumbo, and the word does sound like something said by a "shrink." Yet, inappropriate feelings toward a client, both positive and negative are very common. Here the term *inappropriate* is used advisedly. These feelings are inappropriate because they are felt in the wrong context. Due to our previous relationships, upbringing, cultural background, family of origin, and personality, we react automatically to others before we get to know them.

TABLE 8.2 What Counselors Say Causes the Most (and Least) Stress in Their Jobs

1	2	3	4	5	6	7
Not at All a Source of Stress			*Moderate Source of Stress*		*Major Source of Stress*	
(Least)					*(Most)*	

Rankings from *most to least* amount of stress:	Score
1. Excessive workload	4.10
2. Difficulty working with disturbed people	4.03
3. Organizational politics	3.73
4. Emotional depletion	3.67
5. Responsibilities for patients' lives	3.67
6. Excessive paperwork	3.29
7. Controlling one's emotions	3.28
8. Difficulty evaluating progress	3.28
9. Physical exhaustion	3.10
10. Doubts regarding efficacy of therapy	2.95
11. Inevitable need to relinquish patients	2.88
12. Constraints of the "50-minute hour"	2.57
13. Difficulty leaving "psychodynamics" at office	2.52
14. Professional conflicts	2.46
15. Lack of gratitude from patients	2.38
16. The monotony of work	2.37
17. Social difficulties after work	2.10

In his book, *Love's Executioner* (2000), Irvin Yalom writes about a client he calls the "fat lady." From the beginning, he was repulsed by her, and she notices the fact that he never looks at her and never even shakes her hand. Yalom realizes what he is doing and traces its origins to the obese women in his own family who were very controlling. Thus, the counselor's feelings cannot be truly hidden from the client. We do not always know why we have these prejudices, but we react automatically.

Emotional reactions can be educational if we are aware of them and potentially harmful if we accept them uncritically. Even positive emotions can blur our judgment. For example, consider a client who appears to be a middle-class woman with a husband and three children who is abusing prescription medication. Are

■■■ *Fast Facts* ■■■

The term YAVIS was coined in a 1964 book, *Psychotherapy: The Purchase of Friendship,* by William Schofield to describe the type of client that therapists prefer. YAVIS stands for Young, Attractive, Verbal, Intelligent, and Successful. Schofield argued that counselors favor these clients because physical attractiveness in others is appealing at an unconscious level. Humans (including counselors) equate attractiveness with health, success, and survival.

you likely, because of your own background, to make assumptions about her prognosis (likelihood of getting better)? "She looks just like my aunt," "She's from Long Island just like me," "An attractive woman like that has so much going for her," are some of the potential reactions based on countertransference that can skew our perceptions because they may be based on first impressions, personal histories, or cultural lenses.

Another kind of countertransference reaction is feeling sorry for the client. Sometimes counselors feel their eyes filling up with tears at a client's story. Is this empathy, feeling with the client? Or are you overly identifying with the client's situation? Every counselor has to sort this out personally. It turns out that about 20% of counselors in training are somewhat to very worried about crying with clients because they see it as unprofessional (Curtis et al., 2003). We have found that some people are very likely to cry (even counselors) when they are nervous or when they are exposed to something very sad whether it be a movie or a real story. If you are prone to tears, you will find a way to deal with this countertransference reaction, just as you learn to deal with other emotional reactions to clients like feeling angry. A helpful place to start is by not admonishing yourself for these feelings and by later examining your personal feelings in supervision. Jeffrey Kottler has written extensively on this topic in his book, *The Language of Tears* (1996).

So how should the counselor deal with countertransference or emotions towards the client? The counselor tries to be aware of his or her reaction, recognizing that it is a prejudice and also that others may also react to the client in this way. Becoming a reflective practitioner means making a commitment to being aware of our own reactions so we can grow and so we can analyze what effect we are having on others from our own baggage. Ask yourself questions such as: Why does this client make me angry? Why am I having such a strong reaction (positive or negative) to this client? What is this about? Am I being fair? Am I objective? This leads you to take a second step and discuss every important reaction with a supervisor, sharing these thoughts and feelings to consider how it might be affecting the progress of the client. Reflecting with a supervisor and in your own head helps you become a *reflective practitioner.*

Let us take an example of a client that does not follow through on homework. Week after week he complains about his life and how other people are causing problems for him and do not live up to his expectations. But when the counselor recommends a homework assignment, the client returns the following week with the same complaints and no action. The counselor starts to feel angry and impatient because they are covering the same ground and not making any progress. At such times, it may be useful to confront the client with his lack of follow-through; however, it is equally important for the counselor to recognize his or her own issues that give rise to anger and impatience. These may be the result of frustration—wanting the client to accomplish his goals. But why are we so committed to making the client change that we feel angry? That is a question for supervision and personal reflection.

Responsibility

"I must fix my client's problems." Maybe you do not say this aloud, but you think it and feel it when you are a counselor. After all, the client has come to you, maybe as a last resort. The pressure to make it all better is one of the first barriers a counselor must eliminate before he or she can really help. Feeling totally responsible is not rational, nor is it reasonable to think you are going to solve a client's problems in an hour—issues that the client has been struggling with for a lifetime.

In this chapter's Counseling Controversy, we explore the topic of counselor responsibility through the use of directive versus nondirective counseling. As you read the controversy, consider how your beliefs about the level of responsibility that counselors have for the counseling session might influence your stance on this controversy.

Self-Disclosure

Counselors use self-disclosure to help facilitate an open and trusting therapeutic relationship. When a counselor shares information about him- or herself, clients can begin to see the counselor as an honest, open, and genuine person. In general, counselor self-disclosure is used sparingly and only when the disclosure helps the client. Self-disclosure is never used to develop a social relationship or to make the counselor feel important. Self-disclosures that keep the focus of the discussion on the client are most effective. In other words, disclosures that help clients see the effect of their stories on the counselor (also called self-involving statements) are more effective than disclosures that involve stories about the counselor (Young, 2009). Appropriate self disclosure can help facilitate client self-disclosure, communicate respect and caring, help clients see the impact that their stories have on others, and normalize client behaviors (Anderson & Anderson, 1985). Because counselor self-disclosure is an advanced counseling skill that must be used appropriately, you will learn more about its uses—and misuses—in your counseling skills classes. In general, as with all counseling interventions, before a counselor uses self-disclosure with a client, a good question to ask is, "Whose needs are being met?"

■■■ *Words of Wisdom* ■■■

"A powerful learning experience for me was realizing that I didn't have to have all the answers. I think I was confusing empathy with knowledge. I don't have to be an expert for the client—clients are already experts about themselves."

—Amy P., clinical counseling student
at the end of practicum experience

Counseling Controversy

SHOULD THE COUNSELOR BE DIRECTIVE OR NONDIRECTIVE?

Background: In the early days of counseling, *directive counseling* could also have been described as "test and tell," meaning that the counselor administered tests to the client and then revealed the results. This was the typical scenario for career counseling. For example, the counselor would find a match between the client's personality and a particular career path and make a specific recommendation. Later on, the term *directive* was applied to counseling theories such as Rational Emotive Behavior Therapy (Ellis, David, & Lynn, 2010), which prescribes a healthy way of thinking. In strategic therapy, the counselor gives clients particular directives or tasks to perform (Haley & Richeport-Haley, 2007). In both cases, the counselor is directing the client to act or think in a particular way in order to achieve counseling goals.

Directive counseling contrasts with *nondirective counseling*, which originated with Carl Rogers (1946). The nondirective counselor lets the client take the lead and does not prescribe, give advice, or overtly guide the client. The counselor believes that the answers to the client's problems are within the client, and answers will emerge that are coherent and genuine for the client. A corollary of these ideas has emerged in the newer theories of counseling such as solution focused therapy and narrative therapy, which see the counselor not as expert, but as facilitator.

POINT: THE COUNSELOR SHOULD EMBRACE THE ROLE OF MENTAL HEALTH EXPERT	COUNTERPOINT: THE COUNSELOR'S MAIN PURPOSE IS TO EMPOWER CLIENTS TO FIND THEIR OWN SOLUTIONS
• The counselor has specific training in mental health, relationships, human development, and knows what facilitates change. The counselor should share this knowledge with clients.	• A client's particular problem cannot be easily solved by someone who does not really understand the circumstances.
• People want someone to give them expert knowledge. For example, a client may want to know, "When does substance abuse become dependence?"	• The autonomy of the individual should be respected. It would be wrong for the counselor to impose his or her beliefs on the client.
• The expert role does not force the client to accept a particular suggestion. The counselor is not manipulating the client; he or she is helping the client change in the agreed-upon direction.	• The role of expert sets up a hierarchy between counselor and client. It fosters dependency and mistrust.
• The weight of authority can sometimes help clients do what they have not done for themselves.	• When the counselor falls back on prescribing for the client, the client has not learned anything.
• The counselor who advocates for clients is helping the client and future clients by trying to change the system.	• Advocating for clients such as helping them achieve welfare benefits is depriving them of the opportunity to solve their own problems. It is *ipso facto* disempowering.

(continued)

(Continued)

Questions to Consider:

- Could some counselors provide too much guidance for the clients? What effect would this have on the clients later on in life?
- Could some counselors be avoiding responsibility by hiding behind nondirective approaches so that they do not have to take a stand?
- What approach do you think you would prefer as a counselor?

As with most controversies, there probably is truth on both sides of this argument.

⟵―――⟶

Evidence-based   **Nondirective**

On the continuum, place an "X" where you think you find yourself on this issue.

Fear

As Bion suggests in the accompanying quote, fear is normal and can provide us with the motivation to improve. Fear is often the result of feeling totally inadequate, especially when the client's problems are severe or unusual. Being a counselor should make you humble. The *Diagnostic and Statistical Manual of the American Psychiatric Association* (DSM-IV-R) has over 300 mental disorders and numerous other diagnoses. Within many of them are subcategories. Changes in technology and the social world of teenagers mean that students in schools face stressors and problems that most adults never experienced during their school years. No one can be an expert on all the problems and mental disorders our clients face. So, over time, you begin to recognize that you cannot prepare for every twist and turn in the road. You learn to take your time, understand the problem, listen to the client, and get help from others. On the other hand, in the beginning, sometimes students get so overwhelmed by fear that they cannot properly concentrate on the client. This usually happens about the time you are seeing your first real clients. Your fear makes you sit in stony silence rather than risking making a fool of yourself. You may need some counseling of your own to get past this anxiety, or you may want to learn some stress-reducing techniques so

> ■▪■ *Words of Wisdom* ■▪■
>
> "Anyone who is going to see a patient tomorrow should, at some point, experience fear."
>
> _____
>
> *Source:* Bion (1990, p. 5).

that you can learn to be yourself in the session. At any rate, this is an expected roadblock on the way to becoming a counselor and in many ways it is better than naïve overconfidence. It suggests that the endeavor is important to you and you want to do your best.

Here are some of the common things counselors worry about (Smith, 2003):

1. Saying or doing the wrong thing when dealing with clients from different cultures
2. Dealing with clients who might be considering suicide or who might harm the counselor
3. Getting sued (though very few are)
4. Being overwhelmed by a client's problems and feeling unable to help
5. Crying in the session (Curtis et al., 2003)
6. Being criticized by supervisors or peers

Many of these fears are irrational or overblown. The best reaction to worry is to use it as motivation to learn more by education, workshops, and reading. For example, every counselor should periodically go to training on legal and ethical issues. Knowing what is legal and what is ethical can reduce your fear of practicing out of bounds. The real key to dealing with fear is having a good supervisory relationship. Experienced clinicians and supervisors can help you sort out real concerns from common problems. Even supervision with your peers can help you recognize that many fears are shared by other counselors, and they can help you find solutions. Consider the information included in the accompanying Informed by Research feature. How can knowing the common emotional experiences of beginning counselors help you in your professional journey?

Informed by Research
The Inner Emotional World of Counseling Students

Helping counselors-in-training become more aware of their internalized thoughts, feelings, and beliefs during counseling sessions is an important step toward developing self-reflective practitioners. Counselors' emotional reactions to their clients' stories and to their own responses to their stories can have an effect on the counseling session. Counselors who have extremely negative (self-critical) self-thoughts can become self-focused and lose their ability to empathize with their clients.

In a qualitative study, researchers had 34 first-year master of arts students in counseling record their inner experiences (thoughts, feelings,

(continued)

(Continued)

beliefs) that occurred during counseling directly after their practice counseling sessions had ended (Melton, Nofzinger-Collins, Wynne, & Susman, 2005). They found four predominant affective themes that emerged from the descriptions that the counseling students wrote:

1. Anger/frustration. The beginning counselors were often quick to recognize their own shortcomings or inappropriate counseling interventions.

2. Disappointment/regret. The counseling students in the study expressed regret that they did not know how to connect with their clients or were disappointed with their lack of progress in skill development.

3. Anxiety/fear. The students in the study were often anxious or fearful about trying out their new skills or using the skills to express empathy.

4. Happiness/excitement. Student counselors in the study at times felt happiness or excitement when they used a technique appropriately or believed that their clients were making progress.

An important finding in this study was that all four of these emotional experiences were mixed throughout the sessions, leaving new counselors to feel as though they were on "emotional roller coasters" (Melton et al., 2005, p. 88). Recognizing these internalized emotional states can help beginning counselors distinguish when the emotions are becoming so intense that they are having difficulty focusing on the client. But for now, just knowing that these emotional reactions are a common experience for new counselors can be reassuring. You are not the only one who is experiencing them.

The good news is that these same four themes (anger, sadness, fear, and happiness) have been identified as major components of the change process for clients, too (Hackney & Cormier, 1994). In other words, these emotional states often accompany significant changes in people's lives, and certainly the change that students go through as they become counselors is a significant and exciting part of the journey toward becoming a counselor.

The Skills of Counseling

Becoming a counselor means that you must acquire the skills of the profession. This is an important task and one that your professors will probably encourage you to begin right away. Most counseling programs have separate courses in counseling techniques or skills, and these courses will help lay the foundation for your skill development. It may seem artificial or strange as you first learn your counseling skills, and many beginning counselors struggle when they start to practice them out loud. We encourage you to trust the process and know that the counseling skills you are learning will start to feel more natural with time and practice.

The Therapeutic Relationship

The strength of a therapeutic alliance is defined as the degree of "trust, liking, respect and caring" as well as the sense of being partners committed to achieving therapy goals (Horvath & Bedi, 2002, p. 41). There are things that the counselor and client can do to strengthen the relationship and things that they can do to weaken it. Behaviors that strengthen the relationship include collaborating with the client, being knowledgeable, offering specific techniques to deal with problems, and being professional.

Collaboration involves recognizing that the counselor and client are a team and are committed to the therapeutic goals. Thus, both counselor and client have to agree on goals. Goals that are mutually agreed upon in counseling are more likely to be achieved. In addition, the counselor and client must agree on the methods for achieving those goals. If the technique goes against the client's religious, family, or cultural background, there is little likelihood of success.

Clients find that a judgmental counselor who imposes his or her viewpoint or offers interpretation too soon is not able to create a therapeutic alliance. The use of too much confrontation and too much or too deep self-disclosures can damage the bond. Certainly, not addressing client concerns about how counseling is proceeding can lead to a rupture. Being irritable, cold, negative, competing, or overly directive can weaken the relationship (Horvath & Bedi, 2002).

Skills You Will Learn

Later in your training, you will be learning basic counseling skills. These are generic building blocks *of the relationship* such as focusing on the client's feelings (see Table 8.3). In reality, they are skills that can help you improve your relationship with anyone. Most parenting programs and virtually all marriage/couples education

TABLE 8.3   Basic Counseling Skills

Skill	Example
Open questions (leaves options for the person to respond)	"Tell me more about the blowup at the office."
Encouragers	"Okay." "Uh-huh." "Yes." "Can you tell me more about that?"
Closed questions (can be answered with yes or no or with a brief answer)	"Did you get fired?"
Paraphrase (a rephrasing of the facts)	"So you had to go to another office for several weeks, and there is a strain between you and your supervisor."
Reflection of feeling (identifying the client's emotions)	"You're really embarrassed about what has happened and a little afraid people don't trust you to act professionally."
Reflection of meaning (what the problem means to the client)	"Your identity has always been tied up with your job. Now it is hard to feel good about yourself."
Summary (a distilled version of the whole story, which might include facts, feelings, and meanings)	"Though things have blown over and you have smoothed things out with your supervisor, there are several issues that continue to worry you, including possible promotions and how other people will view you."

programs focus on these helping behaviors. Although they look simple, even basic skills take time to learn (Young, 2009).

Before you take a class on therapeutic communication, there are some preliminary things you can do at this stage. You can begin to observe the effects of your communication on others. In this chapter, we make some suggestions about experiments you might attempt. Your friends and family might think you are acting "shrinky," but you will be able to act more natural in time.

Second, you can practice some basic helping attitudes and helping behaviors that will set the stage for your later practice. We will describe five things you can work on early in your training. These are things that you can practice in your everyday interactions with people when the other person has a problem. We are also including three things to eliminate; habits you may have acquired that you may want to become aware of and replace.

Skills to Work on Now

1. Pay attention.   It is pretty clear that human beings cannot multitask (Rubenstein, Meyer, & Evans, 2001). Although many people believe they can, it turns out that people are more effective when they do one thing at a time. Yet, when someone starts a conversation, what percentage of our attention do we give them? Do we continue watching television or straighten some papers on our desk? Recently a client related that she told a friend, over the phone, that she had been diagnosed with cancer, and after a few minutes noticed that she could hear the friend typing on the keyboard. In this age of electronic distractions, it is difficult to get someone's full attention. Yet attention is a powerful commodity that human beings crave. If you want to gauge the power of attention, the next time someone asks you, drop what you are doing and make eye contact. Just being there with full attention can transmit a very powerful message. It says, "You are important to me." As you begin your training as a counselor, learn to focus wholly and solely on the person in front of you. Through practice, you can learn to channel your full attention in one direction and give the other person the benefit of your presence. Learn to ignore the chattering monkey of the mind and instead pay close attention to what the client is saying. Later on, you will find that this will help you from being distracted by stage fright as you practice your skills. Self-consciousness can be overcome by "other-consciousness" if you can learn to shift your attention.

2. Check your understanding.   Listening is like drawing a picture of the client's problem. Periodically, you hold up your sketch and say, "Is this it?" The client's response makes you draw new lines or erase some of what you have previously drawn until you get it right. Initially, counselors are trying to understand the client's viewpoint, not get at the absolute truth. What gets in our way is the judgments we make, such as, "The client should make a commitment to his girlfriend and get married." Counselors listen for understanding. Counselors believe that we need to understand why the client is dragging his feet, how he sees commitment and marriage before we can make much headway in dealing with his reluctance. We have to create an atmosphere where the client does not feel judged. One way to do this is to provide nonjudgmental feedback to the client regarding what you have heard so far: "So you've been together for seven years and you have not decided that this is the relationship for you?" One way to practice this skill is to start using certain sentence stems that prompt you to check your understanding, such as the following:

"In your mind . . ."

"What I am getting is . . ."

"All right, I am hearing . . ."

"So you are saying . . ."

All of these are far better than saying something like:

"What? Are you crazy, how could you let that woman slip away?"

"Some people never get married."

"How long have you had this commitment problem?"

"There are a lot of fish in the sea!"

3. Use attentive silence.   Attentive silence is not ignoring but rather just accepting what the other person is saying with full attention. Silence can prompt the other person to fill in the gaps, and all good counselors know how to use it effectively. But silence is an art. Counselors use silence so that they do not interrupt the flow of the other person's story, but more often to pressure the client to talk. Have you noticed that pressure when a conversation lags? When a person is telling a story, silence can promote introspection. The counselor learns to live with that silence, using it as a tool to urge the client to disclose. Silence communicates that responsibility for the content of the session is up to the client. He or she is not obligated to answer the counselor's questions but to explore the issue aloud. Here we come to a major fork in the road between therapeutic communication and conversation. It is social to fill in silences and keep the conversation light and breezy. It is *asocial* to use silence, contradict, or focus on topics that are difficult or taboo. The counselor uses asocial communication to let the client know that this is not a social situation (Beier & Young, 1998).

4. Try to imagine what you would be feeling if this happened to you. The ability to share another person's feeling and way of seeing the world is called empathy. **Empathy** is not sympathy or feeling sorry for someone. It is the willingness to transcend one's own situation and see through the eyes of the other. There are many times when imagining how *you* might feel in the client's situation can help you get a handle on what is really bothering him or her.

Perhaps it is not realistic to think we can truly understand someone whose culture, family, and history are extremely different from ours. But think about what happens when we try. If you go to another country and try to learn the language of the locals, you may stumble and you may be awkward, but it is generally appreciated that you have tried. That effort builds a bridge in counseling too.

If you reach out and attempt to enter their world, it has been our experience that clients will help you. One way you might practice this is to make a list of behaviors of other people that you cannot understand. For example,

I can't understand:

- Why it is so important to my roommate that the refrigerator is clean
- Why some men cheat on their wives
- Why people are against abortion but for capital punishment
- Why people have different sexual orientations than me

The answers to these questions are locked up in the minds of the people who do, feel, or believe these things. You will not be able to understand them from your point of view. You will have to get into their perceptions, feelings, and histories, and to do that you must imagine what you would be experiencing in their situation.

Importantly, having empathy does not mean that you must have similar stories or experiences as your clients. Sometimes beginning counselors tell us that they worry that their clients will not want to work with them if they haven't had similar experiences. Counseling students without children may worry that clients who are having parenting problems won't want to work with them. Students working with clients in recovery may question their ability to understand the client's situation. Young counselors may be worried that older clients won't trust them because of their age. We remind our students that empathy is more of an emotional response than a shared experience. In other words, we might remind ourselves, "I don't know what it is like to lose a parent to death, but I know what it is to feel lost and lonely, and on that level, I can connect to another human being." Clients need to feel that connection, and that is the core of empathy.

5. Remain neutral.   Let's say you are having a problem at work with the boss. When you talk to your friend about it, you expect the friend to be on your side, support you, and join you in seeing what an unreasonable jerk the boss is being. But a counselor recognizes that there are two (or more) sides to every story and that the client may be an accomplice in the problem. It takes "two to tango" as the saying goes. Although the counselor is working for the client, he or she remains neutral as to the *cause* of the problem and the *solution* to the problem. If you think about it, the only person you have control over is yourself. You cannot change other people. So, the counselor, much to the dismay of many clients, keeps saying, "Okay, your boss may be a jerk, but what are you going to do about it?" Of course, there are times when counselors must take sides, for instance, when someone is being abused. However, most situations call for the counselor to convey to the client that he or she is listening to the client's version but not necessarily agreeing with the client's interpretation (asocial response). Here is an example:

Client: "My parents won't let me go on Facebook unless they can read what I am writing. It's like the 1950s around them. None of my friends have parents like them. They won't let me go to the beach overnight with my boyfriend, either. It's something we have been planning for months. I can't wait for two years when I can leave."

Counselor: "So, in your mind, your parents don't understand how important this is to you. And you're angry at them for being so restrictive. You think that it doesn't seem fair."

In this response, the counselor is trying to understand what the client is feeling, yet does not fall into the mistake of ganging up on the parents. In the teenage client's mind is the faint hope that the counselor will be able to talk sense into the parents and advocate for her. Can you see that the counselor makes no attempt to solve the problem for the client? Does this fit with your idea of how a counselor talks to a client?

How can you practice this skill of being neutral in your life before you actually work with clients? Believe it or not, family members, friends, and co-workers are often trying to recruit us to the side of the argument. When it seems appropriate, find a way to remain neutral and gauge the effect on the other person. Think about why they might be trying to bring you around to their point of view.

Things to Eliminate Now

1. Give up being a cheerleader.   "That's great!!" "I am so proud of you!" Rah rah, rah. Enthusiastic praise may feel good, but in the world of counselors it is sometimes called "throwing a marshmallow" because, like the unhealthy treat, it does not satisfy us emotionally. It is a judgment that is simple to give and may seem superficial.

Think, instead, about encouragement. Encouragement recognizes the person's effort and offers support, interest, and enthusiasm but does not make a judgment. For example, when your child brings you a picture he or she has drawn, instead of judging it as great art, instead, say what you like about the use of color or some other aspect of the drawing. Note the effort and encourage your child to keep working. Can you see the difference in the relationship between one is giving praise and one who is encouraging? Encouragement is the counseling relationship in a nutshell. Practice encouragement with those around you. Do it in a genuine, non-shrinky way and see how it affects the other person.

2. Give up giving advice.   Advice given to another is seldom useful. It can reinforce a hierarchy in the relationship (one person has the "answer," which the other person seeks), but more importantly, advice sends a message that the person is unable to come to answers on his or her own. When we focus on giving advice and suggestions, we may miss what is most important, such as the feelings the person is experiencing. Giving advice can create distance in a relationship. The person on the receiving end often feels that

---

■■■ *Words of Wisdom* ■■■

"Please give me some good advice in your next letter. I promise not to follow it."

—Edna St. Vincent Millay
(U.S. poet, 1892–1950)

his or her problems were minimized or that the person giving the advice doesn't really understand the situation. Either way, advice is seldom productive.

3. Give up one-upmanship.   Did you ever tell someone about a problem and situation in your own life, only to have it countered with something like, "You think you had a bad day? Let me tell you what happened to me!" When we counter someone's story with a story of our own, we might think we are enhancing a relationship, but we are really creating distance. When our stories are more extreme, more severe, more intense, our goal might be to help others feel less alone in their trouble, but that is seldom the outcome. Instead, they feel misunderstood and minimized, and the emphasis in the counseling session moves away from the client and onto the counselor. Counselors focus on the client and their stories, not on our own.

In the following Spotlight, you can see how the skills that we learn in counseling can enhance our everyday relationships with friends and family.

Roadmap of the Counseling Process

The processes may differ slightly depending on the modality used (individual, group, couples, family) or the setting (community, school, hospital), but despite theoretical differences, most counseling can be described as having five stages. Of course, these stages are not often distinct with a beginning and an end. In each stage, the counselor has a task and the client has a task. Counseling is successful if both partners fulfill their responsibilities.

When we talk about a roadmap of the counseling process, we are usually discussing the most common form of treatment, individual counseling. But group work, couples counseling, and family counseling have their normal stages too. Despite differences, all of them talk about the formation of the relationship being crucial in the early going. For example, in group work, the term *joining* is often used to describe the initial experiences of bonding (Gladding, 2006).

"The roadmap of counseling" (see Figure 8.1) is an analogy that helps counselors and clients remember the basic journey that counseling entails. Although the setting, time line, and specific techniques used in counseling might differ, these five basic stages still apply.

Stage I Establishing the Relationship

Role of the Counselor and the Client: The counselor is empathic and the client opens up.

Every relationship follows a zigzag course. It may start with extreme closeness and then plummet, or it may build over time. The effective, therapeutic counseling relationship may be intense, but it also might be merely pleasant and respectful.

We have already indicated that the counselor must demonstrate warmth, empathy, and professionalism to develop the trust needed for the therapeutic

Spotlight
Using Counseling Skills in Our Everyday Lives

As counselors, we understand that our counseling skills can be useful in all sorts of social interactions, not just in the counseling relationship. Consider this story:

> Last night, about 11:00 p.m., a friend of mine came over to talk to me (Mark) about his marriage problem. What I did was listen as closely as I could and try to reassure him that I would be there to support him. Even without thinking about it, I used quite a few of the basic counseling skills, which had a powerful effect on his ability to sort through his problems. Here are some things I did:

- I gave him my full attention. It was late, and I was tired. But I sat across from him, made eye contact, and listened. I made sure we were in a quiet room when we talked, away from the television and from other members of my family, so he felt comfortable and safe.

- As he spoke, I allowed him time to reflect on his words. I didn't jump in with questions or ideas, but gave him the space and time he needed to fully explore the situation.

- I expressed empathy by letting him know that I understood the feelings that he was having. I didn't take sides in the situation or tell him that I thought either he or his wife was right, but I did make sure he knew that I recognized his pain.

Along the way, I had to restrain myself from doing a number of things I might have really wanted to do, if I wasn't a counselor. These are the things I told myself:

- Don't try to solve the problem. There isn't an easy solution, and even if there were, the solution is not mine to determine. People have within themselves the answers to their problems—talking out loud can help them come to the answers they seek.

- Don't be a superficial optimist. When people are hurting, the last thing they need to hear is empty platitudes. Comments like "I'm sure you two will work it out," or "This, too, shall pass" are unhelpful and distancing. The offer of encouragement and support, "I'll listen whenever you need to talk," is much more helpful.

- Abandon your role as a detective. It's not my role to determine if my friend or his wife (or either of them!) was "right." I don't need all the facts and details, and I don't need to ask a bunch of questions about the minutiae of his story.

- Refrain from advice giving. Clearly, if my friend was struggling enough to come to my house at 11 o'clock at night, then the problem he has is complicated and challenging. It is not something that I can solve after a few minutes of listening to him. Even if I could come up with some answers or advice, it would be far less powerful and useful than anything he could come up with for himself.

When we transfer our basic counseling skills out of the counseling relationship and into our everyday lives, we become better listeners—better friends, partners, family members, and colleagues. We form deeper, more meaningful relationships, because our understanding of others is based on who they really are, not who we want or expect them to be. We encourage you to try these active listening skills in your life. Not only will the practice help you in your journey toward becoming a counselor, you might find that all of your relationships benefit, too.

FIGURE 8.1 The Roadmap of the Helping Process

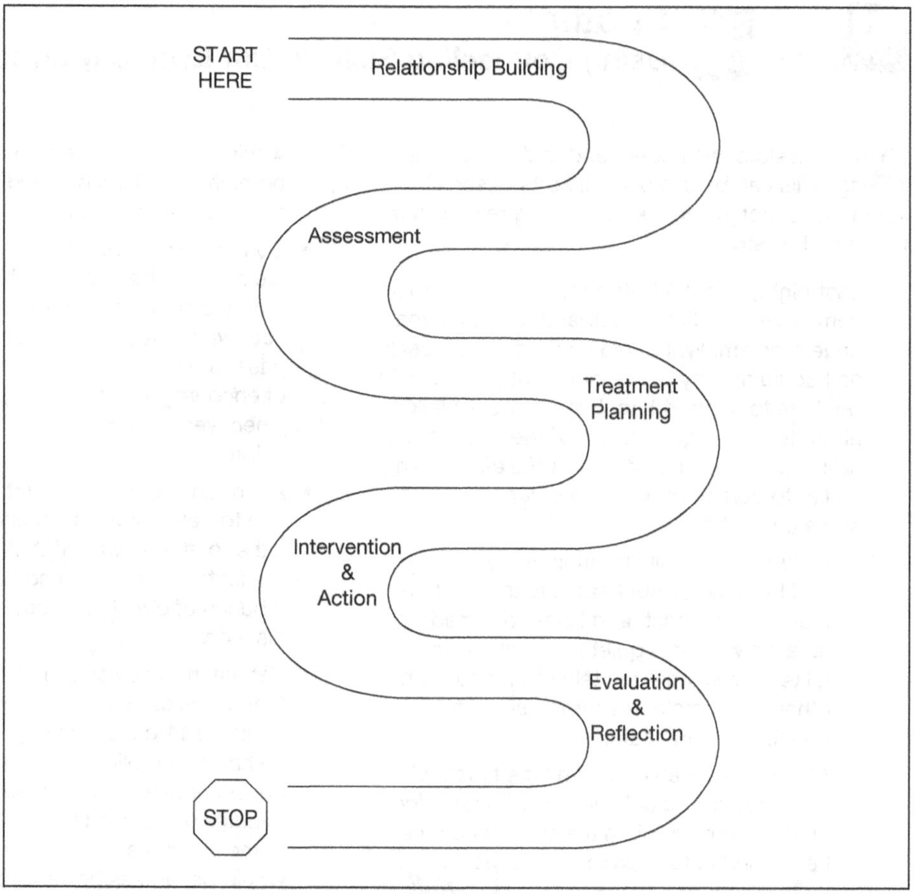

Source: Young, LEARNING THE ART OF HELPING, figure 2.2 "Road Map of the Helping Process," p. 41, 2009. Reproduced by permission of Pearson Education, Inc.

endeavor. But the client also has a job. The client must first be able to show a *willingness* to engage in counseling and second, the necessary abilities to accomplish the basic tasks that the setting requires. Willingness includes the idea that the client's participation is voluntary and that he or she is willing to open up and disclose to the counselor. Clients may be unwilling to do this, and then the counseling process is impeded. Clients may also be *unable* to open up to one degree or another. For example, those who are extremely shy may not open up in group counseling and derive the least benefit from it. Group work is an interpersonal setting, and the lack of interpersonal skills hinders one's ability to grow in that venue.

Stage II Assessment

Role of the Counselor and the Client: The counselor asks the right questions and the client provides information.

Before counseling begins, the client must answer the question, "Where does it hurt?" Most counselors want to know something about the problem, its intensity, frequency, and duration. The counselor wants to list all of the problems the client is experiencing so that in the treatment planning stage, the counseling interventions can address the most critical issues.

The counselor also needs to know a little about the client's background. Counselors might ask questions about the client's living situation, previous counseling, family history, substance use, and the client's potential to harm self or others.

Stage III Treatment Planning

Role of the Counselor and Client: The counselor proposes a schedule for helping the client achieve his or her goals. The client collaborates in identifying the goals and agrees to a plan.

Treatment planning is the process of taking all the gathered client information and sorting it into piles as one might sort playing cards. Let us say that a pile of aces represents the most important problems that a client is facing. They are issues such as finding a place to live, getting a job, or finding a way to pay the rent this month. Usually, the counselor makes a pile of emergency issues like these that the client needs to address first. Treatment planning is the process of determining what to deal with first. Perhaps the client has longer term goals such as becoming more independent, finding a partner, or overcoming the fear of public speaking. These kinds of things go into a longer range pile until all the client's problems and goals are sorted.

Treatment planning allows clients to get a handle on what is bothering them in all areas of life. In and of itself, treatment planning can be very healing. Just having a *To Do* list makes the task seem less daunting and raises one's spirits. Treatment planning takes into account the client's needs to get some pressing issues dealt with and incorporates the counselor's expertise in knowing which problems should be addressed first.

Stage IV Intervention and Action

Role of the Client and the Counselor: The counselor proposes methods to treat the client's problems, and the client puts them into practice.

There are literally thousands of counseling techniques, but most counseling programs expect you to master the basic listening skills first and adopt advanced techniques later. The counselor should choose techniques based on three questions:

1. Has research shown this approach to be effective with this problem?

2. Is this approach acceptable to the client?

3. Do I have the proper training and experience to administer the technique?

The client's role in this stage is to actively change using the proposed technique. For example, the counselor and client in Stage III may have determined that the most pressing problem is the client's difficulty in expressing anger directly and appropriately. If the counselor proposes some assertiveness training

Spotlight
How a Counseling Session Might Look in a School Setting

School counselors recognize that in school settings, counseling can be less formalized, shorter in duration, and less structured than in other settings. School counselors might meet with their students for a few minutes during lunch period to "check in" or have two or three 15- to 20-minute sessions to help a student through a difficult time. It may be tempting to think that because on the surface, the logistics of the counseling sessions look so different, none of the information about the format of counseling sessions in this chapter applies to schools. However, that could not be further from the truth. Whether a counselor sees a client in an agency setting for 20 weekly hour-long individual appointments or for one quick session in a school, the same format applies. Even in a single session, counselors must first establish the relationship (Stage I), which may be done with some basic listening skills and empathetic understanding. Counselors then try to understand the problem (Stage II) that brought the client (student) into the counselor's office and move toward some goal or outcome that both counselor and client can agree with (Stage III). A treatment plan need not be a formalized document, but can simply be a verbal agreement between the counselor and student about what needs to occur to help alleviate the student's concerns. Once the goals are agreed

upon, the counselor uses counseling techniques or interventions to help the student resolve the problem(s) (Stage IV), and then both agree to either set up follow-up sessions if needed, to talk with parents about potential referrals to other resources, or to end the counseling with an understanding that the counselor is available if the student needs more assistance (Stage V).

For example, let's say a high school student peeks her head into a school counselor's office to say that she needs to talk. It might look something like this.

Student: "Ms. Smith? Do you have a minute? I have a question."

Counselor: "Sure, Susie, come on in. [student comes in, sits] What's going on?" (Stage I—relationship)

Student: "Well, um, I guess I'm a little worried about my brother. He's in the military—in the Middle East—and I heard my parents talking about it. I think they are afraid for him. I guess I'm kinda scared, too. Um, you know, I heard my friend say that when people come home from combat, they can be really different, you know, they can just have totally different personalities—be all scary and mean and stuff, because of what they saw in the war."

and techniques in Stage IV, then the client must agree to learning these techniques and using them in his or her life.

Stage V Evaluation and Reflection

Role of the Client and the Counselor: Counselor and client jointly analyze progress, plan further treatment, or terminate counseling.

Sometimes this stage is called *termination*, but that term does not accurately reflect what counselor and client need to do at this juncture. At regular points in treatment, counselors need to call a halt, reflect on progress, and consider new directions. The counselor and client need to look at change from beginning to end and

He's coming home for leave in a few weeks, and I guess I'm kinda scared that he won't be the same guy that he used to be."

Counselor: "Okay, so I'm hearing you say that you are thinking about how things might be different between the two of you when he comes home." (Stage II—assessment of the problem)

Student: "Yeah, what if he's all changed and everything, and he's mean or doesn't want to talk to me or something? I mean, he's my big brother, and I really miss him (voice cracks)."

Counselor: "It sounds like he's really important to you and you really love him. You want to make sure that you do whatever you can to help him adjust back to life here at home." (Stage III—treatment planning or goal setting).

Student: "That's the most important thing. I mean, I know he's going to be different after what he's seen, but I want to help him. He was always there for me when I was little—you know, standing up for me when others kids picked on me and stuff. I want to have my big brother back, but you know, I also want to help him if he needs it."

Counselor: "That's really important, Susie. I'm glad you want to help—it sounds like the two of you have a really special relationship. I wonder what you can do to help him transition back to his life here?" (Stage IV: determining interventions)

Student: "Um, well, I don't know. I guess I could write him an e-mail and tell him that I'm looking forward to seeing him. I thought about that the other day, but it seemed kinda weird—but maybe he'd like it. I also thought I should ask my mom if she has any ideas. I don't know, what do you think?"

Counselor: "It sounds like you already have some great ideas. Telling him that you are excited to see him might help him feel more comfortable about this transition. Is there anything else that you think you might tell him in your e-mail? I also think it's a great idea to talk with your mom. She might have some ideas, too."

Student: "I guess I kinda want to tell him that I want to help him adjust and offer to help . . . do you think that's okay?"

Counselor: "I think that would be really nice."

Student: "Okay, I guess I just wanted to run that by someone before I talk with my mom."

Counselor: "Absolutely, Susie. That's what I'm here for—and please let me know if you want to talk more about this. I have some resources I can share with you about how to help veterans who are returning from the war. Let me know if you want those websites. You can look through them, and then let me know if you have other questions or want to talk some more, okay?" (Stage V: termination)

Student: "Okay, that sounds like a good plan. Thanks!"

either plan further treatment or halt the sessions. Termination is not the only answer. It may be referral to another counselor or another agency. Take, for example, the single mother who comes for help with parenting issues. At the initial session, the counselor sees that, besides her parenting, the mother needs some support and brainstorming to deal with the multiple demands on her time. The counselor supplies this through individual counseling until the client feels more stable. After three or four sessions, client and counselor both agree that the crisis is past but that the client still would benefit from parenting classes. So, a referral is made. The individual counseling sessions are terminated and the client moves on to another agency.

Counselors in all settings use the same basic counseling skills and engage in the same basic format for counseling, although modifications might be necessary to fit the setting or developmental level of the clients. In the preceding Spotlight, we discuss how the format of a counseling session may be adapted to fit within the parameters of a school.

Summary

In this chapter, we discussed the counseling session and what counseling is like for the counselor and the client. We talked about some of the basic counseling skills that counselors use, recognizing that you will learn more about these skills in your counseling techniques courses. These basic listening skills have applicability to all relationships in your life, not just those that occur in the counseling session. Finally, we noted that counselors in all settings provide basic structure for the counseling session through the use of relationship building, assessment, goal setting, interventions, and closure.

End-of-Chapter Activities

Student Activities

1. Now it's time to reflect on the major topics that we have covered in this chapter. Look back at the sections or the ideas you have underlined. What were your reactions as you read that portion of the chapter? What do you want to remember?

_____

_____

_____

_____

2. What do you think makes self-disclosure so difficult for clients? What makes it challenging for you? How can recognizing the difficulty that most people have with self-disclosure make you a more empathetic counselor?

_____

_____

_____

_____

3. Many beginning counselors are discouraged to read about YAVIS and how our clients' appearance can unconsciously affect our counseling relationship. What do you think about the concept that counselors prefer to work with clients who are Young, Attractive, Verbal, Intelligent, and Successful? Do you believe it is true? If not, why not? If so, what can you do to help make sure all of your clients receive fair and equitable treatment in counseling?

_____

_____

_____

_____

_____

_____

 **Journal Question**

1. Think back in your life to a time when you had a strong emotional reaction to someone. It might have been positive or negative. You may feel that there were good reasons for your reaction but rather than think about these reasons, think about and list the characteristics that you liked or did not like about the person. Can you relate this to someone else in your past? How likely are you to have this same reaction to a client?

Topics for Discussion

1. Why is it so important for counselors to remain neutral when they work with their clients? What harm can be done by "siding" with the client?

2. In this chapter, we focused on the satisfactions and stresses of being a counselor. As you look over the satisfactions, which ones do you think are most appealing to you? As you look at the list of stressors, which of these concerns you most? Because you are the expert on yourself, where do you think you will have the most difficulty?

3. How can you incorporate some of your newfound basic listening skills into your relationships with family and friends? How do you think your relationships will change (for better or for worse) if you do?

Experiments

1. Most people who are new to the counseling field think of counselors as advice givers, but counselors know the limitations of this technique. As an experiment, try listening to a friend's problem without trying to fix it. But at the same time, stay involved. Make sure you fully understand all aspects of the problem. How did you feel? What was the friend's reaction? If you are normally prone to advice giving, did your friend notice and feel let down?

2. Talk with counselors who work in different settings about the ways that counseling sessions look for them. Are there common themes that you can uncover? How do counselors maintain the essentials of the counseling relationship when they must adhere to the parameters imposed on them by their settings or clients?

◼◻◼ **Explore More!** ◼◻◼

If you are interested in exploring more about the ideas presented in this chapter, we recommend the following books and articles.

Beier, E., & Young, D. M. (1998). *The silent language of psychotherapy*. New York: Transaction.

> This classic in the field explores the critical role of covert communication, persuasion, and social reinforcement that takes place between counselor and client.

Choate, L. H. (2008). *Girls' and women's wellness: Contemporary counseling issues and interventions*. Alexandria, VA: American Counseling Association.

> This clear, concise book provides a strength-based approach to helping girls and women through the counseling process.

Jourard, S. M. (1971). *The transparent self*. New York: Van Nostrand Reinhold.

> Jourard's book, a foundational work in therapy, reminds all of us why being open and forthcoming is an essential skill toward developing wellness.

Norcross, J., Strausser-Kirtland, D., & Missar, C. (1988). The processes and outcomes of

psychotherapists' personal treatment experiences. *Psychotherapy, 25*, 36–43.

> More than 500 therapists were surveyed to determine their own experiences in therapy, including the lessons they learned as clients that are important for therapists to know.

Powell, J. *(1995). Why am I afraid to tell you who I am? Insights into personal growth*. Allen, TX: Thomas More Publishing.

> This book, appropriate for clients as well as counselors, helps readers become more emotionally open and more self-aware in interactions with others.

Yalom, I. (2002). *The gift of therapy: An open letter to a new generation of therapists and their clients*. New York: HarperCollins.

> Irvin Yalom is a well-known and well-respected therapist and writer whose works are considered essential reading for many developing counselors. This book reminds us all why we entered the field in the first place and gives us strategies for making the most of our interactions with clients.

◼◻◼ **MyHelpingLab** ◼◻◼

To help you explore the profession of counseling via video interviews with counselors and clients, some of the chapters in this text include links to MyHelpingLab at the Pearson.com website. There are some videos that correspond with this chapter, and watching them might challenge you to think about these concepts at a deeper level.

- To learn more about what a counseling session might actually look like, go to Process, Skills, and Techniques, and then

"Engagement" and "Establishing the Therapeutic Relationship"—both of these categories contain video clips for you to explore.

- If you are interested in working with children:

  - Go to Counseling Children and Adolescents, and then "Therapeutic Inventions with Children" to explore more than 50 video clips.

9

Where Does Counseling Take Place?

In this chapter, we will:

- Describe the settings where counseling takes place, including inpatient, outpatient, schools, and nontraditional settings.
- Differentiate between the modalities of counseling, such as group, family, couples, and individuals.
- Identify the major kinds of counseling environments, such as inpatient, outpatient, day treatment, residential treatment, and schools.
- Identify the usual elements of a typical counseling office.
- Learn about three specific environments: a center for treating traumatized children and families, a day treatment facility, and an addictions treatment center.

As you read the chapter, you might want to consider:

- What setting(s) seems most appealing to me?
- Would I like a busy agency or a quiet private practice?
- If I am going into schools, how can I make my office into a place that facilitates the counseling relationship?
- What is it like to work with clients who have a severe mental disorder?
- Would I like to help people with addiction problems or those experiencing a crisis?
- Would I like to help children and practice play therapy?
- Am I attracted to working with couples, families, individuals, or groups?

We start this chapter with the question, "Where does counseling take place?" In order to answer this question we have to consider some other questions: "Who should be in the room?" "What is the best place for my client to receive counseling?" "When is family counseling appropriate?" "When is it best to recommend residential treatment for a client?" "How do I decide when to involve parents?" Before you can make these judgments yourself for a specific and unique client, you need to have an idea about the range of services available. So, in this chapter, we discuss the differences between individual, group, couples, family, and multifamily groups. We then talk about various levels of treatment

■■■ *Words of Wisdom* ■■■

"When I first started my practicum, I was so worried about group counseling. I'm an introvert. Groups sort of overwhelm me. Every time my supervisor suggested that one of my student clients might benefit from group counseling, I found reasons why they needed individual counseling instead. I realize now that I was more worried about what I wanted than what was best for my clients. That was a hard lesson. I try to be more open to my clients now—to what they need, even if it means my groups fill up and I have to set up more of them. I'm still an introvert, but at least I'm an introvert who puts my clients' needs first!"

—Andy S., school counseling
internship student

from inpatient hospitalization to Internet counseling and consider how counselors with different specialties use different types of interventions to help clients obtain optimal functioning. This chapter also includes three Spotlight sections focusing on different counseling workplaces. These are summaries of our visits to real treatment centers that may help you get a feel for what it might be like to work there. They include a center that helps children and families experiencing trauma, a substance abuse treatment center, and a day treatment program for clients with severe and persistent mental disorders. Finally, we include two Snapshots of counselors who work in two very different types of settings: a college counselor and a counselor who faces the realities and satisfactions of counseling in a prison setting.

 ## Who Is in the Room?

One of the first things a counselor does is determine who should come to the counseling session. Some clients really need couples counseling rather than individual counseling. An adolescent client might benefit more if the entire family discusses rules, roles, and communication. The client may have some preference, but the counselor needs to weigh in on this decision and not merely accept the conditions that clients set. Parents who bring in their 4-year-old for therapy because they are going through a divorce may be better served by helping them communicate with each other more productively rather than simply treating the child. By the same token, the school counselor especially needs to be sensitive to the need for family therapy and be able to make referrals rather than trying to solve all the family problems when only the child is receiving help. Consider the following everyday scenarios:

- Parents bring in a 12-year-old girl for counseling because her grades have declined.
- A man comes in to talk about the fact that he is not "in love" with his wife of 20 years.
- A man has difficulty in disclosing himself to others and says that his relationships are shallow and that he is isolated and lonely.
- A 9-year-old girl asks the school counselor how to stop being bullied.
- A single parent wants family counseling because her two children fight "constantly."

Each of these scenarios requires a counselor to make a decision about who should be in the counseling session. In order to make a good decision, the counselor needs more information. Frequently, it is too early to decide who should be in the session when the first appointment is scheduled or when the initial contact is made in a school. Therefore, the first session of counseling, much to the dismay of the beginning counselor, often has little to do with therapeutic progress and more to do with collecting data and sorting out who should attend later sessions. The presenting problem is the key to deciding who should attend counseling. For example, if the problem is poor communication between child and parent, then both should attend a family counseling session. If students are fighting with each other in the halls, it is often productive to bring all of the students into the office to determine if a solution or compromise can be reached. The point is that some problems are best addressed by an individual (even if other people are involved in the conflict), while other situations benefit from multiple perspectives. Differentiating between the two types is something that requires investigation and understanding. For example, an adult client who is frustrated that her mother is overly critical may benefit from a session that includes the client and her parent. It might also be important to work with the client independently, helping her disengage from her mother's attempts to control her through criticism and giving her skills to enhance her sense of self-worth. Counselors first and foremost work to understand the problem before they develop a plan for intervention.

Even when the inclusion of others might benefit the client's problem, this might not be a realistic option. The client's family may refuse to participate in treatment or may live in another state. Further, just because a client's problems involve other people, that does not necessarily mean it is productive (or appropriate) to include the others in counseling. A client who is having difficulty working for an overbearing boss certainly cannot (typically) ask the boss to accompany the client to counseling. A young woman who feels pressured by her boyfriend to have sex even though she is not ready would not necessarily benefit from having the counselor tell the boyfriend to back off. In these instances, clients need to develop the necessary skills to help them navigate difficult interpersonal relationships. Many clients come to counseling and insist that other people need to change so that the client can be happy. They say things like, "My wife nags me all the time," "The other kids won't play with me," or "My son drinks too much and it's ruining his marriage." We remind clients that the only person they can control is themselves. It's a hard lesson, but one we all need to remember. In these instances, counseling is often more about helping clients be proactive about their choices rather than reactive to the behaviors of others.

Of course, even if there are times when having certain individuals in counseling might be beneficial, the individuals do not wish to participate. **Involuntary clients** are

---

■▦■ *Words of Wisdom* ■▦■

"You can only work with the client in front of you."

—Clinical wisdom in counseling

Counseling Controversy

SHOULD WE COUNSEL INVOLUNTARY CLIENTS?

Background: No matter where counselors work, they are asked to work with clients who may not be entirely voluntary. They may be mandated by parents, the courts, the school administration, or student judiciary boards. As with most controversies, there are arguments on both sides of these questions, and specific situations require special solutions. After considering both sides of the argument, think about what you believe about working with involuntary clients.

POINT: COUNSELORS SHOULD NOT WORK WITH CLIENTS WHO HAVE BEEN FORCED INTO COUNSELING	COUNTERPOINT: COUNSELORS SHOULD USE THEIR ROLE TO HELP EVEN INVOLUNTARY CLIENTS ACHIEVE OPTIMAL FUNCTIONING
• It is unethical to change people who do not want to be changed.	• Many clients are involuntary, such as those convicted of child abuse. Involuntary clients should be treated because it leads to a better life for the client and may prevent future abuse.
• The involuntary client has not given consent for treatment, therefore the state, the parents, or an institution is really the client.	• Right now, people with severe mental disorders are not required to take medication or receive counseling. Many of them are homeless. Although their rights are intact, are they really free?
• Involuntary counseling could potentially be misused. For example, one parent in a divorce battle can portray the other as mentally unfit.	• Consider the prison population or those with substance abuse problems. If medication or counseling can help clients obtain release and lead a more normal life, shouldn't they be given the chance for freedom even if they do not initially agree?
• Involuntary clients are unmotivated and defensive. Too much time is spent in cajoling and coaxing.	• Counseling is not a diabolical process of mind control. Suggesting that counselors can force someone to change is not accurate and misrepresents the counseling process.
• Counseling children without their permission is another example of failing to get informed consent. Although it is legal to see children with only parental consent, children should also be asked for their assent, and their wishes should be respected whenever possible.	• Many situations start out as involuntary, such as when parents bring in their adolescents. When clients learn more about the process and what they have to gain, this initial reluctance goes away.
• If we do not allow clients to choose whether they will be in therapy, we are not showing respect for the clients' right to choose. How can we, then, tell the clients that they have the ability to choose a better life?	

As with many controversies, there are valid points on both sides of this argument.

←—————————————————————————————————————→

Do not work with
involuntary clients

Do work with
involuntary clients

On the continuum, place an "X" where you think you stand on this issue.

those who reject or decline counseling but who are mandated to attend by an external authority and who face some type of negative consequence if they refuse. Many counselors struggle with these types of clients, both from a philosophical standpoint (these clients challenge the concept of free will in counseling) as well as from a practical one (involuntary clients can be particularly difficult to counsel). Nevertheless, counselors in many different types of settings will encounter involuntary (or, at the very least, very reluctant) clients. In the accompanying Counseling Controversy, we challenge you to consider your stance on working with these clients. As you read the controversy, consider these scenarios:

- Parents bring their 17-year-old in for counseling because the client is failing his classes. What would you do if the adolescent client refused to participate?
- College counselors are often faced with involuntary referrals from Student Life or Student Judiciary. Do you think it is appropriate to sentence college students to counseling? How would you handle a student referred involuntarily for alcohol abuse or physical violence against another student?
- How do you feel about involuntarily hospitalizing a client if he or she appears to be dangerous to self or others? What sort of training do you think you would need?

 ## Counseling Specialties and Modalities

Remember that the American Counseling Association (ACA) defines professional counseling as "The application of mental health, psychological, or human development principles, through cognitive, affective, behavioral or systematic intervention strategies, that address wellness, personal growth, or career development, as well as pathology" (American Counseling Association, 2007). Further, ACA says that there are *specialties* in counseling that require additional training beyond these basic principles. Some counseling specialties are based on the inclusion of more than one client, and these are sometimes called *counseling modalities*. For example, group counseling, couples and family therapy, and classroom guidance are all counseling modalities that involve more than one client. Beyond the special training required, practicing one of these counseling modalities means making a perceptual shift. For instance, many counselors become discouraged because they first learn individual counseling and then, when confronted with a group, they attempt to work with each individual rather than the group as a whole. Of course, not only is this unproductive, it fails to take advantage of the therapeutic conditions that only group counseling can provide. As another example, the close relationship that forms between the counselor and client in individual counseling seems less powerful in couples work. In order to work with a couple, the counselor cannot obviously side with one member or the other. In this context, the therapeutic relationship is qualitatively different (not more or less, but of a different type) from individual counseling. Thus, counseling modalities are not just different in terms of the knowledge that one must gain but also in terms of *how* the counselor interacts with the clients. These different types of counseling modalities can be used in lots of settings and with many different client populations. In Table 9.1, we summarize our definitions and distinctions of some of the major counseling modalities.

Group Work Including Group Counseling, Group Psychotherapy, and Psychoeducation

Group counseling is a format in which a collection of individuals who were not previously connected meet with a counselor to overcome their problems. Usually the members are carefully chosen to make sure that they can benefit from this form of counseling and the group is an appropriate place for them. Clients with interpersonal problems such as isolation, poor relationship quality, or lack of assertiveness are best suited to group counseling. In school settings, counselors use the power of groups to help children who face interpersonal difficulties, (such as shyness or problems controlling anger), or to help children connect with others who are facing similar challenges (such as parents who are divorcing). Group counseling can be a powerful treatment because it provides clients with a safe interpersonal laboratory in which to try out a new way of interacting.

According to the Association for Specialists in Group Work (ASGW, 2009), groups can be divided into four types: (1) task and work group facilitation; (2) group psychoeducation; (3) group psychotherapy; and (4) group counseling. **Task and work groups** can be facilitated by a counselor who uses his or her understanding of group dynamics to make individuals and work groups and committees function more effectively. **Group psychoeducation** involves a classroom-like setting where group members learn specific skills, such as parenting, couples communication, or assertiveness training and then process their learning with the other group members. Therefore, members of psychoeducational groups usually share the same basic concerns or challenges. **Group psychotherapy**, by contrast, is the use of a group setting to help clients overcome serious problems such as

TABLE 9.1 Counseling Modalities

Modality	Who Is Present?	Relationship of Clients	Best Reason for Choosing This Configuration
Individual Counseling	One client, one counselor	N/A	The client is dealing with personal decisions, values, motivation, career, school problems, disturbing issues from the past, or mental disorders such as depression.
Couples Counseling (also called marriage counseling when applicable)	Two adult clients, one or two counselors	Married, cohabiting, considering commitment, or in a serious relationship	The couple wishes to solve relationship problems affecting both people, or the couple wants to improve their relationship, not the individual issues of each person.
Family Counseling	May be nuclear family, those family members currently living together, extended family, or a client and his/her family of origin. May include children and often two counselors (cotherapy).	Related by blood, marriage through adoption, or see themselves as a family	The problem affects everyone in the family and everyone can help solve the problem. Typical problems include poor communication, rules and roles, adjusting to a family member's substance abuse recovery, death of a family member, etc.
Multi-Family Group Counseling	Members of several families (usually two or three families) and one or two counselors	Families are unrelated except that they may share similar issues.	Families who have common issues such as parenting problems or substance abuse can learn from each other.
Group Counseling	5–12 adults or children, one or two counselors (group leaders)	None	Clients have interpersonal issues such as a wish to improve themselves and to form and maintain relationships.
Group Psychotherapy	5–12 adults or children, one or two counselors (group leaders)	None. Normally clients have different disorders but may have a common symptom such as anxiety.	Clients have serious issues or mental disorders.
Psychoeducation	Normally a group procedure with 5–12 individuals, it may be tailored to individual or couples counseling sessions or with larger groups, one or two counselors (group leaders)	None. Clients are usually experiencing similar problems such as lack of assertiveness, marital problems, parenting issues, etc.	Clients do not have the skills necessary to cope with a particular problem and could benefit from the support of a group.
Classroom Guidance	Counselor and classroom of K–12 students	Students in same class, typically at similar developmental stage	Efficient method to get important information and skills to students within the school structure

depression or anxiety. Clients may have different diagnoses or may all suffer from the same problem, such as eating disorders. Finally, **group counseling** is usually described as a group experience for individuals without mental disorders who want to make specific changes in their life that will make them more effective (see Corey & Corey, 2008).

Couples Counseling

Couples counseling involves helping couples develop better relationships and solve problems in their relationships. Couples are individuals who are married, living together, or committed to a relationship. They may be of the same or opposite sexes. Their problems frequently involve issues of infidelity, poor communication, finances, and dealing with children and sexual difficulties. For example, a couple comes to counseling because they are fighting over money and they cannot agree who will be in charge of making financial decisions. One wants to save and one wants to buy a new car. Although this may seem like an easy problem to solve through compromise, in couples, even the most prosaic problem is deep. Couples may deal with conflict based on their own family histories and can stubbornly refuse to be reasonable because it means relinquishing control. Many couples come to counseling rather late in the game and with problems such as infidelity that take a long time to overcome. Other couples show rapid improvement as they learn methods for better communication and learn to be honest about their needs (see Long & Young, 2007). Couples' problems respond to counseling and to psychoeducational couples education programs, sometimes called Marriage Education.

Family Counseling, Including Multiple Family Groups

Family counseling means seeing members of a family to improve the overall functioning of the family and its individual members. Families often come for help because one member is causing a problem or because the unit is not functioning well together. Communication and distributing responsibilities are common problems. For example, family counseling might be needed when a woman returns home after inpatient substance abuse treatment and feels cut off from the life of the family. Sometimes all family members are asked to attend and sometimes only certain members. Frequently some members cannot or will not attend. That can make it hard for the counselor who is trying to bring everyone together. Family counseling is also challenging to the new counselor because it usually requires the counselor to be more active and to direct the conversation in constructive ways. Counselors who work with families get special training in theories of family therapy and family therapy techniques and learn to recognize special ethical issues associated with family work (see Gladding,

---

■■■ *Words of Wisdom* ■■■

"The couple is a unique dyad, separate from the individual and family, but the couple influences and is influenced by each."

Source: Long & Young (2007, p. 3).

2006). In addition, some counselors, especially in addictions treatment, work in multiple family groups. This is often a hybrid of family counseling and group counseling, with some psychoeducational components. The counselor may work with a particular family and then open up the discussion to the whole group, who give feedback and support. At times, the counselor might offer education on family development, coping with addictions, and the family life cycle.

Classroom Guidance

The American School Counselor Association (ASCA) National Model includes classroom guidance as an important component of school counseling programs. Classroom guidance lessons are an efficient way for school counselors to provide all students with developmentally appropriate knowledge and skills to help them achieve their academic, career, and personal/social competencies (ASCA, 2005). School counselors also use classroom guidance to give students information about available services and resources as well as opportunities for students to learn more about important transitions in their lives, such as preparing for middle school or postsecondary opportunities. Finally, school counselors use classroom guidance as a proactive approach to addressing the needs of students within the school, such as the elimination of bullying; violence prevention; the dangers of tobacco, alcohol, or other drugs; or positive body image or academic competence. The ASCA Model (2005) recommends that elementary school counselors spend 45% of their time in classroom guidance activities. For high school counselors, the recommended allotment of time is 25%.

Counseling Specialties

Counseling specialties can be based on specific types of interventions, for example, biofeedback, narrative therapy, or hypnosis. Counselors can use these interventions in a variety of settings and with different presenting problems. An example of a specific intervention that counselors can learn is play therapy. **Play therapy** is the most commonly used technique for working with young children. Although play therapy is primarily used with kids, it is by no means confined to this population. Many counselors use play techniques with adult individuals, adolescents, couples, and families. For example, with adolescents, the counselor may incorporate games as a way of establishing rapport or use media such as drawing and writing to help clients express themselves. There are also a number of expressive therapy techniques for couples such as asking a couple to draw a picture together. The results can reveal important issues and add an element of spontaneity and fun (see Landreth, 2002). In the accompanying Spotlight, a counselor visits Kids House, a place where abused

Spotlight
Kids House at the Wayne Densch Family Trauma Center

Mark Young

Kids House in Sanford, Florida, is a Children's Advocacy Center where the mission is to aid children by providing all necessary services for children who are victims of abuse, from report and investigation through treatment and prosecution, in a friendly, nonthreatening environment. Kids House is a nonprofit 501(c)3 organization that operates through donations and grants from foundations, concerned citizens, local governments, businesses and corporations, private organizations, and other nonprofit agencies. Without funding support from the community, Kids House would not exist. Kids House is governed by a board of directors comprised of business and community leaders in central Florida. The children walking through the doors of Kids House may have been physically, sexually, or emotionally abused. They may have been victims of medical neglect or witnessed horrible domestic violence. Kids House is a place where forensic interviewers, child advocates, law enforcement, medical staff, and counselors all work together in one place to minimize the impact on clients as they run the gauntlet of agencies and legal entanglements. Over a thousand children and their families are helped here every year. Kids House is a place of support and healing for traumatized people.

Kids House is a warm, friendly environment where the needs of children come first. As you walk past the fountain near the main entrance,

you realize that the physical layout is designed to be calming and at the same time, secure. You must ring the bell and then you can enter if you have an appointment. As soon as they walk in the door, children are invited to explore the playroom, located right in the lobby. Books, movies, and crafts are accessible and their use is encouraged in an effort to make the children feel as comfortable as possible through their ordeal. The center looks nothing like the mental health facilities I am used to. It has bright murals and a very protected outside play area that is highly visible. A lot has been done to deinstitutionalize the facility. It does not feel like a doctor's office.

You travel down a winding hallway to the Mental Health Program wing. Here, Kids House becomes even homier with a series of counselors' offices and play therapy rooms that connect via hallways to a large conference room, which doubles as a play therapy room and family or group counseling room. It is here that the mental health staff meets for case conferences or Treatment Team meetings. The Mental Health Program staff consists of three Licensed Mental Health Counselors, two with master's degrees in mental health counseling and one with a master's degree in clinical psychology; one Registered Mental Health Counselor intern, also with a master's degree in mental health counseling; and a Clinical

children find refuge. You'll read about how hard the staff works to provide an environment that is safe and welcoming for the children as well as supportive for the staff. Could you imagine what it would be like to work in a place like this?

Other counseling specialties are based on client problems or needs, such as rehabilitation counseling, career counseling, sports counseling, gerontological counseling, or addictions counseling. Counselors who work in these specialties recognize that additional training and experience is necessary due to the complexities or specific concerns that their clients face. For example, when beginning counselors work with clients who have addictions, they often discover that their interventions cannot

Social Worker with a master's degree in social work, who is the director of the Mental Health Program. Kids House also offers to share their expertise through an internship program. Usually there are one or two counseling interns who are learning this specialized area of treatment as they finish their master's degrees. As a contracted clinical director, a psychologist in private practice comes in regularly for group supervision.

One of the first things you notice is the camaraderie of the staff. Despite the fact that they are dealing with seriously traumatized kids and disrupted or dysfunctional families, they are positive, optimistic, and collegial. Some of this is probably due to the program director, Nicole Brenenstuhl, who has created an atmosphere of support. A calm and supportive leader is crucial because counselors dealing with trauma are also stressed by what they hear and are faced with secondary trauma and compassion fatigue. When I asked the staff what it was like to work at Kids House, they all mentioned that they feel they can rely on their colleagues for support when they have a difficult case. Nothing could be more important, especially for the beginning counselor. Working with abused children exposes counselors to some of the most complex and difficult counseling situations. There are angry and upset parents, legal messes, and traumatized children. No one can learn this job overnight because there are so many unexpected twists and turns. Children are removed from their homes to foster care, parents divorce, a father or stepfather goes to jail. Sometimes the children themselves are so wounded that they are nonverbal, scared of the counselor, or shut down to protect their parents.

So when these inevitable knotty issues arise, you need someone to talk to right away, not tomorrow. In my interviews with the staff, I found that they all feel that they can easily consult by walking down the hall to another counselor's office or talking with the program director before the day is over. The staff also has facilities for continuing education. When you have the feeling that you are learning new and effective tools, it can give you confidence to face another day. The staff recently completed training in Eye Movement Desensitization and Reprocessing (EMDR), a relatively new treatment for trauma.

The most often used method of treating traumatized kids is play therapy. Play therapy is a way of interacting with children as they play, allowing them to express what is going on inside through their use of toys, sand, games, artistic media, and other activities. The sand tray is a much-used medium in play therapy, allowing kids to envision an environment that they populate with figures to express what they are going through. As children develop, they become more able to verbalize their feelings, and more talk is incorporated into the treatment.

As I left Kids House, I thought about what a blessing this place is for children and their families. I also realized that, in many ways, it is an ideal place for a counselor to work. There is also law enforcement on-site working in collaboration through the investigations, but also providing a sense of security for staff and families. There are opportunities for growth through continuing education and supervision. The stress of working with traumatized individuals is minimized by the opportunities for staff support, collaboration, and an attractive and serene working environment.

operate in isolation but must accommodate the clients' linkages to Alcoholics Anonymous (AA) or Narcotics Anonymous (NA). Gerontological counselors must fully understand the developmental stage of their clients and how developmental concerns interact with the mental health problems they present. Rehabilitation counselors often not only help their clients (consumers) find jobs but help them adjust to life with a disability. In other words, each of these specialties requires additional training and experience to meet the requirements necessary to work with the challenges these clients present. In the accompanying Spotlight, a counselor visits a Center for Drug-Free Living, a setting where the staff focuses on the counseling specialty of addictions. As you read the Spotlight, think about whether you can imagine yourself as an addictions counselor in a setting such as this.

Spotlight
The Center for Drug-Free Living

Tracy Hutchinson, MA, Licensed Professional Counselor

The Center for Drug-Free Living, located in Orlando, Florida, offers a complete range of services from early intervention for those struggling with drug and alcohol dependence, to higher levels of care such as residential treatment and aftercare. There are also services for youth, including community-based prevention and intervention programs in schools. The Center employs 500 staff in more than 30 programs including counselors, behavioral technicians, nurses, doctors, and administrators.

I visited an outpatient chemical dependency facility that is housed in a renovated 1960s motel downtown. The facility hosts a medication assisted program (formerly known as a methadone clinic) for those with an opiate dependency as well as an outpatient counseling program. As I arrive, I move through a waiting area crowded with clients. Many of them are here to receive their methadone before going to work. I walk outside to a courtyard where,

on the second story, you can see the offices of six counselors and three interns along the balcony. The center serves about 200 clients at this location. Jody Scott, the clinical director, explains that most staff have master's degrees, and she adds that many of them are in recovery from some addiction themselves. There is no formal security here and counselors are encouraged not to be at the center alone.

What is it like to work here? The Center is located in a busy, sometimes noisy, urban environment. Counselors are required to see 28 clients per week either in group or individually. Therefore, the daily goal of each counselor is to engage in six direct service activities (client-contact hours) that include new intake sessions, individual counseling, or case management services. Case management is not counseling, but activities by a mental health provider associated with a client's health, legal, job issues, or other practical

An example of a counseling specialty based on client problems or needs is career counseling. **Career counselors** help individuals or groups (for example, in classroom guidance activities) explore career options, make career plans, navigate career transitions, or work through career-related problems. The profession of counseling has its roots in career (vocational) counseling, and Frank Parsons, often called the Father of Vocational Guidance, helped develop the idea of counseling as a mutual process, rather than something done "to" the client. Career counseling has changed significantly from the early days, when selecting a career was thought to be as easy as matching the client to a particular job's environment. Thanks to the work of Donald Super (1910–1994) and others, career counseling is now seen as a lifetime developmental process. Changes and transitions that occur over a person's lifetime, either planned or unanticipated, can greatly affect career choice. Perhaps you have seen this in your own life or the journeys of some of your classmates. People wait to go to graduate school until after the children are grown, or marriages or separations result in geographical moves or changes in finances. All of these experiences and more can alter a career path. Career counseling meets clients where they are in their developmental journey and helps them make appropriate

problems that impinge on treatment. Counselors generally have a caseload of about 30 clients if they work in the outpatient side of the facility and about 50 clients in the methadone clinic. They are also required to facilitate four groups per week. Challenges for the counselor include considerable paperwork and the fact that the Center does not have case managers to advocate and locate services for clients. Therefore, counselors are often faced with helping clients find transportation, housing, and so on.

The starting salary is $28,000 for beginning counselors, and Jody explains that an attractive bonus for beginning counselors is that the clinic offers supervision for those who are seeking licensure. Generally, counselors stay for about two years until they obtain their licenses. Most counselors do not want to work full-time in substance abuse treatment. Thus, turnover is expected by the administration. Supervision is provided weekly in a treatment team format where cases are discussed as a group with all members of the treatment team present including psychiatric nurses, counselors, and supervisors. This provides the opportunity to discuss problems and receive peer supervision.

What kind of clients are seen here?

Many clients may be referred from the highest level of care, the detoxification (detox) unit, a place where clients are unable to leave the premises when they are experiencing the most severe physiological symptoms. There are three levels of intervention based on the client's risk of relapse. The first level of care is outpatient treatment, which is generally 3–4 months in duration following detox. Clients placed in this phase may include those who have received treatment previously and are having problems with their social and occupational functioning as a result of their addiction. Clients in this phase attend two group sessions per week and one session per week with their individual counselor. The second level of treatment is for clients deemed at minimum risk. This treatment consists of six psychoeducation sessions and one individual session. For example, a client in this phase may have been referred by probation or parole officers for an assessment and may not have a chronic chemical dependency concern. Finally, clients who graduate to the third phase of treatment have generally concluded formal treatment and normally attend one aftercare group per week.

career choices for the future. People who are unhappy in their jobs or careers often find that the unhappiness bleeds into other parts of their lives. Those who have conflicts at home or suffer from mental illness discover that their personal problems can affect their careers, too. In short, although career counseling is a separate specialty within the profession, using a holistic approach to understanding clients means that all counselors must understand the integral nature of careers to a client's life.

Finally, some specialties are based on setting, such as school counseling or counselors who work in employee assistance programs (EAPs). These counselors are housed in particular environments that, to some degree, shape the clients and client problems that they will encounter. Some of these environments are highly specialized, such as the life of a forensic counselor, who operates within the legal system, while others, such as counselors in community mental health, have a much broader clientele. Regardless of specialization, it is up to each individual counselor to make sure he or she has the appropriate training and experience to practice a specialty.

An example of a counseling specialty based on setting is the role of the college counselor. **College counselors** work in college- or university-based counseling centers. In general, college counselors spend about two-thirds of their time in direct services to students. The rest of their time is spent in university-wide outreach programming, consultation with faculty and staff, and crisis intervention. College counselors help students navigate both academic and personal/social transitions that occur during college. Some of these concerns are situational in nature, such as adjusting to living with roommates or developing social relationships. Other concerns that bring students into the counseling center are developmental in nature. For traditional-age college students, challenges might include forming intimate romantic relationships or navigating the development of sexual identity. For a significant portion of college students, however, the concerns that bring them into counseling are more deeply entrenched. The last few decades have seen a dramatic increase in serious mental health problems among college students. Nationally, about 20% of students seen at college counseling centers have severe psychological problems, and an equal percentage are on psychiatric medication (in contrast to about 9% in 1994) (Kitzrow, 2003). Between 1990 and 2000, the number of students with depression seen each year at college counseling centers doubled, the number of suicidal students tripled, and the number of students seen after sexual assault quadrupled (Benton, Robertson, Tseng, Newton, & Benton, 2003). The good news is that college counselors can have a significant effect on student mental health. When students receive help for their psychological problems, the counseling they receive can improve not just their overall well-being, but their academic success as well. Among college students who receive counseling, 77% say they are more likely to stay in school because of the counseling and their school performance would have declined without it, and 90% say the counseling helped them meet their goals and reduce stress that was interfering with their schoolwork. Retention rates are 14% higher among students who received counseling (Kitzrow, 2003). College counselors help students learn productive ways to manage their mental health problems and to maintain their highest level of functioning. In the accompanying Snapshot, you will read reflections about the life of a college counselor. As you read her story, consider whether this might be a counseling setting that you would enjoy.

It is clear, then, that there are many different ways that counselors can specialize in their practice, and these specialties can help dictate the environments in which counselors work. As you think about the specialties that interest you, be sure to consider how that specialty can define your work environment. Are the parameters of the specialty interesting to you? You will also need to consider what type of training or experience might be required beyond the graduate training that you are currently receiving. Some specialties, such as those that are based on specific interventions, might require additional courses or workshops, while others require the completion of specific training programs. Still others, such as sex therapy or biofeedback, might be regulated by your state licensure board. Clearly, there are a lot of different counseling specializations for beginning counselors to explore. For example, counselors can receive specialized training to use Dialectical Behavior Therapy (DBT), Gestalt therapy, or Eye Movement Desensitization and Reprocessing (EMDR). They can go to workshops and trainings to be Certified Grief Counselors or Certified Crisis Counselors.

SNAPSHOT

Ximena Mejia, PhD, Licensed Mental Health Counselor

College Counselor

I was born in Quito, Ecuador, and came to the United States to pursue my college education. I graduated with a mental health counseling master's degree from Stetson University and completed my doctorate degree in counselor education at University of Central Florida. I have worked for 15 years supporting college students through their adaptation and development in their college careers in various student services roles, including an admissions counselor, international student advisor, and as the director of a Cross Cultural Center. My counseling experience also includes providing individual, couples, and family therapy with sexual assault victims and people suffering from chronic pain.

There is no average day as a college counselor because it is rewardingly different every day. I provide individual and group counseling, manage cases and crises, do outreach, consult, train and supervise. I also perform various other functions that support and contribute to the counseling center and college's mission statements. As a college counselor, I have to be prepared for any and all clinical needs students might present. Because I work at a small college counseling center trying to optimize services for all students, all of the counselors in our office have to be generalists, working with a full range of situations and problem areas. In a small office such as ours, it would be logistically difficult to match every student who has a particular problem with the counselor who has that kind of expertise. But the main reason is that students' situations are too complex and tangled to be neatly divided in discrete categories. Students who might be abusing substances might also have a diagnosis of depression and anxiety and present with suicidal ideation and academic paralysis simultaneously grieving the recent death of a parent. It is important to understand the complexity of each case as a whole and helping and supporting students requires the perspective and skills of a generalist.

I find it quite satisfying to watch students grow and develop throughout their college journey and to see them navigate their college experiences. Given the small residential campus where I work, I'm able to support students by working together with various other support services on campus such as health center, academic support, ADA office, residential life staff, etc. It is rewarding to be able to refer students to the various offices on campus where they can find support. The pace and volume of my job can be stressful at times. It can also be very demanding in times of crisis and on-call responsibilities. I have to be very intentional about self-care and stress relief routines. In spite of the stressors, though, I absolutely love my job. It is a real honor to be part of students' lives and see them grow and blossom. Overall, being a college counselor is really quite rewarding.

Counselors must be careful to investigate the effectiveness of the different specializations before they engage in advanced trainings or become certified in a particular specialty. Not all specializations or certifications have empirical support to back their claims. In Table 9.2, we briefly describe some of the more common counseling specialties with links to websites with more information.

TABLE 9.2 Some Common Counseling Specializations

Specializations Based on Interventions or Techniques		
Intervention and Definition	**Client Population(s) or Counseling Settings**	**Recommended Uses or Applications**
Play Therapy A counselor uses play and play materials to communicate with a child in developmentally appropriate ways. For more information: www.a4pt.org	Primarily children, but can be used with clients of all ages in all settings	Typically used when the child is young or less verbal, when talk therapy is not working, when parenting help or family counseling is not possible, when the child has experienced a trauma
Art (Expressive) Therapy A counselor uses the creative process to improve and enhance physical, mental, and emotional well-being of clients of all ages. For more information: www.arttherapy.org	Clients of all ages, in all settings	According to the American Art Therapy Association, art therapy is appropriate for use with "children, adolescents, adults, older adults, groups, families, veterans, and people with chronic health issues to assess and treat the following: anxiety, depression, and other mental and emotional problems; substance abuse and addictions; family and relationship issues; abuse and domestic violence; social and emotional difficulties related to disability and illness; trauma and loss; physical, cognitive, and neurological problems; and psychosocial difficulties related to medical illness." (American Art Therapy Association, 2010)

Specializations Based on Client Population or Problem		
Specialization and Definition	**Client Population(s) or Counseling Settings**	**Recommended Uses or Applications**
Addictions Counselor A counselor who works with clients to help overcome addictions, either as part of a larger intervention or as a focus of treatment. For more information: www.iaaoc.org	Clients who have problems with alcohol, drugs, gambling, or other addictions in all counseling settings	Many clients of all ages in all settings have addictions. Most counselors believe that other mental health or interpersonal problems cannot be addressed if a client is actively using substances. Over 9% of people over age 12 have substance abuse or dependence problems, and 50% of people with severe mental illness have a substance abuse problem.

Career Counselor

A counselor who helps clients with career exploration, career change, and personal career development

For more information:
www.ncda.org

Students in schools and universities or adults in community agencies or private settings

Students seeking career direction and clients who are unhappy or unfulfilled in their careers or who are facing unemployment or layoffs benefit from the services of career counselors. In times of economic uncertainty, career counselors can assist clients to find meaningful and secure work.

Gerontological Counselor

A counselor who provides services to elderly clients and their families as they face developmental changes

For more information:
www.aadaweb.org

This specialty is new, but growing fast as Baby Boomers age and demand high-quality mental health care into older age.

Clients who need assistance with the transition into older adulthood and the accompanying lifestyle changes or older clients with mental health problems that can be exacerbated or complicated by old age

Rehabilitation Counselor

A counselor who works with clients who have disabilities to help them maximize their potential, including their personal, social, and vocational goals

For more information:
www.arcaweb.org

Clients with disabilities of all ages who receive services through state and federal vocational rehabilitation agencies or centers, mental health programs, employee assistance programs, insurance companies, correctional facilities, and private practice

Clients with injuries or illness who need assistance with job or career transitions or accommodations, with adjustment to life with a disability, or with developing independence

Specializations Based on Setting		
Specialization and Definition	**Client Population(s)**	**Recommended Uses or Applications**

College Counselor

A counselor who provides direct services to students as well as outreach programming to the university community, crisis prevention and intervention, and consultation with faculty and administration

For more information:
www.collegecounseling.org

College and university students (and in some cases, their families) and consultation to university faculty and staff

College students have significant mental health problems. About 1 in 3 report prolonged periods of depression, 1 in 4 has suicidal thoughts or feelings, and 30% say they have trouble functioning at school due to mental health.

(continued)

(Continued)

Community Counselor

A counselor who works with people in the community who have a variety of mental health concerns and a wide range of mental health functioning.

For more information: www.amhca.org

All ages and all levels of functioning, in many different types of settings, from centers for early childhood development to senior centers, from homeless shelters to domestic violence shelters to crisis clinics and hotlines, to programs funded by the United Way or other charitable organizations

Community counselors help clients through life transitions, through times of crisis, and through many different types of life challenges, including trauma, depression, anxiety, stress, interpersonal violence, social injustice, worksite disruption, and career issues.

School Counselor

A counselors who works in elementary, middle, or high school to provide academic, career, and personal/social competencies to students through comprehensive school counseling programs

For more information: www.schoolcounselor.org

All K–12 students in traditional or online schools, and their parents/families, as appropriate. Consultation with teachers and staff

According to the American School Counselor Association website, school counselors "help *all* students in the areas of academic achievement, personal/social development and career development, ensuring today's students become the productive, well-adjusted adults of tomorrow" (ASCA, 2010).

College Student Personnel

A counselor helps students adjust to campus life through campus student affairs and assists students to develop a journey of lifelong learning and discovery.

For more information: www2.myacpa.org

College and university students

College student personnel provide outreach and advocacy for students to foster college student learning. Many people who work in college student personnel are trained as counselors, although they do not necessarily provide direct counseling services. College student personnel assist students in different ways through offices within universities, such as Disability Services, Wellness Center, Residential Life, University Interfaith, Recreation & Athletics, and Career Centers.

The Environment Where Counseling Takes Place

Much individual counseling does not take place in the counselor's office, although that is what we usually envision when we think about counseling. Counselors also work in recreation centers, schools, treatment centers, and other places where they may share an office or utilize a classroom or a corner of the hallway for counseling sessions. The authors of this book have conducted counseling sessions in agencies, hospitals, and schools, but also in jails, prisons, hospital emergency rooms, domestic violence shelters, and client homes.

Further, some counselors now work exclusively on the telephone (Kenny & McEachern, 2004) or on the Internet. There are advantages, ethical challenges, special skills, and dangers associated with not-in-person counseling (Haberstroh, Parr, Bradley, Morgan-Fleming, & Gee, 2008; Shaw & Shaw, 2006). For example, you may not be able to see nonverbal communications that are indicative of serious problems. Telephone counseling has been researched primarily in the areas of weight loss and physical activity, as well as disease management (Eakin et al., 2009). In spite of limited research on their effectiveness for clients with mental health problems, online and telephonic counseling are increasingly common.

Even within a specific counseling specialty, there are differences in environment and setting. In the accompanying Informed by Research feature, we consider how employment setting affects the job satisfaction of Certified Rehabilitation

Informed by Research
The Job Satisfaction of Counselors

Several research studies have been conducted that have measured job satisfaction of counselors based on setting. One of these studies surveyed more than 1700 Certified Rehabilitation Counselors (CRCs) using a measure of job satisfaction. Respondents were asked to assess their satisfaction regarding daily work activities, pay, opportunities for promotion, supervision, and relationships with colleagues (Armstrong, Hawley, Lewis, Blankenship, & Pugsley, 2008).

A type of statistical test called a univariate logistic regression analysis was used to calculate odds ratios (in other words, given particular characteristics of the person or the position, what are the odds of low or high level of satisfaction compared to other CRCs?). In general, the researchers found that the majority of participants were satisfied with their employment (mean score = 48.02, SD = 11.83 out of potential high score of 54 on overall job satisfaction). However, there were differences based on setting. CRCs who worked in college or university settings had the highest level of overall job satisfaction, and those who worked in state or federal vocational rehabilitation settings had the lowest. In fact, the odds of a CRC in a college setting being satisfied with his or her job was 1.93 times greater than a CRC in a state or federal vocational rehabilitation job. In addition,

there were differences in level of satisfaction with components of the job based on setting. More specifically, CRCs who were in mental health or substance abuse treatment were the most satisfied with the type of work they do (94% indicated high levels of satisfaction). More than 70% of individuals in private rehabilitation (e.g., insurance companies, worker's compensation, private practice) were satisfied with pay (5 times more satisfied than those in vocational rehabilitation). CRCs in mental health or substance abuse as well as those in college and university settings were the most satisfied with opportunities for supervision (82% highly satisfied in each of these settings). Interestingly, regardless of setting, most CRCs were, in general, dissatisfied with opportunities for promotion (more than 50% in all settings indicated dissatisfaction). The study results found that CRCs in all settings tend to be satisfied with their relationships with colleagues, ranging from 87% in private rehabilitation to 92% in colleges and university settings.

The results of this study indicate that employment setting can influence job satisfaction for CRCs. The majority of respondents across all settings indicated general satisfaction with their jobs, but CRCs in college settings were the most satisfied overall.

Counselors. As you read through the description of the research, you may wish to consider how important each of the specific components of job satisfaction is to you (day-to-day work, pay, opportunities for advancement, supervision, and relationships with colleagues). What are you looking for in a counseling job?

A Traditional Counseling Office

There is little to back up claims that a warm, inviting counseling environment helps clients get better (Pressley & Heesecker, 2001). Nevertheless, many counselors believe that the environment can influence a client's willingness to disclose, reduce feelings of anxiety, and imbue a sense of safety. Clinical wisdom and theory suggest that room color, lighting, the presence of plants, art, and the spatial arrangement of furniture can affect both the client and the counselor.

We do know that clients want the counselor to sit (on the average) between 48 and 60 inches away, although cultural background clearly has an influence on this (Stone & Morden, 1976). In addition, privacy of the counseling session certainly affects how much a client is willing to disclose (Holohan & Slaikeu, 1977). In general, warm, intimate settings are preferred by clients over cold, institutional rooms (Chaikin, Derelega, & Miller, 1976). Theory and experience tell us that clients like an orderly, not too homey setting that is private, comfortable, and reflects the credibility of the counselor (Pressley & Hessecker, 2001). For instance, clients seem to like seeing the counselor's credentials displayed but not the picture of the counselor at Disney World with Mickey Mouse. As beginning counselors move into their first offices, they often experiment with setting the appropriate professional tone by bringing in artwork or knickknacks that match their own personal style. It is always appropriate to check out the offices of other professionals in your school or agency to see how they have (or have not) found a balance between a professional and inviting tone.

Obviously, larger rooms are needed for group work. Ordinarily, there should be three chairs: one for the client, one for the counselor, and one for a significant other such as parent, spouse, or partner. A small table with a lamp for soft lighting, along with a carpet, can give a room a more intimate feel that can counteract institutional settings with tile floors and fluorescent lights. A table is also a place to set some papers, a glass of water, and the necessary box of tissues. A key feature is a clock, because most counseling sessions have to run on time. The placement of the clock is important so that the counselor does not have to shift his or her glance too much and disrupt the flow of the session. A white noise machine can preserve privacy by masking the voices of client and counselor from passersby. In general, it is an important safety precaution not to have obstacles (or clients) between you and the door.

Other Settings Where Counseling Takes Place

Although we have identified a generic counselor's individual office, it is also important to look at the larger setting in which the office might be located. In

Table 9.3 we describe the general categories of settings where counseling most often occurs. These range from hospitals to agencies to the client's own home. We believe that clients should be enrolled in the least restrictive treatment environment in which they can participate. Inpatient hospitalization is the most restrictive. Most are locked wards, and although clients have the right to refuse treatment as inpatients, they may be discharged if they are not compliant. At the other end of the continuum, in-home counseling, school-based counseling, Internet, and phone counseling would be considered the least restrictive because there are fewer guidelines enforced by the counselor.

Besides selecting the least restrictive environment, the counselor must consider where the client is likely to make the fastest and most complete recovery. Brief inpatient hospitalization might be the most restrictive, but it may mean that the client will receive intensive daily treatment and medication not available in other settings. For example we once worked with a woman experiencing a major depressive episode. Despite outpatient counseling and medication, she was unable to make a dent in her debilitating mood disorder over a 3-month period. She was admitted to a hospital and within 7 days was significantly improved because her medication could be administered correctly and she could receive daily counseling. As counselors, we have found that some clients cannot make progress in treating their addictions when treated in an outpatient setting. Some need a more controlled environment at first. The selection of the environment also depends on the needs of the client (proximity to support system), the amount of money the client has, the insurance carrier of the client, and in the case of hospitalization, the potential danger to the client or the community. Sadly, as in medical treatment, the client who receives the best care is usually the client who can afford the best treatment facility. In the accompanying Snapshot, we hear from a counselor who works in a very specific specialization based on setting: a prison. As you read her story, consider the unique challenges that she faces in her work with clients. Is this a setting that interests you? Why or why not?

In addition to the practical considerations, the ethical issue of client autonomy comes to the forefront when selecting a treatment location. Clients have the legal and ethical right to refuse a particular treatment. But counselors have an ethical duty to know what the best treatment is likely to be, based on current literature, experience, and consulting with experts. They deliver this information to the client and allow the client to make the decision. In this way, counselors are like all health care professionals. For example, let us say you went to the doctor, who recommends surgery. You ask if there are alternatives, and the doctor indicates that none of the alternatives will actually solve the problem, that medication and diet will only ease the pain for the time being. The doctor can do one of two things in this situation. The doctor can give you the less effective treatment or refuse to go along with half measures. The same

■■■ *Fast Facts* ■■■

About 1.1% of the population of the world has schizophrenia, a persistent debilitating mental disorder characterized by hallucinations and delusions.

Source: The National Institute of Mental Health (2010).

TABLE 9.3 Typical Settings Where Counseling Takes Place

Venue	Treatment	Description	Disadvantages	Best Reason for Choosing This Venue	Length of Treatment
Inpatient Hospitalization	Treatment normally includes medication and individual and group counseling.	A hospital setting. Clients remain in the hospital voluntarily, but most are committed involuntarily due to a danger to self or others. Ward is often locked.	High cost, averaging over $600 per day. Because most are involuntarily admitted, clients may not want treatment.	The client is suicidal, dangerous to others, or needs medication administered in a controlled medical situation.	Depends on the problem, but most are about one to two weeks. Longer term treatment as an inpatient is now rare.
Residential Treatment	The usual treatment is group counseling, psychoeducational sessions, and individual counseling. Clients on medication are monitored.	Most programs are voluntary. Less restrictive than a hospital, but clients normally agree to stay for the entire course of treatment. Residential treatment is commonly used for treatment of addictions, eating disorders, and adolescent behavior problems.	Costs vary depending on facility but may approach the costs of inpatient treatment.	Client needs time away from addictions, family environment, and needs intensive treatment and daily monitoring.	30–120 days
Partial Hospitalization and Day Treatment	Clients receive psychoeducational and therapeutic groups along with some individual counseling and recreation.	These two settings are quite similar except that partial hospitalization takes place in a hospital setting. Day treatment is open to the same kinds of clients but is generally less restrictive. About half the cost of inpatient programs.	Higher cost than outpatient counseling but less than hospitalization.	When clients need a transition from inpatient treatment or needs socialization, a positive way to spend time and skills to help adjust to independent living. Family therapy is usually available. Also provides daily monitoring of client functioning and can prevent hospitalization.	3–6 weeks for clients needing help with transition from the hospital, possibly longer for clients with severe mental disabilities.
Adult Congregate Living Facility (ACLF) for people suffering from chronic mental disorders	There is no formal treatment; however, clients learn to live independently and deal effectively with others. ACLFs usually provide some additional services such as meals.	A home-like environment where several clients reside together. May be public or private.	Fellow residents or lack of oversight may make such homes antitherapeutic or the environment may be dangerous. Usually there is no on-site treatment.	When clients can live independently but need some minimal supervision and assistance to prevent hospitalization.	One month to permanent residence

School Counseling	School counselors provide academic and career counseling as well as counseling for personal and emotional development. These services are provided in individual, group, and psychoeducational classroom sessions. They also consult with parents, teachers and others.	School counseling is primarily to help K–12 students achieve academically and to help them plan for future learning. School counselors also help clients with crises but generally do not provide long-term counseling.	School counselors are usually unable to treat family systems that may be contributing to student issues. Also, school counselor responsibilities may make it difficult to fully address emotional and interpersonal problems as academic issues are foremost.	When student has academic or career issues or difficulties adjusting to the school environment.	The average number of individual counseling sessions for students with behavior problems is about 12 (c.f. Lavoritano & Segal, 2006), but students may receive yearly classroom psychoeducation and intermittent career counseling and advising sessions.
Outpatient Counseling	Clients receive individual, group, couples, family, or multifamily group counseling in the offices of the agency or private practice or college counseling center. Clients make their own appointments and usually arrange for their own transportation.	Counseling takes place in an agency, community mental health center, or private practice. Clients make their own appointments and usually arrange for their own transportation.	Nearly half of first appointments do not show. Clients often fail to keep appointments when they begin to feel better. Counselors have difficulty recognizing signs of deterioration, suicidal or homicidal intentions because clients are usually seen once weekly. The counselor hears only the client's side of the story and is frequently operating in the dark as to the client's academic, work, family, or interpersonal functioning. Transportation can be a problem.	Client is working, raising children, or going to school; does not have a debilitating mental disorder and can function independently without daily monitoring; is not a danger to self or others.	The average number of outpatient sessions is about ten (50-minute sessions). Some clients may utilize outpatient treatment for years, either periodically or continuously.
In-home	Counselor conducts assessments or individual, couples, or family counseling.	The counselor comes to client's home and conducts counseling sessions. Home visits also supply the counselor with a wealth of information about the family.	The environment can be distracting and privacy is difficult to maintain. Counselor materials must be transported.	The client would be unable to make regular counseling appointments unless the counselor came to the home.	May be brief or long term. From three months to a year.

SNAPSHOT
Bonnie Erickson, PhD, Mental Health Counselor

Counseling with Prisoners

I have worked for several years with men and women in county jails and state prisons. Working with inmates can be extremely challenging. Individuals in jail suffer long-term effects of substance abuse, mental health issues, poor relationship skills, and faulty thinking. Most have developed long-term patterns and find it difficult to believe in their potential to change. Working in prisons, you don't have much control over the place and time when you can do counseling. While practicing art therapy, sometimes the women in my groups had to be searched, coming and going, because of the materials that we used. One of the challenges is creating and maintaining good relationships with those who work in the facility. Correctional staff can make it difficult to make treatment accessible to those who need it or they can facilitate access to treatment. Despite the difficulties, working in a jail setting is very gratifying. Though many inmates have severe problems, every effort on the clinician's part is appreciated.

One male resident described his time in jail as a "pause." He saw it as a time to examine the state his life was in and make choices for the future. He participated in an intensive treatment program for substance abuse while in prison, and he claimed that jail had saved his life. With the help of treatment he changed his thinking and lifestyle. After his release, he returned to the same neighborhood where he had been an addict and a drug dealer before prison, maintained his sobriety, and worked to establish his own small business and rebuild his relationship with his daughter. Some of the women I treated in art therapy have contacted me about the changes in their lives, how they have rebuilt family relationships and remained drug free.

You may have heard the story about the starfish on the beach. Something similar happened to me as I was walking on the beach in Clearwater, Florida, between training sessions at a conference in January. The beach was windy, cold, so it was mostly deserted. As I walked, I realized that the beach was covered with conchs. They were still alive but somehow stranded on the sand. I started picking them up, throwing them back into the water to give them a chance to survive. I could only throw them a little way but hoped that it was far enough. For about a half a mile I threw the shells into the water hoping that I could save a few. I was working at the jail at that time and thought about the women in our program. They were a lot like the conchs. They were struggling for life and needed help to get back on track. I was overwhelmed by their numbers and realized that I could only help a few of them and then only help them a little. Hopefully, the boost back into the water was enough to put them back on track. I was also sure that many of them would probably wash back up again, or were too weak to survive. This was also true for my clients. Some returned to the jail over and over again, but a few were able to break the cycle and move on with their lives. As I turned to go back inside, I recognized another counselor at the conference coming from the other direction. We smiled as we realized that we were both trying to save them.

dilemma applies to the counselor. If the client wants a less restrictive, less intensive treatment, the counselor may agree while letting the client know about the potential risks. But the counselor need not accept the client's treatment choice if the counselor feels that it is likely to be harmful or if is likely to be ineffective. In such cases, the counselor is obligated to refer the client to another mental health professional rather than abandon the client. Nevertheless, the counselor is not legally mandated to endorse an ineffective choice. As you can see, these things are a matter of judgment. Judgment means taking the time to consult and think about the issue and not making a split-second decision on an important problem.

In the accompanying Spotlight, a counselor visits a day treatment program. **Day treatment (or partial hospitalization) programs** are an option in the continuum of care for clients with serious mental disorders. These programs typically offer full- or half-day treatment options, but clients either go home or to assisted living facilities at night. Partial hospitalization programs are used to help prevent inpatient hospitalizations, or as a "step down" for clients discharged from inpatient programs. As you read the Spotlight, consider whether this is a counseling environment that might appeal to you.

Some Thoughts About Private Practice

Private practice is, for many, the holy grail of counseling work. In established practices, counselors earn more than in any other setting. Some of the joys of private practice include being your own boss, setting your own schedule, and selecting the clients you are best at helping. For example, some school counselors get licensed as mental health counselors or Licensed Professional Counselors and develop a practice working with children and adolescents and running parenting groups. A marriage and family counselor could specialize in working with couples in groups using a marriage education curriculum. A mental health counselor could develop a niche practice for individuals who have experienced trauma or who want cognitive behavioral therapy.

But private practice is not for everyone, and knowing oneself is a key to deciding whether this is the route for you. Some counselors in private practice find it isolating. Unless you pay for continuing supervision, your work is entirely between you and the clients. You may not have the opportunity to talk to anyone about your cases. Even in a practice with other therapists, time is money, and talking about cases can only occur when there are no clients or other duties to perform. You do not get paid for staff meetings. Co-therapy costs too much. People who do not have insurance or who are financially strapped cannot afford private practice. While some practitioners donate time for those unable to pay, most clients who come to private practices are likely to be white and middle or upper middle class.

Is it too early for you to think about private practice? If it seems attractive, there are some good reasons to begin thinking about it now. First, you need to find out how your state regulates private practice. All 50 states have licensure for counselors, but the ability to practice independently is different in each state. What special training is required? Will you need to be supervised by someone else and pay them?

 ## Spotlight
Turning Point: A Day Treatment Program

Tracy Hutchinson, MA, Licensed Professional Counselor

The Turning Point Program, a division of Seminole Behavioral Healthcare, is a private, not-for-profit agency that serves over 100 clients in the Sanford, Florida, area. This voluntary day treatment program helps clients diagnosed with mental illnesses better understand their condition and learn strategies to function more successfully in the community. Clients who attend this program are diagnosed with severe and persistent mental illness (commonly referred to as the SPMI population). Most of these clients have been struggling for years with chronic mental disorders including schizophrenia, schizoaffective disorder, bipolar disorder, major depressive disorder, borderline personality disorder, and antisocial personality disorder. Medication services are provided weekly by the staff psychiatrist.

Clients come from many areas of the community including family homes, assisted living facilities, group homes, prisons, the streets, and state or local hospitals. In fact, many of these individuals would have been confined to state or "mental" hospitals in the past. Therefore, these clients require a more structured program than weekly outpatient therapy can provide, and really need a daily treatment program where they can learn how to function better in society. For example, clients learn about developing healthy relationships and daily living skills such as dealing with public transportation, dealing with their medication, and maintaining a bank account. Because each client is unique in terms of his or her functioning and severity of symptoms, the staff works closely with clients to reach their individual long-term goals, such as obtaining GED degrees and vocational opportunities ranging from learning job skills to actual job placement.

This day treatment program runs weekdays from 9 a.m. to 2 p.m. Transportation is provided to and from client residences. During this time the program offers meals, psychoeducational groups, individual counseling, and structured and unstructured social time. Clients and staff interact and

What business licenses do you need? In addition, you should probably recognize that your university or college is not really educating you in business administration. You will require additional training. At this stage, you might want to look at some magazines and newsletters such as *Psychotherapy Networker* and *Psychotherapy Finances* to get a feel for the current issues facing private practitioners.

Unless you join a firmly established practice, the beginner in private practice must consider 3–5 years as a minimum time to build a business. And that is what you are: a small business owner. Unless you are successful enough to hire a receptionist/administrator, you will also be dealing with insurance companies, setting up and changing appointments, doing bookkeeping, cleaning the bathroom, and vacuuming the waiting room. You will probably pay 40% of your income for overhead such as office expenses. You will have to figure out how to pay the rent for the first years when you are building a reputation (see Barry, 2005). Do you like dealing with finances?

Beyond money matters, the counselor in private practice has to find ways of getting referrals. This means joining insurance boards and professional organizations and attending the meetings of fellow practitioners and community members

mingle all day long; there is a common area indoors where clients congregate and play games, watch television, and participate in various activities with each other. There are several group rooms along another wing of the building where the various groups are held. These groups range from beginning groups for those who just entered the program to intermediate and advanced groups that focus on social skills, interpersonal skills, and vocational skills. Additionally, there is a large outdoor seating area and parklike environment where clients spend time during their unstructured social time. There is also a full-service cafeteria that serves lunch daily, as well as a snack shop that is operated and stocked by the clients at the center. On the day I visited, clients took a bus trip to the public library. These weekly outings serve as opportunities to apply the skills they are learning in the real world.

The close-knit staff consists of six counselors, four master's-level interns, and one volunteer. The counselors are passionate about their job and working with this population. For example, the program coordinator, John Pitkethly, MA, is a counselor who has worked here for nearly a decade. He explains that counselors generally facilitate two groups per day with clients who are on the counselor's caseload. Each counselor has a caseload of 12–16. While the staff and environment exude warmth and friendliness, clients sometimes have anger outbursts and can become aggressive. For example, during this visit, John was asked to intervene as one of the clients had begun shouting angrily at one of the staff on the field trip and was asked to stay back because of his behavior. Because of his relationship with the client and his conflict resolution expertise, John was able to calm the client down and resolve the conflict that the client was angry about.

Working with clients with severe mental disorders is rewarding. It can be very gratifying to see clients improve their functioning to the point where they can work and have better relationships with their families. Yet stressful situations like the incident with an angry client can make the job challenging and stressful. Clients with severe mental disorders have a high incidence of relapse, and this can be discouraging. For this reason, the staff meets daily at 8:00 a.m. This gives all counselors the opportunity to address concerns about their clients, alert co-workers to clients who are having particular problems, share successes, and get support and ideas from fellow counselors.

who might refer to you. Are you a good self-promoter? Do you have an entrepreneurial spirit? If so, private practice can allow you to build something for yourself free from the red tape and restrictions of agency work (Grodzki, 2009).

 ## Summary

This is a practical chapter designed to expose you to some settings where counseling takes place. In addition, we hope that you have learned some rules of thumb about selecting treatment settings. Rules of thumb suggest that they are not exact or applicable to every setting. They are rough ideas gained from experience. Here is a brief list of what we have suggested:

1. One of the first decisions a counselor has to make is who should come to the counseling session. After doing a thorough assessment, the counselor proposes that the client has an individual, couple, or family problem. The next sessions will then include the key players.

2. There are different modalities of treatment including individual counseling, family counseling, couples counseling, multiple family counseling, psychoeducation, group counseling, and group psychotherapy. Once the players have been chosen, the counselor offers the most helpful modality.

3. There are many different types of specializations in counseling. Some are based on specific interventions, while others are based on client problems or setting. Requirements to practice each counseling specialization vary, and counselors must know the educational and experiential requirements before they engage in these specializations.

4. Counselors must ask, where should the client receive counseling? If the client is dangerous to self or others, a more restrictive environment is appropriate. If the clients are unable to care for themselves, cannot be managed by their families, or are homeless, outpatient counseling does not make sense. In addition, some clients with severe mental disorders require more restrictive environments to manage medication and achieve emotional stability as a prelude to less restrictive treatment. There is also the question of client autonomy to be considered. The client should be able to select the treatment setting he or she wishes, but the counselor as a mental health expert must also make recommendations as to what will be most effective and provide the least risk of failure. Associated with this issue is the knotty problem of counseling people who do not want to be treated, and involuntary clients can be particularly challenging for counselors.

 ## End-of-Chapter Activities

The following activities might be part of your assignments for a class. Whether they are required or not, we suggest that you complete them as a way of reflecting on your new learning, arguing with new ideas in writing, and thinking about questions you may want to pose in class.

Student Activities

1. Now it's time to reflect on the major topics that we have covered in this chapter. Look back at the sections or the ideas you have underlined. What were your reactions as you read that portion of the chapter? What do you want to remember?

_____

_____

_____

_____

_____

2. A counselor's own beliefs and values about couples and families can affect his or her work. For example, if you believe that infidelity means the end of a relationship, or that couples should stay together for the sake of the children, or that blended families can never really get along, you will find that your beliefs will influence your counseling. What are some of your beliefs and values that may affect your work with couples or families?

_____

_____

_____

_____

_____

3. The Spotlight on Kids House highlights a difficult issue within the profession. Counselors are often faced with extremely traumatic situations. We encounter other people in their pain and sorrow, and that can take a toll on the counselor's own emotional health. This is even more challenging for most people when children are involved. What are your thoughts about working with people in pain? How can you take steps to monitor your own reactions to working with people who have survived trauma?

_____

_____

_____

_____

_____

_____

■■■ Journal Question ■■■

A Counselor's Professional Setting. Imagine that you've completed your formal training in counseling and you're in your ideal counseling job. In what type of work setting do you see yourself? What kinds of counseling interventions are you doing, for example, individual? Group? Family? Rehabilitation? Adventure Therapy? Long-term or brief counseling? What does your client population look like (e.g., age, diagnoses, ethnicity)? At this point, when considering your future work setting, are there any clients or populations that you would *not* consider working with or any setting that you would rule out? Why? What is it about these clients/populations/settings that you believe would make it difficult for you to be an effective counselor? Is there anything you could do in the coming weeks and months to expose yourself to this population in order to make sure you haven't ruled them out prematurely?

■■■ Topics for Discussion ■■■

1. In this chapter, we describe a day treatment program where clients might become aggressive. Counselors who work in these environments get training on how to deal with these crises. What are your thoughts about working in this kind of environment? Is it the counselor's job to make sure the place he or she works has adequate security? Is this a part of counselor self-care?

2. We have discussed couples, family, individual, and group counseling as major modalities. Which of these appeal to you most? Many students are reluctant at first to do group counseling. Yet, most workplaces want counselors with this skill. Can you think of some ways that you might become more comfortable with groups?

■■■ Experiments ■■■

1. Pretend for a moment that are the parent of an adolescent who is smoking marijuana and whose grades are slipping. As a parent, where would you go for help in your own community? Choose a specific counselor or treatment center. How did you make your decision? Where did you get the name of the person at the center?

2. Make an effort to notice the visual settings of professional offices you enter or homes you visit. What feelings does the setting evoke? Is the room contemporary or traditional? Are the colors warm or bright? As you take particular notice of these places, consider how the physical environment in your counseling office can affect clients' moods.

■■■ Explore More! ■■■

If you are interested in exploring more about the ideas presented in this chapter, we recommend the following articles.

Barry, P. (2005). Perspectives on private practice: The business of private practice. *Perspectives in Psychiatric Care, 41*(2), 82–84.

Haberstroh, S., Parr, G., Bradley, L., Morgan-Fleming, B., & Gee, R. (2008). Facilitating online counseling: Perspectives from counselors in training. *Journal of Counseling & Development, 86*(4), 460–470.

Pressley, P. K., & Heesacker, M. (2001). The physical environment and counseling: A review of theory and research. *Journal of Counseling and Development, 79,* 148–161.

■■■ MyHelpingLab ■■■

To help you explore the profession of counseling via video interviews with counselors and clients, some of the chapters in this text include links to MyHelpingLab at the Pearson.com website. There are some videos that correspond with this chapter, and watching them might challenge you to think about these concepts at a deeper level.

If you are interested in working with children:

- Go to Counseling Children and Adolescents, and then "Working with Parents" to explore video clips that address working with children and their parents in a variety of settings.

To see examples of how adult clients and their families receive counseling:

- Go to Addictions, Substance Abuse, then "Individual Treatment" or "Family Treatment" to watch the video clips.
- Go to Family Therapy, then "Couple and Marriage Family" to watch the video clips.

How Do Counselors Work
in a Diverse Society?

In this chapter, we will:

- Challenge you to think about your own cultural identity and how your cultural beliefs, values, and experiences might affect your development as a counselor.

- Survey some of the major categories of diversity in the United States and consider what counselors might need to know to work with clients from these groups.

- Introduce you to the Multicultural Counseling Competencies and challenge you to think about how to enhance your own cultural competence.

- Discuss the role of social justice and advocacy in the counseling profession.

As you read the chapter, you might want to consider:

- What are your beliefs and assumptions about the role that culture plays in your life?

- How can you intentionally seek out experiences to enhance your understanding of diversity?

- What can you do to become an advocate for social justice and to help all members of society receive access to mental health services?

The world is a complex, exciting, vibrant, and ever-changing place. It is also big, sometimes overwhelming, occasionally scary, and often chaotic. When we venture out into the world and away from the relative comfort and safety of our day-to-day lives, the challenge of making sense of it all can be stressful. One of the strategies that human beings use to try to navigate the complexity of the world is to categorize or label experiences, places, and people. For example, when we turn on the television during an election campaign and we hear an advertisement for a candidate, our brains instantly tell us "This is a political ad." And, based on that information, we make some assumptions ("This person wants my vote," or "We must be careful not to accept all the information in this ad at face value" or "I'm going to tune this out of my consciousness because I already know who I will vote for"). As another example, if a friend asks us to go with him or her to a jazz concert, we might ask a few questions and then classify the type of experience that it is likely to be and make assumptions about whether we will enjoy it based on that information. ("The concert is a jazz concert by a nationally known group. I like their music. I will probably like this concert." Or "The concert is the local middle school jazz quartet. I do not have a child or sibling in this event, so I am not obligated to go. I will not enjoy a seventh-grade jazz concert.")

In the examples of political ads or jazz concerts, categorizing and labeling is an effective strategy that helps us navigate the world. Taking in all information about everything in our environment and trying to make decisions about each event independently would quickly overwhelm our ability to function. However, that same strategy that helps us in so many situations can harm us when we apply that process of categorizing or labeling to people. This is where stereotypes are born. Consider the following descriptions and think about your *initial uncensored reactions* to each of them. Try not to think about whether your initial reactions are right or wrong, just be open to your initial thoughts and feelings.

- You are in a mall with a friend when around the corner you hear high-pitched laughing and squeals of delight. As you turn the corner, you encounter three young Caucasian girls (11 or 12 years old) looking at a poster announcing that the latest young male heartthrob singer will be putting on a concert in your town. They are dressed in brightly colored clothes, have on lots of bright makeup, and are jumping up and down as they squeal in delight about how cute they think the boy in the picture is and how excited they are about the upcoming concert.
  - What are your immediate reactions? What "category" or "label" would you use for these girls? (Consider your thoughts about their maturity, what you think about the fact that they are wearing makeup, whether you think that their loud voices are appropriate for the mall, whether you have beliefs about the type of people they are, etc.)
- You are out with friends on a Friday night when you turn a corner and find yourself on an unfamiliar street. It is quiet and dark, except for a group of young African American males (ages 18–20) learning against the wall of an abandoned building.
  - What are your immediate reactions? What "category" or "label" would you use for these young men? (Consider your thoughts about their motivations for hanging out where they are, whether you have immediate thoughts about your own safety, whether you have beliefs about the type of people they are, etc.)
- You are downtown on a Saturday night when an expensive car pulls up in front of an upscale restaurant. The valet runs over to open the passenger door and helps a middle-aged woman out of the car. She is wearing a fur coat, and you can see the light from the lamppost in front of the restaurant glimmer off her necklace in a way that makes you believe that she is wearing diamonds.

As she reaches her hand out to the valet, you see the glint of a diamond tennis bracelet on her wrist. The gentleman driving the car is wearing an expensively cut suit. As he passes the valet, he hands him a tip. You see the valet glance at the bill in his hand and look up with an appreciative smile.

- What are your immediate reactions? What "category" or "label" would you use for this couple? (Consider your thoughts about their motivations for driving an expensive car or wearing expensive clothes or jewels, whether you think that their display of wealth is appropriate, whether you have beliefs about the type of people they are, etc.)

In each of these scenarios, most of us immediately begin to make assumptions about the people involved. We may call the young girls "silly," the African American men "scary," and the wealthy middle-aged couple "pretentious." When we do so, we are engaging in stereotypes. **Stereotypes** are simplified and relatively fixed ways we have of making generalizations about groups of people to help us label or classify them. Stereotypes can be positive, but more often than not, they involve negative beliefs about others. Stereotypes are so commonly held that they can become a fixed part of a society's messaging (for example, have you heard of stereotypes such as "dumb jock," "pushy New Yorker," "lazy Southerner," "rude Frenchman," or "frail old lady"?). Stereotypes are not only harmful by themselves, but they are particularly dangerous because they foster prejudice and discrimination. **Prejudice,** as the word implies, is a prejudgment, or making decisions or assumptions about individuals or groups without sufficient knowledge or understanding. **Discrimination** involves putting members of a group at a disadvantage or treating them unfairly because of their group membership. **Racism** is the belief and corresponding set of behaviors that racial groups other than one's own are intellectually, psychologically, and/or physically inferior (Casas, 2005).

Counselors live and work in a world where stereotypes, prejudice, discrimination, and racism are remarkably common and persistent. And, because counselors are first and foremost human beings, we are all susceptible to learning and believing stereotypes and prejudices about others, particularly if we grew up in an environment where these negative messages were dominant and went unchallenged. What differentiates counselors from those who hold onto these negative perceptions about others is that counselors make deliberate and intentional decisions to understand and confront their own beliefs and assumptions about others and to work to eliminate stereotypes, prejudices, and discriminatory behaviors from their lives and challenge these assumptions and behaviors when they exist in society.

In this chapter, we will discuss the challenges, and joys, that counselors face as they live and work in an increasingly diverse society. We will introduce you to some of the basic concepts of multicultural counseling and encourage you to set out on a path of discovery—both of yourself, and of the richness of diversity that exists all around you.

In this text, we continually ask you to reflect on your beliefs and assumptions, to engage in self-assessment and self-understanding, and then to be intentional

about your behaviors. Perhaps there is no
part of your growth as a counselor where this
is more essential to your development.
Understanding your own beliefs, assumptions, and attitudes as well as the early messages you received about diversity, tolerance,
and the role of culture in your life is essential
to becoming a highly functioning counselor.
It is for this reason, that we start this chapter
with an exploration of you!

 ## You: A Culture of One

As you learn to become a counselor who celebrates diversity, the first step is understanding yourself. You are unique. You are a combination of many demographic and
social factors, and understanding these traits about you can help us uncover who
you are. For example, you might be female, White, 22 years old, Irish descent,
Catholic, heterosexual, only child of still-married parents, living in the northeast
United States, single, graduate student, middle class, and so on. But if we were to
find another person who matched you on every one of these characteristics, we
would find both similarities and differences between the two of you. Understanding
the categories a person falls into can only take us so far. For instance, the "you" in
this example might be very much in touch with her Irish heritage or extremely connected to her religion—or she might be these things in name only. When you think
about your own life, what are the beliefs you have about the importance of each of
the "descriptors" about you? Consider descriptors such as race, gender, generation,
work status, religion, disability, social class, geographic setting, sexual orientation,
mental health/illness status, and so on.

- Descriptors of me that I identify with strongly:

  _____

  _____

  _____

- Descriptors of me that I identify with only somewhat:

  _____

  _____

  _____

- Descriptors of me with which I do not identify:

  _____

  _____

  _____

If you were to go to a counselor, based on your appearance and demographic information only, what assumptions might that person make about you? What stereotypes exist about the groups with which you identify? Would the counselor's assumptions and stereotypes about you be accurate?

The most basic element of cultural competence is understanding one's own worldview and one's own culture. Awareness of self as a cultural being is a necessary precondition for emerging from **ethnocentrism** (the belief that one's own culture is the standard by which all other cultures are judged) and becoming culturally competent (Sue, Arrendondo, & McDavis, 1992). Thus, to be a culturally competent counselor, you must first understand who you are.

Culturally competent counselors understand their own assumptions, values, and biases. They engage in active self-assessment to increase their own cultural awareness and to understand their worldview. **Worldview** is defined as how a person perceives his or her relationship to the world, including other people (Richardson & Molinaro, 1996). An individual's worldview is the framework from which the person operates. In the context of counseling, the counselor's worldview influences every interaction with every client, from the formulation of a counselor's theoretical stance to every behavior, word, or nonverbal reaction in a counseling session. Counselors who do not fully understand their own worldview cannot be intentional in their counseling.

Beginning counselors, particularly those whose experiences are congruent with the majority culture, are often challenged when asked to think about their own culture. White Americans have traditionally not been asked to consider themselves as cultural beings, and they may find it easier to acknowledge others' differences without exploring their own cultural value characteristics (Richardson & Molinaro, 1996). Of course, this is exactly the type of thinking that leads to unintentional ethnocentrism—focusing on others and how they are different from me rather than understanding my culture as just one of many that inhabit the world. The more you can adopt an open, inquisitive stance to exploring your own culture and worldview, the more effective your exploration will be. Think of yourself as a cultural anthropologist, trying to investigate and understand you. As you do the hard work of building your self-understanding and self-awareness, take heart that this is a lifelong journey. As you read the accompanying Spotlight about

Spotlight
White Privilege

According to McIntosh, privilege is "an invisible package of unearned assets" that a person can "count on cashing in each day" (2001, p. 95). Whether we are privileged because of our race, gender, sexuality, class, or ability status, most of us are unaware of these privileges because we take them for granted. As members of these groups, we don't see them as privileges—we simply experience them as normal, everyday experiences that everyone has. However, members of minority groups who do not share these same set of privileges recognize them as yet another example of oppression and prejudice.

Researchers have uncovered many different types of White privilege, ranging from advantages in housing and employment to education and self-image. Countless studies find similar results. For example, White and Black applicants for the same job with the same set of skills and training consistently find more job offers go to the White applicants. White applicants are far more likely than Black applicants to have loan applications approved, even with identical credit records. When searching for housing, White buyers are consistently shown far more options than are offered to Black buyers. In schools, minority children are far less likely to be placed in honors classes, even when such a placement is justified by test scores. In other words, White privilege means that:

- I can, if I wish, arrange to be in the company of people of my race most of the time.
- I can be pretty sure that my neighbors will be neutral or pleasant to me.
- I can be sure that if I need legal or medical help, my race will not work against me.
- I can go shopping alone, pretty well assured that I will not be followed or harassed.
- Whether I use checks, credit cards, or cash, I can count on my skin color not to work against the appearance of financial reliability.

- If my day, week, or year is going badly, I need not ask whether each negative situation had racial overtones.
- I can worry about racism without being seen as self-interested or self-seeking.
- I will feel welcomed and "normal" in the usual walks of public life, institutional and social (McIntosh, 1990).

White counselors respond to the concept of White privilege with varying degrees of anger, guilt, confusion, sadness, defensiveness, and a sense of responsibility or need for advocacy (Hays, Chang, & Dean, 2004). But lack of awareness or defensiveness about the concept can lead to resistance about learning about racism or other types of oppression. Awareness of White privilege is essential, however, since there is a strong relationship between White counselors' attitudes toward privilege and the therapeutic process. Specifically, counselors who examine their own racial privilege are less likely to rely on racial stereotypes and impose their own ethnocentric values in the counseling relationship. They are also more likely to view minority clients from a systemic perspective and to recognize and reduce the influence of racial power dynamics in the counseling relationship (Hays, Chang, & Havice, 2008).

What are some of the privileges you may have received in your life because of your membership in a privileged group? As you think about your own development as a counselor, how might the privileges you have received in your life affect your interactions with others? What assumptions might you make about clients and their experiences based on your own ideas of what is "normal" or "typical"? How can you work to actively challenge these assumptions?

_____

_____

_____

SNAPSHOT

Alexis "Lexie" Rae, Licensed Professional Counselor, PhD Student

I am privileged. This is not a bad thing. I grew up in a middle-class suburb as an only child, and I never wanted for anything. I went to private schools, I got the best education, and it was never a doubt that I would get my master's degree. I've been spoiled and taken care of for most of my life. I am White or if you want to use the politically correct terminology, Caucasian. I like who I am and what I do.

When I graduated from my master's program in clinical mental health counseling I was offered a job at my internship site: the Columbus AIDS Task Force. My clients were predominately middle-aged, self-identified homosexual men, who were HIV positive. The majority of people who used the Task Force services were individuals who were low socioeconomic status. I met with men who were prostitutes, in and out of jail, homeless, substance abusers, and in violent relationships. Most of them didn't have any support at all. I worked with people who were in and out of the hospital, who were very sick. When I was there, some of them died and others just stopped coming. I worked with people who wished they were dead and a few who had tried to take their lives.

Perhaps it goes without saying, but I worked with groups of people with whom I had had very little previous interaction. Everything was new. I was constantly on edge, double guessing every word that came out of my mouth. That is one of the risks with being a counselor who is a part of the majority (race, sexual orientation, SES, etc.); you can be so concerned with what you shouldn't say that you don't always say the things that need to be said. Sometimes I would avoid topics altogether because I didn't know how to approach them without being offensive.

I was lucky enough to have an amazing supervisor working at the same agency who could relate to what it was that I was going through. She gave me some advice that I will pass along to you. The people whom you see in counseling are not protected from the evil in this world and you are not doing them any favors by avoiding the difficult conversations in session. Therapy is the place where clients should be able to talk about their worries, concerns, and hurts without being stifled.

So, I started having the clients name or describe what it was that they were going through. Sometimes just exploring the client's world would be more eye-opening for both of us than some specific intervention. I researched and read as much as I could to help me understand the often confusing information given to me by my clients. But all the books and/or journals in the world could never give me the type of information about a client's world as well as just getting them to explain it themselves. I often thought about it like taking a journey with a client, sometimes asking for clarification and guidance but mostly just allowing the individual to show me their world on their terms.

I found that I often needed a great deal of listening and imagination. I would try to picture myself as the client, not just pertaining to what the client was talking about but to really thinking about it as if I had the same background and life experiences. People whom I came into contact with had extremely different childhoods than I did. They grew up with different values, different life lessons, and different needs. I repeatedly tried to learn as much as I could about each client—not the diagnosis, not the presenting problem, but the client.

Each person that sat down with me was phenome-
nally different from each other. I think it helped that
I am a curious individual. I just wanted to know
everything that I possibly could. Upon reflection

I think that this curiosity is what helped me to relate
to different types of people, to be open to the
process as it unfolds, and to honor the dignity of
each person I encountered.

White privilege, take a moment to notice your emotional and cognitive reactions to the concept.

Regardless of our racial or ethnic heritage, we must all learn to think of ourselves as cultural beings and take time to understand how our race or ethnicity
influences how we see the world, and how other people see us. In the first of this
chapter's Snapshots, we hear from a White counselor whose work has brought
her into contact with clients who differ from her in race, social class, sexual orientation, and health status. During her master's clinical counseling internship,
she had to confront her own values and assumptions not only about others, but
about her own experience of being a White, middle-class, heterosexual female in
a society that values these traits. The inclusion of her story in a chapter on diversity raised some eyebrows when we discussed the book with colleagues. Several
people asked us, "Why would you put a story from a White counselor in a chapter on diversity?" One even said, "If you don't know any counselors of color to
include, I'd be happy to help you find some." This is *exactly* the type of thinking
that we are encouraging you to avoid. The counselor in this story *is no less a cultural being* than anyone else. Her inclusion in this chapter is to remind all of us
that we each are a product of complex, sometimes shared, and often unique
experiences that have led us to this place.

The U.S. Population: A Testament to Diversity

In today's America, the idea of encouraging counselors to understand and
respect diversity or to develop culturally competent counseling seems so obvious
that it hardly needs justification. The United States is a nation of diversity in
many different characteristics, including race, ethnicity, religion, sexual orientation, and disability status. **Diversity** is the quality of being different or dissimilar.
Thus, to state that the U.S. population has a lot of diversity simply reports on the
facts without commentary. **Multiculturalism**, on the other hand, is the practice
of acknowledging and respecting the various cultures, religions, races, ethnicities, attitudes, and opinions within an environment. Thus, the concept of multiculturalism carries an inherent value whereas the concept of diversity does not.

Many counseling books and other texts help counselors understand the
major beliefs, values, and worldviews of people from diverse groups in society.

While this level of understanding can be useful, if the information is used incorrectly, it can facilitate the development or maintenance of stereotypes. There are at least three significant errors we can make if we do this.

First, we can make errors of deduction when we believe something to be true in general and apply it to the specific. For example, although it may be important to know that Hispanics typically place high value on the family or that Asian Americans usually value a more restrained display of emotions, it is important not to make assumptions about how (or whether) these values are played out for the client sitting in front of you. This client may be an exception to that general rule and not value these traits at all. Or the client may still value these traits but express them in different ways. There is always an inherent danger of false generalizations when we take broad-based information and apply it to the individual. Can you think of an attribute that is typically associated with your race or ethnicity that does not apply to you?

Second, we can make an error when we assume homogeneity. In other words, when we use a classification such as Asian American, we are essentially lumping together people from more than 70 countries and at least 15 different ethnic groupings. Thus, any statements that we make about what Asian Americans value or how Asian Americans perceive something are clearly bound to be inaccurate for at least part of the population. Discussions about racial groups often cause us to consider differences *between* groups of people, but we must also remember that there is significant variability *within* racial groupings as well. Can you think of an attribute that varies greatly *within* your racial or ethnic group(s)?

A third error we can make is minimization or maximization. We do this when we under- or overemphasize the significance of a person's race or ethnicity. Counselors do this when they make assumptions about the role that race/ethnicity plays in the life of a client without checking for clarity. Sometimes, beginning counselors talk about wanting to be racially color-blind, or not to "see" the client's race at all. They say things like, "I treat all my clients the same" or "When I look at a client, I don't see race—I just see a person." These attitudes, however, make counselors unaware of the effects of racial dynamics and minimize the role of race in a client's life. It is perhaps not surprising, then, that counselors' racial color-blind attitudes have been correlated with low cultural competence in counseling (Chao, 2006). On the opposite side of the spectrum, counselors can maximize the role that a client's race/ethnicity plays for that individual and believe race is *the* defining characteristic of the client's life. Ultimately, there is no way for a counselor to understand the importance of a client's race or ethnicity without asking. Can you think of an attribute typically associated with your race or ethnicity that you value very much? Can you think of one that you do not value at all?

Of course, each of these potential errors can occur for any of the categories of diversity, including race, ethnicity, religion, sexual orientation, gender, socioeconomic status, and so on. It is not difficult to see how these errors can increase the likelihood of stereotyping and prejudice. However, that does *not* mean that counselors do not need to learn about the different groups of people they counsel. Just because this type of information can be used incorrectly does not mean that it is not important. We encourage you to develop your knowledge and understanding of the many different types of diversity within the United States—and then use that information in responsible and appropriate ways to enhance your counseling.

Counseling and Diversity

Counselors who attempt to understand client diversity often consider the following categories to help them understand the client's worldview. Of course, there are many more ways to conceptualize clients, but these ideas will help get you started.

Race and ethnicity. According to the definition used by the U.S. Census Bureau, race and ethnicity are two distinct concepts. **Race** refers to a social definition (as opposed to a biological or genetic test) that allows people to classify themselves with the race(s) with which they most closely identify. Options include White; Black; American Indian, Eskimo, or Aleut; Asian; Mixed; or Other. **Ethnicity** in the United States is essentially divided into two categories: Hispanic/Latino and Not Hispanic/Latino. Thus, in the United States, there are five main racial/ethnic groups: African American/Black, Asian American, Caucasian/White, Hispanic/Latino, and Native American/American Indian/Eskimo.

In 2009, the U.S. Census Bureau reported that 65% of Americans self-identified as White, Non-Hispanic; 15.8% self-identified as Hispanic or Latino ethnicity (any race); 12.4% self-identified as Black; 4.5% self-identified as Asian; and 1% as American Indian/Alaska Native. In 2010, 13% of the U.S. population was foreign-born. For the first time in our nation's history, White, non-Hispanic Americans will be in the minority by 2050 (46.3% of Americans). The number of Hispanic/Latino Americans will more than triple over the next half century, and as a result, the percentage of Americans who self-identify as Hispanic/Latino will nearly double, from 16% in 2010 to more than 30% in 2050. Young children are the most diverse age cohort. Among children age 4 or younger, 25% are of Hispanic origin and 37% are of a race or ethnicity other than non-Hispanic White. Thus, school counselors will face an increasingly diverse student body.

In the second Snapshot of this chapter, Demetra Taylor, a Licensed Professional Counselor, talks about her experiences as an African American counselor working in a setting designed to help clients navigate their mental health problems through the lens of racial identity. As you read her story, think about how her initial assumptions about race had to change in order to best meet the needs of her clients.

Clients typically self-identify as members of race(s) and/or as Hispanic/non-Hispanic (ethnicity), and conceptualizing clients through this lens can help counselors better understand them. **Racial identity** is the client's psychosocial orientation toward membership in his or her race, and models of racial identity development help us understand the client's level of acceptance or rejection of racial identity. There are many different such models that you will learn about in

SNAPSHOT
Demetra Taylor, MA, Licensed Professional Clinical Counselor with Supervising Credential

My internship (and ultimately my first counseling job) was at a place that specialized in working with African American clients. I am African American, so I believed that the clients there would have no trouble listening to me and trusting me because we were of the same race. I wanted to do everything "right" when I began so I started out observing the other counselors, debriefing with them after sessions, and identifying different diagnoses. I thought my biggest challenge would be getting the clients to become more self-aware. But when it came time for me to fully participate and have a caseload of my own, I was challenged in a way I did not anticipate.

I was confronted with the fact that within my own culture, there were subcultures that I was not familiar with. Many of my clients lived in poverty, had broken families, drug problems, and legal problems. I was not familiar with these issues in my personal life and it showed in my interactions with the clients. Instead of the ease and trust that I expected because we were of the same race, my clients put walls up. I heard comments like, "You don't understand because you never . . ." or " I want to talk to someone that didn't learn this in a book." Occasionally, I faced a roadblock because of a male client's feelings regarding having an African American female in a perceived role of authority. These instances were the most challenging as I had to work with men who felt women (especially an African American woman) were beneath them and that I had no business talking to them. Needless to

say, these were the times when I felt stuck and like I would never be able to reach my clients.

During my supervision and debriefings with my co-facilitators during my internship, I learned that even though there were many different subcultures and beliefs within our shared culture, there were actually several similarities that came to light. On a broader level, several recurring issues came up such as basic emotional needs not being met, feeling stigmatized by their diagnoses, and feeling marginalized by society. Because of our shared culture, I was able to relate to my clients when they spoke of being marginalized, stigmatized, and feeling out of place because of our race and in some cases, because of our gender. This was the foothold I needed to be able to work successfully with my clients. As time went on, I also learned to meet clients where they were. I learned to take a step back and instead of trying to find commonalities in which to connect, I began to ask questions. I asked about their experiences, about subcultures I didn't understand, and I showed a genuine interest in how and why my clients took the path that they did. More times than not, this proved to be the best way to connect, build a therapeutic relationship, and get to the important work in front of us.

As I moved forward and became employed at this agency, I also had the pleasure of completing some internship hours at a private practice. Here I was working with counselors and clients of different races and backgrounds as well as other African American clients. I did not feel as out of place when faced with different cultures and subcultures because of my experience at the African American agency. It is easy to assume a commonality between people of the same race. However, I remained open to learning new things and just like within my culture, I was able to understand that not all Caucasian people have the same experiences, not all Hispanic people have the same experiences, and so on. I observed that at times it was easier for clients to talk to me because I was female, or college educated, or they knew I would understand how they felt because I was African American just like they were. What I discovered along the way is that we all have basic human emotions and needs that we want to be met. When this does not happen, and we do not have appropriate coping skills to handle what comes our way, problems arise. I learned to not assume anything about myself or my clients. We are all unique. Learning to appreciate and value that uniqueness allowed me to find the strengths within each person that set them on the path toward mental health.

your graduate program. One of the most commonly used is that of Helms (1995), who identified a six-stage model of racial identity development. The stages in this model, *pre-encounter, encounter, immersion, emersion, internalization,* and *integrative-awareness,* have been used to track both White Racial Identity Development and Racial Minority Identity Development. In general, people move from the pre-encounter stage, characterized by either a lack of awareness about the importance of culture (White Racial Identity) or preference for the dominant culture (Racial Minority Development), through an encounter stage (characterized by crisis or conflict), to immersion and emersion (pride in their own culture and retreat from others) to internalization and integration (a complex understanding of race that involves a commitment to the elimination of all forms of oppression and discrimination). A model of biracial identity development (e.g., Poston, 1990) helps track the complexity of racial identity for individuals who identify with more than one race. In this model, people move through five stages: *personal identity* (identity not connected to a race), *choice of group categorization* (selection of one race or ethnicity over others), *enmeshment/denial* (understanding that selection of one race/ethnicity is incomplete identity), *appreciation* (valuing of multiple racial identities), and *integration* (complete recognition and infusion of all relevant racial identities). Clearly not all individuals actively progress through the stages of these models, but an understanding of a client's (and a counselor's) level of racial identity development helps frame the role of race in the counselor/client relationship.

Another method to track a client's adherence to racial identity is to understand the level of acculturation or assimilation. **Acculturation** occurs when individuals from one culture come into firsthand contact with another culture, as when an immigrant moves to the United States. Within the United States, acculturation has typically meant that the minority group must conform to the dominant culture's values, language, and expectations. **Assimilation** is the acquisition of the traits and characteristics of one culture by another, whereby the minority culture eventually loses all the distinct characteristics that it once had. Assimilation is a more extreme reaction than acculturation to the blending of two cultures, and when people are assimilated into a new culture, their original culture disappears.

Most counselors recognize that some level of acculturation can be beneficial for clients to adjust to living in their new living circumstances, but assimilation is never an appropriate goal.

Gender. Gender is a social construct that emphasizes attitudes, behaviors, beliefs, and relationships that are typically associated with being male or female. Gender is clearly linked to biological sex, but it is not the same thing. The concept of gender varies across cultures, but also varies greatly by individual within each culture. Each of us uses the information and feedback that we receive from the outside world to create a self-image of who we are as female or male and how we should behave. Of course, gender also structures and shapes the expectations of those around us with whom we interact, resulting in self-fulfilling behaviors that help shape our behavior to meet the expectations that are important to others (Worrell & Remer, 2002). Within the field of counseling, gender plays an important role in client conceptualization, assessment, goal setting, and treatment planning, as well as intervention strategies. How counselors see gender issues operating within their clients' lives will have a significant impact on what goals and strategies seem appropriate in counseling (Cook, 1993).

Sexual orientation. A person's sexual orientation describes a pattern of romantic and physical attraction to men, women, both genders, or neither gender. Generally, there are thought to be four categories of orientation: heterosexuality, homosexuality, bisexuality, and asexuality, although these simplified categories do not accurately encompass the fluidity of sexuality that develops over a person's lifetime. Because these categories are not discrete and because there are differences in people's behaviors and self-labels, it is impossible to place percentages of the U.S. population into the different categories. In other words, people might consider themselves bisexual only if they have equal attraction to males and females. Others might consider *any* attraction to same-gendered individuals as bisexuality, even if most or all sexual behaviors occur with those of opposite gender. The U.S. Census Bureau (2010) found that 4.1% of the population (8.8 million adults) identifies as lesbian, gay, or bisexual, although other estimates range as high as 12%. Of course, part of the challenge of identification comes from the stigma that continues to surround sexual minorities. **Stigma** is severe social disapproval of people based on characteristics or beliefs that differ from the norm, and **homophobia** is a specific type of stigma that involves irrational fear or hatred of sexual minorities.

Individuals who are sexual minorities may self-identify as lesbian, gay, bisexual, or transgender (people who do not conform to traditional gender roles), and this group is sometimes referred to as the LGBT population or community. Other terms are adopted by segments of the community to help clarify specific beliefs and practices, such as transsexual (person who identifies with a gender that is different from his or her biological sex and may seek pharmacological or surgical sexual reassignment), questioning (exploring one's gender, sexual identity, and/or sexual orientation), queer (a once negative term that has been reappropriated by members of the LGBT community to demonstrate pride), same-gender-loving (SGL; sometimes adopted by African American males to distinguish themselves from White-dominated LGBT communities), or men who have sex with men (MSM; adopted by men who engage in sexual relationships with other men without identifying or labeling their sexuality). The term *homosexual* is typically not used, as it harkens back to the time before 1973 when homosexuality was included as a mental illness in the *Diagnostic and Statistical Manual of Mental Disorders.* The important take-home message here is that counselors must understand and use the labels and terms that clients prefer rather than imposing their own language and terminology on others.

Within the field of counseling, clients who are LGBT can present with a multitude of concerns, many of which are related to social stigma and the coming-out process. Counselors need to be sensitized to the ways in which the lives of LGBT persons are affected by the stresses of living in a homophobic society with people who believe them to be sick, immoral, or criminal. Additionally, LGBT people are raised in the same homophobia and heterosexist (assuming someone is heterosexual or assuming heterosexual is the standard by which others are judged) society and can believe the messages, resulting in **internalized homophobia**. For young people, bullying and violence, isolation, substance abuse, eating disorders, suicide, depression, and anxiety are all risks associated with coming out, particularly in the early stages of sexual identity. To help LGBT clients navigate their development, Cass (1979) and Coleman (1987) (and others) have developed models of sexual identity development. In general, these models move through the following stages: *identity confusion* (labeling oneself as probably homosexual), *identity comparison* (first exploration of homosexual acts), *identity tolerance* (increasing commitment to sexual orientation), *identity acceptance* (often including selective disclosures to friends or family), *identity pride* (activism and valuing of sexual identity), and *identity synthesis* (integration of sexuality into identity). Just as with racial identity development models, not all individuals move through all stages of this model. Further, because sexual orientation typically requires active disclosure (as opposed to more visible forms of diversity), LGBT individuals must continually navigate the coming-out process in new environments and settings.

In addition to the unique needs that their status as sexual minorities can present, LGBT clients also come to counseling for relationship, family, and parenting issues (or any other mental health or career needs), just like their heterosexual counterparts.

■■■ *Fast Facts* ■■■

When compared to their heterosexual peers, LGBT teens are:

- Bullied at more than three times the rate
- Far more likely to feel unsafe at school (61% fear violence at school)
- More likely to be homeless (20–50% of all homeless youth are LGBT)
- More than twice as likely to drop out of high school
- More than four times more likely to attempt suicide (35% of LGBT youth attempt suicide)
- Far more likely to experience harassment at school (87% of LGBT students)
- 190% more likely to use drugs or alcohol

Source: www.thetrevorproject.org.

From 2000 to 2005, the number of same-sex couples in the United States doubled to more than 777,000 (The Williams Institute, 2006). The danger of maximization (discussed earlier) means counselors may believe sexual orientation is the presenting issue when, in fact, the orientation status of the individual or couple may be simply one of many demographic characteristics that help provide context for counseling. The Association for Lesbian, Gay, Bisexual, and Transgender Issues in Counseling (ALGBTIC) was established in 1997 as a division of the American Counseling Association to promote greater awareness and understanding of gay, lesbian, bisexual, and transgender issues among counselors, clients, and communities (www.algbtic.org).

Religion/spirituality. A 2008 poll of more than 35,000 adults by the Pew Forum on Religion and Public Life concluded that "diverse and extremely fluid" was perhaps the best way to describe the religious life of Americans. More than three-fourths (76%) classified themselves as Christians, and 24% self-identified as part of a religion other than Christianity (9%) or as not part of an organized religion (15%). But these statistics don't tell the whole story. More than 28% had left the faith of their childhood to practice another religion—or none at all, confirming what the survey calls "a remarkable amount of movement." Such movement is most evident in the Protestant community. Fifty-one percent of U.S. adults surveyed identify themselves as Protestant—a significant decline from 65% two decades ago. Catholicism lost more members than any single religion, but the losses have been offset by the number of Catholics who immigrated to the United States. As a result, one-fourth of Catholics in the United States are foreign-born. By contrast, two-thirds of Muslims and 86% of Hindus are foreign-born. Nearly 16% of Americans say they do not belong to any religious affiliation, up from only about 5% at the end of the 1980s. However, it is not accurate to say that this group is not religious. Only about one-quarter of this group (about 4% of the U.S. population) identify themselves as atheist or agnostic.

Many counselors help clients differentiate between religion and spirituality. **Religion** is a formal, structured framework for organizing beliefs and refers to adherence to a particular set of beliefs. **Spirituality** is a search for meaning and purpose that is derived from inner wisdom, higher consciousness, and/or connection to a Supreme Being or life force. For some people, religion and spirituality are the same, but it is clear that spirituality can occur outside of an organized religion.

Within the field of counseling, counselors can help clients integrate their religious and/or spiritual beliefs into their treatment. Although care must be taken not to impose the counselor's religious beliefs on the client, it is also important not to ignore what may be an integral part of the client's life. Just as with all aspects of diversity, the key is understanding the role that religion or spirituality plays in the client's life, the degree to which the client identifies with that role, the client's willingness to explore spiritual or religious needs, and the degree to which religion and spirituality provide comfort, strength, and meaning for the client. Of course, for some clients, religion and spirituality have played a negative role in their identity formation, and this must be acknowledged and (if appropriate) addressed as well. The key is that just as with all aspects of diversity, the role that religion and spirituality plays (or does not play) in counseling is at the discretion of the client. The Association for Spiritual, Ethical, and Religious Values in Counseling (ASERVIC) is a division of the American Counseling Association comprised of counselors who "believe spiritual, ethical, and religious values as essential to the overall development of the person and are committed to integrating these values into the counseling process" (ASERVIC mission statement). In 2009, ASERVIC adopted a list of spiritual counseling competencies that have also been adopted by the American Counseling Association. For more information and a description of the competencies, visit its website (www.aservic.org).

Age/generational status. Perhaps you have heard of the terms associated with different generations of Americans—*Baby Boomers, Generation Xers*, the *Millennials*, and so on. These terms exist because there is a belief that people who are born during particular periods in history tend to share some common cultural reference points, beliefs, and perceptions about the world. In 2010, about 25% of the U.S. population was under age 18, and 12% were over age 65 (1.5% were 85 years or older). The median age in the United States is 35 (50% of people are younger, 50% are older). This compares with the world median age of 28, meaning that the U.S. population is, on average, slightly older than that of most other countries. Some countries, such as Uganda, have a median age of 15, meaning that half of the population in the country are children. The country with the oldest median age is Japan (44.6 years). A country's longevity rate is influenced by factors such as birthrates and access to health care.

From a counseling perspective, age and generational status are important developmental lenses with which to understand our clients and ourselves. Lifespan development issues and life tasks can help provide the context for understanding a client's story. Age tends to have the most significant influence on the counseling relationship when the client is very young or very old, or when the counselor is significantly younger than his or her clients. It is not uncommon for counseling students to be significantly younger than their clients, and many students worry that they will not be taken seriously by clients who are old enough to be their parents or grandparents. Our students sometimes ask, "What do I say if my client asks me how old I am?" We remind students to focus on the underlying message of this question, which is often not about the counselor's chronological age and more about the client's underlying fears and trust ("Can I trust you with my problems?"). Addressing the question at that level, rather than (or in addition to) the chronological level can help allay concerns. Responses might sound something like, "When I hear you ask that question, it occurs to me that what you are really wondering is whether I have the experience or education to assist you, and I think that's an important discussion for us to have. . . ."

In addition, young counselors should remember that professional dress and a professional demeanor will go a long way toward helping clients feel comfortable entrusting you with their concerns.

Finally, we remind all counselors that it is important to have at least a basic understanding of the life tasks facing people of different ages and the historic milestones that people of their generation faced. For example, people growing up in United States in the 1960s may have been influenced by the civil rights movement; those in the 1960s and 1970s lived in the context of the Vietnam War and Nixon's resignation. These experiences helped shape their lives. In the wake of the September 11, 2001, attacks, one of our students expressed to an older client that this was the first time in anyone's memory that our country had been attacked by foreigners. Of course it was not, as anyone alive during the attacks on Pearl Harbor would quickly attest to. The point is that understanding some historical context helps us understand our clients. Alternatively, it is difficult to counsel those younger than you without keeping up with current trends or social movements. A counselor of today's adolescents would want to know the role that Facebook or social media plays in the lives of young people or perhaps even know something about the recent pop icons, if conversations about them would help the counselor and client connect. Just as we cannot be culturally encapsulated and still understand clients of different races or ethnicities, we cannot be trapped in our own generation and age and still expect to connect with older or younger clients. The Association for Adult Development and Aging, a division of the American Counseling Association, is designed to help counselors address the needs of older adults in counseling (www.aadaweb.org).

Dis/ability status. The Americans with Disabilities Act (1990) defines **disability** as physical or mental impairment that substantially limits a major life activity. About 15% of the U.S. population self-identifies as a person with a physical (9%) and/or mental (6%) disability (Brault, 2008). Individuals with disabilities often state that in addition to the hardships imposed by their disability, they face a social stigma that challenges their ability to connect with others in society. In fact, for many people, the attitudes of society often represent a larger barrier than the disability itself (Granello & Wheaton, 2001). In a landmark study on the debilitating effects of stigma, Corrigan (1998) found that persons with severe schizophrenia reported that the stigma associated with having the disease was harder to manage than the disease itself. We find this to be a truly stunning statement. Think about it—people who are living with severe and debilitating psychosis say that the illness is not as bad as the way they are treated by others!

Counselors help people with disabilities face social stigma, discrimination, and prejudice and give them tools to challenge assumptions made about them. Just as with homophobia, persons with disabilities often internalize the stigma, and helping them challenge their own prejudicial assumptions is a critical role for counselors. Rehabilitation counselors help people with disabilities obtain their highest level of functioning and quality of life. Find more information about the American Rehabilitation Counseling Association, a division of the American Counseling Association, at their website (www.arcaweb.org).

Language. English is the de facto language of the United States, and according to the U.S. Census Bureau, 96% of the population claims to speak it well or very well. However, that statistic does not adequately represent the vast number of spoken and signed languages within the U.S. borders. Spanish is the second most common language (spoken by 12% of the population), but this clearly differs by region. Of the 17 million Spanish-speaking Hispanics/Latinos in the United States, 8.3 million either do not speak English or do not speak it fluently. Of the top 10 most common languages in the United States, nine are spoken by more than a million people each (in order: English, Spanish, American Sign Language, Chinese (mostly Cantonese), French, German, Tagalog, Vietnamese, Italian, and Korean). All of the top 20 most common languages are spoken by more than 250,000 people each.

In counseling, shared language creates a common bond and allows for the development of trust. Counseling is, after all, a primarily spoken endeavor, and lack of a shared language can significantly, and often negatively, affect outcomes. When counselor and client speak different languages, the services of an interpreter (sometimes a professional, but often a family member of the client) must be used, often with a corresponding decline in the therapeutic relationship. Language has been identified as a significant barrier in preventing counselors from establishing quality relationships with Spanish-speaking clients and students in schools, and when schools provide counseling services in Spanish, Hispanic/Latino students and their families are more likely to seek help (Smith-Adcock, Daniels, Lee, Villalba, & Indelicato, 2006). In this chapter's Informed by Research feature, two studies highlighting the importance of bilingual school counselors are discussed, emphasizing the important role that language plays in the counselor/client relationship.

Socioeconomic status. The concept of **socioeconomic status (SES)** is an economic and sociological construction that is a combined index of a person's income, education, and occupation. Typically, individuals in the United States are classified into three major SES categories: upper (wealthy), middle (middle class), and low (poor). Others have conceptualized essentially a six-tiered system of SES: upper class (rich and powerful); upper-middle class (highly educated and wealthy); middle class (college educated and employed in white-collar industries); lower-middle class (working class and employed in clerical and blue-collar positions); working poor; and unemployed.

In counseling, SES is correlated with many factors that are often linked to psychological health and wellness. For example, countless studies have found an extremely strong correlation between poverty and mental illness, although determining if one comes first—if being poor renders a person more susceptible to mental illness, or if mental illness pulls a person into poverty—is decidedly more difficult to ascertain. The relationship between poverty and mental health has

Informed by Research

Bilingual School Counselors: Meeting the Needs of Hispanic/Latino Students and Their Families

The Hispanic/Latino population is the largest minority population in the United States and is also the fastest growing, expanding at a rate as much as five times the general population (U.S. Census Bureau, 2009). Approximately half of the Hispanic/Latino population either does not speak English at all or does not speak it fluently. In addition, Hispanic/Latino students and their families may be reluctant to seek assistance, finding it difficult to rely on people other than their family, friends, or community for support. As a result, school counseling services that are available only in English may be ill-equipped to handle the specific needs of the Hispanic/Latino population.

Two studies that specifically addressed the needs of Hispanic/Latino students for bilingual school counselors are discussed in the following paragraphs. As you read through the results of the studies, think about the challenges that the counseling profession might have in supplying the need for bilingual counselors in the schools.

In order to assess the adequacy of culturally responsive services for Hispanic/Latino students and their families, district administrators in Florida were surveyed regarding their perceptions of how well districts provide for the education needs of this population as well as factors influencing administrators' needs to have bilingual school counselors. Florida was selected for the study because of the large growth in the Hispanic/Latino population in the state and because many districts in the state provide for language acquisition programs, translators, and other language programs that target success for Spanish-speaking students. Respondents to the survey included student service administrators from more than half of Florida's 67 school districts ($N = 36$). Study results found that slightly more than half (52%) of administrators believed that Hispanic/Latino students were provided the necessary guidance in the schools, but slightly more than that number (59%) believed that these children and their families are at risk for not getting the needed services. Administrators believed that these students perceived problems of career (69%), academic (65%), and personal success differently than majority children and families because of language and culture differences. The most commonly cited cultural barrier was language (79% of respondents). Finally, administrators perceived a high level of need for bilingual, Spanish-speaking school counselors to address personal (84%), academic (82%), and career (80%) needs. The additional services that were most often suggested by administrators to better meet the needs of the Hispanic/Latino student population were: Spanish-speaking school counselors, family involvement in counseling, cultural awareness training for school staff, and career development programs in Spanish (Smith-Adcock, Daniels, Lee, Villalba, & Indelicato, 2006).

In a second study, in Texas, bilingual school counselors developed Spanish-language *cuentos* (folk tales) to be read to third-grade Spanish-speaking Mexican American students. The students in the *cuento* intervention engaged in 12 1-hour sessions in which stories were first read, paragraph by paragraph, in English, followed by the same paragraph in Spanish. This was followed by role playing the stories' characters and then discussing the relationship of the role play to the students' personal lives. At posttest, participants in the treatment group ($N = 58$), when compared to the control group, had significantly higher scores on measures of global self-esteem, academic self-esteem, and general self-esteem, as well as significantly lower scores on measures of anxiety (Ramirez, Jain, Flores-Torres, Perez, & Carlson, 2009).

These studies taken together highlight the importance of bilingual school counselors for Spanish-speaking Hispanic/Latino students. Both studies reinforce other research that demonstrates that Spanish-speaking students and their families are at risk for failure in the current American educational system, unless significant changes are made. Bilingual school counselors, although certainly not the answer to the entire challenge of meeting the needs of these students, may provide an important mechanism for changing the school system.

long been assumed to be interactive. Children in poor families have higher levels of aggression than their more economically advantaged peers and are instigators and recipients of higher levels of childhood antisocial behavior (bullying, peer violence) than higher income peers. Counselors who understand their clients in the context of their socioeconomic status recognize the powerful effect that the environment plays on the individual.

Other diversity categories. There are, of course, many different ways to classify people into groups. We could make distinctions based on educational level, military status, relationship status, or legal involvement. We classify people by their occupation, hobbies, health care practices, and recreational activities. For example, if we say someone is a Vietnam-era veteran, you may form some immediate assumptions, just as if we said someone was a NASCAR fan, attended polo matches, practiced meditation, worked on Wall Street, or was a juvenile offender. Many people argue that Southerners and Northerners, or residents of the East Coast and the Midwest, are differentiated by their behaviors or values. The classification of urban versus rural also highlights differences, and it is not unreasonable to think that people from different races who live in a large urban area are more alike than people of the same race who live in cities versus farmland. Each of these characteristics (and many more!) help us classify the many different types of diversity in the United States. Each category helps us better understand the worldview of the client, but only if we are open to learning what it means to the client to be a part of the group.

 ## Multicultural Counseling

Looking at the extremely diverse demographics of the United States today, it might be easy to think that counseling has always been tuned in to multiculturalism. Although today's counseling profession celebrates diversity, this attention to multicultural counseling is less than 50 years old. The counseling profession, like all the helping professions, entered the 1960s firmly entrenched in a White, heterosexual male value system. Gilbert Wrenn coined the term "culturally encapsulated counselor" in 1962 to describe White counselors who were ill-equipped to address the needs of minority clients (p. 444). The turmoil of the 1960s and the lessons from the civil rights movement, however, changed the

Spotlight
The Multicultural Counseling Competencies

The Multicultural Counseling Competencies (MCCs) were developed to help guide the interpersonal interactions of counselors engaging in cross-cultural counseling. Originally presented as a position paper in 1982, by 1992 the MCCs had been published as a call to the profession (Sue, Arrendondo, & McDavis, 1992). The MCCs were conceptualized as involving three distinct counselor characteristics and three specific dimensions of cultural competency. As conceptualized by Sue et al. (1992), these are the following:

The Counselor Characteristics

A culturally skilled counselor is one who:

1. Is aware of his/her own assumptions, values, and biases.
2. Actively attempts to understand the worldview of culturally different clients.

3. Actively develops and practices appropriate, relevant, and sensitive intervention strategies and techniques.

The Dimensions

The domains in which counselors develop competence are:

1. Beliefs and attitudes (also called awareness)
2. Knowledge
3. Skills

The counselor characteristics and the dimensions of counseling can be operationalized into a 3 × 3 matrix of cultural competencies. Table 10.1 summarizes these nine areas of competence.

TABLE 10.1   A Summary of the Multicultural Counseling Competencies

	Counselor's Awareness of Own Assumptions, Values, and Biases	Understanding of the Worldview of the Culturally Different Client	Developing Appropriate Counselor Interventions, Strategies, and Techniques
Beliefs and Attitudes (Awareness)	• Moves from being culturally unaware to aware and sensitive of own culture • Aware of how own culture, values, and attitudes influence counseling • Recognizes limits of their competence • Comfortable with differences between self and client	• Aware of negative emotional reactions to other races or cultures • Aware of their own stereotypes of others	• Respects clients' cultural values and beliefs • Respects indigenous helping practices • Values bilingualism

course of the counseling profession. At the national conference in 1969, the American Personnel and Guidance Association (APGA, now the American Counseling Association) governing body approved a petition calling for the organization to become more responsive to the needs of clients of color. Within a few years, the Association for Non-White Concerns (now the Association for

	Counselor's Awareness of Own Assumptions, Values, and Biases	Understanding of the Worldview of the Culturally Different Client	Developing Appropriate Counselor Interventions, Strategies, and Techniques
Knowledge	• Has specific knowledge about own racial heritage • Understands how oppression, discrimination, and stereotypes affect them personally • Possesses knowledge about their social impact on others	• Possesses specific knowledge about group they are working with • Understands how race and culture affect personality, vocation, mental health, etc. • Has knowledge of sociopolitical and economic influences that affect clients' lives	• Understands how traditional counseling interventions may clash with cultural values • Aware of institutional barriers that limit access to mental health • Has knowledge of potential bias in assessment • Has knowledge of minority family structures and community characteristics • Is aware of effects of discrimination on mental health
Skills	• Seeks out education and training to enrich effectiveness with cross-cultural counseling • Constantly seeks to understand themselves as cultural beings	• Familiarizes themselves with relevant research • Actively seeks out educational experiences that enhance cross-cultural skills • Becomes actively involves with minority individuals outside of counseling setting	• Engages in a variety of helping responses • Intervenes at institutional level • Seeks consultation with traditional healers • Interacts in client's language • Has training in traditional assessment methods • Works to eliminate biases and discrimination • Educates their clients about the mental health system

Source: Sue, Arrendondo, & McDavis (1992).

Multicultural Counseling and Development; www.amcdaca.org) and the *Journal of Non-White Concerns* (now the *Journal of Multicultural Counseling and Development)* were established in 1972.

It wasn't until the 1980s, however, that multicultural counseling started to become more than just the concerns of one of the divisions of the association. A 1982 position paper outlined specific multicultural counseling competencies that remain the foundation for culturally competent counseling 30 years later (Sue et al., 1982). A 1992 article in the *Journal of Counseling and Development* called upon the profession of counseling to adopt the standards laid out in the position paper a decade earlier. Within the next decade, the American Counseling Association and six of its divisions endorsed the Multicultural Counseling Competencies. The accompanying Spotlight provides an overview of the Multicultural Counseling Competencies for your exploration. However, although the competencies appear to be rather straightforward, they actually require a lot of effort, education, and self-awareness to implement. Therefore, rest assured that although this may be your first exposure to the Multicultural Counseling Competencies, it certainly won't be your last.

In its 2005 revision of the *Code of Ethics and Standards of Practice*, the American Counseling Association stressed the importance of multicultural counseling competence, and every division of ACA has included multicultural competence in its mission or vision statement, standards, and/or by-laws. In fact, multiculturalism has been called the Fourth Force of the counseling profession (following psychodynamic, behavioral, and humanistic approaches). Social and cultural diversity is one of the eight core areas of the counseling curriculum as outlined by CACREP, and nearly every counseling program includes both classroom and experiential activities to enhance counselor cultural competence. Graduate programs in counseling use one of three strategies to help students become culturally competent: (1) infusion throughout the entire graduate program; (2) a separate course in multicultural counseling; and (3) a combination of #1 and #2. None of these strategies has been demonstrated to be more effective than the others, but many counselor educators would argue that it would be difficult to teach any class in the counseling curriculum without significant attention to multicultural factors.

In spite of the near universal acceptance of the *concept* of culturally competent counseling, there is less agreement about the *content* of the competencies themselves. There is considerable disagreement and confusion within the field about what constitutes a multiculturally competent counselor and, in fact, about the definition of multicultural counseling itself. In this chapter's Counseling Controversy, you will read about the diversity of opinions that surround multiculturalism in counseling.

Although discussions and debates regarding who is included in the competencies and what methods are used to operationalize them are ongoing, no one questions the importance of providing services that meet the needs of diverse clients. Counselors understand that cultural competence is essential to effective practice.

■■■ *Fast Facts* ■■■

In spite of a higher prevalence of psychiatric disorders, African Americans and Americans of Hispanic/Latino ethnicity receive approximately half the amount of outpatient mental health services as non-Hispanic White Americans. These differences persist even after controlling for socioeconomic status and insurance coverage, suggesting that cultural and attitudinal factors drive these disparities.

Source: Shim, Compton, Rust, Druss, & Kaslow (2009).

Counseling Controversy

WHAT IS THE DEFINITION OF MULTICULTURAL COUNSELING?

Background. The Multicultural Counseling Competencies (MCCs) were originally designed to assist White counselors in their interactions with clients representing one of the four major cultural minority groups in the United States. The MCCs define multicultural counseling as follows: "The term multicultural, in the context of counseling preparation and application, refers to five major cultural groups in the United States and its territories: African/Black, Asian, Caucasian/European, Hispanic/Latino, and Native American or indigenous groups" (Arrendondo et al., 1996, p. 43). Since the publication of the competencies, however, many in the profession have argued that the competencies are applicable to a wide range of diversity, not just race/ethnicity (e.g., Weinrach & Thomas, 2002). Others argue that to dilute the original premise of the competencies dilutes their impact. As you read the arguments favoring either of these positions, consider where you stand on the question.

POINT: MULTICULTURAL COUNSELING IS ABOUT INTERACTIONS BETWEEN PEOPLE OF DIFFERENT RACES/ETHNICITIES	COUNTERPOINT: MULTICULTURAL COUNSELING IS BROADLY DEFINED, ENCOMPASSING ALL TYPES OF DIVERSITY
• The MCCs arose in a historical context where racial minorities were invisible in the field of counseling and the contributions and experiences of racial minority clients were considered inferior to those of the majority culture. It is this specific racism that the MCCs were developed to address.	• All counseling is cross-cultural. Every client and every counselor brings a unique historical and sociopolitical context to the counseling session.
• The constituencies who are most often marginalized and about which counselors are least prepared to work are those representing the four major cultural minority groups.	• Making assumptions about another person's experiences based on race alone (or even primarily on race) is racist. We should allow clients the right to determine what culture means to them, whether it is primarily determined by race or by membership in some other group.
• Counseling is a culture-bound profession, and the hallmark of culture in the United States is race.	• The MCCs' emphasis on race is an outmoded idea. In today's climate, race does not provide an adequate explanation of the human condition. Clients experience discrimination because of their inclusion in many different oppressed groups, not just because of their race.
• Although the MCCs focus on race, they recognize multiple identities in Dimension #1, which states that all individuals, not just those from minority racial groups, are cultural beings.	• To include only race in the MCCs is a denial of the realities that many disenfranchised clients from other oppressed groups face every day.

(continued)

(Continued)

• When counselors dilute the MCCs to include all types of identities, they diminish the very real effects that racism has in the lives of clients. Once every descriptor becomes an indicator of multicultural counseling, then multicultural counseling eventually means nothing and no specific competencies are needed.	• Focusing on race denies other aspects of clients' identities. For example, a White lesbian seeking to marry her partner faces discrimination at both the societal and individual level. Her need to have a culturally competent counselor is no less important than that of a Black client.
• The MCCs can be used as a springboard for interacting with clients who suffer from discrimination for reasons other than race, but the competencies themselves must stay focused on race if they are to remain relevant.	• Exaggerating the significance of race or ethnicity to a client's life while minimizing potentially more important characteristics can cause psychological harm to our clients.

As with most controversies, there probably is truth to both sides of this argument.

What should be the definition of multicultural counseling?

←——————————————————————————————————————→

The Multicultural Counseling
Competencies should focus
on race/ethnicity

The Multicultural Counseling
Competencies should use a broad
definition of diversity

On the continuum, place an "X" where you think you stand on this issue.

Strategies to Enhance Your Own Multicultural Competence

Counselors recognize that cultural competence is both something learned during graduate school *and* something that must be attended to throughout a person's personal and professional life. Most professional conferences and journals include information and research on culturally competent counseling, and seeking out opportunities for ongoing learning is essential to your growth in this area. In this section, we highlight five strategies you can use to help enhance your multicultural competence.

1. Attend workshops and trainings. There are many different opportunities available—in person, on the Internet, at your university, and through local and national counseling associations. For example, a quick look at the American Counseling Association 2011 conference program list (which includes over 500 different educational sessions) reveals that many, if not most, of the sessions have a strong multicultural component. In the following list, we provide some examples of some education sessions

from the 2011 conference that have a clear multicultural component *in addition to* their focus on a specific aspect or type of counseling. At the 2011 ACA conference, you could have attended sessions on the following topics:

- Assessment in Counseling
  - Alcohol Screening and Brief Interventions for English- and Spanish-speaking Medical Center Trauma Unit Patients
  - Test Equity for People Who Are Deaf or Hard-of-Hearing: Recommendations for Certification Exams and Other High-stakes Testing
  - Validity and Reliability Evidence of the Intercultural Sensitivity Scale for Turkish University Students
- Career Counseling
  - Career Development Initiatives in Peru
  - Preparing Students with Disabilities for Their Future Careers
  - What Do You Want to Be When You Grow Up? Career Development of African American and Black K–5 Students
  - Career Development of Transsexual Women and Men During Gender Transition
- Child and Adolescent Counseling
  - Pre-, Peri-, and Postmigration Experiences and Adjustment of Adolescent Refugees in the U.S.: Implications for Counselors
  - Growing Up Latina: Interrelations of Ethnic Identity, Acculturation, and Motherhood as a Teen Mom
  - Play and Filial Therapy with Asian American Children and Families Confronting Acculturation Issues
  - Utilizing Native American Spiritual Concepts in Outdoor Adventure Therapy with Adolescents
- College Counseling
  - Lived Experiences of International Students: Immigration, Acculturation, and Resilience
  - The Relationship Between Coping with Humor, Type of Disability, and Quality of Life Among College Students with Disabilities
- Couples, Marriage, and Family Counseling
  - Cultural Dissonance in Intercultural Relationships: Transformative Opportunities for Intercultural Couples and Their Children
  - Daddy and Papa: Evidence-based Strategies for Counseling and Supporting Same-Sex Oriented Fathers
  - The Intersection of Machismo and Marianismo and Its Impact on Latino Couples Counseling

- Mental Health Counseling
  - In the Eye of Recovery: Disaster Interventions and Considerations with Sexual Minorities
  - Allies Walking on White Bison's Red Road to Wellbriety: Developing Culturally Informed Treatments for Native Americans
  - Creative Interventions When Counseling Terminally Ill in Rural Appalachia
- Group Counseling
  - Multicultural Creative Arts: Implications for Group Work Conducive to Healing and Wellness
  - Redefining Anger Management with Underserved Populations: A Leadership-Driven Anger Management Group with Latino Youth
- School Counseling
  - Microaggressions Against African American Middle School Students: Implications for School Counselors
  - Latino/a English Language Learners: Closing Achievement/Opportunity Gaps to Increase College-Going Rates
  - Working with Children with Chronic Illness: An Integrated Approach to Meeting the Needs of the "Whole" Child
  - From the Refugee Camp to the United States School System: The Transition Process for Adolescent Refugees

2. Seek exposure to other cultures. Go to festivals or celebrations of different countries, attend Spanish-language services or visit an African American church, or go to a music festival that celebrates the music of a different culture. While you are there, seek opportunities to interact with others. At your own college or university, talk with classmates and colleagues who represent different perspectives from your own. Initiate conversations. Notice if you are spending time with people who "look just like you" and make intentional efforts to broaden your circle of acquaintances.

3. Read books or scholarly articles. Read a first-person narrative by a person of color with a mental illness or the life of a person with a disability. Seek out scholarly journal articles on diversity or multicultural counseling. As you read, consider how you can apply what you are learning to your own growing sense of cultural competence.

4. Take a class. Use the resources at your university to take a class in culture, religion, disability, gender studies, or military history. Challenge yourself to seek new perspectives in your academic work and work to incorporate your new learning into your development as a counselor.

5. Volunteer. Offer your services at a homeless shelter or other place where you will come in contact with people in poverty. Challenge your preconceived ideas and push yourself to grow.

SNAPSHOT
INTERNATIONAL STUDENTS BECOMING COUNSELORS
Ursula Lau, Diego Lopez-Calleja, Jenny Sheng-Hsin Cheng, and Chieh Hsu

Every year, millions of students make the decision to study abroad in search of a learning experience that extends to the world beyond the classroom walls. Through this endeavor, students immerse themselves in a new culture, master the challenges of learning in a new and different academic environment, and live through the many highs and lows of being a "foreigner." It is a life-transforming decision that results in increased self-confidence and a feeling of achievement that far surpasses any local academic affairs.

Preparation in the field of counseling, in and of itself, entails change. Students don't simply learn how to be counselors—they *become* counselors. It is through this process that many of them discover who they are and form a professional identity. In the case of international students, however, there is an additional layer of complexity that presents numerous challenges both academically and professionally. In this snapshot, Ursula Lau, Diego Lopez-Calleja, Jenny Sheng-Hsin Cheng, and Chieh Hsu, graduate students in the Counselor Education Program at The Ohio State University, share some of their experiences as international students.

"Being an international student in a distant land has reawakened within me the questions related to my own social location and identity. In my training, I am faced with the challenge of finding my own intellectual identity as a counselor-to-be amid the multiple philosophies and theories of human nature. My experiences of both belonging and exclusion within my own country have fostered my own social positioning as a 'politically black' South African Asian woman. In so doing, I feel I am gravitated toward postmodernism as a philosophical approach that not only embraces the tensions of identity and the contradictions of ordinary experience, but also nurtures subjective voices and multiple truths of the clients I would serve in the future."

Ursula Lau

"I have learned that to be an efficient counselor is to know who you are. I was born in Taiwan and immigrated to Canada when I was 13. Now 12 years later, as a Taiwanese-Canadian studying counseling in the United States, I have started to examine the role my dual nationalities play in my identity. The questions I ask myself range from 'Where do I say I am from?' and 'Do I identify with an English or a Chinese name?' to 'How do my cultural perspectives align with different social issues?' It will be some time before I can answer the big question about my identity, but with every small question I answer about myself, I become one step closer to finding out who I am."

Jenny Sheng-Hsin Cheng

"'Where are you from?' asked one of my clients while I opened their file. In that moment I had an important decision to make coming from what seemed like an innocent question. My badge says 'Diego.' However, most people, before looking at my name, assume that I was born in the United States, given that I have no accent, and that I physically do not look like what most people would identify as Hispanic. What happens when I reveal that I am from Costa Rica? Will it be an unimportant detail or will it

(continued)

(Continued)

be a critical piece of information that will instill doubt in my clients about my ability to help them? This is only one of many different challenges I face as an international student every day."

Diego Lopez-Calleja

"Study abroad is like taking an endless ride on a roller coaster where you experience all the ups and downs without knowing the destination. I was born and raised in Taiwan, but I embarked on a journey far away from home to become a counselor. I have been adjusting to this new country and the program, which is a slow but enjoyable process. The language barrier is the primary issue that I have been dealing with. However, my cohort is really helpful and supportive. As a counselor-to-be, I find that the social interaction plays a significant role in my life and

school work. Also, being open to personal feelings and recognizing the purpose of studying in this program are crucial for me to stay positive to all experiences."

Chieh Hsu

These are only some of the many situations that we as international students face in our personal journeys in becoming counselors abroad. Whether it is a challenge during training or out in the field, the learning involved in overcoming any obstacles is an invaluable experience. Each of us brings to the table a diverse set of skills and values, and a unique cultural background that molds our identities as counselors. The challenge then lies in how we capitalize on these contributions to become mental health professionals in the service of humanity.

The point is that there are many, many opportunities to enhance your cultural competence right now as you learn to be a counselor as well as throughout your counseling career. You need only to seek these opportunities and push yourself to learn. We all know that we are not "supposed" to have reactions to interacting with people who are different from ourselves, but we also know that all of us have some level of cultural encapsulation that needs to be challenged. Challenge yourself.

In the third Snapshot in this chapter, four international graduate students in counseling talk about their experiences studying in the United States. As you read through this Snapshot, consider ways in which their perspectives might differ from your own (whether you are an American or international student), and what values and goals you share with these students. How can interacting with students from different countries or cultures enhance your own growth as a multiculturally competent counselor?

 ## Counseling and Social Justice

Over the last decade, counselors have increasingly come to understand that to be a counselor who celebrates diversity and encourages optimal human development for all people means that we cannot sit idly by in the face of systemic oppression and inequality. Counseling does not take place in a social vacuum. In other words, when we focus on helping the individual but ignore the larger social forces around us that limit the freedom and choices of that individual, we miss the boat. Most people get into the profession of counseling because they want to make a difference, but for many clients, individual change is not enough. The social and environmental forces of poverty, oppression, and discrimination shape people's lives. Our clients may live in neighborhoods that are unsafe, attend schools with substandard resources, have limited access to the means to lift themselves out of poverty, and have internalized society's lowered expectations for them. They may be in same-sex partnerships and not have access to the rights and opportunities of their heterosexual peers. Our clients might be migrant workers (or their children) who have limited (or no) access to health care or education. They may have physical disabilities and face discrimination in the workplace. In other words, we need only look around us to see that many of the problems our clients face cannot be handled through counseling alone. We cannot "counsel" someone out of hunger or inadequate housing. Even if we are able to find resources to assist the individual in front of us to survive another day, we still haven't addressed the bigger societal problems that allowed this type of inequality to exist in the first place.

When counselors speak of social justice, they speak of improving society by challenging the systematic inequities that stifle the individual's potential and block opportunities (Lewis, Arnold, House, & Toporek, 2003). **Social justice** involves "promoting access and equity to ensure full participation in the life of a society, particularly for those who have been systematically excluded" (Lee, 2007, p. 1). It is both a personal and professional approach to actively participating in the struggle to eliminate social inequities. Counselors use a social justice approach when they act as advocates in their schools, agencies, or communities for people who are economically or socially disadvantaged. School counselors act from a social justice perspective when they seek to reduce or eliminate the barriers to academic achievement.

Counselors in all settings can work with legislators, policy makers, school administrators, agency leaders, or the media to become advocates for our clients. We can become active in our local (and national) associations that promote mental health for all members of society. Associations such as NAMI (National Alliance on Mental Illness; http://nami.org), Mental Health America (http://mentalhealthamerica.net), and Mental Health Advocacy Coalition (http://mentalhealthadvocacy.org) actively work to reduce stigma and increase access to mental health services for all. Counselors for Social

---

■■■ *Words of Wisdom* ■■■

"School counselors must focus attention on students for whom schools have been the least successful—low income students and students of color. Counselors must concentrate on issues, strategies, and interventions that will help close the achievement gap between these students and their more advantaged peers."

Source: Education Trust, Transforming School Counseling Initiative (2009).

Justice (CSJ) is a division of the American Counseling Association specifically dedicated to helping counselors advocate for systemic change (http://coun selorsforsocialjustice.com). Counselors can make a difference when they team up with these associations and others to fight social oppression.

Those who advocate for a social justice perspective in counseling remind us that improving society by challenging systemic inequities has always been part of the counseling profession. Historical figures in the profession, such as Frank Parsons, Clifford Beers, and Carl Rogers, all recognized that social changes were necessary in order for their clients to thrive. To adopt a social justice perspective, counselors must first recognize that social injustice exists and that it negatively contributes to the mental health of our clients (Crethar & Ratts, n.d.). Once we all accept this reality, it is but a small step to recognizing that we all have a personal and professional obligation to do something. We remind our students that entering into the profession of counseling means that you will have your eyes opened to the painful reality of people who had previously been invisible to you. Beginning counselors who come from middle-class homes and middle-class lives suddenly see firsthand the pain and suffering of people living in poverty, living with severe mental illness, and living without hope. Being a counselor will open your eyes to the world around you, and once your eyes are open, they can never be closed again. For many new counselors, this means giving up some long-held beliefs. For example, counseling students who may have believed that the world was a fair and just place, or that anyone could overcome their circumstances if they just pushed themselves hard enough, are often faced with some cruel and harsh realities when they enter their practicum sites. A social justice perspective, however, gives us the tools to fight back against oppression, racism, and poverty. Rather than throw up our hands and give up, social justice pushes us to be advocates and fight for the dignity and respect of all our clients. Social justice gives us hope.

In Chapter 2, we discussed a social justice approach through "The Many Faces of Advocacy." In that Spotlight, we introduced you to many different types of advocacy and encouraged you to think about ways you could be proactive in changing the world in which you live and work. In the last Snapshot of this chapter, you will read about a graduate student who used his own experience to help him find the strength to significantly improve the lives of others.

Clearly, becoming a social justice advocate, just like becoming a culturally competent counselor, is a lifelong endeavor, and one that requires changes to both our personal and professional world. Counselors who understand the role that social forces play in the lives of their clients recognize that the social and economic status quo is not sufficient. We can do better. We have an ethical, and many would argue moral, obligation to be agents of social change. Are you up for the challenge?

SNAPSHOT
Bowen Marshall, Clinical Mental Health Counseling MA Student

I never thought I would work in "multiculturalism." I don't know why. Being a gay, partially adopted, half-Asian kid from Kansas, I guess I had "diversity" stamped on the back of my head, but of course I couldn't see it. Then I came to The Ohio State University (OSU), where I am a master's student in Clinical Mental Health Counseling and the Graduate Administrative Assistant in charge of Bias Assessment & Response Team (BART) student outreach and engagement.

If you are asking yourself what the heck BART is and what it does, you are not alone. For most of my first year as a Graduate Assistant at the Multicultural Center (MCC), I felt lost. I sat in on meetings and heard a lot of grandiloquent jargon about communities affected by bias incidents, university-sponsored educational responses and sanctions, and all of the university officials I needed to consult with before making a move with BART. This phase of acclimating to a new position was at times disheartening because I felt lost, ineffective, and afraid to make a move for fear of disrupting "the system" and being labeled "the idiot." To compensate, I poured my energy, abilities, and time into the model of the position that others had created for me. While I didn't make any missteps my first year, I also didn't do much of which I could be proud.

That's really what it came down to at the end of the year. I needed work in which I could take pride.

Looking back, becoming an advocate for my profession and my community was easy.

Everything was set up and in place to receive me. Becoming an advocate for me, on the other hand, was one of the hardest things I have ever had to do.

Growing up, I lived in a world that told me I wasn't loved, I wasn't accepted, that I would forever be alone in my misery, and that I would go into an afterlife of eternal damnation. That's a pretty tough pill to swallow, so I didn't. I walled off those comments and the pain and hurt that came with them. I went to the parades, went to the bars, wore my rainbows, and played the part of an out and proud gay man, but I never addressed the ostracism and anguish that underlay it all. I even convinced myself that addressing that underlying stuff was unimportant. As long as I could project the image that everything was fine, what did it matter?

Then came practicum in spring of my first year when I worked with suicidal adolescents and children whose pain and hurt were so powerful they couldn't just push them into a closet and ignore them. Being present with these children and listening to their stories opened me. To grow as counselor and as a human being who is compassionate, accepting and genuine, I was forced to look at that backlog of baggage that I was carrying and experience it even when it meant being angry or drawing attention to a part of myself that is still hated and belittled by some people in our society. Once I began to accept the ways in which I had been mistreated and integrated those truths into my story, I began to see the ways in which love rises up to combat those forces. That is what advocacy is: love working for others.

When the media began to pick up stories in the late summer of 2010 of the suicides of seven beautiful gay men and boys because of hate and prejudice, I no longer felt undirected or powerless. I had the training and Graduate Assistant position to step up and begin to combat

(continued)

(Continued)

hate through counseling, educational engagement, and interviews with the press. As a counselor, that is what multiculturalism means to me. It is a way to show people they are loved and accepted no matter their skin color, sexual orientation, religion, criminal history, or any other reasons the world tries to tell them they don't matter, they shouldn't exist, and that they aren't worthy of love. Advocacy, like counseling, is my love working for others.

Summary

In this chapter, we challenged you to think about yourself as a cultural being, living and working in an extremely diverse and complex society. Through an exploration of your own beliefs and understandings about the world, you can start to make sense of who you will be as a culturally competent counselor. The Multicultural Counseling Competencies will help guide you in that direction, but you must make a concerted and intentional effort to becoming a counselor who understands and celebrates diversity in all its forms. Social justice can be an important component of your personal and professional life, as counselors recognize that clients must live in an environment that promotes their optimal health and wellness.

End-of-Chapter Activities

The following activities might be part of your assignments for a class. Whether they are required or not, we suggest that you complete them as a way of reflecting on your new learning, arguing with new ideas in writing, and thinking about questions you may want to pose in class.

Student Activities

1. Now it's time to reflect on the major topics that we have covered in this chapter. Look back at the sections or the ideas you have underlined. What were your reactions as you read that portion of the chapter? What do you want to remember?

   _____

   _____

   _____

   _____

2. Most people have fairly strong reactions to the idea of privilege and how unearned privileges, by virtue of race, gender, SES, education, and so on,

have affected their lives. What are your reactions to the concept and its application to you? What privileges have you enjoyed by virtue of your membership in privileged groups?

_____

_____

_____

_____

_____

3. You had an opportunity to read Snapshots from the perspectives of members of both majority and minority cultures. As you think about your own cultural identity and your emerging identity of yourself as a counselor, jot down any ideas you might have about how your own understanding of yourself as a cultural being might affect your development as a counselor.

_____

_____

_____

_____

_____

■■■ Journal Question ■■■

Think about your gender, race, ethnicity, sexual orientation, family background, religion, SES, disability status, and other characteristics of you. How do you think you fit with other students in your program? In your college or university? With your faculty? Future clients? How will you capitalize on the similarities and differences between you and others around you to get the most from your program? As an experiment, find a student in your program who is very different from you in at least one of these areas and discuss how your differences and similarities could affect your experiences as counselors-in-training. Reflect on what you learned from this exercise.

■■■ Topics for Discussion ■■■

1. We all are products of social, environmental, and familial messaging. As a result, we have heard, and possibly internalized, many different stereotypes about other groups. How can we acknowledge and then challenge our own internalized prejudice?

2. What do you think about counselors as advocates for social justice? What parts of that role do you embrace? What parts

do you think move us away from our work with clients?

3. What unique cultural groups exist in your community that will require specific education and training for you and your classmates? For example, some communities host specific refugee groups, have large populations of particular immigrant groups, or are located near Native American reservations. How will you learn the necessary skills and information to promote the mental health needs of the populations you will serve?

■■■ Experiments ■■■

1. Think of yourself as a cultural anthropologist exploring the "Culture of You." Develop a PowerPoint or other type of presentation, as though you had just come back from an anthropological expedition to the "Culture of You," and now you need to describe what you learned to a group of people who have never met "You" and have no cultural reference points to understand who you are.

2. Look ahead to your counseling curriculum to discover how multiculturalism will be addressed in your graduate training. Are there separate course(s)? Does your program use an infusion model? How will you be trained to be a culturally competent counselor? Is there anything you need to do to be proactive and take control of this important component of your graduate training?

3. Find out what legislative, policy, or political agendas exist in your state or community that will affect mental health services. Are funding issues being discussed for school services or mental health agencies? Are there legislative initiatives in your state that will affect the delivery of mental health services? What can you do to help influence these discussions and make your voice heard?

■■■ Explore More! ■■■

If you are interested in exploring more about the ideas presented in this chapter, we recommend the following books and articles.

Books

Aldarondo, E. (ed.). (2007). *Advancing social justice through clinical practice.* New York: Routledge.

Anderson, S. K., & Middleton, V. A. (2005). *Explorations in privilege, oppression, and diversity.* Belmont, CA: Thomson Brooks/ Cole.

hooks, b. (1994). *Teaching to transgress: Education as the practice of freedom.* New York: Routledge.

McWhirter, J. J., McWhirter, B. T., McWhirter, E. H., & McWhirter, R. J. (2007). *At-risk youth: A comprehensive response for counselors, teachers, psychologists, and human service professionals* (4th ed.). Belmont, CA: Thomson.

Smith, T. B. (2004). *Practicing multiculturalism: Affirming diversity in counseling and psychology.* Boston, MA: Allyn & Bacon.

Sue, D. W., & Sue, D. (2007). *Counseling the culturally diverse: Theory and practice* (5th ed.). Los Angeles: Wiley.

Tatum, B. D. (2003). *Why are all the black kids sitting together in the cafeteria? A psychologist explains the development of racial identity.* New York: Basic Books.

Articles

McIntosh, P. (1990, Winter). White privilege: Unpacking the invisible knapsack. *Independent School,* 31–36.

Ratts, M. J. (2009). Social justice counseling: Toward the development of a fifth force among counseling paradigms. *Journal of Humanistic Counseling and Development, 48,* 160–172.

Ratts, M. J., & Hutchins, M. (2009). ACA Advocacy Competencies: Social justice advocacy at the client/student level. *Journal of Counseling and Development, 87,* 269–275.

Websites

- The AMCD Multicultural Counseling Competencies on the ACA website: www.counseling.org/Resources/ Competencies/Multcultural_ Competencies.pdf
- Counselors for Social Justice (CSJ) Advocacy Competencies: http://counselorsforsocialjustice.com/ links.html

▪▪▪ MyHelpingLab ▪▪▪

To help you explore the profession of counseling via video interviews with counselors and clients, some of the chapters in this text include links to MyHelpingLab at the Pearson.com website. There are some videos that correspond with this chapter, and watching them might challenge you to think about these concepts at a deeper level.

- Go to Ethical, Legal, and Professional Issues, and "Professional Practice in a Multicultural Society" to check out these video clips:
- Cultural considerations in counseling sessions
  - As you watch this video, think about how culture was introduced into the session. Consider how easy it might be for counselors to ignore the effects of

culture when working with a Caucasian couple.

- A question of values (and the video response to that clip)
  - As you watch this video, think about your reactions to the client's presenting problem. Do you think the counselor is meeting the client's needs? Or, to frame it another way, "whose needs are being met?"
- A cross-cultural miscommunication (and the video response to that clip)
  - As you watch this video, what do you think the counselor could have done differently to encourage the client to explore his career options in a more culturally sensitive manner?

11

How Do Counselors Collect and Use Assessment Information?

In this chapter, we will:

- Differentiate between the process of *assessment,* which is an integral part of the counseling process, and *testing,* which is just a means of assessment.

- Expose you to a case study that illustrates the importance of thorough assessment.

- Introduce you to the concept of personality assessment and its role in counseling.

- Highlight some key ethical issues that may apply during your assessment training.

- Advocate for a scientific attitude toward using and interpreting tests.

- Help you recognize that assessment is not just for the beginning of counseling, but it can help you keep track of the progress of your clients or programs.

As you read the chapter, you might want to consider:

- Assessment is more than testing. It includes information from a variety of sources, including our observations of the client and records from other sources.

- Assessment is not objective. It is full of our own assumptions and the biases of our own culture.

- Assessment is only useful if it helps the client. We are not here to map the client's prison but to help him or her get out.

- For some, it is easy to fall in love with the mystique of assessment, but for the counselor, unless assessment helps the client attain goals, it may be wasted time.

" "Testing is boring." That's what one of our students said to me (Mark) last week. And I have to agree. Giving tests to clients can be boring (test administration). But *assessment* is more than interesting. In fact, it is one of the most fascinating aspects of being a counselor. It is the investigative aspect that allows you to channel Sherlock Holmes in the service of the client. Assessment may include giving paper-and-pencil tests to clients or individually administering tests question-by-question, but assessment is actually the larger enterprise of trying to understand the other person. It involves collecting and analyzing information from at least seven different sources, including the following:

- Results of tests given to the client, including tests of achievement, personality, intelligence, brain functioning, and career development
- Client reports of their problems, background, history of the problem, family issues, and so on
- Reports of family members
- Medical data, including medications and physical problems
- Information from courts, previous counseling services, and agencies, including response to previous counseling, criminal behavior, reports from probation officers, and so on
- Behavior and things that the client says during the session
- Data from schools and teachers, including achievement testing and behavioral information

Counselors use the information they collect to guide their counseling. Without accurate assessment, the entire counseling process is destined to failure. Accurate assessment takes time and patience, and counselors must take care not to assume that the very first thing a client reports is really the problem. Consider this example. Imagine you walk in the door after a long day at school and you are confronted by your roommate (or partner), who says, "You didn't take out the trash last night after supper, even though you said you would. I tripped on it and it spilled in the kitchen, and I had to clean it up." You could respond to the statement, making some promise about being sure to take out the trash in the future, but chances are, that's not really the issue. Seeking to understand the underlying problem will make for a much more productive discussion. Perhaps your roommate or partner feels taken for granted or lonely. Maybe she or he is angry about something else, and the whole story about the trash is just a symptom of an entirely different problem. The point is, accurate assessment helps us determine what intervention is necessary.

 ## What Kinds of Assessments Do Counselors Use?

There are many different types of assessment strategies in counseling, and counselors use a variety of techniques and strategies to gain information about their clients or programs. In general, it is important to understand that assessment is an extremely complex endeavor that requires much education and experience. Counselors in all settings use assessments, primarily in the areas of achievement, career, intelligence, personality/psychopathology, and counseling outcomes. In Table 11.1, we highlight some of the tests most commonly used by counselors.

TABLE 11.1 Types of Tests in Common Use by Counselors

Type	What Do They Assess?	Where Are They Primarily Used?	Example	Controversy?
Achievement	What has been learned?	Schools	Woodcock-Johnson Test of Achievement and various state achievement tests	When teachers are evaluated based on their students' improvement, they teach only to the test.
Tests of Psychopathology	Deficits in emotional adjustment	Mental health clinics, agencies, hospitals, and private practices	Minnesota Multiphasic Personality Inventory (MMPI)	Such tests are time consuming and may not help with diagnosis. No strengths are assessed.
Intelligence	Various areas of intellectual ability and predictions of academic achievement. Usually part of a neuropsychological assessment.	Schools	Wechsler Intelligence Scale for Children (WISC)	The best intelligence tests are individually administered and time consuming. Imaginative thinking is not assessed. Limited usefulness in assessing minorities.
Measures of Counseling Progress	Change as a result of counseling	Mental health clinics, agencies, hospitals, private practices	Outcome Questionnaire 45.2 (OQ45)	May not address the client's specific goals but instead looks at overall functioning.
Neuropsychological Assessment	Impairment in a psychological function such as memory due to problems in the central nervous system	Hospitals, agencies, private practices	Halstead-Reitan Battery and also tests for more specific problems	While dysfunction can be identified, results may not specify treatment.
Personality Tests	The client's personality traits such as introversion versus extroversion	Mental health clinics, agencies, private practices, and in business and industry	California Personality Inventory (CPI) and Myers-Briggs Type Inventory (MBTI)	Personality does not reliably predict behavior. Thus an individual may be an introvert but enjoy working on teams.
Career Tests	Similarity between the client's interests, personality, and values and various career environments, or assesses client's preferences and thoughts about careers		Strong Interest Inventory (SII) and Career Thoughts Inventory (CTI)	Many tests do not predict satisfaction and may pigeonhole women by accepting their interests at face value.

In the following sections, we discuss some of the common assessment strategies used by counselors to gather information and improve their understanding of clients and programs. Among the most common are interviews, standardized or nonstandardized tests and measures, and measures of program effectiveness or accountability.

Interviewing

When we began this chapter, we said that assessment is not just testing. In fact, testing is only a part of the process and not something that every counselor will use with every client. Interviewing, on the other hand, is the most common assessment method among all helping professionals. Interviewing is something a counselor does in the professional relationship with a client that provides information about the client, his or her concerns, and an exploration of client goals. Frequently, this begins in the initial interview, called an *intake session,* during which the counselor elicits background information from the client. Many counselors ask the client to fill out a form and then review the answers with the client. Other counselors prefer an unstructured interview where they use a general outline of topics. Jones (2010) identifies these categories as:

1. General data about the client, including ethnicity, age, referral source, and so on
2. Information about the problem that brought the client to counseling (i.e., symptoms)
3. A history of the problem, including the severity and frequency
4. Family history, including information about whom the client is living with and history with parents and siblings.
5. Relationship history, including close friends, intimate relationships, history of violence in relationships
6. Developmental history, including school problems, diagnostic labels applied, child abuse, and so on
7. Educational history that encompasses success or failure in school, higher education, and other training
8. Work history, which involves present employment, length of employment, and a sketch of the client's successes and failures at work
9. Medical history, including present health, medications, important accidents and illnesses in the past, and chronic conditions
10. Substance abuse history
11. Legal history
12. Previous experiences in counseling

Even counselors who work in settings that do not have formal intake sessions must still elicit information from their clients about what caused them to seek assistance. Initial interviews, whether in-depth and comprehensive, or a few well-articulated questions asked by a school counselor to understand why a student was crying in the stairwell, help counselors focus their interventions.

Diagnostic interviewing is a specialized type of interview that helps counselors arrive at a client's diagnosis. Counselors who seek to form a diagnosis through this process will help the client describe the history of his or her problems, associated symptoms, personal experiences relevant to the problem, current situation, and mental status. Counselors engaging in diagnostic interviews use the DSM-IV-TR as a guide to help ask clarifying questions about specific symptoms or problems. Accurate assessment can facilitate accurate diagnosis, which is essential for appropriate treatment planning. A couple of weeks ago, one of our students in internship class talked about a client who had previously been seen at a college counseling center following the accidental death of his best friend. The previous counselor saw the client for several sessions and marked in the file that he had made good progress. Now, a year later, the client was back in counseling because of recurrent nightmares about his friend, intrusive thoughts about his friend's death, diminished interest in his studies, and blunted affect. Clearly, the student was suffering from Posttraumatic Stress Disorder (PTSD). Because the college counseling center does not require a diagnosis for students to receive counseling, the original counselor had never diagnosed this student and never understood the real problems that the student faced. As a result, the student's problems were never sufficiently or accurately addressed. To quote the internship student, "I enjoyed my assessment and diagnosis classes, but now I get it. I get why assessment and diagnosis matter. Avoiding a diagnosis because of philosophical differences or because it is not a requirement of the site completely misses the point. If the lack of proper assessment means clients do not receive the treatment they need and deserve, then we have the potential to cause great harm."

Questionnaires, Surveys, and Rating Scales

Counselors use surveys to gather information about clients, programs, and needs of a community or school. They can be simple questionnaires that the counselor develops or published surveys that are commercially available. For example, school counselors often use the results of the Youth Risk Behavior Survey (YRBS; http://cdc.gov) to help inform programming in their schools. Or they might use a simple questionnaire with questions that assess students' learning or understanding of material after a group counseling or classroom guidance program. Counselors might also use simple questionnaires, such as a client satisfaction survey, to measure the quality of their programming. In general, we give surveys or questionnaires to our students and clients to help us make sure our programming meets their needs.

Standardized Tests or Instruments

When most people think of assessment, they think of specific tests that are given to individuals or groups to identify problems, assess functioning, measure progress, or determine qualifications for entry into programs or professions. **Standardized tests** are structured instruments that have been developed according to rigorous criteria and allow comparisons to be made across individuals. Most tests that are available for purchase in the field of counseling are standardized. If you took the GRE to get into graduate school or have taken the Myers-Briggs or Strong Interest Inventory, you have taken standardized tests. School counselors are very familiar with standardized tests, primarily the proficiency tests that are commonly used in schools. **Nonstandardized instruments** do not have the same rigorous test development and do not allow for comparisons across individuals. Intake interviews or projective drawings are examples of nonstandardized tests. Both types of tests can be incredibly useful to counselors seeking to better understand their clients, and both can be integral components of the assessment process.

Measures of Program Accountability or Counseling Effectiveness

Although we typically think of assessment as it applies to individuals in counseling, the reality is that many counselors assess the effectiveness of their programs or projects. School counselors, for example, use assessment strategies to demonstrate that their comprehensive school counseling programs are effective. Counselors who oversee large-scale projects, such as alcohol and drug outreach programs at universities or antiviolence campaigns for communities, use assessment strategies to track their effectiveness. In fact, the assessment of program effectiveness is a critical component of many funded projects and programs. Because this type of assessment is so critical to counseling programs, we give it specialized attention in the chapter on the use of research in counseling (Chapter 7).

In the Snapshot in this chapter, you will read about the role of assessment in counseling from a graduate student just starting internship. We thought about sharing the experiences of an expert in assessment, but we believe that the words of a beginning counselor might help you relate even better to the role that assessment plays in every aspect of the counseling process.

Why Should We Spend So Much Time on Assessment?

Counselors know that accurate assessment is important. When asked, they might respond that spending considerable time on assessment is important because assessment

- Provides information to plan realistic goals.
- Allows clients to discover events related to the presenting problem.
- Lets us understand what is unique about our client.

SNAPSHOT

A Student's Perspective on the Role of Assessment in Counseling
Todd Gibbs, Intern, Clinical Mental Health Counseling

I am currently a second-year student in a clinical mental health counseling master's-level program. My first year of education included two courses in assessment. The coursework initially encompassed some basic grounding in statistics and research. We then built upon this foundation to develop applied skills, including psychometric evaluation, clinical interviewing, and writing. Our final task was learning to use all of these abilities to formulate working hypotheses that could help to shape and guide our work with clients. I confess to having felt uncertain as to the value of this work as I made my way through these labor-intensive classes. However, as I have begun to utilize these skills in clinical settings through my practicum and internship experiences, I have grown in my appreciation of how a strong foundation in assessment assists every area of my practice as a counselor.

I have worked in two settings thus far: a residential psychiatric facility offering trauma-informed care for adolescents and a college student counseling center. Both of these sites are multidisciplinary settings, staffed by therapists from a variety of helping professions. Both sites also utilize a combination of standardized instruments and semistructured procedures to conduct initial and ongoing assessment with clients. As soon as I entered practicum, the utility of my education was immediately apparent. I discovered that possessing an understanding of clinical language and interpretative skills not only assisted me to do my work efficiently, but also allowed me to present myself as a competent practitioner, even as a counselor trainee. Metaphorically speaking, a working knowledge of assessment offers counselors a seat at the table and a voice in the conversation with other professionals.

I have even occasionally experienced situations where my assessment training has offered me clinical insight that has helped more seasoned professionals advance their own case conceptualizations. These experiences underscore the value of assessment training on a deeper level than simple practical skills. Developing an investigative approach to counseling has advanced my ability to draw connections and perceive the larger underlying patterns that are present in my interaction with clients. I have an increased ability for discerning and obtaining information that is of value and then integrating this often complex set of stories and data into an understanding of the client's challenges, strengths, and circumstances. This provides me with a baseline for developing a plan of care for the client and shapes every phase of my work.

Effective assessment begins with the first encounter with a client, but it does not end there. Rather, I perceive assessment as an ongoing process that allows me to increase my understanding and tailor my interventions to the needs of the client. Ongoing assessment helps me to avoid jumping to premature conclusions. Instead, the curiosity and compassion that underscore this approach help me to continually engage with my clients. When I encounter situations that are beyond my experience, I can fall back on my research skills that I have gained through my assessment training to seek helpful information. I can state with confidence that research informs my practice, and simultaneously, my practice drives my research.

It is my belief that assessment training has equipped me with skills that are useful in isolation. However, the true value of these skills is that they give me the ability to build upon them and actively scaffold my own knowledge such that I can gain new abilities and insight. A strong foundation in assessment has fostered a stance of compassionate inquiry within me and has helped me to develop and internalize a manner of thinking and practice that benefits every stage of my work with clients.

- Can help us decide if suicide or violence is likely.
- Tells us about the client's strengths as well as weaknesses.
- Makes clients aware of problems that they have ignored.
- Allows us to understand the whole story, not just what the client tells us.
- Lets us track the changes that the client is making.
- Assembles data to make a diagnosis.

Although all of these (and more!) are reasonable and useful reasons to engage in assessment, there are even more important reasons to spend time on and be good at assessment, particularly as we begin our careers as counselors. Beginning counselors are particularly vulnerable to the Three Big Mistakes. We make the Three Big Mistakes when we ignore (or forget to assess):

1. Evidence of a severe mental disorder such as schizophrenia or bipolar disorder that affects all aspects of the client's functioning
2. Evidence that the client is abusing alcohol or drugs
3. Evidence that the client is dangerous to self or others, including failure to assess bullying, suicide, child abuse, and domestic violence.

Ruling out the Big Mistakes is not only clinically prudent, but it is ethically sound. We must ensure that we have done our best to safeguard the client, and we will not waste our time solving minor problems when larger issues are looming in the background. Let us give you an example. Early in my career (Mark), a client came to counseling presumably to deal with feelings of tension and stress. I failed to recognize the symptoms of bipolar disorder and saw him for five or six sessions before a manic episode prompted his hospitalization. During this period of time, he withdrew all of his considerable savings from the bank and was about to invest it in a questionable scheme when his wife recognized the symptoms of his disorder and got him to agree to get inpatient treatment. I made one of the Big Mistakes, which I might have avoided had I been better supervised or done more research on my own. By focusing on the problems that the client presented rather than doing an accurate assessment, I missed the opportunity to understand his situation in a larger context.

Let's Start with a Case Study: What's Wrong with Raymond?

As we consider why we conduct assessments in the first place, let us look at a case study that may illustrate how the counselor uses assessment techniques when he or she gathers information to make a treatment plan. The assessment process may include tests, but important data are also garnered from interviews and observations.

Raymond was a 15-year-old white male who was brought to the session by his adoptive mother after he had been suspended from school following an incident in art class. Raymond had lit a smoke bomb in the trash container, which set off the fire alarm and led to a school evacuation. Raymond was brought to the private practice of a counselor as part of the requirement for him to reenter school. His mother, a social worker, was in favor of counseling and revealed a number of things about his past. Raymond had been adjudicated at age 12 for sexual battery when he fondled a neighbor's child. Raymond himself had been sexually abused by his stepfather, which led to his removal from his family of origin and eventually to his adoption by his foster parents. Once Raymond took the family car for a ride without permission or a driver's license. The adoptive parents have one natural child whom they feel has become fearful of Raymond as he can be physically aggressive. On the other hand, they recognize that to date these incidents are relatively minor and have not resulted in any real injury. Instead, his mother saw them as symptoms of the child's impulsive personality.

Raymond was given a number of tests and was interviewed to arrive at a diagnosis and treatment plan. In an effort to establish rapport, the counselor began with some drawing because, despite his behavior in art class, Raymond had shown some talent. His self-portrait was actually a caricature of the counselor. He was also given a self-esteem measure. Raymond and his mother filled out the Achenbach Child Behavior Checklist (CBCL) (see Achenbach & Ruffle, 2000). The counselor also administered an individually administered intelligence test and a self-esteem scale. A brief self-esteem instrument was not usable because Raymond checked all the items on the test and wrote notes in the margins such as, "Do you think I am crazy?" and "Wouldn't you like to know."

The intelligence test indicated that Raymond was capable of academic success. His scores were in the average range and there were no indications of potential learning disabilities. He was considered to be artistically talented. In contrast, Raymond's grades were poor and he was consistently in danger of failing, which he would usually avert by sporadic efforts just before grades came out. There appeared to be a consistent pattern of Rule-Breaking Behavior and Aggressive Behavior on the CBCL, and his teachers noted a tendency to speak out of turn in class and small skirmishes with fellow students.

Questions to Consider

1. If you were Raymond's counselor, what would be the primary issue that you would focus upon? Make a list of the most important problems.

2. What kinds of assessment methods would you want to conduct before or during counseling?

3. What are Raymond's strengths? How could they help Raymond?

4. What would be the major roadblocks to understanding and communicating with Raymond?

What Should Counselors Assess?

Strengths and Positive Psychology

We have argued that one should avoid the Three Big Mistakes in assessment, but there is another mistake we might make. We might forget to assess the client's strengths and abilities. Notice that the previous section is entitled, "What's Wrong with Raymond?" That is the usual way of stating the problem. We try to find out what is wrong and fix it. Where does it hurt? We often fail to identify what the client is doing well, what is going right, and what resources the client can bring to bear. Solution-focused counselors balk at the idea of spending too much time talking about the origin of a problem, because it steeps the client in the problem-saturated story. According to this theoretical position, we have to shift our focus to what is going well and what works. Thus, in solution-focused therapy, there is little formal assessment.

One area where strengths are being talked about is in the business world. Buckingham and Clifton (2001), in their book, *Now, Discover Your Strengths,* developed an online assessment of 34 strengths. Their list spans tendencies and abilities that range from "Learner" to "Communication," to "Strategic," to "Woo" (winning others over). One of the realizations that comes from thinking about one's strengths is that it is much easier to identify one's weaknesses. Sometimes, we ask clients to identify 10 good things about themselves, and they find it hard. The same clients often can easily list the 10 bad things. It could be said that we have all been trained to look for what is going wrong in us and what is going wrong in the world instead of looking at what is supporting us.

This dichotomy between strengths and disorders underlines a controversy in counseling and in the field of psychology in general. Clinical psychology, psychiatry, and to some extent counseling have focused on defining several hundred mental disorders and finding fixes for those problems. At the same time, there is a burgeoning interest in a "positive psychology" (Seligman & Csikszentmihalyi, 2000), which seeks to study the efficacy of treatments such as hope, forgiveness, gratitude, optimism and happiness, self-efficacy, love, and many others. *The Handbook of Positive Psychology* (Snyder & Lopez, 2009) and its companion, *Positive Psychological Assessment* (Lopez & Snyder, 2004), have documented this movement.

But this controversy is not new. It has raged ever since the humanistic existential theory was first delineated. Abraham Maslow, in his 1954 book, *Motivation and Personality,* named the last chapter of that text "Positive Psychology." Now research seems to be suggesting that positive human traits such as gratitude can become a focal point for counseling, providing clients with a preventive approach and a new set of tools for helping (Young & Hutchinson, in press). In essence, the positive psychology movement reminds us that mental illness is not really a good metaphor for mental disorders. Unlike physical illness, the best approach is not always to focus on eliminating the problem. Sometimes, it is best to boost the individual's psychological immunity to help overcome a problem rather than trying to remove its source. But first, we need to assess an individual's strengths. Earlier, when talking about Raymond, we asked you to think about what resources and competencies he has to draw upon. Although he tended to be impulsive, he has a number of cognitive resources and family supports that might be brought to bear on the challenges he faces. Stop and think for a moment about what those strengths might be, and jot a few notes here:

_____

_____

_____

Counseling has its roots in the humanistic tradition, believing in the resilience and untapped potential of people to heal themselves. In fact, it could be argued that counseling has always been positive psychology in the Maslovian sense. Instead of the phrase "positive psychology," the term *wellness* has entered the counseling lexicon. The WEL Inventory and its successor, the 5F WEL, is an assessment instrument for wellness (an optimal state of health and integrated functioning) (see Myers, Sweeney, & Witmer, 2000) developed by counselors. It originally identified 17 aspects of wellness that can be used to assess strengths, such as: Realistic Thinking, Positive Humor, Exercise, Nutrition, Spirituality, Cultural Identity, Friendship, and Self-Worth.

In summary, the best we can say is that counselors of tomorrow must have double vision, that is, the ability to see both the strengths and the weaknesses in their clients. They cannot ignore the debilitating effects of mental disorders, but they must also be aware that utilizing the client's strengths may be one of the best ways to help the client overcome them. They must assess client problems, but also be searching for solutions. A focus on problems leads to demoralization of counselor and client alike. Hope is an outgrowth of the belief that human beings are also strong, resilient, and capable.

Assessment Is Affected by the Clients That You See

Although all counselors might assess for suicide, substance abuse, and for serious and debilitating mental disorders, frequently the client's needs and special problems point to specific assessment methods. In the following sections, we will consider three counseling specialties: mental health, school counseling, and marriage, family, and couples counseling. Because counselors in these specialties and environments see similar clients with many of the same problems, they frequently select assessment techniques to get at the usual challenges of their clients.

Assessment in School Counseling

School counseling is an assessment-rich environment. School counselors can easily see from school records that their clients have special abilities interpersonally, physically, and intellectually. School counselors must also be able to assess for suicide and substance abuse, looking for the signs and conducting interviews with students. They must be alert to family problems that might be affecting achievement and also aware of the signs of severe mental issues such as depression, because some of these disorders first manifest in the late teens. Counselors must be alert to the signs of child abuse and be able to assess and then report to authorities, because they are legally required to do so in most states.

In the last 10 years, school counselors have been called upon to prevent bullying. Recent news headlines point out that bullied students suffer from ostracism and alienation, and in some cases complete suicide. The assessment issue here is that counselors should attempt to detect and prevent bullying (see Hazler & Denham, 2002; Juhnke, Granello, & Granello, 2011). Crothers and Levinson (2004) identify methods for assessing the potential for physical, verbal, and emotional aggression. They include observations, interviews, peer and teacher ratings and sociometric methods, and even use of standardized tests, such as the Bullying-Behavior Scale (Austin & Joseph, 1996).

One of the most important issues for school counselors to be able to recognize is the learning disabilities and special needs of students, which may interfere with their academic and social functioning. School counselors sit on committees where individualized education plans (IEPs) are formulated based on assessment data from school psychologists, teachers, and behavior reports. School counselors must understand the common mental disorders of childhood as well as the disabilities related to learning, such as those that lead to difficulty in understanding language, reading, and math, those associated with poor attention span, and those that manifest as social and emotional issues.

School counselors conduct, evaluate, and interpret assessment information every day to parents, teachers, and students. Grades are indicators of academic success and also give information about the student's overall functioning. In addition, counselors help students, teachers, and parents understand standardized tests, such as those given by state departments of education. More than half of the states ($N = 28$) have required tests with severe consequences for failure, including not graduating or not being promoted (Dietz, 2010). Frequently, counselors are asked to prepare students for these "high-stakes tests" and even administer them. In addition, college-bound students face the pressures of standardized testing such as the ACT and the SAT. Their scores determine where they might be accepted, and counselors are needed to interpret the scores, help with test anxiety, and find the appropriate college fit.

Assessment in Mental Health Counseling

Of course, mental health counselors working in clinics, hospitals, and private practices will be concerned with screening their clients for substance abuse, suicide, and the existence of severe disorders. Yet they will also be looking at specific symptom groups to evaluate the client's improvement. For example, a mental health counselor might use the Beck Depression Inventory every week with a client to keep track of his or her depressive symptoms. The counselor might also track changes in goal attainment by using client evaluations of progress. For example, if a shy client has set a goal to improve social relationships, the client can report weekly in writing about the number and quality of social contracts, which can help determine if counseling is effective.

Keeping charts and graphs of client progress is useful for both counselor and client. Early in my career I (Mark) was working with a woman named Martha with severe anxiety (panic disorder) and treated her for 8 sessions using progressive muscle relaxation, a technique where the counselor instructs the client to systematically tense and then relax the major muscle groups in the body. I kept track of her fingertip temperature, muscle tension in the forehead, the time it took to reduce her tension, and her subjective units of discomfort (SUD) on a 100-point scale, with 100 being the most tense and 0 being completely relaxed. Overall, she was quite effective in increasing her finger temperature (measure of relaxation) and muscle tension, and decreasing the time it took to achieve a state of relaxation. Yet, as Figure 11.1 shows, her SUD or perceived anxiety at the beginning of each session (before) did not change at the end of the session

FIGURE 11.1 Martha's Progress in Subjective Units of Discomfort over Eight Sessions

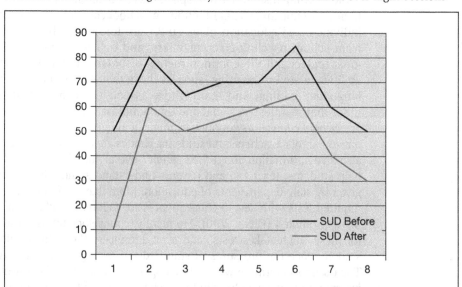

(after), nor did it decrease significantly over the 8 sessions. When, I saw no improvement, I began other treatments, including *in vivo* desensitization, which involved teaching the client to face real-life situations. With the advent of the Internet, we can search for effective treatments on sites such as www.cochrane.org, which reviews treatments for a variety of physical and mental disorders. But because research is based on averages, we still need to use assessment methods to track client progress to see if counseling is working.

Assessment in Marriage, Couples, and Family Counseling

Assessment in couples and family counseling can reveal how the family is functioning, the couple's happiness, whether divorce is likely, and how the family is structured. One of the most commonly used methods of assessment is the genogram (Young, 2009). The genogram is a pictorial family tree that graphically shows the family arrangement through several (usually three) generations. We see the family, individual, or couple within their historical and extended family context. For example, we can see that the client's father was an alcoholic as was his paternal grandfather. The client and counselor can both track family influences on the client's drinking, which may help the client understand the potential consequences and causes of his own problem.

For a couple, assessment can be part of the treatment when couples learn about each other's personality and feelings. For example, in David Olson's PREPARE/ENRICH Programs (Olson & Olson-Sigg, 1999), couples who are married, partnered, or who are considering a permanent relationship take tests to identify areas of compatibility and issues where they will face challenges. Many couples counselors also use a general measure of marital satisfaction, such as the Locke-Wallace (1959) (Marital Adjustment Scale). The scale indicates the general satisfaction of each person and identifies the areas of conflict that can be explored in counseling.

One of the key issues in couples and family counseling is the detection of domestic violence. The definition of domestic violence sometimes includes violence and maltreatment of children. Typically, when we talk about domestic violence, we are discussing only male-perpetrated domestic violence, because most violence in the home is directed at women. All couples should be screened for domestic violence, because approximately 22% of women have been assaulted to varying degrees by a partner (U.S. Department of Justice, 2000). Counseling couples when one member is assaulting the other is not considered to be ethical or effective (Long & Young, 2007). Many clinics and hospitals screen only the female member of the couple so as not to alert a potentially violent

■■■ *Fast Facts* ■■■

The Association for Assessment in Counseling and Education (AACE) is a division of the American Counseling Association that is aimed at promoting research and training in assessment for counselors and related education professionals. Membership is open to students and professionals. AACE publishes the journal *Measurement and Evaluation in Counseling and Development*. The AACE website links to online resources, test reviews, and information about the organization. Website address: www.theaaceonline.com.

husband that the assessment is going on, as this could put the woman at risk. The usual method for assessment is an interview with the victim, who is then given information about how to safely receive help.

 ## Steps in the Assessment Process

Although there are many sources of assessment data, we will focus mainly on the interview and test data to simplify the description of the steps in the process. We use the metaphor of a funnel to describe the method of gathering information and then narrowing down the focus. At the beginning, counselors collect data from a wide variety of sources, like the wide end of the funnel. But eventually, they narrow the focus to work on a few specific issues, just as a funnel narrows as liquid goes through. This is certainly an oversimplification, because assessment is not just conducted in the beginning of the counseling relationship; assessment continues as we try to determine if we are making progress. Still, this metaphor might help us understand the initial steps in assessment when we are first trying to understand the client. We start with an open mind and information assembled from many avenues. Then we make some decisions about what is important.

Selecting Good and Comprehensive Methods

The first step in the process of putting information in the funnel is to make sure you have access to all the sources of information. For some clients, this means contacting their parole officer, asking their mother to come in, or having the doctor fax over the list of medications that the client is taking. For others, it means selecting the appropriate instruments based on the client's age and background. It also means making sure that your instruments are reliable (consistent, free from errors of measurement) and reasonably valid (measure what they say they do).

Next, the counselor needs to see what the referring source wants to know about the client. Is the school trying to determine if a teenager is depressed and that is why she is failing? Are the parents of a 6-year-old trying to find out if their child is adjusting to their divorce? These kinds of questions determine which types of assessment methods you will use.

But assessment is not just testing; it also means selecting the kind of questions and interviewing strategy you are going to adopt. We believe your approach should be dictated by the client. For example, interviewing young children is completely different from interviewing teenagers or adults. Interviewing children has been described as a form of cross-cultural counseling (Sommers-Flanagan & Sommers-Flanagan, 2009). Unfortunately, we tend to think of kids as either just like us or just like us when we were children, which can severely limit our understanding of the children we counsel. Thinking of working with children as a form of cross-cultural counseling reminds us that we need to approach children as if they are from another culture and try to understand the world from their perspective. In short, the interview may or may not be a good source of information, and even when it is, it must be modified to fit the developmental level of the client.

Establishing a Relationship

The relationship between counselor and client during the assessment period is just as crucial as it is in later counseling sessions (Young, 2009). A client who does not trust the counselor will not be honest and open in the assessment process (Gregory, 2010). For example, research has demonstrated that one of the most significant factors in assessing suicide risk and determining the prognosis for success of suicide interventions is the quality of the therapeutic relationship (Bongar, 2002). Sometimes counselors see assessment as a laborious process. Then, the counselor may be tempted to hand the client the requisite forms and disappear. But the best approach is to preview and explain the assessment materials to clients so that they recognize its importance and to emphasize, from the very beginning, that the counselor is trying to help, not just put the client under a microscope.

Administering the Assessment

Whether it is an interview, a test, or filling out an intake form, assessment takes time. For this reason, many counselors try to hurry their clients through the onerous paperwork. Instead of seeing it as a formality, the counselor can utilize the administration time to observe the client's reaction to the assessment. Does the assessment reveal reading or writing problems? Is the client's memory intact? What is the client's reaction to being asked a lot of questions? Does the client answer openly or guardedly? As Yogi Berra said, "You can observe a lot just by watching." In other words, we sometimes fail to appreciate that an individual's response to any task tells us something about the client, and we need to watch. For example, in the case study, Raymond wrote angry notes in the margins during the testing process, which was another example of the behavior that got him into trouble at school.

■■■ *Words of Wisdom* ■■■

"Assessment is treatment. Even the process of assessment itself can begin the healing and start clients on the path of change."

Source: Granello (2010, p. 367).

Interpreting Assessment Data

How you interpret assessment data and what data you pay attention to may be due to your theoretical orientation. Obviously, counselors who adhere to a psychodynamic theory will be more interested in early childhood events, developmental issues, and the influence of the past on the present situation. A behaviorally oriented counselor will focus on behavioral deficits and excesses. What is the client doing too much of, and what behaviors does the client need to increase?

The most important concern when interpreting test data is to make sure that they reflect the context of the person's life. By this we mean that one piece of evidence on a test is not enough to validate an insight about a client. Every piece of data must be compared to what we know about the client. For example, we once administered an IQ test to a 10-year-old boy from rural Appalachia. His response to the question, "What are the four seasons of the year?" was, "Squirrel, Deer, Rabbit, and Fishing." In his world this was technically correct, but according to the scoring sheet, it was not one of the right answers. How do you think clients' responses should be interpreted if English is not their first language? How do you know that they are reading up to the grade level of the test? All of these questions should make us recognize that how the scores are interpreted is based on a number of assumptions about the client. The most important one is that we are basing our evaluation on a comparison with a group of people whom we believe to be like the client. Even when we interview clients, we are essentially comparing our client to someone who is "normal." Thus, the counselor must have multiple sources of data before making bold assertions about the client's personality, family, or problems.

In the age of computerized testing, counselors are sometimes tempted to allow computers to not only score test instruments, but interpret the results as well. For some tests and domains, this may be a reasonable approach. However, for other types of testing, computerized interpretation can fall short of ideal. In the accompanying Counseling Controversy, consider the pros and cons of computerized test interpretation.

Writing Up Assessment Results and Generating Suggestions for Intervention

Of course, the final step in assessment is summarizing the findings of interview and test data. It is this step that can potentially do the most harm to the client, and therefore the counselor must consider his or her words carefully. Will your thoughts prejudice the next counselor who reads this material? How sure are you about your conclusions? There are many manuals and templates that you can utilize to help you organize your reports (cf. Lichtenberger, Mather, Kaufman, & Kaufman, 2005).

Most important, the assessment should yield possible treatment suggestions. In other words, if we find that a middle school student has a reading problem that is affecting her school performance, besides test data, we need a plan to present to the student (and her parents) to help overcome this obstacle to academic success. As opposed to assessment technicians, counselors must be aware of treatment options. They are not just presenting what is wrong but also how to overcome the problem.

What Do You Do After You Have Collected Information?

Section E of the American Counseling Association's Ethical Guidelines identifies some crucial issues regarding letting clients know about the results of their

Counseling Controversy

USING COMPUTERS TO INTERPRET TESTS

Background: Using computers to administer and *interpret* tests is now a common practice, but it is also controversial (Groth-Marnat & Horvath, 2006). It is sometimes referred to as CBTI, computer-based test interpretation. On one side, many believe that allowing the computer to do the test interpretation will result in a better product and will be more efficient and complete, and that it is ethical, if controlled by the counselor. On the other side, some see the danger that could result if counselors are lazy or submissive and merely accept what the computer says without regard to the person of the client. As you read through the arguments on both sides of the controversy, think about what you believe to be the appropriate role of computers in test interpretation.

POINT: COMPUTERS CAN INTERPRET TESTS EFFICIENTLY AND EFFECTIVELY	COUNTERPOINT: TEST INTERPRETATION IS COMPLEX AND CANNOT BE ADEQUATELY HANDLED BY MACHINES
• Computer-based test interpretation (CBTI) is efficient because instead of taking days or perhaps weeks, tests can be administered and interpreted immediately. For clients who need results for court-ordered reports or other official needs, this reduces their stress and expense.	• CBTI does not take into account how the client is presenting himself or herself on the day of testing. Is he or she alert, responsive, antagonistic? All of these states must be factored into how the test is interpreted.
• CBTI is programmed by experts who know more about the test than you will ever know as a general practitioner.	• CBTI does not include the client's history or relevant personal details. The client's history of testing could certainly affect how the results should be considered.
• CBTI is more objective than interpretation by someone who knows the client and who may be prejudiced based on their social class, race, or other personal characteristics.	• Computer read-outs have the look of truth, and they are often accepted without critical thought. Frequently, when reporting test data, information from CBTI is cut and pasted rather than constructed by the counselor. This may be tempting but may also be unethical.
• A good clinician will not merely accept what the computer says, but will match this against all of the other information in the client's record to develop a holistic view of the client.	

Questions to Consider

• If you were having your own assessment results analyzed so that you could make a decision about a career or your feelings of depression, would you rather have an objective computer interpretation of your results or the interpretations of a counselor who knows you?

(continued)

(Continued)

- Do you think that CBTI could induce some counselors to save time and money by just utilizing the interpretations that the computer spits out?
- Is it all right to use CBTI if you are not very familiar with a particular test and you need some help to interpret it?

As with most controversies, there probably is truth to both sides of this argument.

Should Counselors Use Computer-Based Test Interpretation?

←——————————————————————————————————————→

Let the computer do it all   **Only the counselor can realistically and ethically interpret data about a client**

On the continuum, place an "X" where you think you stand on this issue.

assessment. Although it is clear that clients must understand the reasons and types of assessment they are receiving, the guidelines are a little less clear about what we should tell clients about the tests or assessment procedures they have taken. That is because these are complex questions that must be considered in the context of each client and cannot be easily answered in standardized guidelines. Nevertheless, here are some suggestions to consider:

1. Not being told about the results of an assessment procedure can be dehumanizing and make the client feel less a part of the treatment process. Therefore, clients should almost always be fully informed about what the test says.

2. Some tests and assessment methods produce ambiguous or easily misunderstood information. For example, people frequently believe that IQ test scores are very accurate measures of a person's intelligence and that a person with a tested IQ of 105 is smarter than a person with an IQ of 100. This is a complex problem, but counselors should strive to explain as much as possible. That is one obvious way of respecting their clients' right to know about their own performance.

3. When clients are given a diagnosis, the counselor should help the client understand just what that means. For example, the diagnosis of cancer might make many people believe that they are terminally ill. Similarly, a diagnosis of a mental disorder may precipitate fear, shame, and the feeling that the diagnosis suggests a lifelong struggle. Thus, all counselors need to have information that explains common diagnoses in lay terms. School counselors should have handouts about common learning problems.

4. Counselors have to consider the cultural context when explaining assessment results. It may be crucial to have an explanation in the client's native language so that there is no confusion or to have a family member translate when assessment results are explained.

Arthur Kleinman is a psychiatrist and medical anthropologist who has studied the role that culture plays in understanding illness. He developed a list of questions that can be used to help clients communicate their understanding of the problem (Kleinman, 1981). Although the questions were developed for medical illness, they are also used within the counseling profession to help assess the role that culture plays in an individual's understanding of his or her mental illness. The questions remind counselors not to impose their biases on the assessment of clients' problems and that clients must "buy into" the assessment results in order for treatment to work. For example, counselors might ask:

- What do you think the problem is? What is the name you have given it?
- Why and when did it start?
- What does the illness or problem do? How severe is it? How long will it last?
- What should be done (if anything) to treat the problem? What is the prognosis?

When we enter into the world of the client, we make them collaborators in their own treatment. Clients are experts about their own lives, and they often have ideas or have already tried things to help solve their problems before they enter the counselor's office. A collaborative approach to treatment and intervention increases chances for successful outcomes.

 ## Assessment of Personality

In this section, we take some time to discuss the assessment of personality and describe some of the current and historical ways that human nature has been mapped. We do this for three reasons. First, personality is an interesting way to introduce the topic of assessment. We could just as easily described neuropsychological assessment (measuring the degree of impairment of a psychological function such as memory and identifying a location in the brain from which it stems), but we thought personality would be more fun. Second, we address personality assessment because it is all around us in the media and on the Internet. Examining some of these examples illustrates the difference between good assessment and bad. Third, counselors frequently use personality testing to help people choose careers, evaluate their relationships, and assess their preferences. Personality assessment can help people understand themselves and also be more tolerant of others as they recognize the differences.

Personality Assessment Theories

During the 1950s and 1960s theories of personality were of great interest to all helping professionals, and counselors were also enthusiastic about understanding a client's personality as a way of formulating a treatment plan. For example, myriads of personality tests were developed to help counselors identify personality traits. Chief among them were the Minnesota Multiphasic Personality Inventory (MMPI), the California Personality Inventory (CPI), and the Cattell 16 Personality Factors (16 PF). Yet, scads of other tests sprang up in the enthusiasm to map the intricacies of the human mind. For example, the Adorno F-Scale attempted to determine if a person had a fascist personality (Adorno, Frenkel-Brunswik, Levinson, & Sanford, 1950). Personality testing was especially popular in industry and was misused as part of selection procedures for hiring (cf. Gibbey & Zickar, 2008).

Counselors have basic training in psychological testing but philosophically place more emphasis on understanding the client in the process of counseling rather than the assessment of an individual based on paper-and-pencil tests. Nevertheless, personality is a branch of psychology that has relevance for us whether or not we place much emphasis on the major personality tests. The reason is that counselors frequently utilize, read the results of, and refer to some of these tests for understanding couple relationships, career preferences, and to help an individual gain self-knowledge and accept differences in others. For example, knowing that you are an introvert may help you realize why you prefer periods of quiet while your spouse does not. Personality tests also remind us to look deeper than the presenting problems or symptoms that clients discuss. Underlying personality structures that may be outside of clients' awareness can help us figure out why they continue to fall into the same unproductive patterns of behavior. Finally, personality theories are one way of understanding other people, and even without the major theories of personality, human beings seem to develop their own homemade theories. The theories that you hold about life and about people undoubtedly affect your evaluation of them.

What Are Personality Theories?

Personality theories are theories of human nature. *Type theories* say that people can be divided into somewhat distinct categories like introverts or extroverts. *Trait theories* say that all people have the same characteristics or traits to a greater or lesser degree. In trait theory, what makes people unique is the personal combination of these qualities, such as flexibility, trust, sympathy, or rebelliousness.

Personality theories also relate to human *motivation*, because these internal *traits* are believed to direct behavior (Hall & Lindzey, 1978). For example, a sympathetic person is motivated to listen, and an outgoing person is interested in people and things. To understand personality theories a little better, let's start with an ancient Greek type theory: Galen's Four Temperaments. Although mental health professionals rarely talk about these types, the basic principles have made their way into our language, and they are still oddly appealing.

Galen's Four Temperaments

Galen's four psychological types (about A.D. 100) were based on Greek medical theories about bodily fluids. The physicians of that time attempted to restore physical and mental health by keeping a balance between four "humors." This was done by reducing the amount of the fluid in some humors by cathartics, emetics, purgatives, and bloodletting or by eating substances that would increase other fluids. It is said that bloodletting, based on this theory, was the cause of George Washington's death. Although the medical theory has been disgraced, the personality side of the theory has been the subject of study and research for centuries and still inspires interest, probably because the types are intuitively compelling. To illustrate, we have put the names of some U.S. presidents next to these types as examples:

Choleric (yellow bile): excitable, emotional (Teddy Roosevelt)

Melancholic (black bile): sad and inhibited (Abraham Lincoln, Richard Nixon)

Sanguine (blood): active and enthusiastic but changeable (Ronald Reagan, Bill Clinton)

Phlegmatic (phlegm): inactive, calm (Woodrow Wilson, Barack Obama)

Now let's turn to a similarly disgraced trait theory, phrenology, to contrast these two early attempts to understand human nature.

Phrenology

Phrenology is the study of personality traits based on bumps on the head. It began in the 1700s and was initially championed by the Viennese physician Joseph Gall (1758–1828), who reasoned that because human personality traits were distinct, there must be distinct places in the brain that housed these traits. The size and shape of the brain (as evidenced on the skull) could be measured to assess the amount of each trait in an individual. In general, the larger the bump on the head, the more of the specific trait was thought to be present. Phrenology was eventually discredited and now remains something of an embarrassment. Yet, in its time, there were many scholars and lay people who firmly believed in its ability to predict human behavior. One American writer, Ambrose Bierce, is said to have described it as "the science of picking one's pocket through the scalp."

Offshoots of this theory included attempts by Lombroso (1876) and others to investigate the criminal mind based on head and facial features, such as shifty eyes. Lombroso believed that people were born criminals and genetics made them so. It was not a far leap to conclude that certain races were more highly developed than others and that the White race particularly was more highly developed. Although this may seem ridiculous today, this theory was used to support Nazi dogma regarding racial superiority.

Sheldon's Body Types: Type Based on Body Shape

William Sheldon, a psychologist, proposed that physique is associated with personality. During his life, he tried to show that different body types correlated with behavior—especially delinquency (Sheldon, 1942). Sheldon identified the following "somatotypes" or physiques: Endomorphs have soft rounded bodies and love comfort, sociability, food, affection, and people. Mesomorphs are strong, tough, and muscled and love adventure, risk taking, and physical activity. Ectomorphs are thin and lightly muscled and are restrained, secretive, self-conscious, and prefer solitude. To be fair, Sheldon's theory is more complex than we have presented it, and a person is described as having some traits from all three physiques rather than being one specific type. Research has found some confirmation of a link between constitution and personality, if not wholly confirming Sheldon's specific theory (Rees, 1973).

Counselors today do not rely on bumps on the head or bloodletting, but we still use personality theories to classify others. In a previous chapter, we discussed the Myers-Briggs Type Indicator (MBTI), which, though flawed, is a commonly used personality inventory that is still widely used in individual and marriage counseling and in career and business consulting. The inventory looks at introversion versus extroversion; thinking versus feeling; sensing versus intuiting; and perception versus judgment. Based on these traits, 16 potential personality types emerge. One lesson from the MBTI is that by looking at one's own personality and understanding the styles and preferences of others, people can learn to appreciate and tolerate differences and even see them as complementary strengths. For example, can such differences lead you to new solutions and strategies in a work group or in your intimate relationship? Can that help you appreciate rather than clash with colleagues? Could it help you recognize your own preferences and see them as strengths rather than weaknesses? In the next section, we look at the NEO Personality Inventory and John Holland's Self-Directed Search (SDS), which are other personality tests in common use by counselors.

The "Big Five" Theory of Personality and NEO Personality Inventory

The Big Five personality traits are shown in Table 11.2. They are often assessed using the NEO Personality Inventory (Costa & McRae, 1995). These five factors are thought to encompass most of the myriad personality traits that have been proposed by personality tests. The Big Five were identified using a statistical technique called **factor analysis**, which looks at the degree to which the various measures overlap. Factor analysis allows many factors to be grouped together if it looks as if they are measuring the same thing. For example, intelligence has been measured in a variety of ways and with a variety of tests. Factor analysis has shown that many tests seem to be measuring a factor that the researchers named *verbal intelligence* or the ability to understand and use words. The Big Five was the result of this kind of analysis. Of course, these five factors do not

TABLE 11.2 Self-Rating Inventory of the Big Five Personality Characteristics

Name of Dimension	Characteristics	Self-rating (1–10)
Conscientiousness	Responsible and dependable, you are a planner, organized and productive, with a high need for achievement.	
Extraversion & Sociability	Talkative and sociable, you are ambitious, assertive, and active— generally a positive person.	
Agreeableness	You are cooperative, trusting, sympathetic, good-natured, and empathic.	
Neuroticism	Your mood fluctuates a lot; you often feel fed up. You frequently find that you are irritable, guilty, or self-conscious.	
Openness to Experience, Intellectance, & Culture	You are imaginative, artistic, aesthetically interested, curious, and have a need for variety. You are intellectual and feel deeply.	

fully describe the richness of a human being (Paunonen & Jackson, 2002), but it is a good place to start as we become students of personality.

Read over the characteristics of each of the five dimensions in Table 11.2 and rate yourself on a 10-point scale. A self-rating of 1 would indicate that you believe you possess very little of that characteristic; 10 would mean you see yourself as very similar to the characteristics of that dimension. By the way, for simplicity's sake we have not included the opposite poles of each dimension. In other words, if you score low on one of these scales, it may be that you would score high on the opposite dimension. Of course, it is true most people fall in the middle of the two polar descriptors, for example, somewhere between Agreeable and Disagreeable. Our inventory is unscientific because it has not been tested, but it may help you to get a feel for the Big Five.

Now let's take a look back at Table 11.2, Self-Rating Inventory of the Big Five Personality Characteristics. You were asked to rate yourself on each of the characteristics. The purpose was to become familiar with the concepts by thinking about your own personality. But is it not risky to publish this as a test? Could you administer this personality test to your friends and family and analyze them based on their scores? Yes! And it would be a misuse of the test. How do we know that it is really measuring personality? As you answer the following questions about personality tests, think about Table 11.2 as an example:

1. To determine how much oil is in your car, you can use the dipstick, but you could also drain the oil and test the instrument to see if your dipstick is bent or was designed for a different engine. If you wanted to be sure you were measuring a personality trait such as *Extraversion*, what method could you use to validate your test? In other words, what other instruments or

measures could you use to be sure your test is measuring extraversion instead of something else?

_____

_____

_____

_____

2. Our instrument has only one question per personality trait. Do you think one item is enough? Why? Would we get a better measurement if we increased the number of questions?

_____

_____

_____

_____

3. Because personality is supposed to be "a relatively stable and distinctive pattern of behavior that characterizes an individual and his or her reactions to the environment" (Kaplan & Saccuzzo, 2001, p. 405), do you think it would be important for our test to get the same or very similar results next year? In other words, is _reliability_ an important characteristic of all tests?

_____

_____

_____

_____

Figure 11.2 shows a possible profile of Abraham Lincoln on the NEO Personality Inventory. It is an estimate by experts of how he might have answered. Below his profile, a dotted line shows an estimate of the average of all U.S. presidents. Many consider Lincoln our greatest president. The profile shows him as rather neurotic (depressed) but intellectually brilliant and creative. Scores above 65 or below 35 are considered exceptionally high or low. Looking at averages is another way of understanding test scores. Thus compared to the average U.S. president, Lincoln was much more agreeable. This trait was recently described in _Team of Rivals_ (Goodwin, 2005), which documents his ability and willingness to make use of the talents of his archenemies through the use of humor and willingness to share credit. One of the possible implications of looking at these kinds of profiles is that seemingly negative

FIGURE 11.2 Lincoln Analyzed Using the Revised NEO Personality Inventory

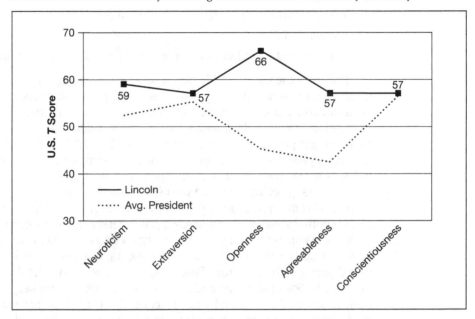

Source: From Rubenzer, S. J., Faschingbauer, T. R., & Ones, D. (2000). Assessing the U.S. presidents using the Revised NEO Personality Inventory. *Assessment, 7*(4), 403–420 (p. 410).

traits such as depression do not necessarily handicap a person and that many traits have a secret strength (Flach, 2002).

John Holland's Self-Directed Search (SDS)

The SDS is a self-adminstered, self-scoring, self-interpreting career interest test. Holland theorized that there are six personality types. When you study career counseling, you will certainly learn about the RIASEC types of John Holland. They are briefly described below.

- Realistic
    - Likes using tools and machines, is physical, is practical, values common sense
- Investigative
    - Scientific, analytical, likes solving problems, values independence and inventiveness
- Artistic
    - Creative, independent, disorganized, values beauty and self-expression
- Social
    - Supportive, helpful, nurturing

- Enterprising
  - Competitive, persuading, achievement oriented
- Conventional
  - Organized, detail oriented, precise, values accuracy and order

Holland's theory, in simple terms, says that a person is more interested in and therefore more satisfied in a career if his or her personality type matches the work environment. Thus, a conventional person is going to be happier working in an accounting firm than in a social environment, such as a day care center where things might get messy. Holland developed the Self-Directed Search (SDS) that matches a person's type with potential work environment. Everyone who takes this test gets scores on each of the six types, and the top three usually guide one to consider a range of work environments. Like those of many counselors, both of the authors' Holland type codes are a combination of Artistic, Social, and Investigative, and we both agree that we could easily have worked as a detective novelist or forensic investigator. Yet it is clear that these types do not predict every possible combination of people and environments. For example, a counselor in private practice would probably benefit from Enterprising tendencies. A school counselor should probably be Social above all and may be happier with record keeping if he or she is Conventional. Thus Holland's theory is flexible enough to recognize that specific work situations call for certain types, despite the general description. We encourage you to take the SDS. It is available online. It may help you understand yourself better and perhaps consider what area of the profession might interest you the most.

Implicit Theories

The term *implicit theory* refers to the fact that we all have ideas about what makes people tick. These personality theories are not formed in our schooling but from our life experience. For example, we frequently hear people described as "down to earth" or "a people person." Yet we often do not recognize that these are assumptions about others and they affect how we interact with them. Perhaps it is because these theories are integral parts of our way of looking at the world (Chiu, Hong, & Dweck, 1997). Allen Greenbaum, a sociologist, believes that he can identify liberalism or conservatism based on how people keep their front lawns (Walker, 2000). Manicured lawns are more likely to be kept by conservatives while more natural lawns with native plants more often belong to "left-leaners." In this same tradition, one of the authors of this text (Mark) has developed a personality assessment tool, the Corn-on-the-Cob Personality Test (COCPT), based on the way people eat sweet corn. Do you randomly *attack* the defenseless ear of corn or *compulsively* eat each kernel separately? Do you *cautiously* cut the kernels off with a knife? Or do you *obsessively* eat from left to right? Right now, the theory is in its infancy, but you see where we are going. People tend to behave in patterns, and we as observers tend to hypothesize about their tendencies to repeat these actions. It seems that human beings have an innate desire to organize what they see to understand and predict the future. Personality theorizing is something we all do.

George Kelly (1963), a well-known personality theorist, believed that everyone is a scientist. We are all constantly theorizing about the world, including other people. Because these implicit theories affect how we see and react to other people, we think it might be useful to become aware of your own implicit theories and assumptions that could affect your counseling relationships— not to mention relationships with family, friends, and co-workers. The dark side to the notion of implicit personality theories is that they are developed without peer review! Thus, we develop a private theory that may be influenced by our prejudices. One objection to personality in general is that it is based on European and American psychologies. The typologies are specific to our culture and our shared language. For example, the notion of conscientiousness is an important principle among White Anglo-Saxon Protestants as it relates to a historic love affair with the work ethic. In Indian personality theory, the notion of the three *gunas* is connected to Hinduism. The three states of life are Raja, Sattwa, and Tamas. Raja is an active state like the sanguine personality. Sattwa is a serene, pure, enlightened state, and Tamas is state of inertia and darkness. Even foods can be divided into Rajasic (spicy), Satvic (vegetables, grains, etc.), and Tamsic (dead foods). Since these states are even mentioned in the *Bhagavad Gita*, the Hindu scripture, they pervade Indian society and consciousness. The point is that our ideas about personality do not arise merely from our scientific data but from our culture and from our own experiences. We need to recognize that the lenses through which we view our clients are not pristine and objective but built from our histories, our families, our biases, and our good and bad experiences with people in our lives.

Role of Personality Theory in Counseling Today

Considerable research suggested that people do not consistently behave in accordance with traits measured on personality inventories. Yet personality theory is still widely studied and used in counseling today. Counselors use personality tests to help clients with career choices and career changes, and to help them better understand and accept themselves and others. As compared to times past, counselors are less apt to give many personality tests such as the Rorschach (inkblots) and the Minnesota Multiphasic Personality Inventory (MMPI) (Butcher, Graham, Ben-Porath, Tellegen, & Kaemmer, 2001) to identify pathology. Yet even thought these kinds of diagnostic instruments are not as influential today, counselors cannot escape their implicit theories of personality, which may affect how they see their clients.

Ethics in Assessment

There are a variety of complex ethical problems in testing and assessment, and you will learn about these during your graduate program. Therefore, we thought it best to discuss the ones that you are apt to run into early in your training, perhaps even before you take your testing or ethics class. In those classes, you will identify ethical principles that are relevant for many different types of assessment situations, and you will learn about all of the legal trouble that counselors can get into if they fail to understand ethics and the law. Rather than scare you with that kind of data, we thought it would be useful to identify some of the issues you may face before you actually start seeing clients. At that juncture, you will have supervision and some ethical training. Right now, you may encounter some ethical pitfalls, including the temptation to assess your friends and family; believe the results of one test, one sign, or one symptom; use photocopies of tests; believe in online tests; and use a test or assessment instrument without any training or supervision.

Learn the Key Ethical Principle by Practicing It

The key ethical principle is confidentiality. In your career class, your assessment class, and even in your introductory classes, you will have the opportunity to give and take tests. You will probably interview fellow students. All of this is assessment data, and you should keep what you learn to yourself. That means that you do not discuss it with your spouse, friends, or other students. You are officially a keeper of secrets and it begins now.

Ethical Issue #1: Evaluating or Testing Your Friends

Is it all right to use assessment instruments with family and friends? It is something like the dilemma of a doctor whose family members want medical help. It is almost always better for the patient to see someone who is quite objective and not emotionally attached. Of course, as a doctor, you would treat a friend or family member on an emergency basis, just as the counselor should recognize suicidal ideation and assist a friend or relation in getting help.

When you analyze your friends with tests or other assessment devices, you are uncovering areas that may hitherto have been unavailable to you. This may influence the way that you look at them in the future and potentially affect your relationship. In order to consent to being evaluated by you, your friend would have to understand all of these implications. Can you keep the results of your assessment secret? What if you find your friend has a substance abuse problem? Would that change things between you? Would you be able to insist that he or she get treatment? These are only a few of the dilemmas that we face when we open up this can of worms, and therefore, counselors avoid diagnosing, evaluating, and testing their friends and relatives.

Consider this example. One of us (Darcy) teaches a personality testing class where graduate students learn to give comprehensive psychological evaluations. Students are asked to practice on volunteers, with the warning that testing family members and close friends can be dangerous to healthy relationships. Nevertheless, a few years ago, one of my students decided to test her mother. She came into my office a few days later, incredibly shaken, because the results of the tests revealed that her mother was having an affair, which was confirmed in the interview she conducted. The student's mother told her, "I'm so glad to be talking to a professional about this—it's really been on my mind, and I feel so guilty. I'm glad to get it off my chest!" Of course, the student did *not* want to know this about her mother, did *not* see herself as a professional in this mother-daughter relationship, and was incredibly upset with having this information. The lesson is an important one. Clear professional and personal boundaries are essential. If we can't establish and maintain good boundaries, why would we be surprised to learn that others cannot make these distinctions with us either?

Ethical Issue #2: Believing the Results of One Test, One Sign, or One Symptom

In my counseling practice, I (Mark) recognized that many of the clients diagnosed with Histrionic Personality Disorder (extreme attention seeking and excessively dramatic behavior) often wore five or six rings. So, I began using that as a sign of the disorder. Although many individuals suffering from Histrionic Personality Disorder do dress dramatically and wear a lot of rings, the converse is not necessarily true. Wearing rings does not mean you have this mental disorder. The *Diagnostic and Statistical Manual* (DSM) identifies *all* of the symptoms that a client must have, and does not allow a diagnosis on a single sign or symptom.

Any client sign or symptom that you identify and the results of any tests have to be taken in context and compared with all the other knowledge you have about the client. One of the related mistakes that counselors can make is to give a client a personality test and consider its results in isolation. Before we can take the results of the test seriously, we have to fit it into an overall picture of the client. So most counselors and other test givers like to give a full range of tests and see if similar results appear from multiple sources.

What relevance does this have for you as a counseling student? Have you ever heard of medical students starting to believe that they have every disease that they study? Similarly, counseling students, as they learn about various pathologies, start to think that they have every mental disorder. Unless you recognize that one symptom does not equal a disorder, you can erroneously assign yourself to a category to which you do not belong. Similarly, as you take tests in your testing or assessment class, you need to keep in mind that they are a single source of information, and your fellow students cannot be diagnosed from one source.

Ethical Issue #3: Using Photocopies of Tests

Many tests are expensive, and it is tempting to photocopy them. Some tests can be copied with the permission of the authors or publishers (see *Measures for Clinical Practice and Research* by Corcoran & Fischer, 2006). So, it is not always necessary to purchase them; however, those that are copyright-protected are like songs. They are the creations of their authors, who deserve to be remunerated just as a popular singer deserves credit for his or her music. Making photocopies of these tests is unethical and illegal.

Ethical Issue #4: Believing Online Tests and Tests in Magazines

There are personality tests, depression and anxiety screening tests, tests for alcoholism, tests for personality disorders, and the list goes on and on. In our section on personality testing, we discuss this foible in more detail. But how do we know that the test measures what it is supposed to measure? If you take it today, will you get the same results next week? If you cannot answer these questions, a test in a magazine should be considered a fun way to pass a plane ride, not something that you can rely on. In the accompanying Informed by Research feature, we consider how these popular surveys can have a real influence on the general population.

Informed by Research
The Effects of Popularized Tests

Surveys have long been a feature of women's magazines and now appear in the new wave of men's magazines such as *Maxim* and *Men's Health*. A recent issue of a popular women's magazine had the following survey: "What's His Intimacy IQ?" Can you really analyze the men you are dating based on your opinion and find out which one has the best potential for an intimate relationship? Not really. But maybe we are taking this too seriously. These tests are primarily for entertainment, right? Even so, is it possible that they mislead readers about what is really important in a relationship? Are you playing on the mistaken belief that all test results are true? Do you think that there is potential damage in disseminating information about health and relationships through surveys that do not really measure what they say they are measuring?

Consider the article entitled "Health Advice in Women's Magazines: Up in Smoke?" by Dr. Elizabeth Whelan (1996), an epidemiologist.

Dr. Whelan complained that surveys in women's magazines failed to identify cigarette smoking as the major health risk for women (the leading cause of premature death) in their health "tests" while overemphasizing other issues. In other words, the content of the test did not include the right questions (this is the problem of test validity). This means that your score on the test is unlikely to relate to longevity, as the articles suggest. Unfortunately, people tend to believe test results even when they come from unreliable sources. Numbers have the power to persuade us even if they are misused. Consider Mark Twain's dictum, "There are lies, damned lies, and statistics." Part of being a counselor today is wading through the statistics and being able to identify the good and the bad research that is coming our way. Counselors, as purveyors of mental health information, must understand research, separating the good from the bad, or risk endangering their clients.

Ethical Issue #5: Using a Test Without any Training or Supervision

You may become fascinated with a particular test and be tempted to go beyond your training. All published tests have specific qualifications that are required to purchase or use them. Typically, Level A tests are surveys and question-naires that anyone can use. Level B tests usually require a college-level course in tests and measurements. Level C tests are the most stringent, requiring an advanced degree, membership in the appropriate professional association, licensure or certification, and training in both the specific test and the testing domain. Of course, there are ways that people access tests inappropriately. A few years ago, for example, a retiring professional was selling all of his Level C tests on eBay. Anyone could have purchased the tests, constituting a serious breach in test security. Although you may be able to get access to highly spe-cialized tests, you should never administer them without proper training and supervision.

Spotlight
Assessing Suicide Risk Through IS PATH WARM?

All clients should be screened for suicide. Some wonder if asking about suicide puts the idea into the client's mind, but there is clear and con-vincing research that says that is not the case. Getting clients to talk about their thoughts will help you determine if some intervention is needed. IS PATH WARM is a mnemonic device that reminds you of the major issues to assess regard-ing suicidal potential. Remember, suicide risk is a complicated type of assessment, and beginning counselors should never try to assess suicide without training and supervision.

- **Ideation:** Does the client think about, write about, or talk about suicide?

  This is the most important criterion and anyone who meets this criterion should be seen by a mental health professional. While the other criteria do increase the chances of suicide, this suggests acute risk.

- **Substance abuse:** Excessive or increased usage of alcohol or drugs.

- **Purposelessness:** Client sees little or no meaning in life or reason to go on.

- **Anxiety:** Client is restless, anxious, sleepless, or sleeping all the time.

- **Trapped:** Client feels that there are few alternatives and no way out.

- **Hopelessness:** Client has no hope for self or the future.

- **Withdrawal:** Client withdraws from usual activities, family, and friends.

- **Anger:** Client feels vengeful because of being wronged or has periods of rage.

- **Recklessness:** Client acts without regard to consequences and may be involved in dangerous behavior. Does not care what happens.

- **Mood changes:** Client experiences extreme mood changes.

Source: Granello & Granello (2007); Juhnke, Granello, & Lebrón-Striker (2007).

 **Spotlight**
Jennifer's Letter

Jennifer, a college student, sent this letter to her professor:

What do I feel? A restlessness. A loneliness. A hurt. Who do I give my love to? Who will love me in return? When I was younger, the loneliness was almost unbearable. It would come at times and be totally engulfing. Sometimes listening to songs does it. Sometimes it doesn't have to be triggered. It just happens. When I was younger the feelings would be worse than being yelled at or getting in trouble. I felt so alone. So desolate. It's hard to put into words. To explain it is really beyond words.

Through the years, I've been able to ward it off. I don't let myself get too close to it. I can feel it coming on. Sometimes it does come and it's just as bad as when I was younger. What's wrong with me? Why am I this way? I want to yell or scream. I want to let it out but I can't. My mind screams with the feelings inside. I scream and scream but no one hears. Everyone thinks I am calm and happy-go-lucky. I want to cry but I can't let anyone see. They'll think I'm crazy because I can't explain. They don't understand. Do they have a feeling like it? It's not good to talk about it.

Why am I so alone? Why is it that when I feel that I have found someone who would understand, things get messed up? Why do I withdraw from people when I get close and they do something I don't like? Why does terror settle in the pit of my stomach? Does anyone care? Can't they listen? Can't they hear? I feel like my insides will explode. I want to let it all out so maybe I will be okay. But will I? Am I normal? I can't be. Nobody else is like this. This can't be. I must be crazy. I need to be locked away. This can't be how others feel.

Who can I talk to? Will they really care? How can they? Please help me. I hurt so bad. The loneliness is unbearable. Tell me I'm not crazy. Tell me I can be loved too. Hear me. See my hurt. I know you can if you'll just look. What does it matter? Nobody would care. All they would say is "Bad thing that it happened." "She was so young and had her whole life in front of her." It's not much of a life if nobody will reach out to me.

Questions to Consider

1. Despite the fact that you do not have much information about Jennifer, if she were your friend, would you consider this a serious problem requiring counseling?

2. Using the Spotlight feature entitled IS PATH WARM, try to get an idea of Jennifer's risk for suicide.

3. Besides being a cry for help, does the note tell us something about Jennifer's thinking that we might use to help her in counseling? What ideas are expressed that give clues to her view of the world, self, and others?

4. What ideas does Jennifer have that might be modified or challenged as part of counseling?

Ethical Issue #6: Thinking You Can Learn to Assess Suicide Later

As soon as you become a student of counseling, your friends, co-workers, family members, and even your fellow students may begin to seek you out for help. You may be flattered at first, but soon you will realize that you are not entirely prepared. One of the areas we are least ready to handle is the unexpected admission by one of these significant others that he or she is considering suicide. You cannot wait to have a plan to deal with such a disclosure. You may wish to keep the person's confidence, but you do not have an ethical responsibility nor a legal right to maintain confidentiality. In fact, you will have to intervene. There is a special Spotlight on suicide risk assessment in this chapter to help get you started.

Now, use the information you have learned in this chapter to consider the case outlined in the accompanying Spotlight. Consider how a letter sent to a teacher includes many clues to understanding the student. Also think about what is left out of the letter—what you would like to ask the student if she were sitting in front of you.

Summary

I n this chapter, we discussed the critical role that assessment plays in the counseling process for counselors in every setting and for every client population. When counseling students think that assessment means only the giving of standardized tests, they miss the essential point of assessment. Assessment means adopting an investigative role in understanding your client. It means taking in information by whatever means available and using that information to develop a full understanding of the client that leads to appropriate and successful interventions. All counselors are investigators, and assessment gives us the tools for this important part of our job.

End-of-Chapter Activities

The following activities might be part of your assignments for a class. Whether they are required or not, we suggest that you complete them as a way of reflecting on your new learning, arguing with new ideas in writing, and thinking about questions you may want to pose in class.

Student Activities

1. Now it's time to reflect on the major topics that we have covered in this chapter. Look back at the sections or the ideas you have underlined. What were your reactions as you read that portion of the chapter? What do you want to remember?

_____

_____

_____

_____

_____

2. As you read the Snapshot by Todd Gibbs, what parts of it could you identify
   with? Were you surprised that a student at the beginning of his internship
   had such strong opinions about assessment? How do your ideas align with,
   or challenge, those presented by Todd?

   _____

   _____

   _____

   _____

   _____

   _____

3. Think about the types of mistakes that counselors might make in assessment (ignoring or not detecting a mental illness, substance abuse, or potential for violence). Why do you think beginning counselors might miss
   these? Most of us have a natural desire to see the good in people. Do you
   think that keeps us from realistically assessing their problems?

   _____

   _____

   _____

   _____

   _____

   _____

■■■ Journal Question ■■■

Think about all the tests that you have taken
during your school years, including an IQ test,
the SAT, and perhaps the GRE or MAT. Your life
may have been drastically affected by these
tests. How crucial is it for you as a counselor to
know about the reliability and validity of tests?

■■■ Topics for Discussion ■■■

1. Much of assessment takes place at the
   beginning of the counseling relationship,
   but few counselors use measurements
   along the way to assess client progress by
   keeping records, charts, and other information. Should counselors spend more time
   learning about methods of tracking client
   progress? What tools are available?

2. Most standardized assessments measure weaknesses, flaws, pathology, and maladjustment. How important is it to identify strengths and competencies? What are your personal strengths that have never been measured in school?

■■■ Experiments ■■■

1. Try making a genogram or pictorial family tree for yourself. Samples and instructions are available from a number of sources, including McGoldrick and Shellenberger (1999) and Young (2009). There is even free genogram software available online. Looking and reflecting on your own genogram is relatively safe; however, if you feel disturbed by thinking about your family history, consider talking to a professional about what you discover.

2. Go to your university career or counseling center and take a career inventory. Discuss the results with a professional. What does it say about you and the possible career of counselor? What other issues besides test results will be useful in making this decision?

■■■ Explore More! ■■■

If you are interested in exploring more about the ideas presented in this chapter, we recommend the following books and articles.

Books

Dana, R. H. (2005). *Multicultural assessment: Principles, applications, and examples.* Mahweh, NJ: Erlbaum.

Drummond, R. J., & Jones, K. D. (2009). *Assessment procedures for counselor and helpers* (7th ed.). Upper Saddle River, NJ: Pearson.

Hood, A. B., & Johnson, R. W. (2007). *Assessment in counseling: A guide to the use of psychological assessment procedures* (4th ed.) Alexandria, VA: American Counseling Association.

Lukas, S. (1993). *Where to start and what to ask.* New York: Norton.

Sommers-Flanagan, J., & Sommers-Flanagan, R. (2009). *Clinical interviewing* (4th ed.). New York: Wiley.

Whiston, S. C. (2007). *Principles and applications of assessment in counseling* (3rd ed.). Pacific Grove, CA: Brooks-Cole.

Articles

Granello, D. H. (2010). The process of suicide risk assessment: Twelve core principles. *Journal of Counseling and Development, 88,* 363–371.

> This article discusses the overarching assessment principles involved in suicide risk assessment, a critical issue for counselors in all settings.

Hays, D., & Emelianchik, K. (2009). A content analysis of intimate partner violence assessments. *Measurement & Evaluation in Counseling & Development, 42*(3), 9–153.

> Intimate partner violence is something that every counselor should know about and any counselor working with couples and families will find essential.

Naugle, K. (2009). Counseling and testing: What counselors need to know about state laws on assessment and testing. *Measurement & Evaluation in Counseling & Development 42*(1), 31–45.

> As the title indicates, this is a starting point for understanding how various states regulate testing and assessment. Your state licensure board is still the most up-to-date source for information.

Willow, R., Tobin, D., & Toner, S. (2009). Assessment of the use of spiritual genograms in counselor education. *Counseling and Values, 53*(3), 214.

> The article highlights assessment issues in assessing religious and spiritual issues in counseling and gives insight into how genograms can be used.

■■■ MyHelpingLab ■■■

To help you explore the profession of counseling via video interviews with counselors and clients, some of the chapters in this text include links to MyHelpingLab at the Pearson.com website. There are some videos that correspond with this chapter, and watching them might challenge you to think about these concepts at a deeper level.

- To explore some of the ways that counselors use assessment in their work, go to

Assessment and Diagnosis, and then "Clinical Assessment" to check out these video clips:

- Multi-modal: Assessments and forming clinical relationships
- Diagnostic Assessment: Assessing key components of presenting issues
- Diagnostic Assessment: Reviewing intake information with clients

12

How Do Counselors Make Legal and Ethical Decisions?

In this chapter, we will:
- Survey the major ethical guidelines of the counseling profession.
- Describe the major legal decisions and their impact on counseling in a variety of settings.
- Consider the role of a counselor's personal values and ethics in the counseling process.
- Discuss ethical decision-making models.

As you read the chapter, you might want to consider:
- What impact might your own personal values and beliefs have on your counseling practice?
- How can you be intentional in your decision to practice counseling in a legal and ethically appropriate manner?
- How will you know when you need assistance in making ethical choices in your practice, and what resources are available for you to consult?

No one enters the profession of counseling with the intention of behaving unethically. In fact, most people enter the profession because they have a deep and heartfelt desire to help others, and the idea of behaving unethically is something they would never consider. Nevertheless, ethical violations among counselors continue to be a major concern in all counseling specializations and in all jurisdictions across the United States.

Counselors who fail to follow the profession's ethical mandates can face serious professional and personal ramifications. Counselors can also find themselves in legal trouble if they fail to follow the state and national legal standards of the profession. The details of the profession's legal and ethical mandates are complex, and the consequences of violations can be severe. In addition, ethical codes and the law are constantly evolving to match changes in the society in which we live, and counselors can find themselves in situations with no clear ethical or legal guidelines upon which to act. As a result, many beginning counselors find themselves feeling overwhelmed with the legal and ethical obligations of their new profession and eager to find quick and definitive answers to their legal and ethical questions. Unfortunately, we cannot provide all of these answers in just one chapter, but we can help you start your journey as a counselor armed with what you need to begin to develop a personal, positive, and practical approach toward becoming an ethical professional counselor.

In this chapter, we take a proactive stance to legal and ethical decision making in counseling. Ethical counselors recognize that they have a personal responsibility to self-monitor and take full responsibility for all of their professional actions. They internalize the values and beliefs of the profession and strive to develop the "habits of character" they need to realize the profession's goals (Welfel, 2005, p. 122). This contrasts with a punitive approach that focuses on the repercussions of violations. In the punitive approach, a counselor might say, "I won't commit an ethical violation because I might lose my license." In a proactive approach, on the other hand, counselors focus on the benefits of ethical practice rather than the punishment for noncompliance. In this approach a counselor might say, "I want to operate as a highly ethical counselor so that I can provide the highest level of service for my clients." This proactive approach aligns with the stance of the American Counseling Association's Code of Ethics (2005), which focuses on developing an ethical approach to practice that benefits clients and fosters professional values that are derived from personal dedication, rather than imposed by an outside force. In other words, the best ethical practice is one that is an outgrowth of the personhood of the counselor and is an integral part of the counselor's personal and professional identity. This type of ethical practice empowers counselors to help their clients grow and develop. Counselors who operate ethically recognize that their primarily responsibility is to their clients, and this responsibility guides all of their professional decisions.

American Counseling Association Code of Ethics (2005)
"**A.1.a. Primary Responsibility** The primary responsibility of counselors is to respect the dignity and to promote the welfare of clients."

American School Counselor Association Code of Ethics (2010)
"**A.1.a.** Professional school counselors have a primary obligation to the students, who are to be treated with dignity and respect as unique individuals."

 # The Purpose of Ethics in the Practice of Counseling

Ethics is the systematic study of value concepts, such as right and wrong, and the principles that are derived from such a study. **Professional ethics** are the standards of good practice, as agreed upon by experts and professionals in a given occupation. Ethics are linked to moral behavior, but professional ethics are not the

■■■ *Words of Wisdom* ■■■

"Competent professionals are competent decision-makers."

Source: Cottone & Tarvydas (2007, p. 13).

same as morals. Professionals develop ethical codes to delineate the standards and rules of good practice, and these standards are based on professional agreement of what is good or right or acceptable, or how professionals "ought" to behave in various situations.

The primary purpose of ethical standards in the field of counseling is to *protect clients and consumers* of counseling services. Clients know that if they go to counselors who are members in good standing of the profession, they will receive treatment that meets the minimum acceptable standard of the profession. Clients have the right to enter into the counseling relationship with specific expectations regarding the counselor's professionalism and practice. Ethical codes protect the rights of clients.

A secondary purpose of the ethical standards is to protect the members of the profession. Professional counselors have ethical codes to guide their practice, and they understand that their colleagues meet these minimal standards of conduct. In this way, counselors are protected, rather universally, from unethical practices of colleagues that would serve to lessen the credibility of the profession in general. Additionally, professionals know that if they adhere to the professional ethics, they are offered some protection from the public against spurious lawsuits.

A third purpose of the ethical standards is to limit government interference in the regulation of the profession. Of course, the government is involved with regulating all the mental health professions, but by drafting their own standards of conduct, professional counselors take a proactive stance in determining the acceptable behaviors for counselors. Thus, members of the profession, who have the most knowledge and insight about the profession, take the lead in drafting the rules of responsible and ethical behavior.

Professional Codes of Ethics

All of the helping professions have established codes of ethics to guide clinical practice. Some of the organizations and associations with ethical codes that regulate practice for counselors are:

- The American Counseling Association (ACA)
- The American School Counselor Association (ASCA)
- The American Association for Marriage & Family Therapists (AAMT)
- The American Mental Health Counselors Association (AMHCA)
- The International Association of Marriage & Family Therapists (IAMFC)

The ethical codes developed by the various counseling associations provide general guidelines for practice and typically represent the minimal standards of conduct. Additionally, the codes tend to be based on past occurrences and therefore cannot anticipate all ethical dilemmas that may occur. For example, any ethical codes that were established more than a few years ago do not address the use of the more recent technologies, such as social media websites or counseling via Skype. Thus, counselors use the ethical codes to guide practice, but they recognize that the codes cannot be blueprints for practice. Adhering to the ethical codes of the profession does not negate the need for use of sound clinical judgment, professional integrity, consultation with other professionals, and ethical reasoning.

We encourage you to become familiar with the ethical code(s) for the counseling specialization(s) you plan to pursue. Typically, these codes are available on the organizations' websites. Although specifics of the ethical codes differ, several common themes have been identified (Koocher & Keith-Spiegel, 2008). These include:

- Promoting client welfare
- Practicing within the scope of one's competence
- Doing no harm
- Protecting client confidentiality and privacy
- Acting ethically and responsibly
- Avoiding exploitation of clients
- Upholding the integrity of the profession

In addition to outlining the ethical principles in the document, some of the professional codes of ethics within the counseling specializations explicitly state the values upon which the code is built. For example, the Code of Professional Ethics for Rehabilitation Counselors (2009) outlines the following foundational values to which all rehabilitation counselors should commit:

- Respecting human rights and dignity
- Ensuring the integrity of all professional relationships
- Acting to alleviate personal distress and suffering
- Enhancing the quality of professional knowledge and its application to increase professional and personal effectiveness
- Appreciating the diversity of human experience and culture
- Advocating for the fair and adequate provision of services

In the accompanying Spotlight, we introduce you to the idea of aspirational ethics, an approach that calls upon counselors to seek to uphold the absolute highest ethical standards of the profession. Aspirational ethics are consistent with the proactive approach we adhere to in this chapter.

Spotlight
Minimal versus Aspirational Ethics

Ethical codes provide only the minimal acceptable standard to which professionals must adhere. If a counselor uses the laws and ethical codes in a strict, prescriptive manner, then he or she follows the minimum guidelines outlined in them. This practice will generally protect a counselor from legal repercussions. This "letter of the law" approach has been called "mandatory ethics," and it is all that is legally required of professionals. The focus of mandatory ethics is discouraging inappropriate practice and protecting clients (Dougherty, 2004). A second approach is a higher level of ethical decision making, called "aspirational ethics." Aspirational ethics refers to "the attempt to accomplish the maximum in moral and ethical outcomes" (Newman, Gray, & Fuqua, 1996, p. 231).

In this approach, counselors do more than simply comply with the codes of ethics or laws. Rather, counselors who use this approach continually scan their interventions and approaches to make sure that they are always aware of the effects of their actions on their clients. Aspirational ethics are less prescriptive and more general than mandatory ethics, which are rooted in specific ethical codes or rules. Examples of aspirational ethics include integrity, social responsibility, and justice (Newman et al., 1996). Maintaining this type of ethical behavior is a continuous active process that involves self-awareness and self-monitoring. Thus, highly ethical counselors follow the minimum guidelines of the mandatory ethics *and* they always work toward the highest levels of aspirational ethics.

The Role of Personal Ethics and Values

Counselors can look to the professional ethical codes to help make sure they are following minimum standards, but the codes cannot provide answers to all ethical dilemmas. There are situations in which the ethical codes are silent. In other situations, the counselor might understand the imperatives within the codes but be less certain as to how to actually carry them out. (For example, counselors know that they cannot accept invitations to date their clients, but what does one *actually say* to a client who asks his or her counselor out to dinner?) In these situations, the personal characteristics of the counselor are critical additions to the professional expertise and identity of the counselor.

Counselors find that many of the positive personality traits that help them be good counselors also help them be ethical counselors (Corey, Corey, & Callanan, 1988). For example, counselors who are open, honest, and willing to take risks are more likely to reach out for help when they need it. Reaching out to colleagues and/or supervisors for advice, support, or feedback is an essential component of ethical decision making. Counselors who believe that there is always something new to learn can be open to new possibilities, including the possibility that just because "that's the way we've always done things here" doesn't mean it's necessarily the best—or most ethical—way of being. Finally, counselors who are able to laugh at themselves recognize that they don't have to be perfect. Counselors who take themselves too seriously run the risk of feeling the need to go to great lengths to cover up mistakes or to make sure that they look like an expert in all situations.

The Role of the Counselor's Personal Values

When counselors seek to integrate their personal and professional selves, one of the most difficult situations to manage can be in the area of values. Because our values are so intrinsic to who we are, we often cannot see when they affect our decision making or influence our work with clients. It is clear that clients are affected by the values of the counselor and may even adopt some of those values as their own (Richards, Rector, & Tjeltveit, 1999). As a result, counselors must be very aware of their own values and beliefs.

Consider these examples.

- A high school counselor working with a bright and capable young woman might be dismayed to learn that she has decided not to accept a scholarship to attend college but instead to move in with her boyfriend and become a waitress. It may be tempting for the counselor to use subtle (or even obvious) means of persuasion to help guide that young person into making a different choice.

- A mental health counselor working with a client with schizophrenia may be frustrated to learn that the client has decided to go off his medication because he misses the voices he was hearing and now finds he is lonely for much of the day. It may be difficult to resist convincing the client to stay on his medication.

- A couples counselor learns that a couple has decided to drop out of counseling, where they were learning how to integrate healthy communication styles into their marriage, deciding that their marital problems are caused by a lack of time devoted to their religious faith. Instead of counseling, they have decided to join a more fundamental branch of their religion and spend more time praying for a resolution of their problems. It may be frustrating for the counselor to discover that the couple has given up on learning a strategy for improved communication in their relationship.

Counselors are faced with countless scenarios like these, and it is often difficult to know when we cross a line between helping clients come to the best decisions they can make and using our power and position to impose our values. There is no clear line here, and ethical counselors recognize the complexity of many of life's dilemmas. Most counselors would argue that in all of these scenarios, the counselor has an obligation to help the client see the potential consequences of their decisions. The question becomes, where is the line between presenting options and imposing values?

In order to sidestep these concerns, beginning counselors sometimes talk about the need to conduct "values-free" counseling. They argue that they will simply be neutral and allow their clients to make their own choices. But even these choices—allowing clients to explore their options and make their own choices—are based on the values of autonomy and freedom. Every choice a counselor makes, from attending to certain parts of a client's story to the selection of certain counseling techniques to the decision to become a counselor in the first place, are all choices that are heavily laden with values. In fact, the "myth" of values-free counseling can actually be dangerous. Counselors who think they are values-free are, in reality, unaware of the effect their own values have on their counseling. One of the most important steps beginning counselors can take is to become keenly aware of their own values and how these values might impact their work as counselors.

Rather than a values-free or even values-neutral approach to counseling, which is impossible, most counselors believe in a "values-aware" approach. That is, counselors should be keenly aware of their own values, understand where those values come from, and recognize how their values might affect the counseling relationship. Although the need for a values-aware approach is often mentioned within the context of multiculturalism and diversity in counseling, the reality is that we must be aware of our values and how they affect our counseling relationships with all of our clients. A consistent theme of this text is the importance of self-awareness and self-discovery for the beginning counselor, and there is no aspect of counseling where this is more important than in the area of counselor values. Counselors impose their values on clients when they attempt to influence or define a client's beliefs, attitudes, or actions. This can be done either actively (such as making overt statements that support one particular value or belief over another), or passively (such as paying attention and responding to only those goals or choices articulated by the client that align with the counselor's values). Importantly, the imposition of values by the counselor can be an intentional choice by the counselor or unintentional and out of the counselor's awareness. Either way, the results are the same.

American Counseling Association Code of Ethics

A.4.b. Counselors are aware of their own values, attitudes, beliefs, and behaviors and avoid imposing values that are inconsistent with counseling goals.

Most counselors can easily think of times when their work with clients put them into discussions where the goals for counseling were in conflict with their own values. For example, I (Darcy) still remember a time when I was working in a clinic in Appalachia. I saw a young woman who was in counseling for panic disorder with agoraphobia (a mental disorder in which people are afraid to leaving the house or go out into crowds for fear they might have a panic attack). The woman came to the first counseling session with her husband, which made sense because her illness made it impossible for her to drive herself. However, within the first few minutes of the session, it became clear that her husband intended to stay in the counseling session with her, and he answered most of the questions that I directed to her. From where I sat, it appeared that their relationship was one in which he

Counseling Controversy

DO COUNSELORS HAVE THE RIGHT TO REFUSE TO WORK WITH CERTAIN CLIENTS?

Background: One of the ethical mandates within the American Counseling Association Code of Ethics is that counselors not condone or engage in discrimination based on sexual orientation of clients, students, employees, or research participants. It is within this context that a series of recent court cases have challenged whether students in counseling programs can be forced to work with gay, lesbian, bisexual, or transgendered clients, or whether this mandate infringes upon their First Amendment rights.

POINT: COUNSELORS HAVE AN ETHICAL MANDATE TO WORK WITH ALL CLIENTS	COUNTERPOINT: COUNSELORS DO NOT HAVE TO WORK WITH CLIENTS WHO EXHIBIT BEHAVIORS THEY DO NOT CONDONE
• A fundamental premise of the counseling profession is to respect the dignity and worth of all clients. The ACA and the ASCA Code of Ethics are both clear that multicultural competence includes protection of gay, lesbian, bisexual, and transgendered (GLBT) clients	• The ethical codes of ACA and ASCA are wrong to force counselors to work with GLBT clients—or any clients who engage in behaviors that the counselor sees as morally wrong. A person's choice of profession should not be allowed to limit that person's free speech or demand that the person engage in behaviors that are contrary to his or her belief system.
• Counseling is about helping clients find their own way, not about forcing the indoctrination of clients into the counselor's beliefs. Prejudice against clients has no place in the counseling relationship.	• The very people who demand that counselors be "nonjudgmental" and "nondisciminatory" are in fact judging and discriminating against counselors who have strong religious injunctions against working with GLBT clients.
• Where personal and professional values are in conflict, professional duty takes precedence. Counselors are licensed by the state and must follow state laws. For example, a Christian Scientist enrolled in medical school could not refuse to give patients medications and still be allowed to practice medicine. Patients (and clients) have a reasonable expectation that their doctor (or counselor) will follow the best practices of their profession, not use the profession to advance their own beliefs.	• Counselors with strong religious beliefs that homosexuality is a sin cannot, and should not, be asked to turn off their beliefs. People of faith cannot pick and choose what parts of their doctrine they will and will not practice in their lives, and to ask them to do so infringes upon their freedom of religion.

• Professional conduct is not the same as individual free speech. Adherence to the code of ethics is a legal and legitimate requirement for state-licensed counselors.	• Counselors have First Amendment rights, which include the freedom to take a strong public stand against a lifestyle to which they are opposed.
• The issue is not about a counselor's personal beliefs or actions outside of the office. It is about the actions of a professional. Every profession has these sorts of mandates. For example, a Realtor couldn't refuse to sell a house to a gay man. Why should counselors be held to lower standards of professionalism than Realtors?	• There has to be room in the counseling profession for many different types of counselors, including those with strong religious beliefs. Diversity of beliefs and practices will only serve to strengthen the counseling profession.
• The option of simply "referring" GLBT clients to another counselor is not sanctioned by the counseling profession and has practical as well as legal and ethical implications. In many schools and social service agencies, other counselors are simply unavailable or overbooked, and referrals are often logically difficult.	• The imposition of "political correctness" (PC) into the counseling profession means that counselors feel threatened to keep silent if their views don't match whatever happens to be PC at the moment, or they risk losing their license.
• Legally, the refusal to work with clients based on their sexual orientation is a form of discrimination. Counselors who attempt to refer GLBT clients based on their orientation can be sued for malpractice.	• Counseling is a blend of the personal and the professional. You cannot separate the two. To ask counselors to be one person when they are at the office and another person when they are at home violates many of the foundational beliefs about counseling, such as integrity, genuineness and congruence. A good counselor is an integration of both the personal and the professional.
• Clients who are referred to another counselor because of their sexual orientation can feel judged or emotionally harmed. This may be particularly true for young people in the "coming out" stage of sexual orientation, who are especially vulnerable and must be protected from counselors who exhibit this sort of prejudice.	• Clients deserve services by counselors who can support and respect their choices. Forcing counselors to work with clients who behave in ways that the counselor believes to be morally wrong and pretend that they respect those choices only means that the client will receive counseling based on a lie. A counseling relationship cannot have this type of deception at its foundation and still be effective for the client.

As with most controversies, there probably is some truth to both sides of this argument.

←——→

**Counselors should be able
to work with all clients**   **Counselors should be
                                                        free to choose their clients**

On the continuum, place an "X" where you think you stand on this issue.

exercised the power and control, and she meekly agreed to whatever he said. My initial reaction was to become angry with the husband, to diagnose the woman with dependent personality disorder (a disorder in which people rely on others to meet their emotional and physical needs), and to set up a counseling goal for her to be more independent and assertive in her relationship. Luckily, I did a quick values-check and was able to stop myself before I said anything. Whose values was I supporting here? Was I expecting this woman to live my values? She hadn't complained about the relationship, and marital equality was not the goal of the counseling. Just because her relationship did not match the type of spousal relationship that I value in my own life did not mean that it needed to be changed. Instead, I recognized that I was about to impose my values on her without her blessing or permission, and I backed away from my own reaction to pay more attention to her story and her perspective and to focus on her goals for the counseling session. I made sure to check in with her independently from her husband (always a good idea, to assess for potential domestic violence), but when I got to know the couple, I saw that they were simply operating from a more traditional framework than my own. As always, when counselors take a moment to ask themselves, "Whose needs are being met?" they can help focus on the values and beliefs of the client, instead of their own.

When Personal and Professional Values Collide

The intersection of personal and professional values can be particularly difficult for counselors who hold strong personal beliefs or values that are in conflict with the stated values of the counseling profession. Professional ethics guide professional behavior. However, a behavior can be professionally ethical, but not morally acceptable to an individual therapist (say, for example, counseling a woman who is getting an abortion). However, personal morals cannot negate professional ethics. For example, if an individual therapist's personal morals support keeping the confidentiality of a child molester (perhaps based on the belief that the therapist can help the client more than involvement in the legal system), that does not free the therapist from the legal and ethical obligation of disclosure. Personal ethics can narrow, but not broaden, the limits of professional ethics, and the ethical mandates of the profession must be upheld regardless of the personal values and beliefs of the counselor. In this chapter's Counseling Controversy, we highlight the challenges that can arise when a counselor's personal values collide with the ethical mandates of the profession.

 # Major Ethical Issues in Counseling

Ethical codes are used to help guide decision making. Counselors should read and understand the ethical guidelines of their profession, and monitor and take responsibility for their own professional actions. The ethical codes of the counseling profession can be organized into several major categories (Swenson,

1997), which can help counselors learn to navigate the complex world of ethics in counseling.

Rules Related to Professional Responsibility

First and foremost, professional counselors have an ethical duty to maintain high levels of integrity in their practice. They have an ethical responsibility to use their professional knowledge and the power of the counseling relationship to help their clients in responsible ways. This responsibility rests with the individual counselor who must uphold ethical practice, even in the face of pressure to engage in unethical practice that may come from clients, employers, insurance companies, or others.

To ensure that the client's needs are being met, counselors are aware of their own personal issues or unfinished business and do not allow personal problems to interfere with the counseling they provide. Counselors should continually engage in self-reflection and be self-aware in order to recognize and correct any counter-transference or symptoms of burnout. Impaired professionals should not work with clients unless they are receiving assistance and supervision.

The ethical imperative of professional responsibility applies in all of a counselor's many roles. Counselors who engage in research adhere to strict rules in their work with human subjects and try to eliminate bias from research. Counselors who teach take care not to allow their opinions to color the presentation of course material. Counselors who supervise beginning professionals understand that their *primary responsibility* is always to the client, but they also have an ethical responsibility to their supervisees, using supervision to enhance the trainee's development and growth.

Rules Related to Competence

Counselors must know and act within their own competence and work to continually maintain and expand their competence. For all professionals, this means keeping current with the latest research in the field, particularly as it relates to their clients and/or specialization. Most licensure laws and certifications carry a legal responsibility for continuing education, but there also is an ethical obligation that counselors have to keep abreast of the latest developments in the field. Counselors must know and recognize their professional limitations and refer clients who have problems that are beyond the scope of their knowledge.

Counselors have an ethical responsibility (as well as a legal one) to inform clients of all of the aspects of their educational backgrounds, licensure, specialization, training, and competence. Counselors who misrepresent themselves or their competence violate the ethical codes and can also be sued for fraud. The legal standard for competence is

■■■ *Words of Wisdom* ■■■

"Primum non nocere" (Above all, do no harm).

—Hippocrates

whether the counselor's skills match an average practitioner in good standing. Thus, the counselor need not be an expert in a particular intervention or with a particular type of client, but must be able to prove training and knowledge, and for some specialized interventions, supervised experience. When counselors use interventions that are not considered the professional standard, they must inform clients that they are using experimental techniques and give the client the option of more conventional interventions.

Rules Related to the Counselor's Own Moral Standards and Values

Counselors are human and have their own personal ethical and moral stances on issues. As mentioned earlier, however, a personal moral stance cannot be used as a defense to violate the profession's ethical standards. Counselors may believe what they wish, but they *behave* in ways that are consistent with the law and the professional ethical codes. For example, counselors may not *engage in* discriminatory behaviors, even if they hold discriminatory beliefs. Counselors are strongly cautioned to monitor their own biases and beliefs for discriminatory or stereotyping thoughts, as these can (even inadvertently) affect behaviors.

The ethical codes also remind professional counselors that they are representatives of the counseling profession in the community at large. They caution that lifestyle choices and behaviors that reflect negatively on the individual also reflect poorly on the profession as a whole.

Rules Related to Confidentiality

Confidentiality is a professional's agreement to respect the privacy of clients and to refrain from disclosing any information about them to others, except under certain agreed-upon conditions. The issue of confidentiality is both an ethical and legal concept and will be discussed in greater detail as a legal issue later in this chapter. Confidentiality is the cornerstone of the counseling relationship, but confidentiality is not absolute.

Rules Related to the Welfare of the Client

Counselors do what is best for their clients. The ethical codes in counseling include rules about promoting the welfare and autonomy of clients and the integrity of the counseling relationship. Counselors put the needs of their clients ahead of their own, consistently asking themselves, "Whose needs are being met?" To help counselors focus on the needs of their clients, the ethical codes include sections on topics such as multicultural competence, advocacy, client dependency, informed consent, termination and referral, dual relationships, and sexual relationships.

Multicultural competence. Counselors have an ethical responsibility to engage in culturally and developmentally appropriate interventions. They recognize and value diversity in cultures and beliefs, and they demonstrate commitment to multicultural counseling competence.

Advocacy. When appropriate, counselors advocate for their clients at the individual, institutional, and societal levels. School counselors are advocates for all students and strive to develop school environments that promote tolerance and respect. They take leadership roles in schools and work to close achievement and opportunity gaps that disadvantage groups of students and deny all students the chance to pursue their educational goals.

Client dependency. Counselors advance the welfare of their clients, whether they are individuals, families, or groups. Counselors use their power to empower others. Fostering client dependency—whether intentionally or unintentionally—is not consistent with ethical treatment. Counseling, which literally translated means "to come alongside," recognizes that counselors assist clients in making decisions, but clients ultimately have the freedom—and the responsibility—to make their own choices.

Informed consent. Informed consent is both a legal and ethical concept and will be discussed in greater detail later in this chapter. Ethically, clients must be empowered to make informed choices about their treatment, and they cannot do so unless they have all the necessary information. Informed consent about the purposes, goals, and techniques used in counseling, as well as the education and licensure of the counselor, and the fees and financial commitments, allows clients to make better choices.

Termination and referral. Because of the potential for clients to be abandoned or neglected by counselors, there are sections of the ethical codes that specifically address issues that can occur at the end of counseling. Counselors ensure that clients have appropriate referrals and emergency information in case interventions are required when the counselor is unavailable. When referrals are made to others or counseling is terminated, counselors keep lines of communication open with their former clients in case they require additional assistance.

Dual relationships. A dual relationship occurs whenever a counselor and client have an additional personal or professional relationship, either prior to or during counseling, or in some cases, after its termination. Dual relationships are inappropriate if they exploit the client financially, sexually, or personally. For example, two people who are friends or business associates should never enter the counselor/client relationship. Likewise, counselors never engage in therapy with members of their families. Professors won't counsel their students. The list goes on and on. Friends, relatives, employees, students, supervisees, research participants, and colleagues can all be inappropriate "clients" for a counselor. It is perhaps not too difficult to understand why dual relationships can be a problem. If you have been asked to practice counseling with one of your classmates in a techniques class, you know that it is important not to delve too deeply into that person's problems. When you visit with family members at holiday get-togethers, you understand that it is inappropriate to practice your new counseling skills with family members as your clients. We cannot be truly objective with our clients if we have multiple relationships with them. Further, the power from the counseling relationship can transfer over into the second relationship, making the nontherapeutic relationship exploitive. When it is impossible to avoid dual relationships (such as in small communities where a counselor and client may be neighbors or belong to the same religious community), counselors make every attempt to make sure that the dual relationship does not cause the client harm.

Sexual relationships. Because of the extreme exploitive nature of sexual relationships, they deserve some extra attention here. Whereas other types of dual relationships are dangerous and should be avoided (or at least managed in cases where it is impossible to avoid them), sexual relationships between counselors and their clients are specifically forbidden in all the ethical codes of the helping professions. Nevertheless, research shows that about 4.4% of all mental health professionals (psychologists, psychiatrists, and social workers—counselors have not been specifically included in these studies) admit to engaging in sexual relations with at least one client (Bernsen, Tabachnick, & Pope, 1994; Borys & Pope, 1989). Offenders are about 4 times more likely to be male (9.4%) than female (2.5%) (Pope, Tabachnick, & Keith-Speigel, 1987). Perhaps the numbers are even higher, as some therapists may not admit to this behavior in self-report surveys.

It is important to note that *more than 90% of therapists admit having a sexual attraction to at least one of their clients* (Rutter, 1989). Counselors are human, and they have natural human reactions to others. Nevertheless, this is a boundary that cannot be crossed. Most therapists who reported having sexual attraction to a client said that they felt guilty, anxious, and confused by their feelings, and more than half said that they had received no guidance or training about how to handle feelings of sexual attraction. Almost 40% said they had no professional with whom they could consult (Pope et al., 1987). Clearly, counselors must have an outlet, for example, their own counseling or peer supervision or consultation with a colleague, to discuss the sexual feelings that can arise during the counseling relationship. If it is impossible to keep sexual feelings in check or to resist responding to a client's seductive behaviors (or perceived seductive behaviors), then the counselor must refer the client. Sexual relationships with

■■■ *Fast Facts* ■■■

More than 90% of clients who become sexually involved with their therapist suffer negative consequences due to the sexual contact, according to a study of 559 clients who slept with their therapists. The most common problems reported were difficulties in personal relationships, hesitation about seeking further help from mental health professionals, depression, and in 11% of the cases, hospitalization or suicide.

Source: Bouhoutsos, Holroyd, Lerman, Forer, & Greenberg (1983).

clients are an ethical violation, and they can be the basis for malpractice suits (or in some states, felony convictions) as well. Laws vary from state to state regarding how long after termination from therapy before counselors and their clients can engage in sexual relationships.

Rules Related to Professional Relationships

Professional counselors recognize that their professional relationships with others in the field of mental health can have a significant impact on their clients as well as on the public perception of the counseling profession. Counselors work to develop positive working relationships in the professional community, and they respect other professionals and their work, even if the counseling approaches employed by their colleagues differ from their own (as long as they are legally permissible).

Clients should never enter into a relationship with more than one counselor simultaneously, and professionals are entrusted to help make sure this does not happen. If a counselor knows that a client is currently seeing another therapist, then the first relationship must be terminated before a new therapeutic relationship can begin.

Counselors who serve as consultants or supervisors have the same requirements for confidentiality, client privacy, and adherence to the ethical codes as counselors who serve in direct service. Clients have the same right to informed consent if consultants, or supervisors, will be reviewing their cases. Counselors seek peer consultation on difficult cases, when they plan to deviate from standard practice, or when they face challenging ethical dilemmas.

Just as dual relationships between counselors and clients are ethically problematic, so too are dual relationships among supervisors and supervisees or students and instructors. This area of ethics, however, is less clear than the rules surrounding the counselor/client relationship. Many argue that supervisors and supervisees should not mix personal and professional relationships, although there are certainly many real-life examples where these boundaries are blurred. Likewise, there are those who say that professors should not have dual relationships with their students (friendships, dating), but this is not universally agreed upon. Although there is little empirical data available on these relationships, two national surveys of graduate students in psychology found similar results. Of those who graduated within the last six years, 13% stated that they had sexual contact with either a professor or a clinical supervisor (or both) during their graduate programs (Pope, Levenson, & Schover, 1979). When only females were included in the analysis, 25% (21% in a 1986 study by Glaser & Thorpe) said they had sexual contact with a professor or clinical supervisor. In the study by Pope and his colleagues, *only 2%* of respondents who had engaged in sexual contact with professors or supervisors reported that they believed such relationships could be beneficial to both trainees and educators.

Finally, the ethical codes underscore the importance of counselors policing our own profession. First and foremost, all professional counselors and counseling students have a responsibility to know and understand the ethical and legal guidelines of the profession. Ignorance of the ethical codes is not a sufficient reason for noncompliance. Welfel (2005) reminds counselors to consistently self-monitor their professional actions and to take responsibility for misconduct.

F.8.a. Standards for Students

Students have the same obligations to clients as those required of professional counselors.

Source: ACA Code of Ethics (2005).

Further, as counselors, we have an ethical obligation to act if we know that other counselors are acting unethically or if they are impaired in any way. Professional counselors monitor the work of their colleagues and step in if there is reason to believe there are ethical or legal violations. Likewise, professors serve as gatekeepers to the counseling profession and do not allow students to practice counseling if they are not sufficiently qualified or if they are impaired.

When counselors suspect that a colleague is behaving unethically, the first step is typically an informal face-to-face meeting. It is possible (and sometimes probable) that the offending professional does not realize that he or she is engaging in unethical acts. Many counselors can recall a time when they took a colleague aside for a quick "heads-up" about a potential ethics violation. For example, one of us saw a professional brochure by a colleague and noticed that the counselor had the letters PhD after her name. The counselor did indeed have a PhD, but it was in a different field. The counselor wasn't aware that the ACA ethical code specifically forbids the use of an educational degree for the purposes of advertising if the degree is not in counseling or a related field. Sure enough, the counselor was unaware of this clause in the code of ethics, the brochure was changed, and there was no reason to go any further. However, if the informal discussion does not result in adherence to the laws and ethics of the profession, it may be necessary to file an official complaint with the offending counselor's professional organization or state licensing board, or when appropriate, a law enforcement agency. Of course, no counselor likes to be in the role of turning in another professional, but policing the profession is an important aspect of our professional responsibility. In this chapter's Snapshot, we introduce you to a lawyer who investigates legal and ethical violations that are brought to the state's counseling licensure board in Ohio.

SNAPSHOT
William (Bill) Hegarty

I have been the deputy director and in charge of the investigations of alleged ethical infractions by licensed mental health professionals for the Ohio Counselor, Social Worker, and Marriage and Family Therapist Board for over 14 years. I am an attorney by profession and try to bring that skill set into investigation situations. Over this time period I have seen the full range of ethical violations, from the more minor types (being late for session on occasion) up to the more serious (client record problems) up to the most severe (having a sexual relationship with a client).

One of the most important things about entering into the mental health profession is the need to be aware there are codes of ethics and, more importantly, laws and rules a licensee must follow. No matter what state you end up practicing in, there are laws and rules that govern the profession. And they change! It is important as a licensed professional that you take a proactive role in your profession by keeping up-to-date on the state laws and rules and by being active in your state or local counseling association. One of the more amazing things I find when I talk to someone under investigation is the total lack of awareness that a set of laws and rules exist—and that they may have changed over the last 10 years!

An equally important part of entering into a new profession or even remaining an integral part of a profession is the understanding that you do not know everything. That is why it is so important a licensed professional seek supervision and peer review. This should not be considered a formality or something you "have to do," but really it is an opportunity for professional growth and development. Seeking quality continuing education opportunities is another important means of learning new things and keeping up with the changes taking place. We all make mistakes, which is why we all need to understand our limitations and abilities and then to seek supervision and peer review when a question arises. The last thing a licensed professional wants to do is inadvertently harm their clients.

As a licensed mental health professional, you must be aware of your scope of practice. This may differ from state to state, so it is incumbent upon you as a professional to know what your scope of practice is and to work within it. If you have a question about whether an action may be outside of your scope of practice, seek supervision and peer review. Talking through issues with other professionals is going to be invaluable to you as you develop your professional competencies.

What I have seen with new counselors entering the profession is that some may be overconfident in their abilities, which prevents them from seeking needed supervision. Others are not organized or cannot manage time effectively, which inevitably leads to problems with client records. Another problem is that some new counselors put so much pressure on themselves to succeed that they lose the ability to empathize with their clients. This can make you less effective as a professional.

In short, the mental health profession can be an exciting, stimulating profession. It also takes hard work every day not to lose sight of your client's best interests. In order to be an effective professional counselor, you must know your limitations, always seek supervision and peer review, and keep abreast of the changes taking place, not only in the profession but in the laws and rules as well. Your counseling education is the first step of your professional journey.

Ethics and the Law

Ethical codes are not the final authority for counselors; counselors must adhere to both the ethical codes and the legal standards of practice. The law and professional ethics clearly overlap, although there are differences between the two. Activities can be legal, for example, but not ethical. An example might be providing counseling to a close personal friend, which, although not specifically prohibited by any law, clearly violates ethical boundaries. In other situations, activities can be ethical, but not legal. For example, a parent may ask a school counselor to share a student's records with a college athletic recruiter, but unless very specific paperwork and legal requirements are met, this is illegal. In many instances, however, decisions have both legal and ethical ramifications, and related principles within the law and ethics complement each other. For example, earlier in this chapter, you learned about the ethical imperative of confidentiality, and in this section, you will learn about the corresponding legal principle of privileged communication. These two concepts are clearly interrelated, but they are not the same thing. Counselors must be able to navigate the complex realms of professional ethics and the law.

In most (but not all) situations, the law and ethics are compatible and both lead counselors to the same (or similar) decisions. Ethical codes exist to clarify and define legal standards or to fill in and offer guidance where the law is silent. However, in all situations, the law takes precedence over any ethical mandates, and counselors must first and foremost follow the legal requirements.

We have taken a stance in this chapter that promotes the counselor's adherence to legal and ethical mandates because of the desire to engage in highly ethical and legally sound practice. However, should a counselor fail to follow these mandates, there is the potential for significant repercussions. Overall, standards of practice in counseling are enforced through four mechanisms: (1) professional ethics committees; (2) state licensure boards or departments of education; (3) civil courts; and (4) criminal courts.

Professional ethics committees are established by counseling associations at the state or national level. Decisions of ethics committees are binding only to members of the association. If a person is a member of a particular association (e.g., ACA, AMHCA, ASCA) or holds a credential (e.g., from NBCC) and violates an applicable code of ethics, then the professional ethics committee of that association can deliver some sort of punishment or sanction, ranging from a letter of warning, to expulsion from the organization, to a referral for possible legal action. Counselors who do not belong to professional associations cannot be sanctioned by them, but the association can notify law enforcement for legal action, when necessary.

State licensure boards regulate the practice of professional counselors in each state, and professional school counselors are regulated by their state's Department of Education. If an ethical or legal violation is reported to the state, the state licensing board or administrative arm of the Department of Education will assess the seriousness of the violation and determine the punishment, which can range from a reprimand, to a period of probation, to a sanction for additional supervision or coursework, to revocation of a license or credential. Persons who do not hold a license or certification in the state cannot be sanctioned by a state licensure board, but they can be referred to law enforcement for legal action, when necessary.

State licensure boards publicize the names of professionals who have been found guilty and have been sanctioned by the board. The names of these professionals and the sanctions that have been imposed are typically listed in board newsletters that go out to members of the profession in that state and/or are posted on the website. Information regarding violations is a matter of public record, and the posting of this information serves to inform the public (and other professionals) about violations and whether a specific professional has been sanctioned by the board.

Regardless of whether the professional association or state boards have taken action on a specific complaint, counselors can find themselves involved in the legal system in either criminal or civil courts. In general, civil law involves an offense to an individual for which there must be compensation to the victim. In counseling, *malpractice* is the most common cause of civil liability. Malpractice is professional conduct that falls below the standard of practice of similar professionals in similar circumstances. Thus, a counselor can be sued for malpractice if he or she operates outside of what reasonable professionals would do in similar circumstances. The remedy for civil violations, such as malpractice, is typically monetary compensation.

Malpractice requires the following three elements:

- The counselor must have a duty to the client (that is, there must be a contract, or implied contract, of a professional relationship between the counselor and client).
- The counselor must have acted in a negligent or improper manner (that is, acted outside of what is the professional standard of practice).
- There must be a causal relationship between negligence and the damage claimed by the client (the counselor's action—or inaction—caused harm to the client).

The final type of enforcement is through the criminal courts. Criminal law for counselors involves conduct that is prohibited to all citizens. The most frequent criminal misconduct by counselors is fraud related to third-party billing. In some states, engaging in sexual contact with clients is considered criminal misconduct. In some instances, legal violations can prosecuted both civilly and criminal, such as failure to report suspected child abuse, which can have both civil and criminal legal ramifications. Criminal misconduct requires punishment by the government, including imprisonment and/or fines.

Legal issues in counseling are determined through state and federal *statutes* and *case law*. Federal and state statutes are determined by governments. In mental health, these laws are often established by legislatures in order to protect client welfare. Examples are state statutes that determine scope of practice or reporting of child abuse. *Case law* is determined by precedent. Judges and juries make legal decisions, which are then codified into case law and are referenced to help determine the legal standing of a particular issue before the courts. Examples of case law include the counselors' duty to warn or duty to protect.

We know that all of this discussion about legal requirements and punishments for legal and ethical violations can be very intimidating, particularly to beginning counselors. Our goal is not to frighten you or to overwhelm you with details. In this introductory text, the goal is for you to be exposed to the major legal and ethical requirements for counselors and to start to learn how to make appropriate decisions in practice. But this chapter is not the final word on the topic during your graduate program. You will have lots of time and opportunities to learn about the nuances of these requirements and to practice their application. You will also have your counseling supervised by more experienced practitioners who can help you navigate the profession's legal and ethical requirements. Remember, counselors are required to have a basic knowledge of their own state statutes and the case law related to their profession, but they are not required to have advanced legal knowledge. Any time there is a legal question, counselors are *strongly urged* to get legal counsel. The statutes and case laws vary from jurisdiction to jurisdiction and change over time.

Major Legal Issues in Counseling

In this section, we will discuss some of the major legal requirements that counselors must follow. In an introductory text such as this, it is impossible to list every legal principle that applies to the counseling profession. Thus, our goal here is to introduce you to the topic and to get you thinking about how to set yourself up to be a legally competent professional counselor.

Legal Principle: Counselor Competency

The legal requirements that regulate the practice of counseling differ from state to state, although all 50 states (and the District of Columbia) have passed legislation that determines who can practice mental health counseling and the scope of practice for counselors in that state. The determination of who can practice school counseling also varies from state to state, and these requirements are determined by the state's Department of Education.

States laws that regulate mental health counseling determine who can conduct counseling (called a **practice act**) or call themselves a counselor (called a **title act**). These laws are supported by a body of rules that interpret and clarify the law. The laws also determine the scope of practice for the profession, which outlines the general areas of competency for counselors, gained through appropriate education and experience. An individual counselor's scope of practice, however, is typically narrower than the scope of practice outlined by law. For example, although a legal scope of practice in a particular state may include psychological testing, if the counselor has not had adequate training and/or practice in testing, then it would be unethical for the counselor to engage in such testing. The law broadly defines the practice, and then the counselor determines his or her own limits, within the boundaries of the law. A counselor's **professional disclosure statement** is used to inform clients of that individual's scope of practice. In most states, mental health counselors are required to provide clients with a copy of this statement and to display a copy of it in a conspicuous location.

State departments of education determine who can practice school counseling. Most (but not all) states require a graduate degree in counseling and a licensure exam. However, in most states, the practice of school counseling is less tightly regulated than the practice of mental health counseling. In many states, school personnel who are not trained as school counselors can engage in the practice of school counseling, particularly as temporary assignments. As a result, the American School Counselor Association (ASCA) and its state divisions have become heavily involved in setting standards for school counselors to ensure the highest levels of professionalism among those who practice.

In general, counselors must operate within the standards of care of the profession. **Standards of care** can be defined as professional conduct as practiced by "reasonable and prudent practitioners who have special knowledge and ability" (Granello & Witmer, 1998, p. 372). These standards are "professional practices followed by others in the same discipline and either considered standard practice or at least accepted by a significant minority of other professionals" (Meyer, Landis, & Hays, 1988, p. 15). Not meeting the professional standards of care is considered negligence, the second criteria for determining malpractice (along with duty to a client and harm caused by the negligence). Thus, when a client is harmed because a counselor fails to follow accepted procedures, it is malpractice.

Ways to Help Protect Yourself from Legal Involvement Regarding Counselor Competency

- Know the license/certification laws in your state that determine who can practice counseling (practice act) and who can use the word *counselor* (or whatever terms are protected) (title act). Many states have both a practice and title act for mental health counselors.

- Operate within your scope of practice. Know what limits the state license or certification places on you and *what limits you need to place on yourself.* Do not engage in interventions that are new—or new to you—without proper training and supervision.

- Keep up-to-date regarding counseling interventions for the clientele with whom you work. Just because something is (or was) a widely heralded intervention does not mean it is effective. Read journals and professional publications and attend professional conferences and workshops that update you on the effectiveness of different interventions and the latest thinking in the field. One good way to help you do this is to join your national (and state) professional organizations.

Legal Principle: Client Rights and Informed Consent

Clients have the right to make informed choices about counseling before they enter into the counseling relationship. Informed consent is both a legal and ethical issue. Clients must fully understand what they can expect from counseling, including potential risks, benefits, and alternatives to counseling.

In school settings (or in any counseling situation with minor clients), school counselors engage in informed consent with parents or guardians. In some school districts, counselors must obtain parental permission before beginning counseling with students, although other districts require such permission only if ongoing counseling is sought. Remley and Herlihy (2007) argue that unless there is a specific school policy or state law to the contrary, school counselors do not need parental permission before they provide counseling to students. This is controversial, however, and it is important for any school counselor to check with the school administration to determine how the legal mandate of informed consent is enforced within each particular school. Regardless of the policy on parental consent, minor students cannot give informed consent. Nevertheless, although it is not a legal responsibility, many school counselors argue that it is important to obtain *assent* from their student clients, meaning that students understand the counseling relationship before they enter into it.

Informed consent is based on three legal requirements. In order for clients (or parents) to enter into counseling as an informed participant, they must have:

1. *Capacity* to make rational decisions. When capacity is lacking (either because the client is a minor or because he or she lacks the cognitive ability to have capacity), typically a parent or guardian must give consent for the counseling relationship to begin.

2. *Comprehension* of the information that is presented by the counselor. That means the information must be presented by the counselor in a clear and unambiguous manner, using common language (not clinical language or psychological terms).

3. *Voluntariness* or the freedom to enter into counseling without coercion or under duress.

Counselors want to give clients the information they need to make informed decisions, yet they must be careful not to overwhelm clients with irrelevant details. Putting information in writing (and having clients or parents sign a copy stating that they have received and read the information, as well as providing a copy for clients to keep) is one way to assist with informed consent. *However, it is not sufficient to simply provide a written informed consent form.* Clients and counselors must also engage in a verbal discussion of informed consent—one that is checked by the counselor for comprehension by the client.

Ways to Help Protect Yourself from Legal Involvement Regarding Informed Consent

- Make sure that all counseling relationships include a discussion of informed consent at the beginning. Check the client for capacity, comprehension, and voluntariness. With involuntary clients, be sure the client understands his or her legal right to refuse treatment and the consequences of that choice.
- Use language that clients understand. One study of informed consent documents found that the majority were written in a language equivalent to upper-level college reading (Handelsman, Martinez, Geisendorfer, & Jordan, 1995).
- Be sure to discuss types of interventions that will be used, particularly if the intervention is not standard practice.
- Revisit informed consent issues during treatment, particularly at "choice-points" in counseling (when considering sending clients to a psychiatrist for medication, when considering termination, etc.).
- Pay attention to cultural issues in informed consent. Clients from some cultures may be inclined to defer to the counselor, rather than consider their own participation or rights in counseling, while others may wish to include community elders or family members in their decisions regarding informed consent.

Legal Principle: Privileged Communication and Confidentiality

Confidentiality is the counselors' ethical duty to keep client information private, and in most states, it is a legal as well as ethical requirement. Privileged communication is a related legal concept that ensures that whatever is discussed in the therapeutic relationship cannot be revealed in a legal proceeding, unless certain criteria are met. Counselors who have their notes subpoenaed should always consult with an attorney. At a minimum, counselors will want to get written consent from their clients authorizing the release of information or a court order from a judge before they release their records (Kennedy, 2008). Counselors are most commonly served with subpoenas in cases related to divorce or parental custody. Only 20 states have granted privilege to school counselors (Haley, 2004). Thus, a school counselor's notes are subject to subpoena (Merlone, 2005). Therefore, only essential data should be contained in these notes, and they should be written in specific, objective, and behavioral terms.

The legal protection of confidentiality cannot be extended to minors, as parents or guardians have the legal right to know what occurs within a counseling session. In general, however, counselors rely upon their professional expertise to determine what information should be shared with parents. The developmental level of the student often plays into this determination, as in general, "the more mature the minor, the greater the measure of confidentiality that young person is given in counseling" (Welfel, 2002, p. 102). However, counselors cannot use the protection of confidentiality to keep information from the parents of any minor child if that information is specifically requested by the parents. Just as with informed consent, school counselors making determinations about student confidentiality should understand their state laws and school policies and consult with more experienced colleagues and supervisors when they have questions.

Even when working with adults, confidentiality is not an absolute guarantee. There are certain situations when counselors are both ethically and legally *required* to break confidentiality. The three major legal exceptions to confidentiality that are present in all states are:

1. Danger to self. If clients are suicidal or pose a danger to themselves, there is no privileged communication or confidentiality. The counselor must place client safety over clients' rights to confidentiality.

2. Danger to others/society (and in some states, danger to property). This exception arose from the *Tarasoff* case (*Tarasoff v. Regents of the University of California*, 1976), in which the court held that a mental health professional must warn a potential victim of a dangerous client, overriding the client's right to confidentiality. In cases where a counselor *reasonably believed or should have believed* that the client posed a serious danger to *an identifiable potential victim* (Anderson, 1996, p. 29), the counselor must warn the potential victim. This is called the *duty to warn*. A more recent case expanded the duty to warn to include any persons who could be foreseeable victims, not just those specifically identified by the client. An extension of the *Tarasoff* case ruled that counselors also have a *duty to protect*, that is, counselors must do everything in their power to protect potential victims, such as hospitalizing dangerous clients, increasing medication, and so on. The *duty to warn* and the *duty to protect* laws are broad, and it is sometimes confusing to understand the specific requirements placed on individual counselors. Because of this, 23 states have passed laws that further define these duties (Cottone & Tarvydas, 2007).

3. Abuse (and in some states, neglect) of children or elder abuse (required in some states). In all instances, child abuse must be reported. This is a legal responsibility. Counselors need only the suspicion of child abuse to make a report. It is not the counselor's responsibility to investigate or substantiate the suspicion, which is the role of child protective services. Mandated reporting of child neglect and elder abuse vary by jurisdiction.

 **Spotlight**
The Special Case of Confidentiality in Group or Family Counseling

When the counselor and client are the only two people in a room, it is fairly easy for the counselor to ensure confidentiality. However, in group, family, or couples counseling, confidentiality becomes a shared responsibility, rather than the sole domain of the counselor. Counselors who work with more than one client simultaneously help educate clients or group members about confidentiality and its role in establishing a trusting and therapeutic environment. Group norms that reinforce confidentiality are important, and counselors can emphasize the need for everyone to respect the privacy of all members of the group. Counselors can ensure their own commitment to confidentiality, but they cannot ensure that other members of the group will honor this commitment. Ultimately, it is up to the group (or family) members to maintain confidentiality.

There are other exceptions to confidentiality that apply in certain legal settings or situations. For example, confidentiality (and privileged communication) can be waived by the client. In these instances, clients agree to have information shared with other professionals (e.g., psychiatrists, social workers), with the court system (e.g., in custody cases), or when suing the counselor. The other exception that applies most directly to counseling students occurs when a counseling student (or new professional) is receiving clinical supervision, and the client is aware that an authorized supervisor will be reviewing case notes or recordings or transcripts of sessions. In all instances, it is important that clients understand the limits of confidentiality before treatment begins (with periodic reminders during treatment). Finally, it is important to note that there are special circumstances, as discussed in the accompanying Spotlight, when confidentiality cannot be guaranteed because there are other people in the room.

Ways to Help Protect Yourself from Legal Involvement Regarding Confidentiality and Privileged Communication

- Make sure clients fully understand confidentiality—and its limits—before beginning counseling. Although most counselors agree that this is important, studies show that fewer than half of counselors actually do so (Simon, 1988).

- Try to involve the client in the process when confidentiality must be broken. Most ethical codes recommend informing clients, and to the extent possible, involving clients in the disclosure.

- Contact a lawyer immediately if you are subpoenaed. Try to maintain client privacy.

- If a client waives privileged communication, make sure the client fully understands the risk of such a move, including any negative evaluations that could be disclosed about that client.

■■■ *Words of Wisdom* ■■■

"If it isn't documented, it didn't happen."

—Common adage related
to documentation in mental health care

Legal Principle: Documentation and Records

Documentation, record keeping, and the handling of client and student records are all components of counseling that have very stringent legal requirements. Some problems with documentation, such as insurance fraud or falsification of records, are very clearly wrong and are legal violations that are obvious to even the most novice counselor. Other legal violations, however, are more nuanced and require a greater understanding of the law.

Documentation is a critical component of the counselor's role. Good case notes allow counselors to be thoughtful and intentional in their interventions because they are forced to stop and think about what they have done, how the session aligned with the client's goals, and where treatment should go next. State requirements differ regarding what should be included in a client's records, but at a minimum, mental health counselors should document the presenting problem, diagnosis, treatment plan, treatment progress, results, and follow-up plan. When working with potentially dangerous or difficult clients, it is important to document abuse and threats to self or others, including actions (such as consultations or reporting to authorities) taken by the counselor (Kennedy, 2008). Documentation by school counselors varies greatly by school district, and school counselors should consult local experts, including colleagues and supervisors, for guidelines.

Legally, counselors must follow the requirements of the Health Insurance Portability and Accountability Act (HIPAA) of 1996. The key requirement of this act is that clients have a reasonable expectation that all health records will be kept private and confidential. This is the same act that regulates all medical professionals. Perhaps you have been to a doctor's office lately and signed legal documents that allow your doctor to submit a bill to an insurance company or to share records with another medical provider. If so, then you have been affected by HIPAA requirements. Counselors, just like all medical professionals, must carefully safeguard clients' Protected Health Information (PHI). All records, both hard copy and electronic, must be carefully secured.

An additional federal requirement for documentation by educators, including school counselors, is the Family Educational Rights and Privacy Act (FERPA) enacted by Congress in 1974. Also called the Buckley Amendments, this law states that federal funds can be withheld from any educational institution that (a) fails to provide parents access to their child's educational records, or (b) disseminates any information from a student's educational records (with a few exceptions) to any third party without the parent's permission. In accordance with FERPA, school counselors cannot share student records with any third party, unless there is an emergency situation when it is necessary to share this information in order to protect the health or safety of other students or individuals (Kennedy, 2008).

Ways to Help Protect Yourself from Legal Involvement Regarding Recordkeeping

- Maintain the security of paper files at all times. Files cannot be left where they can be accessed by unauthorized persons. All trash of a confidential nature must be shredded. If files are stacked on a desktop, they should be kept face down. Keep Protected Health Information separate from other files and locked in a secure cabinet.

- Maintain the security of electronic records. Files on a computer must be password protected. Sign off or lock your workstation when you leave your desk. Set up your computer so the screen faces away from other people.

- Write notes that are clear, objective, and behaviorally based. Include only relevant information. Use nontechnical language. If subjective or opinion statements are made, separate them from the facts and clearly mark them as opinion or professional judgment. Remember: All clients files may someday be seen by the client or the courts. Be very clear about what is written in them.

- In the case of client emergencies or other critical incidents, maintain very detailed notes of all that was done in order to assist the client, particularly in cases where the client is a danger to self or others or when the client refuses treatment. Document extensively.

Other Legal Requirements for Counselors

There are, of course, many laws and legal precedents that have relevance to counselors and the counseling profession, and there are several key factors that make understanding the legal mandates for counselors particularly challenging. First, many of the laws vary from state to state. For example, involuntary commitment of persons who are considered a danger to self or others is regulated by each state. In some states (Florida, for example), mental health counselors are among the list of professionals who have this legal power. Second, the laws related to the practice of counseling are constantly evolving. For instance, in some states, mental health counselors are seeking legal rights for mental health holds, which would allow counselors to have a person considered dangerous to self or others taken into custody and immediately transported to a hospital for a risk assessment. In other states, school counselors are supporting legislation that would put more money— and more accountability—into career planning for middle school students. If the legislation passes, school counselors would be among those required to complete additional paperwork in exchange for more funding. Third, legislation is not the only type of legal mandate counselors must follow. Case law and legal interpretations of the rules to implement legislation at the state and national level also influence counseling. For example, recent suicides by students who were bullied in schools may result in case law that changes how schools respond to reports of bullying in their buildings or online. In other states, courts are scrambling to determine how professionals will be affected by legislation regarding reporting of undocumented immigrants. The point is that laws and legal requirements differ by jurisdiction and are constantly changing. Counselors must keep up-to-date to ensure their practice follows the latest professional and legal standards. Membership in state and national counseling associations is one of the best ways to stay abreast of, and help advocate for, changes and updates to the laws that regulate the profession.

In this chapter's Informed by Research feature, you will read about how school counselors perceive their readiness to adhere to the legal requirements of their job. As you read through the section, think about how often school counselors face dilemmas that have significant legal ramifications and consider what types of strategies you can use to prepare for the legal and ethical requirements of your newfound profession.

Informed by Research
School Counselors and the Law

School counselors encounter many different legal issues in their work, and they must follow the legal mandates that guide the profession. A 2002 study (Hermann) of 273 school counselors assessed the prevalence of certain legal issues and school counselors' perceptions of their ability to respond to these legal concerns in an appropriate manner. Results of the study indicated that many school counselors face difficult legal situations, and respondents varied significantly in their confidence to address these concerns. The top six most frequently cited legal concerns, along with the percentage of counselors who faced the concern in the last 12 months and their perceptions of their level of preparation to handle the problem, are shown in the following table.

Legal Issue	Encountered in Last 12 Months	Well Prepared	Not Prepared
1. Determining whether student was suicidal	90%	72%	6%
2. Determining whether to report suspected child abuse	89%	91%	2%
3. Determining whether student posed danger to others	73%	63%	13%
4. Being pressured to verbally reveal confidential information	51%	57%	14%
5. Being asked to turn over confidential records	19%	52%	22%
6. Being subpoenaed to appear as a witness in a legal proceeding	18%	23%	54%

For the school counselors in this study, years of experience or level of education were not related to confidence in their ability to handle the legal issues that arise in their jobs. Importantly, continuing education was the only factor related to confidence. School counselors who had participated in continuing education in legal and ethical issues within the past year reported that they felt better prepared to address the legal concerns that were part of their jobs. This study provides further support for the need for school counselors (and in fact, all professional counselors) to keep up-to-date through continuing education in legal and ethical issues in counseling.

Several national laws that are of particular importance to counselors:

- The Americans with Disabilities Act (ADA, 1990) prohibits discrimination on the basis of disability and improves accessibility for persons with disabilities in everyday life. Counselors who engage in testing must use tests that are appropriate for persons with a disability or modify or seek alternative assessments, as appropriate.

- IDEA (Public Law 94-142) (1975) guarantees the rights of all children, regardless of severity of disability, to free and appropriate education. The law establishes the use of annual individualized education plans (IEPs) that allow children with physical, emotional, or intellectual disabilities and their parents to participate in the educational process. In 2004, IDEA was reauthorized with updated requirements. School counselors are typically very involved with the provisions of IDEA, particularly in the development IEPs as well as participation in meetings with students and their families.

- Title IX (1972) requires that schools with federal funding provide equal access to students of both sexes. School counselors adhere to these requirements by using gender-neutral, nonstereotypical materials in their counseling and classroom guidance instruction and promoting equality between the sexes in their schools.

- No Child Left Behind Act (NCLB, 2001) was designed to make schools accountable for student learning and to make sure at-risk students were not left behind academically. School counselors have been greatly affected by NCLB, with both positive and negative consequences. Accountability efforts as mandated by NCLB have resulted in more data about the effectiveness of school counseling programs, and that data can be use to demonstrate how school counseling programs support and enhance academic progress for all students. However, NCLB also has led school counselors to become more involved with paperwork and test administration, with less time available for interactions with students (Dollarhide & Lemberger, 2006). School counselors must understand not only the requirements that NCLB places on them directly, but how NCLB affects entire schools and school districts.

Ethical Decision Making in Practice

Learning to counsel at the highest level of legal and ethical practice is an advanced skill. Beginning counselors, who are more black and white in their thinking than more advanced counselors, are often eager to have "answers" about what they "should" do. Some ethical mandates lend themselves to that kind of approach. For example, it is *never* okay to have sex with a client. It is *always* the right thing to do to report suspected child abuse. But other counseling situations are more nuanced and do not have easy answers. For this reason, several models have been developed to help counselors make decisions that follow the best ethical practice when confronted with difficult and challenging ethical dilemmas. These models are intended to supplement, not replace, the codes of ethics, and it is *always* important for counselors to seek consultation and supervision when they encounter ethical challenges, no matter how many years they have been in practice or how advanced their clinical decision-making has become.

One model for ethical decision making (Forester-Miller & Davis, 1996), reminds counselors to first seek a resolution through the relevant ethical codes. If the problem is more complex than can be answered by the ethical codes, the next step is a review of the professional literature and/or consultation with more experienced colleagues or state or national professional associations. Based on these activities, the counselor should generate possible alternatives, carefully considering the potential consequences of each option, seeking additional consultation as appropriate. Once a decision has been made and implemented, the counselor should assess whether the actions had the intended effect and consequences.

In difficult ethical situations in counseling, Kitchener's (1984) seminal work is often used to determine the highest standards of ethical practice. Kitchener believed that five ethical principles can help counselors adhere to the highest level of aspirational ethics.

- **Autonomy** is the right of clients to make their own choices. Unless there is a compelling reason to the contrary (e.g., danger to self or others), clients should be free to act as they desire.

- **Nonmaleficence** can be summed up as "above all, do no harm." It means counselors refrain from intentionally inflicting harm on their clients and refraining from any action that may cause harm.

■■■ *Fast Facts* ■■■

In ethical decision making, consider these three simple tests to determine whether your course of action is appropriate.

1. Test of Justice. Does your decision fit with your own sense of fairness?

2. Test of Publicity. Would you be willing to have your behavior reported to the press? Would you stand up in class (or at a professional conference) and proudly announce what you have done?

3. Test of Universality. Would you recommend the same course of action to another counselor in the same situation?

Source: Stadler (1986).

- **Beneficence** is when counselors act in a way that contributes to the well-being of their clients. It is an obligation to provide aid and assistance, to be proactive, and to help clients.

- **Justice** involves fairness. It means clients have equal access to services and resources, and counselors ensure that they do not discriminate. If counselors treat clients differently, then there must be a therapeutic rationale for doing so.

- **Fidelity** means keeping promises and commitments and being loyal to clients. Fidelity is based on a bond of trust in the counseling relationship. Counselors know that their primary responsibility is to their clients.

There are other models for ethical decision making in practice. For example, a model based on feminist theory gives the client as much power as possible in the ethical decision-making process (Hill, Glaser, & Harden, 1995). Another model uses cognitive counseling theory to develop decision analysis, or a step-by-step procedure to break down an ethical decision into its component parts, testing the logic and rationality of each step (Rest, 1994). Still another model uses a social contructivist approach whereby ethical decision making is a social process that involves an interactive process of negotiating, arbitrating, and reaching consensus (Cottone, 2001). The point is not about which model is correct, but about the importance of using a set of procedures to help guide ethical decision making in counseling. Counselors use these types of models to begin to disentangle the complicated ethical scenarios that are often part of their professional lives.

 ## Summary

Professional counselors must be ever vigilant of their behaviors to ensure that they are conducting themselves in a way that is both legally and ethically appropriate. Aspirational ethics, or striving to achieve the highest level of ethical functioning, is one effective way to minimize risks of engaging in unethical or illegal behaviors. Awareness of the relevant law (both statutes and case law) in the counselor's jurisdiction as well as the ethical codes of the relevant professional organizations is essential to maintaining legal and ethical practice.

Attention to ethical and legal issues in counseling is an on-going concern for counselors, not something to be completed and checked off a "to-do" list. Counselors should continually monitor their practice, consult with colleagues, attend workshops, and read the professional journals to keep abreast of changes in practice as well as changes in pertinent laws and rules. Ethical practice is a way of *being*, and a strong self-awareness, along with an understanding of the laws and rules, is a critical component of ethical behavior.

End-of-Chapter Activities

Student Activities

1. **Reflect.** Now it's time to reflect on the major topics that we have covered in Chapter 12. Look back at the sections or the ideas you have underlined. What were your reactions as you read that portion of the chapter? What do you want to remember?

   _____

   _____

   _____

   _____

2. As you read about all of the legal and ethical requirements for counselors, what are your reactions? Do you find yourself feeling overwhelmed or anxious? How do you think counselors manage to keep up with all the legal and ethical responsibilities for practice?

   _____

   _____

   _____

   _____

3. Some ethical codes, such as the Code of Professional Ethics for Rehabilitation Counselors (2009), include foundational values to which all members of the profession are expected to commit. What do you think of this idea? Is it the place of a professional association to require adherence to personal values from members of the profession? Can personal and professional values be separated?

   _____

   _____

   _____

   _____

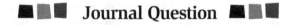 ■ ■ ■ Journal Question ■ ■ ■

Counseling ethics. In any area of your life, have you encountered a professional (e.g., auto mechanic, Realtor, doctor, lawyer, landlord, teacher, supervisor) who acted unethically? Think of a specific situation in which you were the recipient of what you believed to be unethical behavior. As you think of that situation, can you recall many of the details and specifics of how you were wronged? Consider for a moment the experiences of the person who committed the unethical act.

Typically, the person who was unethical does not remember the situation with the same clarity as the person against whom the act was committed. In many situations, in fact, the unethical behavior may seem like "no big deal" to the person who committed it, but remains a lingering and painful memory to the person who was the recipient. How can you relate your experience of receiving unethical treatment to the importance of maintaining ethical behavior as a counselor?

▰▰▰ Topics for Discussion ▰▰▰

1. Take a moment to think about strong values that you hold and how these may affect your counseling. Is there a particular type of client (or presenting issue) that would be difficult for you to counsel? For example, some counselors struggle with clients who have strong religious beliefs, are having an affair, or choose to have an abortion. Other counselors might have more difficulty working with clients who have sexually abused children, harm animals, or use drugs. What are your "hot buttons"—the places where you may have particular difficulty maintaining your clients' rights to pursue their own choices? Remember, this is not about being "values-free," but about being aware of your own values in these challenging areas so you can avoid imposing your values on your clients.

2. As you consider the differences between minimal and aspirational ethics, think about what might make aspirational ethics so much more challenging for counselors in practice.

3. Dual relationships are a particularly challenging component of the ethical codes for most counselors to navigate. What are some of the reasons counselors might give for engaging in dual relationships? Can you think of a time when dual relationships are okay? Why do you think the ethical codes include so many cautions against these types of relationships?

▰▰▰ Experiments ▰▰▰

1. Counselors must post their professional disclosure statements for their clients, and many counselors post their disclosure statements online. Collect some examples of professional disclosure statements and consider how the information contained in them might (or might not) be useful for clients to know before they begin counseling

2. Think about a typical ethical challenge that a counselor might face and consider how Kitchener's model might apply to the scenario. How can a careful consideration of these five ethical principles help counselors make ethical decisions?

3. Go to your state licensure board's website and find the listing of counselors who have engaged in ethical or legal wrongdoing. What are the most common types of violations that counselors in your state are committing, and what can you learn from this experiment?

■ ■ ■ Explore More! ■ ■ ■

Books

Barnett, J. E., & Johnson, W. B. (2010). *Ethics desk reference for counselors.* Alexandria, VA: American Counseling Association.

> A clear and concise reference to help counselors prevent ethical conflicts and to find appropriate responses to ethical situations when they arise.

Remley, T. R., Hermann, M. A., & Huey, W. C. (2010). *Ethical and legal issues in school counseling* (2nd ed.). Alexandria, VA: American School Counselor Association.

> Topics include confidentiality, managing suicidal or potentially violent students, child abuse and neglect, supervision, and navigating the complex legal arena of schools.

Wheeler, A. M., & Bertram, B. (2008). *The counselor and the law* (5th ed.). Alexandria, VA: American Counseling Association.

> Topics include civil malpractice liability, confidentiality, HIPAA, duty to warn, threats of harm to self or others, professional boundaries, records and documentation.

Articles

Granello, P. F., & Witmer, J. M. (1998). Standards of care: Potential implications for the counseling profession. *Journal of Counseling and Development, 76*, 371–80.

> This article provides counselors with an overview of the important legal requirement of standards of care, including

case studies to assist with application of the principle to counseling practice.

Kitchener, K. S. (1984). Intuition, critical evaluation and ethical principles: The foundation for ethical decisions in counseling psychology. *Counseling Psychologist, 12*, 43–55.

> This foundational article describes Kitchener's model, which has now become a standard in the counseling profession.

Welfel, E. R. (2005). Accepting fallibility: A model for personal responsibility for non-egregious ethics infractions. *Counseling and Values, 49*, 120–31.

> Welfel encourages counselors to adopt a self-reflective stance regarding ethics and to monitor their own interactions with a goal toward aspirational ethics.

Websites

Explore the ethical codes of the various counseling specializations, which are available on their websites. They differ in scope, content, and "feel." Some are direct and concise while others are more general, providing overall guidelines rather than specific dictates.

The American School Counselor Association has issued position statements on a wide variety of counseling topics, many of which relate to values, ethics, and the law. These can be found at: www.schoolcounselor.org/files/PositionStatements.pdf.

■■■ MyHelpingLab ■■■

To help you explore the profession of counseling via video interviews with counselors and clients, some of the chapters in this text include links to MyHelpingLab at the Pearson.com website. There are some videos that correspond with this chapter, and watching them might challenge you to think about these concepts at a deeper level.

- Go to Ethical, Legal, and Professional Issues, and then "Boundary Issues" to check out these video clips:
  - An ethical decision (and the video response to that clip)
  - A sexual attraction (and the video response to that clip)
  - A wedding invitation (and the video response to that clip)
    - In all three of these videos, the counselor faces a potential ethical dilemma regarding boundaries. As you think about your future as a counselor, how do you think you will manage your personal and professional boundaries?

There are some additional video clips that may be of interest if you are pursuing a career in school counseling:

- Go to Ethical, Legal, and Professional Issues, and then "Ethical and Legal Issues in School Counseling" to check out these video clips:
  - A teacher asks a student counselor for help (and the video response to that clip)
  - A counselor testifies in a custody dispute (and the video response to that clip)
  - An angry parent (and the video response to that clip)

How Do Counselors Maintain Their Personal Wellness?

In this chapter, we will:

- Give you a very brief history of how the concept of wellness has become part of counseling and how a wellness philosophy can be used in the counseling process.

- Look at how strength-based assessment and counseling can guide practice.

- Discuss the importance of maintaining your own wellness as you go through your journey toward becoming a counselor.

- Discuss the perils of burnout and impairment.

- Outline the challenges to wellness for you and your clients in different counseling settings.

- Make suggestions about how to improve your wellness.

- Help you construct a Personal Wellness Plan (PWP).

As you read the chapter, you might want to consider:

- All helping professions from nursing to dentistry to counseling require practitioners to put their clients first. This can lead to fear of doing the wrong thing, emotional and physical exhaustion, and burnout, a condition of apathy, resentment, and lack of motivation.

- Impairment occurs when counselors are not operating at full capacity due to a mental disorder, substance abuse, or burnout.

- There is a long history in counseling, starting with Maslow, to develop a strength-based, positive approach to helping. Such an approach does not mean ignoring problems but insists that utilizing strengths and developing new coping strategies is just as important.

- Counselors need to make a plan to stay healthy, because they deal with people who are facing extreme loss, anxiety, depression, and family upheaval. Counselors may be traumatized vicariously by their clients' catastrophes.

The foundational principles of the profession of counseling are deeply rooted in the concepts of optimal health and wellness. Counselors believe that all human beings have the capacity for growth and development, and the counseling process is inherently laden with the values of promoting fully functioning human beings. As you begin your journey toward becoming a counselor, consider the reasons that brought you to this path. Chances are, helping other people lead happy and fulfilling lives is at least part of your motivation. As you read through this chapter, you will learn how this relatively recent movement in the counseling profession is, in many ways, an outgrowth of the historical foundations upon which our profession is built. As we begin this chapter, it is a fitting reminder for us to recall that the roots of counseling are based not on giving people answers or advice, but on helping people discover the solutions and the potential that they already possess.

A Brief Historical Sketch of Wellness in Counseling

The earliest identifiable spark that lit the wellness fire in the health care community was the 1947 World Health Organization's definition of health as "a state of complete physical, mental, and social well-being, not merely the absence of disease or infirmity" (World Health Organization, 1958). William Hettler, M.D., was one of the medical pioneers in wellness. In the early 1970s the only term that described this field was "preventive medicine," which really focused mainly on staving off epidemics, providing safety tips, and advocating for good nutrition. At that time, physicians did not study healthy people, only disease. In psychology, George Albee lobbied for the separation of psychology from psychiatry and wanted the profession to focus more on prevention of psychopathology. He was interested in **primary prevention**, which focuses on strategies to avoid the development of pathology, rather than responding to problems after they arise. He believed that psychologists should work at the institutional and governmental level to deal with inequalities and social conditions that produce or contribute to individuals' mental problems.

But it wasn't until the 1980s, as stress became a household word, that mental health professionals realized that psychological factors play a role in physical health. Stress workshops became common in workplaces and agencies, and a new term entered the counseling lexicon: *coping*. Richard Lazarus and colleagues (e.g., Lazarus & Folkman, 1984) found that coping strategies for dealing with stress differ and that people can be taught better ways of dealing with the "hurry sickness." While psychology looked at the effects of stress on mental health, others were developing programs that attempted to look at body, mind, and spirit. This was the beginning of the wellness movement.

One of the pioneers of the wellness movement in counseling was Donald B. Ardell (1976, 1988) at the University of Central Florida (UCF). He created one of the first campus wellness programs for students, and that program is still in operation today. About this same time, J. Melvin Witmer, professor of counselor education at Ohio University, was teaching a class on wellness, which was initially entitled "Stress, Biofeedback and Self-Control." Witmer also wrote about the implications of a wellness philosophy in one of the first books on wellness counseling, *Pathways to Personal Growth* (1985). He linked wellness in counseling to the humanistic movement in counseling and Adlerian philosophy because of their emphases on growth and wholeness (1985). Based on this early work, Myers, Witmer, and Sweeney (1996) developed the WEL Inventory, a multidimensional evaluation of wellness that evaluates the following areas of wellness:

- Spirituality (meaning in life, derived from inner wisdom, higher consciousness, and/or a Supreme Being)
- Sense of Worth (self-acceptance, self-esteem)
- Sense of Control (sense of competence, perceived ability to cope)
- Realistic Beliefs (logical, rational understanding of the world)
- Emotional Responsiveness (willingness to experience and share emotions)
- Intellectual Stimulation (being mentally active, challenging your thinking, engaging in new learning)
- Sense of Humor (ability to laugh appropriately at oneself and the world, to use humor to cope with life's difficulties)
- Nutrition (healthy, balanced eating that maintains one's ideal weight)
- Exercise (engaging in an active, healthy lifestyle)
- Self-Care (limiting exposure to danger by not using substances, by wearing seatbelts or helmets, by seeking preventive health care)
- Stress Management (ongoing assessment of one's coping resources, using methods for stress reduction as appropriate)
- Gender Identity (satisfaction with one's own gender)
- Cultural Identity (satisfaction with one's cultural identity)
- Work and Leisure (activities that contribute to financial resources, feeling satisfaction with work and leisure, ability to engage in work and leisure with high levels of competence)
- Friendship and Love (connectedness to others in both platonic and romantic relationships)

J. Melvin Witmer, Wellness Counseling professor and pioneer

The Wellness Evaluation of Lifestyle (WEL Inventory) is available online at www.mindgarden.com. Since the development of the original WEL, Myers

Thomas J. Sweeney and Jane E. Myers, leading researchers in Wellness Counseling

<table>
<tr><td>

■■■ *Words of Wisdom* ■■■

"The universal striving for wholeness is as old as mankind."

—J. Melvin Witmer

</td></tr>
</table>

and Sweeney (2005a), using factor analysis, developed another research instrument, the Five Factor Wellness Inventory. They identified five major aspects of wellness that encompass the 17 subscales as follows:

- **Creative Self:** Thinking, Emotions, Control, Positive Humor, Work
- **Coping Self:** Realistic Beliefs, Stress Management, Self-Worth, Leisure
- **Social Self:** Friendship, Love
- **Essential Self:** Spirituality, Self-Care, Gender Identity, Cultural Identity
- **Physical Self:** Exercise, Nutrition

Over the years, Witmer, Myers, and Sweeney have continued to be leaders in wellness research. The WEL Inventory and the Five Factor Wellness Inventory have both been used in a number of counseling wellness studies (see Myers & Sweeney, 2005b, 2008).

Definitions and Dimensions of Wellness

Definitions of wellness abound (see Mulvihill, 2003). Frequently, wellness has been described as a state of optimum health, or at least good mental and physical health. Some equate it merely with physical fitness. For example, a former surgeon general, David Satcher (2009), wrote a recent article on "taking charge of wellness programs in schools," but discusses only nutrition and exercise. Thus, the medical community has tended to utilize the concept of wellness as a synonym for physical illness prevention.

On the other hand, some fitness experts and other health practitioners are focused on a "peak health" concept, which suggests that wellness is a pinnacle of total health that we can all attain. The premise is that everyone can become disease free and extremely healthy, which is evidently not true. What is needed is a definition that focuses on people who have developed an intentional plan to be "all that they can be." In other words, wellness is exemplified by the individual who is persistently working on developing a sense of well-being and quality of life in all spheres, even when suffering from acute or chronic mental or physical problems. In this vein, the National Wellness Institute (2010) defines wellness as "an active process through which people become aware of, and make choices toward, a more successful existence" (para. 1).

Wellness involves responsibility and self-actualization. The first aspect of the definition emphasizes a sense of personal responsibility for one's own wellness. Previously, we saw science and medicine as the only route to better health. This statement suggests that our own habits and choices are vitally important. In addition, it also indicates that our goal, connected to the humanistic paradigm, is to be "all that we can be." In other words, to attain our own particular peak of wellness, we must take responsibility for our own choices. We must be intentional. Again and again throughout this text, we use that word: Intentional. When we are intentional in our path toward becoming a counselor, we make decisions that enhance our personal and professional growth. When we are intentional about our own wellness, we make choices about who we want to be, how we want to react, and what actions we want to take to enhance our own lives. In their book, *Choosing Brilliant Health* (2008), Foster and Hicks suggest that rather than respond reflexively to life's stressors and problems, we ask ourselves three questions:

- What is my attitude or behavior right now?
- Is this the most beneficial attitude or behavior?
- Is there a more beneficial attitude or behavior I can choose?

■■■ *Fast Facts* ■■■

Genes account for only about 25% of an individual's health and longevity, while our environment and personal behaviors account for the rest.

Source: Butler (2010).

Counselors know and understand the power of helping clients make intentional choices for optimal living. Clients or students who blame others for their problems are encouraged to focus their energy on what is within their control. Nowhere is this more evident than with clients in in recovery from addiction who look to the Serenity Prayer for guidance: "God grant me the serenity to accept the things I cannot change; courage to change the things I can; and wisdom to know the difference." When we take responsibility for our lives, we move toward wellness.

Holism is an important aspect of the wellness philosophy. Traditionally, we have thought of wellness as a **holistic** phenomenon. That means that the separate parts of human functioning in body, mind, and spirit are thought to be interrelated, each affecting the other. In this way, wellness is like a web (Witmer, 2009). Each strand may be separate, but a vibration in one affects all the others. Let's take the example of sinusitis, a very common physical disorder, which arises when the lining of the sinuses swells. We can identify a number of different causes of sinusitis: viruses, bacteria, fungus, nose blowing (pressure makes the sinuses swell), scuba diving, certain medications, allergies, asthma (preexisting conditions), temperature and humidity, narrow sinus passages (genetic), mucous membranes not functioning properly, dehydration, poor air quality, hormonal imbalance, stress, polyps, tumors, and even sexual activity (Monteseirin, Camacho, Bonilla, Sanchez-Hernandez, Hernandez, & Conde, 2001). Therefore, the causes or ends of the web originate from interpersonal, physiological problems such as hormone imbalance, from the environment, from our genetic history and diet, and from habits and behaviors. Sinusitis is a metaphor for the treatment of mental disorders, too. It is likely that depression has many causes, making it understandable why depression might be treated from physical, mental, emotional, and/or spiritual perspectives. Because of the complexity of causes, frequently we approach treatment in a shotgun approach rather than taking the time to identify the cause. Causes are difficult to identify. So, let us say that a person's depression seems to be associated with a number of irrational thoughts and beliefs about the world, including the depressive triad (negative view of self, the world, and the future) (Beck, 1975). With a holistic view in mind, we might engage the client in cognitive behavioral therapy, but we would also try to get the client to engage in physical activity, refer him or her for antidepressant medication, get the person to activate his or her social support system, and encourage him or her to eat a balanced diet. In other words, because most problems involve many different aspects of a person's life, the solutions ought to include those multiple components as well. As you consider the holistic approach used in wellness, think about your own life. When you are feeling stressed or overwhelmed, do you use one strategy or many to try to help? Chances are, you seldom rely on just one thing. You might organize your work space to eliminate clutter, try to eat better, take a walk, and talk with a friend. The point is, many of us naturally understand the need for multiple inroads into a problem, and a wellness approach makes sure we bring this same holistic model to our work with clients.

■■■ *Words of Wisdom* ■■■

All the evidence that we have indicates that it is reasonable to assume in practically every human being, and certainly in almost every newborn baby, that there is an active will toward health, an impulse towards growth, or towards the actualization.

—Abraham Maslow

Counseling Controversy

STRENGTHS-BASED VERSUS DISORDER-BASED COUNSELING

Background: Abraham Maslow (1966) said, "It is tempting, if the only tool you have is a hammer, to treat everything as if it were a nail" (p. 16). He may have borrowed this quote from Mark Twain. In short, we tend to use familiar tools. Maslow was highlighting the importance of the "law of the instrument," which suggests that if we look through a particular lens, the instrument itself changes our perspective. There is also an Indian saying that the "pickpocket in the crowd only sees pockets." In short, we tend to see what we expect to see, what we have been trained to see, and what we want to see.

The law of the instrument is particularly important in the controversy concerning whether we should primarily diagnose and treat mental disorders. Mental disorders are medical problems and invoke the paradigm of assessment, diagnosis, and treatment. If we subscribe to that training and that point of view, will we begin to see only people's problems and not their strengths? If we fail to study diagnosis, will we miss something crucial in our clients' makeup that could affect their treatment? For example, if we try to strengthen a client's relationships and then find that he or she is suffering from bipolar disorder, it is possible that our attempts to mend the relationships will have been merely a Band-Aid. So, the controversy surrounds how much training and emphasis we should give to psychopathology and how much time and effort we should spend in finding and getting clients to utilize their strengths. Is there a middle ground? Can we find a compromise?

POINT: MENTAL DISORDERS EXIST AND THEY SHOULD BE THE PRIMARY FOCUS OF COUNSELING	COUNTERPOINT: FOCUSING ON ILLNESS KEEPS US MIRED IN THE MEDICAL MODEL AND OBSCURES OUR VISION OF STRENGTHS AND WELLNESS
• Identifying a mental disorder in an individual provides the basis for treatment planning. Without diagnosis, we will not select the best treatments for a particular disorder.	• Clients with similar labels are quite likely to have different treatments.
• In addition, research needs these categories so that we can study what works best and identify evidence-based treatments.	• A person is not merely the sum of his or her problems, and these labels override the client's strengths.
• Merely focusing on a client's strengths when he or she has a major mental disorder may be disastrous if the client's symptoms are not brought under control first.	• A wellness philosophy does not preclude treating mental disorders, but it suggests that utilizing existing strengths and improving overall wellness will be more effective than focusing only on the disorder.
• Counselors need to know how to speak the language of psychiatry and clinical psychology if we are to communicate about clients.	• When all we learn to look for is illness, we will find it. Just as students who learn psychopathology, see symptoms in themselves, they also start seeing them in others.

Questions to Consider

- If you see a client who has been diagnosed with schizophrenia but has been stable on medication for some time, what do you think he or she would be dealing with in a counseling situation?

- Is there a stigma when you have been diagnosed with a mental disorder? How do you think it would affect you if you received such a diagnosis?

- Do you think counselors need more or less training in psychopathology? What is the alternative? Should we be able to speak the language of mental illness as well as mental health?

As with most controversies, there probably is truth to both sides of this argument.

Treat mental disorders   **Focus on strengths and enhance wellness**

On the continuum, place an "X" where you think you stand on this issue.

Wellness is positive and strength-based. Wellness is, by definition, striving toward positive growth. In contrast to traditional psychological approaches that are grounded in a deficit-based medical model, wellness approaches emphasize optimal functioning by discovering and promoting the factors that allow individuals to thrive (Seligman & Csikszentmihalyi, 2000). The counselor with a holistic wellness philosophy tries to identify the client's strengths and utilize them in the service of the client's goals. A recent book on this topic, *Strength-Centered Counseling* (Ward & Reuter, 2011), ties together the philosophy of wellness with postmodern theories, such as solution focused and narrative therapies. The connecting thread is that the client's existing abilities and strengths can be activated when we identify times when the client has met with success and then encourage the client to adapt his or her strengths to a current problem. The approach empowers clients to be experts in their own treatment, reminding them that they have many strengths and positive qualities that they can bring to the current situation. In this chapter's Counseling Controversy, we consider the battle between strengths-based and disorder-based counseling.

Dimensions of Wellness

Although a holistic wellness philosophy recommends a broad approach to counseling and treatment planning, it is also useful to think of the dimensions of wellness separately. A critical look at each component of wellness provides us with a basis for understanding the concept. In addition, it allows for self-evaluation and a place to start developing a personal wellness plan. In other words, you can develop a wellness roadmap for yourself to keep yourself in good shape as you encounter the stresses of helping. Roscoe (2009) looked at nine different theories of wellness and identified eight common components. We believe that six general categories can be built from these.

- **Social Wellness.**   In general, social wellness refers to the amount of support one gives and receives. Social support is the best buffer against stress. Social interaction is crucial to human functioning, gives an outlet for altruism, and combats loneliness and isolation. Adler considered "social interest" to be a prime indicator of mental health. There is a large body of research to support the finding that low levels of social support increase the risk for different types of mental disorders, most commonly depression (Turner & Brown, 2010). Social interest is not extraversion. It is a healthy interest in one's community and in those around you. Do you give in relationships as well as take? Are your relationships intact and of high quality? How do you think "Facebook friends" factor into this definition of social wellness?

- **Emotional Wellness.**   Similar to *Emotional Intelligence* (Goleman, 2004), emotional wellness refers to the ability to be aware of feelings, manage overwhelming negative feelings, and express feelings. Most definitions focus on the ability to control negative emotions, but emotional wellness might also encompass one's ability to experience positive feelings about oneself, others, and life in general. There is a lot of evidence to support the claim that negative emotions (e.g., anger, anxiety, depression) can suppress the immune system or raise blood pressure. Conversely, the ability to express positive emotions has been linked to a strengthened immune system (Kllay, Tincas, & Benga, 2009).

- **Physical Wellness.**   Physical wellness involves regular physical activity to maintain cardiovascular health, flexibility, and strength (Hettler, 1980). In addition, one must be aware of and select a healthy diet, engage in good nutritional practices, maintain regular doctor's appointments, and adhere to medical treatments. In short, physical wellness is not just going to the gym and going on a diet. It means making healthy lifestyle choices such as walking up the stairs rather than taking the elevator and changing one's eating habits to eat more fresh vegetables and fruits. It involves an attitude to stay on top of one's physical condition and actively engage with health care providers. Making healthy choices is not just for the young and able-bodied. Even those who have significant chronic illnesses or disabilities can take charge of at least a portion of their own physical wellness. Although taking the steps may not be an option for a person with a disability, working to keep (or strengthen) whatever mobility is available to you is important. Physical wellness is an approach to taking control over whatever part of your physical health you can manage.

- **Intellectual Wellness.**   We frequently hear that as we age, we need to keep mentally active, do crosswords, keep learning, and generally stimulate the mind. Stimulating the mind means actively and creatively using the mind to solve problems, acquiring new knowledge, and generally developing one's identity as a lifelong learner. Watching television is a passive way of interacting with media, and as one grows older, it is easier for both mind and body to become a couch potato. Intellectual wellness means refusing to accept that you cannot learn, create, or grow because of your circumstances and making a determined effort to stay intellectually fit. Graduate students sometimes tell us that their school work forces them into intellectual wellness and there is no need for more growth. We remind them that intellectual wellness is far more than learning a particular field of study. It involves approaching life in an inquisitive and curious manner, seeking new information and experiences. Do you read the news every day? Do you make an effort to learn something that is outside of your "comfort" zone? Do you engage in lively debates about (noncounseling) topics with people who challenge you to grow? Do you read (or write) fiction or talk to people from other countries or cultures? Intellectual wellness means challenging your mind.

- **Spiritual Wellness.**   Spirituality means one's relationship with God or a higher power, and becoming spiritually well means having a good relationship. Being engaged in religious and spiritual activity such as meditation, prayer, and worship have been shown to positively affect physical and emotional health (Cashwell, Bentley, & Bigbee, 2007; Roach & Young, 2011). Spiritual wellness is a transcendent way for a person to get away from his or her own point of view and see things from a higher perspective.

  Most models of wellness include meaning and purpose in life as part of spiritual wellness. Having a sense of meaning in life can have an impact on your health (e.g., Agardh, Ahlbom, Andersson, Efendic, Grill, Hallqvist, Norman, & Östenson, 2003). For some people, religion and spirituality are the same, while for others, spirituality occurs outside of the context of organized faith. There are a variety of activities that can lead to a sense of meaning, purpose, and coherence in life. These activities may involve a higher purpose, such as working to end poverty or homelessness, creating beauty, caring for animals, and so on. Because these activities connect us to others in deeply meaningful ways, they can be spiritual. But it is also quite possible to have a sense of meaning in life without a religious or spiritual practice. Thus, it appears that meaning and spirituality may be separate entities (Young, 2011). In the accompanying Spotlight, Loving-Kindness Meditation is presented as a technique to help people connect to others and develop their sense of spirituality. As you read through the description, consider how such an approach might be used with clients as they work to incorporate a sense of meaning and purpose into their lives.

Spotlight
Loving-Kindness Meditation

Monica Leppma, PhD, Counselor

Loving-kindness meditation combines mindfulness (i.e., nonjudgmental awareness of the present moment) with the cultivation of warm, compassionate emotions.

It is similar to guided imagery, although the practice involves mindfully focusing on feelings more than visualizations (Fredrickson, 2009). Meditation can be used to improve awareness, self-regulation, well-being, and spiritual development (Walsh & Shapiro, 2006; Young, Cunningham & de Armas, in press). However, loving-kindness meditation is aimed at training the mind to generate feelings of warmth, kindness, and compassion toward ourselves and others (Fredrickson, 2009). This practice seems to be particularly suited to counselors, because our profession requires a great deal of giving and caring on the part of the counselor. Thus, we need ways to replenish ourselves and then joyfully reconnect with others.

The process of loving-kindness meditation begins by sitting in quiet contemplation and focusing on your breath and then your heart. Once you feel centered, you access feelings of loving-kindness by bringing to mind a person or pet that you love a great deal. Visualizing what it feels like to be with this loved one, allow warm, tender feelings to arise. Once you are in touch with these emotions, gently allow the image of your loved one to fade and take ownership of those warm feelings, and then attempt to direct those feelings toward yourself. You are the

source of these feelings, and they can be directed wherever you choose. This can be quite challenging at first but becomes easier with practice (Fredrickson, 2009; Salzberg, 2005; Weibel, 2007).

The next part of the meditation involves slowly expanding those loving, kind, compassionate feelings outward. Typically you begin with people you love and have a connection with, then slowly and gently radiate toward neutral people, possibly people you have had difficulty with, and then your entire community. Ultimately, you extend these feelings to all people, all beings, and eventually the whole planet. As you imagine radiating these feelings in an ever-widening circle, it is customary to *silently* repeat positive intentions such as, "May my friend be happy" or "May my colleagues be happy." Alternately, you may wish health, safety, or the ability to live with ease. You may repeat positive intentions for yourself, others, and eventually all beings. As you end the meditation, you can remind yourself that you have the ability to generate these positive feelings any time you wish (Fredrickson, 2009; Salzberg, 2005; Weibel, 2007). In a major research study, loving-kindness meditation was been shown to be an effective method for increasing positive emotions, increasing feelings of life satisfaction and social support, and decreasing physical symptoms and symptoms of depression (Frederickson, Cohn, Coffey, Pek, & Finkel, 2008).

- **Occupational Wellness.** Counselors recognize the important role that work plays in our lives. Occupational wellness involves the degree of satisfaction one derives from work. At the same time, being occupationally well means being able to strike a healthy balance between the job and personal relationships and other aspects of wellness. For example, work/home spillover is the tendency to let aspects of the job bleed into one's home life until the restorative qualities of being at home are eroded by the frustrations of work. With more and more people working from home, many complain that there is no clear stopping point at the end of the day. Work creeps into the physical space as well as the emotional space that is intended for family and friends. Some people are infected with the obsessive need to stay in contact with their work via cellular phone and e-mail at all hours. Thus, the time they need to recover is diminished by a technology that never sleeps. Coupled with demanding or stressful jobs, the result can be diminished physical health. Occupational wellness reminds us that getting the most satisfaction from one's job helps us feel better in all aspects of our lives. We need not be in high-power or high-status occupations, either. Did you ever notice that some people work hard to make their jobs more fun or more fulfilling, no matter what they do? We certainly have. For example, one of us (Darcy) makes an extra effort to go through the checkout line of a particular grocery clerk, even if the line is a little longer than the others. The clerk is friendly, talkative, and has a great sense of humor. He really enjoys his job, and his positive approach to life is infectious. Occupational wellness isn't just for doctors or lawyers. Deriving satisfaction from work is a healthy approach we all can strive for.

Developing Your Own Personal Wellness Plan

Figure 13.1 is a chart you can use to sketch out a personal wellness plan. Take another look at the six dimensions of wellness described above. They make a general list of the areas of wellness, but now you need to get specific. Identify which areas you need to work on to improve your overall wellness and what obstacles are likely to arise. I (Mark) have filled out an example of the physical dimension on the chart to give you an idea of how it might be used. Although you may have something in each of the dimensions you want to work on, choose one or two. Too many goals can be overwhelming for some people. See what works best for you. The thing about a personal wellness plan is that you need to find a time to regularly review it to see if you are on target. One way to keep yourself honest and on track is to ask a significant person in your life to help you by reminding you or checking in with you about your progress. Put a note on your electronic calendar, PDA, or smart phone and assess how you are doing every 30 days.

Wellness Counseling

Counselors who want to incorporate a wellness approach in their counseling might introduce one of the wellness models to help clients contextualize their lives into this holistic and positive framework. Clients can then make goals to enhance their wellness, just as you did in Figure 13.1. Just as we cautioned you not to try to change *everything* all at once, counselors help clients identify two or three areas within which they can set reasonable goals and work to make changes. As with all counseling goals, small changes that improve wellness in one area of our lives

FIGURE 13.1 Your Own Wellness Plan

Dimension of Wellness	Things I do regularly to strengthen this dimension	One specific goal I have for improving this dimension of wellness	Obstacles to making this a regular part of my lifestyle	Why do I really want to accomplish this goal at all? What is my motivation?	By what date do I expect to make noticeable progress on this goal?	I commit to this goal: (Put your initials here)
EXAMPLE (PHYSICAL)	I swim 3 mornings per week	Walk 10,000 steps daily, 3 days per week	It's hot in the summer and I feel tired at night	I need to reduce my cholesterol and get more fit so I feel better	Nov. 1	MEY
Physical	Power yoga on Fri, try to do spin	Work out for 30min 4x a week	I get caught up at work	Feeling better + getting married	Oct. 15th	GEM
Emotional						
Spiritual						
Intellectual						
Social						
Occupational & Environmental						

often have ripple effects on the other components of wellness. Counselors who help clients enhance their wellness through this approach do not ignore other problems or concerns that a client may have; they simply recognize that a wellness approach can serve as an important complement to more traditional counseling approaches. Using a wellness approach, counselors help clients identify their optimal selves, find the strengths and skills clients already possess to build upon, and then develop strategies to help clients move in the direction of their goals. In the first Snapshot of this chapter, Dr. Paul Granello, a Licensed Professional Clinical Counselor, discusses how he incorporates a wellness perspective into his counseling practice. In his clinical work, Dr. Granello incorporates a wellness perspective

Snapshot
Wellness Counseling

Paul F. Granello, PhD, LPCC

I have been interested in wellness and its role in counseling and mental health for over 20 years. During my doctoral program, I was fortunate to work with Dr. Mel Witmer, a pioneer in wellness counseling. Dr. Witmer has been a wonderful mentor to me, and our collaboration has continued to the present day.

I have been particularly interested in the psychological and social mediators of individual well-being. Much of the research in wellness is focused on the physical aspects of health (for example, exercise, nutrition, sleep), and clearly that is important. But I am fascinated with understanding personality characteristics (optimism, gratitude, hope) and social factors (friendships, connections to others) the help us stay well, too. I try to apply my interest and ongoing learning in the area of wellness to my work with clients. Thus, the Wellness Counseling that I provide to clients can be characterized by a philosophy that stresses several important tenets. First, clients are multidimensional. That is, that they have many domains in which they function including social, emotional, physical, cognitive, and spiritual. I try to assess how the client is getting along in each of these domains, which I believe are interrelated. My assessment encompasses the totality of the client and focuses on client ability and strengths, not just the identification of pathological symptoms for the purpose of diagnosis. Second, I hold a belief that all clients are capable of personal growth in some area of their lives and that improvement in one area will positively impact other areas. Toward that end, the entire lifestyle of the client is a potential target for therapeutic interventions. As a result, treatment planning that comes from a wellness perspective may be a bit broader than it is for counseling that focuses exclusively on the mental and emotional domains. In addition, I understand that when I work from a wellness perspective, I may play a role that includes a bit more emphasis on being a treatment coordinator for the client, particularly if other health professionals are brought in as consultants on the case. For example, when I work with clients with depression, I may encourage them to pursue a nutritional consultation or develop a walking program in consultation with their primary care provider. I believe that helping clients to set reasonable, measureable, and achievable goals is a fundamental component of promoting positive counseling outcomes. Third, when working with clients from a wellness orientation, I am willing to draw from multiple theoretical approaches, apply models for behavior change, and recognize the value of working with professionals in other health care professions. I am open to my clients working with complementary and alternative medicine (CAM) providers, such as massage therapists or acupuncture therapists. I try to provide my clients with quality advice about which CAM procedures have some research behind them and steer them toward quality providers. Fourth, I realize that making any significant change in life is difficult, and I seek to have a very supportive therapeutic relationship with all my clients. Encouragement, support, self and social accountability, and positive feedback are all important elements of counseling from a wellness philosophy. Finally, I believe that everyone can benefit from this type of intervention. I do not believe that a client must have a diagnosable mental illness to benefit from Wellness Counseling. Clients who need help changing a lifestyle habit or those who have a chronic disease and are looking

(continued)

(Continued)

to optimize their health are appropriate for services. Conversely, I have found that even clients with severe and diagnosable mental and emotional disorders can benefit from a wellness perspective. It might be easy when a client has so many pathological symptoms to adopt a problem-based focus. But counseling from a wellness perspective reminds us that all clients, even those with significant obstacles to overcome, are far more than just the sum of their problems.

In my work as a wellness counselor, I incorporate assessment, treatment planning, the selection of appropriate interventions, and a strong supportive relationship, just as I would if I were operating from any successful counseling approach. However, Wellness Counseling has a bit broader focus across multiple domains of client functioning, places emphasis on holistic assessment and recognizing strengths, places emphasis on goal development, and is open to working with a broad range of clients who may or may not have a diagnosable mental disorder. I find that adopting this perspective in my counseling help me—and my clients—get excited about the potential for change and growth that exists within us all.

that helps clients recognize their strengths. He uses individualized wellness plans to work with his clients in both individual counseling and wellness-based workshops entitled "Balance in Life." In this Snapshot, he discusses how his wellness orientation affects his work with clients.

Strengths-Based Counseling

Counselors who adopt a strengths-based approach based on the tenets of positive psychology focus on what is going right in a client's life. Counselors and clients work together to identify past and present successes, and then build on those successes to face current problems or challenges. **Positive psychology** is a relatively new term, but it is based on the historical roots of wellness and thriving in counseling and psychology. Positive psychology focuses on happiness and fulfillment and helping clients achieve their optimal level of functioning. Martin Seligman's (2006) concept of learned optimism (in contrast to learned hopelessness, which has for so long been the focus of behavioral definitions of depression) is a foundational concept of positive psychology.

Strengths-Based Assessment

The first step in strengths-based counseling is identifying the client's strengths so that they can be activated. The Values in Action Inventory of Strengths (VIA-IS; Peterson & Seligman, 2004) is a 240-item inventory that can be taken at authentichappiness.org without cost. There are other strengths inventories, including the StrengthsFinder associated with the book *Now, Discover Your Strengths* (Buckingham & Clifton, 2001). The instrument is available online, and you can also gain access by purchasing the book (used books will not give you access to the test). The test assesses knowledge, skills, and talents primarily focused around 34 themes aimed at business and work settings. Thus, it is easy to see which strengths will work best in a team, committee, or group project setting.

Strengths-based assessment and counseling. Rashid and Ostermann (2009) make a number of observations and suggestions for implementing strengths-based assessment in clinical practice. Among these are the following:

1. Utilize assessments of positive emotions and strengths. For example, assess VIA strengths and other positive psychology instruments online or consult *The Oxford Handbook of Methods in Positive Psychology* (Ong & van Dulman, 2006), which has instruments you can copy. Some of the areas that are very important to assess are the client's level of hope, meaning and purpose in life, and strengths.

2. Use the intake interview to assess strengths as well as problems. For example, include questions like the following:
   - What are you good at?
   - What brings meaning and purpose to life?
   - What holds you together?
   - Who supports you?

3. Help clients identify their own strengths:
   - Discuss famous examples of people with particular strengths, such as Gandhi.
   - Think about books and films that tell stories that clients admire (positive film list in Snyder & Lopez, 2007, pp. 19–22) to allow clients to compare their ideals with their present reality and identify what strengths they wish to use more often.
   - Consider a technique called "Positive Introduction" in which clients introduce themselves in a positive way. The story is about 300 words and it has a beginning, middle, and a positive ending. It should be about a time when the client was at his or her best. The client is taught to discuss particular strengths employed during this incident.

4. Ask family and friends to validate a client's self-assessment of strengths. The client may not be the only one with information about his or her positive traits. Much of an individual's functioning is reflected in the quality of his or her interpersonal relationships, which also serve as a buffer against environmental stress.

5. Assess how a client has handled the most important challenges of life as well as the daily stressors. Sometimes setbacks provide us with the most important growth experiences, especially if we can identify what resources we employed.

6. Assess strengths early in counseling rather than as an afterthought.

■■■ *Fast Facts* ■■■

Even clients with the most severe and debilitating presenting problems can benefit from a strengths-based assessment *in addition to* traditional assessment techniques. For example, Marsha Linehan and her colleagues developed the *Reasons for Living Inventory* to help suicidal individuals and their counselors recognize the important reasons clients have for staying alive, in spite of the internalized pressure they might feel to take their own lives. When used in conjunction with other assessment techniques that measure suicide risk, it can be a powerful tool that helps instill hope while simultaneously assessing risk.

Source: Linehan, Goodstein, Nielsen, & Chiles (1983).

7. Look for signs of flourishing. These are times when the client is operating at a high level of functioning.

8. Develop a plan that suggests that clients use strengths when faced with particular common difficulties. For example, "When I feel anxious, I will utilize my spiritual resources and meditate or pray." Of course, these are individualized based on the client's assessed strengths.

Strengths-Based Interventions

Counselors who use a strengths-based approach use a variety of intervention techniques that complement more traditional approaches. For example, counselors might focus on positive emotions to help negate the harmful effects that negative emotions can have on the body, called the Undoing Effect. Research has demonstrated that positive emotions can help build up a body's resources that have been diminished by stress, including enhancing physical, social, and intellectual well-being (see Fredrickson, 2009).

Counselors might also use a concept called Broaden and Build, whereby positive emotions are used to help broaden an individual's thought-action repertoire, thereby encouraging the person to pursue a wider range of interests, thoughts, and action. The broadened repertoire of thoughts and actions that accompany positive emotions is important because they help build the body's physical and intellectual resources (Fredrickson, Mancuso, Branigan, & Tugade, 2000). In this way, counselors who encourage clients to fully experience their positive emotions (not just concentrate on the negative ones) help their clients develop important resources that can serve as a buffer against future negative emotions and stress.

Other strengths-based interventions include mindfulness (a state of nonjudging, open curiosity), flow (a state of intense absorption in one's work as intrinsically rewarding), and learned optimism (the ability to cultivate a talent for joy and happiness). Each of these interventions helps clients focus on the positive aspects of their world and reminds them that they have the resources and skills to face life's difficult challenges.

The Stress of Counseling and Potential for Burnout

Counselors live in a world of wounds. Like doctors, counselors see horrible accidents and psychological scars inflicted by others. So, every counselor must find a way to deal with two aspects of the job: (1) vicarious trauma, and (2) burnout.

■■■ *Words of Wisdom* ■■■

"Empathy is a double-edged sword; it is simulta-neously your greatest asset and a point of real vulnerability."

Source: Larson (1993, p. 30).

Vicarious trauma is caused when the counselor is significantly affected by the experiences of the client. Vicarious trauma is a process that unfolds over time; it is the cumulative effect of seeing so much pain endured by so many people. All counselors who have been in practice have stories of clients who have deeply affected them, both positively and negatively. Although we take great joy when clients overcome adversity, we are often wounded by the stories our clients tell us. It is impossible to listen to someone's story of abuse, betrayal, or grief and not have it touch your heart. Recognizing and attending to the pain that we can feel when we hear these stories is essential to maintaining our own wellness.

Informed by Research
A National Survey of Counselor Wellness and Impairment

Gerard Lawson, a counselor educator at Virginia Tech, published a survey he conducted with more than 500 counselors in the American Counseling Association (2007). He started with 1000 names and had a return rate of about 50%, which is considered very good. First, he asked participants to complete the Career Sustaining Behaviors Questionnaire (CSB; Stevanovic & Rupert, 2004), which assesses strategies that help a counselor keep a positive attitude and work effectively. The top 12 strategies the counselors identified were the following:

1. Maintain a sense of humor.
2. Spend time with partner/family.
3. Maintain a balance between professional and personal lives.
4. Maintain self-awareness.
5. Maintain a sense of control over work responsibilities.
6. Reflect on positive experiences.
7. Try to maintain objectivity about clients.
8. Engage in quiet leisure activities.

9. Maintain professional identity.
10. Participate in continuing education.
11. Engage in physical activities.
12. Spend time with friends. (Lawson, 2007, p. 28)

Next, Lawson assessed their quality of life using the Professional Quality of Life Scale (ProQOS; Stamm, 2005). The inventory has three scales: Compassion Satisfaction (the degree to which they are deriving satisfaction from their work), Burnout and Compassion Fatigue (the degree to which they are unable to show compassion) and Vicarious Traumatization (the degree to which they are stressed by their clients' problems). He found:

1. About 14% of the counselors were not deriving satisfaction from their work.
2. More than 5% were said to be experiencing burnout.
3. About 11% were showing compassion fatigue or evidence of vicarious traumatization.

Spotlight
Being Well as a School Counselor

Challenges for the School Counselor

The main challenge for the school counselor is the conflict that exists in the role (Burnham & Jackson, 2000; Lambie, 2007). The professional school counselor is pulled between responsibilities to students, teachers, and administrators. For example, consider the example of a high school student who reveals to the school counselor that she has been binging (overeating) and purging (vomiting) at school every day, and two of her friends have also been doing the same because they believe it will help them lose weight. While wanting to help the student, the school counselor is aware that there is more than one student involved and that there is an unhealthy social situation, too. It is also true that the student's behavior is dangerous and potentially life-threatening. Somehow the parents must be notified, and school faculty and staff probably will need to find ways of preventing the spread of misinformation and preventing dangerous practices. In short, the school administration will become involved. Thus, the duty of the counselor to the client competes with larger responsibilities to the other students and the institution.

In addition, a school counselor must deal with crises and unexpected situations including suicide (Juhnke, Granello, & Granello, 2011) and other mental health emergencies and developmental crises. In spite of all of the pressure, most professional school counselors believe that they have an exciting job where every day brings different challenges and successes. Yet, at times, this excitement speeds up the pace of life so much that the school counselor feels that he or she is on a merry-go-round that cannot be stopped. The typical day of a school counselor involves dealing with emergencies, meeting with parents and checking e-mail from parents and administrators, meeting with teachers and administrators, attending meetings about student placement, and lots and lots of paperwork.

Suggestions for Fighting Stress and Burnout as a School Counselor

Like everybody else, school counselors can make a number of personal changes to promote their own wellness outside of the job. But a great deal of most people's stress comes from their work. So, the suggestions here are aimed at helping you, the school-counselor-to-be, think about how you can go into a job and deal with the environmental and

---

Burnout is the term used for long-term exhaustion, which results in diminished interest, low energy, and a reduced sense of personal accomplishment. Counselors are vulnerable to burnout as they manage the pressures and stressors of heavy caseloads, clients with significant pathology, and organizational systems and constraints (e.g., school policies, managed care paperwork, tightening budgets) while trying to maintain a sense of emotional stability for the clients. If not carefully managed, burnout can have negative effects on a counselor's life, both professionally and personally. In the preceding Informed by Research feature, we discuss the findings of a researcher named George Lawson, who studied the role that burnout and vicarious trauma play in the lives of professional counselors.

interpersonal challenges right from the beginning. Our most important suggestion is to know the job and to know your role.

Although you are probably not working as a school counselor right now, there are a few things that we need to highlight as preventive measures. They all fall under the rubric of "being a professional." The school counselor cannot rely on administrators to understand the job of school counselor. The school counselor is a professional and must monitor his or her own stress and advocate for institutional changes that diminish the stressors that push them towards burnout. Young and Lambie (2007) identified some of the things a school counselor can do on an institutional basis to stay vital and prevent burnout. They are the following:

1. Collaborate with the school administration to reduce role ambiguity, role overload, and role conflict. When the school counselor knows what his or her role *should* be, it is easier to advocate for it. A strong professional identity provides a basis for saying "Yes" and for saying "No."

2. One way to clarify the school counselor's role is to advocate for a district-wide school counseling manual that outlines the duties and responsibilities of a school counselor. The ASCA Model (2003) provides a framework for a more consistent professional role. But principals will not be reading the ASCA document. Instead, an internal document is needed to get everyone on the same page.

3. Educate administrators, teachers, students, and parents about what a school counselor does. This is a daily task of the school counselor and should be part of the job so that constituents are not disappointed or expect the school counselor to perform functions outside his or her expertise or role.

4. Insist on supervision. One of the things that can help a counselor deal with the stress of difficult problems, emergencies, and dilemmas is supervision by an experienced counselor. School counselors often have a difficult time getting supervision from other counselors. Most supervisors are not on-site, and therefore supervision is often informal or comes from noncounselors. Therefore, the professional school counselor must become an advocate for himself or herself and ask for clinical supervision.

5. Engage in professional development. This means developing your own learning plan as well as attending conferences and seminars. It also means taking courses to enhance your knowledge and reading the professional literature.

Consider the following story from a counselor, Robert, age 25, who has been working for about two years in a public mental health agency:

Although I was right out of my master's program, my first job was to see all kinds of clients including children, adolescents, and adults. I ran two groups per week. One of my first clients was a 16-year-old girl who was cutting herself nearly every day. Another client was a grieving 58-year-old man who had run over his 2-year-old granddaughter. My third client was very difficult because she had a long history of abuse. She called nearly every day and frequently threatened to commit suicide. I realized that I was under a great deal of stress. I was having trouble sleeping, was thinking about my clients all the time, was irritable with my family, and angry with my supervisors who didn't seem to have any answers. I eventually realized from my friend, who was also a counselor, that I was faced with some pretty severe situations and that perhaps I was suffering from a case of the "myth of omnipotence." I was expecting myself to have all the answers for these long-term and serious problems in just a few short weeks. I had not really accepted the fact that I was a beginner and that I had entered a profession that takes years to learn and where sometimes even vast experience is not enough. One of the things I did was make sure the intake staff knew I was dealing with some difficult cases and to let me have some less severe clients in the next few months. I increased my supervision time and made a concentrated effort not to worry about my clients when I was not at work. Perhaps the biggest change took place when I stopped expecting myself to be a master counselor in my first years.

The case of Robert reminds us that intense pressure can be part of counseling right from the start. Burnout is a response to that pressure. It is a state of depletion, fatigue, and hostility that is a defense against overwhelming stress. Yet the most important symptom is an interpersonal one: The burned-out individual starts seeing people as objects. You have seen this syndrome in retail salespeople and in doctors and nurses. The recognition of burnout in the helping professions began in the late 1970s (Edlewich & Brodsky, 1980; Pines & Maslach, 1978). It was originally conceptualized as a condition of fatigue involving a negative self-concept, a negative view of the job, and a loss of empathy for clients. In the accompanying Spotlight, we discuss some of the special challenges that are part of the life of a school counselor and provide some tips and suggestions to help prevent burnout as a counselor in the fast-paced and challenging world of K–12 education.

Insulating Yourself Against Stress and Burnout

Consider this metaphor. Every time we get on an airplane, the flight attendants give us great advice about helping others: "In the unlikely event that we experience a loss of cabin pressure, oxygen masks will fall from the compartment above. Secure your own mask and breathe normally. If you are traveling with another person who needs your assistance, please put on your own mask before helping others."

As counseling students, when you experience stress, you need to make sure your mask is in place before entering the potentially stressful profession. Do not forget to breathe normally. Your *mask* in this case is all the things that you do to maintain your personal wellness and, as the famous therapist, Virginia Satir said, "to keep your own pot full." Satir's idea of one's "pot" was that

■■■ *Fast Facts* ■■■

Stress in a nutshell:

- Percentage of adults who suffer harm to their health from stress: 43%

- Percentage of all doctor's visits for stress-related complaints: 75 to 90%

- Leading causes of death linked to stress: heart disease, cancer, lung ailments, accidents, cirrhosis of the liver, and suicide

Source: Retrieved September 11, 2010, from http://psychcentral.com/lib/2007/how-does-stress-affect-us.

it represented personal resources that one could call on when depleted. She believed that self-confidence and self-esteem flowed from this kettle that needs constant replenishing (Banmen, 2008). It is a bank account into which you must keep depositing to avoid depletion.

The ACA Code of Ethics (American Counseling Association, 2005) identifies the concept of impairment as an ethical issue for counselors in training (that is you) and established counselors. An important issue here is that counselors are considered impaired when their physical, mental, or emotional issues seem likely to harm a client or others. Such a determination is difficult to make for oneself, and we are often reluctant to report a fellow student or counselor. But ACA ethics make it clear that we have a responsibility to clients that supersedes our own possible embarrassment or fear of confrontation.

Maintaining Your Wellness as a Counseling Student

In this section, we offer strategies, advice, and tips for keeping balance in your life during your graduate program in counseling. The ideas offered in the following paragraphs come from counseling students, counselors, and faculty, and can help you in graduate school as well as later on in your role as a professional counselor.

Physical Wellness

When students are under stress, they often start to ignore their physical wellness. It may be tempting to "save time" by skipping meals, eating junk food, giving up time at the gym, or skimping on sleep. Of course, these are the very strategies that tend to make us work with reduced efficiency, make us sick, or cause us to be so exhausted that we lose interest in what we are doing. Maintaining your physical wellness is essential to optimal functioning as a graduate student.

Maintain your fitness. Physical activity rather than exercise should be the focus for most working adults. In other words, find a fun and regular way to keep moving, whether it be disc golf, walking with a friend, or a daily run. Going to the gym may not always be the best use of time when taking a walk or playing tennis with your significant other can serve two purposes.

Eat well. It is tempting when you have regular appointments or evening classes to skip lunch, wolf down a microwaved meal at dinner, or eat a snack in the car. Eating should be a priority for a counselor because you need regular fuel to keep your energy up during sessions, and it may be some time before you get to eat again. Here are six suggestions for keeping your energy up when you are working as a counselor:

1. Drink juice rather than soda or sports drinks.
2. Eat whole grains rather than white rice and macaroni.
3. Eat fruits and nuts for snacks rather than crackers, or eat an energy bar.
4. Pack a lunch with healthy leftovers rather than eating fast food.

5. Make lunch your biggest meal and do not eat late at night.

6. Drink tea rather than coffee in the afternoon as the caffeine level is lower and tea is less likely to cause stomach upset.

Emotional Wellness

Counselors must be prepared to handle the strong emotions of their clients and, to do so, they must maintain their own emotional wellness. Counseling students can become overwhelmed with the intensity of their clients' emotions. You might have a natural (although unhelpful) reaction, which is the desire to numb yourself to your feelings in order to protect yourself from all the pain around you. Emotional numbing, as you read earlier in this chapter, is one of the signals of counselor burnout. Taking time to care for yourself emotionally will help give you the skills you need to have a long and happy career in the counseling profession.

Reduce emotional arousal. This might mean finding a way to take a five-minute walk during your lunch break or between classes. Find a minute to meditate or pray.

Get counseling for yourself. Until 2005, the British Association for Counselling and Psychotherapy required that members receive 40 hours of therapy as part of their requirements for certification. Now they allow other options for personal development, which can include therapy (Griffiths, 2007). Today, there seem to be fewer counseling programs requiring the student to engage in personal counseling, yet more than 80% of counselors receive personal counseling on their own (Bike, Norcross, & Schatz, 2009). One of the reasons that personal counseling is no longer required in many programs is that requiring a therapeutic relationship goes against a basic idea in counseling: that it is most effective and ethical when it is voluntary. Still, there are good reasons to consider personal counseling as a part of training even if it is not required. Grimmer and Tribe (2001) listed five important reasons why you should consider personal counseling as a student/trainee.

1. **To experience being in the role of the client.** There is no other way to really understand the experience of a client than to sit in the other chair. Early in my own training, I (Mark) went to see a counselor and had to wait for about 20 minutes. I learned a lot from just that one appointment. As I watched the clock, I started wondering if the fee would be reduced or my session would be lengthened, or even if I had showed up at the wrong time and place. I started to consider whether the counselor could really help me if he couldn't even be on time. I became annoyed at the fact that I had to sit in the waiting room with all of the other clients, like a public admission that I couldn't handle my problems. Because of that it experience, if I can avoid it, I never let my clients cool their heels in the waiting room. I try to finish my sessions promptly and began the next session on time.

There is also a sort of humiliation that comes from being in the role of the client. There is often a part of us that feels that help is for everyone else, that it is okay for the weak, but that I am one of the strong. It seems self-indulgent and you feel needy. If you are the kind of person (and we suspect that you are) that others seek out when they need help, then asking or needing help yourself is uncomfortable and unfamiliar.

2. **To feel the impact of counseling interventions and techniques.**   As a client you can really feel certain interventions that as a counselor seemed quite benign. For example, I (Mark) might chide my clients, in the way of Albert Ellis, about their "nutty ideas." Although I want it to be a joke with a message, some people feel that they have just been called a "nut" by a mental health professional. By becoming a client you become more conscious about making such jokes and giving off-the-cuff advice.

More importantly, you can feel it internally when your counselor hits the "nail on the head" and accurately summarizes what you have been saying and thinking and feeling. Everyone wants to be understood, to explain their rationale for their actions and have their intentions understood. They do not merely want to justify themselves or have someone feel sorry for them. When someone truly understands you, it is a tremendous relief. The problem may not be gone, but someone gets it. That is an important part of any intimate relationship.

3. **To increase your personal growth and emotional and mental health.** Counseling stimulates personal growth. When counselors go to counseling, they have the opportunity to explore their own self-defeating patterns and negative ways of interacting with others, and they begin to see that their life can be more than they imagined. The counselor who goes to counseling may be open to trying things and perhaps may want more out of life than before.

4. **To recognize that personal counseling might help you reduce stress when you are in practice.**   When you experience counseling for yourself, you recognize the benefits of having a neutral party to explain yourself to. You experience the reduction in anxiety and tension, and you see the need for a different perspective to help you cope with pressure from inside and from without.

5. **To deal with mental health problems that might be affecting your ability to provide support for the client, whether you are in your internship or in a counseling job.**   When you have an anxiety disorder, substance abuse disorder, are depressed, or are suffering from an episode associated with bipolar disorder, you may be impaired. When one of us (Darcy) faced a physical health diagnosis, a trip to a counselor for a few visits helped manage the complex emotions that accompanied the illness. Processing through the feelings with a counselor allowed me to minimize the possibility that my negative emotions would interfere inappropriately in my work with clients.

Intellectual Wellness

Staying sharp and cognitively engaged is an important part of wellness. Counseling students might argue that they are already intellectually challenged because of their role as students, but intellectual wellness is more about adopting an inquisitive stance to the world around you than it is about meeting the requirements of any particular class assignment.

Stay on the cutting edge. Read the ACA journals. Listen to audiobooks if you have a long commute. Attend conferences and inservice training. Some of the biggest boosts come from your fellow counselors, who know what you are going through and have some ideas to help with that difficult client or a way to adjust your attitude. We are both inspired by a colleague who, in spite of being in the profession for more than 50 years, attends counseling conferences and stays current in the latest research and ideas. He attends workshops by student presenters, goes to sessions on topics that are new to him, and reads journals and books that challenge his thinking. By all accounts, he is an expert in the field, but he is quick to point out, "I always have something new to learn."

Spiritual Wellness

Counselors with a strong sense of meaning and purpose in their lives can find the strength and courage to do the hard work that the profession requires. A sense of spirituality, whether through organized religion, meditation or prayer, or a connection to nature, can provide a contemplative approach that encourages inner peace.

Engage in meditation and prayer. If you make this a regular part of your life, not just a breather at work, the benefits will spill over into your work life. You will be able to remain calm.

Experience nature. When you are not counseling, find ways to commune with nature. Like meditation and prayer, it can give you a peace that you need when you engage others who are not peaceful.

Be ethical. It simplifies your life if you tell the truth, and don't talk about your clients, colleagues, or fellow students behind their backs. The students in your classes are your professional colleagues. If you gossip, you will quickly be seen as unprofessional.

Relationship Wellness

In Chapter 5, we discussed the importance of preparing your family and friends for your life as a graduate student. In this chapter on wellness, we remind you that doing so is important not just because it will help you in your studies, but because you will need the love and support of others to be an effective counselor. Counselors know and understand the importance of other people in their lives, and they work to maintain healthy, strong, and supportive relationships.

Maintain your relationships. Three studies have looked at what problems therapists discuss when they go for personal counseling (Bike, Norcross, & Schatz, 2009; Norcross, Strausser-Kirtland, & Missar, 1988; Pope & Tabachnick, 1994). All three identify marital or couples distress as the leading issue discussed. Like everyone else, counselors have a difficult time maintaining a primary relationship. Yet it is our personal relationships that provide the biggest buffer against stress at work (Andersson-Arntén, Rosén, Jansson, & Archer, 2010). In essence, the reason counselors go to therapy and the potential source of relief are both in their couple relationships. How can we make sense of this conundrum and make some recommendations for beginning counselors? Like all of the recommendations for better wellness in this chapter, all require time and effort. Yet perhaps for romantic reasons, we do not see that our made-in-heaven relationships need maintenance here on earth. Based on research, we would be much better off in terms of stress if we spent as much time mending and sustaining our relationships as we do in the gym. Here are some quick suggestions for relationship wellness that can help you maintain your relationship and improve your overall wellness by decreasing work-related stress.

- **Suggestion 1:** Spend 10 minutes a day, starting now, checking in with your significant other. In the PAIRS program, an educational relationship enhancement curriculum (see http://pairs.org), they have a tool called the Daily Temperature Reading, adapted from the work of Virginia Satir. It involves noticing and appreciating the partner, discussing new information, sharing puzzles and requests for change, as well as going over wishes, hopes, and dreams. Although it may seem overly structured, it is surprising how much couples benefit immediately from even the smallest time spent on talking about what is good in the relationship and how they want it to be. Sharing problems should not be the only interaction that you have with your significant other, nor should a discussion of shared responsibilities take precedence over what you like about him or her.
- **Suggestion 2:** Go ahead and talk about your work but focus on your own feelings, not the problems of your clients or your fellow students. Your clients' problems can be discussed with your supervisor, but do not breach confidentiality, believing that your significant other is bound by confidentiality too.

- **Suggestion 3:**   Seek couples counseling if you need to work on your relationship, not individual counseling. People who seek individual counselor for their marital problems are more likely to break up than those who seek conjoint couples counseling. Find an experienced counselor who has special training and interest in working with couples or go to a relationship or marriage education class. Research is now confirming that relationship psychoeducation can be effective in improving relationships (Halford, Markman, & Stanley, 2008).

Summary

In this chapter, we discussed how counselors use models of wellness and a positive, strength-based approach to counseling to help guide practice. Counselors in all practice settings can find ways to integrate these positive approaches into their work. We also discussed the importance of maintaining a healthy, balanced life, both now as a counseling student and later on as a counselor. Counselors use a wellness approach to help clients achieve their highest level of functioning, but we cannot help clients if we are not willing to work toward wellness ourselves. Because of the potential for burnout and emotional exhaustion that is inherent in the work that we do, counselors must take extra care to maintain their physical, emotional, intellectual, social, and spiritual wellness.

End-of-Chapter Activities

The following activities might be part of your assignments for a class. Whether they are required or not, we suggest that you complete them as a way of reflecting on your new learning, arguing with new ideas in writing, and thinking about questions you may want to pose in class.

Student Activities

1. Now it's time to reflect on the major topics that we have covered in this chapter. Look back at the sections or the ideas you have underlined. What were your reactions as you read that portion of the chapter? What do you want to remember?

   _____

   _____

   _____

   _____

2. Wellness approaches to counseling encourage clients to take responsibility for their own choices. Clearly, counselors are human, and none of us has attained complete and perfect wellness in our lives. Consider your own assessment of your wellness and the goals that you have set for yourself. How can you balance the statement that each of us must take responsibility for our own wellness with the reality that few of us actually do? How can your own striving for wellness help you empathize with your clients?

_____

_____

_____

_____

_____

3. Many counseling students have contact with mental health professionals who are experiencing burnout. Have you met a counselor (or other mental health professional) who demonstrates signs of burnout? If so, how did you know? How did it feel to interact with that person? What lessons can you take for your own professional life from this experience?

_____

_____

_____

_____

_____

_____

■■■ Journal Question ■■■

Think about times as a student or employee when you were overwhelmed with work. What did you do to regain your equilibrium when you experienced symptoms of stress? As a counselor, you may find a parallel situation when you feel incapable of handling the responsibilities and pressures of clients and their needs. You may be pulled by paperwork and by rules and regulations that make your job harder. What strengths do you have and what resources can you call on when that happens?

◼️◼️◼️ Topics for Discussion ◼️◼️◼️

1. Counselors in training have an ethical responsibility to monitor themselves and refrain from offering services when they are impaired by substance abuse, burnout, or any other condition that would potentially cause harm to a client. If you felt that you were suffering from depression, what steps would you take as a student to comply with the ACA ethical guidelines?

2. As you look at the guidelines for keeping yourself well as a counselor, which do you think will be the hardest to implement in your counseling setting? Consider the following: eat well, engage in regular physical activity, maintain your spiritual wellness, develop positive self-talk, go to conferences that refresh you, stay in supervision, get a hobby, and get counseling for yourself.

◼️◼️◼️ Experiments ◼️◼️◼️

1. Go online and use a fitness program or a smart phone application to track your diet or exercise over a five-day period. Many of these programs are quite sophisticated and can give you nutritional information and charts of daily exercise. Keeping track of what you eat and how you exercise increases your awareness and brings about change. What kinds of clients might benefit most from this kind of monitoring? Could keeping track of calories also be a symptom, in some cases, of an eating disorder? Is food monitoring always to be encouraged?

2. Go to the National Institutes of Health Complementary and Alternative Medicine (CAM) website to discover interventions and approaches that have been supported by research (http://nccam.nih.gov). What approach will you take if clients want to engage in CAM activities (e.g., massage, acupuncture, magnet therapy, light therapy, reiki) in addition to the work that you are doing with them?

◼️◼️◼️ Explore More! ◼️◼️◼️

If you are interested in exploring more about the ideas presented in this chapter, we recommend the following books and articles.

Books

Choate, L. H. (2009). *Girls and women's wellness: Contemporary counseling issues and interventions.* Alexandria VA: American Counseling Association.

Granello, P. (Ed.). (2011). *Wellness counseling.* Upper Saddle River, NJ: Pearson.

Ward, C. C., & Reuter, T. (2011). *Strength-centered counseling.* Thousand Oaks, CA: Sage.

Articles

Lambie, G. W. (2006). Burnout prevention: A humanistic perspective and structured group supervision activity. *Journal of Humanistic Counseling, Education and Development, 45*, 32–44.

Myers, J. E., & Sweeney, T. J. (2008). Wellness counseling: The evidence base for practice. *Journal of Counseling & Development, 86*, 482–493.

Roscoe, L. (2009). Wellness: A review of t heory and measurement for counselors. *Journal of Counseling & Development, 87*, 216–226.

14

Counseling Tomorrow

In this chapter, we will:

- Discuss future trends that will affect counseling, including technology, and an aging and more diverse U.S. population.

- Build the Experimental Prototype Counselor of Tomorrow and identify the 14 characteristics of a professional who is equipped to deal with the requirements of a changing profession.

- Look at some cutting-edge issues that counselors should know about as they plan to become lifelong learners.

As you read the chapter, you might want to consider:

- Will technological advances really change the way that counseling is delivered?

- Can technology help the counselor?

- What should you prepare yourself for if your clients are likely to be older, more culturally diverse, and more open to discussing spiritual and religious issues?

- How can you continue to stay professionally involved and enhance your professional identity?

As you have learned throughout this book, counseling is an ever-changing profession. The history of counseling is not just stories from long ago, but is situated in the current complex, challenging, and exciting world in which we live. The counseling profession is changing, and you will be part of, and perhaps take a leadership role, in what happens next. What do you envision for the future? How can counselors and the counseling profession meet the needs of a world that is moving at a break-neck speed? What is needed? Where do we go from here?

It may seem a bit silly to ask you what you think counseling will look like in the future when you are just beginning to learn what it looks like in the present. But the fresh perspective that you bring to the counseling profession makes your input and ideas extremely valuable. You are not entrenched in the "this is the way we've always done it" syndrome, and in many ways, you are more open to possibilities for the future than counselors who have been in the profession for years. As you read through this chapter, consider what trends and ideas you see that will impact the counseling profession—for better or for worse—and think about how counselors can situate themselves to best respond to these trends.

 ## Global and Societal Trends

We have identified three global trends that are fairly certain to change our world. For each trend, we will try to make some guesses about how this will affect counseling, counselors, and clients.

Speeding Up: Technology, More Work, and Stress

The future will be too much for us. There will be too much change, too many choices, too much technology, and too much work. Computer and Internet technology currently allow rapid construction and dissemination of ideas and reports. In the future, the speed of communication will increase. For example, a few years ago, a textbook like this took a year to produce after the authors finished it. Now, that has been cut to half that time because the authors' pages go electronically to the printer, and everyone else communicates faster without mailing big, fat manuscripts back and forth. Faster communication means that the *pace of life* increases, which can result in greater stress. Expectations become higher. Now co-workers seem to demand that you to return their e-mail within 24 hours—or even quicker. Because we can leave text messages and phone messages and posts on social networking sites, there is more pressure to respond. Counselors will feel the pressure to respond rapidly and briefly to clients, parents, and teachers rather than returning their calls in a day or two. The counselors of tomorrow, if they want to connect with their clients, will need to be conversant with all these technologies and be able to help clients who are dealing with the same kind of job stress.

Technophila. There is a saying that "every solution creates new problems." This is certainly true for technology. **Technophilia** is the unhealthy belief that all technology is good for you. You may know, or be, a technophile who spends too much time on the computer away from family and friends, or who answers every call, returns every text, and cannot separate work from family and leisure. Social networking sites allow us to track old flames and manage relationships with hundreds of people simultaneously. The Internet is currently creating problems in committed relationships (Peluso, 2007), just as it has created millions of hours of lost time at work. Although there are many positive aspects of technology, counselors are likely to see many of the negative aspects as well, as clients come to us after their lives and relationships have been harmed by overuse of (or addictions to) electronic devices and the Internet.

It is not just technology that is the problem. It is the fact that we can gain access to work wherever we are, day or night. Right now, Americans work more than people in almost any other country. A corollary is the overscheduling of children who now need a PDA to keep track of their afterschool lives and play dates. It is said that Americans trade the money gained by extra productivity for things that make life easier while we work (for example, eating out or having someone clean the house). Europeans, on the other hand, trade their work for leisure (for example, having less money but more time for leisure), which might be a better idea. Without leisure and time off, there can be an increasing spiral of stress and a feeling that we are not really enjoying life. In the future, career counselors will help people design ways to stop work from taking over their lives.

Connected to the net but technically alone. Recently, on our college campus, we saw a couple holding hands while both talked to other people on their cell phones. Were they together? Technology can separate people as well as bring them together. Certainly one person's love of technology can disrupt a relationship. But technology can also replace relationships of the face-to face variety. It is estimated that at any given moment, there are more than 2 million people in the United States playing a particular fantasy war game online. In such games, the creation of a pseudo-identity is *de rigueur.* Do we know what the effect of living a "second life" will be on adolescents or young adults who are not connected to other people in real-time relationships? We do know that there is a growing subculture of individuals who cannot find love relationships or face-to-face friendships and find a substitute for that in online worlds.

Overchoice. Increasing choice will also be a problem. In his book, *The Paradox of Choice* (2004), Barry Schwartz told how he went shopping for gadgets at a local electronic store. He found 45 different car stereos, 42 different computers, 27 different printers, 110 different televisions, 50 different DVD players, 20 different video cameras, and 85 different telephones. Since his writing, the number of choices has drastically increased. Buying a television and the associated buyer's remorse may not be very distressing, but increasing choices in other areas do make us more stressed when it involves changing our health care coverage, our retirement plan, or buying a house.

Even relationships have more choices. It is not just getting engaged or getting married; it involves deciding when to get married. Should we wait until we finish our degrees, get established in our careers, save enough money to buy a house? Should we live together first? Should we merge our finances? When it comes to careers, whose career should suffer if I get a job here and you get a job there? When should we have children? Counselors in the future will be more involved in helping people make romantic and unromantic relationship choices.

We have named only a couple of areas where increased choices due to technological and societal changes are confronting us. But it is not just the stress of choice that is a potential problem. The way people cope with overchoice may also become an issue. In his book, *Fear of Freedom,* Erich Fromm (1942) predicted that increasing choice and freedom leads to anxiety, and people actually seek to escape this personal freedom by accepting simple solutions, conformity, destructiveness, and authoritarian rule. Freedom and choice can create feelings of alienation and dehumanization. Thus increasing choice and freedom can lead to an increasing allure of simple-minded solutions, harkening to the good old days, and wanting Big Brother to take over. Can we help clients embrace the complexity of modern life without pretending that there are simple solutions to complex problems or worse, escaping into unhealthy ways of life such as substance abuse or extremist religion?

Health, Health Care, and Aging

There is a growing interest in health and wellness in the U.S. population. The counselor of tomorrow will need special training in physical health and wellness, because clients will likely want to work on physical health through counseling. For example, counselors must understand the symptoms of multiple sclerosis so that they can help clients deal with the psychological issues associated with chronic illness. They will need to be able to help individuals with obesity and Type II diabetes. The specialized training a counselor has in helping clients identify and maintain goals will be essential, and an understanding of medications, exercise, and treatment adherence protocols will become part of counselor training in its next transformation. Counselors will need to take care not to operate outside of their scope of practice, but they will want to assist clients in taking greater control of their own health. For example, a counselor cannot (and should not) tell clients to stop taking medication, but counselors *can* help clients develop the necessary skills and assertiveness to speak with their medical doctor about concerns they might have regarding a medication's side effects. The impact of an expanded health care reimbursement system that includes payment for prevention will positively affect counselors, because many of the interventions we are trained in, such as stress management, marriage enrichment, family counseling, parent training, and other psychoeducational procedures, are preventive treatments that will be reimbursed by third-party payers.

The counselors of tomorrow will need to be comfortable working with older people. They will need to understand and devise interventions for a graying clientele. Older people were about 12% of the population in 2000, but by 2030 they will be about 19% of the population as baby boomers will increasingly make up a larger proportion of the population (Administration on Aging, 2010). The American Counseling Association's division, Association for Adult Development and Aging, which was formed in 1986, is the counseling organization that looks at counseling issues in the adult lifespan and publishes the journal *AdultSpan.* Counseling older adults will become a more common specialty, and counselor education programs will include more training for adult issues in the curriculum.

Increasingly Diverse Society

The United States is becoming more racially diverse. Between now and 2030, the percentage of White Americans will decrease, the percentage of African Americans will increase about 1%, the percentage of Hispanics will likely grow from about 12.5% to 24%, and the percentage of Asian Americans will increase by about 200% to 8% of the population. There will also be an increase in the percentage of individuals who are of more than one race (U.S. Interim Projections by Age, Sex, Race, and Hispanic Origin, 2004). Thus, it is incumbent on the counselor of tomorrow not just to be aware of cultural differences but perhaps to be comfortable and familiar with cross-cultural communication. Although most immigrants speak English to some extent, counseling involves subtleties of language that may not be entirely possible to transcend. Therefore, it is expected that as more Spanish-speaking and Hindi-speaking students become counselors, more and more clients will want counseling in their native tongues.

Changing family. American couples and families are changing. Both are becoming more diverse. Counselor educators need to study the intricacies of family dynamics, such as the single-parent family, the role of the father in such families, and the unique characteristics of same-sex couples (Long & Young, 2007). Television is now showing us that couples come in all sizes, married, remarried, unmarried, heterosexual, and homosexual. Families are chosen, blended, adopted, or can be childless. In addition, the age at which couples are marrying, having children, and the effects of older people having children late in life are changes that will affect counselors. Older parents may have different views about childrearing, and dealing with aging parents will overtake individuals who are still attempting to raise their young children.

Religious/spiritual changes. Although there is no apparent upsurge in religious sentiment, the importance of religions and spirituality in counseling is expected to increase as counselors and their clients become more comfortable with the discussion. Americans represent the full spectrum of religions, but there is a growing group of individuals worldwide who consider themselves spiritual but not religious. In a poll conducted by *Newsweek*, 24% of respondents saw themselves this way—believing in a higher power but not in a church or organized religion (Newsweek/Beliefnet Poll, 2005). At the same time, 57% felt that spirituality was very important in their life and 27% felt it was somewhat important. With this kind of response to spirituality, the counselor of tomorrow will have to know more than a person's religion (Robertson & Young, 2011). He or she will need to investigate the importance of spirituality in the client's life and be open to the fact that the client may be a Buddhist Catholic. According to the Pew Forum (2009), research reveals that Americans' religious beliefs no longer fit into neat and traditional categories.

Many Americans are involved in several different religious practices, with 28% of respondents indicating that they attend services outside of their own faith.

 # The Experimental Prototype Counselor of Tomorrow

Walt Disney imagined a futuristic community, which has since become a theme park in Orlando, Florida. He called it EPCOT, for experimental prototype community of tomorrow. He tried to imagine what new technologies and innovations might shape human living. The flagship conference for the Association for Counselor Education and Supervision (counseling professors and supervisors) was held at EPCOT in 1983, and they took up this theme in a publication on the counselor of tomorrow. The individuals who contributed to the book, *Shaping Counselor Education Programs in the Next Five Years: An Experimental Prototype for the Counselor of Tomorrow* (Walz & Benjamin, 1983), were among the most innovative scholars and teachers in the field. They included Robert Nejedlo, Thomas Elmore, Nicholas Vacc, Larry Loesch, Gary Seiler, Glenda Isenhour, Stephen Southern, Patricia Arrendondo, and Barry Weinhold, among others. Their vision about where counseling would go was in many ways prophetic, and most of the needs they identified are still relevant. They identified:

- A need for creative leadership
- A need for a more holistic, developmental approach
- The emergence of health concerns in counseling
- The need for more research skills so that counselors can help the profession stay independent
- The need for a 60-hour master's program for mental health counselors
- The transformation of behavioral approaches into more cognitive behavioral approaches
- The emerging role of meditation and religion in counseling
- The importance of recognizing the impact of culture on the profession
- The trend toward theoretical integration
- The role of technology
- The importance of lifelong learning to combat professional obsolescence

The predictions of these counseling visionaries were made a couple of decades ago. What has changed since then? What, if any, new trends should you be thinking about as you become that future professional? What skills should you possess?

In recent years, the American Counseling Association has undertaken a project to look to the future and consider what the profession of counseling might look like in the decades ahead. In the accompanying Spotlight, "20/20 Vision for the Future of Counseling" outlines the latest thinking about how the profession can adapt to the challenges and opportunities that lie ahead.

Spotlight
The 20/20 Project

In 2005, a scheme was initiated to develop a plan for counseling in the year 2020 (Rollins, 2010). Using a Delphi method, Samuel T. Gladding, a past president of ACA, led a consensual process that yielded a written document endorsed by more than 30 counseling organizations, including the ACA divisions, the American Association of State Counseling Boards, National Board for Certified Counselors, CACREP, the Council on Rehabilitation Education, the Commission on Rehabilitation Counselor Certification, and Chi Sigma Iota. Each organization signed the following statement:

20/20: A Vision for the Future of Counseling Principles for Unifying and Strengthening the Profession

Preamble

As one of the organizations in the counseling profession, our organization supports the premise that strengthening our profession is essential. With this in mind, our organization participated in *20/20: A Vision for the Future of Counseling*. This was a representative process in which 30 counseling associations and organizations worked over a span of 3 years to identify where the counseling profession wants to be in the year 2020 and what it will take to get there.

Rationale

Professional counseling is approaching its 100th anniversary of the founding of the first counseling association. Since this time, we have become an established profession and made significant progress. As the profession expands and develops, continued attention to a unified counselor identity is important. The opportunity to establish a cohesive counseling identity leads to multiple benefits for professional counselors, including the presentation of a clearer image of professional counseling to clients, students, and the general public; and the promotion of

legislative efforts that are in the best interest of the counseling profession and the people we serve. We believe that the seven principles identified in this document constitute a beginning for developing a unifying vision and creating a long-term dialogue regarding these principles. Such a dialogue is important to identify the many approaches toward professionalism that can vary and, at the same time, are common to our profession. The following seven principles provide a foundation for unity and advancing the counseling profession as we progress toward the year 2020.

The delegates of *20/20: A Vision for the Future of Counseling* identified these principles as important in moving the profession forward.

Principles

I.   Sharing a common professional identity is critical for counselors.

II. Presenting ourselves as a unified profession has multiple benefits.

III. Working together to improve the public perception of counseling and to advocate for professional issues will strengthen the profession.

IV. Creating a portability system for licensure will benefit counselors and strengthen the counseling profession.

V.   Expanding and promoting our research base is essential to the efficacy of professional counselors and to the public perception of the profession.

VI. Focusing on students and prospective students is necessary to ensure the ongoing health of the counseling profession.

VII. Promoting client welfare and advocating for the populations we serve is a primary focus of the counseling profession.

Source: Reprinted with permission of the American Counseling Association.

FIGURE 14.1 The Counselor of Tomorrow

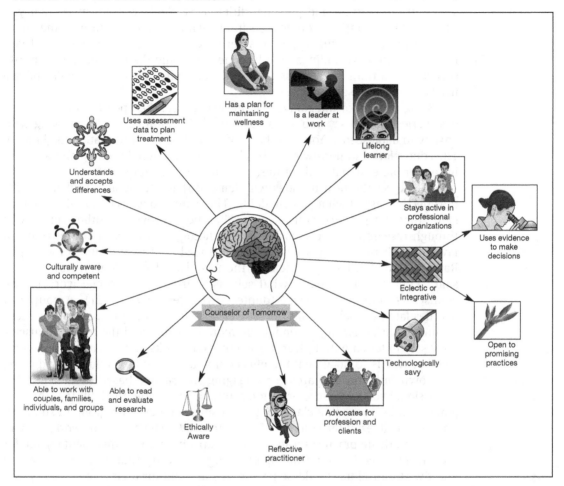

The future counselor we envision has 14 qualities needed to adapt to a new age and develop a professional identity (see Figure 14.1). That may seem to be a lot of areas of skills and knowledge, but, as a beginning counseling student, you are not expected to master them at this juncture. They represent areas of professional and personal development that you will work on throughout your career and that will form an outline for your portfolio of lifelong learning. The counselor of tomorrow will have the qualities we discuss in the following sections.

Eclectic or Integrative

We think that the counselor of tomorrow must be open to new discoveries as research confirms new techniques and also fails to support some older, more traditional approaches. Only an eclectic or integrative approach that can accommodate new thinking is compatible with a scientific perspective and sensitivity to cultural and personal differences. That does not mean that you cannot adopt a major theoretical position such as Adlerian, but you, the counselor of tomorrow, will find that Adlerian counseling has evolved, and you must integrate new findings with basic tenets of the theory. Theoretical purity seems to be a thing of the past as we recognize effective new methods and the needs of our diverse clientele.

Being eclectic or integrative also means you can be open to new ideas and discoveries. Let us say you are a cognitive behavioral counselor working with anxiety in adolescents. You find that biofeedback-assisted relaxation might help. The counselor of tomorrow must be able to get additional training and add it to his or her professional skills or miss potential benefits for clients.

We expect the next decades will demand that you be able to demonstrate the effectiveness of what you are doing. There are two ways to do this. One is to show that the practice you are using has been proven in other settings or through research. The profession of psychology has taken a strong stand in favor of their practitioners relying on evidence-based treatments. For example, Raymond Fowler, past president of the American Psychological Association, said, "Our scientific base is what sets us apart from the social workers, the counselors, and the Gypsies" (quoted in Dawes, 1994, p. 21). A couple of decades later, we believe that Fowler would have a hard time making this accusation stick. Counseling is conducting more research, and the future counselor must stay in touch with it, learning about what works and what does not work. Another way is to document the effects of your own interventions (conducting your own outcome research, or engaging in practice-based evidence). The professional school counselor of tomorrow must be able to show that the programs within a school, a classroom, for a single student or a group of students, improve the lives of the students (Dimmittt, 2009). The counselor working in an agency or private practice setting who sets up a program or treatment regime for a client must collect data on client change to verify that he or she is being effective. Counselors should be prepared to account for their cost efficiency and their treatment effectiveness (Thomason, 2010). That means counselors ought to be better prepared to work with client data and present it in an understandable fashion.

Culturally Aware and Competent

We have suggested that counselors should have appropriate skills, knowledge, and attitudes that increase our ability to work with clients from a variety of cultures. The counselor of tomorrow is much more likely to be Hispanic or represent more than one race. Our clients will be more diverse, too. In tomorrow's world, counselors must be willing to cross social/class boundaries and recognize the needs of those who are economically disadvantaged.

But it is often difficult for counselors to cross racial and cultural boundaries and get the knowledge and skills that they need to function in a competent way.

Although we may have good intentions, it is unlikely that we will find the time to have cross-cultural and immersion experiences unless we make it a priority. A counselor's best source of training is working with clients who are culturally or socially different from themselves, taking a tutorial stance, and learning from them. That is why you owe it to yourself to insist on seeing a wide variety of clients in your practicum and internship experience. Seeking an experience where everyone is culturally similar to you may seem more comfortable, but a more diverse experience will simply make you a more competent counselor. In addition, attending conferences where cultural aspects of counseling are addressed is an easy way to gain information and skills.

Understanding and Accepting of Differences

While talking about cultural and class differences, we suggested that you embrace experiences that put you in touch with people who are different. But besides culture, clients can be different in so many other ways. The most important of these differences have to do with personality, religion, and family background, which often are not covered under the umbrella of multiculturalism. Here are three tips to keep you aware of the importance of recognizing and accepting differences: (1) Take personality tests and compare your results with people you know. You will begin to appreciate the diversity of psychological traits and types that affect how people see the world. (2) Record your own history of your life within your family of origin. Trace the rules and roles you grew up with. Now take a look at the same data from someone you know. Can you see how the family messages affected each of you? (3) Learn about other religions and about denominations in your own faith. Religion and spirituality affect a client's worldview, and finding a sensitive way to understand a client's spiritual background and yearnings is critical to understanding the whole person.

A Leader at Work

Counselors have special training in the right thing to do (ethics) and what is most effective (interventions). Therefore, we have a duty to stand up for these ideals and for what we know in the workplace. That is one form of leadership. Maybe you have not thought of yourself as a leader, but there are many avenues for leadership. Leadership sometimes means going against the grain of what is popular or easy and instead following ethical and legal guidelines. Sometimes it is persuading the powers that be to adopt more effective counseling programs. For a counselor, leadership at work means knowing what is best because of training and research, not just following the rules. The school counselor of the past was a quasi-administrator who took his or her ideas about

---

■■■ *Words of Wisdom* ■■■

"I believe that there are some clients who become a part of me, just as much as the work I do with them becomes a part of them."

—April C., internship student in clinical mental health counseling

what the job should be from the principal. These counselors often did jobs that an untrained clerk could handle, even though they possessed master's degrees. In many situations, that may still seem like a good way to enhance one's career. Today, however, professional school counselors see themselves as highly trained professionals who create new systems rather than react to the job as other people see it. They should set the mental health agendas for the schools, lead efforts to prevent problems like bullying, demand supervision by seasoned counselors, have special training in crisis intervention and suicide, and understand emotional barriers to school achievement. All of these are leadership functions.

All counselors who work in agency settings such as mental health counselors, marriage and family counselors, and rehabilitation counselors must similarly become proactive in identifying unhealthy work situations, such as too many clients, too little time to deal with emergencies, and inadequate supervision (Young & Lambie, 2007). Leadership for the counselor working in an agency means knowing what your training says and comparing this to the way counseling is actually practiced. For example, some new professionals have reported questionable billing practices, and others have found therapists who make clients dependent upon them or who use clients sexually. The professional counselor is sometimes an "army of one" who must speak up, regardless of consequences, especially when clients are being harmed.

A Lifelong Learner

One of the things you face as a counselor at all phases of your career is the fact that you cannot know everything you need to know. The diversity of client problems and their myriad background issues make it impossible to be completely conversant with the full range of client backgrounds and disorders, from eating disorders in children to counseling low-income couples. Lifelong learning is the only answer because, while it would be nice to be able to choose your specialty, sometimes it is prescribed by the clients you see. For example, even if you choose to be a career counselor, you need to recognize (and refer) a client who has significant pathology that is interfering with the ability to hold down a job.

Getting advanced training beyond your formal degree is a good way to improve your skills, especially if you are in a specialized setting such as a substance abuse treatment center. Of course, you can still take university classes in areas you want to explore. Another way people do this is to get "certified" by some organization. A few of these credentials are recognized as requiring lengthy and exacting training such as AAMFT (American Association for Marriage & Family Therapy) Approved Supervisor. Some certifications, however, are money-making ventures for a private institute that require little training beyond sending a check. For example, online you can find individuals who hold themselves out as a

"Nationally Certified Body/Mind Therapist." The home study certification costs $295.00. Although it is legal to put these somewhat bogus letters after your name, it may not be ethical. The ACA code of ethics prohibits us from misleading others about our credentials.

One of the best ways to get advanced training is to attend conferences in an area where you are considering getting training. Different conferences are for different counselors and for different stages of life. As you become interested in a particular area, you find out that there is a specific convention for spirituality in counseling, play therapy, biofeedback, psychodrama, brief therapy, and even a creativity conference. The people you meet at conferences can be sources of information and learning for you. At the American Counseling Association convention, attend a Learning Institute for a day or half-day to get a handle on how to work with couples, help clients with grief, conduct play therapy, assess domestic violence, develop a private practice, use mindfulness, or increase your skills in the DSM. These initial experiences can lead you to more intensive training once you find out what resources are available and which ones are legitimate. In this chapter's Informed by Research feature, you will read about how your professional identity might change and grow over the course of the profession. Notice, however, that these changes don't just happen—you need to make a concerted effort to engage in lifelong learning.

Technologically Competent

The technologies that every counselor should be able to master are e-mail, online library searches, and programs that let you organize and analyze data and make charts and graphs. Counselors will need to have smart phones, because more and more mental health applications will be available. Since the turn of the 21st century, counselor education programs have been increasing their use of distance-based education. Wantz et al. (2003) found 42% of CACREP programs incorporated online learning. Podcasts, video conferencing, and hybrid instruction with some typical classroom instruction blended with online assignments are increasingly popular. The ability to learn online and master the associated technologies will be important in continuing education.

Besides technology that assists counselors in their jobs and in their continuing education, more client applications are becoming popular. Right now, computer programs and home biofeedback devices are available that help clients monitor stress. Self-help programs have also been developed for dealing with psychological problems such as fear of public speaking. Clients can go online each day to chart their symptoms or thoughts and print out reports to share with their counselors or doctors. These technologies allow clients to become more involved with their own treatment, but some technologies can lead clients to believe that assistance from a counselor is no longer necessary. Helping clients navigate the technologies and what they can, and should, do on their own will be an important skill for counselors of tomorrow. In this chapter's Counseling Controversy, we consider the role that technology might play in the counseling

Informed by Research
How Your Professional Identity Grows: A Qualitative Study

Remley and Herlihy (2007) identified six elements that they believed are the core set of knowledge and beliefs that comprise a counselor's professional identity. They include (1) knowledge of the history of counseling; (2) the philosophical underpinnings of the profession; (3) the roles, jobs, and functions of counselors; (4) professional ethics; (5) professional pride; and (6) professional engagement. Can you see that knowledge is part of professional identity, but so is feeling that you are a part of the profession? But how does one actually acquire these qualities? Does it begin during university training?

In 2010, Donna Gibson and Collette Dollarhide, counselor educators, and Julie Moss, a doctoral student, published an article entitled "Professional Identity Development: A Grounded Theory of Transformational Tasks of New Counselors." They conducted 7 focus groups, each of which contained 4–7 students ($n = 43$). A focus group is a recorded discussion of interested individuals on a particular topic. Focus groups have been used in marketing research for many years. Focus group participants in that case would be potential consumers of a product. In the present study, the focus groups consisted of master's degree students at four different phases: (1) before they took courses in the program; (2) before practicum; (3) before internship; and (4) at graduation. The authors asked them 11 questions about their professional identity and recorded their group discussions on audiotape. Based on their reading of the transcripts, the researchers identified three developmental tasks that must be accomplished in order to transform one's identity to that of professional counselor.

The first task they identified was termed "Definition of Counseling." Students' definition of counseling changed as they progressed through their program. Instead of just repeating the definition of authorities, students were able to give personal, internalized views. Task number two was labeled "Responsibility for Professional Growth." Students evolved beyond their original idea that professional growth comes primarily through training by teachers, supervisors, and even professional organizations. As they moved along, they recognized that motivation for growth comes from inside, and they more fully accepted the ideal of becoming a lifelong learner.

The third task is called "Transformation to Systemic Identity." This referred to how the students defined their own identity as a counselor. Students who were just beginning their training talked about certification, job title, and licensure as indicators of their professional identity. Students who were further along in the process saw their identity forming from skills, knowledge, and a relationship with a community of professionals.

In summary, the authors confirmed their hypothesis that new professionals initially rely on authorities and experts for knowledge. In a second phase, they focus on professional and counseling skills and look to supervisors in practicum and work settings. Finally, they develop a more internally focused locus of authority and began to self-evaluate. That is when professional identity crystallizes. An implication for students is that the confusion about professional identity is normal. It is a developmental process that can be accelerated by integrating the views of experts with one's own experiences later on in training. One thought for counselor educators is that they can help facilitate professional identity by focusing on these three developmental tasks in the curriculum by getting counselors in training to personally respond to what they are learning. The authors also recommend allowing students to work with clients earlier in their training to accelerate the transformation process.

Counseling Controversy

SHOULD COUNSELORS PRACTICE TECHNOLOGY-ASSISTED COUNSELING (COUNSELING WHEN THE CLIENT IS NOT PHYSICALLY PRESENT)?

Background: As you read this, a counselor is conducting a group session via the Internet. A client in a wheelchair in a remote part of New Mexico is using Skype to talk to her counselor because she is 150 miles from the nearest town and has difficulty with transportation. Right now, a counselor on a hotline is talking on the phone with a client who is thinking about suicide. In a counseling clinic, a counselor is putting an inventory of current symptoms on a computer that will calculate the client's score and track progress over time. At home, a client who wants to improve his mood is using "Gratitude Rock" on his smart phone to identify things in his life that are going well. Another client is searching for online support groups for her bipolar disorder. In an alternative school, a high school student does all of his assignments online and then consults his school counselor by e-mail.

It is said that the when the printing press was first invented, it met with equal parts excitement and resistance (Einstein, 1983). Similarly, there is caution and optimism in abundance as we look at the role of technology in counseling. There are reasons to be excited and pitfalls to be concerned about (Goss & Anthony, 2009). But like the printing press, technology cannot be stopped, and counselors must be able to recognize good and bad uses. Technology will continue to play a larger role in counseling because it will become the way that we communicate most, not just with friends and family, but with our doctors, vendors, and colleagues. In addition, technology will have a special impact on counseling because of one fundamental fact: Technology can overcome distance.

Counselors have a rule of thumb that if a client lives more than 30 minutes away, he or she will have trouble showing up for the sessions. Without special reminders, clients do not show up in mental health agencies more than 40% of the time (Swenson & Pekarik, 1988). Major reasons for nonattendance are car problems, money for gas, and the time needed to get there. Technology can instantly connect people in a counseling relationship, including those who may be unable or unwilling to travel to see the counselor. There are still remote corners of the United States and even more around the world where face-to-face counseling is simply not feasible.

No matter how good technology becomes and we get high definition and 3-D pictures of the person we are talking to, it is not the same as being there. According to Woody Allen, 80% of success is showing up. This idea is important in the present discussion. Counseling is valued because both people have taken the time and effort to make the meeting happen. Being there in reality is more of a commitment than turning on the computer. The counseling hour becomes important because we have set it aside and excluded the rest of the world.

Keeping this caveat in mind, at the present time, there does seem to be some support for counseling that includes technology such as telephone conversation and therapeutic writing over the Internet (Day & Schneider, 2002). Studies involving online counseling have not been large scale, and few have used random assignment and control groups (randomized control trial) (see Bee, Bower, Lovell,

(continued)

(Continued)

Gilbody, Richards, Gask, & Roach, 2008), yet they have not found a definite advantage for face-to-face counseling. Consider the following points and counterpoints in this controversy.

POINT: TECHNOLOGY-ASSISTED COUNSELING IS THE WAVE OF THE FUTURE	COUNTERPOINT: TECHNOLOGY-ASSISTED COUNSELING SHOULD NOT BE TAUGHT OR PRACTICED
• Technology-assisted practice has been going on for as long as we have had the pen and clients and counselors could write. The telephone and Internet are extensions of communication technology but are only advanced means for connecting client and counselor.	• Previously, technology was an adjunct to counseling, but now it is possible to conduct sessions remotely. The counseling relationship will not be as powerful if we are not physically close to clients.
• Technology allows us to do other counseling practices that were not feasible before. We can alert clients with electronic reminders, cue them to practice, and monitor their progress online. We can send messages via e-mail or text any time of day or night.	• Counseling will lose its special quality in which each member is taking the time to make the meeting happen.
• Clients with disabilities, financial problems, and other barriers caused by distance will still be able to obtain counseling.	• Will the counselor be able to assess suicide risk from seeing the client online? The camera cannot smell alcohol on the client's breath or touch the client on the arm to provide reassurance.
• Potentially client costs can be reduced if a counselor's business is entirely online and he or she does not have to maintain an office.	• Online counseling will be a lonely business for the counselor who sits at home and is deprived of contact with colleagues.
• Some ethical and legal problems will be reduced when a client does not come to an office or is not physically present.	• Counseling sessions that take place remotely on cellular phones, e-mail, and Internet may not be secure from hacking. Clients may record sessions and family members may overhear the conversations.
• Online counseling allows clients to get help when they need it rather than at prearranged times.	• Much of the online counseling is charged by the minute (around $2.00/minute = $120/hour). That could be unethical if clients are not aware of the total amount of their charges before they receive counseling.

Questions to Consider

- What sort of training should a counselor receive in order to competently conduct sessions from a remote location?
- Will the therapeutic relationship be limited by the technology we use?

- Is there an opportunity to exploit clients who pay by the minute?
- What other ethical issues are unique to technologically mediated counseling?

As with most controversies, there probably is truth to both sides of this argument.

◄───►

Technology has important role   **There is no place for**
in counseling   **technology in counseling**

On the continuum, place an "X" where you think you stand on this issue.

process. As you read through the controversy, think about whether you believe counseling is something that can be done entirely, or in part, through the use of technological devices.

Hand-held devices. Hand-held computers such as the iPod Touch or smart phones of all varieties have the most potential for helping both clients and counselors and increasing our ability to provide evidence of our effectiveness (Cucciare & Weingardt, 2010). A hand-held device can deliver reminders and monitor exercise and diet with great efficiency. A recent study showed that hand-held devices can be just as effective for monitoring clients struggling with obesity as the usual group treatment (McDonielab, Wolskeeb, & Shenb, 2010). A smart phone allows access to the Internet from anywhere, giving you information that you or the client may need. Imagine being able to give clients an entrée into a support group that they can access from their own pocket. Smart phones can help clients track homework or moods, and even act as a pedometer or other health monitor. What if we could record a person's social interactions via the smart phones and help socially isolated clients increase the quantity and quality of their relationships? There are clearly many exciting uses for this technology on the horizon.

Video. Another technological arena relevant to counselors and clients is the improved quality and availability of video. Video can, of course, be used in training and supervision, and it is now cheap enough for most counseling clinics and even private offices to record and store video. Although having accurate records of counseling sessions might help with legal issues, it could also help the counselor keep on top of his or her own game by being a source of self-supervision. If the counselor reviews only a small portion of last week's video as preparation, he or she may be better prepared for this week. Live video using smart phones is now a reality, and it becomes possible for supervisors to look in on a counselor's session whenever they wish.

But the use of video goes far beyond supervision or self-evaluation. Video will soon be used to help clients learn skills and evaluate their performance. Video games will be developed with therapeutic themes, and counselors and clients will interact with each other (Ceranoglu, 2010). Video will be used to help clients learn materials for psychoeducational purposes, and it will be delivered over the Internet. For example, video can be utilized to present models of successful behavioral sequences for children and adolescents (see Carr & Fox, 2009; Sansosti & Powell-Smith, 2008). Counselors will soon begin to learn how to use video in their counseling sessions as feedback for clients (Polfai, 2007). Video allows us to get very specific feedback on our performance, just as group counseling can provide feedback on social interactions. Couples can see exactly how they fight unproductively; clients with social anxiety can learn to interact better and with less fear (Parr & Cartwright-Hatton, 2009).

Planful and Intentional in Maintaining Personal Wellness

Counseling can be stressful, and the threat of burnout and vicarious traumatization are real. Burnout makes you see clients as objects and is intensified by hostility and fatigue. Vicarious traumatization can occur to any counselor but especially those who work with physically and sexually abused people. It is not always easy to shake off the stories you hear. In order to be fully present for the next client, the counselor of tomorrow must have a good life on the outside, one that provides positive emotions, emotional security, peace, and fun. Unfortunately, this good life doesn't just happen. We must develop a plan for exercise, fun, time with significant others for social support, relaxation, and spiritual renewal. If you were living with an Olympic athlete, you would expect him or her to have a rather rigid schedule of self-care. Perhaps we need to educate our own significant others about our own limits. Just like an athlete facing an upcoming marathon, we must also have a schedule of self-care that involves taking the time for emotional and physical self-care. Lack of sleep, junk food, and emotional emergencies can affect your work. Self-neglect is not an option for long.

In Chapter 13, we discussed methods counselors can use to develop their own personal wellness plans.

In addition to a plan, a counselor needs a bag of tricks to use at work in order to brush off the negative feelings from the last client and be able to go on to the next. Among these tricks is taking the time to go to lunch with colleagues or just going outside for five minutes. Small breaks like this slow down the pace of life. Learning to enjoy what is happening in the present rather than focusing on mistakes and worries is something we try to teach clients, and we need to focus on it in our work life, too.

Able to Read and Evaluate Research

The counselor of tomorrow must have a strong understanding of research (there is more about how to read and evaluate research in Chapter 7 of this book). When you read a research study that promises to help you in your work, ask yourself the following questions:

- **"Was the study properly designed and carried out?"**   To be a good consumer of research, you should be able to identify a bad study. For example, we saw the published results of a survey that was sent out to supervisors in mental health agencies. They were to copy the survey and administer it to their supervisees. Some of the supervisors sent back surveys; others did not. The researcher did not know who had and who had not responded. It was unclear at the end where the 50 participants came from. In fact, they may have come from a single agency.

- **"How many people participated in the study?"**   The answer about how many subjects make a good study depends on what kind of research you are doing. In general, for quantitative research studies, the more the better, although this is not always the case. Researchers use a formula to identify how many subjects they need before they can boast that their treatment is effective. Still, qualitative studies may utilize only a few subjects but examine their responses in detail. As we will see below, even having a lot of subjects cannot overcome the problem of where you got them.

- **"Who were the subjects?"**   An article in *Self* magazine (Pawlik-Kielen, 2008) has drawn fire because of the fact that the more than 4,000 respondents were readers of the magazine and not the general public. About 75% of the respondents reported eating patterns that could be considered eating disorders (like bulimia). Although the partner researchers tried to explain that these results did not necessarily reflect the general public, the article was written in such a way that makes it seem that most women have these problems. In fact, we can be pretty sure that the people who read a magazine that focuses on beauty were more concerned with dieting and losing weight than the general public.

- **"Who conducted the research and who paid for it?"**   This is the problem with online and social networking site research because the studies may be paid for by advertisers. Yet we recently saw a published journal article about a counseling organization that was sponsored by the organization itself. Guess what? It found that the organization made a difference in people's lives. The companies and individuals who conduct these surveys have something they want to sell or may not allow the publication of findings if they are not flattering.

- **"Where was the research published?**   Was it *Self* magazine or the *Journal of Mental Health Counseling*? Before you believe what you see online about the next great counseling technique, read an article from a respected journal to see whether there is any research behind it. If there is no review of previous research or if the article presents no original research, even if it comes from a worthy source, it may be biased or represent the authors' viewpoints rather than being a scientific look at the effectiveness of a technique.

Active in Professional Organizations

As a student, you might begin to find the benefits of professional groups through Chi Sigma Iota, the counseling honor society, or other student organizations. Leadership and involvement in groups like these prepare you for later work at the local, state, or national level. Why get involved in these groups? Your job may depend upon it. The fact that counselors are now licensed in every state is due to the grassroots work of counselors who knew that opportunities were being denied by legislatures, school systems, and other professional groups. When licensure laws were passed and amended, the real heroes were counselors who went to the state capital, year after year, to testify and lobby for access. It is because of them that counselors are gaining access to the Veterans Administration, Medicare, Tri-Care, and other career options that have been jealously guarded by other professions. Counselors, through their professional organizations, sponsor days on Capitol Hill or in the state capitol to meet with legislatures. Through these events, the ability to use psychological testing instruments, to fund rehabilitation counseling, the ability to get reimbursed by third-party payers, and requiring school systems to hire more counselors have all been achieved.

Besides advocating for counselors, professional groups can provide you two other crucial benefits. First, conferences, both small and large, keep you on the cutting edge and can protect you from burnout. Second, professional groups also have the power to support you. Going to a conference and seeing the universal things we all face helps us recognize that we are not alone and that there are solutions that others have discovered.

■■■ *Words of Wisdom* ■■■

"Never doubt that a small group of thoughtful, concerned citizens can change the world. Indeed, it's the only thing that ever has."

—Margaret Mead

Able to Work with Couples, Families, Individuals, and Groups

Some beginning counselors reject working with groups, couples, or families, feeling sure that they will only see individuals. Then, the first day on the job, they ask you to run a group with families. That is why being widely trained is critical. We cannot be sure what we are going to run into on the job or what we are going to love. We frequently hear beginning counselors say, "I don't think I would like working with middle schoolers," and later hear the exact opposite when the opportunity to work with that age group arises. One area receiving increasing emphasis is working with couples and families, even in the school system.

CACREP training programs do not currently require students to take courses in marriage, couples, and family counseling unless they are in marriage, couples, and family counseling programs. Yet, now and in the future, counselors need to know how to deal with these modalities because couples and family work is now expanding to prisons, the military, and hospices (Doherty & McDaniel, 2010). The school counselor will be dealing with parents and may even run groups for parenting skills. The rehabilitation counselor should know how a family can support a client with a disability. Without a doubt, substance abuse counselors will help their clients' recovery if they know how to conduct family counseling sessions. Even if you are a college counselor and you think you will only be dealing with individuals, college students have relationship issues as well as separation issues from their families of origin.

An Advocate for Clients and the Profession

Counseling's history began in the oppressive conditions of the industrial revolution. It was built on a foundation of societal change, and a thread of that reformer's spirit has remained. Today, there is a movement within the profession to have counselors become more trained in advocacy (Ratts, Toporek, & Lewis, 2010). Advocacy for the counselor means trying to influence political, economic, and social institutions to become more just and more accessible to the needs of all people (cf. Cohen, Vega, & Watson, 2001). Articles on advocacy are appearing in the full range of counseling journals from employment counseling (Chope, 2010) to school counseling (Schaeffer, Akos, & Barrow, 2010). Many believe that advocacy is a crucial skill needed to combat oppression (Holcomb-McCoy & Bryan, 2010). Advocacy can be as simple as helping a client obtain health care reimbursement when unfairly denied or supporting a high school student who has been unfairly victimized by other students.

Advocacy also means being proud of the profession and becoming involved in local, state and national issues and organizations that represent and support counseling. That may mean trying to persuade school administration to offer supervision for school counselors at the system or county level. It may mean going to the state capital to speak in favor of legislation, visiting a legislator, or writing a letter. Professional advocacy opportunities become available when you join listserves or get a newsletter from your professional organization.

A Reflective Practitioner

A reflective practitioner is one who consciously thinks about and evaluates his or her own professional actions and theories and improves his or her practice based on this reflection (Schon, 1987). The idea of a reflective practitioner envisions the learner as an active and engaged participant, not a passive receiver of knowledge (Nelson & Neufeldt, 1998). One of the simplest and most effective ways to begin becoming reflective is to keep a journal where you reflect on what you have learned, your reaction to it based on previous learning, your conscience, prejudices, and feelings (Collins, Arthur, & Wong-Wylie, 2010; Wright, 2005). In this text, we have asked you to keep a journal about your reactions to the material, but every course may not be structured in that way. So, you can continue your journal in other classes, keeping track of your major learning points, growth, and your reactions to the material. If you do, it will help you analyze your resistance to and acceptance of the material you are exposed to. It may help you understand yourself better and help you apply what you are learning when you encounter real-life situations with your first clients in practicum and internship.

Ethically Aware

The problem with a course in ethics is that students tend to memorize ethical standards but may not have the ability to use them as guidelines rather than rules. Ethical guidelines are tools that you use to judge possible courses of action, not commandments. A professional is not a rule follower but must act as a reflective practitioner where ethical guidelines are concerned. The reason is that real problems are too complex to be instantly solved by rules (Tennyson & Strom, 1986). Guidelines are there to help the professional make difficult decisions, not make the right decisions (often because there may not be one right decision, only a best decision). So, beyond learning the ethical guidelines, the counselor of the future must be able to do two other things: (1) reflect, and (2) consult.

Both reflection and gaining knowledge help you grow as a counselor. These activities help you become more cognitively complex as you struggle with ethical dilemmas, real-life situations, and ethical guidelines (Lambie, Hagedorn, & Ieva, 2010). That means you do not spit out simple responses that reflect a right/wrong orientation. You begin to see ethical dilemmas in their full complexity, and you are able to construct solutions that take into account the differences in each situation.

In addition, being ethically aware means that you find that you do not have to react immediately and make snap decisions in most cases. You can take the time to formulate a plan by reflecting with someone about possible alternatives. We call this kind of reflection "supervision." Supervision is the counselor's secret weapon against clinical, ethical, and legal mistakes. As we point out this ongoing need for supervision, we are also aware that ethical issues arise more for school counselors than for those who work in other settings (Remley & Herlihy, 2007), and yet it is the environment in which supervision by a fellow professional is the hardest to obtain.

Able to Use Assessment Data to Plan Intervention and Treatment

At this point in history, many counselors are not trained at the master's level to conduct full-scale psychological assessment batteries. We are taking the point of view that counselors, now and in the future, must be more involved in assessment, especially in the area of risk for suicide and violence (Moran, Sweda, Fragala, & Sasscer-Burgos, 2001) and for monitoring client progress (Young, 2009).

We have advocated for counselors to utilize assessment methods, both formal and informal, to prove to themselves and to others that counseling is working. For both children and adult, brief measures such as the OQ.45 and the YOQ can be given throughout treatment to gauge overall psychological distress in adults and children. Other measures such as the Beck Depression Inventory can be used to identify specific symptoms. In addition, counselors need to keep track of improvement in grades, or of behavior changes as measured by parent and teacher observations. Marriage and family counselors should be able to use observation techniques to identify healthy and unhealthy communication patterns. In short, the future will probably involve more use and more training in assessment if individual counselors and the profession as a whole seek to justify its effectiveness.

In the Crystal Ball

While focusing on proven and promising practices, it is also useful to keep our eyes on the horizon. It is time to go out on a limb and suggest some areas that may emerge in the counselor education program of the future.

The Rise of Ecotherapy

Eco-counseling is a term that has been used by some to talk about family ecology or the relationship between components of a family system (Huber, 1994), and used quite differently by others who want to use counseling expertise to solve environmental problems (Howard, 1993). But *ecotherapy* is something else. In the future, nature will be used, to a much greater degree, as an adjunct to counseling. Many of us are familiar with Outward Bound and other adventure-based counseling programs or wilderness therapy, which pose physical and interpersonal challenges in a natural setting as a therapeutic process (Hill, 2007; Swank & Daire, 2010). That trend will almost certainly continue and expand. The next phase will involve utilizing the wonder, awe, and natural healing qualities of nature rather than just physical/emotional challenge and the development of teamwork skills (Chalquist, 2009). People will spend extended periods in natural locations as a form of therapy. One of the first articles on ecotherapy in the counseling literature appeared in 2004 (Davis & Atkins, 2004, 2009). For more information, see Sackett (2010), who discusses its potential salutary effects on youth.

The Mainstreaming of Japanese Therapies, Meditation, Yoga, and Eastern Perspectives

Japanese therapies are old news in counseling. Morita therapy has been around for some time (see Ishiyama, 1990). Other therapies such as seiza, shadan, and naikan therapy share a similar contemplative approach. They have been labeled the "Quiet Therapies" (Reynolds, 1980) because most involve periods of isolation and reflection, but their primary goal is to spur client action in the face of inaction. Despite the fact that we have become more aware of these therapies (Young & Hutchinson, in press), they have proven difficult to adapt to the Western audience. In the future, that will be less difficult, especially if current research studies confirm their effectiveness. After all, Americans have learned to like sushi.

The prevalence of hatha yoga (the yoga of physical exercises) and an upsurge in meditation are likely to influence counselor practice and theory (Schure, Christopher, & Christopher, 2008; Young, de Armas, & Cunningham, in press). For example, mindfulness has become a buzzword in new approaches to counseling. Mindfulness is a form of meditation in which one keeps attention focused on here and now actions and thoughts. Jon Kabat-Zinn pioneered medical uses of mindfulness in his system, Mindfulness-Based Stress Reduction (which integrates hatha yoga) (Kabat-Zinn, 2003). In the future, therapies that include meditation and mindfulness will increase just as acceptance and commitment therapy, dialectical behavior therapy, and mindfulness-based cognitive therapy are now on the wax (Didonna, 2009).

Increasing Problems with Process Addictions

According to the National Institute of Drug Abuse (2009), marijuana use has leveled off with about 11% of 8th graders, 24% of 10th graders, and 32% of 12th graders reporting use in the last year. These kinds of statistics are alarming, but alcohol remains our most significant drug problem, with millions of Americans in need of treatment and thousands of alcohol-related deaths. On the other hand, in recent years, we have become more aware of *process addictions* or addictions that do not involve a substance but are the result of repetitively engaging in a particular process such as watching Internet pornography, playing a video game, gambling, spending money, and even working too much. They become addictions when they cause disruption in the person's career, finances, and relationships (the same kinds of things that happen with substance addictions). Counselors will need more training in this aspect of addictions.

The Death of Counseling Theories

Beginning in the 1980s counselors and therapists of every ilk showed less allegiance to a particular school of thought compared to earlier decades. The most recent studies have shown that more than 75% of counselors are eclectic or integrative, and tomorrow, that is very likely to increase (Norcross, Hedges, & Prochaska, 2002; Young & Feiler, 1994). Because counselors will want to utilize therapies that have been proven, trainees and experienced counselors will be less likely to accept the premise that one technique or one school of thought is good for everything. It is quite likely that behaviorists and cognitive behaviorists will do more research than anyone else and this will raise the profiles of these methods. Yet we should remember that everything has not been researched. For example, in recent years, the emergence of positive psychology has revealed that research can confirm the effectiveness of a wide variety of neglected techniques including gratitude, hope, and forgiveness (see Lopez & Snyder, 2009). We predict counselors will find ways to organize their treatments using the best of what is available while considering the individual personality, culture, and preferences of the client. Counseling will become more individualized and less driven by theory. Another force that drives this change is the move toward evidence-based treatments, which in the future may not allow a counselor to use his or her favorite theory but may require the counselor (in order to receive third-party reimbursement) to choose treatments from a list.

A Focus on Health, Wellness, Complementary and Alternative Medicine, and Using Discoveries in Neuroscience

The use of complementary and alternative medicines (CAMs) has increased in all areas of medicine, and clients who want to improve their mental health will utilize more of these treatments (Lake & Spiegel, 2007; Micozzi, 2011). Evidence of its growing popularity includes the fact that the federal government has increased its budget to the National Center for Complementary and Alternative Medicine (http://nccam.nih.gov), and Medicare now has codes for preventive health interventions. We can expect that treatments such as acupuncture, homeopathy, osteopathy, chiropractic medicine, yoga, meditation, massage, and others will gain status as evidence-based treatments for mental disorders.

For good or ill, psychopharmaceuticals will become more popular. Drugs will become more specific. Counselors need to understand chemotherapy so that they can alert the supervising physician about the good and bad effects they see. Counselors need to obtain training in basic neuroanatomy if they are to be ready for the next set of biomedical interventions. Just as counselors now use biofeedback devices to identify times when clients are emotionally aroused and when they relax, in the future, feedback from noninvasive scanning technology may allow us to see into clients' brains. Right now biological bases of behavior are largely ignored in counselor education. The counselor of the future must find a way to get training to stay current with medications, CAMs, and health and wellness promotion innovations.

■■■ *Fast Facts* ■■■

In 2007, more than one-third of American adults engaged in complementary and alternative medicines (CAMs) at a cost of more than $34 billion. Some of the most common types of CAMs include chiropractic care, homeopathy (highly diluted drugs made from natural ingredients), acupuncture, and massage therapy.

Source: Barnes, P. M., Bloom, B., & Nahin, R. (2008, December). *CDC National Health Statistics Report #12. Complementary and alternative medicine use among adults and children: United States, 2007.* Downloaded from http://nccam.nih.gov/news/camstats.htm.

Neuroscience has been producing data that is informing counseling. Many of these findings do not have immediate application but are intriguing nonetheless. For example, it turns out the brain changes as it adapts to new experiences and their associated emotions. The brain is adapting to its environment throughout life, not just in childhood. This is sometimes called *neuroplasticity* (Grawe, 2007). Neuroplasticity is merely a buzzword today, but in the future it may be important as we see the ways that the brain changes due to psychotherapy or due to stressful experiences. In the future, we may be able to track brain changes as they react to therapeutic intervention. We may be able to determine how effective a method is by its neurological effects, and we may be able to strengthen weak areas of brain function with psychotherapeutic techniques.

Findings in neuroscience are also expected to have an effect on counseling because of an understanding of "high road" and "low road"—two pathways in which the brain is activated. High-road responses are thoughtful; the low road (limbic response) is quicker, more intuitive, and probably built to protect us from danger. With a low-road response, we can react quickly to a snake in the woods, but the low-road response may not be helpful in human relationships if we react emotionally and irrationally (Fishbane, 2007). Gottman (1999) has discovered that many couples' communication problems are caused when one member is flooded with negative emotions (such as anger) that keeps him or her from connecting verbally. Couples are now being taught to self-soothe and not to activate the other person's emotions so that communication can take place on the high road. On the other hand, Daniel Goleman (2006) points out that attachment and empathy are dependent on low-road responses. Counselors have to "get out of their heads" when they wish to understand another person's emotions. Emotions can help us in our decision making, too. Gut feelings are important information that we need to consider.

The Use of Virtual Reality to Train Counselors and Help Clients Practice

The concept called *transfer of learning* suggests that situations that are more similar to the actual situation you face will allow you to transfer your training to the real situation more easily and completely. Right now, programs are being developed that allow clients to slowly approach feared objects—exposure therapy. Thus, the client who is afraid of spiders, for example, will be able to hear someone say "spider" until he or she is comfortable with that. Later the client will put on special glasses and encounter virtual spiders before trying to face them in real life. Virtual reality has applications for body-image distortion, treatment of posttraumatic stress disorder, testing, and rehabilitation (Riva, 2005). Virtual reality will be enhanced by full-immersion headsets and glove interfaces that allow manipulation of virtual objects (see Goss & Anthony, 2009).

A group of researchers in Spain have recently developed "EMMA's world" (Baños, Botella, Guillen, García-Palacios, Quero, Bretón-López, & Alcañiz, 2009), a virtual world that can be adapted to treat a wide variety of stress-related disorders

SNAPSHOT

Marty Jencius, Associate Professor, Kent State University
(a.k.a. Kimbo Scribe, Dr. Jencius's avatar in the virtual world of Second Life)

I am grateful to be working in a profession where I can mix work with play. Technology is the form of play that I get passionate about. Once I am passionate about an idea, a project, or a piece of scholarship, it ceases to be work and becomes play for me. Play for me is in figuring out how the technology works and then finding applications that can be applied to counseling and counselor education.

I started my work in counseling as a volunteer on a crisis line, communicating care and offering assistance by listening, asking questions, and helping people address their problems using phone "technology." I eventually completed my master's degree and worked as a radio DJ to supplement my income and keep my sanity. Meanwhile, I worked as a counselor for 15 years in addictions, mental health, youth and family services, and in a private employee assistance group. In 1990 I convinced my spouse that I needed to purchase a personal computer to complete my doctoral program. I became fascinated with computers' information and productivity capabilities, but also with e-mail and live chat rooms that were just developing as means of communicating and forming relationships.

In 1994, while still in my doctoral program at the University of South Carolina, I attended a regional counseling conference where healthy academic discussion led the desire of how might we continue these conversations from a distance. I offered to create a listserv for counselor educators, and through the help of my doctoral advisor started the CESNET-L listserv. Over the years, CESNET-L has grown to more than 1,600 counselor educators and supervisors.

I have always been excited about the "next new thing" and have managed to apply technology trends to counseling as my scholarship. In 1995 the next new thing was the World Wide Web and creating a Web presence. I was involved in creating websites for ACES (Association for Counselor Education and Supervision) and ASGW (Association for Specialists in Group Work). In 1997, as a new counselor educator at Columbus State University, I produced course content for student use on CD-ROM. I believe much of what we do in classrooms for instruction can be done using technology, meaning that face-to-face classroom instruction can be used for necessary interactive experiences. I worked with Michael Baltimore to create *The Journal of Technology in Counseling,* a Web-based, peer-reviewed journal on the use of technology in counseling. This was the first online journal in the counseling profession and was the beginning of a current trend to get content from producers (authors) directly to consumers (counseling students and other professionals). I believe that content should be free or at little cost to consumers, so all of my projects are publicly available and free of charge through the efforts and generosity of contributing colleagues.

I moved to my current position at Kent State University in 2000 and during my time here I have served as interview column editor for a journal. When I started listening to podcasts in 2005

(continued)

(Continued)

(to occupy my mind on international flights), I got the idea of creating an audio podcast interview program for counselors, CounselorAudioSource.net (bringing back my radio talents). In 2008 a doctoral student in my college teaching course introduced me to the virtual world of Second Life. Later that year we created Counselor Education in Second Life (SL.CounselorEducation.org) and now the CESL virtual world location has served as a training site for professional conferences and workshops. We have been able to hold professional workshops without the cost of travel, hotels, and conference centers by connecting people through virtual worlds. As a researcher interested in counselor training, I am now passionate about this idea of virtual presence, the visceral connected experience people have when using technology that in our field sets a foundation for therapeutic change.

What does the future hold for technology and the counseling profession? The "real" presence of a counselor will never be eliminated by the virtual presence of an avatar. Humans have a far too complex personal narrative to be replicated or replaced by a computer program. Technology, however, is another way by which people can create a psychological contact that can lead to change.

including post-traumatic stress disorder, adjustment disorder, and pathological grief. The client selects environments and tools that help him or her freely express emotions and review important people and moments in his or her life. Initial trials seemed to decrease negative emotions and increase positive emotions.

Similarly, the creation of a "virtual client" does not seem too far away. Imagine putting on 3-D glasses and seeing a client, a group, or a couple sitting in front of you. Maybe it will just be a holographic image created by multiple projectors. In this method of training, the client responds as you ask questions or reflect feelings. Right now these simulations are being used to help teachers learn classroom management and for a myriad of other training scenarios, especially by the armed services. The virtual client will probably be first used to help train counselors in basic counseling skills and in diagnosis.

In the final Snapshot of this text, Dr. Marty Jencius, an associate professor of counselor education at Kent State University, discusses his lifelong fascination with technology and his application of the latest technological breakthroughs to the world of counseling and counselor training. Dr. Jencius is an internationally known scholar in the field of technological applications to counseling, and his story can help spark your creative ideas about where technology might take the profession of counseling in the future.

 ## Concluding Comments: Where's My Jet Pack?

Yogi Berra once said, "The future ain't what it used to be." It is true. In our childhood we were promised much from science including our own personal airplane, moving sidewalks, self-driving cars, and a 3–4 hour workday. So we ask, "Where's my jet pack?" We were promised that by now we would have one that we could attach to our backs and allow us to zoom around wherever we wanted to go. It turns out change is a lot slower than we thought it would be. The promises of science have not changed life as much as we were told. Is the life of a person today much different than 50 years ago? People wake up, get in their cars and go to work, send their kids to school. Their problems are mostly with other people. They cut the grass and watch TV at night. In other words, we need not see the future as a frightening place that is completely different from the world of today. Rather than envisioning the world as a train that will run us down, it is more likely that the future will probably just creep up on us. That means that we can take a different attitude toward the future. It is something we can prepare for, because it will be a lot like now. A better metaphor than apocalyptic change is the idea that the counselor must stay in touch with the most important and likely changes rather than worrying about the improbable things that may never happen. The other conclusion one can draw is that there may be great truths about counseling and about human nature that are relatively unchangeable, and we should focus on this fundamental understanding of people, as well as what's new and recent.

Counselors, like technology buffs, are on a constant search for the latest and greatest, the technique or theory that will cure everything. In the past 70 or so years since Freud died, there have been enduring contributions and flashes in the pan. Among the enduring contributions, we have to consider person-centered counseling and cognitive therapy, while flashes in the pan are exemplified by primal scream or the use of psychedelics.

So, what can you take from this chapter on the future of counseling? One is that counseling is a growing and expanding profession with challenges, opportunities, and an exciting and promising future. Another is a simple attitude about learning. It is important to be prepared, but it is even better to become a lifelong learner so that you are aware of the changes as they crawl down the pike. It is, after all, quite unlikely that one method, one human invention, or one counseling technique will be discovered that will solve everything. It is more likely that we will rediscover basic truths about helping people. In short, do not expect the kind of rapid change that we have been promised. Rather than merely learn what is newest and most promising, learn from the wisdom of the ages, too. In your papers for class, do not just look at the last five years of literature; go back and read Freud's "On Dreams" and something by Carl Rogers. Despite technological change, societal upheaval, and economic downturns, the profession of counseling will probably remain a meaningful conversation between two or more people about how to change and how to adapt. No technology is required.

 ## End-of-Chapter Activities

The following activities might be part of your assignments for a class. Whether they are required or not, we suggest that you complete them as a way of reflecting on your new learning, arguing with new ideas in writing, and thinking about questions you may want to pose in class.

Student Activities

1. Now it's time to reflect on the major topics that we have covered in this chapter. Look back at the sections or the ideas you have underlined. What were your reactions as you read that portion of the chapter? What do you want to remember?

_____

_____

_____

_____

_____

2. What are your own beliefs about working with clients who represent some of the demographic trends that were discussed in this chapter (for example, clients from different religions or faiths than yours, elderly clients, clients who have English as a second language, clients who have nontraditional families)? Consider how your beliefs about these individuals might affect your work with them.

_____

_____

_____

_____

_____

3. In the last part of the chapter, we argued that change takes place slowly, and counselors must take care not to respond to every trend or fad, but to focus on the big picture of how people change and grow. Do you agree? Do you think that there is evidence to support this? What evidence contradicts this stance?

_____

_____

_____

_____

_____

■■■ Journal Question ■■■

As you look at the 14 characteristics of the counselor of tomorrow, write down a list of those that you feel describe you right now and those that are on your growing edge. Think about one of those that you need to work on. Devise a rough plan to engage in this activity. For example, you might write, "I am just learning how to be a reflective practitioner. I will start a notebook of my reflections on counseling techniques that I learn in my training program, describing my reaction and thoughts about when and with whom this technique might be useful."

■■■ Topics for Discussion ■■■

1. In this chapter, we discussed some of the trends that might influence the profession of counseling. What trends do you see that we have missed?

2. As you read through the 14 characteristics of the counselor of tomorrow, which of these excite or energize you? Which ones do you think will challenge you? Are there any characteristics that counselors of tomorrow will need to have that you think we have missed?

3. There is increasing concern that today's young people may grow up without mastering the skills necessary for face-to-face communication. Do you agree? If so, do you think this is a problem, or is virtual communication simply a new and different (neither better nor worse) way of interacting?

■■■ Experiments ■■■

1. Find someone who is from a faith you know little about. For example, if you know little about Islam, write a paragraph or two about Islamic ideas about mental health and then talk to a practicing Muslim. If you are amazed at your ignorance, it may help to know that you are not alone. For example, only about half of the people in the United States know that the Dalai Lama is Buddhist (Pew Forum on Religion and Public Life, 2010).

2. Search your cell phone or the Internet for free applications that can be used to chart progress with a particular issue such as wellness diaries, blood alcohol content, depression, moods, medication compliance, and so on. Search for programs that allow users to track psychological symptoms and behaviors, such as www.psychtracker.com.

3. Explore the technological applications that are available for counselors to learn more about counseling, such as those suggested by Dr. Marty Jencius or others. What do you think is the role of these types of technologies in counseling or counselor training?

■■■ Explore More! ■■■

If you are interested in exploring more about the ideas presented in this chapter, we recommend the following websites, books, and articles.

Websites
It is always dangerous to put websites in a book, because they change frequently; however, in a chapter about the future of

counseling, much of what is cutting edge is online.

http://counselortech.net

This website was developed and is maintained by Dr. Marty Jencius at Kent State University for counselors who use technology in teaching and practice. If you want to know more about Wiki, blogs, podcasting, social networks, digital storytelling, Second Life, and Twitter (or you have never heard of them), this website has great information.

http://digitalpsyway.net

This website will get you to the American Counseling Association's Web companion to its newsletter, *Counseling Today.*

www.onlinetherapyinstitute.com

The Online Therapy Institute is a site that brings together counseling and technology. The institute publishes *TILT* magazine, which addresses issues such as cybersupervision. They have links to online therapy sites and ideas about ethical use of online therapy.

http://schoolcounselor.com

This site is designed to improve "technological literacy in school counselors and administrators" with a variety of useful links and news.

Books

Goleman, Daniel. (2006). *Social intelligence: The new science of human relationships.* New York: Bantam.

> Goleman's book is an easy way of learning about advances in neuroscience that affect the way we see human relationships. He discusses high-road/low-road responses, the discovery of mirror neurons, and the biological importance of empathy. The book has implications for individual, group, and couples counseling.

Lake, J., & Spiegel, D. (Eds.). (2007). *Complementary and alternative treatments in mental health care.* Washington, DC: American Psychiatric Publishing.

> While written from a conservative, biomedical point of view, this book looks at CAMs and the evidence for effectiveness in treating mental disorders. It includes an examination of Ayurveda, homeopathy, and traditional Chinese medicine.

Articles

Dahir, C. A. (2009). School counseling in the 21st century: Where lies the future? *Journal of Counseling & Development, 87,* 3–5.

> In this introduction to a special section of *JCD*, Dahir outlines the changes that have come about from the Transforming School Counseling Initiative and the ASCA national model. There are five articles in the special section that are worth reading to see how school counseling has changed its direction.

Goss, S., & Anthony, K. (2009). Developments in the use of technology in counseling and psychotherapy. *British Journal of Guidance & Counselling, 37,* 223–230.

> For those interested in the potential application of technology to counseling practice, this article is a comprehensive overview.

Thomason, T. C. (2010). The trend toward evidence-based practice and the future of psychotherapy. *American Journal of Psychotherapy, 64,* 29–38.

> Thomason addresses how the movement toward evidence-based practice will affect counseling practice. He predicts that only evidence-based practice will be reimbursed by third-party payers and that it will be briefer. He also suggests that counseling and psychotherapy will become more a part of the health care system.

■■■ References ■■■

Achenbach, T., & Ruffle, T. M. (2000). The child behavior checklist and related forms for assessing behavioral/emotional problems and competencies. *Pediatrics in Review, 21,* 265–271.

Adler, A. (1907). *A study of organ inferiority and its psychical compensations.* New York: Nervous and Mental Disease Publishing.

Adler, A. (1927). *Understanding human behavior.* Garden City, NY: Garden City Publishing.

Adler, A., Kretschmer, E., Laffan, M. N., Bradley, R. N., Gordon, R. G., Mairet, P., et al. (1999). *The practice and theory of individual psychology.* Philadelphia: Routledge.

Administration on Aging. Aging statistics (2010). Retrieved September 30, 2010, from http://www.aoa.gov/aoaroot/aging_statistics/index.aspx

Adorno, T. W., Frenkel-Brunswik, E., Levinson, D. J., & Sanford, R. N. (1950). *The authoritarian personality.* New York: Harper & Row.

Agardh, E. E., Ahlbom, A., Andersson, T., Efendic, S., Grill, V., Hallqvist, J., Norman, A. & Östenson, C. (2003). Work stress and low sense of coherence is associated with type 2 diabetes in middle-aged Swedish women. *Diabetes Care, 26,* 719–724.

Alexitch, L. R. (2006). Help-seeking and the role of academic advising in higher education. In S. A. Karabenick and R. S. Newman (Eds.), *Help seeking in academic settings: Goals, groups, and contexts* (pp. 175–202). Mahwah, NJ: Lawrence Erlbaum.

Altekruse, M. A., & Sexton, T. L. (Eds.). (1995). *Mental health counseling in the 90's: A research report for training and practice.* Tampa: The National Commission for Mental Health Counseling.

American Art Therapy Association. (2010). Available at: http://www.arttherapy.org

American Association of Christian Counseling. (2004). AACC Christian Counseling Code of Ethics. Retrieved April 8, 2009, from http://www.aacc.net/about-us/code-of-ethics/

American Counseling Association. (2003). *Standards for qualifications of test users.* Alexandria, VA: Author.

American Counseling Association. (2005). *ACA code of ethics.* Alexandria, VA: Author.

American Counseling Association. (2007). Definition of professional counseling. Retrieved April 22, 2008, from www.counseling.org

American Counseling Association. (2008). *Licensure requirements for professional counselors.* Alexandria, VA: Author.

American Counseling Association. (2009). *20/20 statement of principles advances the profession.* Retrieved October 4, 2010, from http://www.counseling.org/PressRoom/NewsReleases.aspx?AGuid = 4d87a0ce-65c0-4074-89dc-2761cfbbe2ec

American Counseling Association. (2009). *Licensure and certification.* Retrieved February 2, 2009, from http://www.counseling.org/Counselors/LicensureAndCert.aspx

American Counseling Association. (2010). Membership statistics. Alexandria, VA: Author.

American Educational Research Association, American Psychological Association, & National Council on Measurement in Education. (1985). *Standards for educational and psychological testing.* Washington, DC: American Psychological Association.

American Mental Health Association. (2010). *Code of ethics.* Available at: www.amhca.org

American Psychiatric Association. (2000). *Diagnostic and statistical manual of mental disorders* (4th ed., text rev.). Washington, DC: Author.

American Psychological Association. (2001). *Publication manual of the American Psychological Association* (5th ed.). Washington, DC: Author.

American Psychological Association. (2010). *Publication manual of the American Psychological Association* (6th ed.). Washington, DC: Author.

American School Counselor Association. (1984). *The school counselor and developmental guidance* [Position statement]. Alexandria, VA: Author.

American School Counselor Association. (2003). *The ASCA national model: A framework for school counseling programs.* Alexandria, VA: Author.

American School Counselor Association. (2004). *Ethical standards for school counselors.* Alexandria, VA: Author.

American School Counselor Association. (2005). *The ASCA National Model: A framework for school counseling programs* (2nd ed.). Alexandria, VA: Author.

American School Counselor Association. (2007). Position statement: Discipline. Retrieved April 16, 2008, from http://www.schoolcounselor.org/content.asp?contentid=203

American School Counselor Association. (2008). The role of the professional school counselor. Retrieved April 22, 2008, from www.schoolcounselor.org

American School Counselor Association. (2010). *Ethical standards for school counselors.* Available at: www.schoolcounselor.org/files/EthicalStandards2010.pdf

Americans with Disabilities Act of 1990, Pub. L. No. 101-336, § 2, 104 Stat. 328 (1991).

Anderson, B. S. (1996). *The counselor and the law* (4th ed.). Alexandria: VA: American Counseling Association.

Anderson, W., & Anderson, B. (1985). Counselor self disclosure. Available: http://www.eric.ed.gov/PDFS/ED268411.pdf

Andersson-Arntén, A. C., Rosén, S., Jansson, B., & Archer, T. (2010). Partnership relations mediate work-stress effects on health. In A. C. Andersson-Arntén (Ed.), Partnership relation quality regulates health through work-stress (pp. 112–127). Saarbrücken, Germany: Lambert Academic Publishing.

Ardell, D. B. (1976). *High level wellness: An alternative to doctors, drugs and disease.* Emmaus, PA: Rodale.

Ardell, D. B. (1988). *Planning for wellness: A commitment to personal excellence* (3rd ed.). Dubuque, IA: Kendall/Hunt Publishing.

Armstrong, A. J., Hawley, C. E., Lewis, A. N., Blankenship, C., & Pugsley, R. A. (2008). Relationship between employment setting and job satisfaction among CRC personnel. *Journal of Vocational Rehabilitation, 28,* 41–51.

Arrendondo, P., Toporek, M. S., Brown, S., Jones, J., Locke, D. C., Sanchez, J., & Stadler, H. (1996). *Operationalization of the multicultural counseling competencies.* Alexandria, VA: American Counseling Association.

Artis, A. B. (2008). Improving marketing students' reading comprehension with the SQ3R method. *Journal of Marketing Education, 30,* 130–137.

Association for Assessment in Counseling. (2003). *Standards for multicultural assessment.* Alexandria, VA: American Counseling Association.

Association for Assessment in Counseling and Education. (1998). Competencies in assessment and evaluation for school counselors. Available at: http://aac.ncat.edu/documents/atsc_cmptncy.htm

Association for Specialists in Group Work. (1991). *Professional standards for the training of group workers.* Alexandria, VA: Author.

Association for Specialists in Group Work (ASGW). (2009). *Professional standards for the training of group workers.* Retrieved from http://www.asgw.org/training_standards.htm

Austin, S., & Joseph, S. (1996). Assessment of bully/victim problems in 8–11 year-olds. *British Journal of Educational Psychology, 66,* 447–456.

Axelson, S. L. (2007). The use and value of student support services: A survey of undergraduate students in online classes. University of Wyoming. *Dissertation Abstracts International Section A: Humanities and Social Sciences.* Vol. 68(5-A), 1766.

Axline, V. M. (1989). *Play therapy.* London: Ballantine Books. (Original work published 1947).

Baillargeon, R. (1992). The object concept revisited. In C. E. Granrud (Ed.), *Visual perception and cognition in infancy: Carnegie-Mellon symposia on cognition* (Vol. 23) (pp. 265–315). Hillsdale, NJ: Erlbaum.

Bakker, A. B., Schaufeli, W. B., Sixma, H. J., & Bosveld, W. (2001). Burnout contagion among general practitioners. *Journal of Social and Clinical Psychology, 20,* 82–98.

Bakker, A. B., Schaufeli, W. B., Sixma, H. J., Bosveld, W., & Van Dierendonck, D. (2000). Patient demands, lack of reciprocity, and burnout: A five-year longitudinal study among general practitioners. *Journal of Organizational Behavior, 21,* 425–441.

Bangert, A. W., & Baumberger, J. F. (2005). Research and statistical techniques used in the *Journal of Counseling & Development: 1990–2001. Journal of Counseling & Development, 83,* 480–487.

Bankart, C. P. (1997). *Talking cures: A history of Western and Eastern psychotherapies.* Pacific Grove, CA: Brooks/Cole.

Banmen, J. (Ed.) (2008*). In her own words: Virginia Satir: Selected papers.* Phoenix, AZ: Zeig, Tucker & Theisen.

Baños, R., Botella, C., Guillen, V., García-Palacios, A., Quero, S., Bretón-López, J., & Alcañiz, M. (2009). An adaptive display to treat stress-related disorders: EMMA's World. *British Journal of Guidance & Counselling, 37*(3), 347–356.

Barry, P. (2005). Perspectives on private practice. The business of private practice. *Perspectives in Psychiatric Care, 41*(2), 82–84.

Bass, B., & Quimby, J. (2006). Addressing secrets in couples counseling: An alternative approach to informed consent. *Family Journal, 14*(1), 77–80.

Baucom, D. H., Epstein, N., & Taillade, J. L. (2002). Cognitive behavioral couple therapy. In A. S. Gurman & N. S. Jacobson (Eds.), *Clinical handbook of couple therapy* (pp. 26–58). New York: Guilford.

Bauman, S. (2004). School counselors and research revisited. *Professional School Counseling, 7,* 141–151.

Bauman, S. (2008). To join or not to join: School counselors as a case study in professional membership. *Journal of Counseling and Development, 86,* 164–177.

Bauman, S., Siegel, J. T., Davis, A., Falco, L. D., Seabolt, K., & Syzmanski, G. (2002). School counselors' interest in professional literature and research. *Professional School Counseling, 5,* 346–352.

Bayne, R. (1993). Psychological type, conversations, and counseling. In R. Bayne & P. Nicolson (Eds.), *Counselling and psychology for health professionals.* London: Chapman & Hall.

Bayne, R. (1995). Psychological type and counselling. *British Journal of Guidance and Counselling, 23,* 95–106.

Beamish, P. M., Granello, D. H., Belcastro, A. L. (2002). Treatment of panic disorder: Practical guidelines. *Journal of Mental Health Counseling, 24*, 224–243.

Beamish, P. M., Granello, P. F., Granello, D. H., McSteen, P., Bender, B. A., & Hermon, D. (1996). Outcome studies in the treatment of panic disorder: A review. *Journal of Counseling and Development, 74*(5), 460–467.

Beck, A. T. (1964). Thinking and depression 2: Theory and therapy. *Archives of General Psychiatry, 10*, 561–571.

Beck, A. T. (1975). *Cognitive therapy and the emotional disorders*. Madison, CT: International Universities Press.

Beck, A. T., Rush, A. J., Shaw, B. F., & Emery, G. (1979). *Cognitive therapy of depression*. New York: Guilford.

Bee, P. E., Bower, P., Lovell, K., Gilbody, S., Richards, D., Gask, L., & Roach, P. (2008). Psychotherapy mediated by remote communication technologies: A meta-analytic review. *BMC Psychiatry, 8*, 1–13.

Beers, C. W. (1908). *A mind that found itself*. London: Longman Greens.

Beier, E. (1962). *The silent language of psychotherapy*. Chicago: Aldine.

Beier, E. G., & Young, D. M. (1998). *The silent language of psychotherapy: Social reinforcement of unconscious processes*. New York: Aldine de Gruyter.

Bellack, A. S., & Hersen, M. (1985). *Dictionary of behavior therapy techniques*. Boston: Allyn & Bacon.

Bem, D. J. (1995). Writing a review article for *Psychological Bulletin. Psychological Bulletin, 118*, 172–177.

Benton, S. A., Robertson, J. M., Tseng, W-C., Newton, F. B., & Benton, S. L. (2003). Changes in counseling center client problems across 13 years. *Professional Psychology: Research & Practice, 34*, 66–72.

Bernard, J. M., & Goodyear, R. K. (2008). *Fundamentals of clinical supervision* (4th ed.). Boston: Allyn & Bacon.

Bernsen, A., Tabachnick, B. G., & Pope, K. S. (1994). National survey of social workers' sexual attraction to their clients: Results, implications, and comparison to psychologists. *Ethics & Behavior, 4*, 369–388.

Beutler, L. E., Consoli, A. J., & Lane, G. (2005). Systematic treatment selection and prescriptive psychotherapy. In J. C. Norcross & M. R. Goldfried (Eds.), *Handbook of psychotherapy integration* (2nd ed., pp. 121–143). New York: Oxford University Press.

Bike, D. H., Norcross, J. C., & Schatz, D. M. (2009). Processes and outcomes of psychotherapists' personal therapy: Replication and extension 20 years later. *Psychotherapy Theory, Research, Practice Training, 46*, 19–31.

Binet, A. (1905). New methods for the diagnosis of the intellectual level of subnormals. *L'Année Psychologique, 12*, 191–244.

Binet. A., & Simon, T. (1916). *The development of intelligence in children*. Baltimore: Williams & Wilkins. (Reprinted 1973, New York: Arno Press; 1983, Salem, NH: Ayer Company).

Bion, W. R. (1990). *Brazilian lectures*. London: Karnac.

Biswas-Diener, R., Vitterso, J., & Diener, E. (2005). Most people are pretty happy, but there is cultural variation: The Inughuit, the Amish, and the Maasai. *Journal of Happiness Studies, 6*, 205–226.

Blocher, D. H. (2000). *The evolution of counseling psychology*. New York: Springer.

Blumenthal, R., & Mosteller, R. (2008, May 18). Voluntary simplicity movement re-emerges. *New York Times*.

Boer, P. M. (2001). *Career counseling over the Internet: An emerging model for trusting and responding to online clients*. Mahwah, NJ: Lawrence Erlbaum.

Bohart, A. (2004). How do clients make empathy work? *Person-Centered & Experiential Psychotherapies, 3*, 102–116.

Bohart, A. C. (2005). Evidence-based psychotherapy means evidence-informed, not evidence-driven. *Journal of Contemporary Psychotherapy, 35,* 39–53.

Bongar, B. (2002). Risk management: Prevention and postvention. In B. Bongar (Ed)., *The suicidal patient: Clinical and legal standards of care* (2nd ed., pp. 213–261). Washington, DC: American Psychological Association.

Borys, D. S., & Pope, K. S. (2001). Dual relationships between therapist and client: A national study of psychologists, psychiatrists, and social workers. In. J. Worell (Ed.), *Encyclopedia of Women and Gender: Sex similarities and differences and the impact of society on gender,* Vol. 2 (pp. 955–962). San Diego: Academic Press.

Bouhoutsos, J., Holroyd, J., Lerman, H., Forer, B., & Greenberg, M. (1983). Sexual intimacy between psychologists and patients. *Professional Psychology, 14,* 185–196.

Bradley, L. J., Sexton, T. L., & Smith, H. B. (2005). The American Counseling Association Practice Research Network (ACA-PRN): A new research tool. *Journal of Counseling & Development, 83,* 488–491.

Brannon, R. (1985). A scale for measuring attitudes and masculinity. In A. Sargent (Ed.), *Beyond sex roles* (pp. 110–116). St. Paul, MN: West.

Brault, M. (2008). Disability status and the characteristics of people in group quarters: A brief analysis of disability prevalence among the civilian noninstitutionalized and total populations in the American Community Survey. Retrieved from: http://www.census .gov/hhes/www/disability/GQdisability.pdf

Brett, J. M., Barsness, Z. I., & Goldberg, S. B. (1996). The effectiveness of mediation: An independent analysis of cases handled by four major service providers. *The Negotiation Journal, 12,* 259–269.

Briggs, C. A., & Pehrsson, D. E. (2008). Research mentorship in counselor education. *Counselor Education & Supervision, 48,* 101–113.

Brigman, G., & Campbell, C. (2003). Helping students improve academic achievement and school success behavior. *Professional School Counseling, 7,* 91–98.

Brookfield, S. D. (1989). Facilitating adult learning. In S. B. Merriam & P. M. Cunningham (Eds.), *Handbook of adult and continuing education* (pp. 201–210). San Francisco: Jossey-Bass.

Brookfield, S. D., & Preskill, S. (1999). *Discussion as a way of teaching: Tools and techniques for democratic classrooms.* San Francisco: Jossey-Bass.

Brown, N. W. (2004). *Psychoeducational groups: Process and practice* (2nd ed.). New York: Brunner-Routledge.

Bruss, K. V., & Kopala, M. (1993). Graduate school training in psychology: Its impact upon the development of professional identity. *Psychotherapy, 30,* 685–691.

Buckingham, M., & Clifton, D. O. (2001). *Now, discover your strengths.* New York: Free Press.

Burgess, D. G., & Dedmond, R. M. (1994). *Quality leadership and the professional school counselor.* Alexandria, VA: American Counseling Association.

Burnham, J. J., & Jackson, C. M. (2000). School counselor roles: Discrepancies between actual practice and existing models. *Professional School Counseling, 4,* 41–49.

Butcher, J. N., Graham, J. R., Ben-Porath, Y. S., Tellegen, A., & Kaemmer, B. (2001). *MMPI–2: Minnesota Multiphasic Personality Inventory–2: Manual for administration, scoring, and interpretation.* Minneapolis: University of Minnesota Press.

Butler, A. C., Chapman, J. E., Forman, E. M., & Beck, A. T. (2006). The empirical status of cognitive-behavioral therapy: A review of meta-analyses. *Clinical Psychology Review, 26,* 17–31.

Butler, R. (2010). *The longevity prescription: The 8 proven keys to a long, healthy life.* New York: Avery.

Capuzzi, D., & Gross, D. R. (2001). *Counseling and psychotherapy: Theories and interventions* (3rd ed.). Upper Saddle River, NJ: Prentice Hall.

Carducci, B. J. (2000). *Shyness: A bold new approach: Managing your shyness at work, making small talk, navigating social situations, parenting a shy child.* New York: HarperPerennial.

Carey, J. C. (2006). Resources for school counselors and counselor educators: The Center for School Counseling Outcome Research. *Professional School Counseling, 9,* 416–420.

Carkhuff, R. R. (1987). The art of helping VI. Amherst, MA: Human Resource Development Press.

Carlson, J., Watts, R. E., & Maniacci, M. (2006). *Adlerian therapy: Theory and practice.* Washington, D.C.: American Psychological Association.

Carr, J., & Fox, E. (2009). Using video technology to disseminate behavioral procedures: A review of functional analysis: A guide for understanding challenging behavior (DVD). *Journal of Applied Behavior Analysis, 42*(4), 919–923.

Casas, J. M. (2005). Race and racism: The efforts of counseling psychology to understand and address the issues associated with these terms. *The Counseling Psychologist, 33,* 501–512.

Cashwell, C. S., Bentley, D. P., & Bigbee, A. (2007). Spirituality and counselor wellness. *The Journal of Humanistic Counseling, Education and Development, 46*(1), 66–81.

Cass, V. C. (1979). Homosexual identity formation: A theoretical model. *Journal of Homosexuality, 4*(3), 219–235.

Ceranoglu, T. (2010). Video games in psychotherapy. *Review of General Psychology, 14*(2), 141–146.

Chaikin, A. L., Derelega, V. J., & Miller, S. J. (1976). Effects of room environment on self-disclosure in a counseling analogue. *Journal of Counseling Psychology, 23,* 479–481.

Chalquist, C. (2009). A look at the ecotherapy research evidence. *Ecopsychology, 1*(2), 64–74.

Champney, T. F., & Schulz, E. M. (1983). A reassessment of the effects of psychotherapy. Paper presented at the 55th annual convention of the Midwestern Psychological Association, Chicago, IL. (Eric document ED237895).

Chao, R. (2006). Counselors' multicultural competencies: Race, training, ethnic identity, and color-blind racial attitudes. *American Counseling Association Vistas.*

Cheung, O., Clements, B., & Pechman, E. (1997). Protecting the privacy of student records. Washington, DC: U.S. Department of Education, National Center for Education Statistics.

Chi, M. T. H., Feltovich, P. J., & Glaser, R. (1981). Categorization and representation of physics problems by experts and novices. *Cognitive Science, 5,* 121–152.

Chi Sigma Iota. (2009). http://www.csi-net.org/

Childs, R. A. & Eyde, L. D. (2002). Assessment training in clinical psychology doctoral programs: What should we teach? What do we teach? *Journal of Personality Assessment, 78,* 130–144.

Chiu, C., Hong, Y., & Dweck, C. S. (1997). Lay dispositionism and implicit theories of personality. *Journal of Personality and Social Psychology, 73,* 19–30.

Choate, L. H. (2008). Girls' and women's wellness: Contemporary counseling issues and interventions. Alexandria, VA: American Counseling Association.

Chope, R. C. (2010). Introduction to the special issue on social justice and advocacy in employment counseling. *Journal of Employment Counseling, 47,* 98–99.

Christopher, J. C., & Maris, J. A. (2010). Integrating mindfulness as self-care into counseling and psychotherapy training. *Counselling and Psychotherapy Research, 10,* 114–125.

Clance, P. R., & Imes, S. A. (1978). The Imposter Phenomenon in high achieving women: Dynamics and therapeutic intervention.

Psychotherapy: Theory, Research, & Practice, 15, 241–247.

Cohen, D., Vega, R., & Watson, G. (2001). *Advocacy for social advocacy: A global action and reflection guide.* Bloomfield, CT: Kumarian Press.

Cohen, L. H., Sargent, M. M., & Sechrest, L. B. (1986). Use of psychotherapy research by professional psychologists. *American Psychologist, 41,* 198–206.

Coleman, E. (1987). *Integrated identity for gay men and lesbians: Psychotherapeutic approaches for emotional well-being.* New York: Harrington Park Press.

Collins, S., Arthur, N., & Wong-Wylie, G. (2010). Enhancing reflective practice in multicultural counseling through cultural auditing. *Journal of Counseling & Development, 88*(3), 340–347.

Commission on Rehabilitation Counselor Certification. (2009). *Code of professional ethics for rehabilitation counselors.* Available at: http://www.crccertification.com

Cook, E. P. (1993). *Women, relationships, and power: Implications for counseling.* Alexandria, VA: American Counseling Association.

Cook, J. M., Biyanova, T., & Coyne, J. C. (2009). Influential psychotherapy figures, authors, and books: An Internet survey of over 2,000 psychotherapists. *Psychotherapy: Theory, Research, Practice, Training, 46,* 42–51.

Corcoran, K., & Fischer, J. (2006). *Measures for clinical practice and research: A sourcebook.* New York: Oxford University Press.

Corey, G., & Corey, M. (2008). *Theory and practice of group counseling* (8th ed.). Belmont, CA: Brooks/Cole.

Corey, G., Corey, M. S., & Callanan, P. (1988). *Issues and ethics in the helping professions* (3rd ed.). Pacific Grove, CA: Brooks/Cole.

Corey, G., Corey, M. S., Callanan, P., & Russell, J. M. (2004). *Group Techniques.* Pacific Grove, CA: Brooks-Cole.

Corey, M. S., & Corey, G. (2006). *Groups: Process and Practice* (7th ed.). Belmont, CA: Wadsworth.

Corrigan, P. W. (1998). The impact of stigma on severe mental illness. *Cognitive and Behavioral Practice, 5,* 201–222.

Corsini, R. J. (Ed). (2001). *Handbook of innovative psychotherapies.* New York: Wiley.

Costa, P. T., & McCrae, R. R. (1995). Solid ground in the wetlands of personality. *Psychological Bulletin, 117,* 216–220.

Coster, J. S., & Schwebel, M. (1997). Well-functioning in professional psychologists. *Professional Psychology: Research and Practice, 28,* 3–13.

Cotton, D. H. G. (1990). *Stress management: An integrated approach to therapy.* New York: Brunner/Mazel.

Cottone, R. (2001). A social constructivism model of ethical decision making in counseling. *Journal of Counseling and Development, 79,* 39–45.

Cottone, R., & Mannis, J. (1996). Uncovering secret extramarital affairs in marriage counseling. *Family Journal, 4*(2), 109–115.

Cottone, R. R., & Tarvydas, V. M. (2007). *Counseling ethics and decision making* (3rd ed.). Columbus, OH: Merrill/Prentice Hall.

Cottraux, J., Note, I., Yao, S. N., de Mey-Guillard, C., Bonasse, F., Djamoussian, D., Mollard, E., Note, B., & Chen, Y. (2008). Randomized controlled comparison of cognitive behavior therapy with Rogerian supportive therapy in chronic post-traumatic stress disorder: A 2-year follow-up. *Psychotherapy and Psychosomatics, 77,* 101–110.

Council for Accreditation of Counseling and Related Educational Programs (CACREP). (2008). *CACREP Standards.* Retrieved August 24, 2008, from www.CACREP.org

Crethar, H. C., & Ratts, M. J. (n.d.). *Why social justice is a counseling concern.* Available: http://www.txca.org/images/tca/Template/

TXCSJ/Why_social_justice_is_a_counseling_concern.pdf

Crites, J. O. (1981). *Career counseling: Models, methods, and materials*. New York: McGraw-Hill.

Crothers, L., & Levinson, E. (2004). Assessment of bullying: A review of methods and instruments. *Journal of Counseling and Development, 82*(4), 496–503.

Cucciare, M., & Weingardt, K. (2010). *Using technology to support evidence-based behavioral health practices: A clinician's guide*. New York: Routledge/Taylor & Francis Group.

Cummings, N.A. (2006). Psychology, the stalwart profession, faces new challenges and opportunities. *Professional Psychology: Research and Practice, 37*(6), 598–605.

Curtis, R., Matise, M., & Glass, J. S. (2003). Counselling students' views and concerns about weeping with clients: A pilot study. *Counselling and Psychotherapy Research, 3*, 300–306.

Dahir, C. A., Sheldon, C. B., & Valiga, M. J. (1998). Vision into action: Implementing the national standards for school counseling programs. Alexandria, VA: American School Counselor Association.

Dahlstrom, W. G. (1995). Pigeons, people, and pigeon holes. *Journal of Personality Assessment, 64*, 2–20.

Dana, R. H. (2003). Assessment training, practice, and research in the new millennium: Challenges and opportunities for professional psychology. *Ethical Human Sciences and Services, 5*, 127–140.

Dana, R. H. (2005). *Multicultural assessment: Principles, applications, and examples*. Mahweh, NJ: Lawrence Erlbaum.

Davis, H. V. (1969). *Frank Parsons: Prophet, innovator, counselor*. Carbondale, IL: University of Southern Illinois Press.

Davis, K., & Atkins, S. (2004). Creating and teaching a course in ecotherapy: We went to the woods. *Journal of Humanistic Counseling, Education & Development, 43*(2), 211–218.

Davis, K., & Atkins, S. (2009). Ecotherapy: Tribalism in the mountains and forest. *Journal of Creativity in Mental Health, 4*(3), 272–282.

Dawes, R. M. (1994). *House of cards*. New York: The Free Press.

Day, J. M. (1994). Obligation and motivation: Obstacles and resources for counselor well-being and effectiveness. *Journal of Counseling and Development, 73*, 108–110.

Day, S. X., & Schneider, P. L. (2002). Psychotherapy using distance technology: A comparison of face-to-face, video and audio treatment. *Journal of Counseling Psychology, 49*, 299–503.

deJong, P., & Berg, I. K. (2002). *Interviewing for solutions* (2nd ed.). Pacific Grove, CA: Wadsworth.

Didonna, F. (2009). *Clinical handbook of mindfulness*. New York: Springer Science + Business Media.

Dietz, S. (2010). *State high school tests: Exit exams and other assessments*. Washington, DC: Center on Education Policy.

Dimmitt, C. (2009). Why evaluation matters: Determining effective school counseling practices. *Professional School Counseling, 12*, 395–399.

Dimmitt, C., Carey, J. C., McGannon, W., & Henningson, I. (2005). Identifying a school counseling research agenda: A Delphi study. *Counselor Education and Supervision, 44*, 214–228.

Dobson, K. S. (1989). A meta-analysis of the efficacy of cognitive therapy for depression. *Journal of Consulting and Clinical Psychology, 57*, 414–419.

Doherty, W. J., & McDaniel, S. H. (2010). *Family therapy*. Washington, DC: American Psychological Association.

Dollarhide, C. T., & Lemberger, M. E. (2006). "No Child Left Behind": Implications for school counselors. *Professional School Counseling, 9*, 295–304.

Dougherty, A. M. (1990). *Consultation: Practice and perspectives*. Pacific Grove, CA: Brooks/Cole.

Doughterty, A. M. (2004). *Psychological consultation and collaboration in school and community settings* (4th ed.). Pacific Grove, CA: Brooks/Cole.

Eakin, E., Reeves, M., Lawler, S., Graves, N., Oldenburg, B., Del Mar, C., Wilke, K., Winkler, E., & Barnett, A. (2009). Telephone counseling for physical activity and diet in primary care patients. *American Journal of Preventive Medicine, 36,* 142–149.

Echterling, L. G., Cowan, E., Evans, W. F., Staton, A. R., Viere, G., McKee, J. E., Presbury, J., & Stewart, A. L. (2002). *Thriving: A manual for students in the helping professions.* Boston: Lahaska Press.

Edelwich, J., & Brodsky, A. (1980). Burn-out: Stages of disillusionment in the helping professions. New York: Human Services Press.

Education Trust. (2009). *The new vision for school counseling.* Available: http://www.edtrust.org/dc/tsc/vision

Ehrenwald, J. (1991). *The history of psychotherapy.* Northvale, NJ: Jason Aronson.

Einstein, E. (1983). *The printing revolution in early modern Europe.* Cambridge, UK, Cambridge University Press.

Ekstrom, R. B., Elmore, P. B., Shafer, W. D., Trotter, T. V., & Webster, B. (2004). A survey of assessment and evaluation activities of school counselors. *Professional School Counseling, 8,* 24–30.

Elliott, M., & Williams, D. (2003). The client experience of counselling and psychotherapy. *Counselling Psychology Review, 18,* 34–38.

Elliott, R., & Freire, E. (2007). Classical person-centered and experiential perspectives on Rogers (1957). *Psychotherapy: Theory, Research, Practice, Training, 44,* 285–288.

Ellis, A. (1962). *Reason and emotion in psychotherapy.* New York: Lyle Stewart.

Ellis, A. (1989). Rational-emotive therapy. In R. J. Corsini & D. Wedding (Eds.), *Current psychotherapies.* Itasca, IL: F. E. Peacock.

Ellis, A. (1999). Early theories and practices of rational emotive behavior theory and how they have been augmented and revised during the last three decades. *Journal of Rational-Emotive & Cognitive-Behavior Therapy, 21,* 69–93.

Ellis, A. (2003). Helping people get better rather than merely feel better. *Journal of Rational-Emotive and Cognitive-Behavior Therapy, 21,* 169–182.

Ellis, A., David, D., & Lynn, S. (2010). Rational and irrational beliefs: A historical and conceptual perspective. *Rational and irrational beliefs: Research, theory, and clinical practice* (pp. 3–22). New York: Oxford University Press.

Elmore, P. B., Ekstrom, R., Shafer, W., & Webster, B. (1998, January). *School counselors' activities and training in assessment and evaluations.* Presented at the Assessment 1998, Assessment for Change—Changes in Assessment, St. Petersburg, FL.

Emerson, S., & Markos, P. A. (1996). Signs and symptoms of the impaired counselor. *Journal of Humanistic Education and Development, 24,* 108–117.

Eriksen, K. (1996). Making an impact: A handbook on counselor advocacy. Washington, DC: Accelerated Development.

Erikson, E. (1950). *Childhood and society.* New York: Norton.

Erikson, K., & Kress, V. E. (2006). The DSM and the professional counseling identity: Bridging the gap. *Journal of Mental Health Counseling, 28,* 202–217.

Eron, J. B., & Lund, T. W. (1998). *Narrative solutions in brief therapy.* New York: Guilford.

Etringer, B. D., Hillerbrand, E., & Claiborn, C. D. (1995). The transition from novice to expert counselor. *Counselor Education and Supervision, 35,* 4–17.

Ewing, K. M., Richardson, T. Q., James-Myers, L., & Russell, R. K. (1996). The relationship between racial identity attitudes, worldview, and African American graduate students' experience of the Imposter Phenomenon. *Journal of Black Psychology, 22,* 53–66.

Eysenck, H. J. (1970). *The structure of human personality*. London: Methuen.

Facebook Statistics. (2010). Available: http://www.facebook.com/press/info.php?statistics

Fall, M. (1994). Developing curriculum expertise: A helpful tool for school counselors. *School Counselor, 42*, 92–100.

Falvey, E. (1989). Passion and professionalism: Critical rapprochement for mental health research. *Journal of Mental Health Counseling, 11*, 86–95.

Farber, B. A., Berano, K. C., & Capobianco, J. A. (2004). Clients' perceptions of the process and consequences of self-disclosure in psychotherapy. *Journal of Counseling Psychology, 51*, 340–346.

Farber, B. A., & Heifetz, L. J. (1981). The satisfactions and stresses of therapeutic work: A factor analytic study. *Professional Psychology, 12*, 621–630.

Federal Register (Thursday, July 26, 2001). 34 CFR Part 99, Part V, Family Education Rights and Privacy, Final Rule. Office of Family Policy Compliance, Family Education Rights and Privacy Act (FERPA). Retrieved from http://www.ed.gov/print/policy/gen/guid/fpco/ferpa/index.html

Fishbane, M. D. (2007). Wired to connect: Neuroscience, relationships and therapy. *Family Process, 46*, 395–412.

Flach, F. (2002). *The secret strength of depression* (3rd rev. ed.). New York: Hatherleigh Press.

Flanagan, D. P., Genshaft, J., & Harrison, P. L. (1997). *Contemporary intellectual assessment*. New York: Guilford.

Folkman, S., & Lazarus, R. S. (1980). An analysis of coping in a middle-aged community sample. *Journal of Health and Social Behavior, 21*, 219–239.

Forester-Miller, H., & Davis, T. (1996). *A practitioner's guide to ethical decision making*. Alexandria, VA: American Counseling Association.

Foster, J. (2008). An exploration of voluntary simplifiers: Characteristics, motivations and relevant research. Unpublished manuscript.

Foster, R. & Hicks, G. (2008). *Choosing brilliant health*. New York: Penguin.

Fowler, J. W. (1995). *Stages of faith: The psychology of human development and the quest for meaning*. San Francisco: Harper.

Frank, J. D. (1961). *Persuasion and healing*. Baltimore: Johns Hopkins University Press.

Frank, J. D. (1974). Therapeutic components of psychotherapy. A 25-year progress report of research. *Journal of Nervous and Mental Disease, 159*, 325–324.

Frank, J. D., & Frank, J. B. (1991). *Persuasion and healing: A comparative study of psychotherapy* (3rd ed.). Baltimore: Johns Hopkins University Press.

Franklin, C., Moore, K., & Hopson, L. (2008). Effectiveness of Solution-Focused Brief Therapy in a school setting. *Children and Schools, 30*, 15–26.

Fredrickson, B. L. (2009). *Positivity: Groundbreaking research reveals how to embrace the hidden strength of positive emotions, overcome negativity, and thrive*. New York: Crown Publishers.

Fredrickson, B. L., Cohn, M. A., Coffey, K. A., Pek, J., & Finkel, S. M. (2008). Open hearts build lives: Positive emotions, induced through loving-kindness meditation, build consequential personal resources. *Journal of Personality and Social Psychology, 95*, 1045–1062.

Fredrickson, B. L., Mancuso, R. A., Branigan, C., & Tugade, M. M. (2000). The undoing effect of positive emotions. *Motivation and Emotion, 24*, 237–258.

Freeman, M., Hayes, B., Kuch, T., & Taub, G. (2007). Personality: A predictor of theoretical orientation of students enrolled in a counseling theories course. *Counselor Education & Supervision, 46*(4), 254–265.

Freud, S. (1952). *On dreams*. New York: Norton.

Fromm, E. (1942). *The fear of freedom*. London, UK: Routledge.

Gearhart, J. A. (2005). School records and case notes. *Connections: Colorado Department of Education, 17*. Available: http://www.cde

.state.co.us/cdesped/download/pdf/nurSchoolCaseNotes.pdf

Gelso, C. J., & Fretz, B. R. (1992). *Counseling psychology*. Fort Worth, TX: Harcourt Brace.

Gelso, C. J. (2006). On the making of a scientist-practitioner: A theory of research training in professional psychology. *Training and Education in Professional Psychology, 1*, 3–16.

Gelso, C. J., & Carter, J. A. (1985). The relationship in counseling and psychotherapy: Components, consequences, and theoretical antecedents. *The Counseling Psychologist, 13*, 155–244.

Germain, C. A., & Horn, L. (1997). *Evaluating Internet websites*. Available online at: http://library.albany.edu/usered/webeval/

Geyer, P. (2002). An MBTI history. Retrieved May 31, 2002, at: http://members.ozemail.com.us/~alchymia/library/history.html

Gibson, D. M., Dollarhide, C. T., & Moss, J. M. (2010). Professional identity development: A grounded theory of transformational tasks of new counselors. *Counselor Education & Supervision, 50*(1), 21–38.

Gilbert, W. (1952). Counseling: Therapy and diagnosis. In *Annual Review of Psychology* (Vol. 3) (pp. 357–380). Palo Alto, CA.: Annual Reviews.

Gilligan, C. (1982). *In a different voice: Men, women, and relationships*. Cambridge, MA: Harvard University Press.

Ginter, E. J. (1991). Mental health counselor preparation: Experts' opinions. *Journal of Mental Health Counseling, 13*, 187–203.

Gladding, S. T. (2002). *Becoming a counselor: The light, the bright, and the serious*. Alexandria, VA: American Counseling Association.

Gladding, S. T. (2006). *Family therapy: History, theory and practice*. Upper Saddle River, NJ: Prentice Hall.

Glaser, R. D., & Thorpe, J. S. (1986). Unethical intimacy: A survey of sexual contact and advances between psychology educators and female graduate students. *American Psychologist, 41*, 43–51.

Glasser, W. (1965). *Reality Therapy: A new approach to psychiatry*. New York: Harper & Row.

Glasser, W. (1998). *Choice theory: A new psychology of personal freedom*. New York: HarperPerennial.

Glauser, A. S., & Bozarth, J. D. (2001). Person-centered counseling: The culture within. *Journal of Counseling & Development, 79*, 142–147.

Gold, J. R. (1996). *Key concepts in psychotherapy integration*. New York: Springer.

Goldberg, C. (2002). The secret that guilty confessions fail to disclose. *American Journal of Psychotherapy, 56*(2), 178.

Goldfried, M. R. (1980). Toward the delineation of therapeutic change principles. *American Psychologist, 35*, 991–999.

Goldfried, M. R. (1995). *From Cognitive-Behavior Therapy to psychotherapy integration: An evolving view*. New York: Springer.

Goleman, D. (2006). *Social intelligence: The new science of human relationships*. New York: Bantam Books.

Goodwin, D. K. (2005). *Team of rivals: The political genius of Abraham Lincoln*. New York: Simon & Schuster.

Gordon, V. (2006). *Career advising: An academic advisors' guide*. Manhattan, KS: NACADA.

Goss, S., & Anthony, K. (2009). Developments in the use of technology in counseling and psychotherapy. *British Journal of Guidance & Counselling, 37*, 223–230.

Gottman, J. (1999). The seven principles for making marriage work. New York: Crown.

Gottman, J., & Notarius, C. (2000). Decade review: Observing marital interaction. *Journal of Marriage & the Family, 62*(4), 927–947.

Granello, D. H. (2000). Encouraging the cognitive development of supervisees: Using Bloom's Taxonomy in supervision. *Counselor Education and Supervision, 40*, 31–46.

Granello, D. H. (2002). Assessing the cognitive development of counseling students: Changes in epistemological assumptions. *Counselor Education and Supervision, 41*, 279–293.

Granello, D. H. (2003). Influence strategies in the supervisory dyad: An investigation into the effects of gender and age. *Counselor Education and Supervision, 42,* 189–202.

Granello, D. H. (2007). Publishing quantitative manuscripts in *Counselor Education and Supervision*: General guidelines and expectations. *Counselor Education and Supervision, 47,* 66–75.

Granello, D. H. (2010). Cognitive complexity among practicing counselors: How thinking changes with experience. *Journal of Counseling and Development, 88,* 92–100.

Granello, D. H. (2010). The process of suicide risk assessment: Twelve core principles. *Journal of Counseling and Development, 88,* 363–371.

Granello, D. H., Beamish, P. M., & Davis, T. E. (1997). Supervisee empowerment: Does gender make a difference? *Counselor Education and Supervision, 36*(4), 305–317.

Granello, D. H., Granello, P. F., & Lee, F. (2000). Measuring treatment outcome in a child and adolescent partial hospitalization program. *Administration and Policy in Mental Health, 27*(6), 409–422.

Granello, D. H., & Granello, P. F. (2001). Counseling outcome research: Making practical choices for real-world applications. In G. R. Walz & J. C. Bleuer (Eds.), *Assessment: Issues and challenges for the millennium.* (pp. 163–172). Greensboro, NC: ERIC/CASS.

Granello, D. H., & Granello, P. F. (2007). *Suicide: An essential guide for helping professionals and educators.* Boston: Allyn & Bacon.

Granello, D. H., & Hazler, R. (1998). A developmental rationale for curriculum order and teaching styles in counselor education programs. *Counselor Education and Supervision, 38*(2), 89–105.

Granello, D. H., & Wheaton, J. E. (2001). Attitudes toward persons with physical disabilities and mental illnesses. *Journal of Applied Rehabilitation Counseling, 32*(3), 9–16.

Granello, P. F. (2011). *Counseling for wellness.* Upper Saddle River, NJ: Pearson.

Granello, P. F., & Granello, D. H. (1998). Training counseling students to use outcomes research. *Counselor Education and Supervision, 37*(4), 224–237.

Granello, P. F., & Witmer, J. M. (1998). Standards of care: Potential implications for the counseling profession. *Journal of Counseling and Development, 76,* 371–380.

Grawe, K. (2007). *Neuropsychotherapy: How the neurosciences inform effective* psychotherapy. Mahwah, NJ: Erlbaum.

Gredler, M. E. (1996). *Program evaluation.* Englewood Cliffs, NJ: Merrill/Prentice-Hall.

Greenberg, L. S., Elliott, R. K., & Lietaer, G. (1994). Research on experiential psychotherapies. In A. E. Bergin & S. L. Garfield (Eds.), *Handbook of psychotherapy and behavior change* (pp. 509–539). New York: Wiley.

Greenhill, L. L., & Osman, B. B. (Eds.). (2000). *Ritalin: Theory and practice.* Larchmont, NY: M. A. Liebert.

Gregory, R. J. (2010). *Psychological testing: History, principles, and applications* (6th ed.). Upper Saddle River, NJ: Prentice Hall.

Griffiths, A. J., (2007). The requirement for personal therapy in BACP accreditation schemes. *Therapy Today, 18,* 54–55. http://web.ebscohost.com.ucfproxy.fcla .edu/ehost/detail?vid=16&hid=104&sid= f9fd527e-7290-44ca-bd13-ea4ac86b548c%40 sessionmgr107-bib5up#bib5up

Grimmer, A., & Tribe, R. (2001). Counselling psychologists' perceptions of the impact of mandatory personal therapy on professional development—an exploratory study. *Counselling Psychology Quarterly, 14*(4), 287–301.

Grodzki, L. (2009). *How to crisis proof your private practice: How to survive and thrive in an uncertain economy.* New York: Norton.

Groth-Marnat, G., & Horvath, L. (2006). The psychological report: A review of current controversies. *Journal of Clinical Psychology, 62*(1), 73–81.

Gulliver, P. H. (1979). *Disputes and negotiation: A cross-cultural perspective.* New York: Academic Press.

Gummere, R. M. (1988). The counselor as prophet: Frank Parsons, 1854–1908. *Journal of Counseling and Development, 66,* 402–405.

Gumz, E. (2004). An administrator's perspective of trends in community mental health: An interview with Norman J. Groetzinger. *Families in Society, 85,* 363–370.

Gysbers, N. C., & Henderson, R. (2000). *Developing and managing your school guidance program* (3rd ed.). Alexandria, VA: American Counseling Association.

Haberstroh, S., Parr, G., Bradley, L., Morgan-Fleming, B., & Gee, R. (2008). Facilitating online counseling: Perspectives from counselors in training. *Journal of Counseling & Development, 86*(4), 460–470.

Habley, W. R., and Crockett, D. S. 1988. The third ACT National Survey of Academic Advising. In W. R. Habley (Ed.), *The status and future of academic advising: Problems and promise.* Iowa City: American College Testing Program.

Hackney, H., & Cormier, L. S. (1996). *The professional counselor: A process guide to helping.* Boston: Allyn & Bacon.

Hadley, R. G., & Mitchell, L. K. (1995). *Counseling research and program evaluation.* Pacific Grove, CA: Brooks & Cole.

Hadwin, A. F., Kirby, J. R., & Woodhouse, R. A. (1999). Individual differences in notetaking, summarization and learning from lectures. *Alberta Journal of Educational Research, 45*(1), 1–17.

Haggbloom et al. (2002). The 100 most eminent psychologists of the 20th century. *Review of General Psychology, 6,* 139–152.

Haley, J., & Richeport-Haley, M. (2007). *Directive family therapy.* New York: Haworth Press.

Haley, M. (2004). *School counseling: Professional ethics and legal issues.* Available: http://www.ablongman.com/helpingprofessions/coun/ppt/school/profethicslegaliss.ppt#395, 2,ProfessionalEthicsandLegalIssues

Halford, W. K., Markman, H. J., & Stanley, S. M. (2008). Strengthening couple relationships with education: Social policy and public health perspectives. *Journal of Family Psychology, 22,* 497–505.

Halibur, D. A., & Vess Halibur, K. (2006). *Developing your theoretical orientation in counseling and psychotherapy.* Boston, MA: Allyn & Bacon.

Hall, C. S., & Lindzey, G. (1978). *Theories of personality* (3rd ed.). New York: Wiley.

Hamberger, L. K., & Stone, G. V. (1983). Burnout prevention for human service professionals: Proposal for a systematic approach. *Journal of Holistic Medicine, 5,* 149–162.

Handelsman, M. M., Martinez, A., Geisendorfer, S., & Jordan, L. (1995). Does legally mandated consent to psychotherapy ensure ethical appropriateness? *Ethics and Behavior, 5*(2), 119–129.

Hansen, J. T. (2003). Including diagnostic training in counseling curricula: Implications for professional identity development. *Counselor Education and Supervision, 43,* 96–107.

Hanshew, E. R. (1998). An investigation of the wounded healer phenomenon: Counselor trainees and their self-conscious emotions and mental health. *Dissertation Abstracts International Section A: Humanities and Social Sciences.* Vol. 58(10-A), 3846.

Harvey, J. C. (1981). *The Imposter Phenomenon and achievement issues of sex, race, and self perceived atypicality.* Paper presented at the Annual Convention of the American Psychological Association (89th, Los Angeles, CA, August 24–26, 1981). ERIC Document Reproduction Service No. ED212966

Hawkins, P., & Shohet, R. (1989). *Supervision in the helping professions.* London: Open University Press.

Hays, D. G., Chang, C. Y., & Dean, J. K. (2004). White counselors' conceptualization of privilege and oppression: Implications for training. *Counselor Education and Supervision, 43*, 242–257.

Hays, D. G., Chang, C. Y., & Havice, P. (2008). White racial identity statuses as predictors of white privilege awareness. *Journal of Humanistic Education, Counseling, and Development, 47*, 234–246.

Hazler, R. (1988). Stumbling into unconditional positive regard. *Journal of Counseling and Development, 67*, 130.

Hazler, R., & Denham, S. (2002). Social isolation of youth at risk: Conceptualizations and practical implications. *Journal of Counseling & Development, 80*(4), 403–09.

Hazler, R. J., & Kottler, J. A. (2005). *The emerging professional counselor: Student dreams to professional realities* (2nd ed.). Alexandria, VA: American Counseling Association.

Health Insurance Portability and Accountability Act (HIPAA) of 1996, P.L. 104-191, 119 Stat.

Healy, C. C. (1989). Negative: The MBTI: Not ready for routine use in counseling. *Journal of Counseling and Development, 67*, 487–488.

Helms, J. E. (1995). An update of Helms' white and people of color racial identity. In J. G. Ponterotto, J. M. Casas, & C. M. Alexander (Eds.), *Handbook of multicultural counseling* (pp. 181–198). Thousand Oaks, CA: Sage.

Henning, K., Ey, S., & Shaw, D. (1998). Perfectionism, the Imposter Phenomenon and psychological adjustment in medical, dental, nursing, and pharmacy students. *Medical Education, 32*, 456–464.

Herink, R. (1980). *The psychotherapy handbook: The A to Z guide to more than 250 therapies in use today*. New York: New American Library.

Hermann, M. A. (2002). A study of legal issues encountered by school counselors and perceptions of their preparedness to respond to legal challenges. *Professional School Counseling, 6*, 12–19.

Herr, E. L., Heitzmann, D. E., & Rayman, J. R. (2005). *The professional counselor as administrator: Perspectives on leadership and management in counseling services.* New York: Routledge.

Hershenson, D. B., Power, P. W., & Waldo, M. (1996). *Community counseling: Contemporary theory and practice.* Boston: Allyn & Bacon.

Hettler, B. (1980). Wellness promotion on a university campus. *Family and Community Health, 3*(1), 77–9.

Hick, S. F. (Ed.). (2009). *Mindfulness and social work.* Chicago: Lyceum.

Hill, C. E. (2004). *Helping skills: Facilitating exploration, insight, and action* (2nd ed.). Washington, DC: American Psychological Association.

Hill, M., Glaser, K., & Harden, J. (1995). A feminist model for ethical decision making. In E. J. Rave & C. C. Larsen (Eds.), *Ethical decision making in therapy: Feminist perspectives* (pp. 18–37). New York: Guilford.

Hill, N. R. (2003). Promoting and celebrating multicultural competence in counselor trainees. *Counselor Education and Supervision, 43*, 39–51.

Hill, N. (2007). Wilderness therapy as a treatment modality for at-risk youth: A primer for mental health counselors. *Journal of Mental Health Counseling, 29*(4), 338–349.

Hinkelman, J. M., & Luzzo, D. A. (2007). Mental health and career development of college students. *Journal of Counseling and Development, 85*, 143–147.

Hirschfeld, M. (1982). *The imposter phenomenon in successful career women.* Paper presented at the Annual Convention of the American Psychological Association, 90th, Washington, DC, August 23–27, 1982. ERIC Document Reproduction Service No. ED226264.

Hjelle, L. A., & Ziegler, D. J. (1982). *Personality theories: Basic assumptions, research, and applications.* New York: McGraw-Hill.

Holcomb-McCoy, C., & Bryan, J. (2010). Advocacy and empowerment in parent consultation: Implications for theory and practice. *Journal of Counseling & Development, 88*(3), 259–268.

Holloway, E. L. (1992). Supervision: A way of teaching and learning. In S. D. Brown & R. W. Lent (Eds.), *Handbook of counseling psychology* (2nd ed.) (pp. 177–214). New York: John Wiley and Sons.

Holohan, C. J., & Slaikeu, K. A. (1977). Effects of contrasting degrees of privacy on client self-disclosure in a counseling setting. *Journal of Counseling Psychology, 24,* 55–59.

Horvath, A. O., & Bedi, R. P. (2002). The alliance. In J. C. Norcross (Ed.), *Psychotherapy relationships that work* (pp. 37–69). New York: Oxford University Press.

House, R. M., & Hayes, R. L. (2002). School counselors: Becoming key players in school reform. *Professional School Counseling, 5,* 249–256.

Houser, R. A. (2008). *Counseling and educational research: Evaluation and application* (2nd ed.). Thousand Oaks, CA: Sage.

Howard, G. (1993). Ecocounseling psychology: An introduction and overview. *The Counseling Psychologist, 21*(4), 550–559.

Huber, C. (1994). Ecocounseling: Focus or fringe? *Family Journal, 2*(3), 246–249.

Individuals with Disabilities Education Act of 1975 (Pub. L. No. 94-142).

International Association of Marriage & Family Therapists. (2001). *Code of Ethics.* Available: http://www.iamfc.org

Ishiyama, F. I. (1990). A Japanese perspective on client inaction: Removing attitudinal blocks through Morita therapy. *Journal of Counseling and Development, 68,* 567–570.

Ivey, A. G. (1976). The counselor as teacher. *Personnel and Guidance Journal, 54,* 431–434.

Ivey, A., & Authier, J. (1971). *Microcounseling.* Springfield, IL: Charles C. Thomas.

Jackson, S. W. (1999). *Care of the psyche: A history of psychological healing.* New Haven, CT: Yale University Press.

Jones, K. D. (2010). The unstructured clinical interview. *Journal of Counseling and Development, 88,* 220–226.

Jourard, S. M. (1971). *The transparent self.* New York: Van Nostrand Reinhold.

Juhnke, G. A., Granello, D. H., & Granello, P. F. (2011). *Suicide, self-injury, and violence in the schools: Assessment, prevention, and intervention strategies.* Los Angeles: Wiley.

Juhnke, G. A., Granello, P. F., & Lebrón-Striker, M.A. (2007). *IS PATH WARM? A suicide assessment mnemonic for counselors* (ACAPCD-03). Alexandria, VA: American Counseling Association.

Jung, C. (1962). *The stages of life.* In *Collected works* (Vol. 8, pp. 387–403). Princeton, NJ: Princeton University Press. (Original work published in 1931).

Kabat-Zinn, J. (2003). Mindfulness-based interventions in context: Past, present, and future. *Clinical Psychology: Science & Practice, 10*(2), 144–156.

Kalb, C. (2000, March 6). Drugged-out toddlers. A new study documents an alarming increasing in behavior-altering medication for preschoolers. *Newsweek, 135,* 53.

Kaplan, L. S. (1995). Principals versus counselors: Resolving tensions from different practice models. *The School Counselor, 33,* 261–267.

Kaplan, R. M., & Saccuzzo, D. P. (2001). *Psychological testing: Principles, applications and issues* (5th ed.). Belmont, CA: Wadsworth.

Kapoun, Jim. Teaching undergrads WEB evaluation: A guide for library instruction. *C&RL News* (July/August 1998): 522–523.

Kellogg, S. H., & Young, J. E. (2008). Cognitive therapy. In J. L. Lebow (Ed.), *Twenty-first century psychotherapies: Contemporary approaches to theory and practice* (pp. 43–79). Hoboken, NJ: John Wiley & Sons.

Kelly, A. E. (1998). Clients' secret keeping in outpatient therapy. *Journal of Counseling Psychology, 45*(1), 50–57.

Kelly, A. E., & Yip, J. J. (2006). Is keeping a secret or being a secretive person linked to psychological symptoms? *Journal of Personality, 74*(5), 1349–1370.

Kelly, A. E., & Yuan, K. H. (2009). Clients' secret-keeping and the working alliance in adult outpatient therapy. *Psychotherapy Theory, Research, Practice, Training, 46*, 193–202.

Kelly, G.A. (1963). *A theory of personality.* New York: Norton.

Kennedy, A. (2008). Proactive protection pointers. *Counseling Today Online.* Available at: http://www.counseling.org/Publications/ CounselingTodayArticles.aspx?AGuid= 009cbf12-1de8-4a45-85fe-01bd894f1d2e

Kenny, M., & McEachern, A. (2004). Telephone counseling: Are offices becoming obsolete? *Journal of Counseling & Development, 82*(2), 199–202.

King, J. E., & Cooley, E. L. (1995). Achievement orientation and the Imposter Phenomenon among college students. *Contemporary Educational Psychology, 20*, 304–312.

Kirk, E. E. (1996). *Evaluating information found on the Internet.* Available online at: http://www.library.jhu.edu/researchhelp/ general/evaluating/index.html

Kirschenbaum, H. (2004). Carl Rogers' life and work: An assessment on the 100th anniversary of his birth. *Journal of Counseling and Development, 82*, 116–125.

Kirschenbaum, H. (2007). *The life and work of Carl Rogers.* United Kingdom: PCCS Books.

Kirschenbaum, H., & Henderson, V. (Eds.). (1989). *The Carl Rogers reader.* Boston: Houghton Mifflin.

Kiselica, M. S. (2004). When duty calls: The implications of social justice work for policy, education, and practice in the mental health professions. *Counseling Psychologist, 32*(6), 838–854.

Kiselica, M. S. (2005). Matters of the heart and matters of the mind: Exploring the history, theories, research, and practice of multicultural counseling. *Journal of*

Multicultural Counseling and Development, 33, 118–128.

Kiselica, M. S., & Look, C. T. (1993). Mental health counseling and prevention: Disparity between philosophy and practice? *Journal of Mental Health Counseling, 15*, 3–14.

Kitchener, K. S. (1984). Intuition, critical evaluation and ethical principles: The foundation for ethical decisions in counseling psychology. *Counseling Psychologist, 12*, 43–55.

Kitzrow, M. A. (2003). The mental health needs of today's college students: Challenges and recommendations. *NASPA Journal, 41*, 167–181.

Kleinman, A. (1981). *Patients and healers in the context of culture: An exploration of the borderland between anthropology, medicine, and psychiatry.* Berkeley, CA: University of California Press.

Kline, W. B. (2008). Developing and submitting credible qualitative manuscripts. *Counselor Education & Supervision, 47*, 210–217.

Kllay, V., Tincas, I., & Benga. O. (2009). Emotion regulation, mood states, and quality of mental life. *Cognition, Brain, Behavior: An Interdisciplinary Journal, 13*, 31–48.

Koegel, P., Burnam, M. A., & Morton, S. C. (1996). Enumerating homeless people/ alternative strategies and their consequences. *Evaluation Review, 20*, 378–403.

Kohlberg, L. (1975). The cognitive-developmental approach to moral development. *Phi Delta Kappan, 56*, 671–675.

Kohn, A. (2000). The case against standardized testing: Raising the scores, ruining the schools. Portsmouth, NH: Heinemann.

Kolb, D. M. (1983). *The mediators.* Cambridge, MA: MIT Press.

Koocher, G. P., & Keith-Spiegel, P. (2008). *Ethics in psychology and the mental health professions.* New York: Oxford University Press.

Kottler, J. A. (1996). *The language of tears.* San Francisco: Jossey-Bass.

Kramen-Kahn, B., & Hansen, N. D. (1998). Rafting the rapids: Occupational hazards, rewards, and coping strategies of psychotherapists. *Professional Psychology, Research and Practice, 29*, 130–134.

Kreiser, J. S., Ham, M. D., Wiggers, T. T., & Feldstein, J. C. (1991). The professional "family": A model for mental health counselor development beyond graduate school. *Journal of Mental Health Counseling, 13*, 305–314.

Kush, J. C. (1997). Relationship between humor appreciation and counselor self-perceptions. *Counseling and Values, 42*, 22–29.

Kuther, T. L. (2008). *Surviving graduate school in psychology: A pocket mentor*. Washington, D.C.: American Psychological Association.

Kwartner, P. P., & Boccaccini, M. T. (2008). Testifying in court: Evidence-based recommendations for expert-witness testimony. In R. Jackson (Ed.), *Learning forensic assessment* (pp. 565–588). New York: Routledge.

Lafleur, L. B. (2007). Counselors' perceptions of identity and attitudinal differences between counselors and other mental health professionals. *Dissertation Abstracts International Section A: Humanities and Social Sciences*. Vol. 68(5-A), p. 1877. ProQuest Information & Learning.

Lake, J., & Spiegel, D. (Eds.). (2007). *Complementary and alternative treatments in mental health care*. Washington, DC: American Psychiatric Publishing.

Lambert, M. J., & Barley, D. E. (2001). Research summary on the therapeutic relationship and psychotherapy outcome. *Psychotherapy, 38*(4), 357–361.

Lambert, M. J., & Cattani-Thompson, K. (1996). Current findings regarding the effectiveness of counseling: Implications for practice. *Journal of Counseling and Development, 74*, 601–608.

Lambert, M. J., Dejulio, S. J., & Stein, D. M. (1978). Therapist interpersonal skills: Process, outcome, methodological considerations, and recommendations for future research. *Psychological Bulletin, 85*, 467–489.

Lambert, M. J., & Ogles, B. M. (2004). The efficacy and effectiveness of psychotherapy. In M. J. Lambert (Ed.), *Bergin and Garfield's handbook of psychotherapy and behavior change* (5th ed., pp. 139–193). New York: Wiley.

Lambert, M. J., & Okiishi, J. C. (1997). The effects of the individual psychotherapist and implications for future research. *Clinical Psychology: Science and Practice 4*, 66–75.

Lambie, G. W. (2006). Burnout prevention: A humanistic perspective and structured group supervision activity. *Journal of Humanistic Counseling, Education and Development, 45*, 32–44.

Lambie, G. W. (2007). The contribution of ego development level to burnout in school counselors: Implications for professional school counseling. *Journal of Counseling & Development, 85*, 82–88.

Lambie, G., Hagedorn, W., & Ieva, K. (2007). Social-cognitive development, ethical and legal knowledge, and ethical decision making of counselor education students. *Counselor Education and Supervision, 49*(4), 228–246.

Landreth, G. (2002). *Play therapy*. New York: Routledge.

Langford, J., & Clance, P. R. (1993). The Imposter Phenomenon: Recent research findings regarding dynamics, personality and family patterns and their implications for treatment. *Psychotherapy: Theory, Research, Practice, Training, 30*, 495–501.

Langman, M. C. (2001). The process of becoming a counselor or psychotherapist and the effects that personality has on this process: A qualitative study. *Dissertation Abstracts International Section A: Humanities and Social Sciences*. Vol. 61(7-A), 2606.

Larson, D. G. (1993). *The helper's journey*. Champaign, IL: Research Press.

Lavoritano, J., & Segal, P. B. (2006). Strategies in behavioral change: Evaluating the efficacy of a school counseling program. *Psychology in the Schools, 29*, 61–70.

Lawson, G. (2007). Counselor wellness and impairment: A national survey. *Journal of Humanistic Counseling, Education and Development, 46,* 20–34.

Lazarus, A. A. (1971). *Behavior therapy and beyond.* New York: McGraw-Hill.

Lazarus, A. A. (1981). *The practice of multimodal therapy.* Baltimore, MD: Johns Hopkins University Press.

Lazarus, R. S., & Folkman, S. (1984). *Stress, appraisal, and coping.* New York: Springer.

LeBlanc, P. M., Bakker, A. B., Peeters, M. C. W., van Heesch, N. C. A., & Schaufeli, W. B. (2001). Emotional job demands and burnout among oncology care providers. *Anxiety, Stress, & Coping: An International Journal, 14,* 243–263.

Lee, C. C. (1998). Counselors as agents of social change. In C. C. Lee & G. R. Walz (Eds.), *Social action: A mandate for counselors* (pp. 3–14). Alexandria, VA: American Counseling Association and ERIC/CASS.

Lee, C. C. (2007). Social justice: A moral imperative for counselors. ACAPCD-07). Alexandria, VA: American Counseling Association.

Lee, C. C., & Remley, T. P. (1992). Counselor membership in ACA. ERIC document retrieved August 19, 2008, from http://find articles.com/p/articles/mi_pric/is_199212/ai_267487088/pg_1?tag = artBody;col1

Levy, S. (August 20–27, 2007). Facebook grows up. *Newsweek,* 41–46.

Lewin, K. (1952). *Field theory in social science: Selected theoretical papers by Kurt Lewin.* London: Tavistock.

Lewis, J, Arnold, M. S., House, R., & Toporek, R. L. (2001). *Advocacy competencies: American Counseling Association Task Force on Advocacy Competencies.* Retrieved August 19, 2008, from http://www.counseling.org/Counselors/

Lewis, J., & Coursol, D. (2007). Addressing career issues online: Perceptions of counselor education professionals. *Journal of Employment Counseling, 44,* 146–153.

Lichtenberger, E. O., Mather, N., Kaufman, N. L., & Kaufman, A. S. (2005). *Essentials of assessment report writing.* New York: Wiley.

Linehan, M. (1994). *Cognitive behavioral treatment of borderline personality disorder.* New York: Guilford.

Linehan, M. M., Goodstein, J. L., Nielsen, S. L., & Chiles, J. A. (1983). Reasons for staying alive when you're thinking of killing yourself: The Reasons for Living Inventory. *Journal of Consulting and Clinical Psychology, 51,* 276–286.

Locke, H. J., & Wallace, M. (1959) Short marital adjustment and prediction test: Reliability and validity. *Marriage and Family Living, 21,* 251–259.

Loesch, L. C., & Ritchie, M. H. (2005). *The accountable school counselor.* Austin, TX: Pro-Ed.

Loesch, L. C., & Vacc, N. A. (1994). Setting minimum criterion scores for the National Counselor Examination. *Journal of Counseling and Development, 73,* 211–214.

Loevinger, J. (1987). *Ego development: Conceptions in theories.* San Francisco: Jossey-Bass.

Lombroso, C. (1876). *L'Uomo delinquente (The criminal man).* Turin, Italy: University of Turin.

Long, L. L., & Young, M. E. (2007). *Counseling and therapy for couples.* Belmont, CA: Brooks/Cole.

Lopez, S. J., & Snyder, C. R. (Eds.). (2004). *Positive psychological assessment: A handbook of models and measures.* New York: Oxford University Press.

Lopez, S., & Snyder, C. (2009). *Oxford handbook of positive psychology* (2nd ed.). New York: Oxford University Press.

Lorr, M. (1965). Client perceptions of therapists: A study of therapeutic relationships. *Journal of Consulting Psychology, 29,* 146–149.

Mahoney, M. (1991). *Human change processes*. New York: Basic Books.

Manthei, R. J. (2007). Client-counsellor agreement on what happens in counseling. *British Journal of Guidance and Counselling, 35*, 261–281.

Markus, H., & Nurius, P. (1986). Possible selves. *American Psychologist, 41*, 954–969.

Marlatt, G. A., & Donovan, D. (2005). *Relapse prevention* (2nd ed.). New York: Guilford.

Maslach, C., & Leiter, M. P. (1997). *The truth about burnout*. San Francisco: Jossey-Bass.

Maslow, A. (1954). *Motivation and personality*. New York: Harper & Row.

Maslow, A. H. (1966). *The psychology of science*. New York: HarperCollins.

Matthews, C. R., & Skowron, E. A. (2004). Incorporating prevention into mental health counselor training. *Journal of Mental Health Counseling, 26*, 349–359.

May, R. (1995). *Existence*. Lanham, MD: Jason Aronson.

McCarthy, H., & Leierer, S. J. (2001). Consumer concepts of ideal characteristics and minimum qualifications for rehabilitation counselors. *Rehabilitation Counseling Bulletin, 45*, 12–23.

McCarthy, J., & Holliday, E. L. (2004). Help-seeking and counseling within a traditional male gender role: An examination from a multicultural perspective. *Journal of Counseling & Development, 82*, 25–30.

McCurdy, K., & Murray, K. (2003). Confidentiality issues when minor children disclose family secrets in family counseling. *Family Journal, 11*(4), 393–398.

McDaniels, C., & Watts, G. (Eds.). (1994). Frank Parsons [Special issue]. *Journal of Career Development, 20*(4).

McDonielab, S. O., Wolskeeb, P., & Shenb, J. (2010). Treating obesity with a novel hand-held device, computer software program, and Internet technology in primary care: The SMART motivational trial. *Patient Education & Counseling, 79*, 185–101.

McGlothlin, J. M, & Davis, T. E. (1999). Perceived benefit of CACREP (2001) curriculum standards. *Counselor Education and Supervision, 43*, 274–285.

McGoldrick, M., Gerson, R., & Shellenberger, S. (1999). *Genograms: Assessment and intervention* (2nd ed.). New York: Norton.

McIntosh, P. (1990). White privilege: Unpacking the invisible knapsack, *Independent School*, Winter, 31–36.

McIntosh, P. (2001). White privilege and male privilege. In M. L. Andersen & P. Hill Collins (Eds.), *Race, class, and gender* (4th ed., pp. 95–105). Belmont, CA: Wadsworth/Thomson Learning.

Melton, J. L. Nofzinger-Collins, D., Wynne, M. E., & Susman, M. (2005). Exploring the affective inner experiences of therapists in training: The qualitative interaction between session experience and session content. *Counselor Education & Supervision, 45*, 82–96.

Merlone, L. (2005). Record keeping and the school counselor. *Professional School Counseling*, 372–376.

Merry, T. (2000). Person-centred counseling and therapy. In C. Feltham & I. Horton (Eds.), *Handbook of Counselling and Psychotherapy*. London: Sage.

Meyer, G. M., Landis, E. R., & Hayes, J. R. (1988). *Law for psychotherapists*. New York: Norton.

Micozzi, M. (2011). *Fundamentals of complementary and alternative medicine*. London: W. B. Saunders.

Miller, G. (2003). *Incorporating spirituality into counseling and psychotherapy*. New York: Wiley.

Miller, J. B. (1976). *Toward a new psychology of women*. Boston: Beacon.

Miller, W. R., & Rollnick, S. (2002). *Motivational interviewing: Preparing people for change*. New York: Guilford Press.

Mirin, S. M., & Namerow, M. J. (1991). Why study treatment outcome? *Hospital and Community Psychiatry, 42*, 1007–1013.

Monteseirin, J. Camacho, M. J., Bonilla, I., Sánchez-Hernández, C., Hernández, M., & Conde, J. (2001). Honeymoon rhinitis. *Allergy 56*(4): 353–354.

Moran, M., Sweda, M., Fragala, M., & Sasscer-Burgos, J. (2001). The clinical application of risk assessment in the treatment-planning process. *International Journal of Offender Therapy and Comparative Criminology, 45*(4), 421–435.

Moreno, J. L. (1951). *Sociometry, experimental method and the science of society: An approach to a new political orientation*. Beacon, NY: Beacon House.

Mulvihill, M. (2003). The definition and core practices of wellness. *Journal of Employee Assistance, 33*(3), 13–15.

Murphy v. A. A. Mathews, 841 S.W. 2d 671 (Mo. 1992).

Murphy, P. M., Cramer, D., & Lillie, F. J. (1984). The relationship between curative factors perceived by patients in their psychotherapy and treatment outcome: An exploratory study. *British Journal of Medical Psychology, 57*, 187–192.

Myers, I. B. (1962). *The Myers-Briggs Type Indicator*. Princeton, NJ: Educational Testing Service.

Myers, J. E. (1992). Wellness, prevention, development: The cornerstone of the profession. *Journal of Counseling and Development, 71(2)*, 136–139.

Myers, J., Emmerling, D., & Leafgren, F. (Eds.). (1992). Wellness through the life span [Special issue]. *Journal of Counseling & Development, 71*(2).

Myers, J. E., & Sweeney, T. J. (2001). Specialties in counseling. In D. C. Locke, J. E. Myers, & T. J. Sweeney (Eds). *Handbook of counseling* (pp. 43–54). Thousand Oaks, CA: Sage.

Myers, J. E., & Sweeney, T. J. (2004). Advocacy for the counseling profession: Results of a national survey. *Journal of Counseling and Development, 82*, 466–471.

Myers, J. E., & Sweeney, T. J. (2005a). *The Five Factor Wellness Inventory*. Palo Alto, CA: Mindgarden.

Myers, J. E., & Sweeney, T. J. (Eds.). (2005b). *Wellness in counseling: Theory, research, and practice*. Alexandria, VA: American Counseling Association.

Myers, J. E., & Sweeney, T. J. (2008). Wellness counseling: The evidence base for practice. *Journal of Counseling & Development, 86*, 482–493.

Myers, J. E., Sweeney, T. J., & White, V. E. (2002). Advocacy for counseling and counselors: A professional imperative. *Journal of Counseling and Development, 80*, 394–402.

Myers, J. E., Sweeney, T. J., & Witmer, J. M. (2000). The Wheel of Wellness counseling for wellness: A holistic model for treatment planning. *Journal of Counseling & Development, 78*, 251–266.

Myers, J. E., Witmer, J. M., & Sweeney, T. J. (1996). *The Wellness Evaluation of Lifestyle Inventory*. Palo Alto, CA: Mindgarden.

Myrick, R. D. (1997). *Developmental guidance and counseling: A practical approach* (3rd ed.). Minneapolis: Educational Media Corporation.

National Center for Education Statistics. (2008). Data analysis system. Retrieved from: http://nces.ed.gov/dasol/

National Endowment for the Arts. (2007). *To read or not to read: A question of national consequence*. Washington, DC: Author.

National Institute of Drug Abuse (June, 2009). *NIDA infofacts*. National Institute of Institutes of Health, U.S. Department of Health and Human Services. Washington, DC: Author.

National Institute of Mental Health. (2010). The numbers count. Available at: http://www.nimh.nih.gov/health/publications/the-numbers-count-mental-disorders-in-america/index.shtml

National Wellness Institute. (2010). Defining wellness. Retrieved July 14, 2010, from:

http://www.nationalwellness.org/index
.php?id_tier = 2&id_c = 26

Neilsen Ratings and the *Wall Street Journal*.
(2010, October 14). *YU luv texts, H8 calls*.
Retrieved from: http://online.wsj.com/
article/SB1000142405274870367360457555
0201949192336.html

Nelson, M., & Neufeldt, S. (1998). The pedagogy
of counseling: A critical examination.
Counselor Education & Supervision, 38(2), 70.

Neukrug, E. S., & Williams, G. T. (1993).
Counseling counselors: A survey of values.
Counseling & Values, 38, 51–62.

Newman, J. L., Gray, E. A., & Fuqua, D. R.
(1996). Beyond ethical decision making.
*Consulting Psychology Journal: Practice
and Research, 48,* 230–236.

Newsweek/Beliefnet Poll (2005). Newsweek/
Beliefnet poll results. Retrieved on
September 30, 2010, from http://www
.beliefnet.com/News/2005/08/Newsweek
beliefnet-Poll-Results.aspx

No Child Left Behind (NCLB) Act of 2001,
20 U.S.C.A. § 6301 *et seq.*

Norcross J. C., & Goldfried, M. R. (Eds.).
(2005). *Handbook of integrative psychotherapy.* New York: Oxford University Press.

Norcross, J. C. (1990). Commentary: Eclecticism
misrepresented and integration misunderstood. *Psychotherapy, 27*(2), 297–300.

Norcross, J. C. (2002). *Psychotherapy relationships that work: Therapist contributions
and responsiveness to patients.* New York:
Oxford University Press.

Norcross, J., Hedges, M., & Prochaska, J.
(2002). The face of 2010: A Delphi poll on
the future of psychotherapy. *Professional
Psychology: Research and Practice, 33*(3),
316–322.

Norcross, J. C., & Newman, C. F. (2003).
Psychotherapy integration: Setting the con-
text. In J. C. Norcross & M. R. Goldfried,
Handbook of integrative psychotherapy
(pp. 3–45). New York: Oxford University
Press.

Norcross, J. C., Strausser, D. J., & Faltus, F. J.
(1988). The therapist's therapist. *American
Journal of Psychotherapy, 42,* 53–67.

Norcross, J. C., Strausser-Kirtland, D., & Missar,
C. D. (1988). The processes and outcomes
of psychotherapists' personal treatment experiences. *Psychotherapy, 25,* 36–43.

North Carolina School Counselor Survey.
(2000). *How North Carolina school counselors spend their time.* Retrieved April 22,
2008, from http://www.dpi.state.nc.us/
docs/curriculum/guidance/scos/school
counselor.pdf

Nugent, F. A. (2008). *Introduction to the profession of counseling* (5th ed.). Upper Saddle
River, NJ: Merrill.

Ohio Counselor, Social Worker, and Marriage
and Family Therapist Board. (2009). Ohio
ethics violations. Available at: http://
www.cswmft.ohio.gov/ethics

Olson, D. H., & Olson-Sigg, A. K. (1999)
PREPARE/ENRICH Program: Version
2000. In R. Berger and M. Hannah (Eds.),
*Handbook of preventative approaches in
couple therapy.* (pp. 196–216). New York:
Brunner/Mazel.

Ong, A. D., & van Dulmen, M. (Eds.). (2006).
*The Oxford handbook of methods in posi-
tive psychology.* New York: Oxford
University Press.

Orlinsky, D. E., Grave, K., & Parks, B. K. (1994).
Process and outcome in psychotherapy—
Noch einmal. In A. E. Bergin, & S. L. Garfield
(Eds.), *Handbook of psychotherapy and
behavior change* (pp. 247–310). New York:
Wiley.

Parloff, M. B. (1979, February). Shopping for the
right therapy. *Saturday Review,* 134–142.

Parr, C., & Cartwright-Hatton, S. (2009). Social
anxiety in adolescents: The effect of video
feedback on anxiety and the self-evaluation
of performance. *Clinical Psychology &
Psychotherapy, 16*(1), 46–54.

Parsons, F. (1909). *Choosing a vocation.* Boston:
Houghton Mifflin.

Patterson, C. H. (1973). *Theories of counseling and psychotherapy*. New York: Harper & Row.

Patterson, C. H. (1985). *The therapeutic relationship: Foundations for an eclectic psychotherapy*. Monterey, CA: Brooks/Cole.

Paunonen, S. V., & Ashton, M. C. (2002). The nonverbal assessment of personality: The NPQ and the FF-NPQ. In B. De Raad & M. Perugini (Eds.), *Big Five assessment* (pp. 171–194). Goettingen, Germany: Hogrefe and Huber.

Pawlik-Kienlen, L. (April 24, 2008). New research on eating disorders. *Self Magazine*.

Pedersen, P. B. (1991). Multiculturalism as a generic approach to counseling. *Journal of Counseling and Development, 70*, 7–12.

Peluso, P. (2007). *Infidelity: A practitioner's guide to working with couples in crisis*. New York: Routledge.

Pennebaker, J. W. (1989). Confession, inhibition, and disease. *Advances in Experimental Social Psychology, 22*, 211–244.

Pennebaker, J. W. (1990). *Opening up: The healing power of confiding in others*. New York: William Morrow.

Perry, W. (1970). *Intellectual and ethical development in the college years*. New York: Holt, Rinehart and Winston.

Pérusse, R., Goodenough, G. E., Donegan, J., & Jones, C. (2004). Perceptions of school counselors and school principals about the National Standards for School Counseling Programs and the Transforming School Counseling Initiative. *Professional School Counseling, 7*, 152–161.

Peterson, C., & Seligman, M. E. P. (2004). *Character strengths and virtues: A handbook and classification*. New York: Oxford University Press/Washington, DC: American Psychological Association.

Pew Forum on Religion and Public Life. (2008). *U.S. Religious Landscape Survey*. http://religions.pewforum.org/pdf/report-religious-landscape-study-full.pdf

Pew Forum. (2009). Many Americans mix multiple faiths. Retrieved September 30, 2010, from: http://pewforum.org/Other-Beliefs-and-Practices/Many-Americans-Mix-Multiple-Faiths.aspx

Pew Forum on Religion and Public Life. (2010). Religious knowledge questionnaire. Retreived October 2, 2010, from, http://pewforum.org/uploadedFiles/Topics/Belief_and_Practices/religious-knowledge-questionnaire.pdf

Piaget, J. (1964). *Judgment and reasoning in the child*. New York: Viking.

Pines, A. M., & Maslach, C. (1978). Characteristics of staff burnout in mental health-settings. *Hospitals and Community Psychiatry, 29*, 233–237.

Plante, T. G., Couchman, C. E., & Diaz, A. R. (1995). Measuring treatment outcome and client satisfaction among children and families. *Journal of Mental Health Administration, 22*, 261–269.

Polfai, F. (2007). Watching a video of themselves experiencing delirium tremens reduces relapse rates for up to three months in people with severe alcohol dependence. *Evidence-Based Mental Health, 10*(4), 120.

Pope, K. S., Levenson, H., & Schover, L. R. (1979). Sexual intimacy in psychology training: Results and implications of a national survey. *American Psychologist, 34*, 682–689.

Pope, K. S., Tabachnick, B. G., & Keith-Spiegel, P. (1987). Ethics of practice: The beliefs and behaviors of psychologists as therapists. *American Psychologist, 42*, 993–1006.

Pope, K. S., & Tabachnick, B. G. (1994). Therapists as patients: A national survey of psychologists' experiences, problems, and beliefs. *Professional Psychology: Research and Practice, 25*, 247–258.

Pope, V. T., & Kline, W. B. (1999). The personal characteristics of effective counselors: What 10 experts think. *Psychological Reports, 84*, 1339–1344.

Poston, W. S. (1990). The biracial identity development model: A needed addition. *Journal of Counseling and Development, 60*, 152–155.

Powell, J. (1995). *Why am I afraid to tell you who I am? Insights into personal growth.* Allen, TX: Thomas More Publishing.

Prediger, D. J. (1994). Multicultural assessment standards: A compilation for counselors and graduate students. *Journal of Marital and Family Therapy, 19*, 68–73.

Presbury, J., McKee, J., & Echterling, L. (2007). Person-centered approaches. *Counseling and psychotherapy with children and adolescents: Theory and practice for school and clinical settings* (4th ed.) (pp. 180–240). Hoboken, NJ: John Wiley & Sons.

Pressley, P. K., & Heesacker, M. (2001). The physical environment and counseling: A review of theory and research. *Journal of Counseling and Development, 79*, 148–161.

Prochaska, J. O., Norcross, J. C., & DiClemente, C. C. (1994). *Changing for good.* New York: Avon.

Prochaska, J. O., & Norcross, J. C. (2010). *Systems of psychotherapy: A transtheoretical analysis* (7th ed.). Pacific Grove, CA: Brooks Cole.

Radeke, J. T., & Mahoney, M. J. (2000). Comparing the personal lives of psychotherapists and research psychologists. *Professional Psychology: Research and Practice, 31*, 82–84.

Ramirez, S. Z., Jain, S., Flores-Torres, L. L., Perez, R., & Carlson, R. (2009). The effects of Cuento Therapy on reading achievement and psychological outcomes of Mexican-American students. *Professional School Counseling, 12*, 253–262.

Rashid, T., & Ostermann, R. F. (2009). Strength-based assessment in clinical practice. *Journal of Clinical Psychology, 65*, 488–498.

Raskin, N. J., & Rogers, C. R. (1989). Person-centered therapy. In R. J. Corsini &

D. Weddings (Eds.), *Current psychotherapies* (4th ed., pp. 155–194). Itasca, IL: Peacock.

Ratts, M., Toporek, R., & Lewis, J. (2010). *ACA advocacy competencies: A social justice framework for counselors.* Alexandria, VA: American Counseling Association.

Rees, L. (1973). Constitutional factors and abnormal behavior. In H. J. Eysenck (Ed.,), *Handbook of abnormal psychology* (pp. 344–392). New York: Basic Books.

Reicherts, M. (1998). Gesprachspcyotherapie. In U. Baumann & M. Perrez (Eds.), *Lehrbuch klinische psycholgie* (2nd ed.). Bern, Switzerland: Hans Huber.

Reinecke, M. A., & Freeman, A. (2005). Cognitive therapy. In A. S. Gurman and S. B. Messer (Eds.), *Essential psychotherapies: Theory and practice* (pp. 224–271). New York: Guilford.

Remley, T., & Herlihy, B. (2007). *Ethical, legal, and professional issues in counseling* (2nd ed.). Upper Saddle River, NJ: Prentice Hall.

Rest, J. R. (1994). Background: Theory and research. In J. R. Rest & D. Narvaez (Eds.), *Moral development in the professions: Psychology and applied ethics* (pp. 1–26). Hillsdale, NJ: Erlbaum.

Reynolds, D. K. (1980). *The quiet therapies: Japanese pathways to personal growth.* Honolulu, HI: University of Hawaii Press.

Rice, L. N. (1988). Integration and the client-centered relationship. *Journal of Integrative and Eclectic Psychotherapy, 7*, 291–302.

Richards, P. S., & Bergin, A. E. (2005). *A spiritual strategy for counseling and psychotherapy* (2nd ed.). Washington, DC: American Psychological Association.

Richards, P. S., Rector, J. & Tjeltveit, A. (1999). Values, spirituality, and psychotherapy. In W. R. Miller (Ed.), *Integrating spirituality into treatment: Resources for practitioners* (pp. 133–160). Washington, DC: American Psychological Association.

Richardson, T. Q., & Molinaro, K. L. (1996). White counselor self-awareness: A prerequisite for developing cultural competence. *Journal of Counseling & Development, 74*, 238–242.

Riessman, F. (1965). The "helper" therapy principle. *Social Work, 10*, 27–32.

Riva, G. (2005). Virtual reality in psychotherapy: A review. *CyberPsychology & Behavior, 3*, 220–240.

Roach, L., & Young, M. E. (2011) Spirituality and wellness. In P. Granello (Ed.), *Wellness counseling*. Upper Saddle River, NJ: Pearson.

Robertson, L., & Young, M. E. (2011). Spiritual competencies. In C. Cashwell & J. S. Young (Eds.), *Integrating spirituality in counseling: A guide to competent practice* (2nd ed.). Alexandria, VA: American Counseling Association.

Robinson, F. P. (1946). *Effective study* (2nd ed.). New York: Harper & Row.

Rogers, C. R. (1942). *Counseling and psychotherapy*. Boston: Houghton Mifflin.

Rogers, C. R. (1946). Significant aspects of client-centered therapy. *American Psychologist, 1*(10), 415–422.

Rogers, C. R. (1955). Persons or science: A philosophical question. *American Psychologist, 10*, 267–278.

Rogers, C. R. (1957). The necessary and sufficient conditions of therapeutic personality change. *Journal of Consulting Psychology, 21*, 95–103.

Rogers, C. R. (1961). *On becoming a person*. Boston: Houghton Mifflin

Rogers, C. R. (1980). *A way of being*. Boston, MA: Houghton Mifflin.

Rogers, C. R., Gendlin, E. T., Kiesler, D. J., & Truax, C. B. (1967). *The therapeutic relationship and its impact. A study of psychotherapy with schizophrenics*. Madison: University of Wisconsin Press.

Rogers, C. R., & Stevens, B. (1967). *Person to person: The problem of being human; a new trend in psychology*. Walnut Creek, CA: Real People Press.

Rollins, J. (June, 1, 2010). Making definitive progress: 20/20 delegates reach consensus on definition of counseling. *Counseling Today Online*.

Romano, J. L. (1984). Stress management and wellness: Reaching beyond the counselor's office. *Personnel & Guidance Journal, 62*, 533–537.

Rønnestad, M. H., & Skovholt, T. M. (1991). En model for profesjonell utvikling og stagnasjon hos terapeuter og radgivere [A model of the professional development and stagnation of therapists and counselors]/*Tidsskrift for Norsk Psykologforening [Journal of Norwegian Psychological Association]. 28*, 555–567.

Rønnestad, M. H., & Skovholt, T. M. (1993). Supervision of beginning and advanced graduate students in counseling and psychotherapy. *Journal of Counseling and Development, 71*, 396–405.

Rønnestad, M. H., & Skovholt, T. M. (1997). Die professionelle entwicklund und supervision von psychotherapeuten/psychotherapeutinnen [Professional development and supervision of psychotherapists]. *Der Psychotherapeut, 42*, 299–306. (In German)

Rønnestad, M. H., & Skovholt, T. M. (1999). Om terapeuters profesjonelle utvikling og psykoterapiveiledning I et utviklingsperspektic [Psychotherapists' professional development and psychotherapy supervision in a developmental perspective]. In M. H. Ronnestad & S. Reichelt (Eds.), *Psykoterapiveiledning [Psychotherapy supervision]* (pp. 71–102). Oslo: Tano Aschehoug. (In Norwegian)

Ronnestad, M. H., & Skovholt, T. M. (2003). The journey of the counselor and therapist: Research findings and perspectives on development. *Journal of Career Development, 30*, 5–44.

Roscoe, L. J. (2009). Wellness: A review of theory and measurement for counselors. *Journal of Counseling and Development, 87*, 216–226.

Roysircar, G. (2003). Counselor awareness of own assumptions, values, and biases. In

Association for Multicultural Counseling and Development (Eds.,), *Multicultural Counseling Competencies 2003* (pp. 17–38). Alexandria, VA: American Counseling Association.

Rubinstein, J. S., Meyer, D. E., & Evans, J. E. (2001). Executive control of cognitive processes in task switching. *Journal of Experimental Psychology: Human Perception and Performance, 27*(4), 2001, 763–797.

Rutter, P. (1989). Sex in the forbidden zone. *Psychology Today, 23*(10), 34–38.

Sackett, C. R. (2010). Ecotherapy: A counter to society's unhealthy trend? *Journal of Creativity in Mental Health, 5,* 134–141.

Sagan, C. (1980). *Broca's brain: Reflections on the romance of science.* New York: Ballantine.

Sain v. Cedar Rapids Community School District, 626 N.W.2d 115 (Iowa 2001).

Salzberg, S. (2005). *The force of kindness: Change your life with love & compassion.* Boulder, CO: Sounds True.

Sampson, J. R., Vacc, N. A., & Loesch, L. C. (1998). The practice of career counseling by specialists and counselors in general practice. *The Career Development Quarterly, 46,* 404–415.

Sansosti, F., & Powell-Smith, K. (2008). Using computer-presented social stories and video models to increase the social communication skills of children with High-Functioning Autism Spectrum Disorders. *Journal of Positive Behavior Interventions* [serial online], *10*(3), 162–178.

Satcher, D. (2009). Taking charge of school wellness. *Educational Leadership, 67*(4), 38–43.

Schaeffer, K., Akos, P., & Barrow, J. (2010). A phenomenological study of high school counselor advocacy as it relates to the college access of underrepresented students. *Journal of School Counseling, 8*(2), 1–35. Retrieved October 10, 2010, from http://www.jsc.montana.edu/pages/articles.html

Schmidt, J. J. (1999). Two decades of CACREP and what do we know? *Counselor Education and Supervision, 39,* 34–45.

Schofield, W. (1964). *The purchase of friendship.* Englewood Cliffs, NJ: Prentice Hall.

Schon, D. A. (1987). *Educating the reflective practitioner. Toward a new design for teaching and learning in the professions. The Jossey-Bass Higher Education Series.* Retrieved from ERIC Database, October 14, 2010.

Schottenbauer, M. A., Glass, C. R., & Arnkoff, D. B. (2005). Outcome research on psychotherapy integration. In J. C. Norcross & M. R. Goldfried (Eds.), *Handbook of psychotherapy integration* (2nd ed.). New York: Oxford University Press.

Schure, M., Christopher, J., & Christopher, S. (2008). Mind-body medicine and the art of self-care: Teaching mindfulness to counseling students through yoga, meditation, and Qigong. *Journal of Counseling & Development, 86*(1), 47–56.

Schwartz, B. (2004). *The paradox of choice: Why more is less.* New York: HarperCollins.

Seligman, M. (2006). *Learned optimism: How to change your mind and your life.* New York: Vintage.

Seligman, M. E. (1999, July–August). Teaching positive psychology. *APA Monitor on Psychology, 30*(7). Available from www.apa.org

Seligman, M. E. P., & Csikszentmihalyi, M. (2000). Positive psychology. *American Psychologist, 55,* 5–14.

Selye, H. (1974). *Stress without distress.* New York: New American Library.

Sexton, T. L. (1996). The relevance of counseling outcome research: Current trends and practical implications. *Journal of Counseling & Development, 74,* 62–63.

Sexton, T. L. (1999). Evidence-based counseling: Implications for counseling practice, preparation, and professionalism. ERIC Digest. ERIC Clearinghouse on Counseling and Student Services. Greensboro, NC (ED 435948).

Sexton, T. L., & Whiston, S. C. (1996). Integrating counseling research and practice. *Journal of Counseling and Development, 74,* 588–589.

Sexton, T. L., Whiston, S. C., Bleuer, J. C., & Walz, G. R. (1997). *Integrating outcome research into counseling practice and training.* Alexandria, VA: American Counseling Association.

Sharf, R. S. (2000). *Theories of psychotherapy and counseling: Concepts and cases* (2nd ed.). Belmont, CA: Brooks/Cole.

Shaw, H., & Shaw, S. (2006). Critical ethical issues in online counseling: Assessing current practices with an ethical intent checklist. *Journal of Counseling & Development, 84*(1), 41–53.

Shaw, L. R., Leahy, M. J., Chan, F., & Catalano, D. (2006). Contemporary issues facing rehabilitation counseling: A Delphi study of the perspectives of leaders of the discipline. *Rehabilitation Education, 20,* 163–178.

Sheldon, W. H. (1942). *Varieties of temperament: A psychology of constitutional differences.* New York: Harper & Brothers.

Sherman, C. F. (1992). Changing practice models in managed health care. *Psychotherapy in Private Practice, 11,* 29–32.

Shim, R. S., Compton, M. T., Rust, G., Druss, B. G., & Kaslow, N. J. (2009). Race-ethnicity as a predictor of attitudes toward mental health treatment seeking. *Psychiatric Services, 60,* 1336–1341.

Shuman, D. W., & Greenberg, S. A. (2003). The expert witness, the adversary system, and the voice of reason: Reconciling impartiality and advocacy. *Professional Psychology, Research, and Practice, 34,* 219–224.

Simon, C. (1988). Boundaries of confidence. *Psychology Today, 22*(6), 23–26.

Simpson, D. E., Dalgaard, K. A., & O'Brien, D. K. (1986). Student and faculty assumptions about the nature of uncertainty in medicine and medical education. *The Journal of Family Practice, 23,* 468–472.

Sink, C. A., & Stroh, H. R. (2006). Practical significance: The use of effect sizes in school counseling research. *Professional School Counseling, 9,* 401–411.

Skinner, B. F. (1972). *Beyond freedom and dignity.* New York: Vantage.

Skovholt, T. M. (2001). *The resilient practitioner: Burnout prevention and self-care strategies for counselors, therapists, teachers, and health professionals.* Boston: Allyn & Bacon.

Skovholt, T. M., Jennings, L., & Mullenbach, M. (2004). Portrait of the master therapist: Developmental model of the highly functioning self. In T. M. Skovholt and L. Jennings, *Master therapists: Exploring expertise in therapy and counseling* (pp. 125–146). Boston: Pearson.

Skovholt, T. M., & Rønnestad, M. H. (1992). Themes in therapist and counselor development. *Journal of Counseling and Development, 70,* 505–516.

Skovholt, T. M., & Rønnestad, M. H. (1995). *The evolving professional self: Stages and themes in therapist and counselor development.* New York: John Wiley & Sons.

Skovholt, T. M., Rønnestad, M. H., & Jennings, L. (1997). Searching for expertise in counseling, psychotherapy, and professional psychology. *Educational Psychology Review, 9*(94), 361–369.

Small, J. (1990). *Becoming naturally therapeutic: A return to the true essence of helping.* New York: Bantam.

Smith, D. (1982). Trends in counseling and psychotherapy. *American Psychologist, 37*(7), 802–809.

Smith, H., Sexton, T. L., & Bradley, L. (2005). The practice research network: Research into practice, practice into research. *Counselling and psychotherapy research, 5,* 285–290.

Smith, M. (2003). The fears of the counsellors: A qualitative study. *British Journal of Guidance and Counselling, 31,* 229–240.

Smith, M. L., Glass, G. V., & Miller, T. L. (1980). *The benefits of psychotherapy.* Baltimore: Johns Hopkins.

Smith, R. J., & Steindler, E. M. (1983). The impact of difficult patients upon treaters:

Consequences and remedies. *Bulletin of the Menninger Clinic, 47,* 107–116.

Smith-Adcock, S., Daniels, M. H., Lee, S. M., Villalba, J. A., & Indelicato, N. A. (2006). Culturally responsive school counseling for Hispanic/Latino students and families: The need for bilingual school counselors. *Professional School Counseling, 10,* 92–101.

Snyder, C. R., & Lopez, S. (Eds.). (2009). *Handbook of positive psychology.* New York: Oxford University Press.

Snyder, R. C., & Lopez, R. J. (2007). *Positive psychology: The scientific and practical explorations of human strengths.* Thousand Oaks, CA: Sage.

Sodowsky, G. R., Kuo-Jackson, Y. P., & Loya, G. J. (1997). Outcome of training in the philosophy of assessment: Multicultural counseling competencies. In D. B. Pope-Davis & H. Coleman (Eds.), *Multicultural counseling competencies: Assessment, education and training, and supervision* (pp. 3–42). Thousand Oaks, CA: Sage.

Softas-Nall, B., Baldo, T. D., & Williams, S. C. (1997). Counselor trainee perceptions of Hispanic, Black, and White teenage expectant mothers and fathers. *Journal of Multicultural Counseling and Development, 25,* 234–244.

Sommers-Flanagan, J., & Sommers-Flanagan, R. (2009). *Clinical interviewing* (4th ed.). New York: Wiley.

Sperry, L., & Shafranske, E. P. (Eds.). (2005). *Spiritually oriented psychotherapy.* Washington, DC: American Psychological Association.

Stadler, H. A. (1986) Making hard choices: Clarifying controversial ethical issues. *Counseling and Human Development, 19,* 1–10.

Stagnitti, M. (2005). Antidepressant use in the US civilian non-insitutionalised population, 2002. Statistical Brief #77. Rockville, MD: Medical Expenditure Panel, Agency for Healthcare Research and Quality.

Stamm, B. H. (2005). *The ProQOL manual. The Professional Quality of Life Scale: Compassion Satisfaction, Burnout & Compassion Fatigue/Secondary Trauma scales.* Pocatello: Idaho State University and Sidran Press.

Stevanovic, P., & Rupert, P. A. (2004). Career-sustaining behaviors, satisfactions, and stresses of professional psychologists. *Psychotherapy: Theory, Research, Practice, Training, 41,* 301–309.

Stoltenberg, C. D., & Delworth, U. (1987). Developmental models of supervision: It is development—response to Holloway. *Professional Psychology: Research and Practice, 19,* 134–137.

Stone, C. (2002). Negligence in academic advising and abortion counseling: Courts' rulings and implications. *Professional School Counseling, 6,* 28–35.

Stone, G. L., & Morden, C. J. (1976). Effect of distance on verbal productivity. *Journal of Counseling Psychology, 23,* 486–488.

Strupp, H. H., Fox, R. E., & Lessler, K. (1969). *Patients view their psychotherapy.* Baltimore, MD: Johns Hopkins.

Sue, D. W., Arrendondo, P., & McDavis, R. J. (1992). Multicultural counseling competencies and standards: A call to the profession. *Journal of Counseling & Development, 70,* 477–486.

Sue, D. W., Bernier, Y., Durran, A., Feinberg, L., Pedersen, P. B., Smith, E. J., & Vasques-Nuttal, E. (1982). Position paper: Cross-cultural counseling competencies. *The Counseling Psychologist, 10,* 45–52.

Sullivan, T. A. (1991). Making the graduate curriculum explicit. *Teaching Sociology, 19,* 408–413.

Sullivan, W. P. (2006). Mental health leadership in a turbulent world. In J. Rosenberg & S. Rosenberg (Eds.), *Community mental health: Challenges for the 21st century* (pp. 247–258). New York: Routledge.

Swank, J., & Daire A. (2010). Multiple family adventure-based therapy groups: An innovative integration of two approaches. *The Family Journal, 18*(3), 241–247.

Swenson, L. C. (1997). *Psychology and law* (2nd ed.). Pacific Grove, CA: Brooks Cole.

Swenson, T. R., & Pekarik, G. (1988). Interventions for reducing missed initial appointments at a community mental health center. *Community Mental Health Journal, 24*, 205–218.

Szasz, T. (1961). *The myth of mental illness.* New York: Harper.

Tennyson, W., & Strom, S. (1986). Beyond professional standards: Developing responsibleness. *Journal of Counseling & Development, 64*(5), 298.

The Williams Institute. (2006). Same-sex couples and the gay, lesbian, bisexual population: New estimates from the American Community Survey. Retrieved from: http://www.law.ucla.edu/williamsinstitute/publications/SameSexCouplesand GLBpopACS.pdf

Thomason, T. C. (2010). The trend toward evidence-based practice and the future of psychotherapy. *American Journal of Psychotherapy, 64*, 29–38.

Thompson, W., & Hickey, J. (2005). *Society in focus.* Boston, MA: Pearson.

Title IX of the Education Amendments, 20 U.S.C. sec. 1681 (1972).

Travis, J. W. (1981). *Wellness workbook* (2nd ed.). Berkeley, CA: Ten Speed Press.

Truax, C. B., & Carkhuff, R. R. (1967). *Toward effective counseling and psychotherapy: Training and practice.* Chicago: Aldine.

Trusty, J., & Brown, D. (2005). Advocacy competencies for professional school counselors. *Professional School Counseling, 8*, 259–265.

Tubesing, D. A. (1981). *Kicking your stress habits.* Duluth, MN: Whole Person Press.

Tuckman, B. (1965). Developmental sequence in small groups. *Psychological Bulletin, 63*, 384–399.

Turner, R. J., & Brown, R. L. (2010). Social support and mental health. In T. L. Scheid & T. N. Brown (Eds.)., *A handbook for the study of mental health: Social contexts, theories, and systems* (2nd ed., pp. 200–210. New York: Cambridge University Press.

Tymofievich, M., & Leroux, J. A. (2000). Assessment in action: Counselors' competencies in using assessments. *Measurement and Evaluation in Counseling and Development, 33*, 50–59.

U.S. Bureau of Labor Statistics. (2008). *Occupational Outlook Handbook.* Retrieved August 23, 2008, from http://www.bls.gov/oco/reprints/ocor001.pdf

U.S. Census Bureau. (2009). *Census: More diversity, slower growth by 2050.* Retrieved January 21, 2009, from http://www.imdiversity.com/villages/asian/reference/census_2050_asian_projections.asp

U.S. Census Bureau. (2010). Projections of the population by sex, race, and Hispanic origin for the United States: 2010 to 2050. Available at http://www.census.gov/population/www/projections/files/nation/summary/np2008-t4.xls.

U.S. Department of Justice (2000). Extent, nature and consequences of intimate partner violence. NCJ 181867. Washington, DC: Author.

U.S. interim projections by age, sex, race, and Hispanic origin (2004). Retrieved October 2, 2010, from http://www.census.gov/ipc/www/usinterimproj/

U.S. Surgeon General. (1999). Mental health: A report of the Surgeon General. Retrieved July 24, 2008 from http://www.surgeongeneral.gov/library/mentalhealth/toc.html

Ulloa, E. C., & Herrera, M. (2008). Strategies for multicultural student success: What about grad school? *The Career Development Quarterly, 54*, 361–366.

University of Georgia Graduate School. (2006). Success in graduate school for minority students. *The Five Minute Mentor, 4*(4), 1–2.

Vanpelt-Tess, P. (2001). Personality characteristics of counselor education graduate students as measured by the Myers-Briggs

Type Indicator and the Bem Sex Role Inventory. *Dissertation Abstracts International Section A: Humanities and Social Sciences, 61*(10-A), 3910.

Venable, M. (2008). Online delivery of career choice interventions: Preferences of first-year students in higher education. *Dissertation Abstracts International Section A: Humanities and Social Sciences.* Vol. 69(4-A), 2008, 1338.

Vera, E. M., & Speight, S. L. (2007). Advocacy, outreach, and prevention: Integrating social action roles in professional training. In E. Aldarondo (Ed.), *Advancing social justice through clinical practice* (pp. 373–389). Mahwah, NJ: Lawrence Erlbaum.

Vernberg, E. M., & Ewell, K. K. (1995). Aversive exchanges with peers and adjustment during early adolescence. *Child Psychiatry and Human Development, 26,* 43–59.

Wachtel, P. (1977). *Psychoanalysis and behavior therapy: Toward integration.* New York: Basic Books.

Wadsworth Cengage Learning. (n.d.). *How to read a research article and evaluate the research.* Available at: http://college .cengage.com/psychology/shared/ exercises/nl/nl-howtoread_frame.html

Walker, R. (2000, August 31). Lawn-chair theories of personality. *Christian Science Monitor.*

Walsh, R., & Shapiro, S. L. (2006). The meeting of meditative disciplines and western psychology: A mutually enriching dialogue. *American Psychologist, 61*(3), 227–239.

Walz, G. R., & Benjamin, L. (1983). Shaping counselor education programs in the next five years: An experimental prototype for the counselor of tomorrow. Ann Arbor, MI: ERIC Counseling and Personnel Services Clearinghouse. ED 237 867.

Wantz, R. A., Tromski, D. M., Mortsolf, C. J., Yoxtheimer, G., Brill, S., & Cole, A. (2003). Incorporating distance learning into counselor education programs: A research

study. In J. W. Bloom, & G. R. Walz (Eds.), *Cybercounseling & cyberlearning: An encore* (pp. 327–344). Alexandria, VA: American Counseling Association.

Ward, C. C., & Reuter, T. (2011). *Strength-centered counseling: Integrating postmodern approaches and skills with practice.* Thousand Oaks, CA: Sage.

Watkins, C. E. (1983). Combatting student burnout: A structured group approach. *Journal for Specialists in Group Work, 8,* 218–225.

Watson, J. B. (1913). Psychology as the behaviorist views it. *Psychology Review, 20,* 158–177.

Watson, Z. E. P., Herlihy, B. R., & Pierce, L. A. (2006). Forging the link between multicultural competence and ethical counseling practice: A historical perspective. *Counseling and Values, 50,* 99–107.

Watts, R. E. (2003). Reflecting "as if": An integrative process in couples counseling. *The Family Journal: Counseling and Therapy for Couples and Families, 11,* 73–75.

Watts, R. E., Peluso, P. R., & Lewis, T. L. (2005). Expanding the acting as if technique: An Adlerian/constructive integration. *Journal of Individual Psychology, 61,* 380–387.

Watzlawick, P., Weakland, J. H., & Fisch, R. (1974). *Change: Principles of problem formation and problem resolution.* New York: W. W. Norton.

Weaver, K. M. (2000). The use of the California Psychological Inventory in identifying personal characteristics of effective beginning counselors. *Dissertation Abstracts International Section A: Humanities and Social Sciences, 60*(12-A), 4334.

Weibel, D. (2007). A loving-kindness intervention: Boosting compassion for self and others. Doctoral dissertation, Ohio University). *Dissertations & Theses: Full Text.* Retrieved from ProQuest Digital Dissertations database. (Publication No. AAT 3292869).

Weinrach, S. G., & Thomas, K. R. (2002). A critical analysis of the Multicultural

Counseling Competencies: Implications for the practice of mental health counseling. *Journal of Mental Health Counseling, 24*, 20–35.

Weisz, J. R., Weiss, B., Han, S. S., et al. (1995). Effects of psychotherapy with children and adolescents revisited: A meta-analysis of treatment outcome studies. *Psychological Bulletin, 117*, 450–468.

Welfel, E. R. (2002). *Ethics in counseling and psychotherapy: Standards, research, and emerging issues* (2nd ed.). Pacific Grove, CA: Brooks/Cole.

Welfel, E. R. (2005). Accepting fallibility: A model for personal responsibility for none-gregious ethics infractions. *Counseling and Values, 49*, 120–131.

Wettersten, K. B., Lichtenberg, J. W., & Mallinckrodt, B. (2005). Relation of working alliance to outcome in brief solution-focused and interpersonal therapy. *Psychotherapy Research, 15*, 35–44.

Wheaton, J. E., Bruno, M., & Granello, D. H. (unpublished manuscript). The multicultural counseling competencies of practicing school counselors.

Wheeler, S. & Elliott, R. (2008). What do counsellors and psychotherapists need to know about research? *Counselling and Psychotherapy Research, 8*, 133–135.

Whelan, E. (1996). Health advice in women's magazines: Up in smoke. Available at: http://www.acsh.org/publications/priorities/0803/advice.html

http://web.ebscohost.com.proxy.lib.ohio-state.edu/ehost/detail?vid = 35&hid = 7&sid = 8c740d5b-4529-4dbe-8ef5-c04cde2e0f11 % 40sessionmgr4&bdata = JnNpdGU9ZWhvc3QtbGl2ZQ % 3d % 3d-bib47up#bib47up

Whiston, S. C. (2003). Outcomes research on school counseling services. In B. T. Erford (Ed.), *Transforming the school counseling profession* (pp. 435–447). Upper Saddle River, NJ: Merrill Prentice-Hall.

Whiston, S. C. (2005). *Principles and applications of assessment in counseling* (2nd ed.). Belmont, CA: Brooks/Cole.

Whiston, S. C., & Coker, J. K. (2000). Reconstructing clinical training: Implications from research. *Counselor Education and Supervision, 39*, 228–253.

Whitney, J. (2007). The self-perceived multicultural counseling competencies of licensed professional counselors. *Dissertation Abstracts International Section A: Humanities and Social Sciences.* Vol. 67(10-A), 2007, 3726.

Wilkins, P. (1997). *Personal and professional development for counsellors.* Thousand Oaks, CA: Sage.

Wilkinson, L., & the Task Force on Statistical Inference. (1999). Statistical methods in psychology journals. *American Psychologist, 54*, 594–604.

Wilks, D. (2003). A historical review of counseling theory development in relation to definitions of free will and determinism. *Journal of Counseling & Development, 81*(3), 278–284.

Williams, S. C. (1999). Counselor trainee effectiveness: An examination of the relationship between personality characteristics, family of origin functioning, and trainee effectiveness. *Dissertation Abstracts International: Section B: The Sciences and Engineering.* Vol. 59(8-B), 4494.

Witkin, B. R., & Altschuld, J. W. (1995). *Planning and conducting needs assessments.* Thousand Oaks, CA: Sage.

Witmer, J. M. (1985). *Pathways to personal growth.* Muncie, IN: Accelerated Development.

Witmer, J. M. (2011). Evolution of wellness. In P. Granello (Ed.), *Wellness counseling.* Upper Saddle River, NJ: Pearson.

Witmer, J. M., & Sweeney, T. J. (1992). A holistic model for wellness and prevention over the life span. *Journal of Counseling & Development, 71*(2), 140–148.

Witmer, J. M., & Young, M. E. (1996). Preventing counselor impairment: A wellness approach. *Journal of Humanistic Education and Development, 34*(3), 141–155.

Worell, J., & Remer, P. (2002). *Feminist perspectives in therapy: Empowering diverse women.* Los Angeles: Wiley.

World Health Organization. (1958). *Constitution of the World Health Organization.* Available at: http://www.who.int/governance/eb/who_constitution_en.pdf

World Health Organization. (n.d.). Ten facts on mental health. Available at: http://www.who.int/features/factfiles/mental_health/mental_health_facts/en/index.html

Wrenn, C. G. (1954). Counseling methods. In *Annual Review of Psychology*, Palo Alto, CA: *Annual Reviews, 5*, 337–357.

Wrenn, C. G. (1962). The culturally encapsulated counselor. *Harvard Educational Review, 32*, 444–449.

Wright, J. (2005). "A discussion with myself on paper": Counselling and psychotherapy master's student perceptions of keeping a learning log. *Reflective Practice, 6*(4), 507–521.

Wright, T. L., Ingraham, L. J., Chemtob, H. J., & Perez-Arce, P. (1985). Satisfaction and things not said: Clinical tools for group therapists. *Small Group Behavior, 16*, 565–572.

Yalom, I. D. (1970). *The theory and practice of group psychotherapy.* New York: Basic Books.

Yalom, I. D. (1989). *Love's executioner and other tales of psychotherapy.* New York: Harper.

Yalom, I. (2002). *The gift of therapy.* New York: HarperCollins.

Yalom, I. D. (2005). *The theory and practice of group psychotherapy* (5th ed.). New York: Basic Books.

Young, M. E. (2009). *Learning the art of helping* (4th ed.). Upper Saddle River, NJ: Prentice Hall.

Young, M. E. (2011). Wellness and meaning. In P. Granello (Ed.), *Wellness counseling.* Upper Saddle River, NJ: Pearson.

Young, M. E., de Armas, L., & Cunningham, L. (in press). Using meditation in addictions counseling. *Journal of Addictions & Offender Counseling.*

Young, M. E., Cunningham, L., & de Armas, L. (under review). Meditation in addictions counseling.

Young, M. E., & Feiler, F. (1994). Trends in counseling: A national survey. *Guidance and Counselling, 16*, 108–113.

Young, M. E., & Hutchinson, T. S. (in press). The rediscovery of gratitude. *Journal of Humanistic Education and Development.*

Young, M. E., & Lambie, G. W. (2007). Wellness in school and mental health systems: Organizational influences. *The Journal of Humanistic Counseling, Education and Development, 46*(1), 98–113.

Zinbarg, R. E., & Griffin, J. W. (2008). Behavior therapy. In J. L. Lebow (Ed.), *Twenty-first century psychotherapies* (pp. 8–42). Hoboken, NJ: John Wiley & Sons.

■■ Index ■■

Index

Index